An Exposition of

EZEKIEL

An Exposition of

EZEKIEL

by

Patrick Fairbairn

SOVEREIGN GRACE PUBLISHERS
Grand Rapids, Michigan 49506

1971

CONTENTS

CONTENTS

INTRODUCTION.

It will not be necessary to detain our readers long at the threshold, nor would it be proper to go here into discussions which might presuppose and require an intimate acquaintance with the writings of our author. The purposes of a general introduction will be served, if we present a brief but distinct view of the personal position and circumstances of Ezekiel, the more distinctive features of his prophetical character, the nature of his style and diction as a sacred writer, the order and classification of his prophecies, and the literature connected with their interpretation.

I. On the first of these points it is not necessary to say much, for the whole that is known with certainty of Ezekiel is furnished by his own hand, and is so closely interwoven with his discharge of the prophetical office, that it is only by following him through the one we can become properly acquainted with the other. We know nothing of what he was or did as a man, but only of what he saw and spake as a prophet. That he was the son of Buzi, a priest, and entered on his prophetical career by the river Chebar or Chaboras, in the fifth year of Jehoiachin's captivity, which was the same also of his own (comp. chap. 1:1,and 33:21), he has expressly informed us; and Josephus transmits the additional information (Ant. 10:6, 3) that he had become a captive when he was still a young man. This, however, has been as often questioned as believed; and among recent commentators, while Ewald sees reason to conclude that the prophet "was pretty young when he was carried into exile," Havernick, on the other hand, thinks that "the vigorous priestly spirit which prevails throughout his prophecies furnishes evidence of a greater age, and that he had undoubtedly for some considerable time performed the service of a priest in the temple" before he left Judea. These diversities of opinion show that the precise age of Ezekiel at the period of his exile can at most be only a matter of probability. But from certain considerations that will be adduced on the dates mentioned in the opening verses of his book, there is ground to believe that the probability is mainly on the side of his having been at the time of his removal to Chaldea a comparatively young man – in the twenty-fifth year of his age. And as one of his later prophecies makes mention of the twenty-seventh year of his captivity (chap. 29:17), this, added to the original number of twenty-five, brings him to an advanced stage of life, though still not to the close of his prophetical agency. For some of his later predictions appear to have been uttered at a period subsequent to the time to which the prediction in chap. 29 belongs. There is reason, therefore, to conclude, that Ezekiel's public life both began early, and was prolonged to the season of mature age.

But of the absolute cessation of his prophetical gift, we have no difinite chronological information; nor, except from incidental notices sometimes introduced into his communications, do we learn anything of the experiences and results that attended its exercise. The direct historical notices in his writings, apart from the record of the visions he saw, and the messages of good and evil he received from above, are comparatively few. But in the messages themselves references are not unfrequently made to the circumstances amid which he was placed, and the trials or sorrows connected with his official ministry. From those scattered notices we can easily gather, that as the time was marked by the fearful prevalence of evil in a moral, not less than in an outward and worldly respect, so there was the application, on his part, of an unwearied activity, and the energy of a devoted zeal, striving against gigantic difficulties and vexing discouragements. He had to plead the cause of God in an atmosphere of rebellion; prove himself to be faithful amidst many faithless; and, without palliation or reserve, lay open evils in the condition of his companions in exile, which they sought most anxiously to cover out of sight. Hence, while he appears as one tenderly sympathising with them in their depression and gloom (chap 3:15), there is nothing to indicate that they ever properly sympathised with him in his contendings for truth and righteousness. They recognise him, indeed, as a prophet of the Most High, and collect around him, from time to time, to hear what message he might have received for their behoof, or to make inquiry through him concerning the mind of God (chap. 8:1, 11:25, 14:1, etc.); but it was never without having a rebuke administered to them on account of the frame of mind in which they appeared, or some intimation given respecting the light and captious humor they were wont to exhibit towards him (chap. 14:1, 18, 33:30-33, etc.). So that his official career, we can have no doubt was connected with much that was trying and painful; and, like too many of our Lord's prophetical types, he also in no slight degree had to *"endure the contradiction of sinners against himself."*

Yet this must not be understood of his connection with the whole band of exiles, nor probably of the later period of his public ministry nearly so much as of the earlier. For amid the prevailing iniquity there are not wanting occasional indications of a better spirit among the captives (chap. 11:16; Jer. 24); and at a period not very distant from the close of his ministrations, a very marked and general amendment had undoubtedly taken place among them. It could not greatly, if it did at all, exceed thirty years from the cessation of his active labors, when the decree was issued for the return of the captives; and notwithstanding the corruptions which still lingered among them, and which soon began to appear in the infant colony, there was a general repudiation of idolatry, and an adherence to the law of Moses, very different from what had existed at the era of the captivity, or for a considerable time previous to it. Nor can there be any doubt, that among the agencies which contributed to effect this beneficial change, a prominent place must be ascribed to the ministry of Ezekiel. Thus by the results that appeared, decisive evidence was borne to the fact, that a prophet had been among them, who had not labored in vain; and we can scarcely doubt, from the whole circumstances of the case, that the satisfaction was afforded our prophet – a satisfaction which was denied to his great contemporary Jeremiah – of witnessing the commencement of the spiritual renovation for which he so earnestly labored.

II. It naturally follows, from what has been said of the position and circumstances of Ezekiel, that, in respect to his prophetical agency, one of the leading characteristics was that of active and energetic working. He had, almost single-handed, to begin and direct the process of a general reformation, which no one can do with effect, even now, without force of character and energy of action; and still less could it be done then, when writing and reading were so much less in use, and practical effects on communities were necessarily more dependent upon the instrumentality of the living voice. This consideration is of itself sufficient to disprove the idea entertained by Ewald, and more recently espoused by Hitzig, of the comparatively quiescent and chiefly literary character of Ezekiel as a prophet. "As we see him in his book," says Ewald, "he appears more as a writer than as a prophet taking part in public life. The writer may have his individual peculiarities of a kind quite foreign to a prophet of the elder sort; and so, in point of fact, Ezekiel as an author surpasses all the earlier prophets, in particular Jeremiah, in finish, beauty, and completeness; but the more the man grows as an author and a cultivator of learning, he loses in the same proportion as a genuine prophet." He therefore contemplates the great book of Ezekiel as "proceeding almost entirely from the study of a learned retreat;" and Hitzig, following in the same track, and speaking as from the most intimate acquaintance with the facts of the case, tells us that, as Ezekiel was driven from the external world by the badness of the times, he "but cultivated the more the internal world – he flew to his books, and gave himself up to literature, leading a kind of dusky retirement in the law and his own past reminiscences (Vorbem. 2). If so, we might certainly affirm, never did an author's course of life present a greater contrast to the character of his writings, or appear less adapted to the aim he professes to have in view. The work to which he owns himself to have been called, from its very nature, required the most resolute and devoted agency: he was expressly called to do the part of a watchman in the midst of abounding danger and corruption, where success in any degree must have seemed utterly hopeless, excepting as the result of unwearied diligence and self-denying labor. And though, it is true, in his writings, as in those of the prophets generally, we have the record of little else than his direct communications with Heaven, and his more special messages to the people, yet these breathe throughout such a living earnestness and practical vigor, as clearly bespeaks the man of active labor, not the learned leisure and meditative quiet of the recluse.

This moral δεινότης, or fervent energetic striving after a practical result, is stamped upon the whole of Ezekiel's writings, although it comes out more palpably in some portions than in others. The book possesses much of a rhetorical character, and has, in a manner, but one aim – that of moral suasion. Hence the more peculiar difficulties connected with its interpretation are not those which attach to the meaning of the words or the construction of sentences, but such rather as inhere in the general form and substance of the prophet's communications. Though the former are occasionally found, it is the latter which chiefly prevail; and some even of the most profound and enigmatical portions are remarkable for the perfect plainness and simplicity of the style. At the same time, while we thus maintain the essential incorrectness of the view given of Ezekiel's prophetical character by Ewald and Hitzig, we are not insensible to a difference, in the line indicated by them, between the writings of this prophet and the other prophetical books; this book is characterized in a quite peculiar manner by a tendency to minute, detailed, and, as might seem, elaborate descriptions. But this arose from the native bent of the prophet's mind – not from the retired and studious character of his life.

For, as another distinctive peculiarity in Ezekiel, there appears a very marked individuality in his cast of mind – such as gives a kind of uniqueness to his writings, and plainly distinguishes them as productions from those of the other prophets. It is true that in the one as well as in the other we have the inspired utterances of men speaking as they were moved by the Holy Ghost. But it is not the less true, that in thus moving them, the Spirit of God had respect to their diverse natural characteristics, and allowed their constitutional peculiarities to give their full impress to the form and method of the messages they delivered. The doctrine of inspiration does not imply, however often it has been so represented, that the persons who were the subjects of it should be wrought upon by the Spirit as a kind of mechanical instruments, whose natural faculties were suspended under the violent and impulsive agency of a higher power. On such a supposition, we could never account for the diversities of manner which characterize the sacred oracles, and which not only shed over them the charm of an instructive and pleasing variety, but also endow them with a manifold adaptation to the different tastes and capacities of men. The Spirit did not suspend, or imperiously control, but most wisely and skilfully used the mental peculiarities and individual relations of his human instruments of working. And as through the employment of these the Divine Author of the communications has sought to find his way more thoroughly to our understandings and our sympathies, so it is by making due account of the same that we must endeavor to find our way to what, in the communications themselves, may be the mind of the Spirit.

In the simply literary department of the religious sphere, we readily concede a full play to the varied idiosyncrasies of mind, and the diversified methods they naturally fall into in the exhibition of Divine truth. A clear and solid judgment, practical wisdom and sagacity, rapt fervor of spirit, logical accuracy, the playful sportings of fancy or the bolder flights of imagination; the direct and the veiled, the homely and the refined, the historical and the allegorical – all find here their peculiar province, and have each their appropriate use. And in reaping the benefit which they are severally fitted to render to the cause of truth, and to minister of personal instruction, every one knows that they must each be treated after their own kind, and judged by their distinctive characteristics of thought and expression. Now there is the same variety in the natural gifts and endowments of the inspired writers; and they must be dealt with in the same manner, if we would catch aright their spirit, and receive just impressions from the discourses they delivered. For example, in the case more immediately before us, in the prophet Ezekiel we have an example of the Spirit's theopneustic agency in one of the more uncommon and eccentric class of minds, – a mind susceptible of deep emotions, possessed of an aerial fancy, and intensely energetic in its aims and movements; a mind, therefore, strongly realistic in its tendencies, so that it must be ever striving after the living presence or the life-like representation of things, beholding the unseen mirrored in the seen, and arraying the dim perspective of the future in the familiar garniture of the past or present. To such a mind, the distinctions, in a manner, vanish between history and prophecy, symbol and reality, flesh and spirit; the one seems insensibly to merge into the other, or to be related to it only as the exterior form of the life that dwells within. And the Spirit of God, in serving Himself of such a mind, as a channel of Divine communications to the Church, must be understood to have left these marked peculiarities to their native operation, and only to have given them the proper impulse, and furnished them with the necessary materials of working. It was, in truth, precisely such a mind that was needed in the crisis at which the affairs of the covenant-people had then arrived, when, the external framework of the Divine kingdom having fallen to pieces, the interest of God seemed ready to perish, and the very foundations of the faith were tottering to their base. No ordinary man, at such a time, was fitted anew to raise the standard of God's truth, and rally the prostrate forces of the kingdom. One was needed who should be capable of living alike in the past and the future, and who could see as with open eye, and grasp as with a giant's hand, the hidden realities of faith.

The peculiarities, therefore, of Ezekiel's mental constitution stood in very close connection with his special calling as a prophet; and due account must be made of them by all who would either understand aright his mission to the Church, or read in an intelligent and discerning spirit the book of his prophecy. If we should expect to find there, as in some of the other prophets, fine displays of tender feeling, or descriptions remarkable for their flow of pleasing sentiment and artistic beauty of composition, we shall certainly be disappointed. This is not the field for gems of such a nature. The mind of the prophet was concentrated upon one great object, – to give life and reality, body and freshness, to the objects of faith, so as thereby to reanimate an expiring Church, and recall men's confidence to an almost forgotten and unknown God. Whatever might serve this purpose, whether in the real or ideal world, in the symbols of religion or in the facts of sacred history, he freely lays under contribution to effect it. Even strange combinations and grotesque forms are often resorted to, when by means of them he can add to the graphic power and moral force of his delineations. And comparatively regardless of the mode, intent mainly on the effect of his communications, he indulges in frequent reiterations, and invests his imagery with such specific and minute details as one naturally connects with a felt and present reality.

The characteristics now noticed in the prophetic agency of Ezekiel seem to call for a species of commentary which shall be more paraenetical and exegetical; in other words, which shall rather handle the different communications as doctrinal or practical discourses on particular subjects, than break them up into detached fragments for minute explanatory remarks. There would otherwise be a want of fitting correspondence in form between the text and the kind of interpretation subjoined to it. And this it is our purpose to keep steadily in view, not slurring over difficulties in the text, or refusing any aid we can find for elucidating its import; yet, at the same time, dwelling chiefly on the great principles of truth and duty, to which all that is either more common or more peculiar in the prophet is rendered principally subservient.[1]

It is impossible not to notice, as another distinguishing element in Ezekiel's prophetical character, his strong priestly feeling. For the most part the prophets belonged either to the priestly or the Levitical order; and sometimes, as in the cases of Samuel and Jeremiah, prominence is given to the fact of their having been by birth connected with those more select portions of the community. But in Ezekiel alone of the later prophets does the priestly element become so peculiarly prominent and pervading as to give a tone and impress to the general character of his ministrations, and to render ever his prophetical labors a kind of priestly service. His thoughts seem perpetually to linger about the temple, and even delight to find in its symbolical materials and forms of worship the channels through which to unfold the truths he was commissioned to declare. This, however, it must be remembered, was less owing to any individual peculiarity or personal choice, than to the circumstances of his position and the nature of his calling. It sprang more immediately from the desire of satisfying the spiritual want occasioned first by the absence, and then by the destruction of the outward temple, which it was of importance to meet by something of a corresponding nature. But of this more will be said under the opening verses.

Still further, the prophetical gift itself possessed and exercised by Ezekiel was of the higher kind. Beyond all question, he belongs to the first rank of those who, under the old covenant, were called to the regular discharge of the prophetical office. As with the prophets generally, his gift was exercised as well in regard to the present as the future; and in both respects it proved itself to be, as Witsius terms it, "incomparable."[2] It enabled him to form a correct estimate of the existing state of matters, not less than a clear apprehension of what was going to take place. His spiritually enlightened eye takes the true gauge and measure of what was around him; looks through the appearances into the realities of things; so that, with the assured confidence of one who knew the mind of God, he gives forth the judgment of Heaven respecting them. His anticipations of the future are not less remarkable. Even De Wette admits that not only are there here actual predictions, but that "in none of the ancient prophets are there found such definite predictions as in this." The last part of the statement may certainly be questioned by those who believe in the genuineness of Daniel's prophecies; yet the predictions of Ezekiel are both of great variety, and singularly minute and faithful in their delineations of coming events. Partly, however, from some of the events referred to in them lying not far remote from the utterance of the predictions, and partly also from the strongly figurative form into which not a few of the others are cast, their apologetical value in the present day, against the adversaries of the faith, is not altogether in proportion to their number or their definiteness. Of many of them it must be said, that they are fitted rather for confirming the faith and strengthening the convictions of those who already believe, than for removing the doubts of such as are still opposed to the truth. Yet we should deem it impossible for any one, in a spirit of candor and sincerity, to peruse the wonderful and discriminating predictions contained in his writings, respecting either the Jews themselves (those, for example, in chap. 5,6,11,17,21), or the neighboring nations, more particularly those of Tyre and Egypt – predictions which foretold in regard to the subjects of them very different and varying fortunes, and such as necessarily required ages for their accomplishment; – we should conceive it impossible for any one in a proper spirit to examine these, and compare them with the facts of history, without being persuaded that they afford indubitable evidence of a supernatural insight into the far distant future. No spirit of human divination, or mere worldly sagacity, could possibly have enabled him to descry events at once so remote in time, and so different from what might, on many accounts, have been supposed likely to happen.

III. In respect to the style and diction of Ezekiel, different estimates have been formed by different writers, and exaggerated representations, as well of a favorable as of an unfavorable kind, are still to be met with. The comparative estimate of Lowth may certainly be characterized as in some respects overdrawn; but he says, with substantial correctness, "that in his images he is fertile, magnificent, harsh, and sometimes almost deformed; in his diction grand, weighty, austere, rough, and sometimes unpolished; abounding in repetitions, not for the sake of ornament or gracefulness, but through indignation or violence" (Praelec. 21). His diction, he adds, is sufficiently perspicuous, almost all his obscurity lying in the matter; and notwithstanding the obvious want of parallelism which pervades the greater part of the book, Lowth is disposed to claim most of it as poetical, although, he admits, "the sentences are often so rude and void of composition, that he was often doubtful what to determine in that respect." In truth, he was here trying the productions of the prophet by a somewhat mistaken standard. And altogether the view taken and the estimate formed by Ewald are much more correct. The latter says (Propheten, p. 212): "Considered simply as a writer, this prophet exhibits great excellences, especially as living in so dismal a period. His mode of representation, indeed, like that of most of the later writers, has a tendency to length and expansion, with sentences often very much involved, and rhetorical breadth and copiousness; yet it seldom dwindles down like that of Jeremiah, readily recovers itself, and usually makes a fine conclusion. His language has scattered through it several Aramaic and foreign expressions, in which one may perceive the influence of his exiled condition; though, for the most part, it is formed after the elder and better models. His diction, besides, is rich in rare comparisons, often alike attractive and striking, full of varied terms, and commonly wrought out with much beauty (for example, chap. 32). Where the discourse rises higher to the delineation of the sublime visions presented to him (as in chap. 1 and 10), it exhibits the vividness of genuine dramatic composition. It has also a certain evenness and repose, a quality which distinguishes this prophet from Jeremiah; he but seldom soars into lyrical strains (chap. 7), or becomes vehemently moved (chap. 21)." It is added, that the verse is often rough, and the strophe-arrangement much obscured, on account of the tendency to lengthen out the sentences; but they are still regarded as to some extent existing, though they are only to be found in a distinct and regular form in a few select portions, such as chap. 7 and 21).

In one respect Ewald also has given an erroneous view of the character of Ezekiel as a writer – representing this as in a certain sense interfering with his character as a prophet. This is done more especially in respect to the symbolical actions and parabolical discourses, which abound so much in his writings. "The writer here," he says, "overpowers the prophet. The writer seeks for excellent images, similitudes, and enigmas, and the merely literary prophet finds therein the readiest helps and supports to his fancy; and so Ezekiel very commonly sets out from an image, conducts this with all possible varieties of form and embellishments, and then unfolds it in proper discourse; or he draws long delineations marked by genuine poetic beauty: but the point and keenness of the prophetic style suffer much thereby," etc. This line of remark proceeds on the misapprehension already noticed respecting the prophetical character of Ezekiel. It has been well met, as to the particular point now under consideration, by Havernick, who says: "It is quite correct that a certain amount of skill is discoverable in this mode of representation; but it is to misapprehend the nature of prophecy, when this artistic impulse is viewed as the productive power of such compositions. Prophecy has its root in quite other soil; and were it after this fashion drawn into the mere province of art, it should cease to be genuine prophecy, and should belong to the class of degenerate productions – spurious imitations of the true. The writer's skill evinces itself here rather in giving forth with the greatest vividness and fidelity his internal perceptions with the full impress of their immediateness and originality. It is the historical skill of the narrator of internal facts, a simply reproductive and not a productive faculty, which must be conceded to the prophet, and in which he shows a perfect mastery" (Comm. p. 24).

We simply add, under this head, that the darkness to a certain extent inseparably connected with our prophet's delight in the use of parable and symbol, was, when rightly contemplated, by no means at variance with his great design as a prophet. His primary object was impression, – to rouse and stimulate, to awaken spiritual thoughts and feelings in the depths of the soul, and bring it back to a living confidence and faith in God. And for this, while great plainness and force of speech were necessary, mysterious symbols and striking parabolical delineations were also fitted to be of service. They showed the prophet's mind to be on the stretch to arrest the attention of his people, and lead them to penetrate into the deep things of God. To the great majority of them such things appeared deep, chiefly on account of that superficial habit of mind which rests satisfied with looking at the exterior, and mistakes shadows for realities, – the same habit substantially which has led the modern Jews to magnify to such a height the obscurities of this book of Ezekiel, ordaining that no one should read it till he had passed his thirtieth year, with other foolish and extravagant things of a like nature. Had either the earlier or the later Jews understood it aright, they would have felt that the profound and enigmatical character of some of the visions, especially when viewed in connection with the awful directness and pungency of others, was itself a witness against them, and formed a call to serious consideration and anxious inquiry. And thus in respect to the more peculiar part of the form and clothing, as well as the matter of his revelations, wisdom is here also justified of her children.

IV. The order and classification of his prophecies next demand some notice. And here it ought first of all to be borne in mind, that whatever arrangement may be made respecting them as to their subjects, an order and progression belongs to them as a whole, as well as a homogeneousness of nature, which fits them for mutually throwing light on each other; and in particular, one large portion of them (chap. 1-32), which is mainly conversant with sin and judgment, in a great degree supplies the key, by which the later announcements – more cheering in their tone, but more remote in their objects – are to be interpreted. There is in this respect a unity in the character of the book which calls for an orderly and progressive perusal of its contents. And should any one, heedless of this characteristic, overleap all the earlier portions of the prophecy, and proceed at once to grapple with some of the later and more peculiar visions, he would only take the course most likely to involve himself in perplexity or disappointment.

A general classification of the contents of the book, as has just been noticed, may be made into those which have respect predominantly to sin and judgment, and those which are more peculiarly appropriated to the revelation of grace and mercy. We can only, however, speak of prevailing, not by any means of exclusive, characteristics of this sort. For in the one part mercy is often found intermingling with the judgment, as in the other judgment occasionally alternates with the mercy. The more specific, and at the same time quite natural divisions are commonly indicated by the prophet himself, in the several dates which he has, at certain intervals, placed as superscriptions to the messages he successively received. These are altogether eight. 1. The first is introductory, containing a description of the first vision, and in connection with it of the call of the prophet – (chap. 1-3:15). 2. The next portion, embracing the remaining verses in chap. 3, and reaching to the close of chap. 7, is occupied chiefly with a more explicit announcement of the prophet's commission and charge, and his entrance on the work it devolved upon him, by setting forth the enormous guilt of the people, the certainty of the coming destruction of Jerusalem, with still subsequent calamities, and the prostrate condition of the whole affairs of the kingdom. 3. The next section embraces chap. 8-19, but falls into two parts. The first, including chap 8-ll, contains still further revelations of the people's sinfulness, especially as connected with the profanation of the temple and the corruption of the priesthood; the determination of God, in consequence, to forsake his sanctuary, with severe executions of vengeance on the wicked, though not without gracious interpositions for the safety of the few who remained faithful; and then, the twofold work of destruction and preservation being (symbolically) done, his actual departure from the temple-mount, that he might go and reveal himself in tenderness and power to an inquiring and afflicted people in exile. In the second part of this division, which includes chap. 12–19, the prophet prosecutes in detail his exposure of the sins which were bringing down such inflictions of judgment, and shows how all classes as well as the priests – prophets, princes, and the people generally – had corrupted their ways, and should severally share in the destruction that was impending. 4. In chap. 20-23 the same subject is continued, though, as the time of judgment had approached nearer, there is an increased keenness and severity in the prophet's tone; he sits, as it were, in judgment upon the people, brings out in full form the Divine indictment against them, and with awful distinctness and frequent reiteration, announces both their consummate guilt and its appropriate judgment. 5. Then comes, in chap. 24, the actual announcement of the end, as regards Jerusalem and its guilty people, with a representation of the behavior

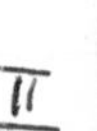

suitable for such as survived the calamity; the prophet himself being required to share in the confusion and silence which were proper at such a time. 6. Chap. 25-32 form a group by themselves, containing the announcements respecting sin and judgment, which, during the interval of the prophet's silence towards his own people, he was commanded to utter against the surrounding nations. The great object of them was to show, that if judgment had begun at the house of God, it would assuredly embrace, and visit with still more overwhelming calamities, the ungodly world. There are various headings in this section; and some of the revelations were given at periods considerably later than others; but they began to be uttered immediately after the doom of Jerusalem, and all manifestly relate to one great theme. 7. In chap. 32-39 we have a series of predictions given to the prophet in the twelfth year of the captivity, after the appearance in Chaldea of the remnant that had escaped from Jerusalem (chap. 23:21); a series which points more particularly to the better times in prospect, and unfolds, with considerable fulness and variety, the revival of God's cause among the covenant-people, the re-establishment of the Divine kingdom, and its sure and final victory over all the sources of evil, which had prevailed so much against it in the past. 8. Then, after an interval of thirteen years, comes the closing vision, in chap. 40-48, disclosing, under the symbolical representation of a new temple, city, and commonwealth, the restored condition, with the perfect order and beauty, of the people and kingdom of God.

V. All that is necessary for the present time to be said on the literature of the subject may soon be told. Our own country had done comparatively little in relation to it. The bulky and tedious work of Greenhill, reprinted some years ago in a cheap form, is, like most of the Puritan writings, of small account in an exegetical respect; and is rather a collection of commonplaces founded on Ezekiel, with a multitude of parallel passages from other Scriptures, than a commentary in the proper sense. The only English work calling for special notice here is the Translation, with Notes, by Archbishop Newcome, published in 1788. The notes are of a very brief description; chiefly explanatory of the meanings given in the translation; and both the translation and the notes proceed to a large extent on the vicious principle, very prevalent at the time, of getting rid of difficulties in the sense by proposed emendations of the text. This false and superficial style of criticism has now deservedly fallen into discredit; although Ewald, and after him Hitzig, still pursue, to some extent, the same course, and not seldom, like Newcome, would correct the Hebrew text from the Septuagint. How little confidence can be placed in emendations derived from such a source, no one can need to be told who is in the least degree acquainted with the character of the Septuagint translation generally, and, in particular, with its translation of this book. Hitzig himself admits that many of its variations from the true sense have arisen from palpable mistakes; and that, as a whole, it is pervaded by frequent and systematic deviations from the correct import, while the Hebrew text is remarkable for its degree of purity, are among the surest results of a sound biblical criticism. We have, therefore, but rarely paid any regard to the diverse readings derived from the Septuagint, and with the rarest exceptions have adhered to the existing text.

By far the most elaborate work ever published on the prophecies of Ezekiel was the joint production of two Spanish Jesuits, Pradus and Villalpandus, in three huge folios (Rome, 1596). The first volume, which, with a slight exception, was executed by Pradus, and reaches to the close of chap. 28, is the best portion of the work; now, however, chiefly valuable as a repertory of the opinions of the Fathers. The two other volumes are occupied with interminable discussions in reference to the temple, and, as will appear from our preliminary remarks to chap. 40-48, proceed throughout on a wrong principle. The expository discourses of Calvin extend only to the first twenty chapters, and are distinguished by his usual acumen and discrimination, also by his hearty appreciation of the great moral principles exhibited by the prophet; but afford little help in regard to some of the more peculiar difficulties connected with the interpretation of the book. The same also may be said of the commentaries of Rosenmuller and Maurer, though both are deserving of consultation, – the former more especially for the judicious and extensive use it makes of existing materials; the latter (which, as to the sense, very commonly follows Rosenmuller), for its grammatical exactness and acute remarks on particular passages. The translation of Ewald, with its brief notes, forming part of his Hebrew Prophets, though unsatisfactory as a whole, is yet of considerable value, and has frequently been consulted. But a much more valuable contribution to the study of Ezekiel appeared very shortly after it – that of Havernick, which issued from the press in 1843, a year to two before the lamented death of its author. Though I cannot always adopt the views and conclusions arrived at in this work, yet I gratefully acknowledge my deep obligations to it. The commentary of Hitzig, of still later date (1847), is the production of an accurate scholar, but of a very inferior mind to that of Havernick; and while it is entitled to an honorable place as regards the grammatical sense and connection, it has added nothing to the general elucidation of the book, or done aught to enhance its value as part of the Inspired Volume. In this respect it is rash and superficial, and partakes of the wonted leanness and spiritual poverty of Rationalism. The few passages of Ezekiel examined by Hengstenberg in his Christology are treated with his usual accuracy and penetration.

CHAPTER I.
THE TIME AND MANNER OF HIS ENTERING UPON THE PROPHETICAL OFFICE.

[1] Now in the thirtieth year, in the fourth *month*, in the fifth *day* of the month, as I was among the captives by the river Che-bar, the heavens were opened, and I saw visions of God.

[2] In the fifth *day* of the month, which was the fifth year of king Je-hoi-a-chin's captivity,

[3] the word of the LORD surely came[1] to E-zek-iel[2] the priest, the son of Bu-zi, in the land of the Chal-de-ans by the river Che-bar. And the hand of the LORD was on him there.

The information contained in these introductory verses, respecting the person of Ezekiel, and the time at which he entered on his prophetical calling, is very explicit upon some points, but indefinite or doubtful upon others. It tells us that he was of the priestly order, and that his father's name was Buzi; but it does not indicate with what particular family of the priesthood he was connected; nor does it state that he had ever personally discharged the duties of the priestly office in the temple. The more special part of the description has respect to his position and calling as a prophet to his exiled countrymen on the banks of the Chebar. He was, indeed, the only individual raised up among them to fulfil there the prophetical office. Daniel, it is true, flourished during the same period in exile, and was also richly furnished with prophetical gifts; but Daniel might more fitly be called a seer than a prophet, since the spirit of prophecy imparted to him was not given to fit him for the discharge of a spiritual office, but for the purpose of enabling him to disclose beforehand coming events in the providence of God. Chosen by the king of Babylon from that portion of his countrymen who were distinguished by their superior rank and accomplishments, the sphere which Divine Providence marked out for him in the land of exile was one that required his application to the affairs of worldly business, not to the employments of a sacred ministry. His lot was to dwell in king's palaces; and in giving counsel to princes and directing the movements of empire, he found his proper vocation. Hence the revelations vouchsafed to him had respect chiefly to the outward relations of God's kingdom, – its connection with the kingdoms of this world, and their ever-shifting dynasties. It is on this account, and not for the fanciful reasons sometimes alleged, that the later Jews place the book of Daniel not among the prophetical scriptures, – the writings of strictly prophetical men, – but among those of a more general character, – the Hagiographa, or sacred writings.

The sphere which Ezekiel was called to occupy was entirely different. His was the distinctive work and calling of a prophet. Himself of priestly origin, and hence devoted from his birth to the peculiar service of God, he had to do more especially with the inward concerns of the Divine kingdom; and it was in connection with this essentially spiritual vocation that the high calling and supernatural gifts of a prophet were conferred on him. When sent into exile, his duty of service was but transferred from the visible temple in Jerusalem to the spiritual temple in Chaldea, as it was also withdrawn from ministrations of a more common and formal, to those of a more select and elevated kind. Therefore, as it was Daniel's part to guide the machinery of government, and transact with affairs of state, it was Ezekiel's to deal in God's behalf with the hearts and consciences of men. And as the one was called to raise the standard of truth and

righteousness in the high places of the world's pomp and corruption, so the other had to battle with the forms of evil that were nestling in the bosom of the Jewish community, and contend against the abominations which were laying waste the heritage of God.

The place where Ezekiel was called to discharge the functions of this high ministry is said to have been *"in the land of the Chaldeans, by the river Chebar"* (ver. 3), – which Chebar is universally agreed to have been the river that is more commonly known by the name of Chaboras, a river in Upper Mesopotamia, flowing into the Euphrates near the ancient Carchemish, or Circesium, at the distance of about two hundred miles above Babylon. It was among the captive Jews settled there that Ezekiel's lot was cast, and for them more immediately that he had to do the work of a prophet. But whence came those captive brethren? and when had they settled there? They consisted, mainly at least, of that portion of the captivity which was carried away with Jehoiachin, on the second occasion that the Babylonian army made reprisals upon the land and people of Judah. The first occasion was about eight years earlier, in the third or fourth year of the reign of Jehoiakim, the father of Jehoiachin; of which there is no particular account in the historical books of Scripture, though, from being the occasion on which Daniel was carried into exile, it has found an explicit record at the commencement of his book.[3] The captives, however, of this first successful expedition of the Chaldeans against Judea, appear to have been few compared with those who suffered in the second expedition, when, having first quelled Jehoiakim's rebellion, and put him to death, the army proceeded to carry off his successor, Jehoiachin, with all the flower of the people. The kingdom was then left in a feeble and dependent state, and so continued for about eleven years longer, when the infatuated revolt of Zedekiah provoked a third incursion of the Chaldeans, who now reduced Jerusalem to a heap of ruins – the remaining inhabitants being partly killed, partly taken captive to Babylon, and partly, also, dispersed to other regions.

It is not expressly said that the whole of the captives who had been carried away with Jehoiachin were settled near Carchemish, on the banks of the Chebar, though the probability is that the great body of them had been located there. Ezekiel's call was to labor among *"the captivity,"* – or, as we prefer rendering it, the captives, – and he constantly represents these captives as having their local habitation on the banks of the Chebar. If there was any considerable number of captives taken from Judea on the first incursion of Nebuchadnezzar, it is probable that the most of them were settled there after the battle of Carchemish; these would form the whole portion of the Jewish settlers on the banks of the Chebar. And as the leading object of those deportations were evidently to consolidate the Chaldean empire, by what seemed a wise allocation of its subjects, it could scarcely fail to be regarded as a politic arrangement, to attach the succeeding and much larger companies of captive Jews to those already settled there, as they would thus more readily feel at home in their new habitations, and with less difficulty become reconciled to the change that had passed over their condition. So that when we hear of the Jews, time after time, being carried to Babylon, or again delivered from it, we are not to understand by this the city of Babylon itself, in which, apparently, a mere fraction of their number was appointed to dwell, but the Chaldean region at large, and especially this particular district of it on the banks of the Chebar. The place of exile was identified with Babylon merely because the centre of power and influence was there, and the fortunes of the whole region were necessarily bound up with those of the capital.

In a moral point of view, the situation of the exiles on the Chebar was peculiarly trying and perilous, and never more so than during the eleven years' reign of Zedekiah, – the period that elapsed between the captivity of the chief part of them and the utter prostration of their country. Encompassed, as they now were, by the atmosphere of a triumphant heathenism, the more degenerate portion were in imminent danger of burying themselves in the world's darkness and corruption; while those who had attained to more correct views both of Divine truth and of their own position, were exposed to a variety of influences, which tended to nourish false expectations in their bosom, and to take off their minds from what should have been their grand concern, – the work of personal reformation. The kingdom seemed now to have become in some degree consolidated in the hands of Zedekiah; and why might they not hope, after a few years more had elapsed, to get permission from the king of Babylon to return and dwell peaceably in their native land? Even without any express leave on his part, the matter did not seem entirely hopeless – relief might still possibly come through the intervention of Egypt; for though that power had sustained a severe blow by its defeat at Carchemish, it was not so far broken as altogether to exclude the prospect of its again taking the field against the king of Babylon. It was precisely this expectation which misled Zedekiah to his ruin; for it induced him to enter into a treacherous alliance with Egypt, which proved the forerunner of his utter discomfiture and final overthrow. Nor were persons wanting, as we learn from Jeremiah and Ezekiel, who sought to inspire the exiles at Chebar with the same delusive hopes. And it is more than probable, though we have no explicit information on the subject, that some of the earlier predictions, especially those of Isaiah and Habakkuk, which so clearly foretold the downfall of Babylon, were employed to countenance and support them in the false prospects they entertained. Then, for the small remnant of sound believers who existed there, like a few grains of wheat among heaps of chaff, how much was there, if not to betray them into those vain confidences, at least to fill their souls with depression and gloom? Cut off, as by an impassable gulf, from the temple of the Lord, while their more favored brethren in Judea were still allowed to frequent its courts, how apt must they have been to feel that thev were cast out of God's sight, and to mourn, in the plaintive strains of the Psalmist, "*Woe is me that I sojourn in Mesech, that I dwell in the tents of Kedar.*"

We find that Jeremiah, amid the severe and painful struggles which beset his course in Judea, was not unmindful of these endangered and forlorn exiles in the land of the enemy. On the occasion of an embassy going from King Zedekiah to Babylon, he despatched communications to them by the hand of Seraiah, such as their circumstances required. One of these – the prophecy contained in Jer. 51 – announced the certain downfall of Babylon, but was probably committed to Seraiah in confidence, that he might impart its tidings only to such as were likely to profit by them. The other was a letter addressed to the captives generally, in which he warned them not to believe the false prophets, who held out flattering hopes of their speedy and certain return to the land of their fathers; assured them that there should be no return till the period of seventy years had been accomplished in their captivity; and exhorted them to submit themselves to the hand of God, and to seek him with all their hearts (chap. 29). So far were the views expressed in this letter from coinciding with those prevalent on the banks of the Chebar, that one of the captives, we are informed, wrote back to the high priest at Jerusalem, and even complained of his allowing Jeremiah to go at large, since he was acting more like a madman than a prophet (chap. 29:24-28). And it was in immediate connection with these transactions, and for the purpose of giving a full utterance and a pointed application to the truths and lessons which have been expressed in the communications of Jeremiah, that one was raised up among the captives themselves to do the work of a prophet, – the fervent and energetic Ezekiel. For as it was in the fourth year of Zedekiah's reign that those communications went from Jeremiah to the captives (Jer. 51:59), so it was very shortly after, namely, in the fifth year and fourth month of the same reign, or, which is all one, of Jehoiachin's captivity (Ezek. 1:2), that Ezekiel was called to the prophetical office; whence he begins with the usual historical formula, "*And it came to pass,*" as if what was going to be recorded was merely the resumption of a thread that had somehow been broken or suspended, a continuation in a new form of the testimony that had been delivered by other servants of God. In him the truth found a most important witness, both as regards the nature and variety of the communications with which he was charged. By his very name and call to the prophetical office, he was a witness of the Lord's faithfulness to his people, as, by the tone and character of his ministrations, he gave strong expression to the high and holy principles of God's government over them; for, as has been justly said, "He was one who raised his voice like a trumpet, and showed to Israel his misdeeds; whose word, like a threshing machine, passed over all their sweet hopes and purposes, and ground them to the dust; whose whole manifestations furnished the strongest proof that the Lord was still among his people; who was himself a temple of the Lord, before whom the apparent temple, which still stood for a short time at Jerusalem, sunk back into its own nothingness, a spiritual Samson, who with a strong arm seized the pillars of the temple of idols, and dashed it to the ground; an energetic, gigantic nature, who was thereby suited effectually to counteract the Babylonish spirit of the times, which loved to manifest itself in violent, gigantic, grotesque forms; one who stood alone, but was yet equal to a hundred scholars of the prophets."[4]

We have referred as yet only to the more explicit date assigned by Ezekiel for his entrance on the prophetical office, viz. the fifth day of the fourth month of the fifth year of Jehoiachin's captivity. Before this, however, he mentions another, which he simply designates *"the thirtieth year"* – a date which has been very variously understood. Some, in the first instance, Jewish authorities, in particular Kimchi and Jarchi; recently, in this country, the Duke of Manchester, in his *"Times of Daniel,"* p. 35, and on the Continent, Hitzig – regard the prophet as reckoning from the last jubilee. By some misapprehension, the Duke of Manchester represents Jerome and Theodoret as being of this opinion; both, on the contrary, reject it. Jerome's words are: "Tricesimus annus, non ut plerique aestimant, aetatis prophetae dicitur, nec Jubilaei, qui est annus remissionis, sed a duodecimo anno Josiae," etc. The chief objection to this view is, that it rests entirely on hypothesis, there being no historical notice of a jubilee about the time referred to, nor any other instance of such an occurrence being taken by a prophet as an era from which to date either his own entrance on the prophetical office, or any other event of importance to the Church. It seems the more unlikely that Ezekiel should fix upon an era of that description, since it already lay so far in the distance; and so many painful and humiliating events had occurred in the interval, that no one almost would naturally think of it, or feel as if, in existing circumstances, anything had depended on it. Of what moment was it to Ezekiel or his countrymen that thirty years ago there had been a jubilee in the land of Judah, when now the whole nation was in bondage, and the best of its people were miserable captives in a foreign land? The more common opinions are, that the thirty years date either from the eighteenth year of Josiah's reign, when, with the finding of the book of the Law in the temple, a notable reformation began – so the Chaldee, Jerome, Theodoret, Grotius, Calov, Piscator, Ideler, Havernick (some also of the Rabbinical writers combine their idea of the jubilee with this period) – or from the Nabopolassarian era, at the commencement of the reign of Nebudchadnezzar's father, and of the Chaldean dynasty – so Pradus, Scaliger, Perizonius, Michaelis, Rosenmuller, Ewald. Of these two epochs, it is quite certain that the eighteenth of Josiah's reign did stand at the distance of thirty years from the fifth year of Jehoiachin's captivity (14 of Josiah's reign, 11 of Jehoiakim's, and 5 of the captivity); and recent chronological investigations have rendered it probable that the Nabopolassarian era must also have nearly, if not altogether, coincided with it. But it unquestionably seems strange that either of these epochs should have been indicated by giving only the number of years that had elapsed, with no explicit mention of the point from which they commenced to run. Neither of them could then possess so marked and settled a character in history that, without being expressly named, the one or the other might have been expected at once to present itself to the mind. The very circumstance that two seem almost with equal right to claim the distinction, implies that neither of them stood so prominently forward as to render the specific mention of them unnecessary. If it were established, however (though it cannot possibly be so), that the Chaldean era had then come into general use, the opinion which would date the thirty years from it would be the most probable, as the era would, in that case, have formed a definite note of time, which it had been quite natural for a prophet in Chaldea to point to; while no period of internal reformation, like that in Josiah's reign, is ever taken by the prophets as a chronological starting-point. In this uncertainty as to any reference to a public historical epoch, we cannot but think more weight is due than has latterly been given to an ancient opinion, that the prophet had respect to himself in this number, and meant simply to denote by it the thirtieth year of his own life. It was customary for the Levites, and we may infer, also for the priests, to enter on their duty of service at the temple in their thirtieth year; and though the prophets were not wont to connect the period when they received their predictions with their own age at the time of their receiving them, yet the case of Ezekiel was somewhat peculiar. As the Lord, by his special presence and supernatural revelations, was going to become a sanctuary of the exiles on the banks of the Chebar (see especially chap. 11:16), so Ezekiel, to whom these revelations were in the first instance made, was to be to the people residing there in the room of the ministering priesthood. By waiting upon his instructions they were to learn the mind of God, and to have what, situated as matters now were in Jerusalem, would prove more than a compensation for the loss of the outward temple service. It seems, therefore, to have been the intention of the prophet, by designating himself so expressly a priest, and a priest that had reached his thirtieth year, to represent his prophetic agency among his exiled countrymen as a kind of priestly service, to which he was divinely called at the usual period of life. And then the opening vision which revealed a present God, enthroned above the cherubim, came as the formal institution of that ideal temple, in connection with which he was to minister in things pertaining to the kingdom of God. Such appears to me, on full and careful consideration, by much the most natural view of the subject; and it seems chiefly from overlooking the distinctive character and design of Ezekiel's agency as a prophet, that the difficulty respecting the thirtieth year has been experienced. The prophet wished to mark at the outset, by what he said of his own position and calling, the priestly relation in which he stood both to God and to the people. And thus also the end fitly corresponds with the beginning; for it is as a priest delineating the rise of a new and more glorious temple that he chiefly unfolds the prospect of a revived and flourishing condition to the remnant of spiritual worshippers among whom he labored.

In regard to the revelation itself, which formed at once the call of Ezekiel to the prophetical office, and the commencement of his mission, there are altogether four expressions employed, – the three first having respect to what was objectively presented to the prophet, and the other to his internal fitness for apprehending what was presented. *"The heavens were opened"* – *"he saw visions of God"* – and (in connection with these Divine visions, as the aim and object of them), *"the word of Jehovah did verily come to him,"* – all indicating, and that in the first instance, the reality of the supernatural manifestation, both in action and speech, that was made to him. Without such actual appearances and communications on the part of God, nothing in the state of the prophet himself would have been of any avail as to the certain revelation of God's mind and will. At the same time, a corresponding state of spiritual excitation was needed on his part, to fit him for perceiving what was exhibited in the Divine sphere, and for being the organ of the Holy Spirit in making known the truth of God to the Church. Hence the prophet adds in respect to this, *"And the hand of Jehovah was upon him;"* as in the case of St. John (Rev. 1:17, *"And he laid his right hand upon me saying, Fear not"*), and of Daniel (chap. 10:10,18), the Lord now, by a Divine touch, invigorated his frame and endowed him with strength of eye and elevation of soul for the lofty sphere he was to occupy. And thus raised on high by the immediate agency of God, he was in a condition for witnessing and reporting aright what passed in the region of his inner man.

[4]And I looked, and behold, a whirlwind came out of the north, a great cloud, and a fire unfolding itself, and a brightness around it, and out of the middle of it, (like the color of brass, out of the middle of the fire).[5]

[5]Also out of the middle of it *came* the likeness of four living creatures. And this was how they looked; they had the likeness of a man.

[6]And each one had four faces, and each one had four wings.

[7]And their feet were straight feet; and the sole of their feet was like the sole of a calf's foot; and they sparkled like the color of

polished brass.[6]

[8]And *they had* the hands of a man under their wings on their four sides; and the four of them had their faces and their wings.

[9]Their wings were joined to one another. They did not turn when they went; they went, each one, straight forward.

[10]As for the likeness of their faces, the four of them had the face of a man, and the face of a lion, on the right side; and the four of them had the face of an ox on the left side; the four of them also had the face of an eagle.

[11]So their faces were. And their wings were stretched upward; two *wings* of each one were joined to one another, and two covered their bodies.[7]

[12]And each one of them went straight forward. Where the spirit was to go, they went; *and* they did not turn when they went.

[13]As for the likeness of the living creatures, they looked like burning coals of fire *and* like lamps. It went up and down among the living creatures. And the fire was bright, and out of the fire went forth lightning.

[14]And the living creatures kept running and returning, like a flash of lightning.[8]

[15]Now as I looked at the living creatures, behold, one wheel was on the earth by the living creatures, with its four faces.

[16]The wheels and their work looked like the color of a beryl,[9] and the four of them had one likeness. And they and their work looked like a wheel in the middle of a wheel.

[17]When they went, they went on their four sides; and they did not turn when they went.

[18]As for their rings, they were so high that they were fearful; and their rings were full of eyes all around the four of them.

[19]And when the living creatures moved, the wheels moved beside them; and when the living creatures were lifted up from the earth, the wheels were lifted up.

[20]Wherever the spirit was to go, they went; there *their* spirit would go; and the wheels were lifted up along with them. For the spirit of the living creature was in the wheels.[10]

[21]When those went, *these* went; and when those stood still, *these* stood still. And when those were lifted up from the earth, the wheels were lifted up along with them. For the spirit of the living creature was in the wheels.

[22]And there was a likeness over the heads of the living creature – an expanse, like the color of the awesome crystal, stretched out over their heads above.

[23]And under the expanse their wings were straight, the one toward the other. Each one had two *wings* which covered *their bodies* on this side, and each one had two *wings* which covered on that side of their bodies.[11]

[24]And when they went, I heard the noise of their wings, like the noise of great waters, like the voice of the Almighty, the voice of speech like the noise of an army.[12] When they stood still they let down their wings.

[25]And when they stood still *and* had let down their wings, there was a voice from the expanse that was over their heads.

[26]And above the expanse that was over their heads was the likeness of a throne, looking like a sapphire stone. And on the likeness of the throne was a likeness which looked like a man above on it.

[27]And I saw *him*, like the color of brass, looking like fire all around within it. From the likeness of his loins even upward, and from the likeness of his loins even downward, I saw *him*, looking like fire, and it had brightness all around.

[28]As the bow that is in the cloud in the day of rain looks, so the brightness all around looked. This was how the likeness of the glory of the LORD looked. And when I saw *it*, I fell on my face, and I heard a voice of One who spoke.

To gather up now the leading features and symbolic purport of this wonderful vision, we can easily perceive that the groundwork of it was derived from the patterns of Divine things in the most holy place in the temple; yet very considerably modified and changed, to adapt it to the present occasion. Here also there is the throne of the Divine Majesty, but not wearing the humble and attractive form of the mercy-seat; more like Sinai, with its electric clouds and pealing sounds, and bursting effusions of living flame. Here, too, are the composite forms about the throne – the cherubim with outstretched wings touching each other: but instead of the two cherubic figures of the temple, four, each with four hands, four wings, four faces, looking in so many directions – doubtless with respect to the four quarters of the earth, toward which the Divine power and glory was going to manifest itself. These four are here further represented as peculiarly living creatures, full of life and motion, and not only with wings of flight, but wheels also of gigantic size beside them, revolving with lightning speed, and all resplendent with the most intense brightness. The general correspondence between what Ezekiel thus saw in the visions of God, and what was to be found in the temple, indicated that it was the same God who dwelt between the cherubim in the temple and who now appeared to his servant on the banks of the Chebar; while the differences bespoke certain manifestations of the Divine character to be now at hand, such as required to be less prominently displayed in his ordinary procedure.

1. That he appeared specially and peculiarly as the God of holiness; this, first of all, was intimated by the presence of the cherubim. For here, as in the temple, the employment ot these composite forms pointed back to their original destination in the garden of Eden, to keep the way to the tree of life, from which man had been debarred on account of sin; ideal creatures, as the region of pure and blessed life they occupied, had now become to men an ideal territory. Yet still they were creatures, not of angelic, but of human mould; they bore the predominant likeness of man, with the likenesses superadded of the three highest orders of the inferior creation (the lion, the ox, the eagle). "It is an ideal combination; no such composite creature as the cherub exists in the actual world; and we can think of no reason why the singular combination it presents of animal forms should have been set upon that of man as the trunk or centre of the whole, unless it were to exhibit the higher elements of humanity in some kind of organic connection with certain distinctive properties of the inferior creation. The nature of man is immensely the highest upon earth, and towers loftily above all the rest by powers peculiar to itself. And yet we can easily conceive how this very nature of man might be greatly raised and ennobled by having superadded to its own inherent qualities those of which the other animal forms here mentioned stand as the appropriate types." – "These composite forms are here called חַיּוֹת; for which the Septuagint, and John in the Apocalypse, use the synonymous term *ζῶα* – living ones. The frequency with which this name is used of the cherubim is remarkable. In Ezekiel and the Apocalypse together it occurs nearly thirty times, and may consequently be regarded as peculiarly expressive of the symbolical meaning of the cherubim. It presents them to our view as exhibiting the property of life in its highest state of power and activity, – as forms of creaturely existence, altogether instinct with life. And the idea thus conveyed by the name is further substantiated by one or two traits associated with them in Ezekiel and the Apocalypse. Such, especially, is the very singular multiplicity of eyes attached to them, appearing primarily in the mystic wheels that regulated their movements, and at a later stage (chap. 10:12) in the cherubic forms themselves. For the eye is the symbol of intelligent life, the living spirit's most peculiar organ and index. And to represent the cherubim as so strangely replenished with eyes could only be intended to make them known as wholly inspirited. Hence, in ver. 20, *"the spirit of the living creatures"* is said to have been in the wheels; where the eye was, there also was the intelligent, thinking, directive spirit of life. Another and quite similar trait is the quick and restless activity ascribed to them by Ezekiel, who represents them as *"running and returning"* with lightning speed; and then by John, when he describes them as *"resting not day and night."* Incessant motion is one of the most obvious symptoms of a plenitude of life. We instinctively associate the property of life even with the inanimate things that exhibit motion – such as fountains and running streams, which are called living, in contradistinction to stagnant pools, that seem comparatively dead. So that creatures which appeared to be all eyes, all motion, are, in plain terms, those in which the powers and properties of life are quite peculiarly displayed. But life, it must be remembered, most nearly and essentially connected with God, – life as it is, or shall be held by those who dwell in his immediate presence, and form in a manner the very enclosure and covering of his throne – pre-eminently, therefore, holy and spiritual life."[13]

2. But this idea of holy and spiritual life, as connected with the presence and glory of God, was greatly strengthened in the vision by the appearance, as of metallic

brightness and flashes of liquid flame, which shone from and around all the parts and figures of the vision. It denoted the intense and holy severity in God's working, which was either to accomplish in the objects of it the highest good, or to produce the greatest evil. Precisely similar in meaning, though somewhat differing in form, was the representation in Isaiah's vision (chap. 6), where instead of the usual name cherubim, that of seraphim is applied to the symbolical attendants of God, – the burning ones, as the word properly signifies, burning forms of holy fire, the emblems of God's purifying and destroying righteousness. Hence their cry one to another was, *"Holy, holy, holy is the Lord God of Hosts."* And in token of the twofold working of this holiness, it was by the application of a burning coal to his lips that the prophet, as the representative of the elect portion of the people, was hallowed for God's service, while in the message that follows, the ungodly mass are declared to be for burning (as the word literally is in ver. 13). The same element that refined and purified the one for God's service was to manifest itself in the destruction of the other. And it is this also that is symbolically taught here by the dazzling light, the glowing embers, and fiery coruscations, with which all was enveloped and emblazoned. It made known God's purpose to put forth the severer attributes of his character, and to purify his Church by *"the spirit of judgment and by the spirit of burning."*

3. Even these fiery appearances, however, in the cherubim and the other objects of the vision did not sufficiently express what was here meant to be conveyed; and therefore, to make out the idea more completely, wheels of vast proportions were added to the cherubim. The prophet would thus render palpable to our view the gigantic and terrible energy which was going to characterize the manifestations of the God of Israel. A spirit of awful and resistless might was now to appear in his dealings; not proceeding, however, by a blind impulse, but in all its movements guided by a clear-sighted and unerring sagacity. How striking a representation did such a spirit find for itself in the resolute agency and stern utterances of Ezekiel! In this respect he comes nearest of all the later prophets to Elijah.

4. Finally, above the cherubim of glory and their wonderful wheel-work was seen, first, the crystal firmament, and then, above the firmament, the throne of God, on which he himself sat in human form, – a form, as here displayed, beaming with the splendor of heavenly fire, but at the same time bearing the engaging aspect of a man, and surrounded with the attractive and pleasing halo of the rainbow. In this shone forth the mingled majesty and kindness of God, – the overawing authority on the one hand, and the gracious sympathy and regard on the other, which were to distinguish his agency, as now to be put forth for the reproof of sin among the covenant-people, and the establishment of truth and righteousness. The terror which the manifestation was fitted to inspire was terror only to the guilty; while, for the penitent and believing, there was to be the brightest display of covenant love and faithfulness. Especially was this indicated by the crowning appearance of the rainbow; which, from being the token of God's covenant with Noah, in respect to the future preservation of the earth, was like the hanging out from the throne of the Eternal of a flag of peace, giving assurance to all that the purpose of Heaven was to preserve rather than to destroy, and to fulfil that which was promised in the covenant. Even if the Divine work now to be carried forward in the spiritual world should require, as in the natural world of old, a deluge of wrath for its successful accomplishment, still the faithfulness and love of God would be sure to the children of promise, and would only shine forth the more brightly at last, in consequence of the tribulations which might be needed to prepare the way for the ultimate good.

Such, then, was the form and import of this remarkable vision. There was nothing about it accidental or capricious; all was wisely adjusted and arranged, so as to convey beforehand suitable impressions of that work of God to which Ezekiel was now called to devote himself. It was substantially an exhibition by means of emblematical appearances and actions of the same views of the Divine character and government which were to be unfolded in the successive communications made by Ezekiel to the covenant-people. By a significant representation, the Lord gathered into one magnificent vision the substance of what was to occupy the prophetic agency of his servant; as in later times was done by our Lord to the Evangelist John in the opening vision of the Apocalypse.

CHAPTER II.-III. 1-11.

CALL TO THE PROPHETICAL OFFICE.

[1] And He said to me, Son of man,[1] stand on your feet and I will speak to you.

[2] And the Spirit entered into me when He spoke to me and set me on my feet, so that I heard Him who spoke to me.

[3] And He said to me, Son of man, I send you to the children of Israel, to a nation of rebels,[2] who have rebelled against Me; they and their fathers have sinned against Me, to this very day.

[4] For *they are* children with brass foreheads and hard hearts. I send you to them; and you shall say to them, Thus says the Lord GOD.

[5] And they, whether they will hear or whether they will stop *hearing* (for they are a rebellious house,) shall yet know that there has been a prophet among them.

[6] And you, son of man, do not be afraid of them. Do not be afraid of their words, though briers[3] and thorns are with you and you dwell among scorpions. Do not be afraid of their words or frightened by their looks, though they are a rebellious house.

[7] And you shall speak My words to them, whether they will hear or whether they stop *hearing*. For they are most rebellious.

[8] But you, son of man, hear what I say to you. Do not be rebellious like that rebellious house; open your mouth and eat what I give you.

[9] And when I looked, behold, a hand was sent to me; and lo, a roll of a book was in it.

[10] And He spread it before me; and it was written inside and out. And *there were* written in it weepings, and mourning and woe.

CHAPTER 3

[1] Besides He said to me, Son of man, eat what you find. Eat this roll, and go speak to the house of Israel.

[2] So I opened my mouth, and He caused me to eat that roll.

[3] And He said to me, Son of man, cause your belly to eat, and fill your bowels with this roll that I give you. Then I ate *it*; and in my mouth it was like honey for sweetness.

[4] And He said to me, Son of man, go! Go up to the house of Israel and speak to them with My words.

[5] For you are not sent to a people of a strange speech and of a hard language,[4] *but* to the house of Israel –

[6] not to many people of a strange speech and of a hard language, whose words you cannot understand. Surely, if I had sent you to them, they would have listened to you.

[7] But the house of Israel will not listen to you, for they will not listen to Me – for all the house of Israel have brass foreheads and hard hearts.

[8] Behold, I have made your face strong against their faces and your forehead strong against their foreheads.

[9] I have made your forehead as an adamant harder than flint. Do not fear them. Do not be frightened by their looks, though they are a rebellious house.

[10] And He said to me, Son of man, receive all My words which I shall speak to you in your heart, and hear with your ears.

[11] And go! Go to those of the captivity, to the children of your people, and speak to them, and tell them, Thus says the Lord GOD – whether they will hear or whether they will stop *hearing*.

The most striking thing in this section is the strong delineation that is given of the backslidden state and confirmed degeneracy of the people. Not only are they compared to such noxious productions as briers and scorpions, but with painful and emphatic reiteration they are declared to be altogether infected with the spirit of rebellion, setting their face, with determined and insolent effrontery, against the will and purpose of

Heaven. No doubt the description is to be taken with some limitation, as applicable in its full sense to the greater portion of the captives, though not absolutely to the whole. But that such a general description should have been given of them by the God of truth was a clear indication that they were in a most sunk and degraded condition, and that the remnant who were animated by a better spirit must have been comparatively few.

How distinguished a proof of covenant love and faithfulness in God, that he should condescend to deal with such people, and send a prophet yet again to instruct them! And for that prophet, with an arduous and vexing enterprise, to prosecute among them the business of a faithful ambassador of Heaven!

But to render him more fully alive to what awaited him in this respect, a symbolical action was added. Looking up, he saw a hand stretched out toward him, and in the hand the roll of a book, written within and without, but written only *"with lamentations, and mourning, and woe."* This was significant of the heavy things which were to form the chief burden of his communications to the people. For, broken and afflicted as they already were in their condition, they were not yet weaned from their false hopes, nor had they reached the darkest period of their history. Troubles and calamities still more disastrous than those which had yet been experienced were needed to crush their proud refractory spirit; and in such a time of spiritual disorder and corruption, it was only through a season of midnight darkness that light could arise to the people of God. Therefore the prophetic roll delivered into the hands of Ezekiel was necessarily much written with the dark forebodings of tribulation and sorrow. And as God's representative at such a time, and to such a people, he must eat it (chap. 3:1,2), – not of course literally swallow the roll, but so receive and appropriate its unsavory contents, that these should infuse themselves, as it were, into his very moisture and blood, and imbue his soul with a feeling of their reality and importance. Hence the bitter as well as the sweet which followed in the experience of the prophet (chap. 3:3,14), – *"sweet as honey in his mouth,"* yet afterwards causing him to go *"in bitterness, in the heat of his spirit;"* – bitter indeed, because he had to announce a message and prosecute a work which was to be peculiarly painful and arduous; but sweet notwithstanding, because it was the Lord's service in which he was to be engaged, and a service which had the full consent and approval of his own mind. It was sweet to be the representative and agent of the Most High, however contrary to flesh and blood might be the special embassy on which he was sent; as Jeremiah also says, chap. 15:16, *"I found thy words and ate them; and thy words were to me the joy and rejoicing of my heart: for I am called by thy name, O Lord God of Hosts."* "The action denotes that the prophet, being carried in a manner out of himself, entered into the room of God; and divesting himself of carnal affection, rising into the region of pure and spiritual contemplation, whatever the will of God might call him to do for magnifying the justice as well as goodness of God, he was thoroughly to approve in his own mind, and derive pleasure from the words of God, whatever might be the tenor of their announcements."[5] In short, like every true reformer, and every faithful ambassador of Heaven, it must henceforth be his to count God's glory his own highest good, and to make all subordinate to the one end of fulfilling with joy the ministry he had received from above.

And most nobly did this man of God execute his high commission, proving himself to be an Ezekiel indeed – a man strengthened with the might of God – a most powerful and effective instrument of Divine working. In the resolute and devoted spirit of his pious ancestry, *"he said not unto his father and to his mother, I have seen them; neither did he acknowledge his brethren, nor know his own children, that he might teach Jacob thy judgments, and Israel thy law"* (Deut. 33:9). How valiantly did his heroic bearing rebuke the general spirit of despondency, and against hope still inspire the hope of better days to come! And even now, when he has so long since rested from his labors, may it not be an instructive and soul-refreshing thing to look back upon the struggle which he so vigorously maintained, – to see him lifting his giant form above the deep waters of adversity that were surging around him, and the more the evil prevailed, nerving himself.

in God's name, to a more determined and strenuous resistance against it! In such a spiritual hero we recognise a sign of the ever-during strength and perpetual revirescence of the cause of God, which, like its Divine author, carries in its bosom the element of eternity – survives all changes – amid all death, lives. If this cause should for a season be found to droop and languish, let us never doubt that it shall again clothe itself with freshness and vigor. Its winters are sure to be succeeded by returning springs. And standing, as it pre-eminently does, in the righteous principles which have a witness and an echo in every bosom, there only needs the consecrated energies of courageous hearts and strenuous arms, like those of Ezekiel, to raise it from the most depressed condition, and infuse into it the warmth of a renovated life. Lord God of Ezekiel, imprint the image of this thy faithful and devoted servant deep upon our hearts! Let the thought of his holy daring and triumphant faith put to shame our cowardice and inaction! And do thou find for thyself, in these days of evil, many who shall be willing, like him, to make Heaven's cause their own, and shall count nothing so dear to them as its prosperity and progress!

CHAPTER III. 12-27.

EZEKIEL'S ENTRANCE ON HIS MISSION, AND THE FIRST MESSAGE IMPARTED TO HIM.

[12]Then the Spirit took me up, and I heard behind me a voice of a great rushing, *saying*, Blessed be the glory of the LORD from His place.

[13]I also *heard* the noise of the wings of the living creatures that touched one another, and the noise of the wheels along with them, and a noise of a great rushing.

[14]So the Spirit lifted me up and took me away, and I went in bitterness, in the heat of my spirit – but the hand of the LORD was strong on me.

[15]Then I came to those of the captivity at Tel-a-bib, who lived by the river Che-bar. And I sat where they sat and remained there stricken dumb among them seven days.

[16]And at the end of seven days the word of the LORD came to me, saying,

[17]Son of man, I have made you a watchman to the house of Israel. Then hear the word of My mouth and give them warning from Me.

[18]When I say to the wicked, You shall surely die – and you do not give him warning, nor speak to warn the wicked from his wicked way, to save his life – the same wicked *man* shall die in his iniquity; but I will require his blood at your hand.

[19]Yet if you warn the wicked, and he does not turn from his wickedness or from his wicked way, he shall die in his iniquity – but you have delivered your soul.

[20]Again, when a righteous *man* turns from his righteousness and commits iniquity, and *when* I lay a stumblingblock before him, he shall die. Because you have not given him warning, he shall die in his sin, and his righteousness which he has done shall not be remembered; but his blood I will require at your hand.

[21]But if you warn the righteous *man*, so that the righteous does not sin, and *if* he does not sin, he shall surely live because he is warned, also you have delivered your soul.

[22]And the hand of the LORD was on me there. And He said to me, Arise, go into the plain and I will talk with you there.

[23]Then I arose and went into the plain; and, behold, the glory of the LORD stood there, like the glory which I saw by the river Che-bar. And I fell on my face.

[24]Then the Spirit entered into me and set me on my feet and spoke with me. And He said to me, Go, shut yourself inside your house!

[25]But you, O son of man, behold, they shall put bands on you and shall bind you with them, and you shall not go out among them.

[26]And I will make your tongue cling to the roof of your mouth, so that you shall be

dumb and shall not be one who warns them. For they are a rebellious house.

[27]But when I speak with you, I will open your mouth, and you shall say to them, Thus says the Lord GOD: He who hears, let him hear; and he who stops *his ears*, let him stop – for they are a rebellious house.

This section, which should have formed a separate chapter, records the entrance of Ezekiel on his high vocation, and contains the first message delivered to him respecting it. His former place of abode, it would seem, was not the most advantageously situated for prosecuting with success the work committed to him; and in consequence, he removed to Tel-abib, which is nowhere else mentioned, but was in all probability the best peopled locality, or the chief town of the Jewish colony. When he came and saw the captives dwelling there in a dejected and mournful condition, he sat down among them for seven days continuously – sitting being the common attitude of grief (Ezra. 9:3; Lam. 1:1-3), and seven days being the usual period for the manifestation of the heaviest sorrow (Job. 2:13). By thus spending, at the outset, so many days of desolation and sadness, he gave proof of his deep fellow-feeling with his exiled brethren in their depressed condition, and showed how entirely he entered into their state. Thus sorrowing in their sorrow, and breathing the tenderness of a sympathizing spirit toward them, he sought to win their confidence and secure a favorable hearing for the words of mercy and of judgment which he was, from time to time, to press upon their notice.

The prophet, however, did not go alone to this mournful field of prophetic agency. He was borne thither under the conscious might of the Spirit of God, and was attended by the symbols of the Divine presence and glory. When he rose to proceed on his course, the whole machinery of the heavenly vision began also to move; and amid the crashing or tumultuous noise which broke upon his spiritual ear, he heard the words, *"Blessed be the glory of Jehovah from his* (or its) *place,"* – certainly a somewhat peculiar utterance, and one not found in any other part of Scripture; yet not materially different from another in frequent use, *"Blessed be the name of the Lord."* The glory of Jehovah here was that manifested glory which had appeared in vision to the prophet, and which was, in other words, a revelation of his glorious name. To pronounce it blessed from its place was in effect to bless God himself, as thus and there revealing his adorable perfections and Divine will. And as the prophet was going to be the representative and herald of these in a sphere where there was much to damp his spirit and withstand his faithful agency, it was fit that he should go with the solemn word pealing in his ears, from those ideal ministers of heaven, *"Blessed be the glory of the Lord;"* as much as to say, Let this above all be magnified; whatever is experienced or done, let nothing interfere with that pure and majestic glory of Jehovah, which has now in emblem been exhibited.

In regard to the message communicated to the prophet, after the seven days of sadness had expired, there is also something peculiar in it; for it is only Ezekiel among the prophets who is described as a watchman appointed by God, to give timely and faithful warning to the people. Habakkuk speaks of standing upon his watch-tower (chap. 2:1), but this was only in respect to his eager and anxious outlook for the manifestations he was expecting of Divine power and faithfulness. Ezekiel alone is represented as called to do for others the part of a watchman; and in doing it, he was most strictly charged, on the one hand, to receive all his instructions from God as to the existence of whatever danger there might be in the condition of the people, and, on the other, to sound a loud and solemn alarm when he might perceive it actually besetting them. That such should have been the distinctive character given to his position and calling, manifestly bespoke the very perilous condition of those to whom he was sent. It indicated that he had something else to do than merely to sympathize with them in their afflicted state, and speak soothing words to their downcast and drooping spirits. It was to be his rather to open their eyes to the profounder evils that encompassed them, to break the spell of inveterate and cherished delusions, and raise the cry of danger where none was suspected. So that the very form of the commission given to him was like the deliverance of a strong and impressive testimony to the people of the latent corruptions and imminent perils with which they were beset.

If we look also to the substance of the communication, or to the particular instructions given to the prophet concerning the discharge of his office, we see at once the grand principle disclosed on which the destiny of Israel was to turn. The question, whether life or death, blessing or cursing, was to be their portion, hung upon another, whether they were to make righteousness or sin their choice? Their return to righteousness was the indispensable condition of their restoration to blessing. If in despite of this wicked should persevere in his evil ways, or even the righteous man should turn aside and practise iniquity, a visitation of wrath must be looked for, – the original sentence against sin, to which the language designedly points, that the purpose of God in this respect might be seen to be fixed and unalterable – the sentence that he who transgresses *"shall surely die,"* must take effect; for God is unchangeably the same, and what he appointed at first as the wages of sin must continue to be its wages still.

But while this part of the charge cut off all hope from a backsliding and impenitent people, the other part of it held out ample encouragement to such as remained stedfast in the covenant of God, or repented of their evil ways. The man who continued to love the paths of righteousness, and the man also who, after having forsaken, again returned to them, was to be assured of the blessings of life; these should as surely live as the others should die. For the prophet, as God's watchman, was to represent the mercy as well as the justice of God's administration; he was to have a wakeful eye upon the good, not less than the evil, that appeared among the people; and was to stretch out the hand of fellowship, and display the banner of Divine love and protection in behalf of all who might be inclined or moved to cleave to the service of Heaven. Thus were they to know from the outset, that for the people as a whole, and for each individual amongst them, this one path lay open for their return to peace and blessing.

We shall not go into the question too often raised from this representation, as to the possibility of the righteous falling from a state of grace. For it seems to us a misapplication of this passage to introduce it in such a connection. Its direct and immediate bearing had respect only to the inseparable connection between righteousness and life, sin and death. And certainly by the former is meant a real participation of the Divine likeness and blessing, and by the latter the loss of both. Calvin plainly errs in maintaining the contrary. But whether this loss may ever be sustained by any who have properly enjoyed the good, – whether those who have been truly renewed by grace ever fall back again into the corruption and ruin of nature, – this is not to be determined by a passage like the present, which being intended only for a direction to the prophet in regard to his public ministrations, of necessity spake of the appearances, rather than the absolute realities of things. Unquestionably there were persons then, as there are persons still, who to all human appearance have lived for a time in the fellowship and favor of God, and yet afterwards turn again to folly. Such are known by their fruits to be not of the true fold of Christ. But it is well that the possibility of what looks so much like a falling from grace should be borne in mind both by pastors and people, that there may be exercised a wakeful jealousy in regard to the vital bond which connects life with righteousness, and death with sin. Even the most established believer is not safe, unless he keep constantly in mind the dangers of his condition, and, with a godly jealousy over himself, perpetually watch and pray lest he fall into evil.

At the very outset, therefore, and by the terms of his Divine commission, the prophet seeks to recall the people to the main point at issue, and urges them to a right settlement of the controversy between them and God. Individually and collectively they must come to be at one with him in respect to the love of righteousness and the hatred of iniquity. This is the grand turning-point on which hangs the destiny that awaits them, as it is also the vital thread that runs through all the prophet's future ministrations and announcements. Once and again he presses it on their notice in the same terms that he does here, only with more fulness of detail, and greater urgency in the application (chap. 18, 33), while, in one form or another, the subject is perpetually referred to throughout the book of his prophecy. Here also he was reminded of the necessity of this repeated earnestness in the matter, and of the arduous and difficult task that was given him to accomplish in respect to it. For, immediately after he has received his charge, the hand of the Lord was upon him, and he was ordered to go forth into the plain, that the Lord might there talk with him alone (ver. 22). And when there, and favored again with a manifestation of the Divine glory, as at the first, the spirit enters into him, and directs him to go and shut himself up in his house; thus giving him to understand, that in the work he had to do he must look for no sympathy and support from man, but must be alone with his God, reverently hearing his word, and receiving strength from his hand. The reason follows: *"And thou, son of man, behold, they lay bands upon thee, and bind thee with them, that thou mayest not go forth amongst them;"* that is, their obstinate and wayward disposition shall be felt upon thy spirit like fetters of restraint, repressing the energies of thy soul in its spiritual labors, so that thou shalt need to look for thy encouragement elsewhere than from fellowship with them. For that the imposition of bands must be understood spiritually of the damping effect to be produced upon his soul by the conduct of the people, can admit of no doubt. It is a marked specimen of the strong idealism of our prophet, which clothes everything it handles with the distinctness of flesh and blood. *"And I will make thy tongue* (it is added) *cleave to the roof of thy mouth, and thou shalt be dumb, and shalt not be to them for a reprover; for they are a rebellious house."* So deeply rooted and inveterate is the evil in them, that it shall prevail over thee; thou shalt not prevail over it; after thou hast plied every weapon, thou shalt need to sit down in silence, as one baffled of his purpose; but still not as if the work were altogether in vain, or the cause absolutely hopeless. It is Jehovah's word that is to be spoken, and this cannot for ever be in vain: *"And when I speak to thee, I will open thy mouth, and thou shalt say to them, Thus saith the Lord Jehovah, Let him hear that will hear, and let him forbear that will forbear; for they are a rebellious house."* The word is true, and must ultimately prevail, because it is Divine; and however those may deal with it to whom it is immediately addressed, it is thine to utter it with unswerving faithfulness as the Lord's true message.

A salutary lesson is conveyed here to all who are put in trust with souls, as well in regard to the nature of the charge itself, as to the manner in which it ought to be fulfilled. It is emphatically the work of God they have to do, and the instrument to be wielded in the doing of it is his own word. Let this be plied with unwearied diligence, with affectionate tenderness and fervency of spirit; for the work is of infinite importance, and results past reckoning depend on it. Eternal weal or woe grows out of it to all who come within the field of its operations. And for oneself – whatever may be the result for others – the path of duty is the only path of safety; faithfulness to God must be the supreme rule, and his glory the chief aim. *"I have a commission to fulfil, I must deliver my own soul,"* – let this be the one answer to all counter-solicitations from the flesh or the world; and it will also be the best guarantee of ultimate success. For it is to the labors of those who thus supremely eye and honor God that the harvest of souls is usually given; and the more that any one proves himself to be such a workman, the less he shall need to be ashamed either here or hereafter.

CHAPTER IV.

THE VISION OF THE SIEGE AND THE INIQUITY-BEARING

[1] You also, son of man, take a tile to yourself and lay it before you, and portray on it the city Jerusalem.

[2] And lay siege against it, and build a fort[1] against it, and cast a mound against it. Also set the camp against it, and set *battering* rams against it all around.[2]

[3] And take an iron pan to yourself and set it *for* a wall of iron between you and the city. And set your face against it, and it shall be under attack. And you shall set a battle against it. This shall be a sign to the house of Israel.

[4] Also lie on your left side, and lay the iniquity of the house of Israel on it; *according* to the number of days that you shall lie on it, you shall bear their iniquity.

[5] For I have laid on you the years of their iniquity, according to the number of days, three hundred and ninety days. So you shall bear the iniquity of the house of Israel.

[6] And when you have fulfilled them, lie again on your right side, and you shall bear the iniquity of the house of Judah forty days – a day for a year – a day for a year;[3] I have set for you.

[7] Therefore you shall set your face toward the siege of Jerusalem, and your arm shall be uncovered, and you shall prophesy against it.

[8] And, behold, I will lay bands on you, and you shall not turn yourself from one side to another until you have ended the days of your siege.

[9] Take also to yourself wheat, and barley, and beans, and lentiles, and millet, and spelt, and put them in one vessel, and make bread of them for yourself. *According* to the number of the days that you shall lie on your side, three hundred and ninety days, you shall eat of it.[4]

[10] And your food which you shall eat shall be by weight twenty shekels a day; from time to time you shall eat it.

[11] You shall also drink water by measure, the sixth part of a hin. From time to time you shall drink.

[12] And you shall eat it *as* barley cakes, and you shall bake it with dung that comes out of man, in their sight.

[13] And the LORD said, Even so shall the children of Israel eat their defiled bread among the Gentiles, where I will drive them.

[14] Then I said, Ah Lord GOD! Behold, my soul has not been defiled. For from my youth up, even till now, I have not eaten of that which dies of itself or is torn in pieces. And no unclean flesh has come into my mouth.

[15] Then He said to me, Lo, I have given you cow's dung for man's dung, and you shall prepare your bread with it.

[16] And He said to me, Son of man, behold, I will break the staff of bread in Jerusalem. And they shall eat bread by weight and with care. And they shall drink water by measure, and in silence,

[17] so that they may lack bread and water, and be stricken dumb with one another, and waste away for their iniquity.

The prophet is here commanded to take a tile or brick, and engrave on it an outline of the city of Jerusalem. Having done this, he is instructed to direct against the city the usual means and appliances of a siege,—to build a tower of observation, to cast up a mound against it, to prepare battering-rams, or instruments for effecting breaches in the walls; and with an iron frying-pan, set up between him and the city, and as with a wall of metal separating him from it, to carry on a close and vigorous seige. At the same time, and while this action was proceeding (see ver. 7 and 8), the prophet is enjoined to lie first on his left side for 390 days, bearing for so long a time the iniquity of the house of Israel; then turn to the other side, and for 40 days more to bear the iniquity of the house of Judah. These days of iniquity-bearing, he is also given to understand, represent so many years, during which the people whom he personified were destined to bear their iniquity. Nor was there to be any release from the appointed doom; for in token of the Divine determination to execute what was decreed, bands were to be laid upon him, to hold him

in his place till the whole was accomplished. Still further, he is directed to take different kinds of grain, from the richest to the poorest (wheat, barley, beans, lentils, millet, spelt or dhourra, the three last being the poorer kinds of grain), and mix them all together for bread, as if no choice was to be exercised about the quality, but the worst as well as the best had to be turned to account. He was also to bake them with the foulest and most offensive ingredients; and eat what was baked in scanty portions, with an accompanying pittance of water, as is usual in times of straitness and scarcity. This he was to do for the period of *"390 days, – the days he was to lie upon his side;"* for thus, it is added by way of explanation, *"even thus shall the children of Israel eat their defiled bread among the Gentiles, whither I will drive them."* And after having complained of the defilement necessarily connected with the order (*"Ah! Lord God, behold, my soul hath not been polluted!"*), and having obtained a slight modification of the order, though the bread was still to be scant and abominable, the Divine communication was thus briefly and mournfully wound up: "*And he said to me, Son of man, behold I break the staff of bread in Jerusalem; and they shall eat bread by weight, and with care; and they shall drink water by measure, and in desolateness; that they may want bread and water, and be desolate one toward another, and pine away in their iniquities.*"

In this singular communication there is fortunately no difficulty worth naming as regards the meaning of the words or the construction of the sentences. And in regard to the part required to be played by the prophet himself, however it may have been understood in former times, we should suppose few now will be disposed to doubt that the successive actions spoken of took place only in vision, and are no more to be ranked among the occurrences of actual life than the eating of the prophetic roll mentioned in the preceding chapter. Indeed, such actions as are described here, though well fitted when rehearsed as past, and read as narratives of things ideally done, to make a strong and vivid impression upon the mind, would plainly have had an opposite effect if transacted in real life. It would have been impossible for ordinary spectators to see Ezekiel conducting a miniature siege with a tile and a sauce-pan, and such like instruments of war, without a feeling of the puerile and ludicrous being awakened; and the other symbolical actions mentioned, especially his lying for 390 days motionless on one side, if literally understood, can scarcely be regarded as coming within the limits of the possible. And along with the physical impossibility of one part of the requirement, there was the moral impossibility of another; since to eat bread composed of such abominable materials would have been (if performed in real life) a direct contravention of the law of Moses,– that law, respectful submission to which was ever held to be the first and most essential characteristic of a true prophet (compare Deut. 14:3, 23:12-14, with 13:1-5). Besides, we find the prophet (chap. 8:1) represented as sitting in his house before the number of the days to be spent in a lying posture could have been completed.[5] So that, on every account, it is necessary to consider the actions to have taken place in vision, as indeed was usually the case in prophetical actions, and uniformly so, as we shall find, in Ezekiel.

But if there is little room for diversity of opinion as to the visionary nature of the scene described in this chapter, or to the import of the terms employed, when we look to the message itself contained in the vision, there is something so peculiar and enigmatical in its structure, that it would be difficult to point to a single chapter in the whole prophetical scriptures where our commentators have found themselves so entirely at sea, and so unable to satisfy either themselves or their readers. It is of great importance, however, to find the right clue here, as a good deal depends on it for a correct understanding of the peculiar manner of our prophet generally, and for the satisfactory explanation of the more obscure portions of his writings. Nor is there any insurmountable difficulty in the way, if only we view the different parts of the vision in their due connection one with another, and give to the language of the prophet its fair and legitimate import.

1. Let it first be noted, then, for a right interpretation of the vision, that the several parts form but one great whole. What is first symbolized by the prophet's laying seige to Jerusalem is not to be regarded as something diverse and apart from what is afterwards

indicated by his lying so many days upon his side, and eating scant and abominable bread; for the two actions are distinctly represented as contemporaneous. It is while in the act of lying upon his side that he is to set his face toward Jerusalem, and to stretch out toward it his uncovered arm, as a sign of the Lord's displeasure manifested against it (vers. 7,8). Nor is he allowed to change his posture *"till the days of the siege are ended."* So that the second line of action must have been designed to be supplementary to the first, and was merely added to bring out more fully and distinctly the instruction sought to be conveyed. But such being the case, the action of the siege, which forms the first part of the vision, cannot have been intended to depict the calamity of an actual siege of Jerusalem; for then, by the other and contemporaneous actions, it must needs have been protracted for centuries, and must also have been a calamity in which the house of Israel shared as well as the house of Judah. We must, therefore, dismiss from our minds the thought of an actual siege (which has so commonly embarassed the views of interpreters), excepting in so far as that may have formed a constituent part of the contemplated troubles. Jerusalem, the common mother, the centre of the whole covenant-people, appearing as a besieged city, assailed with all the means and implements of war, and these plied by the immediate direction and agency of the living God, – this stands here as an image of the people themselves lying under the ban of Heaven, given up as a prey to the powers of evil, and doomed to experience at their hands the most severe and painful indignities. Hence, also, as the siege itself was comprehensive of the whole that was to be experienced, we are told merely of its continued pressure, but not of its result; for, in the present case, nothing really depended on that, and the mention of it might even have tended to convey a false impression, by leading us to fix our minds simply on a literal siege and overthrow of Jerusalem.

2. It must be noted again, in regard to the second action in the vision, that by the bearing of the people's iniquity must be understood the punishment due to their sins. If the expression had been in itself a doubtful one, the instruction we have seen to be imparted by the action of the siege would have obliged us to take it in the sense now mentioned. But the expression is one that very frequently occurs in Scripture, and always in the sense of sustaining the punishment due to sin. We point only to a few examples out of many which might be given: Num. 14:33; Lev. 19:8; Isa. 53:12; and in Ezekiel himself, chap. 18:19,20, 23:35.[6] The corresponding years, therefore, on the part of the people, represented by the days of iniquity-bearing in the prophet, must be years of trouble and affliction, – years not of committing sin, but of receiving chastisement for sin already committed, – years during which the Divine judgment, rather than the Divine mercy and forbearance, came into exercise. The same also appears still further from the kind of treatment they were to receive during the period in question, which has its most prominent representation in the destination to eat defiled bread, and that only in small portions, among the Gentiles. What could more impressively denote a people bearing a load of unpardoned guilt, and groaning under the rebuke and chastisement of Heaven? It implies that Israel's peculiar distinction, as compared with others, was to be virtually abolished, and that as they had degraded themselves spiritually to a level with the heathen, so the Lord would make their condition outwardly to correspond, by subjecting them to a base and dishonorable treatment before the world. This is said with respect more immediately to the house of Israel; but of entirely similar import is the other and less prominent part of the representation, which points more directly to the house of Judah: that they should *"eat bread by weight and with care; and drink water by measure and in desolateness, and consume away in their iniquities."* In respect to both departments alike of the covenant-people, it is manifestly the infliction of a penalty that is meant by the evil suffered, – the just desert of sin.

3. These things being premised and explained, we come now to what may be called the grand difficulty of the scene, – the time during which the iniquity-bearing was to proceed with its humiliating and afflicting treatment: 390 years for the house of Israel, and 40 for the house of Judah. It is clear from the remarks already made, that the period mentioned

can have no respect to the time that may have actually been consumed to the last siege of Jerusalem by the Chaldeans. For it is not a literal siege at all which the vision properly contemplates; and if it could be proved (which it never can with certainty) that the time actually spent by the Chaldeans in besieging Jerusalem precisely corresponded with the number of days during which the prophet was to lie on his two sides, what should thereby be gained? These days have no independent worth in themselves; they merely represented the number of years during which the people were to be dealt with for their sins. Neither can the periods mentioned bear respect to the times during which the houses of Israel and Judah respectively pursued their course of rebellion, provoking, but still not properly experiencing, the execution of Heaven's judgments: as if it might be enough to verify the prophetic delineation, could 390 years be ascertained of open defection for the house of Israel, and 40 for the house of Judah, before the destruction of Jerusalem. It was palpably the reverse, at least in the case of Judah; for the vigorous reformation of Josiah took place within these last forty years, and the history of the period does not present such a continued prosecution of rebellious courses as the supposition would require. But besides this evident failure in respect to the one house, such a line of inquiry leads entirely in the wrong direction for both houses, as it refers to the time of iniquity being committed, not of iniquity being borne, – to the contracting of the guilt, not to the enforcing of the penalty. Calculations, therefore, of the kind just referred to tend only to mislead; and we must look elsewhere altogether for the proper clue to this part of the vision.[7]

The 390 years for the house of Israel and 40 for the house of Judah, it will be observed, make up together 430 years, – a period famous in the earlier history of the covenant-people, being the term of their sojourn in the land of Egypt (Ex. 12:40,41). The thought of a reference to this could scarcely escape the notice of a Hebrew scholar or careful student of the prophet; and accordingly we learn from Jerome, in his notes on the passage, that the Jews of his time understood the prophet to intimate that, "as the children of Israel had been 430 years in Egypt, so in the same number would their final captivity be completed." The commencement of this final captivity, he further tells us, they dated from the second year of Vespasian, when Jerusalem was taken by the Romans, and the temple destroyed; and they were living in the hope that when 430 years from that memorable era had run their course, a career of uninterrupted prosperity was to be entered on by the Jewish people. In this anticipation, however, they showed but too clearly that they had already lost the key to the right interpretation of the mystery, – which requires us, indeed, to connect the whole time specified with the 430 years formerly spent in the house of bondage, yet so as not to overlook the division of this term into the two unequal portions of 390 and 40. For in the 40 years assigned to the house of Judah, there is the recurrence of another remarkable period in the history of ancient Israel, – that of the sojourn in the wilderness. We can the less suppose this latter period to have been overlooked by the prophet, as in the very structure of this part of the vision – in the adoption of the principle a day for a year – there is an evident reference to that passage in Numbers which records the doom of the Israelites to their long sojourn in the desert: *"And your children shall wander in the wilderness for 40 years, and bear your whoredoms, until your carcases be wasted in the wilderness. After the number of the days in which ye searched in the land, forty days, each day for a year, shall ye bear your iniquities, even forty years; and ye shall know my breach of promise"* (Num. 14:32-34).[8]

Keeping in view, then, this twofold allusion in the periods before us to the earlier history of the covenant-people, the solution of the prophet's enigma will not occasion any extreme difficulty. But it will open itself out more easily and naturally to our view, if we first point to one or two prior revelations, which in a simpler form set forth the principle of the representation, and prepared the way for its development in the more hidden and enigmatical shape it assumes in the hands of Ezekiel. The first is the word of Moses, in Deut. 28:68, where, speaking of the evils which were likely to befall the people for their sins, he says: *"And the Lord shall bring thee into Egypt again with ships, by the way whereof I spake to thee, Thou shalt see it no more again: and there ye shall be sold to your enemies for bondmen and bondwomen, and no man shall buy you."* This striking announcement of Moses had already proved a fertile word for Hosea, who says, with manifest reference to it, *"Now will he remember their iniquity, and visit their sins: they shall return to Egypt."* And again: *"They shall not dwell in the Lord's land; but Ephraim shall return to Egypt, and they shall eat unclean things in Assyria"* (Hos. 8:13; 9:3). This last clause shows beyond a doubt that when the prophet speaks of the Israelites being sent back to Egypt, it is not the exact country, but the state of bondage and misery with which, from past experience, that country had become identified in their minds, that he has in view. For as the power that was now in readiness to do the part of the oppressor was the proud Assyrian, so it was in this direction, the opposite one to where it formerly had been, that the new Egypt was to be found; they were to *"eat unclean things in Assyria."* That such was really the meaning of Hosea is rendered still more manifest by another passage (chap. 11:5): *"He shall not return into the land of Egypt, but the Assyrian shall be his king."* He shall return there, and yet not return. What can this mean? what but that the Egypt-state shall once more become his, the prevalence of sin calling for another house of bondage with its oppressions and miseries, though the place where the evil was to be endured should no longer be the same: or should be transferred to Assyria? Nor, indeed, did the original announcement of Moses mean otherwise; for in the same chapter in which he held out the threat of a return to Egypt, he also speaks of their being brought to a nation *"which neither they nor their fathers had known,"* and of their being *"scattered among all people, from one end of the earth to the other."* So that what was indicated by the return to Egypt might be found in any region of the earth where God was pleased to drive them in his anger. And the same also substantially holds of another prophecy of Hosea (chap. 2:14,15), where the Lord speaks of bringing Israel again into the wilderness, of giving them their vineyards from thence, and rendering the valley of Achor to them a door of hope; that is, he was to deal with them much as he had dealt with their forefathers, when he tried and humbled them in the wilderness.

Now, Ezekiel here resumes these earlier announcements of prophecy, and with that minuteness of detail and vividness of coloring which so remarkably characterize his prophetical delineations, throws the ideas they embody into a specific and numerical form. The covenant-people, as a whole (for they must still in some sense be regarded as one), were now again to suffer for their sins the same sort of hardship and discipline which had of old been laid upon their fathers during the period of their servitude in Egypt; the doleful past was again substantially to repeat itself in the future; the dark season of oppression and exile was again to come back with its sad and sorrowful experiences. Yet, with this general similarity, there was also a difference, – a difference first in the respective spiritual conditions of the two branches of the covenant-people, and requiring to be met by a corresponding difference in the dealing they might expect from God. The house of Israel were spiritually in a much worse case than Judah; for from the time of their revolt they threw off their allegiance to God, and separated themselves from his life-giving ordinances of worship; in defiance, also, of God's appointment, they renounced their connection with the house of David, to which, by an everlasting covenant, he had given the power and the dominion. Therefore, by much the greater part, not far from the whole of the period which symbolized the Egypt-state of bondage and exile, is assigned to this house of Israel; for with them, all, in a manner, was out of course – they were on the borders of perdition – they virtually needed to be again redeemed.

But with the house of Judah, notwithstanding their many sins and backslidings, there was redemption, although they had greatly impaired its value, had well-nigh rendered it of no effect, by their continued obstinacy and perverseness. They had the covenant of promise, and the tabernacle of David, with which God had irrevocably associated the good of the world. The elements of life, the true grounds of hope were theirs, yet mixed up with so much that was false and perilous, that severe and painful experiences were needed to fit them for enjoying the good that was within their reach. Therefore, if not precisely the Egypt-state of bondage in all its rigor, yet that which was most nearly akin to it, what was indeed but a continuation of it in a modified form, and in more hopeful circumstances, – the course of trial and discipline in the wilderness: this must now again substantially become the portion for a season of the house of Judah. They needed it much as their fathers of old, who, even after they were redeemed from the house of bondage, still required the forty years of additional troubles and discipline in the wilderness to prepare them for the inheritance and service of God. So these degenerate children of the house of Judah, who could not be moved by all they had experienced of the goodness and severity of God to forsake their evil ways, who had seen their brethren of the house of Israel sent anew into the Egypt-state of worldly oppression and seemingly hopeless exile, and yet would not be warned to abandon the paths of ungodliness and corruption, – for them now there was of necessity coming a relegation of privations and trials like those of the wilderness, through which they must be made to know, after the manner of their forefathers, the determination of God to have a people cleansed from the abominations of sin, before they could be raised to the sunshine of his favor and blessing.

Thus understood, the several parts of the vision receive a perfectly natural and harmonious meaning. Jerusalem in a state of siege represents the covenant-people as a whole straitened and oppressed by the powers of this world, as the instruments of God's just displeasure. And the prophet being appointed to bear, during its continuance, the iniquity of the people, with stinted and foul provisions, points in another form to the same visitation of evil – only with a more particular respect to the cause from which it was to spring, and the penal character it should wear. That the time specified should have been in all 430 years, denoted that the dealing was to form a kind of fresh Egyptian exile and bondage to the elements of the world; but much more so in the case of the one house than in that of the other. The house of Israel having cast off nearly all that was distinctive in the position and privileges of the covenant-people, they had consequently sunk into a condition of greatest danger, one bordering on heathen darkness and perdition – nigh unto cursing. What they might expect was to be bruised and crushed to the dust, as if under the rod of Egypt. But Judah was not so far gone; she had the true priesthood to minister at her altars, and the house of David to rule by Divine right over the heritage of God; so that her subjection to the powers of evil was only to be like the time of chastisement and trial in the wilderness, out of which she might again emerge into a state of peace and blessing. As the prophet also again declared in a later prophecy, *"And I will bring you into the wilderness of the peoples"* (not the wilderness merely, but the wilderness of the peoples, to show that it was to be the same only in character as of old, but not in geographical position), *"and there will I plead with you face to face; like as I pleaded with your fathers in the wilderness of the land of Egypt, so will I plead with you, saith the Lord God"* (chap. 20:35-38). A new time of chastisement, but mingled as of old with mercy; severe and earnest dealing, but for a gracious result, – that they might be refined and purified, so as to become fit for enjoying the good, which as a redeemed people was secured to them for a heritage of blessing. And if any hope remained for the other branch, the house of Israel – if they were ever to escape from their state of Egyptian darkness and bondage, it must be by their going to join their brethren of Judah in the wilderness, and sharing in their peculiar treatment and prospects. On which account it is not the whole of the 430 years of the Egypt-state that is appointed toward the house of Israel in the vision, but this shortened by the 40 years of the wilderness sojourn; to teach them that a way still lay open for their return to life, but only by their having the Egypt-state merged into that of the wilderness; in other words, by ceasing from their rank idolatries and open apostacy from the way of God, and coming to seek, along with Judah, through God's covenant and ordinances, a restoration to righteousness, and peace, and blessing.[9]

4. But why should the prophet, in thus announcing the future dealings of God, have thrown the delineation into so peculiar, so enigmatical a form? Why should he have presented it to the view as a returning again *"of the years of former generations?"*

Not, certainly, on the principle of a bald and meagre literalism, as if he meant us to understand that the clock of Providence was actually to be turned back, and the identical ground trodden over again, the precise measures of time filled up anew of which we read in the earlier history of the chosen race. He who would interpret in such a style the symbolical visions of an Ezekiel, is incapable of entering into the rapt emotions of such a mind, and must necessarily flounder at every step. For here we have to do not only with a lively and fervid spirit, which is ever breathing life, as it were, into the dead, but that spirit in a state of ecstatic elevation, in which the mind naturally served itself of the more remarkable facts and providences in the past; yet only as aids to the utterance of prophetic thought, – appropriate forms wherein to clothe the new things concerning God's kingdom, that were through the Spirit imaging themselves to the prophet's vision. And, indeed, the very imperfection that usually appears in the frame of such historical visions as compared with the past realities, – the partial mingling together here, for example, of the two great consecutive periods of past judgment and trial in the history of the covenant-people, so as to make the second begin before the first had ended, – this very imperfection shows, as it was doubtless intended to do, that an exact reproduction of the past was not in the eye of the prophet; and that the nature of God's contemplated designs, rather than any definite bounds and limits respecting them, was imaged under those ancient periods of tribulation in Egypt and the wilderness.

There were three reasons chiefly why the prophets in general, and this prophet in particular, might be often led to speak of the future under the form and image of the past. In the first place, as the meaning obviously did not lie upon the surface, it called for serious thought and inquiry regarding the purposes of God. A time of general backsliding and corruption is always a time of superficial thinking on spiritual things. And just as our Lord by his parables, that partly veiled while they disclosed the truth of God, so the prophets by their more profound and enigmatical discourses, sought to arouse the careless from their security, to awaken inquiry, and stir the depths of thought and feeling in the soul. It virtually said to them, You are in imminent peril; direct ordinary discourse no longer suits your case; bestir yourselves to look into the depths of things, otherwise the sleep of death shall overtake you.

Then, again, it conveyed in a few words, by means of a brief allusion, what the most lengthened description without it could scarcely have accomplished. It was employing a device which the most powerful and effective orators have sometimes resorted to with the greatest effect, – as in the memorable words of Mirabeau, when, wishing to repel the thought of danger, he flashed out the pregnant interrogation, "Is Hannibal at the gates?" In like manner the prophet here, seeking to impress upon his countrymen the certainty and the awfulness of God's impending judgments on account of sin, carries them back to the past; he brings up to their view Egypt and the wilderness as ready to renew themselves again in their experience. What thoughts of terror and alarm were these fitted to awaken in their minds! Centuries of bondage and oppression! A wearisome sojourn amid drought and desolation! And then this foreshadowing of the future, not only rendered more distinct, but also strengthened as to its credibility, authenticated by those stern realities of the past! It assuredly has been, shall it not be again?

But this suggests another and indeed still deeper reason for such a mode of representation having been adopted. For such renewed exhibitions of the past were among the means specially chosen by God for the purpose of enforcing on men's notice the uniformity of his dealings, and teaching them to regard the providential facts of one age as substantial predictions of what are to be expected in another. It told men then, and it tells us now (only it was more peculiarly adapted to those who lived in ancient times, as the revelations they possessed consisted, much more than now, in the records of history – yet it tells all alike), that the forms alone are transitory in which Divine truth and righteousness manifest themselves, while the principles embodied in these forms are eternal, and can never cease, amid all outward varieties, to be giving forth similar exhibitions of their life and power to those which have already appeared. The eye that can thus look through the shell into the kernel may see the future things of God's administration mirrored in the past, – not, indeed, the exact copy and image of what is to be, yet its essential character and necessary result. Even those very periods of bygone tribulation and chastisement, which the prophet here represents as coming to life again in his day, have they not also a voice for other times? Are they not still reiterating their lessons, and perpetually renewing their existences, in the case of impenitent transgressors, now as well as formerly, in that of drooping exiles in the cities of the Medes, or on the banks of Chebar? One of these periods – the sojourn in the wilderness – the Baptist still finds prolonging itself to the era of his own ministry. His word of stern expostulation and solemn warning makes itself heard as *"the voice of one crying in the wilderness;"* for he sees everywhere around him trackless deserts, where ways of God need to be opened up, – elements of corruption working which require to be purged away by the searching application of Divine righteousness, before the Canaan of God's inheritance can be properly entered and enjoyed. And the lukewarm and fruitless professor still, so long as he cleaves to the ways of iniquity, and refuses to yield a hearty surrender to the will of God, what else is his condition? He is in bondage to the elements of the world, and therefore can have no part in that good inheritance which floweth with milk and honey. The doom of Heaven's condemnation hangs suspended over his head; and if not averted by a timely submission to the righteousness of God, and a cordial entrance into the bond of the covenant, he shall infallibly perish in the wilderness of sin and death.

CHAPTER V. VI.

THE VISION OF THE SHORN HAIR AND ITS FORESHADOWING DESOLATIONS.

[1]And you, son of man, take a sharp knife to yourself, take a barber's razor and cause it to pass on your head and on your beard. Then take scales to weigh, and divide the *hair.*

[2]You shall burn a third part with fire in the middle of the city, when the days of the siege are fulfilled – and you shall take a third part *and* beat around it with a knife – and you shall scatter a third part in the wind, and I will draw out a sword after them.

[3]Also you shall take a few of them in number, and tie them up in your skirts.

[4]Then take of them again, and throw them into the middle of the fire, and burn them in the fire; *for* a fire shall come forth from them into all the house of Israel.

[5]Thus says the Lord GOD; This is Jerusalem. I have set it in the middle of the nations and countries *that are* all around her.

[6]And she has changed My judgments into wickedness[1] more than the nations, and My laws more than the countries that are all around her – for they have refused My judgments and My laws; they have not walked in them.

[7]Therefore thus says the Lord GOD: Because you multiplied more than the nations that are all around you,[2] *and* have not walked in My laws, neither have kept My judgments, nor have done according to the judgments of the nations that are all around you;

[8]therefore thus says the Lord GOD; Behold, I, even I, am against you, and will carry out judgments in the midst of you in the sight of the nations.

[9]And I will do in you that which I have not done, and the like of which I will never do again, because of all your idolatries.

[10]Therefore the fathers shall eat the sons in your midst, and the sons shall eat their fathers. And I will execute judgments in you, and I will scatter the whole remnant of you into all the winds.

[11]Therefore, *as* I live, says the Lord GOD, surely, because you have defiled My sanctuary with all your detestable things, and with all your idolatries, therefore I will also cut *you* off.[3] And My eye shall not spare *you*, nor will I have any pity.

[12]A third part of you shall die with the plague and with famine they shall be destroyed in the midst of you. And a third part shall fall by the sword all around you; and I will scatter a third part into all the winds, and I will draw out a sword after them.

[13]So My anger shall be fulfilled, and I will cause My fury to rest on them, and I will be eased. And they shall know that I the LORD have spoken *it* in My zeal, when I have fulfilled My fury in them.

[14]And I will make you a waste and a curse among the nations that are all around you, in the sight of all who pass by.

[15]So it shall be a curse and a mocking, a

teaching and a wonder to the nations which are all around you, when I shall execute judgments in you in anger and in fury and in angry rebukes. I the LORD have spoken it.

[16]When I shall send on them the evil arrows of famine, which shall be for *their* ruin, which I will send to destroy you; and *when* I increase the famine on you, and break your staff of bread;

[17]and *when* I send on you famine and evil beasts, and when they have taken away your *loved ones*; and when pestilence and blood shall pass through you; and when I bring the sword on you – *you shall know that* I the LORD have spoken.[4]

CHAPTER 6

[1]And the word of the LORD came to me, saying,

[2]Son of man, set your face towards the mountains of Israel and prophesy against them.

[3]And say, Mountains of Israel, hear the word of the Lord GOD. Thus says the Lord GOD to the mountains, and to the hills, to the rivers and to the valleys: Behold, I, *even* I, will bring a sword on you, and I will destroy your high places.

[4]And your altars shall be wasted, and your images shall be broken. And I will cast down your dead before your idols.

[5]And I will lay the dead bodies of the children of Israel before their idols; and I will scatter your bones around your altars.

[6]In *all* the places where you live, cities shall be laid waste, and the high places shall be deserted – so that your altars may be laid waste and ruined, and your idols may be broken and cease, and your images may be cut down, and your works may be wiped out.

[7]And the slain shall fall in the midst of you, and you shall know that I am the LORD.

[8]Yet I will leave a remnant so that you may have *some* who shall escape the sword among the nations, when you shall be scattered through the countries.

[9]And those of you who escape shall remember Me among the nations where they shall be carried captives, because I was broken with their idol-worshiping heart which has departed from Me, and with their eyes which go lusting after their idols. And they shall despise themselves for the evils which they have committed in all their idolatries.

[10]And they shall know that I am the LORD *and that* I have not said in vain that I would do this evil to them.

[11]Thus says the Lord GOD: Strike with your hand and stamp with your foot, and say, Alas for all the evil idolatries of the house of Israel! For they shall fall by the sword, and by the famine, and by the plague.

[12]He who is afar off shall die of the plague; and he who is near shall fall by the sword; and he who remains and is under siege shall die by the famine. So I will fulfil My fury on them.

[13]Then you shall know that I am the LORD, when their dead shall be among their idols all around their altars, on every high hill, in all the tops of the mountains, and under every green tree, and under every thick oak, the place where they offered sweet perfume to all their idols.

[14]So I will stretch out My hand on them and make the land a waste, yes, more wasted than the wilderness toward Dib-lath,[5] in all the places where they live; and they shall know that I am the LORD.

In the vision of the siege and the iniquity-bearing, a heavy burden of troubles, partly in progress, and partly still impending, had been announced by the prophet as determined against the covenant-people. The afflictions of Egypt and the trials of the wilderness were, in a manner, to pass over them again. But even that was not enough; for as their guilt exceeded the guilt of their forefathers, so the chastisement now to be received from the hand of God was to surpass all that had been experienced in the history of the past. This more severe message is unfolded in the next vision, that recorded in these chapters, – in which the prophet is commanded (after having finished the days of the siege, i.e. spent in vision, not in real life, the time during which it was to be prosecuted) to take a sharp sword, and also a razor, to shave off the whole hair of his head and beard, – itself a symbol of violent and humiliating treatment. For the priests were enjoined to nourish their hair, and avoid baldness, in token of their peculiar consecration to the Lord (Lev. 21:5). Therefore, to have this hair, which was at once the natural ornament of the head and the symbol of sacredness, cut off by an instrument of war, plainly bespoke a work of severe and desolating judgment. But the same was still more strikingly indicated by the use to be made of the hair, – of which one-third part was to be burned in the fire,

another smitten about with a sword, and the last scattered to the winds and pursued by a drawn sword. A few of this last division the prophet was instructed to bind in the skirts of his garment, in token of safe preservation, – for even of these, a portion only were to be saved, – while others were to be again cast into the fire and burned, a flame issuing from the conflagration which was to *"come forth against all the house of Israel."*

In these last words, which form the conclusion of ver. 4, the description of the symbol, as sometimes happens in the prophets, passes into the reality, the house of Israel being substituted for the hairs which represented it. This is followed, however, by an express and pointed application of the different parts of the vision to the circumstances and prospects of the covenant-people. Jerusalem, we are again told, was the object of the whole; but Jerusalem, as in the former vision, standing for the people at large, of which it was the proper centre and natural representative. For the prophet presently proceeds to speak of this Jerusalem as a people set in the midst of surrounding heathen; and in the two following chapters, which are merely a continuation and further enlargement of what is contained in chap. 5, we find substituted for the name of Jerusalem, *"the mountains of Israel," "the land of Israel,"* and *"the children of Israel."* There can be no doubt therefore, that the prophecy has the most extensive bearing, and that we are no more in this case, than in that of the siege, to think of the single city of Jerusalem, – though, from being the appointed centre of the whole, both the city itself, and that portion of the people more immediately connected with it, might expect their full share in the judgments announced.

The judgments themselves are distributed into three classes, according to the threefold division of the hair: the sword was to devour one-third of the people; famine and pestilence, another; and that which remained was to be scattered among the nations. The strongest language is employed to describe the calamities indicated under these various heads, and everything is introduced that might have the effect of conveying the most appalling idea of the coming future. Amid the horrors to be produced by famine and pestilence, the dreadful words of Moses, that *"their fathers should eat their sons in the midst of them,"* are reiterated, with the addition of the still darker feature, that *"the sons should also eat their fathers"* (ver. 10). The wild beasts of the field, too, were to embitter by their ravages the calamities produced by the evil arrows of famine; and the sword was to pass through the land in such fury that none should be able to escape, rendering all a desolate wilderness (chap. 6:14), destroying also their idols, and scattering around them the dead carcases of the people, so that the things in which they had foolishly trusted should only in the day of evil prove the witnesses and companions of their ruin (chap. 6:3-6). Finally, in respect to those who should escape the more immediate evils, not only should they be scattered far and wide among the nations, but should there also meet with taunting and reproaches; nay, a sword should be drawn out after them, as had already been predicted by Moses (chap. 5:12; Lev. 26:33); they too were to be for burning (so also Isa. 6:13); for the anger of the Lord was still to pursue after them with *"furious rebukes,"* until he had completely broken their rebellious hearts, and wrought in them a spirit of true contrition for sin and perfect reconciliation of heart with God (chap. 6:9).

Nothing of a definite nature is mentioned as to time and place in this dark outline of revealed judgments. That the doom of evil was by no means to be exhausted by the troubles connected with the Chaldean conquest is manifest; for that portion of the people who were to go into exile and be dispersed among the nations were appointed to other and still future tribulations. There was to be a germinating evil in their destiny, because there would be, as the Lord clearly foresaw, a germinating evil in their character; and so long as this root of bitterness should still be springing up into acts of rebellion against God, it should never cease to be recoiling upon them with strokes of chastisement in providence. In this there was nothing absolutely singular as to the principle on which the Divine government proceeded; only, as God had connected himself with Israel in a manner he never had done with any nation before, nor would with any other again, there should be a certain singularity in their case as to the actual experience of suffering on account of sin. In their history as a people, the footsteps of God's righteous judgment would leave impressions behind it of unexampled severity, according to the word here uttered: *"And I will do in thee that which I have not done, and whereunto I will not do any more the like, because of all thine abominations."*

But there is no caprice in the dealings of God. When he afflicts with the rod of chastisement and rebuke, it is only because the righteous principles of his government demand it; and the fearful burden of evils here suspended over the heads of ancient Israel sounds also a warning note of judgment to all nations and all ages of the world. There have been, it is true, such changes introduced into the outward administration of God's kingdom as render it, for the most part, impossible to trace the execution of his judgments with the same ease and certainty with which we can mark their course in the history of ancient Israel. But it is not the less certain that the principles which produced such marked effects then are in active operation still; and whenever Israel's guilt is incurred anew, there will infallibly be experienced a renewal of Israel's doom. For the gospel has brought no suspension of God's justice any more than of his mercy. It contains the most glorious exhibition of his grace to sinners, but along with this it contains the most affecting and awful display of his righteous indignation against sin. Both features, indeed, of the Divine character have reached under the gospel a higher stage of development; and so far has the introduction of the new covenant been from laying an arrest on the severity of God, that not till it appeared did the Jews themselves experience the heaviest portion of the evils threatened against them; then only did the wrath begin to fall upon them to the uttermost, and the days of darkness and tribulation come, such as had not hitherto been known. This vision of woe, therefore, extends alike over both dispensations, and speaks to men of every age and clime; it is a mirror in which the justice of God reflects itself for the world at large, with no further alteration for gospel times than such as is implied in the words of the apostle: *"Of how much sorer punishment, suppose ye, shall he be thought worthy who hath trodden under foot the Son of God, and hath counted the blood of the covenant, wherewith he was sanctified, an unholy thing, and hath done despite unto the Spirit of grace?"*

Such being the case in respect to the execution of Divine judgment, it becomes the more necessary that we should mark distinctly the nature of the guilt on account of which the judgment was to be executed. We are the rather called to be particular in marking this, as the prophet so emphatically and repeatedly presses the circumstance, that the treatment to be given to Israel in the way of punishment was to be a dealing with them after their own ways, or a meting back to them of their own measure. The passages which more particularly refer to this portion of the subject are the following: – *"This is Jerusalem: in the midst of the nations I set her, and she rebelled against my judgments, for wickedness about the heathen and against my statutes more than the countries that are round about her," etc.* And again: *"Surely because thou hast defiled my sanctuary with all thy detestable things, and with all thine abominations, therefore will I also withdraw, neither shall mine eye spare, neither will I have any pity."*

The stress laid here upon defilement of the sanctuary is intended to single out this profanation as the very climax of the prevailing iniquity, and the sign that it had now reached the last stage of Heaven-daring wickedness. But the grand charge which the prophet evidently means to bring against them, was the utter discordance which appeared between their conduct and their calling; they had failed to maintain the position and fulfil the ends for which more especially they had been settled in Canaan, and had acted so as to cause the name of God to be blasphemed in them rather than honored. Let us glance for a little both at what the calling itself was, and at this unfaithfulness in regard to it, that we may thus more clearly perceive the reasonableness of this severity which the Lord exercised toward them, and discern the lessons of instruction which the whole furnishes to future times.

1. In respect to the peculiar calling of the Israelites, the prophet represents than as having been placed by God, with the charge of his statutes and judgments, in the midst of the nations. This is not, certainly, to be understood in the sense adopted by some of the earlier commentators, that Jerusalem stood precisely in the centre of the natural world, and on this account was chosen to be the peculiar dwelling-place of God. But neither is it

to be understood, with many later ones, as simply meaning that Israel in Canaan alone possessed as a nation the true knowledge of God, and that the surrounding nations were all plunged in heathenish darkness and corruption. It rather indicates that the land of Canaan did form a kind of centre for the nations of heathen antiquity, and was designed on that account to be a position of power and influence in respect to the knowledge and worship of God. Viewing the world as it existed at the time of Israel's settlement in Canaan, and for a thousand years afterwards, we believe it would be impossible to fix upon a single region so admirably fitted at once to serve as a suitable dwelling-place for such a people, and to enable them, as from a central and well-chosen vantage-ground, to act with success upon the heathenism of the world. It lay nearly midway between the oldest and most influential states of antiquity, – on the one side Egypt and Ethiopia, with their dependencies; on the other, Babylon, Nineveh, India, – the seats of art and civilisation when the rest of the world still lay in comparative barbarism, and to which the much later, but ultimately more powerful, commonwealths of Europe were primarily indebted for their skill, and even their philosophy and religion. Then, in the immediate neighborhood were the Phoenician mariners, whose sails frequented every harbor of the civilised world; and all around the Ishmaelite tribes, the great inland traders, who kept up a perpetual and most extensive intercourse among the different communities of southern Asia and northern Africa. So that, isolated as the land of Canaan in some respects was, it was the very reverse of being withdrawn to a corner; and no region in the whole ancient world could have been selected that afforded more obvious and varied facilities for exerting a beneficial and commanding influence on the mind of ancient heathendom.

That the children of Israel, by being appointed to occupy such a central position, were also called to take advantage of it for making known the character and extending the worship of Jehovah, was to be understood of itself from their being the chosen depositories of God's will, and the peculiar seed *"in whom all the families of the earth were to be blessed."* The distinguished marks of Divine favor they were to enjoy, and the political ascendancy that was to be granted them over the nations of the earth, were made expressly to depend upon their remaining stedfast to the covenant of God, and being faithful witnesses of its truth and holiness. *"This,"* said Moses, in Deut. 4:6, when urging them to fidelity in keeping God's statutes and judgments, *"this is your wisdom and your understanding in the sight of the nations, which shall hear all these statutes, and say, Surely this great nation is a wise and understanding people."* And again, in chap. 28, he holds out to them the elevated prospect, if they would only keep the commandments of God and walk in his ways, of being *"the head only and not the tail, above only and not beneath,"* and of causing *"all the people of the earth to see that Jehovah had established them to be an holy people to himself, and called them by his name."* How thoroughly David and other pious men in the better periods of Israel's history understood the high calling they thus held of God, is evident from many passages in the Psalms. For example, in Ps. 9: *"Thou hast rebuked the heathen, thou hast destroyed the wicked . . . Sing praises to the Lord, which dwelleth in Zion, declare among the people his doings."* In Ps. 59, perhaps one of the earliest of David's compositions: *"O Lord God of hosts, the God of Israel, awake to visit all the heathen . . . Consume them (mine enemies) in wrath; consume them that they may not be; and let them know that God ruleth in Jacob unto the ends of the earth."* So again in Ps. 68, probably one of his latest, *"Because of thy temple in Jerusalem shall kings bring presents unto thee. Princes shall come out of Egypt; Ethiopia shall soon stretch out her hands to God. Sing unto God, ye kingdoms of the earth,"* etc. And in the Psalm immediately before this, the inspired writer, in the name of the true Israel, and in the most enlarged spirit of philanthropy, entreats God to make his face to shine upon them, that so his way might be known upon earth, and his saving health among all nations. He desired an increased manifestation of Divine goodness, not so much for its own sake, as for the ulterior good of which it might be productive: *"God shall bless us, and all ends of the earth shall fear him."* Undoubtedly this wide-spreading effect may, in such cases, have been contemplated as very much a result that was to grow spontaneously out of the good that should appear in Israel, the mere exhibition of God's rich blessing upon them being expected to prompt and allure the nations of the earth to seek that the same might be realized also in their own experience. But still the personal good for Israel was viewed as strictly subservient to the more general good for the nations; and such desires and expectations toward the world at large could not possibly be cherished without the obligation being recognised and felt to employ every available means for extending the true knowledge of God in the world. So utterly false is the idea – the spurious brood of an unscriptural and exclusive Pharisaism – that the Israelites were placed in Canaan for their exclusive benefit, and in a sort of unfriendly antagonism to the other nations of the earth! On the contrary, they were placed there as on a high vantage-ground, for acting the part of the world's benefactors; placed aloft as God's lights in the earth, that through them the nations around might learn his will, and come to obtain an interest in his blessing.

This calling of Israel in respect to the nations of the world is precisely that which now rests upon the Christian Church. There is no difference between the two in nature, though, in regard to the manner of its execution, the change that has meanwhile entered into the character of God's kingdom, and the general aspect of the world's condition, naturally gives rise to corresponding differences. It was necessary that the impulse should be communicated more nationally before, more individually now. And as the religion of God's ancient people was predominantly of a symbolical, outward, and national character, so, in the manner of its propagation in the world, fleshly weapons, outward prosperity, the visible sunshine of Heaven's favor and loving-kindness, necessarily played an essential and prominent part. But now, on the other hand, when the discoveries of the gospel have laid open Divine realities themselves to the eye of faith, and thereby given a more spiritual and elevated tone to the true religion, there is greatly less need of those external appliances. The grand element of power now lies in the truth itself; and by means of this, exhibited in the lives of God's people, and plied on every hand by their instrumentality, is the triumph of righteousness chiefly to be sped forward in the world. With such differences, however, as to the method of working, the obligation itself remains substantially the same. The Christian Church is now, just as Israel was of old, set in the midst of the nations, and charged in all her members to give faithful testimony to the truth, by which she has herself been blessed, that others may come and partake of the blessing. What a noble function! and, as the result of its faithful discharge, what an unspeakable good has to be realized! Nothing less than the possession of the world under Christ as the field which the Lord doth bless! The right to this possession is Christ's, who has received from the Father the heritage of the earth; and he commits it to his Church as the instrument of his working, to make good the title. With her people, therefore, lies the weighty responsibility of the world's regeneration; they are individually and collectively the light of the world; they are the salt of the earth. Happy if they are so in reality! but if not, heavy above all others must be their condemnation.

2. In the case of ancient Israel, it was their misfortune to incur the condemnation. They failed to take advantage of their favorable position for extending the knowledge and glory of God among the nations; but, imbibing the corruptions they should have striven to abolish, they dealt more treacherously toward the true religion than the surrounding nations did toward their false ones. That, in charging them with an excess over these very nations, the prophet meant that they went absolutely beyond them in the practice of abominable idolatries, we can scarcely suppose. But in sinning against such privileges and obligations, their guilt was unquestionably much greater; and in going so readily over to the corruptions of heathenism, they so far did worse than others, that they betrayed a looser attachment to their religion than those heathens did to their respective idolatries. *"They have not walked in my statutes, neither have kept my judgments, neither have done according to the judgments of the nations that are round about you;"* neither adhered to the one, nor wholly espoused the other, – therefore inferior in point of religious principle to those wretched idolaters who cling with inveterate fondness to their several superstitions. Jeremiah had already called attention to this singular fact, and mourned over the amazing infatuation it displayed: *"Pass over the isles of Chittim and see and send unto Kedar, and consider diligently, and see if there be such a thing: Hath a*

nation changed her gods, which yet are no gods? but my people have changed their glory for that which doth not profit" (chap. 2:10,11).

There must have been some ground in the nature of things for this apparent anomaly, – some very powerful and constraining impulse which so incessantly led Israel, in the face of all remonstrances and warnings in providence, to prefer and fall in with the Gentile superstitions – where shall we seek it? Undoubtedly the main and fundamental reason is to be sought in their own prevailing carnality and corruption of heart, which the mere nature-religions of heathenism did nothing to check, but rather fostered and sanctified Outward and carnal as the Jewish worship was in its character compared with the Christian, it still was immeasurably less so than the idolatrous religions of Paganism, in which not only every god had its representation in a visible idol, but the gods themselves were precisely such as the natural heart desires, – gods *"whose attributes were pride, revenge, and lust."* In Judaism, on the contrary, amid all that was outward and showy in its observances, there still was in the bosom of every service a spiritual and holy God as the sole object of veneration, and a conformity to his righteous will as the one great end to be aimed at. Therefore, whenever the people lost the true spirit of piety, they of necessity lost, at the same time, their relish for the pure service of Jehovah; they became at once unfit for its duties and ashamed of its sanctity, and gladly accepted from the hands of their neighbors what might render their religion more palatable to their ungodly dispositions.

Shall we wonder at such behavior in Israel? We may, indeed, wonder at it when we think of their singular advantages, and the astonishing things which God had done in their behalf; but the same perversity which ran such a career of wickedness in them, lives still in the Christian Church; nor is there a country in Christendom where Israel's folly is not on a large scale perpetually repeating itself. What are the corruptions of Popery but so many accomodations of the pure spirit of the gospel to the grovelling tendencies of the flesh? And even in Protestant lands, with by far the greater proportion of worshippers, the religion actually embraced is not that of the Bible, but this moulded and shaped into a form more agreeable to the natural heart. It borrows from the thoughts and maxims of the world fully as much as it derives from the gospel; and gathers up from the two such a compound of flesh and spirit, purity and corruption, as the natural man finds little occasion either to quarrel with or to be ashamed of. Hence the spiritual languor, the worldly-mindedness, the numberless forms of vanity and pollution, which are so commonly seen going hand in hand with a religious profession, and which have at once robbed the Church of her power to conquer and bless the world, and miserably curtailed her own inheritance of good. The spiritual adversary who sought in vain to strangle Christianity in her birth has too well succeeded in impeding her progress, by corrupting the purity of her worship, and replenishing her with the means of worldly honor and enjoyment. Nor can she ever fulfil aright her destiny, or be safe from the rod of chastisement and rebuke, till the foul admixtures she has contracted from the world are purged out, and, in the simple spirit of an implicit reliance on the Divine word, and an unswerving adherence to the cause of truth and righteousness, she goes forth to resist and put down whatever is opposed to the will of Heaven.

It may be proper, before closing our remarks on the vision contained in these three chapters, to refer to a style of interpretation which is unhappily too current in the present times, and which is equally remarkable for the groundlessness and the confidence of its assertions. "Look," says a popular writer, in a discourse on Ezekiel 9:4-6, "into the fifth chapter of Ezekiel, ver. 12, and you will see a passage which was not fulfilled in the days of Zedekiah. There it was predicted that a third part of the nation should die by pestilence, that a third part should die by the sword, and that another third part of the nation should be scattered unto all the winds, and a sword sent after them. In the days of Zedekiah no such thing occurred. There was nothing of famine or pestilence; there was no destruction of a third part with the sword; and those that were carried captive, instead of being scattered unto all the winds, were taken into one country, and were kept in one country all the time of their captivity."

It is not saying too much of this passage ,that it contains as many errors as sentences. For, (1) in regard to the threefold destination of the people to the pestilence, the sword, and dispersion, it might be as correct to affirm that no such thing was spoken by Ezekiel of the days of Zedekiah, as that no such thing occurred then. The prophet, as we have already shown, is not here speaking of Jerusalem alone, or even of the people of Judah alone, but of the covenant-people at large, as inhabitants of the land of Canaan; so that we are to take in not simply what happened in the days of Zedekiah, but what all Israel had been suffering, or were still to suffer, by means of the calamities which the Lord sent against them for their sins. (2) It is a rash and utterly groundless affirmation to say, even of those who lived in the days of Zedekiah, that a third part were not destroyed by pestilence, and a third by the sword; for that vast numbers perished by both causes is manifest from the fact of the history – and where did the author learn that it was less than two-thirds? As for the remaining third being all carried captive to one country, and kept there, we have simply to ask whence, then, came the Jews mentioned in the book of Esther, who were scattered through all the provinces of the Persian empire? Or how should the decree of Cyrus, authorizing their return to Palestine, have been addressed to the seed of Israel throughout the whole kingdom, to *"every man in the place where he sojourneth"*? Or why should a special curse have been pronounced over Edom, because they sought to cut off, and to some extent did cut off, the miserable fugitives from the land of Israel, who, in the day of their calamity, fled from the face of the adversary? (Obad. 5:14) In short, it is a mere assertion, and utterly opposed to the well-known facts of history, to affirm that all who survived the Chaldean desolation were carried to the region of Babylonia and kept there. The larger portion were so, but by no means the whole; there was a scattering to the winds of heaven.[6] (3) It is quite untenable, and is in fact betraying the truthfulness of the prophet into the enemies' hands, to assert, regarding such a vision as this, that the infliction of those calamities, which it marks as presently to be expected, was to be postponed for many centuries, and not to take place till an entirely different state of things had entered. For, in the prophecy, the calamities announced are not merely predicted as events, but threatened as Divine judgments for the sins of that particular period; and if they were not inflicted in connection with that period, they were plainly not inflicted at all; the penalties threatened against the prevailing sinfulness were not enforced; the prophecy, as it stands here, lies unfulfilled. Besides, when the prophet so distinctly indicates a certain series of judgments, and so solemnly and repeatedly declares that the time was close at hand for their taking effect, – if, after all, they were not to take effect till seven hundred years had elapsed, and the condition of things in Israel had become so essentially changed that the special characteristics here given – the copying after the ways of the heathen, and the erection of many altars – were precisely those most carefully avoided at that later period, – then it is manifest we must have different rules for interpreting such portions of Scripture from those we would adopt in regard to any other book. The process of interpretation, in short, becomes a matter ot caprice, and the manner of fulfilment is simply what the interpreter himself thinks fit, not what the writing itself seems to indicate. If the prophetical scriptures really needed such arbitrariness of interpretation to preserve their conformity with the course of things, sceptics would require nothing more to justify their unbelief. But in the present case it is merely the interpreter, and not the prophetic word, that is at fault. Amid the desolations of long sieges and bloody conquest, produced by the invading hosts of the Assyrians and Chaldeans, beyond all doubt one large portion of the people perished by famine and pestilence, and another large portion by the sword; and that the remaining portion was scattered into many countries, and even amid these was subjected to ever-recurring troubles and calamities, is as certain as anything of which a credible record has been handed down to us from ancient times. To deny this is at once to throw discredit on the plainest utterances of prophecy, and bring into doubt the most unquestionable facts of history.

CHAPTER VII.

LAMENTATION OVER THE GUILT AND FALL OF ISRAEL.

This chapter does not contain anything properly new. It simply describes the mournful feelings and reflections which the preceding revelations of guilt and judgment had awakened in the mind of the prophet; and it hence naturally takes the form of a poetical dirge or lamentation over the unhappy case of his infatuated country. Some particular words and allusions require explanation; but otherwise the sentiments uttered are so simple and appropriate, that no comment is needed to exhibit their import.

[1]And the word of the LORD came to me, saying,

[2]Also, son of man, thus says the Lord GOD to the land of Israel: An end! The end has come on the four corners of the land.

[3]Now the end has come on you, and I will send My anger on you and will judge you according to your ways and will lay on you all your idolatries.

[4]And My eye shall not spare you, nor will I have pity. But I will repay your ways on you, and your idols shall be in your midst; and you shall know that I am the LORD

[5]Thus says the Lord GOD: An evil:[2] Behold, an only evil has come!

[6]An end has come, the end has come. It awakes against you; behold, it has come.

[7]The morning has come to you,[2] O dwellers in the land. The time has come, the day of trouble is near, and not the echo of the hills.[3]

[8]Now I will soon pour out My fury on you, and fulfil My anger on you. And I will judge you according to your ways and will repay you for all your idolatries.

[9]And My eye shall not spare, nor will I have pity; I will repay you according to your ways and your idols that are in the midst of you. And you shall know that I am the LORD who strikes.

[10]Behold the day! Behold, it has come; the morning has gone forth; the rod has blossomed; pride has budded.

[11]Violence has risen up into a rod of wickedness. None of them *shall remain*, none of their multitude, not of any of theirs – nor *shall there be* wailing for them.[4]

[12]The time has come; the day draws near. Let not the buyer rejoice, or the seller mourn; for wrath is on all the multitude of it.

[13]The seller shall not return to that which is sold, although they were still alive; for the vision is about the whole multitude of it, *which* shall not return. No one shall strengthen himself in the iniquity of his life.

[14]They have blown the trumpet,[5] even to make all ready; but none goes to the battle, for My wrath is upon all the multitude of it.

[15]The sword is outside, and the plague and the famine inside. He who is in the field shall die with the sword; and he who is in the city shall be devoured by famine and plague.

[16]But those who escape from them shall slip away and shall be like doves of the valleys on the mountains, all of them mourning, each one for his iniquity.

[17]All hands shall be feeble and all knees shall be weak as water.

[18]They also shall wear sackcloth, and horror shall cover them; and shame shall be on all faces, and baldness on all their heads.

[19]They shall throw their silver in the streets, and their gold shall be removed. Their silver and their gold shall not be able to deliver them in the day of the wrath of the LORD. They shall not satisfy their souls nor fill their bowels, because it is the stumblingblock of their iniquity.

[20]As for the beauty of His ornament, He set it in majesty. But they made the images of their idols and of their hateful things in it; therefore I have set it far from them.

[21]And I will give it into the hands of the strangers for a prize, and to the wicked of the earth for a spoil; and they shall defile it.

[22]I will also turn My face from them, and they shall defile My secret *place*; for the robbers shall enter into it and defile it.

[23]Make a chain; for the land if full of bloody crimes, and the city is full of violence.

[24]Therefore I will bring the worst of the heathen, and they shall possess their houses. I will also make the pomp of the strong to cease; and their holy places shall be defiled.[7]

[25]Ruin comes; and they shall seek peace, and *there shall be* none.

[26]Evil shall come on evil, and rumor shall be on rumor. Then they shall seek a vision from the prophet; but the law shall perish from the priest, and wisdom from the elders.

[27]The king shall mourn, and the prince shall be clothed with misery, and the hands of the people of the land shall be troubled. I will do to them according to their way, and according to their deserts I will judge them; and they shall know that I am the LORD.

CHAPTER VIII.

THE IMAGE OF JEALOUSY AND OTHER ABOMINATIONS AT JERUSALEM.

[1]And in the sixth year, in the sixth *month*, in the fifth *day* of the month, as I sat in my house and the elders of Judah sat before me, the hand of the Lord GOD fell on me there.

[2]Then I looked, and behold, there was a likeness which looked like *a fire* – from his loins and downward *he* looked like fire; and from his loins and upward *he* had a look of brightness, like the color of copper.

[3]And he put forth the form of a hand, and took me by a lock of my head. And the Spirit lifted me up between the earth and the heavens, and brought me in the visions of God to Jerusalem, to the door of the inner gate that looks toward the north. There was the seat of the image of jealousy, which provokes to jealousy.

[4]And, behold, the glory of the God of Israel was there, according to the vision that I saw in the plain.

[5]Then He said to me, Son of man, lift up your eyes now the way toward the north. So I lifted up my eyes the way toward the north, and behold, northward at the gate of the altar, this image of jealousy was in the entrance.

[6]Then He said to me, Son of man, do you see what they do, *these* hateful things which the house of Israel is doing here, that I should go far off from My sanctuary? But turn once again; you shall see more disgusting things.

[7]And He brought me to the door of the court; and when I looked, behold, a hole in the wall.

[8]Then He said to me, Son of man, dig in the wall now. And when I had dug in the wall, behold, a door.

[9]And he said to me, Go in and see the wicked idolatries that they do here.

[10]So I went in and saw. And behold, every kind of creeping thing, and hateful beast, and all the idols of the house of Israel, were portrayed on the wall all around.

[11]And there stood before them seventy men of the elders of the house of Israel, and in the midst of them stood Ja-az-a-ni-ah the son of Sha-phan, with each man having a censor in his hand. And a thick cloud of incense went up.

[12]Then He said to me, Son of man, have you seen what the elders of the house of Israel do in the dark, each man in his image room? For they say, The LORD does not see us; the LORD has forsaken the earth.

[13]He also said to me, Turn yet again, *and* you shall see greater evils which they do.

[14]Then He brought me to the door of the gate of the LORD's house, which was toward the north. And behold, there sat women weeping for Tam-muz.

[15]Then he said to me, Have you seen this, O son of man? Turn yet again, *and* you shall see greater evils than these.

[16]And He brought me into the inner court of the LORD's house, and behold, at the door of the temple of the LORD, between the porch and the altar, were about twenty-five men with their backs toward the temple of the LORD and their faces toward the east – and they worshiped the sun toward the east.

[17]Then He said to me, Have you seen *this*, O son of man? Is it a light thing to the house of Judah that they do the hateful things which they do here? For they have filled the land with violence and have turned to provoke Me to anger. And lo, they put the branch to their nose.

[18]Therefore I will also deal in fury; My eye shall not spare. I will not have pity. And though they cry in My ears with a loud voice, I will not hear them.

A new stage of the prophetic agency of Ezekiel, and of his spirit-stirring communications to the captives on the banks of the Chebar, opens with this chapter, and proceeds onwards in an uninterrupted strain to the end of the eleventh. These four chapters form one discourse (as the preceding portion had also done, from chap. 3:12 to the close of chap. 7), and a discourse somewhat more specific in its character and bearing than the revelations previously made. The vision of the siege and of the iniquity-bearing, described in chap. 4, had respect to the covenant-people generally – including, indeed, the inhabitants of Jerusalem, yet so as also to comprehend the scattered portions of Judah and Israel. This, too, was the case with the vision of the shaven hair, and its foreshadowing desolations, contained in chap. 5-7. The burden there delivered was an utterance of Divine judgments against the whole covenant-people on account of sin; because, having been planted as the witnesses and heralds of God's truth in the midst of

the nations, they had already fallen before the heathen corruptions, which it was their special calling to have resisted to the uttermost. Therefore in just retribution for the betrayal of God's cause into the enemies' hands, the heathen were become his instruments of vengeance, to inflict on the whole house of Israel the various forms of a severe and prolonged chastisement. But now, in the section of prophecy which commences with chap. 8, the people of Jerusalem, and the small remnant of Judah who, under Zedekiah, continued to hold a flickering existence in Canaan, form the immediate object of the prophet's message, not only as apart from the Babylonish exiles, but even as standing in a kind of contrast to them. And it is of essential moment to a proper understanding of the purport of the vision, that we rightly apprehend and estimate the circumstances which led to so partial and specific a direction in the message now delivered.

In the sixth year of the captivity, the sixth month, and the fifth day of the month, the prophet was sitting, we are told, in his own house; and the elders of Judah, namely, of that portion of Judah who sojourned with him on the banks of the Chebar, sat before him. No express reason is assigned for their sitting there, though we can have little doubt that it was for the purpose of receiving from his lips some communication of the Divine will. The Lord also was present, to impart suitable aid to his servant; but lo! instead of prompting him to address his speech directly to those before him, the Spirit carried him away in the visions of God to the temple at Jerusalem, that he might obtain an insight into the state of corruption prevalent there, and might learn the mind of God respecting it. The message delivered to the elders who sat around him consisted mainly in the report of what he witnessed and heard in those Divine visions; and it falls into two parts, – the account given of the reigning abominations contained in chap. 8, and the dealings of judgment and of mercy which were to be pursued toward the respective parties in Israel, as unfolded in the three succeeding chapters.

Now what should have led the prophet to throw his message into such a form as this, but that some connection existed between the exiles of Chebar and the remnant in Jerusalem, which made the report of what more immediately belonged to the one a seasonable and instructive communication to the other? We formerly had occasion to notice, that among the exiled portion there were some who still looked hopefully toward Jerusalem, and, so far from believing things there to be on the verge of ruin, were persuaded that ere long the way would be opened up for their own return thither in peace and comfort. Among those also who were still resident in Jerusalem and its neighborhood, it appears there were some who not only looked upon themselves as secure in their position, but eyed their exiled brethren with a kind of haughty indifference or contempt, as if these had no longer anything in common with them! That it was this latter state of feeling which more immediately led to the present interview between the elders and the prophet, and the revelations which ensued, we may not doubtfully gather from the allusion made to it near the close of the vision (chap. 11:15), where the inhabitants of Jerusalem are represented as saying to the exiles, *"Get you far* (rather, Be ye far, continue in your state of separation and distance) *from the Lord; unto us is this land given in possession."* As much as to say, "It may well befit you to be entertaining thoughts of evil and dark forebodings of the future; your outcast condition cuts you off from any proper interest in God, and renders such sad anticipations natural and just. Abide as you are; but as for us, we dwell near to God, and by his good hand upon us have the city and land of our fathers in sure possession." It is not improbable that this taunting declaration of their own fancied superiority and assured feeling of safety had been called forth by the tidings reaching Jerusalem of the awful judgments announced in Ezekiel's earlier predictions; as, on the other hand, the express and pointed reference made here to that declaration leaves little room to doubt that the rumor of it had been heard on the banks of the Chebar, and had led the elders of Judah to present themselves in the house of the prophet. For in their unhappy circumstances, the knowledge of such thoughts and feelings being entertained toward them at Jerusalem must have exercised a most depressing influence on their minds, and could not but seem an adequate occasion for their endeavouring to ascertain the mind of the Lord as between them and their countrymen in Judea.

Raised, therefore, by the Spirit into a state of Divine ecstasy, the prophet forthwith beheld in vision the Lord of glory, though in human form, yet glowing with celestial fire from his loins downwards, and radiant with the splendor of light in the upper parts; that is, as well explained by Zullig at Rev. 8:2, *"below, toward the earth, the person on the throne appeared in the glowing fire of his function as judge and avenger, above, in the pure splendor of his calm, untroubled, heavenly majesty."* In the presence of this glorious majesty the prophet was suddenly transported, by a Divine hand, to the north entrance into the temple at Jerusalem. There, at the altar-gate, as it is called in ver. 5 (because the gate that opened into the inner court, and led straight to the altar of burnt-offering), he sees in vision the glory of the Lord as it had formerly appeared to him on the plain of Chebar, viz. in the parts standing nearest to the earth, the Divine likeness with the appearance of fire, indicating that he came in the fervent heat of his indignation; while still the upper parts of the form presented the aspect of the holy majesty of heaven in its pure and unsullied brightness. The vision appeared a little to the north of *"the seat of the image of jealousy which provoketh to jealousy."* What precisely is to be understood by this image of jealousy has long been matter of dispute, or rather of various conjecture, among commentators. The more common opinion has been that Baal was meant, while some have understood it rather of the Syrian Venus, called the Aschera or Astarte (the word used in the original for that Queen of Heaven in 2 Kings 21:3,7, 23:4,7, where, unhappily, the translation grove has been adopted in our version). Havernick, however, has recently advanced the opinion that it was an image in wax or clay of the Tammuz or Adonis mentioned afterwards, and called *"the image that provoketh to jealousy,"* with special reference to the youthful and attractive beauty of the object it represented; and that all the scenes of idolatrous worship described in the chapter were but the several and successive portions of the grand festival held shortly before at Jerusalem in honor of Adonis. Some show of support for this idea is derived from the view presented of the Adonis-festival by recent writers on the mythology of the ancients; but it is still entirely fanciful, and on many accounts to be rejected. For, first, it is against all probability to suppose, that when disclosing the abominations which were ready to bring down the consuming judgments of Heaven upon the land, those only should have been delineated which were connected with a single occasion, and that the festival of a comparatively inferior object of idol-worship. Then the idolatrous scenes described one after another have manifestly the appearance of separate and cumulative proofs of the people's appetite for heathenish pollutions, rather than the united and consecutive parts of some one religious festival. And still further, as the scenes in question were those submitted to the eye of the prophet in the visions of God, what we are naturally led to expect in them is, not a plain matter-of-fact description of things literally enacted at any set time in the temple, but rather a combined and concentrated view of the prevailing idolatries gathered from every side, and portrayed, as in one dark and revolting picture, within the temple at Jerusalem. That temple was the image as well as the centre of the whole kingdom. As the heart of the nation had its seat there, so there also, in the mongrel and polluted character of the worship celebrated, the guilt of the people found its representation; and hence, when the object was to give a clear and palpable exhibition of the crying abominations that existed in the land, the scene was most fitly laid in the temple, and assumed the form of things seen and transacted in its courts. But we are no more to regard the things themselves in the precise form and combination here given to them, as all actually meeting together at any particular moment in the temple-worship, and simply transcribed by the prophet from the occurrences of real life, than to regard the instructions that immediately follow – to set a mark for preservation on the foreheads of some, and to destroy the rest with weapons of slaughter – as actually put in force at the time and in the manner there described. In both cases alike the description is of what took place in the visions of God; therefore not the mere outward and naked literalities which the bodily eye might have perceived, and the pen of history noted down, but a representation so contrived and arranged as might serve most fitly to express to the apprehension of the mind, and render in a manner palpable to the sight, the realities of Israel's guilt and judgment.[5]

While, then, we see ample reason for holding that by *"the image of jealousy"* the statue of Adonis is not to be understood, we are further disposed to think, from the ideal character of the representation, that it should not be limited to any specific deity. The prophet, we are persuaded, purposely made the expression general, as it was not so much the particular idol placed on a level with Jehovah as the idol-worship itself which he meant to designate and condemn. So sunk and rooted were the people in the idolatrous feeling, that where Jehovah had an altar, there some idol-form must have its *"seat,"* – a fixed residence, to denote that it was no occasional thing its being found there, but a regular and stated arrangement. And whatever it might for the time be, – whether it was Baal, or Moloch, or Astarte that the image represented, – as it was necessarily set up for a rival of Jehovah, to share with him in the worship to which he alone was entitled, it might justly be denominated *"the image of jealousy,"* as it provoked that jealousy, and called for that visitation of wrath, against which the Lord had so solemnly forewarned his people in the second commandment. That *"he should go far off from his sanctuary"* was so certainly the result of such an abomination, that in ver. 6 it is represented as its very aim; and the moment of his departure must also be the signal for the execution of vengeance.

That we do right in thus taking into account the ideal element in the representation appears yet more obviously from the next scene, of which no clear and satisfactory explanation can be rendered but by ascribing to some of the leading traits a non-literal or symbolical meaning. Being commanded to turn again, that he might see other great abominations, the prophet presently finds himself at the door of the court, where he espies a hole in the wall, and after digging as he was enjoined, he discovers a door (a door, of course, not patent or accessible from without, as it only became visible when the wall was cleared away); and entering within, he saw *"every form of creeping things, and abominable beasts, and all the idols of the house of Israel portrayed upon the wall round about. And there stood before him seventy men of the ancients (elders) of the house of Israel; and in the midst of them stood Jaazaniah, the son of Shaphan, with every man his censer in his hand; and the prayer of a cloud of incense went up."* Now, that the prophet could not mean this to be understood of any actual exhibition that was wont to be made in the temple is evident, first, from the entire seclusion of the chamber in which the idolatrous scene is laid, – a recess so hidden from public view, and so closely walled up, that an entrance could only be made good by a process of digging; an inexplicable mystery if understood as a chamber actually frequented by temple-worshippers, but plain enough if regarded as a symbol of the conscious guilt and cunning secrecy with which the foul rites in question were sought after among the covenant-people. It is also evident from the kind and variety of the objects said to have been portrayed against the wall, – *"every form of creeping things, and all the idols of the house of Israel,"* – necessarily a huge hyperbole if taken literally, but a perfectly intelligible trait if regarded as an ideal representation of the prevailing tendency to idolize after the manner of Egypt, where the portraying of such objects was so usual, and at the same time so peculiar to that country among the nations of antiquity, that it might with the utmost propriety be given as the characteristic mark of an Egyptizing spirit in religion. It is evident, once again, from the persons who are described as occupying the chamber, and filling it with the incense of devotion – the seventy elders. A reference is plainly had here to those passages in the Pentateuch where the same number of elders appear in connection with Israel, and especially to Ex. 24:1, where seventy elders as representatives of the congregation go up with Moses to the mount, to behold the glory of Jehovah, and be witnesses of the more secret transactions which related to the establishment of the covenant. By mentioning, therefore, precisely this number of elders, the prophet sets before us a representation of the whole people, – an ideal representation, and of such a kind as to indicate the strong contrast that existed between former and present times, the original seventy being employed in immediate connection with God's glory and covenant, while these here were engaged in an act which bespoke the dishonoring of God's name and the virtual dissolution of his covenant. To render the contrast still more palpable between what was and what should have been, the prophet singles out one from among the seventy, and places him in the midst – Jaazaniah, the son of Shaphan. This he does not from any natural or official superiority in that person above the rest, but from the expressive import of his name, which means Jehovah hears, while by their deeds the whole company were intimating, what in the next verse they are reported to have said, *"The Lord seeth us not, the Lord hath forsaken the earth."* The very prominence given to this person on account of his name – the representation of the people by the primitive number of seventy elders – the attributing of an act of worship to these elders, the offering of incense in censers, which was one of the most distinctive prerogatives not of the elders, but of the priesthood – and the express declaration that what they were collectively doing there was just what *"every man was doing in the chambers of his imagery,"* – all plainly denote that it is no actual service which is here described, but an ideal or pictorial representation of the debasing idolatries which the people had begun secretly to practise in their own dens of pollution, beyond what they were willing to own and exhibit in the light of day. In a word, we are told their idolatrous spirit had outrun even their public defections, and was already drinking up the rank poison of Egypt, though in nothing did the transactions of their earlier history raise a louder and more emphatic protest than against such a retrograding to the foul region of Egyptian idolatry.

From the secret abominations practised in the chambers of imagery, the prophet's attention was next turned to a scene in the outer court, at the north door, where he beholds women sitting in an attitude of grief and weeping for Tammuz. We have the explicit testimony of Jerome that this was the Hebrew and Syriac name for Adonis, the fancied paramour of Venus, who was fabled to have been killed by a boar, and restored to life again; in which the mystery is said to have been couched of the sun's yearly declension and return, or, more generally, nature's annual decay and renovation. However that may have been, there can be no doubt that the Adonis-festival, which had first its original seat at Byblos in Phoenicia, was celebrated by doleful lamentations, as for one lost or dead, and then by extravagant libidinous rejoicings, on again finding the object of affection. This fantastical and impure piece of worship bore in its nature so strong a resemblance to the Egyptian orgies connected with the lost and recovered Osiris, that not a few both earlier and later mythologists are disposed to trace the matter up to this source; although there seems no reason to question the Phoenician caste of the superstition, as practised in Asia and Greece. And the women seen in vision by the prophet sitting and weeping at the outer gate on the north, betokened that it had now also found its way into Judea. It was but a fragment, as it were, of the idolatrous scene which met his eye, but enough to indicate, in accordance with the pictorial style of the whole description, that this Phoenician abomination had become one of the festering sores of Judah's disease.

But turning from this, the prophet is once more directed to another, and what is expressly called a greater abomination, – greater, not as betokening a worse idolatry, but implying, on account of the persons and the place connected with it, a more direct and flagrant dishonor to God. In the inner court of the Lord's house, and immediately before the door of the temple, between the porch and the altar, – where only the most solemn services should have been conducted, and where the priests never advanced but on some rare and extraordinary occasions, when the most earnest cries were to be put forth for sparing mercy (Joel 2:17), – there the prophet sees twenty-five men. The place where they were seen could be trodden only by the priests; and beyond doubt, the right idea was expressed by Lightfoot (in his Chronica Temporum), when he understood by them the leaders of the twenty-four classes into which the priests were divided by David, with the high priest at their head. With reference, apparently, to the same division, and the presidency of the several classes naturally connected with it, Isaiah speaks (chap. 43:28) of *"the princes of the sanctuary,"* and Jeremiah (chap. 35:4) of *"the chamber of the princes,"* while in 2 Chron. 36:14 we not only read of *"the chief of the priests,"* but are also told of their having *"polluted the house of the Lord which he hallowed in Jerusalem."*

Therefore twenty-five men of priestly rank, *"the princes of the sanctuary,"* would be the precise number to represent the whole priesthood, just as the seventy elders were the proper representation of the whole people, and for that purpose had been employed in an earlier part of the vision. But how melancholy the appearance presented here by the elite of the priesthood! Their backs toward the temple, at the very threshold of which they stood (the reverse position of all devout worshippers, 1 Kings 8:44; Dan. 6:10), and their faces toward the east, doing obeisance to the rising sun! Thus they bore witness that the highest places in the land had become infected with the Parsee element of fire-worship And not then, indeed, for the first time; for in the reformation effected by Josiah, we are told of his putting away those who burnt incense to the sun, and moon, and other heavenly bodies, with the horses and chariots that had been consecrated to the sun (2 Kings 23:5,11). But the corruption had taken too deep root to be thus destroyed; it again revived with other heathenish customs, and now, in the days of Zedekiah, had attained to a high ascendancy.

Thus, from the various scenes that met the eye of the prophet in his ideal walk through the precincts of the temple of Jerusalem, it was but too clearly manifest, that so far from the worship of God being preserved there in its purity, the land had become the common sink of heathenism. There was to be seen, side by side with the altar of Jehovah, the image of the Syrian lord of nature, whether known by the name of Baal or Moloch, or aught besides, the abhorred rival of heaven's real King; there also was the Egyptian beast-worship, with the foul rites of Phoenician licentiousness, and the more refined but still idolatrous and corrupting services of the Eastern fire or sun worship. Yet even these heathenish pollutions, the Lord proceeds to testify in the ears of the prophet, were not enough to satisfy the people's depraved appetite for evil; it was but a light thing, as it were, that they should thus dishonor God in the things immediately connected with his service; they had, besides, filled the land with violence, trampling as flagrantly upon the second table of the law in their dealings one toward another, as by their heathenish abominations they were trampling on the first. *"And they have returned,"* the Lord concludes, *"to provoke me to anger; and lo! they put the branch to their nose. Therefore will I also deal in fury; mine eye shall not spare, neither will I have pity; and though they cry in mine ears with a loud voice, yet will I not hear them."* Even the most fervent supplications, such as those recommended by Joel, would be of no avail.

But to revert now to the occasion of these fearful disclosures, how does this state of heathenish corruption and rampant iniquity in Judah and Jerusalem comport with the proud satisfaction the people there are represented to have felt regarding their own case, as compared with that of their exiled brethren? It was well with themselves, they had been saying, because they were near to the Lord, and this made them sure of the continued possession of the land; while, according to the vision now delineated, they seemed to be rejoicing in anything rather than the conscious presence of God – nay, were giving vent to the impious sentiment which is again, with marked emphasis, ascribed to them in the next chapter, *"The Lord seeth us not, the Lord hath forsaken the earth."* There was certainly a deep practical inconsistence between the two states of feeling indicated, if tried by the truth of God's word; but not such an inconsistence as ought to shake our belief, or even greatly excite our wonder. Among the false religionists of our Lord's time, the very same inconsistence again reappears, only somewhat modified and chastened by the altered circumstances of the times. In them also we see both the elements above noticed very prominently displayed. There was proud self-complacence, as of persons who plumed themselves on their peculiar nearness to God, not without feelings of settled scorn toward such as seemed to stand at a remoter distance. Yet along with this there was the absence of any real love to God, and a plentiful distrust of his power and goodness, appearing in their vain traditions, their secret wickedness, their fleshly confidences, their manifold idolatry of a present world, and expectations of mere earthly deliverances; so that with the most perfect truth it might be said of them, they were cherishing the spirit and doing the deeds of their fathers in the days of Zedekiah. And wherever religion loses its true childlike spirit of faith and love, and degenerates into a superstition, the same practical inconsistence is sure, in some form or another, to manifest itself. For there being

in such cases no genuine love of God in the heart, but a slavish dread of him, the affections of the soul will naturally flow into forbidden channels, while the very pains and services to which it is prompted by that slavish dread will as naturally tend to beget a feeling of presumptuous confidence toward God, and contemptuous behavior toward those who take another mode of serving him. Is not this precisely what we see in the deluded votaries of Rome? On the one hand the most perfect conviction that they are peculiarly the people of God; and on the other, the most flagrant corruptions of the simplicity of his truth and worship, ways and services, such as seem rather to bespeak their sense of an absent or angry, than of a near and loving Father. Or look to the superstitious man generally. Did not Milton correctly delineate him when he said, "In very deed the superstitious man by his good will is an atheist [since, having only a dread of God, he would rather that God were not, and, as often as he can, strives to keep God away from his thoughts and feelings]; but being scared from thence by the pangs and gripes of a boiling conscience, all in a pudder he shuffles up to himself such a God and such a worship as is most agreeable to remedy his fear; which fear of his, as also is his hope, fixed only upon the flesh, renders likewise the whole faculty of his apprehension carnal; and all the inward acts of worship issuing from the native strength of the soul run out lavishly to the upper skin, and there harden into a crust of formality"? In a word, the inward desires and spontaneous movements of minds given to superstition, as well as many of their outward actions, virtually declare that God – the spiritual and holy God of the Bible – either does not exist, or, at least, is not near enough to regard them in their perverse and crooked ways. But yet if any one should talk to them of salvation, none apparently are so sure of it; for this to their view is inseparable from the formal ritualism in which they have encrusted themselves. Such a religion is a vain as it is contrary to the whole genius of the gospel. We err from the simplicity of the faith whenever we resort to other means and influences for obtaining life and peace to the soul than those which God has himself sanctioned and approved in his word. And we err not less plainly from its spirit of childlike confidence and devoted love, if we are not giving to the God and Father of our Lord Jesus Christ the undivided homage of our hearts, and habitually realizing his gracious presence as alike our safeguard from evil, and our most inspiring motive to faithfulness in every good work.

CHAPTER IX.

THE VISION OF THE SEALING.

[1]He also cried in my ears with a loud voice, saying, Cause those who have charge over the city to draw near, even every man *with* his destroying weapon in his hand.

[2]And behold, six men came from the way of the upper gate which lies toward the north, and every man *had* a weapon of slaughter in his hand. And one man among them was clothed with linen, with a writer's inkhorn by his side. And they went in and stood beside the bronze altar.

[3]And the glory of the God of Israel had gone up from the cherub on which it was, to the doorstep of the house. And He called to the man clothed in linen, who *had* the writer's inkhorn by his side.

[4]And the LORD said to him, Go through the midst of the city, through the midst of Jerusalem, and set a mark on the foreheads of the men who sigh and who cry because of all the abominations that are done in the midst of it.

[5]And to the others He said in my hearing, Go after him through the city and strike. Let not your eye spare, neither have pity.

[6]Fully destroy old men, young men and virgins, and little children and women. But do not come near any man on whom is the mark. And begin at My sanctuary. And they began at the old men who were before the house.

[7]And He said to them, Defile the house, and fill the courts with the dead. Go forth! And they went out and killed in the city.

[8]And while they were slaying them, and I was left, I fell on my face and cried, and said, Ah Lord GOD! Will You destroy all the rest of Israel in Your pouring out of Your fury on Jerusalem?

[9]Then He said to me, The iniquity of the house of Israel and Judah is exceeding great, and the land is full of blood, and the city is full of perverseness. For they say, The LORD has forsaken the earth, and the

LORD sees not.

[10]And as for Me also, My eye shall not spare, nor will I have pity, *but* I will put their way on their head.

[11]And behold, the man clothed with linen, who *had* the inkhorn by his side, reported the matter, saying, I have done as You have commanded me.

The vision depicted in chap. 8 was intended to lay open the various workings of that apostate and rebellious spirit which had infected the people of Judah and Jerusalem. And as such a wide-spread and leprous state of guilt manifestly called for the interposition of a righteous God, the prophet proceeds to unfold the course of procedure which was to be adopted regarding it.

1. He first of all hears the Lord crying with a loud voice, as in a matter of great urgency, and in a state of vehement indignation, summoning the officers or overseers of the city into his presence, and ordering them to bring each in their hand a weapon for slaughter. The persons who answered to this summons were six in number, but along with these, and in the midst of them as being the leader of the party, there was one in different habiliments – clothed in linen, and with a writer's inkhorn at his side. That these should have been in all precisely seven in number is chiefly to be accounted for from the sacredness attached to that number in ancient times, and especially in the Hebrew Scriptures. It indicated that the action now to be proceeded with bore that sacred character which belongs to everything that comes from the hand of God. With reference to the same import, we read in Zechariah of the seven eyes of the Lord (chap. 3:9), and in the Apocalypse of the seven spirits before the Lord (Rev. 5:6). The persons in question, although called men, are evidently to be regarded as the inhabitants of a higher sphere – the special messengers of Jehovah; and they appeared in the character of officers, who had the charge of the city committed to them, because they had come to execute the judgments of righteousness, which the proper officers should have put in force. Their approach was from the north, where also the different forms of idolatry had been seen by the prophet; and they stood beside the brazen altar, waiting to receive the command of Jehovah. It was there, as we said before, that the people's guilt lay unpardoned; and according to the principle, *"where the carcass is, there will the eagles be gathered together,"* from the same quarter must proceed the work of judgment. "While those ministers of the Divine justice," says Hengstenberg excellently,[2] "tread beside the brazen altar, the glory of the Lord moves toward them out of the holy of holies, and appears to them at the threshold of the temple. It imparts to him who is clothed in linen the commission to preserve the pious, to the others to destroy the ungodly without mercy. Now who is the one clothed in linen? No other than the angel of the Lord. This appears from Dan. 10:5, 12:6,7, where Michael, but another name for the angel of the Lord, is designated in the same way, – a remarkable agreement in two contemporary prophets. It is also evident from the subject itself. The clothing is that of the earthly high priest; but the heavenly high priest and intercessor is the angel of the Lord (Zech. 1:12). He who was clothed in linen is not, however, to be regarded as solely engaged in the work of delivering the pious; not as standing in contrast with the six ministers of righteousness. These are rather to be considered as subordinate to him, as accomplishing the work of destruction only by his command and under his authority. The punishment proceeds from him no less than the prosperity. This appears even from general grounds. Both have the same root, the same object – the prosperity of the kingdom of God. The six cannot be regarded as evil angels. This would be in contradiction to the whole doctrine of Scripture on the subject. It uniformly attributes the punishment of the ungodly to the good angels, and the trial of the pious, under God's permission, to the evil; as is seen, for example, in the trial of Job, the temptation of Christ, the buffeting of Paul by a messenger of Satan. If this, then, be established, it is equally so that the judgment on this occasion belongs to the angel of the Lord. For all inferior angels are subordinate to him, the prince of the heavenly host, so that all they do is done by his command. But in addition to these general grounds, there are special reasons, which are entirely decisive. It deserves consideration that he who was clothed in linen appears in the midst of the six. They surround him as his followers, his servants. Still more weighty, however, and of

itself sufficient, is chap. 10:2,7: *"And the Lord spake to the man clothed in linen, and said, Go between the wheels under the cherubim, and fill thy hand with coals of fire, which are between the cherubim, and scatter them over the city; and he went before mine eyes. And a cherub stretched out his hand between the cherubim, to the fire that was between the cherubim, and took and gave it into the hands of him who was clothed in linen. And he took it and went forth."* The fire is an image of the Divine anger. The angel of the Lord is here, therefore, expressly designated as the one who executes the judgments of the Divine justice. The importance of the transaction extends beyond the explanation of the passage before us. We have here the Old Testament foundation of the doctrine of the New, that all judgment has been committed to the Son; and a remarkable example of the harmony of the two Testaments, which in recent times has been but too much overlooked. (Comp. Matt. 13:41, 25:31).

In regard to what was ordered to be done on the present occasion by the angel of the covenant and his attendant ministers of righteousness, a few particulars deserve to be noted. (1) It was pre-eminently a work of judgment against sin. Of this the moving of the Divine glory from the inner sanctuary to the threshold without was itself an impressive sign, indicating that God was rising out of his place to punish the inhabitants of the land; yet even in doing this, the Lord showed the care and fidelity with which he watched over his own. For the first part of the charge given to the presiding angel has respect to the safety of the good – the small remnant of faithful ones, who, so far from going along with the prevailing tide of evil, were daily sighing and crying for the abominations that were proceeding around them. These were to be kept under the shadow of the Almighty, while destruction, like a whirlwind, was sweeping on every side of them. So has it ever been in the history of God's judgments. The angels who were charged with the overthrow of Sodom and Gomorrah declared they could do nothing till righteous Lot had made good his escape. Nor was the destroying angel sent forth to slay the first-born in Egypt till the families of Israel found time to sprinkle on their door-posts the blood of reconciliation. So also in Revelation, before the great tribulations begin, the peremptory command was given, *"Hurt not the earth, neither the sea, nor the trees, till we have sealed the servants of God in their foreheads."* Refreshing thought! The Divine faithfulness still abides sure to the true children of the covenant, even though they should exist but as a few grains of wheat among heaps of chaff destined to destruction. Let such, therefore, trust in the Lord at all times, and fear not that it shall be well with the righteous.

(2) In respect, again, to the method taken to separate between this faithful remnant and others, though there is something peculiar in it, yet it evidently points to the preservation of Israel in Egypt by the sprinkling of the paschal blood on the door-posts. Here, however, as it was not for families, but for individuals that the sign was needed, a change in the mode was necessarily adopted. *"Set a mark* (literally, mark a mark) *upon their foreheads,"* is the command given to the angel of the covenant. What kind of mark is not specified, and indeed would scarcely have been suitable, as it was a mere symbol of the personal security of the individuals referred to – not a mark to be actually imprinted and seen upon their persons, but as an indication of the place they held in the watchful oversight and directing agency of God. And that the forehead is named – the most prominent and conspicuous part of the person – as that on which the mark was to be set, this was simply to show how clear and certain their interest was in the guardianship and protection of Heaven; it was as if God would have all men to take notice of their connection with his service, and their sure inheritance of blessing from his hand.[3]

(3) Further, we cannot but perceive in regard to the sentence of judgment executed upon the rest of the community, that it is ordered so as most fitly to express the utter loathing and abhorrence with which the sins of the people had filled the mind of God. The work of slaughter was appointed to begin at the sanctuary, that all its courts might be defiled with the blood of the slain. In consequence of the aggravated and shameful guilt of the worshippers, it had already lost the reality of holiness, and in accordance with its true character, the appearance of an abominable place must now be given to it. Not only so, but the very first persons whose blood is reported to have been shed there was

that of *"the ancient men before the house,"* – the seventy elders mentioned in the preceding chapters, themselves the more aged and venerable portion of the worshippers, and those who might naturally be regarded as occupying the foremost rank among the people at large. The slaying of such persons first was an indication of the unsparing severity with which the Divine judgment was to proceed, involving alike in destruction *"old and young, maids and little children, and women."* So terrible was the sight, that the prophet himself for the moment forgets the assurance that had been given by the act of sealing a preserved remnant; and, overcome by his intense feelings, falls down and exclaims, *"Ah, Lord God! wilt thou destroy all the residue of Israel in the pouring out of thy fury upon Jerusalem?"* A cry for mercy which has no other effect than to call forth a fresh declaration from the Lord of the greatness of the people's guilt, and of the necessity of vengeance being executed against it.

So very broadly marked in this portion of the vision is the distinction between the righteous and the wicked! In the ideal territory which the vision occupies, the treatment awarded to each is as different as the character respectively belonging to them; but was the distinction equally preserved amid the real transactions that followed? In the calamities that so soon fell like an overwhelming flood on the city, did the wicked alone suffer, and the good escape unhurt? Such, certainly, we are warranted to infer would in general be the case, as we see in Jeremiah and the false prophets – the one faithfully guarded, though surrounded on every hand with instruments of destruction, while the others miserably perished. Yet we cannot suppose the line of demarcation would be preserved with such perfect exactness, as that all the wicked should be destroyed, and all the righteous defended from evil. The records of history prove, indeed, the reverse. "But it must be noted," as Calvin justly remarks, "that while God apparently sends trouble to his people in common with the wicked, there is still this distinction on the side of the former, that nothing befalls them but what shall turn to their salvation. When God, therefore, forbids the Chaldeans to touch his faithful servants, he does not mean that they should be free from all trouble and annoyance, but promises that matters should be ordered so differently with them, as compared with the wicked, that they should know in their own experience God had not forgotten his faithful word. It may be, indeed, that God shall not spare his own so as to exempt them from having their faith and patience exercised; yet he will spare so far as not to allow anything deadly to befall them, – so far as always to prove himself their faithful guardian. But when he appears to extend pardon to the wicked, this only tends to their destruction, because they are rendered by it more and more inexcusable."

CHAPTER X.

THE VISION OF THE COALS OF FIRE.

As soon as the prophet's attention was withdrawn from what had for the time completely absorbed it, – the proceedings connected with the preservation of the good and the destruction of the wicked, – he was favored with another vision of the glory of Jehovah, such as he had already beheld on the plains of Chebar. The scene only of the Divine manifestation was different, the manifestation itself was substantially the same. Here also there were, as had formerly been seen, the cloud of glory and the dazzling splendor filling the field of vision – the cherubim with the likeness of a throne above, surmounted by the sapphire firmament – gigantic wheels by the side of the cherubim, full of eyes round about, instinct with life and motion, and themselves moving in the midst of the glowing fire – the voice, from time to time, of these cherubim, pealing in the ears of the prophet as the voice of the Almighty, – all serving by the nature of their appearance and the character of their movements to shadow forth the mind and will of Him who, amid such accompaniments of Divine majesty, occupied the throne. The presentation of this glorious vision to the eye of the prophet took place in the midst of the appointed executions of judgment – one part being already past, while another was still to come. And the leading object of it seems to have been to bring distinctly into view the immediate agency of God in the matter, and to show how all proceeded, as by a law

of imperious necessity, from the essential holiness of his nature. But let us first give the prophet's description of the scene itself:

1 Then I looked, and behold, in the expanse that was over the head of the cherubim, something looking like a sapphire stone came over them, *and* it was in the form of a throne.

2 And He spoke to the man clothed with linen, and said, Go in between the wheels, under the cherub, and fill your hands with coals of fire from between the cherubim, and scatter *them over* the city. And he went in as I watched.

3 Now the cherubim stood on the right side of the house when the man went in; and the cloud filled the inner court.

4 Then the glory of the LORD went up from the cherub *and stood* over the doorstep of the house. And the house was filled with the cloud, and the court was full of the brightness of the LORD's glory.

5 And the sound of the cherubim wings was heard to the outer court, as the voice of the Almighty God when He speaks.

6 And when He had commanded the man clothed with linen, saying, Take fire from between the wheels, from between the cherubim, he went in then and stood beside the wheels.

7 And *one* cherub stretched out his hand from between the cherubim to the fire that was between the cherubs. And he took it and put it into the hands of him who was clothed with linen. He took *it* and went out.

8 And there appeared in the cherubim the form of a man's hand under their wings.

9 And when I looked, behold, the four wheels by the cherubim, one wheel was by one cherub, and another wheel by another cherub; and the wheels looked like the color of a beryl stone.

10 As to how they looked, the four of them had one likeness, as if a wheel had been in the midst of a wheel.

11 When they went, they went on their four sides. They did not turn as they went, but they went to the place where the head looked. They did not turn as they went.

12 And their whole body, and their backs, and their hands, and their wings, and the wheels were full of eyes all around, *even* the wheels that the four of them had.

13 As for the wheels, it was cried to them in my hearing, O wheel!

14 And each one had four faces. The first face was the face of a cherub, and the second face was the face of a man, and the third was the face of a lion, and the fourth the face of an eagle.

15 And the cherubim were lifted up. This is the living creature that I saw by the river of Che-bar.

16 And when the cherubim went, the wheels went beside them; and when the cherubs lifted up their wings to mount up from the earth, the same wheels also did not turn from beside them.

17 When they stood still, *these* stood still, and when they were lifted up, *these* lifted themselves also. For the spirit of the living creature was in them.

18 Then the glory of the LORD moved from the threshold of the house and stood over the cherubim.

19 And the cherubim lifted up their wings and mounted up from the earth in my sight. When they went out, the wheels also were beside them, and *each one* stood at the door of the east gate of the LORD's house. And the glory of the God of Israel was over them.

20 This is the living creature that I saw under the God of Israel by the river Che-bar, and I knew that they were the cherubim.

21 Every one had four faces each, and every one four wings. And the likeness of the hands of a man was under their wings.

22 And the likeness of their faces was the same *as the* faces which I saw by the river Che-bar, their appearances and themselves. Each one of them went straight forward.

The Divine manifestation here described as having been presented in vision to Ezekiel is distinctly connected with the one previously given on the banks of the Chebar. It is substantially a renewal of the former vision, though differing as to the locality where the manifestation was given, and the symbolical actions with which it was accompanied. Looking to the two manifestations in their common features, and with respect to their general design, we can have no difficulty in perceiving both the propriety and importance of such displays of the Divine presence and glory having been vouchsafed to the prophet especially near the commencement of his career. They were needed to qualify him for the discharge of his high function, and for maintaining the arduous conflict he had to wage against unbelief and corruption. "The Divine presence," to use the words of Havernick, "was discovered to him in such glorious manifestations, – first, for the purpose of calling

him to do the part of a witness of that glory in the midst of his God-forgetting people; then for the purpose of taking leave of the visible locality with which the old manifestations of Deity were connected, and with which they were never to be associated in the ancient manner again. These two occasions of a Divine manifestation so peculiarly glorious were periods never to be forgotten in the life of Ezekiel; to exhibit them in their harmonious agreement was what he could on no account omit. Twice had his spiritual eye beheld the very God of Israel upon the cherubim; this was the seal of truth which he stamped on his announcements; this for himself was the dearest pledge of the Divine condescension – an inexpressible grace, which he felt constrained by a lively sense of the Lord's presence to record with candor and delight."

When we look to the differences between this vision and the earlier one, the appearances themselves, and the actions connected with them, for the most part admit of a ready explanation. The particular feature mentioned here respecting the cherubim, that they were in every part full of eyes, and not mentioned in the former description, can scarcely be regarded as a difference; for it seems to be merely a more specific detail, which the prophet's second and closer inspection of the appearance enabled him to observe and note. He expressly states that the living creature was the same that he had seen at first; which implies that it had each time the same composite and peculiar structure. Here, however, the throne which appeared above the cherubim is without the accompaniment of the rainbow, for, on this particular occasion, it is the work of judgment alone that is symbolized. The sign of returning grace after floods of wrath might still, indeed, be said to be there, in the background, for the judgment was not to be utterly annihilating; a remnant was still to be spared, and a door left open for fresh manifestations of covenant-love and faithfulness. But this had already been indicated in the preceding part of the vision (chap. 9), by the action of the sealing of those who had kept aloof from the reigning abominations, and reserving them for a purpose of mercy in the future. What is unfolded in the present chapter is simply the following out to its proper conclusion of the work of judgment. The sinners in Zion were already slain; their carcasses are seen lying throughout the streets of the city, and some of them were defiling the house which their rampant iniquity had so fearfully profaned. And now it only remained that the work of severity should be consummated, by destroying the city itself where all the abominations had been practised. The Lord therefore appears on his throne of judgment; and, to make it more manifest that the judgment is in vindication of his injured holiness, and on account of the sins which had been committed against his covenant, the scene of the judicial action is laid in the temple itself. The cherubic machinery, moved close to the threshold of the house, and the glory of the Lord not only stood above it, but also pressed inwards, so that the whole house was filled with the cloud – the emblem of God's awful majesty and hot displeasure. There, in immediate contact with the sanctuary, a cherub, at the Divine command, gives a portion of the fire which glowed between the wheelworks of the cherubim to the man clothed in linen – the angel of the covenant – that he might scatter it over the city and reduce the whole to ashes. This fire may certainly, with Hengstenberg (on Rev. 8:5), be called elemental fire, since the purpose for which it was given was to consume the devoted city. But this surely does not render it less (as he conceives) a symbol of the holy wrath and judgment of God, for that consumption of the city was no merely natural operation, but a solemn act of judgment, in vindication of the honor and majesty of God. Nothing here, either in the vision itself or in the actions represented as proceeding, belongs simply to the natural sphere; even the natural powers and agencies, of which the cherubic appearances and the wheel-work were partly symbolical, have their place in the vision, from their subservience to the moral ends and purposes in progress. But it deserves to be noted, with Calvin (though he errs, we think, in other parts of his explanation), that the fire is represented as being taken not from the altar of God, which had so much to do with the work of reconciliation for iniquity, but from the ideal source specially provided for purposes of judgment suited to the occasion. And that a man's hand supplied this material element of fire for the work of destruction may naturally be regarded as indicating that human agents should not be wanting, at the

proper time, to carry into effect the judgment written; the Lord would not need, as in the case of Sodom and Gomorrah, to rain down fire and brimstone from heaven, but would find among men instruments properly fitted for executing his purpose. The whole prophetic burden contained in this and the preceding chapter is to be found in plain language, and with much detail, in many parts of Jeremiah's writings, and indeed was comprised long before in the following brief but awful passage of Isaiah (chap. 23:12 sq.): *"The people shall be as the burnings of lime, as thorns cut up shall they be burned in the fire. The sinners in Zion are afraid; fearfulness hath surprised the hypocrites. Who among us shall dwell with the devouring fire? who among us shall dwell with everlasting burnings?"*

Another scene of destruction, however, was yet to be presented to the eye of the prophet, before the revelation could properly be made of the purpose of mercy that was in reserve; a special work of judgment must prepare the way for its accomplishment. This we have in the earlier part of the next chapter, after which, in the latter part, comes the exhibition of the purpose of mercy.

CHAPTER XI.

DESTRUCTION OF A CORRUPT PRIESTHOOD, WITH THE PROMISE OF GRACE AND BLESSING TO A BELIEVING REMNANT AMONG THE EXILES.

[1]And the Spirit lifted me up and brought me to the east gate of the LORD's house, which looks eastward. And behold, twenty-five men were at the door of the gate – among whom I saw Ja-az-a-ni-ah the son of A-zur, and Pel-a-ti-ah the son of Be-nai-ah, chiefs of the people.

[2]Then He said to me, Son of man, these are the men who plot evil and give wicked advice in this city –

[3]who say, *It is* not near; let us build houses; this city is the pot, and we are the flesh.

[4]Therefore prophesy against them; O son of man, prophesy!

[5]And the Spirit of the LORD fell on me and said to me, Speak: Thus says the LORD: Thus you have said, O house of Israel. For I know the things that come into your mind, *every one* of them.

[6]You have multiplied your dead in this city, and you have filled the streets of it with the dead.

[7]Therefore thus says the Lord GOD: Your slain whom you have laid in its midst, They are the flesh, and this *city* is the pot. But I will bring you out of the midst of it.

[8]You have feared the sword, and I will bring a sword on you, says the Lord GOD.

[9]And I will bring you out of its midst and deliver you into the hands of strangers, and I will execute judgments on you.

[10]You shall fall by the sword. I will judge you in the border of Israel, and you shall know that I am the LORD.

[11]This *city* shall not be your pot, nor shall you be the flesh in its midst. I will judge you in the border of Israel,

[12]and you shall know that I am the LORD – for you have not walked in My statutes, nor have you done My judgments, but have done as the nations who are around you do.

[13]And when I prophesied, Pel-a-ti-ah the son of Be-nai-ah died. Then I fell down on my face and cried with a loud voice, and said, Ah Lord GOD! Will You make a full end of the remnant of Israel.

[14]Again the word of the LORD came to me, saying,

[15]Son of man, your brothers, even your brothers, the men of your family and all the house of Israel as a whole, are those to whom the people of Jerusalem have said, Go far away from the LORD. To us is this land given in possession.

[16]Therefore say, Thus says the Lord GOD: Although I have cast them far off among the heathen, and although I have scattered them among the countries, yet I will be to them as a little sanctuary in the countries where they shall come.

[17]Therefore say, Thus says the Lord GOD: I will even gather you from the people and assemble you out of the countries where you have been scattered, and I will give you the land of Israel.

[18]And they shall come there, and they shall take away all its hateful things and all its abominations from it.

[19]And I will give them one heart, and I will put a new spirit within you. And I will

take the stony heart out of their flesh, and will give them a heart of flesh,
[20]so that they may walk in My statutes and keep My ordinances, and do them. And they shall be My people, and I will be their God.
[21]But *as for* those whose heart walks after the heart of their hateful things and their idols, I will put their way on their own heads, says the Lord GOD.
[22]Then the cherubim lifted up their wings and the wheels beside them. And the glory of the God of Israel was over them above.
[23]And the glory of the LORD went up from the midst of the city and stood on the mountain which is on the east side of the city.
[24]Afterwards the Spirit took me up and brought me in a vision by the Spirit of God into Chal-de-a, to those of the captivity. So the vision that I had seen went up from me.
[25]Then I spoke to those of the captivity all the things that the LORD had shown me.

When the prophet was going to witness the new scene of destruction with which this chapter opens, he was made to change his position. For the manifested glory of God had fixed its residence at the entrance of the east gate of the Lord's house (chap. 10:19), the principal entrance to the temple, as through that the way lay straight into the sanctuary The Spirit lifted the prophet up, and placed him at that gate, in the immediate presence of the Divine glory. There the first thing that met his eye was a company of twenty-five men, two of whom also are expressly named, and called *"princes of the people."* This number naturally leads us to think of the twenty-five mentioned in chap. 8, whom we identified with the heads of the twenty-four classes into which the families of the priests were divided, with the high priest as their superior, – the natural representatives of the whole priesthood. Nor is there anything in what is said here to prevent us from supposing that the same persons are again brought into notice. That they should be called, not as in Isa. 43:28, *"princes of the sanctuary,"* or in 2 Chron. 36:14, *"chief* (princes) *of the priests,"* but *"princes of the people,"* is sufficiently explained from the light in which they are here contemplated, as ringleaders in the general profligacy and corruption. Hence it is immediately added, *"These are the men that devise mischief, and give wicked counsel in this city;"* for they had taken advantage of their influential position to lead the people astray from God, and infuse perverse counsel into their minds; and on this account might justly be called, though not perhaps without some mixture of irony, *"princes of the people."*

This view is also confirmed by the place assigned to these twenty-five men in the vision. Already has the wrath of God come forth with consuming power against the people as represented by the elders, who were then worshipping in the courts of the Lord's house. Not only this; but the glory of the Lord has also been seen leaving its proper habitations in the most holy place, and like the cherubim of old, and the flaming sword in the garden of Eden, has gone forth to occupy the gate that leads into the now deserted sanctuary. Of what use, then, any more the ministrations of an apostate and polluted priesthood in this sanctuary? Nay, is it not time that judgment should alight upon such a priesthood? and that the glory of the Lord should break forth upon them before they are again permitted to enter the sacred precincts? This is precisely what we should expect to take place from the order of the Divine vision, and the point at which things had arrived; and when viewed in connection with what had been previously said of the twenty-five, as to their ministering on peculiarly holy ground, and now of their appearing at the eastern approach to the temple, leaves no proper room to doubt that these were the representatives of the priesthood in Judah.

The two who are named in this representative company of priests appear to have been singled out, as was formerly done in the case of the seventy elders, on account of the peculiar significance of their names, and to mark the contrast that now existed between the idea and the reality. *"Jaazaniah* (God hears), *the son of Azur* (help); *and Pelatiah* (God delivers), *the son of Benaiah* (God builds)." Such names should have been regarded as perpetual monitors, reminding them where they should have sought, and where also they should have found, their confidence and safety. Had they but remained stedfast in the covenant of God, he would assuredly have heard and helped them in the time of need, delivered them from danger, and built them up. But now it was their very relation to God which proved the source of their greatest danger, and the immediate cause of their overwhelming destruction. For not only the corruptions they had introduced into his service, but also their insolent contempt of his authority, had reached such a height that he could no longer refrain from manifesting his righteousness in their punishment. Setting themselves in direct opposition to the will of God, they had given wicked counsel to the people, and said, *"Not in the nearness is the building of houses; this is the caldron, and we are the flesh."*

It is not quite obvious, at first sight, how these words convey so bad a meaning as the connection in which they are introduced leads us to expect; for it is in them, apparently, that the extreme wickedness of the priesthood expresses itself, while the words themselves might seem to imply nothing particularly bad. This alone suggests to us the propriety of seeking for some covert reference in the language, such as might impart to it a peculiar force and intensity of meaning. And the connection between the prophecies of Ezekiel and those of Jeremiah, formerly adverted to, supplies here precisely what we need; for it enables us to perceive, in the short speech here put into the lips of a corrupt priesthood, an insolent and scornful parody of words that had been previously uttered by Jeremiah. In the letter that prophet sent to the captives among whom Ezekiel lived, the very first announcement was, *"Build ye houses, and dwell in them"* (chap. 29:5); because the time of their sojourn there was not to be, as the great majority of the people thought for a brief space, but for the long period of seventy years. On the other hand, in regard to the people at Jerusalem, and indicative of the short respite that was to be allowed them there, Jeremiah had seen in a vision a caldron or seething-pot (chap. 1:13), with its mouth towards the north; which was interpreted to mean, that the kingdoms of the north, with Babylon at their head, would come and take possession of Jerusalem. Now it is these two speeches – the one bearing respect more immediately to the exiles, the other to the remnant in Judah – which the impious and ungodly priesthood are represented here as parodying; they take the words of the Lord's servant into their mouth, but only for the purpose of showing how they could make light of the most solemn messages: *"Those who are far off in the land of exile may, if they please, take the prophet's advice and set about building houses for themselves; that does not concern us, it is too remote a thing for our needing to be at all careful about it. And as for the pot you have seen, which is ready to smoke and boil under the fury of a hostile invasion from the north, let it be so – the Jerusalem be the pot, then we shall be the flesh within it; its strong fortifications and sure defences shall preserve us against any flame of war that may kindle around us. We know our ground, and have no occasion to be terrified with such visions."*

Such plainly appears to have been the spirit in which the words were uttered by the priesthood, and the sense they conveyed. And viewed thus, the language reveals as by a flash of lightning the real state of the priesthood in Jerusalem, – showing not only how contemptuously they eyed their brethren in exile (the circumstance which gave rise to the whole of this series of visions), but how completely their heart had departed from the Lord, and gone to rest in fleshly confidences. The threatenings of the Lord's servant were now bandied about as idle words, or twisted into any shape that might suit their own perverse inclinations. And as if the Lord had indeed forsaken the earth, or was destitute of means to execute his own word, they looked to the bulwarks of their city as amply sufficient to protect them from all the assaults that could be made against it. Nay, they had the presumption to intimate, by the turn they gave to the prophet's similitude, that the city must stand for their sakes, even as the pot exists for the safety and due preparation of the flesh that is put into it. In like manner, because they must as a matter of necessity continue to abide and flourish, the city cannot but stand them in good stead against the coming evil![2]

It was impossible that a holy God could permit such a presumptuous and scornful degree of impiety to pass unpunished, especially when it appeared in those who stood nearest to God, and held the highest places of influence in the land. Therefore the Divine judgment is immediately announced. As perfectly cognisant of their vain imaginations and their wicked courses, the Lord declares that he is ready to take vengeance on their inventions. Their miserable sophistries and external defences would be equally unavailing in the day of rebuke. Those whom they had cunningly deceived or violently overborne to their ruin, these would really be as the flesh in the midst of the caldron, the hapless victims of destruction; but the treacherous and wicked priesthood would have to answer for their blood, and as an abhorred race would be driven from their imagined sanctuary, and slain by the hands of heathen in the borders of the land, – thus finding, as they deserved, a violent death and a polluted grave. (Comp. Jer. 39:4,5.)

As soon as the communication was made of this purpose to execute judgment on the corrupt priesthood, Pelatiah (God delivers) fell down dead, – a manifest sign that now all hope of a better issue was gone, that their defence was departed from them, and that the doom pronounced was sure of taking effect. The prophet at once perceived the meaning of this sign; and, overwhelmed with the fearful carnage that now burst in prospect upon his view, he again prostrated himself, and exclaimed, *"Ah, Lord God! wilt thou make a full end of the remnant of Israel?"* Shall this be a final and exterminating judgment? Must all perish, and the name Pelatiah henceforth be a lie?

It is this question that brings out the gleam of hope that still lingered amid all those dark and dismal proceedings. But this was not to be found in any mitigation of the purpose to execute judgment upon Jerusalem and to destroy the confidences of those who lived there. There must be, in that respect, a sweeping desolation; and in that very exile, which the priests and princes of Jerusalem affected to look upon with such disdain, it was that the hope of Israel now lay, and from thence was the prospect of better days to begin. *"Son of man, thy brethren, thy brethren, are the men of thy redemption (thy Goalim – redemption-men), and all the house of Israel, the whole to whom the inhabitants of Jerusalem have said, Be ye far from the Lord: to us is this land given in possession. Therefore say, Thus saith the Lord God,"* etc., vers. 15-21.

The full import of the first part of this declaration has been considerably obscured by regarding the Goalim spoken of at the beginning as simply the relations or kindred of the prophet (which the word never properly means), and by mistaking the precise object of the affirmation made respecting them. The prophet, by birth a priest, felt when he saw the priesthood in Jerusalem doomed to destruction, as if his own nearest kinsmen were given up to ruin; so that it behoved him to do for them the part of the Goel, and plead or vindicate their cause. According to the law of Moses, the right of the Goel belonged only to the brother, or, failing him, to the relative who stood nearest in blood, and so might fitly be regarded as the proper advocate, deputy, or avenger of the individual (Lev. 25:25,48). Hence it was quite natural for the priest Ezekiel to identify himself with the priesthood in Jerusalem, so far as to feel called upon to espouse their cause, and even to regard his own interest as, in a manner, bound up with theirs. But that natural feeling, the Lord now taught him, must give way to a higher one. *"Thy brethren, thy brethren"* – the repetition of the word indicating, as very commonly in Hebrew, the stress that was intended to be laid upon the relationship – *"thy proper, thy real brethren, these are no longer the priests in Jerusalem, with whom thou art bound by the natural ties of blood and a common right to serve in the temple; in place of these, doomed to destruction for their incorrigible wickedness, a new brotherhood must henceforth become known to thee, – a royal priesthood, which the Lord is going to form for himself out of the wreck of the natural community. Look no more to Jerusalem, but to thine expatriated countrymen, thy fellow-exiles on the banks of the Chebar, and the house of Israel generally, the whole of them that survive. And in them, despised as they are by the inhabitants of Jerusalem, see the true brethren, whom the Lord is preparing as a spiritual seed for the glory of his name. Go and do for them the Goel's part; seek their deliverance."*

The great evangelical principle comes out here, that not those who are most highly esteemed among men, or who may appear to themselves nearest to the kingdom, are those whom God chooses, but rather the poor and despised, and such as, in a sense, are not. A spiritual priesthood, such as the Lord sought, could only be found among the broken hearts of the captivity. Weaned there from their fleshly confidences, humbled in the dust, nay, melted and fused in the hot furnace of affliction, they were in a condition to receive the riches of Divine grace, and repair anew to God for strength and blessing. And so then, as continually since, *"the last were first"* – for only through tribulation could the kingdom be entered. No door of hope at such a time but in the valley of Achor.

The Lord did not overlook the contrariety which his word to Ezekiel presented to outward appearances, and to the taunts which had been thrown out by the priest respecting the exiles, as to their being far from the Lord. *"Therefore, say to them,"* the Lord continued, *"because I have cast them far off among the heathen, and because I have scattered them among the countries, and have been to them for a sanctuary during a little season in the countries whither they have come; therefore I also will gather you from the peoples,"* etc. As much as to say, It is true, they are in a sense far removed, and miserably scattered; but that by no means necessarily involves their being also in a state of distance from God. They have lost access to the outward temple, where fellowship with God has chiefly been maintained; but God himself has come near to them; he has become their sanctuary; and as his presence can make any place a temple, so it has proved a present sanctuary to them, in the room of that which has become an abomination of desolation at Jerusalem. Therefore these are the true priesthood, and in due time shall be gathered again, and reinstated in the land.

A great truth unfolds itself here for all times, – that the Lord is not confined to temples made with hands, and that if there be but the lowly and spiritual heart, he is to be found in the most remote and lonely regions, not less than in the place more especially consecrated to his service and glory. Yea, though it may be their own sins which have conducted them into such regions, and in their very position they can discern too plainly the signs of an offended God, yet, if even then they cry to him, they need not doubt that he is near to give the blessing. But in so particularly unfolding this truth here for the people in exile, it is impossible not to see how the Lord was preparing the way for the better times of the gospel, when the material temple should pass away, and the spiritual alone should rise into view. It was the peculiar temptation of those who loved under the old economy, that even when not chargeable with corrupting the service of God, their minds were apt to contract themselves to the earthly pattern of sacred things exhibited before them, and they could scarcely realize a present God apart from the outward temple and the land of Canaan. So natural and so strong was this tendency, that we find the prophet Jonah attempting to evade the Lord's presence by endeavouring to withdraw to Tarshish. And if the feeling had been allowed to grow unchecked – if some great dispensation in Providence had not been sent in time, to loosen in some degree the tie that bound them to the outward and material, to expand and elevate their conceptions of God, we can easily conceive how alien and repulsive to the views of the most devout worshippers must have been the idea of Christ's spiritual kingdom and universal Church.

In this respect the dispersion, besides being a just chastisement on acocunt of sin, and a salutary discipline to lead the heart of the people back to God, had an important end to accomplish as a preparatory movement in Providence for opening the way for Messiah's kingdom. It was very far from an unmixed evil. As a mere external arrangement, it was destined to be of great service in diffusing the knowledge of God, and providing materials for the first foundations of the Christian Church, by giving the bearers of God's truth a place and an influence in many of the most commanding positions in the heathen world. But still more important and necessary was the end it had to serve in spiritualizing the views of the better part of the Jews themselves, and training them to the knowledge and service of God, without the help of a material temple and an earthly kingdom. Practically it had the effect of indefinitely widening the bounds of Canaan, or of giving to the world at large somewhat of its distinctive characteristics, since the devout worshipper at Babylon, Alexandria, Rome, or wherever he might be placed, found himself a partaker of God's presence and blessing as well as in Jerusalem. What a mighty advance did the kingdom of God thus make toward the possession of the world! And in rendering the dispersion of his people instrumental to the attainment of such a result, how strikingly did the Lord manifest his power to overrule a present evil for the accomplishment of an ultimate good! Nor were it, perhaps, too much to say, having respect to the issues of things, that the dispersion of the Israelites among the nations was fraught with as much blessing for the Church and the world, as even their original settlement in Canaan.

At the time, however, of this vision, when the old economy had still ages to run before it could give way to a better, the Lord could not allow the chosen land and the outward temple, with which it was so essentially connected, to lie long in a state of desolation. The separation of the covenant-people from them could only be temporary. And the very circumstance of God's promising to be a sanctuary to his people in exile – ready to meet them there with tokens of his presence – with refreshments and gifts of the Spirit – was itself an assurance that a restoration could not be far distant. Hence the Lord couples with the promise a limitation in respect to time: he was to be to them a sanctuary for a little – not a little sanctuary, as in our common version and many others, which gives a sense derogatory to the majesty of God, and one also unsuited to the connection. The thought expressed is, that God would be to his people in exile, instead of the temple, a sanctuary so long as that exile lasted; but bounds were to be set to it – it would not need to continue for a long period, as a return must again be opened up for them to the land of the covenant. Therefore the Lord immediately proceeds to declare his purpose to gather them out of the nations among which they had been scattered; and to do so expressly on the ground that he had been to them for a sanctuary in their dispersed and scattered condition. Their scattering, in one sense, had been in another a gathering; it had driven them to take up their refuge in God, thereby preparing and fitting them for being again restored to the land of their fathers. And so, as their sanctuary, God proceeds to make promise of his grace to renew and sanctify their natures, to change their hearts as from stone to flesh, that when they returned they might put away all the abominations which had brought such floods of judgment on the land. These abominations had rendered it what it originally was when its inhabitants were given up to the curse of Heaven; but, returning to it with a heart utterly opposed to such defilements, they would make it again a holy and blessed habitation. Yet only in the event supposed – only if they hearkened to the voice of God, and cherished the spirit of holiness and love he sought to implant within them. If any among them were still bent upon going after the heart of their vile and abominable things, they must reap in bitterness the fruit of their doings, and a threatening to that effect closes the communication.

The promise of a return to Canaan, therefore, was not given to the exiles here, no more than its original possession had been granted, as an absolute and unconditional good. What it should be would still depend upon the spiritual condition of the people themselves, whether they received or frustrated the grace brought to them through such messengers as Ezekiel and Daniel, and the other men of God raised up from time to time among the people. And comparing the promise of what should have been with the record of what actually was, we find that the word received but a partial fulfilment – just because the spiritual renovation had been so partially undergone; and Canaan, as occupied by the restored remnant, was not the region of holiness here represented. Still the promise did not fail; the Lord did provide for himself a spiritual offspring from the captivity, and plant them anew as a seed of blessing in the land of their fathers, – enough to show that he was mindful of his word, and enough also to furnish a pledge that the sum of all promise – the work of reconciliation in Christ, and the inheritance by a redeemed people over his everlasting kingdom – would, in due time, be brought to completion.

Thus closes this remarkable series of visions. As soon as the last communication was uttered, the glory of the Lord, with the attendant cherubim, withdrew altogether from the temple and its courts, *"leaving the house to them desolate,"* and retired even beyond the bounds of the city to the Mount of Olives, there to watch upon the evil that was to befall the city. The prophet is borne back again in spirit to the elders who sat before him, and descending from his state of ecstasy, reports to them what had passed in vision before the eye of his mind. That report itself formed the message which their present circumstances required; and it certainly contained much that was fitted to cheer them under the gloom that hung around their condition, as well as to awe and solemnize their hearts, by the thought of such appalling judgments ready to be executed against the guilty.

CHAPTER XII.

THE VISION OF EZEKIEL'S TYPICAL REMOVING AS AN EXILE, AND ACCOMPANYING INSTRUCTIONS.

[1]The word of the LORD also came to me, saying,

[2]Son of man, you dwell in the midst of a rebellious house, who have eyes to see and see not. They have ears to hear and hear not, for they are a rebellious house.

[3]Therefore, son of man, prepare stuff for moving, and move by day in their sight. And you shall move from your place to another place in their sight. It may be they will consider, though they are a rebellious house.

[4]Then you shall bring forth your stuff by day in their sight, like stuff for moving. And you shall go forth at evening in their sight, as those who go forth into captivity.

[5]Dig through the wall in their sight, and carry out through it.

[6]In their sight you shall carry *it* on *your* shoulders, *and* carry *it* out in the twilight. You shall cover your face so that you do not see the ground, for I have set you *as* a sign to the house of Israel.

[7]And I did as I was commanded. I brought forth my stuff by day, as stuff for captivity, and in the evening I dug through the wall with my hand. I brought *it* forth in the twilight, *and* I carried *it* on *my* shoulder in their sight.

[8]And in the morning the word of the LORD came to me, saying,

[9]Son of man, has not the house of Israel, the rebellious house, said to you, What are you doing?

[10]Say to them, Thus says the Lord GOD: This burden *concerns* the king in Jerusalem and all the house of Israel who are among them.

[11]Say, I am your sign: As I have done, so it shall be done to them. They shall move *and* go into captivity.

[12]And the king who is among them shall carry *burdens* on *his* shoulder in the twilight, and shall go forth. They shall dig through the wall to carry out by it. He shall hide his face so that he does not see the ground with *his* eyes.

[13]I will also spread My net on him, and He shall be taken in My snare. And I will bring him to Babylon, the land of the Chal-de-ans. Yet he shall not see it, though he shall die there.

[14]And I will scatter to every wind all who are around him to help him, and all his bands; and I will draw out the sword after them.

[15]And they shall know that I am the LORD, when I shall scatter them among the nations and scatter them in the countries.

[16]But I will leave a few men of them from the sword, from the famine, and from the plague, so that they may declare all their hateful things among the heathen where they come. And they shall know that I am the LORD.

[17]And the word of the LORD came to me, saying,

[18]Son of man, eat your bread with quaking and drink your water with trembling and with carefulness.

[19]And say to the people of the land: Thus says the Lord GOD of the people of Jerusalem *and* of the land of Israel: They shall eat their bread with carefulness and drink their water in dumb silence, so that her land may be deserted of her fullness, because of the violence of all those who dwell in it.

[20]And the cities that have people shall be laid waste, and the land shall be deserted. And You shall know that I am the LORD.

[21]And the word of the LORD came to me, saying,

[22]Son of man, what is that proverb that you have in the land of Israel, saying, The

days will go on and every vision shall fail?

[23]Therefore tell them, Thus says the Lord GOD: I will make this proverb to cease, and they shall no more use it as a proverb in Israel. But say to them, The days are at hand, and the fulfilment of every vision.

[24]For there shall never again be any vain vision nor flattering fortunetelling within the house of Israel.

[25]I am the LORD. I will speak, and the word that I shall speak shall come to pass. It shall no more be delayed; for in your days, O rebellious house, I will say the word and will do it, says the Lord GOD.

[26]Again the word of the LORD came to me, saying,

[27]Son of man, behold, the house of Israel says, The vision that he sees is for many days *to come*, and he prophesies of the times *that are* far off.

[28]Therefore say to them, Thus says the Lord GOD: There shall none of my words be delayed any more, but the word which I have spoken shall be done, says the Lord GOD.

There is nothing absolutely new in this portion, if viewed simply in regard to the great objects of the tidings it conveys. The burden of some of the preceding visions is again resumed, and several striking particulars added, to confirm the certainty of the coming evil, and beget, if possible, a deeper impression of its fearful nature. The elders, it would seem, had withdrawn, to whom the prophet had communicated the visions already imparted to him respecting the crying abominations and approaching doom of Jerusalem. He is to all appearance alone at the time of the Spirit's next descent upon him; and indeed, the persons immediately interested in the revelation given were not those around him on the banks of the Chebar, but those still residing in Jerusalem, – *"the rebellious house,"* as they are described in ver. 2, in words originally addressed by Moses to their fathers (Deut. 29:4). *"who have eyes to see, and see not; and ears to hear, and hear not."* Yet he is spoken of as dwelling in the midst of them, and is commanded to exhibit in his own person a typical representation of what was to happen. *"It may be,"* said the Lord, *"they will see, though they are a rebellious house."*

Two things were to be done by Ezekiel. He was, first, in open day, and in the sight of his neighbors, to provide for himself the articles usually taken by one who was going to flee as for his life, or be dragged as a captive to a foreign land. Then being thus provided, he was ordered to wait till the evening, and depart *"as they that go forth into captivity."* The expression in the original refers properly not to the persons of such as went into exile, but to the period usually chosen for their doing so; it is literally, *"as the goings forth of the exile,"* viz. amid the darkness and silence of night, when he can most easily effect his escape. If more exactly defined, the period intended would be certainly the earlier part of the night, yet still not simply the evening, nor the twilight, as is improperly given by our translators in ver. 6, but rather by night, after it had become dark. When it is said, therefore (in ver. 3), that the prophet was to remove *"by day before their eyes,"* the meaning is, not that he should then actually change his abode, but that he should be employed in the business of removing, so as to give clear evidence to all that this was his object, which he only waited for the shades of evening to carry into effect. Nor was this all; the nocturnal departure was not of itself sufficient to indicate the approaching future; he must also effect his escape through a hole in the wall, as one too closely watched by hostile parties to adventure into the open street, and must cover his face, as too sorrowful or abashed even to look upon the ground.

The instructions thus given are reported to have been faithfully complied with by the prophet; and on the morrow the word of the Lord came to him in explanation of the action, telling him, that in all that he had done he was merely foreshadowing, as in a type, what was presently to take place with Zedekiah and his people at Jerusalem. And then he goes on to portray, with an apalling distinctness of vision and minuteness of detail, the disasters that had been prefigured, first and most prominently in the case of Zedekiah, and then in the case of the people at large. In this detail he specifies not only the fact of Jerusalem's approaching overthrow, but also the king's hurried and disgraceful flight under cover of night – the failure of his attempt to escape – his seizure by the Chaldeans

– his deportation to Babylon, though in a state in which he should not be able to see it – the utter prostration of his host – the dispersion of his people among the nations – and the miserable desolation of the whole land. The variety of particulars mentioned in this prediction, coupled with the confirmation given to them in the subsequent history, as recorded in 2 Kings 25 and Jer. 52, is of a very striking nature, and entitles the prophecy to a place among the more remarkable delineations of coming events in Scripture. Nor can we wonder at the statement made by Josephus (Ant. b. 10. c. 7), though we have no other evidence of its truth, that Ezekiel sent a copy of it to Zedekiah. The report carries the more probability with it, as Jeremiah's letter of sympathy and counsel to the captives on the river Chebar was what instrumentally called forth at first the agency of Ezekiel; and it was no more than might be expected that he should endeavour to strengthen the hands of his spiritual father in the land of Judah, by sending in turn a message to Jerusalem, confirmatory of the warnings already uttered there by Jeremiah. On the supposition of this having been actually done by Ezekiel, the further report of Josephus, as to the effect produced upon Zedekiah by the communication, readily commends itself to our belief. He states that the infatuated prince, instead of simply receiving the word of God, began to compare together the predictions of Jeremiah and Ezekiel, and finding that the one declared he should be carried to Babylon, while the other affirmed he should indeed be brought to Babylon, but should not see it, he presently concluded that the two predictions were at variance with each other, and rejected both as false. In this he but showed the captious disposition of superficial inquirers and shallow unbelievers of all ages, who no sooner discover some obvious difficulties on the surface of revelation, than they conclude the whole to be a cunningly devised fable, or treat it as unworthy of their serious consideration. Would they but search a little deeper, and survey, in a spirit of impartiality, the entire field of revelation, they would find that the things which at first stagger their belief disappear on closer inspection, or remain only as difficulties inseparable from communications which bear respect to the character and purposes of Godhead. They would not unfrequently find, what was found by Zedekiah too late for his own good, that the very things which are most apt at first to create a feeling of distrust or suspicion are those which contain the most undoubted evidences of the finger of God. Human sagacity might possibly have foreseen, or by a happy conjecture anticipated, the coming rupture between Zedekiah and the Chaldeans, and the consequent overthrow of the city of Jerusalem; but that Zedekiah should endeavour to make his escape from it by night, should be caught in the attempt, should meet face to face with the king of Babylon, should himself be carried to Babylon, though (from his eyes having been meanwhile put out) should not actually behold the place, – that such a train of peculiar circumstances should have been delineated beforehand by the hand of a prophet manifestly bespoke the directing agency of that Spirit who sees the end from the beginning.

The circumstance that the burden contained in this Divine communication had direct reference to the king and people of Jerusalem, alone renders it highly probable that the symbolical action here also took place not externally but in vision. So far as the parties immediately interested were concerned, the representation would have been equally significant if confined to that region within which the prophet's soul properly moved when supernaturally acted on by the Spirit of God, as if exhibited under the form of an outward and ordinary transaction. Indeed, the action is described as proceeding among the very people for whom the instruction was peculiarly intended, *"the rebellious people among whom he dwelt,"* as if his abode had actually been transferred from Chebar to Jerusalem. So, too, when the action was done, it was still the same *"rebellious house, the house of Israel,"* who are represented as saying to him, *"What doest thou?"* Throughout the representation the prophet appears present in the spirit at Jerusalem, and transacting there directly with its people; but how he could be and transact there, while personally resident on the banks of the Chebar, otherwise than in vision, it seems impossible to understand. Besides, if the action had taken place on the territory of real life, how could it have appeared to be other than an incongruous thing for an individual, himself living in exile, to personate, by his removal, the going of his brethren into exile from their proper home in Judea? The action would rather have carried a contrary import – would most naturally have signified the return of his fellow-exiles to Judea – unless it proceeded on the supposition of his being for the time located, of course as an ideal inhabitant, in his native land. At the same time, holding the action to have taken place in vision, as it certainly bore respect more immediately to the king and people of Jerusalem, we are not to imagine that the instruction was without meaning for the prophet's fellow-captives in Chaldea. For many of these, probably by much the larger portion of them, were still hanging their hopes upon the fallacious confidence that matters should ere long right themselves with the house of David, so as to admit of their returning again to the land of their fathers. They were but externally dwelling at a distance, for Jerusalem still lived in their hearts, the delusions which were reigning at the one place had found a home also in the other; and, just as in the preceding visions the communications given to the prophet for the behoof of his fellow-captives were fitted also to admonish and warn the people at Jerusalem, so now, inversely, the word received, and most probably sent as soon as received, for the use of the people of Jerusalem, was fraught with wholesome instruction to those among whom he lived and labored on the Chebar.

If anything could have broken the spell of delusion which lay upon the minds of Zedekiah and his counsellors, or their adherents in Chaldea, one might suppose this instructive action of the prophet would have done it, especially when followed up by such a minute and varied detail of approaching calamities. Nor was it merely the certainty of those calamities being appointed which he thus sought to impress upon them; he was equally explicit in regard to their nearness. For, well knowing how some were ready to treat the message with scorn, and others, though not prepared utterly to despise it, were yet disposed to put away from them the evil day, the Lord spake further in the ears of the prophet, "*Son of man, what is that proverb ye have in the land of Israel, saying, The days are prolonged, and every vision fails? Tell them, therefore, saith the Lord Jehovah, I will make this proverb to cease, and they shall no more use it as a proverb in Israel; but say unto them, The days are at hand, and the word of every vision.*" It would seem the class of themselves, that as the evil had so often been threatened and still postponed, the evil itself had no reality; the experience of God's forbearance had effaced their impressions of his truthfulness; so that on hearing such an unwelcome message as that contained in the earlier part of this chapter, they were ready to dispose of it by the slighting remark, "*Ah, we have heard many words like these before, yet matters have not turned out so bad!*" They not merely thought much time had still to elapse before the prophetic roll discharged its burden of woe, but a spirit of unbelief had taken possession of their minds regarding the reality of the burden itself; it seemed to them but a dream of the prophet's own mind. And there were others who simply presumed upon the delay they expected to intervene, and, as is said in Amos 6:3, "*put far from them the evil day.*" They did not deny that a day of evil was coming, but indulged the hope that it might still be at a considerable distance. They were disposed to say, as Ezekiel himself reports their words in ver. 27, "*The vision that he sees is for many days to come, and he prophesies of the times that are far off.*" But to them also the prophet was commanded to reply, "*There shall none of my words be prolonged any more, but the word which I have spoken shall be done, saith the Lord.*"

The incredulous and secure feeling which is here ascribed to the people of Jerusalem, growing as the hour of destruction approached, is in perfect accordance with the testimony recorded in other prophetical scriptures. Thus Zephaniah declares the Lord's determination "*to search Jerusalem, and punish the men that are settled on their lies; that say in their heart, The Lord will not do good, neither will he do evil*" (chap. 1:12). In a spirit of practical atheism, they had grown into the conviction that there should be no special interposition of Heaven at all, and that, whatever the people might do, events would take their natural course. But still more expressly Jeremiah, "*Behold, they say unto me, Where is the word of the Lord? Let it come now"* (chap. 17:15). That this was said in a feeling of scornful disbelief regarding the evil he had so often foretold, is evident from the vindication he immediately presents for himself, protesting before God that *"he had not desired the evil day,"* but spake only that which God had put into his lips. And again, in chap. 20, he describes the anguish of soul he experienced on account of the treatment that was given to the word of God, which had nearly prevailed on him to yield to the temptation of ceasing to utter it any more. *"I cried out, I cried violence and spoil; because the word of the Lord was made a reproach to me, and a derision daily. Then I said, I will not make mention of Him, nor speak any more in his name. But it was in mine heart as a burning fire shut up in my bones, and I was weary with forebearing, and I could not stay."* No wonder, then, that Ezekiel, in his distant exile, should have sympathized with his afflicted brother in Judah, and should have sought to strengthen him in his conflict with evil, by levelling a word of severe reproof against the vain presumptions and false confidences which were so offensively rearing their head among the people of Jerusalem. The one prophet did for the other the part of a true fellow-laborer in the service of God. He came boldly to his help in the day of blasphemy and rebuke, and gave fresh support to the cause of righteousness and truth, by proclaiming from another watch-tower the faithful, though despised, warning note of danger.

We cannot but think with wonder, when we look back upon the times of these Old Testament prophets, of the obstinate incredulity and measureless content in which so many of the people seem to have shut themselves up, alike in defiance of the most solemn warnings of God, and in spite of several lowring appearances in Providence, which seemed to give no doubtful indications of a coming storm. So too, doubtless, thought the next generation of the Jews themselves, when, in the language of Zechariah, they saw how *"God's words and statutes, which he commanded his servants the prophets, had taken hold of their fathers"* (chap. 1:6). But it is well for us to bear in mind, that the spirit of unbelief and false security which prevailed so extensively then is ever springing forth anew, and is plainly announced in New Testament Scripture as destined to form a distinguishing characteristic of the last times. It was a significant question of our Lord, and evidently pointed to the great defect in this respect that should discover itself before the consummation of all things, *"When the Son of man comes, shall he find faith in the earth?"* Such faith, namely, as he had been speaking of, – faith realizing in firm confidence the certainty of the Lord's manifestation to put a final end to the evils that afflict his Church, and in this confidence waiting, hoping, praying to the last. The Apostle Peter also still more distinctly intimates in his second epistle what might be looked for: *"There shall come in the last days, scoffers, walking after their own lusts, and saying, Where is the promise of his coming? for since the fathers fell asleep, all things continue as they were from the beginning of the world."* It will readily be understood that the danger from this source to this faith of God's elect will always be the greater, the more the time is lengthened out that is to intervene between the first and second coming of the Lord. For time, which is justly said to try all things, in this respect also tries faith, that it silently impairs in men's minds the foundation on which faith rests – the word of God. In common with other things of meaner value, this, too, seems to wax old as time proceeds, and to become, the longer it is in use, the less in power and value. Even already it is looked upon by many as comparatively antiquated, out of date; the facts of which it testifies are but faintly described in the distant past; centuries have rolled away since they took place and were put on record; and the record itself has been so long in existence, so frequently handled, and so fully discussed, that with those to whom nothing is interesting but what possesses the freshness of novelty, the sacred volume, so far from being able to nourish and support a living faith, has itself become stable and dead.

Thus it is that natural men judge of God's word, as if, like their own productions, it were subject to wasting and decay. They know not that this word of God, being the expression of his own eternal nature, has in it what lives and abides for ever, – what is as new and fresh to the heart of faith still as the very moment when, ages ago, it proceeded from the lips of those who spake as they were moved by the Holy Ghost. Then, along with a prevailing ignorance or forgetfulness of this great truth, there is the fascinating influence which is apt to be wielded over men's minds by the onward movements of society in knowledge and civilisation. Here they find an attractive contrast to the stationary character of the ground and objects of faith. For everything in this lower field seems constantly in progress, and big with hope for the future. It is deemed incredible that while such vital powers are at work, and such a career of advancement is in prospect, God should lay a sudden arrest on the vast machinery, and wind up the affairs of the world by bringing in the fixed and final issues of eternity. Nay, the belief of a personal God, separate from the workmanship of his own hands, and capable of suddenly introducing a state of things altogether new, is in many quarters fast giving way. In a new and peculiarly subtle form, the old carnal and idolatrous tendencies are reviving, impiously commingling the Divine and human, identifying the creature with the Creator. And judging from present appearances, there is too much reason to conclude that, precisely as before Christ came to execute judgment upon Jerusalem a rage for worldly saviors was one of the reigning delusions of the time, so, as the period draws on for his coming to execute judgment upon the world, a like rage will prevail for a worldly gospel, – one that will seek to confound heaven and earth, God and man, and, in a manner possibly even more daring and presumptuous than in the Papacy, will dispose man to *"exalt himself in the temple of God, and show himself that he is God."* What need, then for those who would escape the condemnation of the wicked to look well to the foundation of their faith, and to see that this stands not in the wisdom of man, but in the word of God! How careful should each be to dwell beside the fountain of Israel! For times of trial manifestly are coming, in which they only who are taught of God, and kept by the power of his Spirit, can expect to resist the swelling tide of delusion, and maintain even the appearance of godliness.

CHAPTER XIII.

THE FALSE IN PROPHECY, ITS CHARACTER AND DOOM.

A very close connection exists between the subject of this chapter and the one immediately preceding. The former had denounced the false expectations of the people respecting the safety of Jerusalem; this denounces the persons who were the chief instruments in feeding these expectations. And in this case, still more directly than in the other, Ezekiel stretches out the hand to Jeremiah, and comes forward as a second, though perfectly independent witness, to reiterate and confirm the testimony already delivered in substance by his fellow-servant in Judea. One of the sorest trials – and, indeed, one of the most baffling difficulties Jeremiah had there to contend with – arose from the false pretenders to the prophetical gift, who were constantly delivering, in the name of God, messages which tended only to foster prevailing sins, and to lend the appearance of a Divine sanction to the popular delusions. *"Mine heart within me is broken,"* he says in chap. 23:9, *"because of the prophets; all my bones shake; I am like a drunken man."* It is more than probable that most of these false prophets were perfectly conscious of the fraud they were practising upon the people, and laid claim to Divine communications only as a pretext for more readily securing their own selfish though short-sighted purposes. But it seems evident, especially from what is written in Jeremiah, that there were at least some who had become the dupes of their own delusions, and were fully as much fanatics as knaves. A crafty diviner, who plays upon the credulity of others for the sake of his own gain or aggrandizement, will always be careful to make his announcements run in such a strain, that while they obviously tend to feed the desires and prejudices of the persons he addresses, they at the same time furnish no clear and definite grounds for detecting his hypocrisy. And whenever such vain pretenders to a supernatural insight into the Divine will begin to hazard deliverances which admit of being distinctly falsified as well as confirmed by approaching events in Providence, we may be sure that the spirit of fanaticism has risen to the ascendant in their bosoms, and that, if they deceive others, they have themselves already been deceived.

Such, unquestionably, was the case at Jerusalem in the time of Jeremiah. Not only were there persons in considerable numbers who prophesied falsely, and gave forth general assurances of continued peace (Jer. 5:31, 6:14, 14:13), but there were also those who, in the most confident tone, held out the promise of specific events in the immediate future, and fixed the period of their fulfilment. Thus Hananiah of Gibeon said to Jeremiah in the house of the Lord, in the presence of the priests and of all the people: *"Thus speaketh the Lord of hosts, the God of Israel, saying, I have broken the yoke of the king of Babylon. Within two full years will I bring again into this place all the vessels of the Lord's house, which Nebuchadnezzar took away from this place and carried them to Babylon. And I will bring again to this place Jeconiah, the son of Jehoiakim, king of Judah, with all the captives of Judah that went into Babylon, saith the Lord: for I will break the yoke of the king of Babylon"* (chap. 28:2-4). No man in his senses would have ventured on such a circumstantial prediction, unless he had himself firmly believed it; for he was plainly prevailed in Judea, it had also extended to the banks of the Chebar. There is no doubt over which he had no control, and which might shortly take a turn that would expose him to reprobation as an arrant impostor. By whatever process the persuasion may have been reached, we cannot doubt that he had become thoroughly persuaded in his own mind of the truth of his prediction before he proclaimed it in the public ear. And we must keep in mind the fact that there were such self-deceived impostors at Jerusalem, – a fact, as we shall see, pointedly referred to in this chapter of Ezekiel, – both to understand correctly the circumstances of the time, and to derive from them the improvement they are fitted to convey.

It is to be further borne in mind, that while the spirit of false prophesying chiefly prevailed in Judea, it had also extended to the banks of the Chebar. There is no doubt existed in comparative feebleness, having few of the outward stimulants to nurse it into activity and strength which were supplied in abundance by the peculiar position and circumstances of Jerusalem; and it probably did little more than re-echo the utterances which proceeded from its centre of influence in Judea. Yet that there was such a spirit at work also on the banks of the Chebar is manifest alone from the letter addressed by Jeremiah to the captives, in which he charged them *"not to be deceived by their prophets and their diviners that were in the midst of them, for they prophesied falsely in the Lord's name;"* and he even mentioned three persons by name, Ahab, Zedekiah, and Shemaiah, who were acting the part of false prophets among them (chap. 29:8,9,21,etc.). So that the evil against which the communication in this chapter is directed was not without its abettors in the immediate neighborhood of Ezekiel, although, in the rampant and offensive form here delineated, it was to be found only in Jerusalem, and the word, therefore, must be regarded as directly and primarily intended for the use of those who still resided there. For this reason, also, it is that the word of Ezekiel joins itself so closely to similar words previously delivered to Jeremiah on the spot, and, in the very language employed, bears unmistabeable references especially to the 23rd chapter of that prophet's writings.

But it is time to come to the more particular examination of the passage itself. It naturally falls into two principal parts, – the one bearing respect to the false prophets, and the other to the false prophetesses. Each of these again admits of a twofold division, – a first part, delineating the operations and symptoms of the false spirit in question, and a second, disclosing the judgment of God upon those who yielded themselves to its sway.

[1] And the word of the LORD came to me, saying,

[2] Son of man, prophesy against the prophets of Israel who prophesy. And say to those who prophesy out of their own hearts, Hear the word of the Lord:

[3] Thus says the Lord GOD, Woe to the foolish prophets who follow their own spirit and have seen nothing!

[4] O Israel, your prophets are like the foxes in the deserts.

[5] You have not gone up into the breaks,

nor built the wall for the house of Israel, that it might stand in the battle in the day of the LORD.

6 They have seen vanity and lying fortune-telling, saying, The LORD says. And the LORD has not sent them; and they have made *others* to hope that they would confirm the word.

7 Have you not seen a vision, and have you not spoken a lying prophesy, yet you say, The LORD says, although I have not spoken?

8 Therefore thus says the Lord GOD: Because you have spoken vanity and seen lies, therefore, behold, I am against you, says the Lord GOD.

9 And My hand shall be on the prophets who see vanity and who prophesy lies. They shall not be in the meeting of My people, nor shall they be written in the writing of the house of Israel, nor shall they enter into the land of Israel. And you shall know that I am the Lord GOD.

10 Because, even because they have led My people astray, saying, Peace – and there was no peace – and one built up a wall, and, lo, others daubed it with chalk;

11 say to those who daub it with chalk that it shall fall. There shall be an overflowing rain, and you, O great hailstones, shall fall, and a stormy wind shall tear.

12 Lo, when the wall has fallen, shall it not be said to you, Where is the daubing with which you have daubed?

13 Therefore thus says the Lord GOD: I will even tear with a stormy wind in My fury. And there shall be an overflowing rain in My anger, and great hailstones in *My* fury to destroy it.

14 So I will break down the wall that you have daubed with chalk, and bring it down to the ground, so that the foundation of it shall be uncovered. And it shall fall, and you shall be destroyed in the midst of it; and you shall know that I am the LORD.

15 So I will fulfill My wrath on the wall and on those who have daubed it with chalk, and will say to you, The wall is not, nor those who daubed it –

16 *that is,* the prophets of Israel who prophesy concerning Jerusalem, and who see visions of peace for her, and *there is* no peace, says the LORD.

17 Likewise, son of man, set your face against the daughters of your people, who prophesy out of their own heart. And prophesy against them,

18 and say, Thus says the Lord GOD: Woe to the *women* who sew pillows to armholes, and make handkerchiefs of every size to put on the head in order to hunt souls! Will you hunt the souls of My people, and will you save alive the souls *that come* to you?

19 You will defile Me among My people for handfuls of barley and for pieces of bread, to kill the souls that should not die, and to save alive the souls that should not live, by your lying to My people who hear *your* lies.

20 Therefore thus says the Lord GOD: Behold, I am against your pillows with which you hunt the souls there, to make *them* flee. And I will tear them from your arms and will let the souls go, the souls that you hunt in order to make *them* flee.

21 Also I will tear your handkerchiefs and deliver My people out of your hand, and they shall no more be in your hand to be hunted. And you shall know that I am the LORD.

22 Because with lies you have saddened the heart of the righteous, whom I have not made sad; and have made the hands of the wicked strong, so that he should not turn from his wicked way, by promising him life.

23 Therefore you shall never see vanity any more, nor tell fortunes. For I will deliver My people out of your hands; and you shall know that I am the LORD.

I. We look first at the case of the false prophets.

1. These are variously described; and first, in regard to the fundamental distinction that existed betwixt them and the true. *"Son of man, prophesy against the prophets of Israel that prophesy, and say thou unto the prophets out of their own hearts, Hear ye the word of Jehovah: Thus saith the Lord Jehovah, Woe unto the foolish prophets that follow their own spirit, and have seen nothing."* A threefold error, – first, in regard to the source from which their messages were derived, *"their own hearts"* (so also in Jer. 23:16,17); then in the point aimed at, going *"after their own spirit,"* or following the bent on their natural inclinations; and finally, in the result attained, *"they saw nothing,"* and yet spake as if they had seen something. Expressed in philosophical language, the whole was subjective merely without any objective reality – hence, but a vision in the air, a baseless and shadowy superstructure. The true prophet differed in each particular from the false one: He prophesied not from his own heart, but form the heart of God, in conceiving and uttering his message, he followed not his own spirit, but the Spirit of God; and consequently, the message he delivered was charged with a Divine reality. There was, first

of all, something objective in his experience, something presented to his soul from above, which gave rise to whatever belonged to him of a subjective character – at once lighted and fed the flame. Hence the expression we sometimes meet with in the prophets, of their seeing as a vision what they had to utter: *"The vision of Isaiah, the son of Amos, which he saw;" "The burden which Habakkuk the prophet did see;"* and the still more peculiar expression, which is frequently employed, of seeing the Word of the Lord (Isa. 2:1; 13:1; Mic. 1:1). "The perception of the Word, which God communicated to the prophets, was made by means of the spiritual sense, the apprehension of which is named, in reference to the noblest of the natural senses, a seeing. For what enters into the consciousness of the prophet as such, is not the product of his own natural power of reflection, but an object presented to him by the Spirit of God as from without, and by himself discerned through the opened spiritual eye. The Word itself, indeed, is not seen, inasmuch as it is the body, in a manner, of the thought which has come into the region of his sensible apprehensions. But as the communication of the Divine Word to the prophet is to be conceived of as a purely internal, not a corporeally audible one (unless the contrary is distinctly specified), and the Divine idea presents itself not mediately through the natural sense, but directly to the spirit of the prophet, so the notion of seeing is in its proper place; the prophet perceives that which thereafter forms itself in his soul, as the cover (veil) of the external word."[6]

Here, then, lay the grand characteristic of the true prophet, as distinguished from the false. There was exhibited objectively to his soul, through the operation of the spirit of God, a thought or succession of thoughts – an action, perhaps, revealing the mind and will of God; and then taking up this in the apprehension of his mind, he went forth to declare it to others, as from his own inward consciousness, clothed in such words as fitly expressed what had been seen within. With the false prophet, on the other hand, even supposing him to be perfectly sincere in what he uttered, all proceeded from the impulse of his own inflated imagination or excited feelings; the whole was from within merely, nothing from without, from above. Yet with this distinction so clearly traced, and traced for the express purpose of drawing the line of demarcation between the true and the false in prophetic utterances, we are still presented with views and theories of inspiration, which, in the case of inspired men generally, prophets as well as evangelists and apostles, if they do not altogether discard the objective, render the subjective alone prominent, – make so much account of the internal consciousness or intuitional sense of the subject of inspiration, as necessarily to throw into the background the Divine communication made to him from above. But in the two classes of prophets here presented to our notice, the one could lay claim, as well as the other, to the internal consciousness of some spiritual thought or idea; the only question was, whence came the idea? Did it spring up from within, as of itself? or was it presented there by the Spirit of God? Was the mind's consciousness of the thoughts and feelings it experienced of its own awakening, or was it awakened by a Divine and formal communication from above? If we lose sight of this important distinction, we virtually make no account of what constitutes the fundamental element of a Divine revelation, and leave ourselves without a fixed landmark between the movements of God's Spirit and the capricious workings of human fancy. And confounding thus things that essentially differ in regard to the origin of a revelation, we lay ourselves open to the further error of disparaging the value of a revelation when made; we totally change it indeed, and lower its character, and assign it only a kind of higher room among the views and cogitations of men's own imagining.

The Church of God will do well to watch with the utmost jealousy against any attempts in this direction, from whatever quarter, and under whatever show of reason or piety they may be introduced. How well had it been for Germany had the churches there listened to the warning voice which the learned Bengel in his day lifted against the evil, when it was just beginning to appear among them, though still only in its infancy and breathing the odor of an elevated devotion! "What some," says he, in his work on the Apocalypse, "are forward to teach about the inward word, is likely to occasion much fearful evil, as soon as philosophy shall officiously take such a subject in hand. Persons who are always dwelling upon that subject are impatient to get possession of the kernel without its fostering shell; every such appurtenance is with them an impertinence; in other words, they would have Christ without the Bible. But notwithstanding this favorite refinement, they are insensibly approximating to an opposite extreme, and they will arrive at it. For as it often happens that extremes meet, so are fanaticism and gross deism found at last to coincide; and mischiefs symptomatic of the one and of the other may already be seen occasionally in one and the same beclouded mind."

It is only, however, at the commencement of a process of this kind that there is likely to be the appearance of extremes meeting; for the fanatical or hypocritical spirit can never be very long in betraying its essential agreement with the deistical, or, at least, worldly spirit, by its visible distaste for the pure and elevating character of those revelations which come from God. Here also the tree is known by its fruits. The Spirit of God must have a holy vessel for the subject and channel of his Divine communications, – even for such as are of a more ordinary kind; but how much more when he comes to put forth his loftier breathings in the soul, and make it, in a peculiar manner, the oracle of Heaven's counsels! The true prophet, therefore, unlike the false one, who lived and breathed merely in the element of his own corruption, behoved to be in the strictest sense a man of God, – one who was accustomed to tread the higher walks of the spiritual life; for thus only could he possess the necessary adaptation for the Spirit's agency in his soul, – the receptive faculty, or, as we may rather call it, the spiritual sympathy to apprehend aright what was communicated from above, and appropriate it as his own. If at any time this spiritual adaptation was wanting, or but imperfectly attained, the agency of the Spirit could not fail to exhibit something fitful and irregular, or even violent, in its working, – as we see especially in the case of Balaam, when he was constrained to do the part of a true prophet. Nor could it be otherwise with the inspired writers of the New Testament Scriptures; in their case, the personal adaptation must rather be of a higher, more regular, and equable kind. For the Spirit's work in them did not so much consist, as formerly in the case of the prophets, in raising them at times with rapt emotion above present objects, and giving them a supernatural insight into particular circumstances and events, as in enabling them to stand upon the elevated platform of the objective realities of the gospel dispensation, and thence to read forth, according to the mind of the Spirit, the manifold views of Christian truth, and obligations, and hope, which spring from those realities as from their common ground. But for this it was plainly necessary that they should habitually live in the region of the Spirit's presence, and not merely as in a few ecstatic moments, but in the regular tone and temper of their minds, he prepared for entertaining and uttering the thoughts of the Spirit. And if *"holy men of old"* were needed as instruments of Divine communication to *"speak as they were moved by the Holy Ghost,"* still more, may we say, were such needed at the beginning of the gospel, to declare with infallible certainty, and in *"words which the Holy Ghost teacheth,"* the things that are now freely given us of God. The Spirit's work must reflect itself in the character of the agents he employed, as well as in the nature of the communications they imparted.

But to return to the charge of Ezekiel against the false prophets. Having exposed the hollowness of their pretensions in regard to God, he now unfolds the pernicious results of their course in relation to the people. He compares them to *"the foxes in the deserts,"* and adds, *"Ye have not gone up into the breach, neither have drawn a wall around the house of Israel, to stand in the battle in the day of the Lord."* The description proceeds upon a silent comparison between the covenant-people and a vineyard, a similitude already in established use (Isa. 5:1-7, 27:2; Jer. 2:21; Ps. 80). It was the special duty of the prophets to do the part of watchmen and overseers in this spiritual vineyard. By their quick discernment in the fear of the Lord, and their faithfulness in disclosing his mind and will to the people, they should have protected the sacred enclosure against the assaults of the adversaries, repaired the breaches as they arose, and repressed, with holy energy, the first risings of corruption. But the reverse of all this was done by the false prophets, while they consulted merely their own ease, and humored the perverse inclinations of the people. In respect to the safety and well-being of the commonwealth they did the part of foxes, *"which spoil the vines"* (Song 2:15), – nay, foxes in waste or desert places, the most savage and insatiable of their species. Yet no suspicion of this seemed to have crossed their own minds; they looked with the most perfect complacence upon the success of their mission, and *"hoped,"* as is said in ver. 6, *"to confirm* (or establish) *their word."* The subjective existed with them in full vigor, though utterly destitute of everything objective; for, in the just retribution of God, they had been given up to such strong delusion that they came to believe their own lie.

2. The punishment threatened against these false prophets is one exactly suited to the nature of their sin. They had sought, by making high pretensions to communion with Heaven, to become persons of great note and influence among the people, while still the true foundation for such greatness was wanting. Therefore the Lord declared his determination to make their fate answer to their condition; he would unmask their hypocrisy and discover their nothingness, cast them out of his kingdom as empty and worthless creatures, and, as with a destroying and desolating blast, lay all their pretensions and hopes in the dust. Instead of ruling the counsels of the nation, they should not, he tells them (vers. 8, 9), be so much as found in the assembly of his people; their names should not even be written in the roll of the house of Israel, nor their persons be permitted any more to enter the land of Israel inheriting the curse of the covenant *"they should be cut off from among their people."* Then, in regard to their work of vanity and delusion, a similar visitation of severe judgment and exterminating ruin is foretold. By that work they had but ministered to the foolish desires and vain confidences of the people; so that while the one was like the builders of a loose and incompact wall, the others were as persons coming after and daubing it over with a thin and showy, but still feeble and unsubstantial covering. Wherefore, it must be assailed with the storm of the Lord's fury, – a storm that is represented as combining the three most destructive agents of the lower heavens – wind, rain, and hailstones. Particular stress is laid upon the hailstones, because these were more out of the usual course of nature in those parts of the world, and on that account were sometimes in reality given as tokens, as they are also often poetically referred to as emblems, of the most severe expression of God's displeasure upon the adversaries (Ex. 9:18; Jos. 10:10; Job 38:22; Ps. 18: 12, 13, etc.). Here, too, to give the reference to them a more intense form, and render the emblem more strikingly expressive of the unsparing judgment that was to be executed, the prophet employs, instead of the usual epithet for hailstones, what is literally ice or crystal stones. And like one who actually beheld the devastation made by these and the other emblematical instruments of vengeance, he winds up the whole description by a kind of solemn attestation to the effect produced: *"Thus I accomplish my wrath upon the wall, and upon them that plastered it with whitewash, and say unto you, The wall is not, nor they that plastered it, – the prophets of Israel who prophesy concerning Jerusalem, and who see a vision of peace for her, and there is no peace, saith the Lord Jehovah."*

II. Such is the interpretation given in this vivid picture of the character and doom of the false prophets; and we turn now to the closely related delineation of the false prophetesses, which occupies the remainder of the chapter.

1. These are plainly represented here as also playing an important part in strengthening the reigning delusions of the time, and lulling the people into a false security. It is somewhat singular that in no other passage are they spoken of in such a connection; probably because the pernicious influence they exerted was more from the seductive courses they pursued than from the false prophecies they uttered. For mention is frequently enough made, both in this prophet and Jeremiah, of the active share the women took at that time in introducing and maintaining the evil practices of idolatry, but only in this place of the guilt they incurred by pretending to supernatural revelations; and here also it is coupled with strong representations of the deceitful and corrupt practices

they followed. That they should, however, have made pretensions of this kind, and in such numbers as to call for the special rebuke of Heaven, is itself a convincing proof of the great excitement which prevailed at the period; since it was not in the ordinary course of things, but only in peculiar emergencies, that either the Lord might be expected to bestow on women the gift of prophecy, or that men would be disposed to receive from their lips the revelation of God's will. There were not wanting instances in the history of the past which warranted the supposition that God might sometimes employ female instruments in making known his purpose to men, – such as Miriam, Deborah, Huldah, – though the rareness of these instances, and the extraordinary nature of the occasions which gave rise to them, tended considerably to aggravate the guilt of those who falsely pretended to a Divine commission. Like the false prophets, these are also represented as prophesying *"out of their own hearts;"* and being themselves of one mind and spirit with the people at large, no higher result was achieved, or was aimed at by the prophesyings, than to strengthen and confirm the prevailing delusions.

In the case of these prophetesses, however, the false direction given, assumed, if the common view be correct, a more palpably effeminate and luxurious character; it aimed not only at encouraging the people in their false security, but also at pampering their love of fleshly ease and personal indulgence. They are described as *"sewing pillows for all arm-holes,"* or making soft cushions for all arm-joints – apparently articles of some sort to be used in reclining, so as to give to the person using them the softness of an agreeable repose. Not content with this, they made also *"kerchiefs,"* or coverings, *"upon the head of every stature,"* – some kind of fashionable and attractive head-dress, fitted to act as a lure in winning others to their corrupt and sinful ways. For the great object they had in view in making such articles of luxury was to *"hunt,"* or *"catch souls;"* so that, with their high pretensions to communion with Heaven, the real design and tendency of their arts was no other than that of the profligate characters described in Prov. 6 and 7 – to ensnare and ruin the unwary. It is possible, however, and indeed, we think, most probable, that the prophet, in his description of the conduct of these women, is not to be understood literally, but that he unfolds the design and tendency of their deceitful ways under the image of gay and luxurious clothing. So was it with his description of the false prophets, when he spoke of them as acting the part of foxes, and whitewashing an unsubstantial wall, – that is, ministering to a false security, as the prophetesses here did to a false comfort and delight. In this case, it was their fair speeches and lying divinations which were the cushions and the tapestry mentioned by the prophet. But this makes no alteration on the nature of their conduct: they acted a most wicked part. Therefore the prophet turns on them with a question of fiery indignation and sharp rebuke, *"Will ye hunt (catch) the souls of my people, and save your own souls alive? And will ye pollute me among my people for handfuls of barley, and for pieces of bread, to slay the souls that should not die, and to save alive the souls that should not live, by your lying to my people that hear a lie being of themselves inclined to listen to falsehood)?"* Acting the part of soul-destroyers to others, it was vain to expect that they should themselves escape the coming vengeance. And the less so, as it was for so paltry a consideration they were carrying on the infamous traffic of decoying others to destruction. Of course, the largest prospects of personal gain would have been totally insufficient to justify them in such practices; but that they should have been ready to prostitute the name of God, and ply the arts of hypocrisy and deceit for such miserable pittances of present good, showed the grovelling debasement and intense selfishness of their spirits. It stamped them as in the strongest sense *"lovers of pleasure more than lovers of God."*

In regard to the punishment threatened, there is nothing peculiar or difficult, so far as the act of Divine retribution is concerned. The Lord simply declares his purpose to defeat the crooked and carnal policy of those false prophetesses, and, by terrible things in righteousness, to put it beyond their power to employ much longer their pernicious arts. He would rend in pieces their articles of luxury, or defeat the corrupt and captivating wiles which they used as gins to ensnare and catch men's souls, so that these might find an escape from their foils; though still nothing is said as to the particular way in which the retribution was to be effected. But as it had been plainly enough indicated in the case of the false prophets that the work of punishment was to be accomplished by weapons of awful violence and unsparing destruction, it was naturally to be inferred, that these female associates would share the same fate, and that their power to use the seductive arts they had hitherto plied with such fatal success was to cease and determine, because they should themselves be involved in the common ruin, and the vanity of their pretensions would become manifest to all.

It is a part of Satan's policy to avoid a formal repetition of exploded errors, and to shift and adapt his stratagems as the ever-changing temper of the times may require. We may not, therefore, expect to see exactly the same devices resorted to, and the same scenes enacted over again, which have passed under our review in this chapter. But we may not the less certainly expect that the evils here depicted shall be perpetually recurring, with such modifications in respect to manner and form as may be likely to render them more effectual in their mischievous operation. Our Lord plainly forewarned the Church of false prophets, who should arise and deceive many. And the working of the Antichristian power, of which Paul spake so distinctly, was represented to be *"with signs and lying wonders, and with all deceivableness of unrighteousness in them that perish."* But, as in all ages, and under all forms alike, the object of Satan is to corrupt and overthrow the truth of God, so it ever remains the sure, as it also is the only effectual, safeguard against his delusions, to hold by that truth in the simplicity and confidence of faith. The danger in such cases is merely, as the apostle intimated, to those who will not believe the truth, and receive it in love. And whether it be in the form of pretended revelations concerning the things of God that the temptation comes, or in the more common but not less dangerous arts of fleshly indulgence and worldly allurement, let there be but an enlightened knowledge of the word of God, and a lively apprehension of its great doctrinal and moral principles, and there will be no material difficulty in distinguishing between the evil and the good. Satan may transform himself for a time into an angel of light; his agents may assume, when prosecuting their work of delusion, the most lamb-like and winning appearance; but there still is one thing too hard for them to accomplish – they cannot identify the saving truth of God with falsehood and corruption; and the childlike spirit, the soul that is taught of God and abides in the simplicity of the faith, has a rock beneath its feet which cannot be moved, and a way of peace and safety which no force or stratagem can turn into a pathway of ruin.

CHAPTER XIV.

HYPOCRITICAL INQUIRERS AFTER GOD – THEIR WICKEDNESS DISCOVERED AND REBUKED.

[1] Then some of the elders of Israel came to me and sat before me.

[2] And the word of the LORD came to me, saying,

[3] Son of man, these men have set up their idols in the heart, and put the stumbling-block of their iniquity before their face. Should I at all be inquired of by them?

[4] Therefore speak to them and say to them, Thus says the Lord GOD: Every man of the house of Israel who sets up his idols in his heart and puts the stumbling-block of his iniquity before his face, and comes to the prophet; I the LORD will answer him who comes according to the multitude of his idols;

[5] so that I may take the house of Israel in their own heart, because they are all cut off from Me through their idols.

[6] Therefore say to the house of Israel, Thus says the Lord GOD: Repent and turn from your idols, and turn away your faces from all your hateful things.

[7] For every one of the house of Israel, or of the stranger who lives in Israel, who separates himself from Me and sets up his idols in his heart, and puts the stumbling-block of his iniquity before his face, and comes to a prophet to ask of him concerning Me – I the LORD will answer him by Myself.

[8] And I will set My face against that man,

and will make him a sign and a proverb, and I will cut him off from the midst of My people; and you shall know that I am the LORD.

[9]And if the prophet is deceived when he has spoken a thing, I the LORD have deceived that prophet, and I will stretch out My hand on him and will destroy him in the midst of My people Israel.

[10]And they shall bear the punishment of their iniquity; the punishment of the prophet shall be just like the punishment of him who seeks *to him* –

[11]so that the house of Israel may never again go astray from Me, nor be at all defiled with all their transgressions, but that they may be My people, and I may be their God, says the Lord GOD.

[12]The word of the LORD came again to me, saying,

[13]Son of man, when the land sins against Me by trespassing grievously, then I will stretch out My hand on it and will break the staff of its bread and will send famine on it. And *I* will cut off man and beast from it.

[14]Though these three men, Noah, Daniel and Job were in it, they should deliver *only* their own souls by their righteousness, says the Lord GOD.

[15]If I cause destroying beasts to come through the land, and they spoil it so that it is deserted, so that no man may pass through because of the beasts,

[16]though these three men were in it, *as* I live, says the Lord GOD, they shall deliver neither sons or daughters. They only shall be delivered, but the land shall be deserted.

[17]Or *if* I bring a sword on that land and say, Sword, go through the land – so that I cut off man and animal from it –

[18]though these three men were in it, *as* I live, says the Lord GOD, they shall deliver neither sons or daughters, but they only shall be delivered themselves.

[19]Or *if* I send a plague into that land and pour out My fury on it in blood, to cut off man and animal from it;

[20]though Noah, Daniel and Job were in it, *as* I live, says the Lord GOD, they shall deliver neither son nor daughter. They shall deliver *only* their own souls by their righteousness.

[21]For thus says the Lord GOD: How much more when I send My four sore judgments on Jerusalem, the sword, and the famine, and the destroying beast and the plague, to cut off man and animal from it!

[22]Yet, behold, there shall be left a remnant in it that shall be brought out, sons and daughters. Behold, they shall come out to you, and you shall see their way and their doings. And you shall know that I have not done without cause all that I have done in it, says the Lord GOD.

This chapter opens with a statement that *"certain of the elders of Israel came to the prophet and sat before him."* By these elders we are certainly to understand persons holding that dignity among the exiles of Chebar, and not, as some have erroneously supposed, deputies from the people still resident in Judah and Jerusalem. For what purpose they came – whether to ask counsel from the prophet regarding some point of difficulty that had occurred to themselves, or to hear what he might be prompted by the Spirit to communicate of seasonable instruction – we are not expressly told. But that they came in the character of inquirers may be almost certainly inferred from ver. 3, where the Lord at once proceeds, through his servant, to repudiate the idea of his being inquired at by persons of such a character, – persons who had *"set up their idols in their heart, and put the stumbling-block of their iniquity before their face."* After this it is scarcely possible to doubt that they came in the character of inquirers; though what might be the precise object of their inquiry is nowhere indicated in what follows, unless we can suppose (what is in the highest degree probable) that the message of the prophet was so framed as in some part to meet the proposed subject of inquiry, and thus incidentally to discover what the subject itself really was. This supposition is confirmed by the fact, which strikes us the moment we glance over the contents of the chapter, that it falls into two parts, – the first (vers. 3-ll) referring to the preliminary point respecting the character of the inquirers, and the remaining portion addressing itself to a subject entirely distinct, – God's method of dealing with a land and people when they have reached a state of hopeless corruption and depravity. It is more than probable, therefore, that while God refused to give any formal answer to such inquirers as those who now sat before the prophet, he yet, in this latter portion of the message, gave a substantial deliverance on the question about which their anxiety had been raised.

The previous communications of the prophet had disclosed an amazing degree of wickedness prevailing generally among the people of Judah, and extending even to those who should have set themselves vigorously to check and reform it, – the priestly and prophetical orders. It was not to be denied, however, with all the truth there might be in such representations, that there still were some noble expectations. Among the prophets there was, at least, the faithful and unflinching Jeremiah; and there were others, beyond doubt, of a kindred spirit, both in the priesthood and among the laity. How naturally, then, in such a case might the thought arise, that possibly after all, the existence of this faithful remnant would tell favorably upon the procedure of God, and throw a kind of shield over the land of Judah for its preservation! It is even conceivable, that the thought might assume in the minds of some a more decided form, and that they might be tempted to ask, how, with such an admixture of righteousness in the midst of them, God could justly proceed to pour down his exterminating judgments on the land! Such cogitations and inquiries were by no means unnatural at the time, especially when it is known how loath the people were – as well that portion of them which was already in exile, as those who still dwelt in Jerusalem – to think of the nation going to ruin. And if these were the points respecting which the elders on this occasion came to confer with the prophet, the message delivered in the latter division of the chapter might certainly be regarded as forming a most direct and explicit deliverance upon their intended inquiries.

1. But there was a strong reason for the prophet addressing himself, in the first instance, to the preliminary point connected with the character of the inquiries, on account, more especially, of the close relation that subsisted between such an exhibition of character in them, and the false spirit of prophecy which had already been so severely condemned, However they might wish, by coming to the Lord's true prophet, to be regarded as of a different spirit from the false prophets and their deluded followers mentioned in the preceding chapter, they were in reality of one spirit with them, and, under another form, pursuing the same infatuated course. Therefore, when the word of the Lord came describing them as persons who were each setting up their idol in their heart, and putting the stumbling-block of iniquity before their face, their hypocrisy was at once unmasked, and they were themselves identified with the corrupt idolaters and incorrigible backsliders in Judea. *"You,"* the prophet virtually said to them, discerning through the Spirit the real state and purposes of their heart, *"you also are living in idolatry, and differ only in outward semblance from those who are openly worshipping false gods; you have not yet returned in truth to the living God, but are each bent on the love and pursuit of things which are utterly opposed to his mind and will. And that you may be encouraged in these, not that you may learn with childlike docility what God would have you to do, is the object tha lies nearest to your heart. In such a state, what presumption is it not in you to expect any friendly communications from God?"*

The expression of *"setting up their idols in their heart"* (lit. making their idols to go up upon their heart), as Calvin justly remarks, implies a silent comparison between God and idols. For, as God erects the seat of his empire in our hearts, when we set up idols there we of necessity endeavour to subvert the throne of God, and to render his supremacy of no account. So also in the other expression, *"putting the stumbling-block of iniquity before their face,"* a contrast is implied between the law of God and the perverse inclinations of their own hearts. What should have been set before their eyes for their constant observance was the law of God, respecting which the exhortation had been given, *"Let it not depart from thine eyes; then shalt thou walk in thy way safely, and thou shalt not stumble"* (Prov. 3:21,23). But displacing this unerring rule of Divine counsel and direction, and adopting in its stead the course dictated by their own selfish and corrupt passions, they were as surely running into mischief as if they had deliberately placed a stumbling-block in their path. So that, in both respects, they were warring with the mind of God – being at once idolatrous at heart and perverse in their ways.

For such persons to come and inquire of God, at the mouth of his servant, was plainly but a mockery of God; it was professing to have a desire to know God's will, and a heart ready to fall in with its requirements, while in reality their mind was made up to a plan and purpose of its own, which set at nought the Divine authority. No wonder, then, that the Lord should at once have repelled the thought of his being inquired at by such persons; since, to use the words of Jerome, "he does not deserve to hear the truth who seeks for it in a fradulent manner, but ought to be taken in his own heart." Seeing, however, in these elders types of a class unhappily very numerous among the Jews, both in Judea and in exile, the prophet proceeded to inform them how, if they persisted in their course, they might expect to be dealt with. They should certainly find an answer to their inquiries, and that answer in a sense also from the Lord; but one, at the same time, after their own heart's lusts, not in conformity with the truth of things – "*that I may take,*" it is added, "*the house of Israel in their own heart, because they are all estranged from me through their idols.*"

Yet, that this was not what the Lord properly wished – that the giving of such an answer, and the ruinous consequences it was sure to entail, was a judgment which the Lord would fain avert, if he righteously could, he again charged the prophet to say to the house of Israel, "*Thus saith the Lord Jehovah, turn, and come back from your idols, and turn away your faces from your abominations.*" He wished them distinctly to understand that if they really sought to be on terms of friendship with God, and to obtain answers of peace to their inquiries, there was one thing essential to be done: they must thoroughly reform their ways, and abandon the polluted objects on which they had set their hearts. On this condition alone could they expect to be graciously dealt with by God; and if they refused to comply with the terms, they might indeed go to a prophet, and receive an answer to their inquiries, but it must be with a sure reversion of evil; their own measure would be meted back to them. They should, in that case, be dealing deceitfully toward God, and the prophet in turn would deal deceitfully toward them. Both subjects of a common delusion, they should also at last become the victims of a common ruin. "*And they shall bear the punishment of their iniquity; the iniquity of the prophet shall be even as the iniquity of him that inquires at him; that the house of Israel may go no more astray from me, and may no more be polluted with all their transgressions; but that they may be to me a people, and I may be to them a God, saith the Lord Jehovah.*"

The point chiefly to be noticed in this deliverance of the mind of God is the connection between the self-deceived people and the deceiving prophet; regarding whom it is said, in peculiarly strong language, "*I the Lord have enticed (or deceived) that prophet.*" It is an example in the highest sphere of the lex talionis. If the people were sincere in their desire to know the mind of God, for the purpose of obeying his will, the path was plain. They had but to forsake their idolatries, and the Lord was ready to meet them with direction and blessing. But if, on the other hand, they were bent on playing the hypocrite, professing to inquire concerning him while their hearts in reality were cleaving to corruption, punishment was sure to overtake them, and that too, in the first instance, after the form of their own iniquity. God would chastise their sin with a corresponding sin; and as they had rejected the safe direction of the true light, he would send the pernicious delusion of a false one. Prophets would be given them, who should re-echo the deceitfulness that already wrought in their own bosom, so that their iniquity should prove their ruin.

The people themselves had no reason to complain of such a procedure, for they had from the first been distinctly forewarned of it by Moses. At the beginning of the 13th chapter of Deuteronomy, the supposition is made of a false prophet arising, who, by dreams and visions, should attempt to lead away the people from the true worship and service of Jehovah. In that event they were expressly discharged from hearkening to his words – nay, were commanded to put him at once to death; and were instructed to regard such occurrences as among the means of trial which the Lord appointed for the purpose of proving and purifying them. "*For the Lord your God proveth you,*" it is said, "*to know whether ye love the Lord your God with all your heart, and with all your soul."* The very appearance of such characters, then, was a judicial act on the part of God. It implied that he detected the existence of sin among the people, and required, for the ends of his righteous government, to apply a touchstone, by which to effect a separation between the precious and the vile. Not as of itself, but as a form of chastisement under the hand of God, did the false spirit of prophecy arise – a sure indication that the day of visitation had begun. So, too, it had happened in the case of Saul, when an evil spirit was sent to trouble him, in the room of that blessed Spirit whose guidance he had rejected; a messenger of Satan, indeed, but one that should not have been suffered to appear unless there had been a call for judgment! It was the Lord's instrument of correction for indulged sin.

The most notable and striking example of this sort in ancient history, and one to which the prophet here evidently refers, is that recorded in 1 Kings 22:19, etc., where the prophet Micaiah says to Ahab: *"Hear thou, therefore, the word of the Lord: I saw the Lord sitting on his throne, and all the host of heaven standing by him, on his right hand and on his left. And the Lord said, Who shall persuade Ahab, that he may go up and fall at Ramoth-Gilead? And one said on this manner, and another said on that manner. And there came forth a spirit, and stood before the Lord, and said, I will persuade him. And the Lord said unto him, Wherewith? And he said, I will go forth; and I will be a lying spirit in the mouth of all his prophets. And he said, Thou shalt persuade him, and prevail also; go forth and do so."* Here it is plain, the spirit of falsehood, entering into and working in the false prophets, appears to come elsewhere than from God; but not less plain, also, that the giving up of Ahab and his people to the influence of such a spirit was of God, – an act of judgment, standing midway between the sins of a past life and the approaching doom of a fearful retribution. It was God who, in righteousness, fixed the doom, and who also appointed this particular mode of carrying it into execution. Yet the power by the immediate instrumentality of which it was to be effected was no magical one, such as might fascinate and control the minds of Ahab and his people, independently of their own free will. On the contrary, it was their voluntary adherence to the spirit of delusion, and their obstinate surrender to its influence, which led God to abandon them to this new and more fatal subjection to its power. And hence, both in the case of Ahab, and here again in the representation of Ezekiel, the yielding to that spirit, whether in the way of persuading or of being persuaded, is treated as a crime, drawing after it its appropriate punishment: the Lord stretches out his hand, and punishes both the prophet and him that inquires at him.

The facts and statements now referred to clearly imply something more on the part of God than that bare permission, by which many commentators, both in earlier and later times, have sought to explain his entire connection in such cases with evil. "I have deceived that prophet," that is, says Dr. Adam Clarke, "He ran before he was sent; he willingly became the servant of Satan's illusions; and I suffered this to take place, because he and his followers refused to consult and serve me." So also, Maurer, who explains the statement thus: "I will suffer him to be deceived; I will not hinder him from being so: I will surrender him to his fate." True, no doubt, as far as it goes, but a portion of the truth still remains to be told. There is not merely a negative, but also a positive relation on God's part to sin, inasmuch as he controls and directs its operations, so that they may fit suitably into his Divine plan, and may develope themselves in such forms and ways as are demanded by the order and rectitude of his administration. Should a spirit of delusion, for example, break out in any particular place or time, it is certainly in itself to be regarded as an emanation from the prince of darkness; but that it should appear in the precise form it does, at such a time, or with such results, must be ascribed to the directing agency and overruling providence of God. So the apostle evidently teaches, when, speaking of what, in Christian times, should correspond to the false prophesying of an earlier period, he says: *"And for this cause"* – viz. because they received not the love of the truth, that they might be saved – *"God shall send them strong delusion, that they should believe a lie; that they all might be damned who believe not the truth, but had pleasure in unrighteousness"* (2 Thess. 2:11,12). "God punishes sin with sin. Therefore upon the lost who in their guilt would not cherish a love of the truth in their hearts, he sends forth a powerful delusion, that they might believe a lie. The force of the expressions must not be weakened, so as to describe anything less than a judicial hardening. The *'strong delusion,'* as to its ultimate ground, points to Antichrist himself, who in *'the working of Satan,'* sets forward his deceit; but the *'sending'* indicates the coming of Antichrist to be of God. The Lord does not make Antichrist, so far as he is evil, but he certainly does make him, in so far as he manifests himself in this particular shape and form, under these circumstances and relations."[3]

II. But we pass on to the second part of the chapter, which, as before noticed, speaks to a case entirely different, and one that probably coincided with the inquiry proposed by the elders. It has respect to the question, what effect the existence of a few righteous persons among the Jewish people might be expected to have at such a time on the purposes of God? The Lord had already told Jeremiah that the guilt of the people was too great to be pardoned on account of his intercession, and that even if Moses and Samuel, to whom the Lord had lastened on former occasions of grievous backsliding and apostasy (Ex. 32; Num. 14; 1 Sam. 7), were not present to lead in their behalf, it would be altogether in vain (Jer. 14:2, 15:1). It was in immediate connection with the forms of evil, which are so prominently exhibited in this portion of Ezekiel's writings, viz. the prevalence of the spirit of false prophecy, and the readiness of the people to listen to its lying divinations, which called forth in Jeremiah that strong declaration of the utter inefficacy of prayer to meet and remedy such a case as this. And as in regard to the subject itself Ezekiel treads in the footsteps of Jeremiah, so also, in the judgment pronounced upon it, he merely supplements the representation previously given by Jeremiah, by bringing another moral element into play, and declaring also its incompetence to prevent or rectify the evil in such a time of apostasy and rebuke. The two most powerful and honored intercessors, Moses and Samuel, could not do it by their intercession, Jeremiah had said, No, responds Ezekiel from the banks of the Chebar; nor could three of the most righteous men that have ever lived, either in past or present times, do it by their righteousness. Though Noah, Daniel, and Job were all at this moment in the land, they could not stay the judgment of God from proceeding.

Many frivolous reasons have been assigned, especially to the Fathers, why these three men in particular should have been singled out for such distinguished honor on this occasion. But the real reasons are not far to seek. For these three individuals were all eminently distinguished for their personal righteousness, and, on account of this, were saved from overwhelming calamities which destroyed others. Yet not without some striking diversities of circumstance, evidently in the eye of the prophet. Noah was saved amid the wreck and desolation of a world, and had the members of his family, but these alone, given to him. Daniel was saved from the unreasonable fury of the king of Babylon, and prevailed also to shield from destruction a few companions of kindred spirit, though inferior standing to himself (Dan. 2). But Job was stript even of his family and household, not a son nor a daughter left to him; and of the three, therefore, was the most striking monument of the simple righteousness of God preserving the good and punishing the bad. On this account, probably, his name comes last in order, since, in his case, the principle under consideration found its most stringent application. In all these cases, God had signally stamped their righteousness with his approbation; yet if the whole three should now stand before him, they could not alter his determination to inflict the sore judgments which were impending over the king and people of Judah; the cup of iniquity was full; the stroke of vengeance must come down; and the utmost that the righteousness of such men could do, would be to deliver their own souls – only a Job's escape could be given to them, without either son or daughter.[4]

The manner of the prophet in unfolding this sentiment is highly rhetorical. He first puts the case in the form of a general supposition, – the case of a land sinning grievously, and liable to one of the grievous judgments threatened in the law against hardened transgressors (Lev. 26:22,33); he repeats successively the four different kinds of Divine judgment, as ready to be executed, and in respect to each affirms the impossibility of the three righteous men arresting the course of justice, or prevailing to deliver more than their own souls. Then, at ver. 21, concentrating the whole of the supposed cases, with their corresponding judgment, as in one mass of condemnation and woe upon Jerusalem, he proceeds: *"How much more when I send my four severe judgments upon Jerusalem, the sword, and the famine, and the noisome beast, and the pestilence, to cut off from it man and beast!"* As much as to say, "This land has now reached such a state of utter abandonment and hopeless depravity, that it deserves to have not one merely, but the whole of my sore judgments let loose upon it in combined fury; and if those righteous men could not save a land, when one only was due, how foolish to think that they could save such a land as this!"

And even this does not reveal the whole of the severity that was to be exercised upon Jerusalem; for the two concluding verses, while they point to a remnant escaping the flood of judgments, points at the same time to the necessity of still further severity being made to follow them. It is a word of threatening, not of promise, as the great majority of commentators suppose, and our translators also appear to have understood it. *"And, behold, therein shall be left a remnant that shall be brought forth, sons and daughters: behold, they shall come forth unto you, and ye shall see their way and their doings; and ye shall be comforted concerning the evil that I shall have brought upon Jerusalem, in all that I shall have brought upon it. And they shall comfort you, when ye see their ways and their doings; and ye shall know that I have not done without cause all that I have done in it, saith the Lord Jehovah."* The word is formally addressed to the people already in exile, who are regarded as viewing the destruction about to be executed on Jerusalem with astonishment, and some degree of dissatisfaction. The prophet tells such there would certainly be a remnant – not, however, in the proper sense, as if they were themselves deserving persons, or spared for blessing for the sake of the pious among them, but a remnant still so wedded to sin, and so manifestly deserving of severe chastisement, that every one would recognise the justice of God's dealings toward them. "Ye shall see," to use the language of Calvin, who here caught the real meaning of the prophet, "the men to be so wicked, that ye shall be forced to confess the city was deserving of destruction, and the men themselves worthy of death. And instead of murmuring and fretting against God, ye shall be satisfied, it could not have been otherwise ordered, their wickedness was of so desperate a nature; so that, with soothed and tranquil minds, ye shall henceforth proclaim my righteousness, and cease any more to utter the complaints which now disturb your minds."

This, we have no doubt, is the correct view of the passage, for it has respect simply to God's justice in visiting them with such severity; and there is not a word dropped, either of their being brought to repentance when in exile, or of God's extending mercy to them when there. It is the severe aspect of the Divine procedure that is exhibited throughout. Doubtless the view given is to be understood with certain limitations; there was mercy, to some extent, to be found mingling with the judgment, as there would also be some grains of wheat concealed among the heaps of chaff that were to be driven forth into Chaldea. Other prophecies speak also of these; but the word here has to do only with the work of judgment on account of sin. Yet, even in regard to that, it challenges the concurring judgment and approval of all who should be at pains to acquaint themselves with the entire circumstances. For God must ever be justified when he is judged with knowledge and impartiality. Dissatisfaction with his ways, or quarrelling with his purposes, springs up only where ignorance and sinful prejudice exist. And when all things shall at last be made manifest, there is not an act in his administration, however stern and severe, which shall not call forth the response from every intelligent bosom: He hath done all things well; his ways are righteousness and truth.

CHAPTER XV.

THE GUILT AND CONDEMNATION OF ISRAEL PARABOLICALLY REPRESENTED.

[1]And the word of the LORD came to me, saying,

[2]Son of man, What is the vine tree more than any tree, or than a branch which is among the trees of the forest?

[3]Shall wood be taken from it to do any work? Or will *men* take a pin from it to hang any vessel on it?

[4]Behold, it is thrown into the fire for fuel. The fire devours both its ends, and its middle is burned. Is it fit for work?

[5]Behold, when it was whole, it was fit for no work. How much less shall it be fit for any work when the fire has devoured it, and it is burned!

[6]Therefore thus says the Lord GOD: As the vine tree among the trees of the forest, which I have given to the fire for fuel, so I will give the people of Jerusalem.

[7]And I will set My face against them. They shall go out from *one* fire and *another* fire shall devour them. And you shall know that I am the LORD when I set My face against them.

[8]And I will make the land a ruin, because they have committed a trespass, says the Lord GOD.

This chapter is so closely related to the following, that the one may be regarded as a kind of introduction to the other. It represents briefly, and by way of parable, what chap. 16 exhibits at length, and with all the minuteness of historical detail. The subject of both alike in the inveterate and incorrigible wickedness of the covenant-people is the two branches, Israel and Judah, which had defeated the ends of their high calling, and rendered them obnoxious to the severest penalties.

In this introductory chapter the prophet begins with asking, *"What is the vine-tree more than any tree – the branch that is among the trees of the forest?"* The point of comparison lies in the wood belonging respectively to the vine and the forest-trees, – what is the vine-wood more than any forest-wood? In this respect it has nothing to entitle it to any pre-eminence above the others, but quite the reverse; it is inferior to them all. Its soft and brittle nature renders it unfit for being made into any useful implements, even of the most common kind; not so much as a pin can be made from it; it is fit only for fuel to the fire. Such were the chosen people of God, if viewed simply as a people of this world, who had no longer any peculiar connection with the higher purposes of the Divine government. They have often been compared to the vine, and sometimes even to vines of the choicest kind (Deut. 32:32; Isa. 5; Ps. 80; Jer. 2:21; Hos. 10:1), but always with respect to the fruitful qualities of the vine, as significant of the prolific goodness that ought to have been found in them, as the people whom God had chosen. Destitute of this, what were they better than others? Nay, in respect of those things which constitute the natural greatness of kingdoms, – antiquity of origin, extent of territory, abundance of resources, attainments in arts and science, – what could they boast of, in comparison of Egypt, Ethiopia, Babylon, and the greater kingdoms of the earth! Their inferiority was palpable; and whenever they lost their distinction as the nation that kept the truth of God, and wrought righteousness in the earth, they were no longer capable of holding a place of power and influence in the destinies of the world. On the contrary, like salt that had lost its savor, they had become fit only to be cast out, or committed as a piece of vine-wood to the fire.

Such is the representation here given of the covenant-people as a whole, considered even in their state of undiminished fulness and noontide glory. But they were far from being in that state when Ezekiel wrote; and in vers. 4 and 5 he modifies this description of the worthless vine, so as exactly to suit their case: *"Behold, it is given to the fire for fuel; the fire has consumed both the ends of it, and its middle part is on flame. Is it* (viz. the scorched part that still remains) *fit for work? Behold, when it was entire, it did not serve for work; how much less when the fire has devoured of it, and it is on flame, shall it still be taken for work!"* The allusion is to the impoverished and reduced state of the covenant-people, it was with them as if the two ends were already consumed in the fire, and the middle portion that remained also very severely scorched. The ten tribes had been carried away into Assyria, and the nation, not large or powerful at the best, had been brought to the brink of ruin; they existed only as a brand plucked from the burning, or rather with the fire still kindling around them. Therefore, if incapable on merely natural grounds, and in respect to purposes of an inferior kind, of coping with other kingdoms, they were immeasurably more so now; and it might be evident, even to the most careless and unreflecting, that they were in danger of complete destruction. *"And I set my face against them; from the fire they go out, and the fire still devours them; and ye shall know that I am Jehovah when I set my face against them. And I make the land a desolation, because they have acted most treacherously, saith the Lord."*

The parable indicated, in a very striking manner, the strictly moral nature of the ends for which God chooses a people out of the world, and teaches them to expect in immediate connection with these all their security, and power, and glory. It is the same truth, only applied to other times and altered circumstances, which is brought out by John the Baptist, when he says in regard to the approaching work and kingdom of Messiah: *"And now the axe is laid to the root of the trees; therefore every tree with bringeth not forth good fruit is hewn down and cast into the fire."* The same also which our Lord himself taught in the parables of the wicked husbandmen and of the fruitless fig-tree in the vineyard (Matt. 21:33-41; Luke 13:6-9), and which he still further embodied in the parabolical action of the cursing of the fruitless fig-tree by the way-side (Mark 11:12-14). The truth, therefore, is for all times and stages of the Church's history. It matters not that her members are not intermingled with the world, and not, as of old, placed in a state of visible separation and distance from it. They still are a chosen seed, distinguished with the highest privileges and most elevating hopes, but all for the single end of withdrawing them from the pollutions of the world, and rendering them to God a peculiar people, zealous of good works. If they only pursue after this high end with undeviating purpose and steady aim, they shall be found full of the favor and strong in the might of God; they shall successfully contend with principalities and powers, and will prove themselves the appointed channels of conveying life and blessing to a perishing world. But if they are themselves drawing back to the ways of corruption; if they begin to breathe the spirit of the world, and do its works, as they must be of all men the most guilty, so are they also the most sure to inherit the woes of condemnation. They oppose and frustrate the very end for which they have been called to the enjoyment of such distinguished privileges, and so belong to the unhappy class of whom our Lord has said, that it shall *"be more tolerable for Sodom and Gomorrah in the day of judgment than for them."*

Having prepared the way, by the parabolical delineation of the fifteenth chapter, , the prophet proceeds, in the long historical detail of the next chapter, to make application of its principles to Israel. In this ideal narrative the covenant-people are personified as a single individual, – the daughter Jerusalem, under the image of whose life the most vivid picture is presented of the history of God's connection with them, and their behavior toward him.

CHAPTER XVI.

THE STORY OF ISRAEL'S GUILT AND PUNISHMENT.

1 Again the word of the LORD came to me, saying,

2 Son of man, cause Jerusalem to know her idolatries.

3 And say, Thus says the Lord GOD to Jerusalem: Your origin and your birth is of the land of Canaan. Your father was an Amorite, and your mother a Hittite.

4 As for your birth, in the day you were born, your navel was not cut, nor were you washed with water to cleanse *you;* you were not salted at all, nor swaddled at all.

5 No eye pitied you, to do any of these to you to have compassion on you. But you were thrown out into the open field, because your life was despised in the day you were born.

6 And when I passed by you and saw you in your own blood ready to be trampled, I said to you in your blood, Live! Yes, I said to you in your blood, Live!

7 I have caused you to multiply like the bud of the field, and you have multiplied and become great, and you have come to excellent ornaments. Your breasts are formed, and your hair is grown, yet you were naked and bare.

8 Now when I passed by you and looked on you, behold, your time was the time of love. And I spread my skirt over you and covered your nakedness. Yes, I swore to you and entered into a covenant with you, says the Lord GOD, and you became Mine.

9 And I washed you with water. Yes, I thoroughly washed away your blood from you, and I anointed you with oil.

10 I also clothed you with embroidered work and made shoes for you of badgers' skin, and I dressed you with fine linen, and I covered you with silk.

11 I also adorned you with ornaments, and I put bracelets on your hands and a chain on your neck.

12 And I put a jewel on your forehead, and earrings in your ears, and a beautiful crown on your head.

13 So you were adorned with gold and silver. And your clothing was of fine linen and silk and embroidered work. You ate fine flour and honey and oil. And you were exceedingly beautiful, and you went on to a kingdom.

14 And your fame went out among the heathen, because of your beauty – for it was perfect in My beauty, which I had put upon you, says the Lord GOD.

15 But you trusted in your own beauty and played the harlot because of your fame, and *you* poured out your fornications on everyone who passed by – it was his.

16 And you took from your clothes and adorned your high places with different colors and played the harlot on them. Such thing have not come, nor ever shall be.

17 You have also taken your beautiful jewels of My gold and My silver, which I had given you, and made images of men to yourself, and committed adultery with them.

18 And *you* took your embroidered dresses and covered them, and you have set My oil and My incense before them.

19 Also My food which I gave you, fine flour and oil and honey *which* I fed you, you have even set it before them for a sweet smell. And *so* it was, says the Lord GOD.

20 And you have taken your sons and your daughters, whom you have borne to Me, and you have sacrificed these to them for food. Is it a little thing that because of your fornications

21 you have killed My children and delivered them to cause them to pass through *the fire* for them?

22 And in all your hateful deeds and your fornications you have not remembered the days of your youth, when you were naked and bare and were ready to be trampled in your blood.

23 And after all your wickedness, woe, woe to you, says the Lord GOD!

24 You have also built yourself a high place; yes, you have made yourself a high place in every street.

25 You have built your high place at every head of the way and have made your beauty to be despised, and *you* have opened your feet to everyone who passed by and have multiplied your fornications.

26 You have committed fornication with the E-gyp-tians, your lustful neighbors. And *you* have multiplied your fornications to provoke Me to anger.

27 Behold, therefore I have stretched out My hand over you and have withdrawn your share of *food,* and have delivered you to the will of those who hate you, the daughters of the Philistines, who are ashamed of your wicked way.

28 You have also played the harlot with the Assyrians, because you could never be satisfied. Yes, you have played the harlot with them, and yet could not be satisfied.

29 And you have multiplied your fornication in the land of Canaan to Chal-de-a, and yet you were not satisfied with it.

30 How weak is your heart, says the Lord GOD, since you do all these *things,* the work of an overbearing, lustful woman –

31 in that you build your high place in the head of every way, and make your high place in the head of every street – and you have not been as a harlot, in that you scorn hire,

32 but like a wife who commits adultery, *who* takes strangers instead of her husband!

33 They give gifts to all harlots, but you give your gifts to all your lovers and hire them so that they may come to you from every side for fornication.

34 And you were just the opposite from *other* women in your adulteries, in that no one goes after you to commit adulteries. And in that you give a gift, and no gift is given to you, in this way you are different.

35 Therefore, O harlot, hear the word of the LORD.

36 Thus says the Lord GOD: Because your filthiness was poured out and your nakedness was discovered, through your fornications with your lovers and with all the idols of your idolatries, and by the blood of your children whom you gave to them.

37 behold, therefore I will gather all your lovers, with whom you have taken pleasure, and all whom you have loved, with all whom you have hated – I will even gather them all around against you and will uncover your nakedness to them so that they may see all your nakedness.

38 And I will judge you as women who break wedlock and shed blood are judged. And I will give you blood and fury and jealousy.

39 And I will also give you into their hand, and they shall throw down your high place. Yes, *they* shall break down your high places. They shall also strip you of your clothes, and shall take your beautiful jewels and leave you naked and bare.

40 They shall also bring up a company against you, and they shall stone you with stones and thrust you through with their swords.

41 And they shall burn your houses with fire and execute judgments on you in the sight of many women. And I will cause you to cease from playing the harlot, and you shall also give no hire any more.

42 So I will make My fury toward you to rest, and My jealousy shall depart from you, and I will be quiet and will be angry no more.

43 Because you have not remembered the days of your youth, but have troubled Me in all these – behold, therefore I will also repay your way on *your* head, says the Lord GOD. And you shall not commit this fornication above all your idolatries.

44 Behold, everyone who uses proverbs shall use this proverb against you, saying, As the mother is, *so* is her daughter.

45 You are your mother's daughter, who despises her husband and her children. And you are the sister of your sisters, who despised their husbands and their children. Your mother was a Hittite, and your father was an Amorite.

46 And your old sister is Samaria, she and her daughters who live at your left hand. And your younger sister, who lives at your right hand, is Sodom and her daughters.

47 Yet you have not walked according to their ways, nor done according to their hateful deeds. But, as *if that were* a very little *thing,* you were corrupted more than they were in all your ways.

48 As I live, says the Lord GOD, Sodom your sister, she nor her daughters, has not done as you have done, you and your daughters.

49 Behold, this was the iniquity of your sister Sodom: pride. Fullness of bread and abundance of idleness was in her and in her daughters. Nor did she strengthen the hand of the poor and needy.

50 And they were haughty and did hateful things before Me. Therefore I took them away as I saw *fit.*

51 Samaria has not committed half of your sins, but you have multiplied your idolatries more than they, and have justified your sisters in all your hateful acts which you have done.

52 You also, who have judged your sisters, bear your own shame for your sins which you have committed more hateful than they. They are more righteous than you. Yes, blush and bear your shame, since you have justified your sisters.

53 When I shall bring again their captivity, the captivity of Sodom and her daughters, and the captivity of Samaria and her daughters, then *I will bring again* the captivity of your captives in the midst of them –

54 so that you may bear your own shame and may blush in all that you have done, in that you are a comfort to them.

55 When your sisters, Sodom and her daughters, shall return to their former state, and *when* Samaria and her daughters shall return to their former state, then you and your daughters shall return to your former state.

56 For your sister Sodom was not mentioned by your mouth in the day of your pride,

57 before your wickedness was uncovered,

as at the time of *your* your reproach of the daughters of Syria, and of all her neighbors, the daughters of the Philistines (who despise you on every side).

[58]You must bear your fornication and your abominations, says the LORD.

[59]For thus says the Lord GOD: I will even deal with you as you have done, *you* who have despised the oath in breaking the covenant.

[60]But I will rmember My covenant with you in the days of your youth, and I will establish to you an everlasting covenant.

[61]Then you shall remember your ways and be ashamed, when you shall receive your sisters, your older and your younger. And I will give them to you for daughters, but not by your covenant.

[62]And I will establish My covenant with you. And you shall know that I am the LORD;

[63]so that you may remember and be ashamed, and never open your mouth any more because of your shame, in that I have received an atonement for all that you have done, says the Lord GOD.

1. The history recorded so graphically in this chapter naturally falls into several successive portions; and of these, the first, which ends with ver. 7, unfolds Israel's beginnings as a people – when they were struggling into national existence. It takes its commencement with the birth of the female child, and terminates with her advancement to womanhood. The two features that are brought prominently out in this portion of the history are the naturally helpless, unpromising, and polluted condition of Israel, and the wonderful mercy and loving-kindness of God in preserving their existence and nursing them to maturity. *"The origin and the birth"* of this child are said to have been *"in the land of Canaan;"* and it is added, *"Thy father was the Amorite, and thy mother the Hittite."* To connect the chosen people with such a parentage was one of the most impressive ways that could be taken to mark their inveterately depraved and sinful character. The original inhabitants of Canaan, and in particular the Amorites and the Hittites, who, from being the most important and powerful tribes, are sometimes named as representatives of the whole,[20] were so hateful in the sight of God, on account of their sinful and corrupt ways, that he had decreed their utter extermination from the land, which was given as a possession to the children of Israel. Therefore, to represent these Israelites now as the legitimate offspring of the very outcasts they had supplanted, was in the strongest manner to identify the state and manners of the one with those of the other. It was adopting substantially the same figure when John the Baptist called the Scribes and Pharisees of his day *"a generation of vipers"* – the serpent's brood; and when our Lord charged many others with being *"of their father the devil, and doing the lusts of their father."*[21] Even Hosea, whose language is tame compared to Ezekiel's, had already addressed Israel on one occasion by the name of Canaan (chap. 12:7, where we should read, *"Canaan! the balances of deceit are in his hands"*); and Isaiah, earlier still, had gone to the utmost length in the use of the figure when, in proclaiming the word of the Lord to his countrymen, he addressed them as the *"rulers of Sodom, and the people of Gomorrah!"* (chap. 1:10.) It was virtually saying, the people no longer deserved the name of the seed of Abraham, but were rather to be classed with the worst and vilest portion of mankind.

When the prophet has thus marked the native vileness and depravity of the people, by ascribing to them a Canaanitic origin, he proceeds to exhibit, under a few striking traits, the miserable helplessness and destitution out of which their national existence had emerged. The child that personifies them is represented as a despised and neglected infant, that was denied the commonest acts of parental regard – its very life a miracle – neither bandaged, nor washed, nor salted, nor swaddled, at its birth, but cast forth as a worthless and polluted thing on the face of the earth, and mercilessly abandoned to the elements of nature. So wretched and forlorn in the first stage of being, had Israel been left to their own resources, they would certainly have perished under the adverse influences against which they had to struggle, or, which is all one in this connection, would have failed to reach an independent national existence. But here now appears, in striking contrast to the evil, the other prominent feature of the description, – the wonderful grace and mercy of God, which prevailed over all that was abject and repulsive in their condition, and fostered the feeble life into full-grown maturity. His eye pitied the poor and wretched little one, and with a word of power he bade it live; and not only live, but grow and strengthen to its full proportions. *"I made thee,"* as the words literally and properly are in ver. 7, *"a myriad, like the increase of the field, and thou didst multiply, and wax great, and became most beautiful; they breasts formed, and they hair grew, and thou (still) wast naked and bare."* The idea obviously is, that under the protecting and fostering care of God, the small and despised people, who had been at first ready to perish, rapidly grew into considerable numbers and strength, capable of being used for some important purpose, though still, from their low and impoverished state, the aid of a gracious and powerful hand would be needed to bring it into accomplishment.

The period of Israel's history embraced in this part of the description is undoubtedly that of the sojourn in Egypt; for it was then, properly, that their existence as a people began. It was a beginning, however, impressed with the most humiliating marks of feebleness and contempt. Even when the family of Jacob were, for Joseph's sake, treated to distinguished favor, it was not without accompanying tokens of a contrary description: on account of their occupation as shepherds, they were eyed with disdain by the Egyptians, and had to dwell by themselves as an inferior caste. But this natural antipathy soon expressed itself in a more actively offensive form, and a tide of undisguised hatred and cruel oppression set in against them, which, with few interruptions, continued to flow for centuries. Everything was done which an unscrupulous tyranny could devise to depress their condition, and even extinguish their existence. Yet so carefully did the Lord watch over them during this long season of peril, that not only was their being preserved, but their growth also was supernaturally increased: *"They were fruitful,"* it is said, *"and swarmed, and multiplied, and increased most exceedingly"* and *"the more they afflicted them, the more they multiplied and grew"* (Ex. 1:7,12). This paternal kindness and watchful oversight on the part of God was the more striking, and should have produced the deeper impression on the national mind of Israel, as it was exercised not merely amid destructive influences working from without, but also in the face of much spiritual corruption prevailing within. The families of Israel had become most deeply infected with the foul leprosy of Egypt; and to the contempt arising from their political feebleness, there was also to be overcome the disgust which could not fail to be produced by their sensual idolatries. Doubtless there was then, as through all subsequent periods of their history there still was, a faithful remnant, in whose bosoms the hidden life of faith was maintained. The covenant of Abraham, pledging to him in perpetuity a spiritual seed, indispensably required this; and the brief notices of the period abundantly testify that it was not altogether wanting. Still, viewed as a whole, the people were in a most degenerate and polluted condition. The general meanness and poverty of their external circumstances was but the symbol of their spiritual state; and while in respect to number they had now become suited to the higher purposes of God, they still lacked what was most essentially needed to fit them for the execution of his will. But in all this, believers of every age must see the image of their own state by nature, and the ground of their infinite obligations. What have they of their own? Only, like Israel, the elements of weakness, pollution, and death. It is the grace of God alone that breathes life into the soul, and at once reveals the things that are to be received and done in God's service, and confers the power for receiving and doing them aright. Whence the first and last feeling in every regenerate bosom must be one of deep abasement, and entire renunciation of self, spontaneously yielding the praise and glory to God.

2. The second stage of this allegorical history, exhibited in vers. 8-14, represents the singular honor and glory conferred on the ideal virgin in her exaltation to the rank of spouse to the King of Zion, and her decoration with apparel suited to her elevated station. Here, again, everything is fragrant with the matchless grace and loving-kindness of God. She has nothing of her own to entitle her to such an ennobling distinction, and nothing of her own to fit her for adorning it. It is not she that makes the advance to God, but God that makes the advance to her; *"the Lord passes by her"* now as he had done at the

first, and fixes on her the regard of his love. And that love not a mere general benevolence but such a special affection as one cherishes toward the person he would betroth for his wife; for when the Lord passed by her, *"he spread his skirt over her;" "Yea,"* he adds, explaining more distinctly what was meant by the transaction, *"I sware unto thee, and entered into a covenant with thee, saith the Lord Jehovah, and thou becamest mine."* That is, she became his in the same sense in which a woman becomes a man's when united to him by the marriage oath and covenant, in respect to which, as usually connected with the solemnization of marriage, the proper wife of an Israelite is called, in Mal. 2:14, *"the wife of thy covenant."* And as it was customary for brides, when entering into union with earthly kings and potentates, to pass through a period of purification (Esth. 2:12), so this betrothed spouse of the king of Zion, all unfitted as she naturally was for such a glorious union, is declared to have been specially prepared for the occasion: *"And I wash thee with water, and I rinse they blood from off thee* (that, namely, of her original impurity still cleaving to her), *and I anoint thee with oil."* When thus personally prepared for the solemnity, she is furnished with all the usual articles of a bride's apparel, – raiment of rich embroidery, shoes of tachash, silk and fine linen, ear-rings, jewels, ornaments of silver and gold, and a beautiful crown upon the head; for, being the spouse of a king, she was raised to the highest dignity, and must bear the emblem of royalty. And as the consequence of this instalment in high and honorable state, she was furnished with the best provisions – with flour, and honey, and oil – and prospered, and became great, so that the fame of her comely and beautiful appearance spread all around, and she attracted the admiration and envy of her heathen neighbors.

The description presents a vivid and impressive image of the singular goodness of God to Israel, from the time that he visited them in Egypt, and raised them from the low and depressed condition which they held there, to the nearest fellowship with himself, and the highest place among the kingdoms of the earth. The relation formed between Jehovah and Israel at that interesting period had already been more than once represented under the image of the marriage-union. To say nothing of various descriptions founded on this image of Isaiah (such as chap. 1:1, 54:1), it forms the basis of the whole series of representations given by Hosea in the three first chapters of his writings; and Jeremiah, referring expressly to the period of the deliverance from Egypt, and what immediately followed, says in one of his earliest prophecies (chap. 2:2): *"I remember thee, the kindness of thy youth, the love of thine espousals, when thou wentest after me in the wilderness, in a land not sown."* Indeed, no earthly relation could so fitly have been employed as that of marriage to exhibit the nature of that hallowed union, in virtue of which the Lord not only conferred upon them the rich dowry of temporal good, but also graciously condescended to maintain with them a most intimate and endearing interchange of love. For, as Havernick justly remarks, while the external greatness and glory afterwards imparted to Israel are not excluded from the representation, they are by no means (as Grotius, and interpreters of a kindred spirit imagine) alone intended. It is the internal relationship established between them and God, and the spiritual blessings immediately growing out of it, which are here primarily and chiefly referred to. Even the outward temporal blessing secured in the covenant, and in part also realized, should never have been viewed as an ultimate and independent good, but rather as the expression and emblem of something higher and better. They were not properly blessings at all, except in so far as they were held in connection with the favor of Heaven, and bespoke the fellowship of love that subsisted between Jehovah and his people. Canaan itself derived its chief value as a covenant-good from its being the Lord's possession – the land which he claimed as peculiarly his own, and in which his people dwelt as *"sojourners with him."* It is, therefore, their close relationship to God, and their high place in respect to the affairs of his spiritual kingdom, which is most directly indicated under the idea of their marriage-union to the Lord. The same, substantially, which is otherwise expressed by their being made a kingdom of priests; and still again by their having put upon them the name of Israelites – God's wrestlers.

But considering the state in which they were found in Egypt, they much needed to undergo a process of purification, to fit them for bearing aright so high and ennobling a character. That many rites of cleansing should have been prescribed to them, and a long course of preparatory discipline appointed, only betokened the Lord's earnest desire to have them qualified for the exalted state and destiny he wished them to fill. And throughout, nothing was wanted of tender compassion and faithful dealing on his part. From the first he crowned them with marks of his goodness. A fulness of power and glory rested on them, far surpassing what their numbers alone might have warranted them to expect. And when the kingdom at last rose to meredian splendor, and received the confirmation and enlargement given to it, especially in the days of David and Solomon, the surrounding heathen were compelled to own that there is a great reality in the favor and blessing of Heaven. They saw in Israel, as a people, living monuments of the mighty efficacy of Divine grace, how it can exalt the feeble, and lay the powers of the world, as well as the bounties of nature, under contribution to the furtherance of its beneficent designs. And assuredly, the children of grace should be such monuments still; nor, if true to their principles, and faithful to their heavenly calling, can they fail to be so. *"Washed, sanctified, and justified in the name of the Lord Jesus, and by the Spirit of our God,"* they are admitted into the very secret of the Lord's presence; and all things become theirs – all things needful for their present and final welfare. They dwell *"where angels visit," "where beams descend from the Eternal Sun,"* where flows that river of life which makes glad the city of God, – partakers even now of a blessing which the world may well envy, but which, blessed be God, it can as little take away as it can give.

3. In the preceding section, the prophet has magnified the grace and goodness of God to Israel, and in the next, embracing vers. 15-34, he exhibits, in the most pungent terms, the ungrateful and treacherous conduct of Israel toward God. The much-beloved spouse, who has been treated to such high honors, and replenished with so many precious and costly gifts, proves unfaithful to her husband, employs the very ornaments and provisions he has conferred on her to the shameful purpose of feeding her wanton disposition and compassing her sinful ends; and instead of seeking, as in duty bound, to promote his credit and renown in the world, acts rather as if her object were to show how low a place he held in her esteem, and how much she preferred others before him.

In this part of the narrative the allegorical style is perhaps as closely preserved as it could have been consistently with vividness and accuracy in the representation; but it is impossible not to notice at various points how the fictitious garb drops off, and the plain reality discovers itself, – as when mention is made of the children being sacrificed by passing through the fire (ver. 21), and the Egyptians and Assyrians are specified among those with whom a forbidden intercourse was carried on (vers. 26,28). We can only view the representation generally, and with respect to its leading features; as from the very nature of the image it is impossible to be minute without, at the same time, falling into indelicacy. But we see at a glance that the primary evil charged, and the spring of all the abominations that followed, was the misappropriation of God's goodness – viewing the gifts conferred apart from the bounteous Giver, and applying them to selfish purposes. *"Thou didst trust in thine own beauty, and didst play the wanton upon thy name,"* or renown: such is the first crime laid to her charge. Instead of holding, as Israel manifestly should have done, all their mercies and privileges in humble dependence on God, and using them for his glory, they looked upon them as in the strictest sense their own, and turned them into instruments and occasions for exalting themselves in the eyes of others. They became vain in their imaginations, and seemed to enter into a sort of senseless rivalry with their neighbors, for the countenance and support of their false gods. It may possible appear as if the picture were somewhat overdrawn, when Israel is represented as courting the attention of those foul divinities, and, for that purpose, turning to account her beautiful ornaments and stores of plenty. But a deep truth lies at the bottom of the representation. For what were the false gods in question but the personification of those carnal desires and affections which the good things so amply poured into Israel's lot had but served to feed? defied human nature in its manifold varieties of lust and earthliness? So that their zeal in worshipping such gods and lavishing on them costly tokens of their regard, very much resolves itself into an anxiety to have the countenance of Heaven upon the gratification of their own grovelling and earthly propensities. And hence it was that, when replenished with a fulness of worldly comforts, Israel so naturally preferred the worship of idols to that of Jehovah, and, like a treacherous spouse, breaking loose from the holy restraints of wedlock, yielded themselves to the service of these impure rivals; for thus they could give freer play to the corrupt affections of nature. Their conduct in this was simply an example of the native effect of the world upon the heart, according to the circumstances of the time; and when our Lord, speaking for all times, sets before us the prodigal son, selfishly coveting his portion of goods, and going to spend them in alienation from his father's house, he but presents us with another exhibition, differently modified, of the same great truth. Let the heart of nature be fed to the full with gifts, and there will never fail to appear, in one form or another, the idolatry of self and the world.

The fervid and glowing character of Ezekiel's mind, however, is not satisfied with this general description of the idolatrous spirit that discovered itself in Israel's history. It must give stroke after stroke, and heap one particular upon another, to make the impression complete. And therefore he goes on to tell how everything that Israel had received of good, – her garments of divers colors, jewels of gold and silver, oil, flour, honey, incense, – were all employed in the service of corruption; and how new ways were sought out, and special places erected for the prosecution of her unhallowed purposes. Nor does he fail to notice, in thus filling up the picture of evil, one or two revolting traits, which give a peculiar hideousness to the character of Israel's degeneracy. The sacrificing of the children, by making them pass through the fire, is one of these; and the Lord calls them his own children, rather than hers, – *"my children,"* - because they had been born under his covenant with Israel, and bore the sign of the covenant upon them. Another also is given toward the close of the description, when, after having declared the readiness of Israel to take up with every form of idolatry in Canaan and all round to Chaldea, on the one hand, and Egypt on the other, the cutting remark is brought in, that none of these nations followed her – the treacherous and wanton dealing was all on Israel's part – she conceded everything to them, they yielded back nothing in return to her – her wickedness was gratuitous and unrequited folly. A solemn and pregnant truth, which the Church of God should never forget. She loses all, and the world gains all, when she foolishly stoops to impair the testimony of God, or adjust the claims and services of religion to the tastes and practices of the carnal mind. A nominal advance or apparent reconciliation may possibly be achieved by the manoeuvre, but it can be no more than nominal and apparent; the interests that really profit by such a policy are those of the flesh and the world. It is only when the Church is faithful to her testimony – when she stands in the truth of Christ, and in that truth shines forth *"bright as the sun, clear as the moon,"* that she is found also, in her conflict with evil, *"terrible as an army with banners."*

4. The next section – vers. 35-52 – is chiefly occupied with the denunciation of judgment, though at different places, and especially toward the close, the peculiar greatness of Israel's sin is again brought into view, to justify the awful severity of the punishment. Here also, as in the other parts, the prophet indulges in considerable amplification, and descends to much minuteness of detail. But the substance of the representation consists in denouncing against the faithless spouse the sentence of death written in the law against conjugal infidelity, and this to be executed by the hand of her guilty paramours. In the law there were two modes sanctioned of capital punishment, – the one for individuals, the other for communities; in the first case, stoning; in the other, destroying with the sword. As adultery belonged to the first of these classes, the appropriate punishment for it was stoning to death.[22] And as the conjugal infidelity in this case was coincident with two other heinous crimes, – apostasy from the true worship, and the sacrificing of children to Moloch, – which were also adjudged to the

same punishment (Deut. 13:10; Lev. 20:1-5), the doom might be said here to be doubly due. But a single form of punishment, even though a capital one, does not seem adequately to express the full measure of condemnation that was provoked by such aggravated guilt; and therefore the other also, which was decreed against an apostate city (Deut. 13:15), is conjoined with it, though the consistence of the allegory suffers by the conjunction: *"They shall bring up a company against thee, and they shall stone thee with stones, and thrust thee through with their sword."* For the same purpose of rendering what was done more fully expressive of the Lord's sore displeasure against the sin, the execution of the doom is coupled with all manner of indignities, – exposing the faithless spouse to shame before others, demolishing her high places, spoiling her of her jewels and apparel, burning her houses, and reducing her in all respects to the most abject and humiliating condition. And that the whole was to be accomplished in the presence and by the instrumentality of those nations whose evil manners Israel had followed, and whose treacherous alliance she had courted, is intended to mark the dealing of God toward her as more signally exemplifying the Divine law of recompense. It was to bring prominently into view, through her melancholy experience, the grand lesson, that *"God will make him who leaves God for the world, disgraced even in the eyes of the world, and indeed the more so, the nearer he formerly stood to himself."*[23]

The result of this sever execution of judgment is intimated in a peculiarly strong manner of expression, though already in substance employed at chap. 5:13: *"I will make my fury to rest in thee, and my jealousy shall depart from thee, and I will be quiet, and will be no more angry."* The meaning is, that the Divine vengeance called forth by people's sins should then have run its course; God's holiness and majesty should have unfolded themselves in measures of justice toward the people, corresponding to their extreme and incorrigible wickedness toward him. The one followed upon the other by a close and stringent necessity; since, for God to have acted otherwise would have been to show himself indifferent to the interests of holiness, or rather to appear as the patron of sin. Hence the very singular and too commonly misunderstood asseveration, with which the Lord winds up this part of the description: *"And also I, behold, I recompense thy way on thy head, saith the Lord Jehovah, and will not do what is scandalous upon all thine abominations."* I thus vindicate myself from any participation in the guilt, and show that I do not act the shameful part of countenancing thee in thy abominable ways, but by these judgments raise a solemn and effective protest against them.

Yet, as if there might seem an undue severity in the judgments pronounced, the prophet again dwells at some length on the greatness of the provocation. And to give his discourse here more pungency and force to those whom it immediately respected, he narrowed the application to that portion of the covenant-people with whom alone he had properly to do – those of the kingdom of Judah. Viewing Jerusalem now in this restricted sense, he charges her with having exceeded in the measure of her criminality the very worst and guiltiest of her neighbors. The legitimate daughter of a Hittite mother and an Amorite father, she had also proved herself the genuine sister of Samaria (called the elder, because in a moral respect more nearly related) on the north, and Sodom on the south. For she had trodden anew in their polluted ways, but with still greater perverseness of disposition and wantonness of behaviour, so that she might even be said to have justified them; they could shelter themselves when accused of sin under her worse example. Not that the unrighteous and perverse ways followed in Judah were in themselves of a darker and more abominable character than those which had already given such an unhappy notoriety to Samaria and Sodom. This had well-nigh been impossible. But the evil deeds here having been committed on holier ground, in the midst of more distinguished privileges, and in defiance of warnings and protestations altogether peculiar, bore upon them a far deeper impression of guilt. It was simply on the territory of heathenism, and from being carried away by the full tide of worldly prosperity poured into their lot, that Sodom and her daughter cities of the plain became to an unusual degree immersed in the vices of pride, carnality, and lust. And even Samaria, though occupying higher ground than Sodom, and sinning against greater privileges, still held, in comparison of Judah, a much inferior position. For it was the peculiar distinction of Judah, that she had in her very bosom the temple of God, a legal priesthood, the order of government which God himself had appointed, kings often of eminent piety, prophets endowed with the richest gifts of the Spirit, and in addition to all, the spectacle before her eyes of God's judgments resting both on Samaria and Sodom – on each hand appalling monuments of Divine vengeance! Her sins, therefore, were relatively of a much deeper dye than those of her erring neighbors, and it was in the highest degree impossible that she should escape the righteous judgment of God. But if she, in comparison of them, incurred such pre-eminent guilt and condemnation, much more, again, sinners under the gospel in comparison of her; for now it is emphatically that the clear light shines, and that the many talents of knowledge and grace are held in God's kingdom. Sin committed in such circumstances acquires its darkest character, and the judgment that alights must come with corresponding severity. As our Lord, indeed, intimated in that solemn word to the Jews, which may still be substantially addressed to every impenitent transgressor: *"If I had not come and spoken to them, they had not had sin, but now they have no cloak for their sin."*

5. The last portion, which reaches from ver. 53 to the close of the chapter, subjoins a word of promise to the long series of expostulation and threatening, and lets in a gleam of hope as to the future condition of the people. Of course, this again could only be done at the expense of the allegorical representation; for on the supposition of the faithless spouse having been actually stoned to death, and thrust through with the sword, all hope must of necessity have been cut off. But truth required that the form in this case should be sacrificed to the substance of the delineation. It was absolutely necessary to show that, however severe the judgments of God were to be against the apostasy of Judah, they were not to be utterly exterminating, and that a people of God should still survive for honor and blessing.

The particular form given to this more cheering part of the representation was chosen with an especial view to the lowly and abased spirit, which the prophet would have them to understand was absolutely necessary before they could find a return of the Lord's favor and goodness. Even the humiliating providences and manifold tribulations, which were to pass over the remnant of the house of Judah, would fail to be sufficiently productive of the desired effect; it would come only with the returning showers of the Divine goodness. For this end, to render the spiritual result in question more certain, the offending sisters, who had shared before Judah in the punishment, are also named before her as partakers of the benefit, that self-boasting on her part might be excluded; *"And I shall turn again their captivity, the captivity of Sodom and her daughters, and the captivity of Samaria and her daughters, and the captivity of thy captivities* (i.e. thy very grievous captivity) *in the midst of them. And thy sister, Sodom and her daughters shall return to their former state, and Samaria and her daughters, shall return to their former state, and thou and thy daughters shall return to your former state:"* they not less than thou; even Sodom too, though she, as is presently mentioned in ver. 56, *"was not for a report in thy mouth* (not viewed and spoken of as a case, of which thou shouldst have been mindful, and from which thou shouldst have learned wisdom) *in the day of thy glory."* She has disdained to be admonished by her example and even afterwards by the chastisements she personally received at the hand of the Syrians, the Philistines, and other warlike neighbors, whom the Lord occasionally employed against her as instruments of rebuke; for her sin was still not fully discovered, she did not yet see to the depth of it, and would not receive correction (ver. 57). Whence it became necessary to have the whole brought clearly to light, and judgments corresponding to it laid on her (vers. 58,59).

But what precisely is to be understood of the returning, or bringing back of the captivity, here promised? The expression, as we have stated in a previous note, is used proverbially for the removal of an afflicted condition in general, and the appointment of a happy and prosperous one. Its application to the case of Job – *"and the Lord turned the captivity of Job"* (chap. 42:10) – puts this beyond a doubt. And even here, though the import of the phrase appears to be rendered more express by specifying a return to the former state, yet when it is spoken of Sodom and her neighbor cities, as well as Samaria and Jerusalem and their neighbor cities, it manifestly could not be intended to intimate specifically and properly a return from exile, and a re-inhabitation of the old places. This was obviously impossible in the case of Sodom and the cities of the plain. The promise is simply one of restored prosperity; the approaching tide of desolation should again be turned back, and a state of prosperity and happiness as of old, be appointed. Not that exactly which had been, line for line; but what, in the altered circumstances of another time, might be regarded as corresponding to it. "The safe and prosperous conditions of former times," says Havernick justly, "is the determinate form under which the prophet descries also the future; but presently, again, this appears arrayed in so ideal a splendor, that that very form bursts asunder, and a new world in reality comes into view. There is the old God, with his old gifts of love; but the subjective condition has became quite different, and hence the old blessings are also of a new kind, and the whole state, in consequence, rises into something far more elevated and glorious than the old one." It is as if an assurance were given to a child, whose family had become enveloped in misfortune, that he should live to see the former prosperity return again; but meanwhile he himself springs to manhood, and having now other wants to satisfy, and higher relations to fill than formerly, the revived prosperity must bring new and nobler gifts within his reach, to place him on the same relative position he originally occupied. In short, the bringing back of the captivity, and returning to the former state, as applied to the covenant-people, indicates nothing as to the outward form of things to be enjoyed, but points only to their nature and character, as similar to what already had been. And in regard to the manner of accomplishing the promised good, by coupling Sodom and Samaria with Jerusalem in the happy prospect, it must be borne in mind that the representation is figurative; it is the truth represented and embodied in an ideal history; and nothing more can fairly be deduced from the particular trait now referred to, than that the covenant-people, as they had, in the aggravation and magnitude of their guilt, sunk below the most depraved nations around them, so they might expect the return of God's favor and blessing only when they came to view their case in its real enormity, and cherish on account of it a suitable feeling of abasement. They must be ready to put themselves on a level with the lowest, as the necessary condition of their being visited anew with honor and enlargement. Hence it is entirely out of place here to move any question, with some commentators, as to the building anew of Sodom and the other cities of the plain. This were to turn the figure into a reality, and also to transfer the subject itself from the moral region of God's government toward men, to the merely natural region of his providential arrangements respecting the material world. And if it is out of place to move such a question regarding Sodom, it is equally unnecessary, at least, regarding Samaria and Jerusalem. It is the kind, not the precise form of things, which is to be kept in view; and the promise of good here given for the future might be brought to a full accomplishment, and carried even to its highest perfection, though the cities of Judah and Israel should continue, like those of the plain, monuments of desolation and ruin. For the happiness and glory of the covenant-people, which alone is to be regarded here, however it might be connected with them, might also be attained without them; and so far from being necessarily tied to them, may even be found in largest measure while the old things in that respect are gone into utter oblivion.

The closing verses, while they carry forward substantially the same line of thought, in respect especially to the necessity of profound humiliation on the part of the people, and the proposed manifestation of rich grace on the part of God, also render prominent a remarkable difference between those represented by this ideal woman and others. With all her guilt and baseness, she still had what they had not, and what in the day of returning grace would bring them to her, rather than send her to them for blessing, – she had the covenant of God, which, however it had been suffered to fall into abeyance, had never been repudiated by him. *"And I remember,"* the Lord says, *"my covenant with thee in the days of thy youth, and I establish for thee an everlasting covenant."* That covenant made with them in the days of their youth, as to its promise of blessing, was God's word, which he could not suffer to pass unfulfilled. And though there was in this respect an Old and a New, yet so little was there of contrariety between them, when rightly understood, that the one was properly, as here represented, the root of the other; the Old, the germ out of which all the coming good was to spring and develope itself. A glorious rise, indeed, was to take place from a lower to a higher, when the Old passed into the New; but by no means an antagonism, as from bad to good. The better things to come, when they appeared, merely filled up and completed what had been shadowed forth and promised in the Old; and precisely by being thus filled up and completed, did the covenant become what it is here called, an everlasting one. Grace reigns now in a manner it never did before, and the blessing rests upon better promises, because there is a much fuller manifestation of Divine power and goodness associated with them. And on this account there is no longer the same room for the former breaches and desolations to enter; the inheritance is made sure for ever to all the seed of blessing.

But the more that everything appears to stand in the grace and loving-kindness of God, the more there is to abase and humble the partakers of the blessing; especially when they consider the freeness with which grace not only comes from the bosom of God, but also sheds forth its abundance on the worst and the vilest. Those who had been sisters to Judah in guilt and punishment were now also to become partners with her in experiences of blessing, and were to be given to her for daughters – because through her they should attain to the inheritance of blessing. Yet *"not by thy covenant,"* it is added, lest she should again arrogate the glory to herself; not by virtue of any transaction or league of her own framing, such as of old she was ever attempting to form; not by any such covenant of thine, but by mine – the Old, and yet New – the everlasting covenant, which I make with you, and establish for the good of the world.[24] And so, as the result of all, *"Thou shalt know that I am the Lord; to the end thou mayest remember, and be confounded, and never open thy mouth any more because of thy shame, when I am pacified toward thee (or, when I grant forgiveness to thee) for all that thou hast done, saith the Lord Jehovah."*

So ought it to be also in our experience. The humbling and salutary lessons, so strikingly brought out in this wonderful history, should take such deep and abiding hold of our hearts that we shall ever be careful to avoid the evils against which it warns us. And especially since God has now laid open to us the marvellous riches of his grace, and called us to the inheritance of his kingdom, we should strive to remember how unworthy we naturally are of such singular goodness, and how often, by our light and sinful behaviour, we have provoked him to withdraw it agian; so that we may give to him all the glory, and may set our hearts more upon that better country, where imperfections shall be for ever done away, and the strivings between nature and grace shall be wholly unknown.

CHAPTER XVII.

THE PARABLE OF THE TWO GREAT EAGLES, AND THE CROPPING OF THE CEDAR OF LEBANON.

[1] And the word of the LORD came to me, saying,

[2] Son of man, put forth a riddle and speak a parable to the house of Israel.

[3] And say, Thus says the Lord GOD: A great eagle with great wings, long of wing and full of feathers, who had different colors, came to Leb-a-non and took the highest branch of the cedar.

[4] He plucked off the top of its young twigs and carried it into a land of traders. He set it in a city of merchants.

[5] He also took of the seed of the land and planted it in a fruitful field. He placed *it* by great waters, setting it *as* a willow tree.

[6] And it grew and became a spreading vine

of low stature, whose branches turned toward him. And its roots were under him. So it became a vine and brought forth branches and shot forth springs.

[7]There was also another great eagle with great wings and many feathers. And, behold, this vine bent its roots toward him and shot forth its branches toward him, that he might water it, away from the beds of its planting.

[8]It was planted in a good soil by great waters, that it might bring forth branches, and that it might bear fruit, that it might be a goodly vine.

[9]Say, Thus says the Lord GOD: Shall it prosper? Shall he not pull up its roots and cut off its fruit, so that it shall wither? It shall wither in all the leaves of its spring, even without great power of many people to pluck it up by its roots.

[10]Yes, behold, being planted, shall it prosper? Shall it not utterly wither when the east wind touches it? It shall wither in the beds where it grew.

[11]And the word of the LORD came to me, saying,

[12]Say now to the rebellious house: Do you not know what these *mean?* Tell *them,* Behold, the king of Babylon has come to Jerusalem and has taken its king and its princes and brought them to himself to Babylon.

[13]And *he* has taken of the king's seed and has made a covenant with him, and has taken an oath from him. He has also taken the mighty of the land,

[14]so that the kingdom might be low, that it might not lift itself up, *but* that by keeping his covenant it might stand.

[15]But he rebelled against him in sending his ambassadors into Egypt, that they might give him horses and many people. Shall he be blessed? Shall he who does such *things* escape? Or shall he break the covenant and be delivered?

[16]As I live, says the Lord GOD, surely in the place the king *lives* who made him king, whose oath he despised and whose covenant he broke, *even* with him in the middle of Babylon he shall die.

[17]Pharaoh with his mighty army and great company shall not work for him in the war, by casting up mounds and building forts, to cut off many persons.

[18]Since he despised the oath by breaking the covenant, when, lo, he had given his hand, and has done all these *things,* he shall not escape.

[19]Therefore thus says the Lord GOD: As I live, surely My oath that he has despised, and My covenant that he has broken, I will even repay it on his own head.

[20]And I will spread My net on him, and he shall be taken in My snare, and I will bring him to Babylon, and I will judge him there with his sin which he has sinned against Me.

[21]And all his fugitives with all his bands shall fall by the sword, and those who remain shall be scattered toward all winds. And you shall know that I the LORD have spoken.

[22]Thus says the Lord GOD: I will also take of the highest branch of the highest cedar and will set *it;* I will crop off from the top of its young twigs a tender one, and will plant *it* on a high and lofty mountain.

[23]In a mountain, in a high place of Israel I will plant it. And it shall bring forth boughs and bear fruit, and be a beautiful cedar. And under it shall dwell all birds of every wing; in the shadow of its branches they shall dwell.

[24]And all the trees of the field shall know that I the LORD have brought down the high tree, have exalted the low tree, have dried up the green tree, and have made the dry tree to flourish. I the LORD have spoken and have acted.

The prophet is here commanded to put forth to the house of Israel a parable or similitude; which is also denominated a riddle, because it was to be fraught with a meaning that should by no means discover itself at first sight, and, even with the aid of an accompanying explanation, would require the most careful thought and consideration to be understood in its profound and wide-reaching import. A great eagle first presents itself in vision to the eyes of the prophet (literally, the great eagle, emblem of the well-known, pre-eminently great king), large and long of wing, very full and variegated in its plumage – the noblest of its kind. He sees it directing its course to Lebanon, and when there, plucking off the topmost shoot of the cedar, and the summit of its young branches, which it thence carried away to a land of traffic, and placed in a city of merchants. He sees the same eagle taking of the seed of the land – not a foreign production, but one native to the region – and planting it in a fruitful field, in the immediate vicinity of great waters, where it possessed every natural advantage for growth and fruitfulness. Yet still only within certain limits. Its growth was not to be like that of the strong and lofty cedar, but such merely as belonged to the low and spreading vine, – and a vine whose branches were instinctively turned toward the eagle that planted it, and whose roots shot under him, as if doing fealty to the power to which it owed its separate existence and its flourishing condition.

But another eagle now comes on the field of vision, also of great bulk, with large wings and many feathers, though not of such long pinions and richly-colored plumage as the former. Yet the vine, as if it descried an attractive beauty in this bird, which the other had not, presently begins to bend its roots, and turn its branches toward him, that he might water it out of the garden-bed in which it was planted. It was ambitious of getting a larger growth, and reaching a greater altitude than it was likely to attain as it stood; and, with this view, sought the agency of a new power to supply it more abundantly with the means of refreshment. An extravagant and vain imagination! For it was already planted in a good soil, on the banks of a copious river, and with everything necessary to render it heathful and flourishing. Therefore, going against nature in this new attempt after enlargement, so far from succeeding according to its wishes, it should be made to feel the withering blast of the east wind, nay, should be plucked up by the roots, and left to perish and die; and that not as a matter of arduous achievement, but without great power, or multitudes of people, as a thing of easy accomplishment.

Such is the parabolical delineation contained in the first section of the chapter, vers. 1-10; and in the next, vers 11-21, the interpretation is given. The first eagle, is the king of Babylon, who had come to Jerusalem, the seat of civil honor and dignity in Canaan, as Lebanon was of external elevation and forest grandeur. Like the eagle, in plucking off and carrying away the tops of the highest branch, and of the young shoots of the cedar, so the king of Babylon had taken away the head of the royal house, Jehoiachin, to Babylon, a place renowned from the earliest times for its merchandise; and, along with him, many of the younger members of the seed-royal, the princes of Jerusalem. But while he thus humbled the house of David, he did not entirely overthrow it; he still conceded to it a certain degree of honor; and with one of the king's seed, his uncle Zedekiah, he made a covenant, and set him on the throne. The kingdom was now unquestionably in a comparatively enfeebled and dependent state, – no longer like a tall and stately cedar, king of the forest; but rather as a low and creeping vine, incapable of rising high, or standing altogether alone. Yet still it was capable of such strength and prosperity as is characteristic of the vine, – if only they had been content with the measure of good allotted them by God, – if they had but seen the overruling Providence of his hand in their depressed condition, and had bowed with chastened hearts to his will. In that case they had resembled a vine-tree planted beside flowing streams, and in a fertile soil. But they acted in an entirely different spirit. Fretting under the thought of their dependence on Babylon, they eagerly grasped at the proffered alliance of the king of Egypt, – represented by the other eagle, less strong in pinion and rich in plumage; and so provoked their former master to visit them with a severe and merciless retaliation. By acting thus, the house of David gave, in its earthly relations, a new manifestation of that treacherous and deceitful spirit which it had already so often and so perversely displayed in regard to the covenant of God. Indeed, as the covenant with Babylon had been sworn to in the Lord's name, it also was virtually his covenant (ver. 19); and he must himself revenge the breach of it, and prevent the infatuated policy from succeeding. *"And I will spread my net upon him,"* – it is now future time, for the prophecy dates upwards of three years at least before the final downfall of Jerusalem;[3] *"and he shall be taken in my snare, and I will bring him to Babylon, and will reckon with him there for his treacherous dealing toward me. And all his fugitives, with all his bands, shall fall by the sword, and those that are left of them shall be scattered to every wind; and ye shall know that I, Jehovah, have spoken."*

In the charge that is here brought against the house of David, the radical error evidently stood, first, in their not humbling themselves sufficiently on account of the chastisement they had received, in being subjected to the yoke of Babylon; and then, in what was the natural consequence of this, their resorting to deceitful courses and wretched contrivances of their own to recover their lost standing. Destitute of the true fear of God, they looked upon the disasters that had taken place as the result merely of untoward circumstances, and as such, capable of being retrieved by some more skillful manoeuvre, or more propitious turn of the world's affairs. God, therefore, must keep a jealous and watchful eye upon their movements, and utterly defeat their crooked policy. He must constrain them in deep prostration and abasement of spirit to feel, that as his hand had brought them down, so his hand alone could lift them up again; and that never should the lost glory return to the house of David, or to the people of God through it, till they had effectually learned to cease from man, and had come to put their trust wholly in the grace and power of Jehovah.

But it is from this point of depression that the new and better turn of affairs takes its rise. When the execution of deserved judgment should have accomplished the utter prostration of the house of David, and scattered all their false confidences and hopes to the wind, – when matters should have been reduced so low, that to the eye of man everything would seem finally and irretrievably gone, the Lord himself re-appears upon the scene, to rectify the evil, and in the concluding portion (vers. 22-24) gives the assurance of a restoration to the greatest honor and prosperity. *"Thus saith the Lord Jehovah, And I take (or, I too take) of the topmost branch of the high cedar, and set – from the top of its shoots I pluck off a slender one, and I plant it upon a mountain high and elevated. Upon the mountain-height of Israel I will plant it; and it shall raise aloft its branch and bring forth fruit, and become a glorious cedar: and under it shall dwell as birds of every kind, in the shade of its branches shall they dwell. And all the trees of the field shall know that I, Jehovah, bring down the high tree, exalt the low tree, dry up the green tree, and make the dry tree to flourish: I, Jehovah, speak and do."*

Here the Lord presents himself as the rival of the king of Babylon, and the doer of a work precisely opposite in its character and effects to that which the earthly potentate had accomplished. Nebuchadnezzar had been allowed for a time to wield a magisterial power and authority regarding the house of David, which, in the nature of things, could yield nothing more than an inferior and temporary good, and in reality issued in a complete prostration. Now, however, the Lord manifests himself for the gracious purpose of reviving the house of David from the state of apparent hopelessness to which it had been reduced, and even of raising it to a degree of power and glory hitherto unknown. But in doing this he would not infuse new vigour into that particular branch of it which Nebuchadnezzar was seeking to protect and foster, the native seed he had planted in a fruitful field – Zedekiah; this was doomed to certain perdition. He would neither revive that, nor take an altogether new seed, but would pluck a slender twig from the summit of the same lofty cedar, which had previously been pluckt by the king of Babylon; that is, a scion of the house of David, to which the kingdom belonged by an everlasting covenant, and of no new or secondary formation, but in the old, direct, and proper line. This tender twig Jehovah would plant upon Mount Zion–by pre-eminence the high and elevated mountain, because morally the grand centre of grace and glory to the world.[4] And there it springs and rises aloft, and becomes a tree so magnificent in stature, and so ample in foliage, that it commands the admiration and homage of the world; every tree of the field owns its superiority, every fowl of heaven seeks its shelter; in other words, all rival powers, and all intelligent creatures, unite in regarding this as the wonderful impersonation of Divine power and glory in the earth.

It is vain to seek the realization of this prophetic image anywhere but in the Messiah. In no other individual do the lines meet of the prophet's delineation; but in him they meet with the greatest possible exactness–and in him, as the whole tenor of the representation might have led us to expect, primarily as an individual, though not without respect also to his character as the head and representative of the Divine kingdom. The earlier features in the description had each pointed to individuals,–to Jehoiachin, Zedekiah, and through them also to Nebuchadnezzar and Pharaoh,–but to these as individuals, in whose outward state and condition were reflected those of the whole commonwealth of Israel. So, certainly, it is Messiah as an individual that is here indicated; first, as a tender scion of the house of David, in the direct and proper line, then grown into a stately tree, and, finally, risen to the highest place of honour, and power, and glory. But the Messiah, who was to appear on earth only for the sake of the Divine kingdom, could not be regarded as apart from the kingdom itself; its fortunes must stand inseparably bound up with his history, and partake along with it of evil or of good. So that here, as in our Lord's own parable of the mustard-seed, the smallness of the promised beginning tells at once of the lowliness of his appearance, and the depressed condition of the kingdom at the time; and the surpassing greatness afterwards to be reached, while it announces his personal elevation to the highest rank of honour and glory in the heavenly places, makes promise also of the world-wide extension of his kingdom, and the prolific fulness of its blessings to all who might seek shelter in its bosom. But when it is said so emphatically, that God himself should do all this, and that all the trees of the field (the other nations or powers of the earth) should thereby be constrained to own that he exalts the humble and abases the high, what could this import? Certainly, that the whole should be effected in a way different from that of nature, and superior to it,–not by fleshly weapons, or any means and appliances of a worldly kind, but by the peculiar operation of the power of God, securing for his own kingdom a gradual and growing ascendancy over everything earthly and human. Whatever glory should come from the accomplishment of the Divine plan, must redound to God, not to man; the pride of all flesh should be stained by it.

Such is the vision here presented to us of God's future purposes in respect to his kingdom among men–how truly the vision of a Divine seer! What a subline reach and elevation of soul must have been attained by him who could appear thus at home with the far distant future, and, with such clear foresight and firm assurance, could tell of things that were not as if they were! It is greatness of spirit, too, the more surprising, that it was possessed by one whose outward condition seemed so deeply marred with depression and gloom. Himself but a poor exile on the banks of the Chebar, with the cry perpetually sounding in his ears of shattered fortunes and ruined expectations; yet, like the royal bird, of which he here serves himself as an image, he wings his flight aloft, and in the bright radiance of heaven's own light looks afar upon the field of Providence, and brings up to view the very shape and aspect of its yet undeveloped movements. If we look to the unerring skill and precision with which he drew so long beforehand the pattern of what was to come, we might have supposed him a mere automaton, unconsciously obeying the impulse of a higher hand; but if we regard the manner in which he does it, never did a poet's fancy seem to move with more natural and unconstrained freedom in framing its conceptions, or selecting the most appropriate imagery for their expression. And then how divinely strong the faith which could pierce through the dark and portentous cloud of evils that then overhung the spiritual firmament, which could still hold its confidence in the Divine faithfulness, and, instead of being staggered with the signs of approaching desolation, could descry in these but the necessary condition and presage of ultimate good? What a noble superiority does it show him to have reached above that weakness of nature, which is ever apt in times of trouble to raise doubt and despondency in our minds! May such an example of the higher gifts of grace not pass before us in vain! And especially, may the conviction settle itself in our minds, as an abiding ground of consolation, that the word of God is unfailingly true, even in its most peculiar announcements, and that none who trust in it ever can be disappointed!

CHAPTER XVIII.

THE RETRIBUTIVE RIGHTEOUSNESS OF GOD.

[1]And the word of the LORD came to me, saying,

[2]Son of man, set your face toward Jerusalem and drop *your word* toward the holy places, and prophesy against the land of Israel.

[3]And say to the land of Israel, Thus says the LORD: Behold, I am against you and will draw out My sword from its sheath and will cut off from you the righteous and the wicked.

[4]Since then I will cut off the righteous and the wicked from you, therefore My sword shall go out of its sheath against all flesh from the south to the north,

[5]so that all flesh may know that I the LORD have drawn out My sword from its sheath. It shall not return any more.

[6]Therefore sigh, son of man, with the breaking of *your* loins; and sigh with bitterness before their eyes.

[7]And when they say to you, Why do you sigh? You shall answer, Because of the news. Because it is coming; and every heart shall melt, and all hands shall be feeble, and every spirit shall faint, and all knees shall be weak *as* water. Behold, it comes, and *it* shall be brought to pass, says the Lord GOD.

[8]Again the word of the LORD came to me, saying,

[9]Son of man, prophesy and say, Thus says the LORD. Say, A sword! A sword is sharpened and also polished!

[10]It is sharpened to make a grievous slaughter; it is polished so that it may flash like lightning. Should we then rejoice? It despises the rod of My son, along with every tree.

[11]And He has given it to be polished so that it may be handled. This sword is sharpened, and it is polished, to give it into the hand of the slayer.

[12]Cry and howl, son of man. For it shall be on My people. It shall be on all the princes of Israel. Because of the sword, terrors shall be on My people. Therefore strike on *your* thigh.

[13]Because it is a trial, and what if *the sword* even despises the rod of power? It shall not be any more, says the Lord GOD.

[14]Therefore, son of man, prophesy and strike *your* hands together. And let the sword be doubled the third time, the sword of the slain. It is the sword of the great men who are slain, which enters into their secret rooms.

[15]I have set the point of the sword against all their gates, that *their* heart may faint and *their* ruins may be multiplied. Ah, *it* is ready to flash like the lightning; it is wrapped up for the slaughter.

[16]Go one way or the other, either on the right hand or on the left, wherever your face is set.

[17]I will also strike My hands together, and I will cause My fury to rest. I the LORD have spoken.

[18]The word of the LORD came to me again, saying,

[19]Also, son of man, choose yourself two ways that the sword of the king of Babylon may come. Both of them shall come out of one land. And choose a place, choose *it* at the head of the *highway* to the city.

[20]Choose a way that the sword may enter into Rab-bah of the Am-mon-ites and into Judah, into fortified Jerusalem.

[21]For the king of Babylon stood at the parting of the way, at the head of the two highways, to ask of images. He made arrows bright; he asked of images; he looked in the liver.

[22]At his right hand was the divining for Jerusalem, to choose captains, to open the mouth in the slaughter, to lift up the voice with shouting, to choose *battering* rams against the gates, to cast a mound and to build a fort.

[23]And it shall be to them as a false divining in their sight, to those who have sworn oaths. But he will call iniquity to memory, that they may be taken.

[24]Therefore thus says the Lord GOD: Because you have made your iniquity to be remembered, in that your transgressions are discovered so that your sins are revealed in all your doings; because you have come to memory, you shall be taken with the hand.

[25]And you, ungodly, wicked king of Israel, whose day has come when iniquity shall have an end,

[26]Thus says the Lord GOD: Remove the diadem and take off the crown. This shall not be as it was. Lift up the low one and put down the high one.

[27]I will overturn, overturn, overturn it! And this shall never again be until the coming of Him whose is the right. And I will give it *to Him*.

[28]And, son of man, prophesy and say, Thus says the Lord GOD concerning the Am-mon-ites and as to their shame. Even say: The sword, the sword is drawn, polished to flash like lightning and to destroy –

[29]while they see false visions for you, while they divine a lie to you, to bring you on the necks of *the* slain, of the wicked whose day has come when iniquity shall have an end.

[30]Shall I cause it to return into its sheath?

I will judge you in the place where you were created, in the land of your birth.

[31]And I will pour out My fury on you. I will blow the fire of My wrath against you, and deliver you into the hands of beastly men, able to destroy.

[32]You shall be as fuel for the fire. Your blood shall be in the midst of the land. You shall be remembered no more. For I the LORD have spoken. 1

The prophet passes from the purposes of God respecting the future establishment of his kingdom and glory in the world–as disclosed in the preceding chapter–to an expostulation with the people on account of sin, and an earnest pleading on behalf of righteousness. He wished them to understand that, however gracious the intentions of Heaven might be, and however certainly they would reach their destined accomplishment, they were not to move as in an orbit of their own, independently of the condition of the people; nor might the people expect any benefit from them, if wedded to the love and practice of sin. While, on the one hand, God might confidently be expected to do what he had promised, they, on the other, should not be entitled to look for any blessing, unless they applied themselves in earnest to do what he required at their hands.

The chapter preserves throughout the form of a controversial pleading; because the people are contemplated by the prophet as in a self-righteous condition, disposed to shift off themselves the blame of what was evil in their lot, and lay it partly on their fathers, partly on God himself. We suffer, it is true, they were complacently saying among themselves, under the rod of chastisement, but that we do so is our misfortune, rather than our sin; it is not we, but our fathers, who ate the sour grapes, and now, inheriting what was justly due to their transgression, our teeth are set on edge. What was it but in effect to say, God can have no proper quarrel with *us?* We are dealing faithfully by the commandments of his law, and we can no otherwise account for his subjecting us to punishment than on the principle of our being made to bear the iniquities of those who have gone before us.

The mere fact of their taking up such a view of their case, and putting it forth in vindication of themselves, was obviously a proof of some sort of reformation having been accomplished. The feeling could not have sprung up, and taken shape in their minds as a ground of defence, without at least an ostensible justification in the present, as compared with the past. To what extent this might actually be the case, either with the remnant at Jerusalem, or with the captives on the Chebar, we have no very specific data for ascertaining. Reckoning from the period of Manasseh's reign, when the practice of all manner of corruption seemed to have reached its climax, we can have no reasonable doubt that in both divisions of the Jewish people a visible reform had taken place – more particularly with the captives, as their actual experience of God's judgments would naturally have forced on them a more serious and thoughtful examination of their ways. But ample grounds exist, both in this prophet and Jeremiah, for holding that in each division alike there still was no thorough and general renunciation of iniquity. The partial improvements that had been made were chiefly of a superficial nature, and seem to have had no other effect than in fostering the self-righteous spirit, which induced them to seek elsewhere than in themselves the cause of their troubles and calamities. Therefore, in a word of severe expostulation and rebuke, which, if called forth by what then existed, has been no less applicable to succeeding generations of the Jewish people, the prophet exposes the vanity of their imaginations, and declares them to be still at war with the principles of God's righteous administration.[2]

In doing this, Ezekiel first announces the general principle of God's righteousness as a principle of fair and impartial dealing with each individual according to his actions; then he explains and illustrates the operation of this principle in a series of supposed cases; and finally calls the people to repentance and amendment of life, as being still far from righteousness, and in danger of perdition.

1. There is, first, a general announcement made of the principle of God's righteousness; which is declared to be a principle of fair and impartial dealing with each individual,

according to his actions: *"As I live, saith the Lord God, ye shall no longer use this proverb in Israel. Behold, all the souls are mine; as the soul of the father, so also the soul of the son is mine; the soul that sinneth, it shall die"* (vers. 3,4); – it alone shall die, as having, through sin, incurred the law's penalty; others, who have lived righteously, shall be treated according to their desert, not as persons appointed to die, but rather as entitled to the blessings of life. And this on the broad and comprehensive ground that God is alike the maker of all, and can have no reason for adjudging some to a punishment from which he exempts others, except the different manner in which they conduct themselves toward him.

Here, of course, the question naturally arises, whether such has always been the principle of God's dealing? or, whether the announcement made by the prophet marked a change in the Divine administration? There can be no doubt that the law did sanction the principle of a certain visitation of the sins of the fathers upon the children: *"I the Lord thy God am a jealous God, visiting the iniquities of the fathers upon the children unto the third and fourth generation of them that hate me, and showing mercy unto thousands of them that love me and keep my commandments."* But then this principle, it would seem, remained still in active operation, neither suspended, nor in any way materally affected, by what is written here. For the prophet Jeremiah expressly connects the judgments which were shortly afterwards to alight upon Judah and Jerusalem with the sins of Manasseh's time in the preceding generation (chap. 15:4); and again in Lam. 5:7, after the judgments had actually been inflicted, *"our fathers have sinned, and are not; and we have borne their iniquities."* Even in gospel times we find our Lord speaking of the principle as still in force, nay, as ready to be acted on with such fearful severity in the case of that generation, that upon them was to be charged and visited the righteous blood shed in all preceding ages of the Church's history (Matt. 23:34-36).

Yet neither our Lord in later, nor the prophets in earlier, times, seem to have had the least suspicion of any contrariety existing between the principle which thus connected the child with the parent in visitations of evil, and the direct and proper responsibility of each person for the actions merely of his own life. How thoroughly the gospel is pervaded by this latter principle requires no particular proof; there every one is made to feel that his condition and destiny depend upon the course he himself takes in respect to the will of God. And the prophet Jeremiah, when addressing God as *"recompensing the iniquity of the fathers into the bosom of the children after them,"* in the very next breath celebrates his impartial administration of justice to all according to their doings: *"Great in counsel and mighty in work; for thine eyes are upon all the ways of the sons of men, to give every one according to his ways, and according to the fruit of his doings"* (Jer. 32:18,19). In the law itself, indeed, there is as strong an assertion of this principle of individual responsibility as anywhere in Scripture, in the charge that is given to the judges: *"The fathers shall not be put to death for the children, neither shall the children be put to death for the fathers; every man shall be put to death for his own sin"* (Deut. 24;16); a charge which never would have been given to God's representatives on earth, unless it were in full accordance with the character of his own administration. It is clear, therefore, from these distinct and unambiguous testimonies, that the two principles in question must have been perfectly consistent with each other, and that only the perversenéss or misapprehensions of the people could have led to their being viewed as in any sort of antagonism. Nor is the ground of the reconciliation far to seek. The principle of a descending curse to families on account of sin proceeds on the assumption of a descending guilt as the reason of the appointment. The iniquity was to be visited from father to son, because the iniquity itself was viewed as passing with cumulative force from the one to the other. Hence the line of descent is characterized as *"the generation of them that hate God,"* while the superabundant flow of mercy on the other side is declared *"to thousands of them that love him."* In truth, the principle which has its connection with the jealousy of God, as most intently watching the movements of sin, is just the manifestation of God's righteousness in respect to the tendency of sin to spread and perpetuate itself in the world, and especially to go downward from parent to child as a growing and swelling tide of corruption. So that, if successive generations, yielding to this tendency, should become known as a hereditary band of evil-doers, God must in turn unite them in a bond of chastisement, and proportion his visitations of wrath to the degree of perverseness and obstinacy shown in pursuing the course of iniquity. But respect was ever had, at the same time, to the personal responsibility and behavior of each, and only because the son was regarded as consenting to his father's iniquity, and deliberately choosing it as his own inheritance, did the Lord visit him for both together.[3]

When the Lord, then, declares in this passage that the people should no longer have occasion to use the proverb of the fathers having eaten the sour grapes, and the children's teeth being set on edge, allusion is not made to any projected change in the government of God, but merely to the sharp, personal dealing he was going to hold with each, which would not permit them any more to throw upon others the blame that was properly their own. "It was just as if he had said," to use the excellent words of Calvin, "I will drive out of you this boasting, by laying bare your iniquity, in such a manner that the whole world shall perceive you to suffer the punishment you yourselves deserve, and you shall not be able, as you have been hitherto endeavoring, to cast the burden on your fathers." It was to be made fully manifest that their punishment only corresponded to their own guilt. And the circumstance of the Lord prefacing this declaration with his oath, *"As I live, it shall be done,"* was like a solemn and earnest protest against the injurious and blasphemous character of the thought, which led them to impute to him a partial and arbitrary principle of dealing with his people.

This very protest, however, against the wrong principle of dealing falsely imputed to God, carried along with it a strong assertion of the necessity of the opposite principle – that of holding those liable to punishment who were guilty of sin. If it is abhorrent to the mind of God to render the just desert of sin in the wrong quarter, because contrary to the essential principles of justice, it must be equally abhorrent, and for the same reason, to withhold punishment from the quarter where it is due. For to protect and countenance the sinner is all one with discouraging and depressing ; the righteous. Therefore, the soul that sinneth must die; and the less God can punish the innocent for the guilty, the less also can he refrain from dealing with the guilty according to their transgressions. Thus, the severe impartiality of God, while it is a wall of security and defence for the good, becomes of necessity like a consuming fire to the wicked; and if death is not yet actually their portion, it can only be because the long-suffering of God is still waiting for their repentance.

2. So much for the principle itself of fair and impartial dealing, which the prophet here asserts for God in his government toward men. Let us now glance for a moment at the series of supposed cases, by which the prophet explains and illustrates the operation of the principle. There are altogether four distinct cases specified, which are also followed up toward the close by a renewal vindication of the Lord's method of dealing in respect to them.

(1) The first case supposed is that of a righteous man, who applies with sincere and honest purpose of heart to keep the ways of the Lord (vers. 5-9). And because very lax and imperfect notions prevailed concerning God's ways, the prophet enters into some particulars, with the view of exhibiting clearly the nature of the requirements which the Divine law made at the hands of men, and thereby administering a reproof for prevailing evils. His enumeration of excellences was, doubtless, chosen with a respect to existing circumstances, that the mass of his countrymen might perceive how far they were deviating in their conduct from the character they ought to have maintained. And if, in one of two features of the representation, undue prominence seems to be given to points which in themselves were less important than others that might have been mentioned, a ready explanation is to be found in the prevailing character of the times. The prophet must adapt his description to the persons whom he sought more especially to benefit by

it. And when he has thus delineated one who stood aloof from the reigning corruptions, and gave ample proof of having the law of God within his heart, the prophet draws the conclusion in his favor, that he shall live: *"He is just; he shall surely live, saith the Lord God."*

Perhaps what will strike most readers in the present day as chiefly peculiar in the description given of the righteous man, is the stress laid upon his abstaining from usury: *"He hath not given forth upon usury, neither hath taken any increase."* We find the same prominence, however, given to this feature in the still briefer description of the righteous by the Psalmist in the 15th Psalm: *"Putteth not out his money to usury."* It arose in both cases from the strict prohibition in the law against lending money for interest to an Israelite (Ex. 22:25; Lev. 25:35,37; Deut. 23:19,20). In several of the passages it is clearly implied that the money to be lent was to the poor, which consequently ought to have been done in a spirit of brotherly love, and not for the purpose of taking advantage of their necessities, and turning the loan into an occasion of trouble and oppression. The word denoting usury, נֶשֶׁךְ (from the verb to bite or eat), has respect to this vexatious and selfish mode of dealing with a brother's poverty – making gain out of the distress of the borrower. But as the law permitted the lending of money on usury to strangers, it of course indicated that the practice was not in all circumstances improper. The law had respect to a very simple state of society, and a polity which was designed to form a check on speculation in trade and commerce, and diffuse a general well-being and comfort; hence it was important to encourage liberality to the poorer members of the commonwealth, and, on the part of the richer, repress the tendency to undue exactions; though, in corrupt times, the spirit of selfishness was always breaking through the restrictions. In the artificial and complicated affairs of modern times, the prohibitions of the law against usury cannot fairly be stretched farther than to regard them as involving the imperative obligation of dealing in a kind and liberal spirit toward our poorer brethren, lending to them when they have need, without expecting anything again, and to discourage the spirit of rash and ambitious speculation.[4]

We notice, in regard to another part of the description, *"the not eating upon the mountains,"* in ver. 6, that it has respect to the tendency, which so naturally and so frequently also manifested itself in the history of the Israelites, of holding their sacrificial feasts upon the neighboring mountains, instead of repairing to the place God had chosen. Even when these feasts were held in honor of Jehovah, they were contrary to the express enactments of the law (Deut. 12:13, etc.), but of course they became much more so when they were coupled, as they too commonly were, with the worship of false gods. The righteous man is described as not so much as *"lifting up his eyes to these false gods,"* that is, not cherishing any wistful desire toward them in his heart. And with this shrinking abhorrence of idolatry, or abstinence from whatever is idolatrous and sensual in the services of religion, he is further described as carefully shunning any manifestation of such a spirit in his earthly relations; he is sober, chaste, and faithful. (Upon the last clause in ver. 6 Cocceius well: "notatur castitas observanda in matrimonio; nam etiam propria conjuga potest quis abuti.")

(2.) The next case supposed is precisely the reverse of the preceding one; it is that of a son refusing to follow the example of a righteous parent, and turning aside to the ways of vanity and corruption. Here, again, to make the charge pointed and specific, the prophet descends to an enumeration of the particular deeds in which he held the unrighteousness to consist. But it differs in nothing material from that already given – the son being simply represented as doing the bad things, which were shunned by the father, and leaving undone the good which he did. Therefore, being guilty of such flagrant offences against the Divine law, this ungodly son must bear his own doom; his pious parentage, which only aggravated his guilt, cannot be allowed to screen him from judgment; *"he has done all these abominations; he shall surely die; his blood shall be upon him."*

(3.) The third supposition, again, presents a reverse picture; it is the case of a son of such an unrighteous person as the one just described, seeing the evil of his father's doings, and turning from them to do the will of God. Having more respect to the authority of God than to the pernicious example of a degenerate parent, he obtains an exemption from the heritage of evil; though *"the father dies in his iniquity,"* yet *"the son shall not die for the iniquity of the father; he shall surely live."*

Here the people are introduced objecting to the word of the prophet, and in their objection apparently seeking for a continuance of that which they had originally preferred as a complaint. It seemed to be their burden that the son was made to bear *"the iniquity of the father,"* as to that principle in the Divine government they ascribed their present suffering condition (ver. 2). But now when they have heard the prophet, in the Lord's name, repudiating this alleged principle, and asserting the Divine impartiality in dealing with each according to his ways, they interpose and say: *"Wherefore? Doth not the son bear the iniquity of the father?"* or as we might read, *"Wherefore doth not the son bear the iniquity of the father?"* Is not such actually the case? We had thought this was an undoubted principle of the Divine government, and on it alone could account for what otherwise was quite inexplicable to us. It seems now as if it would be a consolation for them to think that the son might suffer for the father's misdeeds, or, in the language of the proverb, that, while the fathers ate sour grapes, the children's teeth should be set on edge. And the reason, no doubt, was that they found it more agreeable to their carnality, and more soothing to their pride, to regard themselves as innocent sufferers for sins they had not personally committed, than to ascribe their troubles to their own departures from the law of righteousness. For in the one case they were furnished with an excuse for continuing to live on still as they had been doing in the past; while in the other, as the evil came to be traced up to their own misdeeds, the necessity forced itself upon them of striving, if they really wished to get rid of it, to realize the high pattern of righteousness set before them in the descriptions of the prophet. This, however, they were by no means inclined to do; and hence it came upon them rather as a disappointment, to have the querulous complaint taken out of their mouths, that the innocent children were suffering for the sins of their guilty parents. But the prophet will not allow them to enjoy this miserable solace, or to rest in a confidence so utterly groundless. He must convince them of their own sinfulness, and lead them to repentance and amendment of life, as the one way of escape from their depressed and abject condition. Therefore, in reply to their query, he again reiterates the great truth of each man's treatment being according to his personal condition and character before God: *"When the son hath done that which is lawful and right, hath kept all my statutes and hath done them, he shall surely live. The soul that sinneth shall die; the son shall not bear the iniquity of the father, neither shall the father bear the iniquity of the son: the righteousness of the righteous shall be upon him, and the wickedness of the wicked shall be upon him."*

(4.) And now, having repudiated the false imagination of the people, as to the innocent suffering for the guilty, and asserted anew the great principle of God's impartiality in dealing with each according to his desert, the prophet comes to his last hypothetical case – the case, namely, of a supposed change, not, as hitherto, in the character of one generation as compared with another, but in the character of one and the same individual, from bad to good and from good to bad. This was more especially the practical case for the persons here addressed by the prophet, and therefore he reserved it to the last; as it enabled him to shut them up to the alternative of either abandoning at once their sinful ways or of charging upon their own hardened impenitence all that they might still experience of the troubles and afflictions that pressed upon them. For the message here is, that so far from laying to men's charge the burden of iniquities that had been committed by others, the Lord would not even visit them for their own, if they sincerely repented and turned to the way of righteousness; while on the other hand, if they should begin to fall away into transgression, they must not expect their earlier goodness to screen them from judgment, – because in that case, having taken up with a new condition, it was just and proper that a corresponding change should be introduced into the Divine procedure toward them: *"If the wicked will turn from all his sins that he has committed, and keep all my statutes, and do that which is lawful and right, he shall surely live, he shall not die. None of his transgressions that he has committed shall be remembered against him : in his righteousness that he has done he shall live. Have I any pleasure at all that the wicked should die? saith the Lord Jehovah, and not that he turn from his way and live? But when the righteous turns away from his righteousness, and commits iniquity, and does according to all the abominations that the wicked does, shall he live? Nothing of all his righteousness that he has done shall be remembered: in his trespass that he has trespassed, and in his sin that he has sinned, in them shall he die."*

What a beautiful simplicity and directness in the statement! It is like the lawgiver anew setting before the people the way of life and the way of death, and calling upon them to determine which of the two they were inclined to choose. Then, what a moving tenderness in the appeal, *"Have I any pleasure in the death of the wicked? saith the Lord God."* You think of me as if I were a heartless being, indifferent to the calamities that befall my children, and even delighting to inflict chastisement on them for sins they have not committed. So far from this, I have no pleasure in the destruction of those who by their own transgressions have deserved it, but would rather that they turn from their ways and live. Thus he presents himself as a God of holy love, – love yearning over the lost condition of his wayward children, and earnestly desiring their return to peace and safety, – yet still exercising itself in strict accordance with the principles of righteousness, and only, in so far as these might admit, seeking the good of men. For however desirous to secure their salvation, he neither can nor will save them, except in the way of righteousness.

The people, however, being still wedded to their own sinfulness, continued as before to find fault; and, looking superficially to the outward diversity that appeared in God's dealings with men, they raised the objection, *"The way of the Lord is not equal."* An outward inequality the prophet, indeed, had admitted; it was the very design of his expostulation to prove that such must have place according to the varying conditions of those with whom he had to do; but only so as to establish a real equality in a moral point of view. Therefore the prophet turns the accusation against the people themselves: *"Hear, now, O house of Israel! is not my way equal? Are not your ways unequal?"* My way is equal, he virtually affirms, because I deal with the guilty backslider and the penitent transgressor, each according to his behavior – the one as deserving of death, the other as a proper subject of life and blessing. But your ways are unequal, since, living in idolatry and corruption, you expect to be dealt with as if you were following the paths of uprightness.

3. Therefore, finally, having driven the people from all their false imaginations and captious objections – having shut them up to the conclusion, that as they were in a depressed and suffering, they must also be in a sinful condition, the prophet closes his expostulation by urging them to repent and turn from all their unrighteous ways, that so they might not perish in their sins: *"Therefore I will judge you, O house of Israel, every one according to his ways, saith the Lord God. Return, and come back from all your transgressions, and iniquity shall not be your ruin* (more properly: and iniquity shall not be for a snare to you, the occasion of restraining you from good, and entangling you in ruin). *Cast away from you all your transgressions, whereby ye have transgressed; and make you a new heart and a new spirit; and why will ye die, O house of Israel? For I have no pleasure in the death of him that dieth, saith the Lord Jehovah; but turn ye, and live."*

The charge is given to the whole house of Israel; for the people, as a whole, are regarded by the prophet as in a state of apostasy and alienation from God. And it was no slight or partial reformation that was needed to restore them to the favor and blessing of God, but an entire and radical change. Therefore they are called upon not only to repent and cast away their transgressions, but also to get possession of a new heart and a new spirit, nay, even to make such to themselves, as if it were a matter that lay within the compass of their own responsible agency. This has an appearance of strangeness, as already, in chap.

11, and again in chap. 36, the imparting of such a new heart and spirit is represented as the great boon which at some future period they were to receive from the grace and mercy of God. Nor, indeed, is there anything more clearly announced, or more frequently stated in the word of God, than that a regenerated condition can only be reached through the quickening power of his grace; he must himself be the author of this new creation, wherever it is brought into being, as he was at first of the old. But why then should God call upon men to make to themselves a new heart, seeing he alone is able to produce it? Does not such a call but seem to mock men's impotence, or to beget in them false expectations? By no means. It was rather intended to set before them what was necessary to rectify their state in so strong and startling a manner, that from the very height of the requirement they would despair of themselves, and betake to the promised grace of God. For, as Calvin justly remarks, "it must always be considered for what end God speaks in such a manner, viz. that being convinced of their sinfulness, men may cease to lay the blame elsewhere, as thev constantly endeavor to do, there being nothing to which we are more prone than shifting the ground of our condemnation away to some other quarter, that we ourselves may seem to be just, and God unjust. Therefore, because this perversity recourse to the promised aid of the Spirit; so that the outward command becomes the occasion or instrument which God employs for conferring the grace of his Spirit . . . . As often, therefore, as such passages meet us, let the well-known saying of Augustine come to our mind, *'Da quod jubes, et jube quod velis'* (give what thou requirest, and require what thou pleasest). For otherwise, if God should lay upon us the least tittle of commanded duty, we shall not be able to bear it; while, on the other hand, our strength shall suffice for whatever he may exact of us, if only he himself shall give the supply, and we shall not be so foolish as to suppose that nothing more is demanded in his precepts than what we have power in ourselves to do."

Such, then, is the case which the prophet presses on the covenant-people as the result of this long and earnest expostulation with their sinfulness. The Lord demands of them a renovated condition – a heart that should dispose them to yield a sincere and ready obedience to his commandments. Never till such a spiritual change was effected could they expect his judgments to be turned into blessings. Never could they hope to see and reap the accomplishment of that promise of renewed prosperity at the close of the preceding chapter, according to which the little twig of the Lord's planting was to become a mighty tree, with fowl of every wing lodging in its branches. And never can the Church of God in any age justly expect to be safe and prosperous in her condition, and to be a fit instrument in the hand of the Lord for executing his righteous purposes, till she becomes possessed through all her members of such a spirit of obedience as shall prompt her to embrace heartily his Divine will, and keep the way of his commandments. Oh! need we wonder, when we see how little this is really possessed, that the flow of the Divine goodness should be arrested, and that we should seem so often to be dwelling among the tombs, instead of basking, as we should be, in the sunshine of life and blessing? In how many forms is the controversy still maintained with the righteousness of God? and with all her privileges of grace, how far is the Church of Christ, either individually or collectively, from the measure of perfection that ought to be reached? How much cause still for the prayer, Turn us again, Lord God of hosts, and cause thy face to shine, and we shall be saved! Rekindle in the bosoms of thy people the love of holiness, which so sadly languishes and droops; and let not iniquity and death prevail, where only righteousness and blessing should be found!

CHAPTER XIX.

THE LAMENTATION OVER THE DOWNFALL OF THE ROYAL HOUSE.

The expostulation contained in the last chapter was held with the covenant-people as a whole, and its final aim was to put them on the only way of recovering the prosperity they had lost, namely, by a sincere and hearty return to the paths of righteousness. But in this chapter the vision of the prophet is confined to the more distinguished portion of Israel, the princes of the house of David (for the spirit of prophecy recognises no other princes besides those who belonged to that house); and the only word he receives concerning them is one of doleful lamentation over their inevitable ruin. In expostulating with the people, it was taken for granted that a period of revival and blessing still awaited them, and that the only question was as to the course of procedure on their part which might warrant them to expect its arrival. But no ray of hope mingles with the sombre representation he gives respecting the princes of Israel; in what had already befallen, and what was yet to befall them, there was room only for the wail of sorrow and despair.. It is true the royal house was not to become utterly extinct; it was still destined to furnish a head to the people of God, under whom the cause of righteousness and truth was to attain a glory it had never reached before. This had been most distinctly announced by our prophet himself at the close of the seventeenth chapter, under the image of a tender shoot plucked by the hand of Jehovah from the topmost bough of the cedar of Lebanon, and planted on the lofty mountain of Israel. But the very character of the description thus given of a coming glory – that it was to be a tender shoot, which was to be plucked, and that its plantation on the mountain of Israel, its marvellous growth, and ultimate unparalleled greatness, were so peculiarly to mark the overruling power and sovereignty of God – clearly implied that the prospect was to be realized in a way quite different from the ordinary course and expectations of nature, and in defiance, as it might seem, of all outward appearances. And the melancholy dirge contained in the present chapter may be regarded as supplying the further information, that now and henceforth appearances were indeed to be of the most humiliating kind as concerned the members of the royal house, that their outward glory was waning to extinction, and that they forfeited all claim to any restoration of the worldly greatness which they had hitherto enjoyed. Viewed simply as princes in the earth, their place was lost beyond recovery.

[1]And take up a weeping for the princes of Israel,

[2]and say, What is your mother? A lioness. She lay down among lions; she nursed her cubs among young lions.

[3]And she brought up one of her cubs; it became a strong lion and learned to catch the prey. It ate men.

[4]The nations also heard of him. He was taken in their pit, and they brought him with chains to the land of Egypt.

[5]Now when she saw that she had waited *and* her hope was lost, she took another of her cubs and made him a strong lion.

[6]And he went up and down among the lions. He became a young lion and learned to catch the prey, *and he* ate men.

[7]And he knew their deserted palaces, and he laid their cities waste, and the land and its fullness was wasted away, because of the noise of his roaring.

[8]Then the nations set against him on every side from the provinces and spread their net over him. He was taken in their pit.

[9]And they put him under guard in chains and brought him to the king of Babylon. They brought him into strongholds, so that his voice should never again be heard on the mountains of Israel.

[10]Your mother is like a vine in your blood, planted by the waters. She was fruitful and full of branches because of many waters.

[11]And she had strong rods for the scepters of those who bore rule, and her stature was exalted among the thick branches. And she appeared in her height with the multitude of her branches.

[12]But she was plucked up in fury. She was thrown down to the ground, and the east wind dried up her fruit. Her strong rods were broken and withered; the fire burned them

up.

[13]And now she is planted in the wilderness, in a dry and thirsty ground.

[14]And fire has gone out from a rod of her branches, licking up her fruit so that there is no strong rod in her to be a scepter to rule. This is a mourning and shall be for a mourning.

Thus we see that, in order to make the import of his message more plain and palpable, the prophet gives it the benefit of a twofold representation. But in each case the representation is so highly figurative, that to seek a very close and minute correspondence between the symbol and the reality cannot be necessary, and may even tend to mislead. Interpreters have commonly run into this error, when at the outset they begin to inquire, who is to be understood by the mother? As might be expected, very different answers are given to the question, – some, as Pradus, answering Jerusalem; others, as Lowth, the land of Israel; others again, as Havernick, the theocratic Israel at large; and still others, as Hitzig, the more peculiarly regal portion, the tribe of Judah. To descend upon limitations of this sort is to lose sight of the bold and luxuriant character of Ezekiel's style; and one might as well have asked, in regard to the figurative representation of the sixteenth chapter, which of the progenitors of the Jewish people could be meant, when it was said that their father was an Amorite and their mother a Hittite. We must keep in view the general object of the representation, which, in the case now before us, was to exhibit the princes of Israel in such a light as sufficiently to account for their being allowed to fall into overwhelming and hopeless ruin. For instead of feeling, as they should have done, that they were set up in the high position they occupied, as sons of God in particular, to carry out in all things his will, and promote the interests of truth and righteousness, they acted in such a wild, lawless, arbitrary manner as might seem to befit only those who were possessed of the most savage and ungovernable natures. It seemed, judging from their behavior, as if a lioness had been their mother – a lioness who had herself lived among the other wild beasts of her species, and who had reared her young amid the ravening and ferocious tenants of the forest. Hence, when they ceased to be under the mother's care, and began to act for themselves, it was after the capricious and unruly manner of such fierce and untamed natures – without regard to any will but their own, and with no desire but the gratification of their own selfish purposes. The particular course followed would, of course, differ in each, according to their natural temperaments, though the prophet simply represents it, according to the image he has chosen, as a catching of prey, devouring men, and spreading around scenes of horror and desolation. We are not to suppose from this that the princes, more particularly in the eye of the prophet, were all alike remarkable for the ferocity of their disposition, and the heartless manner in which they sported themselves with the calamities and ruin of others, or, indeed, that any of them did so. There is nothing in the history to countenance the idea that either Jehoahaz first, or afterwards Jehoiakim and Zedekiah, were peculiarly characterised by such a disposition. The whole we are to understand by the representation is, that like the lion among beasts, so they among men followed recklessly the bent of their own minds, and pursued, without let or hindrance, their sinful courses, regardless of the mischief which they might thereby bring upon the people they were bound to watch over and protect. Their conduct was as wayward, and the disastrous consequences that flowed from it were as great, as if their object had been to tear in pieces and spread desolation throughout the land. So that it was simply to mete to them according to their own measure, and reward them after their own doings, to allow the surrounding nations, first Egypt (in respect to Jehoahaz), and then Babylon, with her multitudinous hosts (in respect to the rest), to come and snare them as wild beasts, and lay them under perpetual arrest, *"that their voice should no more be heard upon the mountains of Israel."* Thus these two foreign kingdoms, and more especially Babylon, became in a manner the grave of the earthly pomp and dominion of the princes of Israel.

The figurative representation now given has respect more immediately to the character of the princes, and the punishment it both provoked and was destined to receive. But to complete the gloomy picture, the prophet adds another, taken from the vine, chief of the fruit-bearing trees, as the lion is of the beasts of prey; having respect more especially to the royal house itself, and the contrast between its original and its now altered and doomed condition. This royal house, the source of all the individual princes that sprung from it, as represented as, from the first, like a healthy and fruitful vine, planted beside streams of water for abundance of nourishment, so that she shot forth her branches, which were like so many royal sceptres, aloft in the air, and drew upon her the eyes of all on account of her imposing attitude and flourishing appearance. But without saying how, – it is to be understood from the preceding delineation, on account of the corrupt fruit that was borne by those rods of command and rule, – this vine becomes the object of irresistible fury, which plucks her up from the fertile situation she had hitherto occupied, dries up her fruit, breaks off and burns in the fire her once vigorous branches; and not only this, but transplants the tree itself into a dry and sapless region, where it could no longer flourish, and where the little fruitfulness that still appeared in it was to be devoured by a fire coming out of itself. For such was the wilful infatuation and folly of the royal house, that even when reduced and crippled on every hand by the punitive justice and restraining providence of God, it acted so as only to provoke further visitations of wrath, until it was rendered, like the vine-tree of the prophet, without either fruit to yield or a rod of sufficient strength to form a sceptre to rule. In other words, the royal house of Israel, as to this earthly power and glory, becomes utterly wasted and gone; the fit theme only of a present and coming lamentation.

A doleful picture indeed, but how exactly accordant with the truth of things! Who but the unerring Spirit of God could have guided the hand of the prophet to exhibit so faithful a representation of the coming future? It might have been clear enough to a discerning mind, from the signs of the times in which Ezekiel lived, that the princes of Israel were likely to be further shorn of their power by the king of Babylon, and possibly even removed to other parts of his dominions; but that their princely power and glory should thus actually expire, that the royal house of Israel itself should finally lose its place among the princedoms of the world, while yet the Lord should one day bring out of its seeming ruin a king, that should rise to the dominion in spite of all the powers of this world, and ultimately gather them all under his universal sway, – a train of events so peculiar and extraordinary as this, and so entirely corresponding with the future issues of Providence, could only have been tracked out beforehand by him who sees the things that are not as though they were. But still, let us keep all in its proper place. This wonderful anticipation of the future regarding the house of David was not intended merely, nor even primarily, as a proof of Divine foresight to the Church and the world, but rather as a grand demonstration, reaching from the past into the future, of the righteous principles of God's administration. It was to embody and exhibit these principles in connection with the highest power and authority in the realm, that God originally chose out of Israel a royal house, to which he delegated, in a measure, his own rightful supremacy. But the seed of royalty forgot the nature of their calling, and abused, to purposes of selfishness and corruption, the honor they had received from above. And as, in the case of the people at large, their falling away from the righteous purposes, for which especially they were planted in the land of Canaan, carried along with it the forfeiture of all their blessings, so in the house of David, their inveterate attachment to sinful and worldly aims must of necessity involve the extinction of all its rank and consideration among men. It must go down, engulphed in that worldly element to which it had so fondly and perversely wedded itself; and there must it lie, till, through the special interposition of Heaven, it should again revive in One, in whom the spiritual should so clearly bear the ascendancy over the earthly – One who should make himself so peculiarly known as loving righteousness and hating iniquity, that none could fail to regard him as of one mind, in this respect, with God, and God himself should forever anoint him with the oil of gladness above his fellows. We must ever keep this in view, as the main key to the mystery of God's work, the fundamental and all-pervading element of those wonderful and otherwise unaccountable evolutions in providence, which prophets were so early instructed to disclose to the people. And let it never be forgotten, that precisely as men enter into God's mind, and embrace the righteous principles on which the government of his kingdom is conducted, are they prepared either to fulfil the part assigned them as members of the kingdom, or to enjoy the benefits which it provides for those who are destined to inherit it! For, as it is in righteousness the King of Zion is to reign and prosper, it can only be in proportion as we are embued with his spirit of righteousness that we are fitted for taking part with him in what concerns the affairs of his kingdom, and for rising to a proper inheritance in his blessings.

CHAPTER XX.

A DISPLAY OF THE PEOPLE'S LONG-CONTINUED SINFULNESS AND THE LORD'S LONG-SUFFERING MERCY AND GOODNESS.

A new series of prophecies begins here, and stretches to the close of the twenty-third chapter. It commences with a definite period of time, marked as the seventh year, fifth month, and tenth day of the month (nearly a year later than the last previous date given), and took its rise in a specific occasion. The entire series is of a peculiarly dark, objurgatory, and threatening character, interspersed with only some occasional gleams of light and distant prospects of a still coming good. No substantial amendment had been produced by the earlier communications of the prophet, and the contemporary efforts of other servants of God. Hence the guilt having become so much greater, and the time drawn nearer for the execution of judgment, the burden which the prophet had to deliver was but the more fearfully charged with intimations of brooding woe.

The occasion of this series of discourses was furnished by certain of the elders of Israel coming to inquire of the Lord at the mouth of the prophet. What might be the precise object of their inquiry is kept in the background, as it was also on a former occasion (chap. 14). There can be little doubt, however, that it had respect in some shape to the then depressed and suffering condition of the covenant-people, and implied, at least, if it did not openly express, a desire to ascertain something more definite about God's purposes respecting them. But here, again, a preliminary objection arose from the moral state of the persons inquiring, which was such as precluded them from any right to expect a friendly response from God to their desire for further information. Regarding, as they did, iniquity in their heart, the Lord could not hear them. He therefore, at the outset, denounced the presumption of such persons in coming to inquire at his servant, and called upon the prophet to do toward them the part of a judge, by charging upon them the rebellious spirit of their fathers, and showing how little either they or their fathers had received in chastisement from God compared with what they had deserved.

[1] And in the seventh year, in the fifth *month* the tenth of the month, some of the elders of Israel came to ask of the LORD and sat before me.

[2] Then the word of the LORD came to me, saying,

[3] Son of man, speak to the elders of Israel and say to them, Thus says the Lord GOD: Have you come to ask of Me? *As* I live, says the Lord GOD, I will not be inquired of by you.

[4] Will you judge them, son of man, will you judge? Cause them to know the idolatries of their fathers.

[5] And say to them, Thus says the Lord GOD: In the day that I chose Israel and lifted up my hand to the seed of the house of Jacob, and made Myself known to them in the land of Egypt; when I lifted up My hand to them, saying, I am the LORD your God;

[6] in the day I lifted up My hand to them, to bring them out from the land of Egypt into a land that I had searched out for them, flowing with milk and honey, which is the glory of all lands,

[7] then I said to them, *Let* each man throw away the idols of his eyes and do not defile

yourselves with the idols of Egypt. I am the LORD your God.

8 But they rebelled against Me and would not listen to Me. They did not each one throw away the idols of their eyes, nor did they forsake the idols of Egypt. Then I said, I will pour out My fury against them to fulfill My anger against them in the middle of the land of Egypt.

9 But I worked for My name's sake, that it should not be polluted before the heathen among whom they were, in whose sight I made Myself known to them in bringing them out of the land of Egypt.

10 Therefore I caused them to go out of the land of Egypt and brought them into the wilderness.

11 And I gave them My statutes and showed them My judgments, which if a man do, he shall even live in them.

12 And also I gave them My sabbaths to be a sign between Me and them, that they might know that I am the LORD who sets them apart.

13 But the house of Israel rebelled against Me in the wilderness; they did not walk in My statutes and they despised My judgments – which if a man do, he shall even live in them. And they greatly polluted My sabbaths. Then I said, I will pour out My fury on them in the wilderness to destroy them.

14 But I worked for My name's sake, so that it should not be polluted before the heathen in whose sight I brought them out.

15 Yet also I lifted up My hand to them in the wilderness, that I would not bring them into the land which I had given *them,* flowing with milk and honey, which is the glory of all lands;

16 because they despised My judgments and walked not in My sabbaths, for their heart went after their idols.

17 Nevertheless My eye spared them from destroying them; I did not make an end of them in the wilderness.

18 But I said to their children in the wilderness, Do not walk in the statutes of your fathers, observe not their judgments, do not defile yourselves with their idols.

19 I am the LORD your God. Walk in My statutes and keep My judgments, and do them,

20 and keep My sabbaths holy; and they shall be a sign between Me and you, that you may know that I am the LORD your God.

21 But the children rebelled against Me. They did not walk in My statutes, nor kept My judgments, to do them – which, *if* a man do, he shall even live in them. Then I said I would pour out My fury on them, to fulfill My anger against them in the wilderness.

22 But I withdrew My hand and worked for My name's sake, that it should not be defiled in the sight of the heathen in whose sight I brought them out.

23 I also lifted up My hand to them in the wilderness, that I would scatter them among the heathen and scatter them through the countries,

24 because they had not done My judgments, but had despised My sabbaths and had defiled My sabbaths, and their eyes were after their father's idols.

25 Therefore I gave them also laws *that were* not good, and judgments by which they should not live.

26 And I defiled them in their own gifts, in that they caused all that open the womb to pass through *the fire*[3] that I might make them a waste, to the end that they might know that I am the LORD.

27 Therefore, son of man, speak to the house of Israel and say to them, Thus says the Lord GOD: Yet in this your fathers have blasphemed Me, in that they have committed a sin against Me.

28 When I had brought them into the land *for* which I lifted up My hand to give it to them, then they saw every high hill, and all the thick trees, and they offered their sacrifices there. And there they offered their provoking gifts. There also they made their sweet perfume and poured out their drink offerings there.

29 Then I said to them, What is the high place to which you go? And the name of it is called Ba-mah to this day.[4]

30 Therefore say to the house of Israel, Thus says the Lord GOD: Are you defiled in the same way as your fathers? And do you commit fornication after their idols?

31 For when you offer your gifts, when you make your sons to pass through the fire, you defile yourselves with all your idols, even to this day. And shall I be inquired of by you, O house of Israel? *As* I live, says the Lord GOD, I will not be inquired of by you.

32 And that which comes into your mind shall not happen at all, that you say, We will be like the nations, like the families of the countries, to serve wood and stone.

33 As I live, says the Lord GOD, surely with a mighty hand and with a stretched out arm, and with fury poured out, I will reign over you.

34 And I will bring you out from the people, and I will gather you out of the countries in which you are scattered, with a mighty hand and with a stretched out arm and with fury poured out.

[35]And I will bring you into the wilderness of the people, and there I will enter into judgment with you face to face.
[36]Just as I entered into judgment with your fathers in the wilderness of the land of Egypt, so I will enter into judgment with you, says the Lord GOD.
[37]And I will cause you to pass under the rod, and I will bring you into the bond of the covenant.
[38]And I will purge out from among you the rebels and those who sin against Me. I will bring them forth out of the country where they live. And they shall not enter into the land of Israel. And you shall know that I am the LORD.
[39]As for you, O house of Israel, thus says the Lord GOD: Everyone go and serve his idols, and *do so* from now on if you will not listen to Me. But never again defile My holy name with your gifts and with your idols.
[40]For in My holy mountain, in the mountain height of Israel, says the Lord GOD, there all the house of Israel, all of those in the land, shall serve Me. There I will receive them, and there I will ask for your offerings and the first fruits of your oblations, with all your holy things.
[41]I will receive you with your sweet perfume when I bring you out from the people and gather you out of the countries into which you have been scattered. And I will be sanctified in you in the eyes of the nations.
[42]And you shall know that I am the LORD, when I shall bring you into the land of Israel, into the country *for* which I lifted up My hand, to give it to your fathers.
[43]And there you shall remember your ways and all your doings in which you have been defiled. And you shall despise yourselves in your own sight for all your evils which you have committed.
[44]And you shall know that I am the LORD when I have worked with you for My name's sake, not according to your wicked ways nor according to your corrupt doings, O house of Israel, says the Lord GOD.

I. The chapter naturally falls into two great portions, the first of which consists of what fell from the prophet in the execution of his office of judgment. It extends to the close of ver. 32, and proceeds historically, dividing the entire course of Israel into so many sections, in each of which substantially the same spirit of rebelliousness is charged upon the people, and the same purpose of severity is ascribed to God, but constantly tempered and restrained by manifestations of mercy. Five distinct periods are thus rehearsed in order, – the first, when the Lord came to visit the children of Israel in Egypt; the second, when they were brought into the wilderness; the third, when, near the close of their sojourn there, a new generation had come into being; a fourth, when they were settled in the land of Canaan; and the last, the period comprehending the generation now addressed by the prophet. There is no difficulty in discovering the import of what is said, either with respect to the people's behavior during those successive periods, or to the manifestations of God's mind and will concerning them. The language throughout is remarkably plain, and free from ambiguity or darkness of any sort, so that verbal criticism has here scarcely any occasion for its exercise. But, on the other hand, there is not a little that calls for explanation or remark in the things that are affirmed both respecting the people's sinfulness and the manner in which this was dealt with on the part of God. We must therefore look at what is written of each period in succession.

1. In regard to the earliest period named, we find a very specific charge not only of idolatry, but even of obstinate and perverse attachment to the corruptions of idolatry, brought against the Israelites as a people. In that mere infancy of their national existence, *"the day,"* **as it is called,** *"when God chose Israel, and lifted up his hand (or swore) unto the seed of Jacob, and made himself known unto them in the land of Egypt, to bring them forth out of the land of Egypt into a land that he had espied for them,"* **then he said to them,** *"Cast ye every man away the pollutions of his eyes, and defile not yourselves with the idols of Egypt: I am Jehovah, your God. But,"* **it is added,** *"they rebelled against me, and were not willing to hearken to me; they did not every man cast away the pollutions of their eyes, neither did they forsake the idols of Egypt. And I said that I would pour out my wrath upon them, that I would accomplish my anger in them within the land of Egypt"* **(vers. 5-8).**

There is nothing in the history of the period referred to, to countenance the idea that the words here attributed to the Lord were actually spoken to the Israelites in Egypt, or that the injunctions upon the one side and the disobedience on the other took the formal and definite shape here given to them. The description is according to the prophet's usual manner, whose vivid imagination, when transporting him either into the past or the future, constantly seeks to give a living and embodied form to the truths exhibited to his view. Moses has not even left any direct notice of the people's addictedness to idolatry in Egypt, nor has he spoken of any resistance made by them to the Divine injunctions issued regarding it. The only kind of resistance to the word of God, which he expressly mentions, is that which arose out of the cruel treatment practised upon them. *"They hearkened not unto Moses for anguish of spirit and for cruel bondage"* (Ex. 6:9). In more than one passage, however, he has given no doubtful indication of the real state of matters in this respect; as when in Ex. 32 he represents the whole people as so speedily lapsing again into the practice of Egyptian idolatry; or when, in Lev. 17:7, contrasting what should now be done with what had previously existed, he says, *"And they shall no more offer their sacrifices unto devils (literally, Seirim, he-goats), after whom they have gone a lusting."*[5] Indeed the very form given to the commission of Moses, to go and vindicate the children of Israel for God that they might come forth and serve him, was itself a proof how much the worship of Jehovah had fallen into abeyance, and how generally the people had allowed themselves to sink into the prevailing idolatries. They must go out of the polluted region, where other lords, spiritual as well as temporal, have had dominion over them, that they may stand free to worship and serve Jehovah. And so the whole design and purport of the commission of Moses might be regarded as a protest against their connection with the abominations of Egypt, and a call, not only to Pharaoh to let the people go, but also to the people themselves to come out and be separate, as a seed whom the Lord had chosen.

Now that they did not properly respond to this call of God – that, oppressed and afflicted as they were, they would rather have remained where they were than gone forth to join themselves to the pure worship and service of Jehovah – is but too manifest from the subsequent history. They were not themselves, indeed, at the time fully aware of the contrariety that existed in their heart and ways to what was to be required of them in the Lord's service; for as yet their views were very crude and imperfect. But the Lord knew well how matters actually stood, and could easily descry, through the apathy, the impatience, and partial opposition that discovered themselves in their behavior, the signs of a deep-rooted opposition to his righteous and just demands. Nor can we doubt, especially from what afterwards occurred, that the thing most grievous to the eye of Jehovah during the whole of that dreadful conflict which was maintained with the powers of evil in Egypt, was the debased and corrupt state of those in whose behalf it was more immediately maintained – the comparatively slight difference, in a spiritual respect, that existed between them and the people of Egypt. They evinced no intelligent or hearty sympathy with the high ends and purposes for which such a conflict was waged; so that if the Lord had acted toward them according to the strict requirements of justice, he would even have poured out his anger upon them. And nothing but a regard to his own name, – that he might appear true to the promises he had made to the seed of Israel, and that the heathen themselves might see what a glorious thing it was to have an interest in his covenant-love and faithfulness, – nothing but this could have moved God in such circumstances to work so marvellously for the deliverance of his people from the house of bondage. Such is the testimony of the prophet regarding the first period brought under consideration.

2. The next period embraces the first part of the sojourn in the wilderness. When conducted thither, the Lord gave them, it is testified, *"his statutes, and showed them his judgments, which if a man do, he shall live in them."* There is nothing properly new or peculiar in this part of the statement, though it has not unfrequently been perverted to a wrong purpose. The same thing substantially had been said by Moses, when in respect to

the laws and ordinances, which through his ministration had been imposed on Israel, he declared he had set before the people life and death, – life if they loved the Lord, and walked in his ways, and kept his commandments and statutes and judgments, but if otherwise, death (Deut. 30:16). But neither Moses nor Ezekiel, it is obvious, meant that the life spoken of, which comprehends whatever is really excellent and good, was to be acquired by means of such conformity to the enactments of Heaven; for life in that sense was already theirs, freely given and secured by the goodness of God in the covenant of promise. What they meant was, that only thus could the children of Israel retain possession of what was given, or attain to the secure and continued enjoyment of it. For as the statutes and ordinances, which God enjoined them to keep, were to constitute the outward form and expression of their spiritual being, so by the measure of their conformity to these must necessarily be determined what should belong to them, either of the goodness or of the blessedness of life. If life existed at all, this was the channel through which it was to flow, these were the signs and exhibitions which it was to give of itself. And just as in the natural sphere the exercise and discharge of all the appropriate functions is the way to sustain and invigorate, as well as to exhibit, the principle of life; so it might be said of Israel in respect to their covenant life, that by following the appointed channel of God's institutions, it was to preserve itself in healthfulness and vigor. Doing those things, they lived in them; because life thus had its due exercise and nourishment, and was in a condition to enjoy the manifold privileges and blessings secured in the covenant. And the very same may be said of the precepts and ordinances of the gospel: a man lives after the higher life of faith, only in so far as he walks in conformity with these; for though he gets life by a simple act of faith in Christ, he cannot exercise, maintain, and enjoy it but in connection with the institutions and requirements of the gospel.

It was manifestly the design of Ezekiel here, as also of Moses in the passage referred to in Deuteronomy, in coupling life so expressly with the observance of the laws and ordinances of the old covenant, to show the necessary connection between what was required of God and what was to be enjoyed by the people. They were thus taught to regard it as an act of kindness that he should have set before them such laws and ordinances and could not fret and turn aside from them without wronging their own souls. But there is one ordinance in particular, of which special mention is made by the prophet, in connection with this period of Israel's history: *"And also my Sabbaths I gave them, to be a sign between me and them, that they might know that I am Jehovah who sanctifies them."* Along with Neh. 9:14, this passage is often appealed to as a proof of the later origin of the Sabbath, and its essentially Jewish character, as if from its being given to the Israelites, and made to stand as a sign between the Lord and them, it must then for the first time have come into existence. But one might as well affirm, that up till that period they were altogether without the statutes and judgments by which they could live; for these too are connected with the same period, and of necessity were also, to a certain extent, signs between God and Israel. The proper view rather is, that the Sabbatical institution was then brought more prominently out, and more formally enacted, than it had hitherto been; and that, from its very nature, as requiring for its proper observance the general ascendancy of religious principle, it was specially fitted to serve as a sign of the people's faithfulness to the covenant of God. If they kept the Sabbaths of the Lord, whether in their weekly recurrence, or as connected with the annual feasts, as he required them to be kept, it would be a living and palpable proof of their having entered into the spirit of the dispensation they were under, while their neglect and profanation of the Sabbath would equally serve as a proof of their unfaithfulness. Hence the observance of the Sabbath is here so expressly mentioned in connection with their sanctification: *"a sign between me and them, that they might know that I am Jehovha who sanctifies them."* It was, in truth, their sanctification, or their holiness in heart and conduct, which was the grand sign and evidence of Israel's being the chosen people of God. In so far as they complied with the exhortation, *"Be ye holy, for I am holy,"* they possessed the mark of his children. And the proper observance of the Sabbatical rest being so specially designated a sign in this respect, could only have arisen from its singular importance to the interests of religion and morality. These, it was virtually said, would thrive and flourish if the Sabbath was duly observed, but would languish and die if it fell into desuetude. And for this reason the prophet Isaiah, at the close of a long expostulation with the people regarding sin, presses the dutiful observance of the Sabbath, as sure to carry along with it the remedy of the evil: *"If thou turn away thy foot from the Sabbath, from doing thy pleasure on my holy day; and call the Sabbath a delight, the holy of the Lord, and honorable; and shalt honor him, not doing thine own ways, nor finding thine own pleasure, nor speaking thine own words: then shalt thou delight thyself in the Lord; and I will cause thee to ride upon the high places of the earth, and feed thee with the heritage of Jacob thy father: for the mouth of the Lord hath spoken it"* (Isa. 58:13,14). This passage may justly be taken as an explanation of the sense in which the Lord meant the people to regard his Sabbaths as a sign between them and him. Such paramount importance could never have been attached by the prophet to this sacred institution, nor could it have been so peculiarly connected with the blessing of the covenant, if the mere outward rest had been all that the institution contemplated. This is what those who hold mistaken views on this subject almost uniformly take for granted, as if the people should have been properly sanctified by simply resting every Sabbath from their usual labors. The command must have had a far deeper import, and required a great deal more at the hands of the people, in order to prove an adequate sign between them and God. It must have been, and it was, intended not only to separate them from their worldly employments, but also to call out their hearts in suitable exercises of faith and love to God, and in brotherly acts of kindness and good-will toward those around them. On no other account could its faithful observance be represented as indicative of a sound and healthful state of religion generally. And we might ask, without the least fear of contradiction, if the same practical value is not attached to the careful observance of the Lord's day now by those who have an enlightened regard to the interests of religion? When this day ceases to be devoutly observed, all experience and observation testify that there never fails to ensue a corresponding decline in the life and actings of religion.[6]

But, to return to the subject more immediately before us, the prophet brings, in regard to these statutes and ordinances which the Lord imposed upon the Israelites, as soon as he had led them into the wilderness, substantially the same charge that had been already brought against them in regard to the period of their sojourn in Egypt. He declares that they showed the same spirit of rebellion as formerly, but in a more directly offensive manner, as there was now more of positive precept to transgress. They did not walk in his judgments, they despised his statutes, they polluted his Sabbaths, of which the historical records of the period contain but too ample evidence. These also relate how, as is testified here, the Lord once and again threatened to pour out his fury upon them, and consume them, but was again restrained by a regard to his own glory, that his name might not be polluted among the heathen, especially those of them in whose sight he had brought out Israel, and set them in a state of freedom (Ex. 32:10,11; Num. 14:11, etc.). So far he did allow his righteous displeasure to proceed, that he would not permit the generation that came out of Egypt to enter the land of Canaan, but caused them to sojourn and die in the wilderness, though he did not there make an end of the people themselves. There was a visitation of judgment, but one so light when compared with the sins which provoked it, that it might rather be characterised as the triumph of mercy over judgment!

3. The next period of special dealing mentioned by the prophet is that which comprises the latter part of the sojourn in the wilderness, and has respect to the younger generation, the children of those who had come out of Egypt as full-grown men. To them, it is said, the Lord repeated the charge he had given to their fathers respecting his statutes and judgments and Sabbaths, and had also distinctly warned them not to follow the ways, nor defile themselves with the idols, of their fathers. But neither did this new generation keep

the charge of the Lord; they rebelled against him, by setting at nought his commandments and ordinances, so that the Lord again said he would pour out his fury upon them, to accomplish his anger against them in the wilderness. There is apparent contrariety in what is thus said of the generation that grew up in the wilderness, to the testimony borne partly respecting them, and partly respecting the former generation, by Jeremiah, at the beginning of the second chapter of his writings: *"I remember thee, the kindness of thy youth, the love of thine espousals, when thou wentest after me in the wilderness, in a land that was not sown. Israel was holiness to the Lord, the first-fruits of his increase; all that devour him shall offend; evil shall come upon them, saith the Lord."* But this testimony is not to be understood of the actual condition of Israel; it rather indicates what they were in appearance, what, in the freshness and ardour of their youthful zeal, they professed and seemed to be, than what they really were. At the very most, it cannot be regarded as more than a comparative statement; for the prophet himself, immediately afterwards, represents them as beginning to defile the land, as soon as they entered it; and the historical records also of the period too clearly show, that the congregation as a whole were far from being what they should have been. It was near the close of the sojourn in the wilderness that the rebellion of Korah and his company appears to have taken place; as also the murmuring for water in Kadesh, which proved the occasion to Moses and Aaron of their losing the prospect of entering Canaan. And worse than all, the fearful apostasy on the plains of Moab belongs to this period, and did not occur till after the congregation had finally left the wilderness. Such facts decisively show, that however this new generation excelled the one that had come out of Egypt, elements of corruption were still plentifully at work in it; and it was not without ample reason that Moses spoke of them as, notwithstanding the many signs and wonders they had witnessed, not having got a heart to perceive, or eyes to see, or ears to hear, unto this day (Deut. 29:4). It was also to that generation peculiarly, and no doubt because they needed the warning, that the threatening was proclaimed of a future dispersion among the heathen, as recorded in Deut. 28, and referred to here by Ezekiel in ver. 23.

Our prophet, however, not only represents God as lifting up his hand, threatening a dispersion to them on account of sin, but adds further: *"Wherefore I gave them also statutes that were not good, and judgments whereby they should not live,"* – words which from the earliest times have been variously misunderstood. Among the Fathers, the opinion was so common as to be almost universal (Jerome alone tries to qualify it), that the law in general, and in particular its sacrificial rites, must be understood by those statutes not good, and judgments in which men could not live – although the prophet expressly opposes them to those which God had given in the wilderness, and which must have comprehended all the sacrificial institutions. Others, again, have sought to distinguish between one part of the new law and another, giving to the decalogue especially the honor of being accounted good and life-sustaining; while the other and more burdensome parts of the ritual are assigned to the class of not good, and tending to death (so Spencer, Warburton, etc.). As if only the decalogue had been given to the generation that had come out of Egypt, and at the commencement of the wilderness sojourn, while all the rest had been reserved to the close, and made known to the generation that succeeded! On the contrary, all the distinctive laws and ordinances of the old covenant were imposed during the first and second year after the deliverance from Egypt; and consequently were given, not principally to the generation here spoken of by the prophet, but to their fathers, who had been brought out of Egypt. It was also of these laws and ordinances, of the whole legislation of God by Moses, that Moses himself spake when he told the people that they had therein the way of life set before them.

It must therefore be something quite diverse and opposite; it can only, indeed, be the polluted customs and observances of heathenism that the prophet here characterizes as statutes not good, and judgments in which life was not to be found. By a strong expression (and yet not so strong as that in Isa. 63:17: *"O Lord, why hast thou made us to err from thy ways and hardened our heart from thy fear?"*), God is said to have given death-bringing ordinances to the Israelites, when he saw their wayward and perverse behavior in regard to the commandments and duties of his service; since, to punish their unfaithfulness, he subjected them to influences which carried them still farther astray, and brought on, first spiritual, then also, in due time, outward desolation and ruin. We have precisely the same process described, and in still stronger language, in 2 Thess. 2, where, of those who *"received not the love of the truth,"* it is said, *"And for this cause God shall send them strong delusion, that they should believe a lie, and that they might be damned,"* – first, the corrupting influences that bring spiritual blighting and disaster let loose upon them, and then, when these have wrought their full effect, the doom executed upon them of final perdition. Such entirely was the case with the Israelites, who were led into the land of Canaan. And as a proof of what might be expected there – a solemn pre-intimation and warning of the future – the troubles were allowed to befall them, which took place on the plains of Moab, in the matter of Baal-peor. It was in chastisement for existing unfaithfulness to God's covenant that the votaries of Baal were permitted on that occasion to ply them with solicitations to apostasy, as is but too clearly evinced by the melancholy success which attended the experiment; a widespread degeneracy alone could have accounted for this. The very direction of events, therefore, so as to expose them to this unhappy temptation, was itself an act of judgment, and a judgment exactly of the kind now under consideration; it surrendered the people to influences which were sure, as matters then stood, to entangle them in the abominations of heathenism, as these, again, were sure to bring down upon them the stroke of Divine retribution. The first step in the Divine procedure was necessary to render manifest the corruption they were secretly harboring in their bosom; and the second, to drive it out by the rod of chastisement. Would that succeeding generations had sufficiently considered the solemn lesson! How many renewals of the same severe and wholesome discipline might have been spared them! But to their own shame and confusion, they constantly forgot the works of the Lord, and remembered not his judgments.

That the view now given of ver. 25 is the correct one, becomes still more evident when we look at the next verse, which ought to be regarded as explanatory of the other: *"And I polluted them in their gifts* (viz. as the results of the bad statutes and judgments now brought in upon them); *in the presentation of all their firstborn, that I might make them desolate, that they might know that I am the Lord."* When the Lord speaks of polluting them in their gifts, something more is to be understood than Havernick's, "I declared them to be impure, I treated them as such." They really were impure, and God had, in righteous judgment, ordered his providence so as to render this impurity palpable. He speaks, therefore, as if he himself had polluted them, that he might lead the people to regard the blindness and infatuation of mind, which disposed them to submit to heathenish influences, as the result of his just displeasure. Whence also it further came to pass that the Lord's face was turned away from them – that even when they brought their gifts according to the law, in particular when they presented their firstborn, by which each succeeding generation should have been consecrated to the Lord, all was regarded by him as defiled through the heathenish admixture, nor would he even own it as properly done to himself. But in proportion as such feelings were entertained by God, he must make it manifest by the outward executions of judgment; he must render their condition desolate, that, thus chastened and humbled, they might come to know the Lord, and return to him in truth.

4. The next period in this religious history is the somewhat indefinite one that followed the settlement in the land of Canaan; it comprehends generally the procedure of the fathers of the generation who lived in the prophet's time, from the era of their settlement in Canaan downwards. It is characterized as substantially of the same nature with those which had preceded it; their fathers still went on, it is stated by the prophet, trespassing against God, and blaspheming his name: *"For when I had brought them into the land, which I lifted up my hand to give to them, then they saw every high hill, and every thick tree, and they offered their sacrifices, and there they presented the provocation of their*

offering, and there they set forth their sweet savours, and there they poured out their drink-offerings. And I said to them, What is the high place to which ye come? And its name was called Bamah (high-place) unto this day." That is, their worship (viewed generally) has been still a mere high-place celebration, a mongrel combination of the false and the true; and that wherever performed, whether on Mount Zion or on the other places chosen for the purpose throughout the land, the scene of their devotions has ever been, in my sight, but a high-place – its name is Bamah – it has no proper sacredness about it, nor have the services presented come with acceptance before me.

5. Nothing more is said of the fathers who had hitherto been occupying the land of Canaan. The prophet is impatient to get at the children, – the generation who then lived, and with whom he had more immediately to do. He is anxious to bring home to them the charge of being of the same spirit with their fathers, and therefore having no right to expect that the Lord would deal with them on friendly terms, and return a peaceful answer to their iniquities. *"Therefore say unto the house of Israel, Thus saith the Lord Jehovah, In the way of your fathers ye have polluted yourselves; and after their abominations have ye wantonly gone. And in the offering of your gifts, in the making pass (or presentation) of your children through the fire, are ye defiled with all your idols to this day. And shall I be inquired of by you, O house of Israel? As I live, saith the Lord Jehovah, I shall not be inquired of by you. And that which comes up into your mind shall not be at all, in that ye say, We shall be like the heathen, like the families of the nations, to serve wood and stone"* (vers. 30-32).

Thus he describes the spirit of apostasy as reaching its climax in the existing generation. They were not satisfied with treading generally in the footsteps of their fathers, but they must even aspire to a perfect conformity to heathen customs, as if it was a privilege they were ambitious to reach, or a consummation they desired. And so the dedication of the children, which of old had been done with so much of foreign admixture that the Lord could not own it as done to him, now takes the hideous form of a committing of them to the flames in honor of their false deities; and instead of simply mingling up Jehovah and Baal together, as their fathers had done, they must now be altogether on a footing with the wretched idolaters, who bowed down to wood and stone.

II. Now, having thus fulfilled the office of judgment, and disclosed with all plainness the estimation in which the Lord held the people of Israel, represented by the inquiring elders before him, the prophet thenceforth proceeds to the second great division of his message. It stretches from vers. 33 to 44, where, in the Hebrew Bible, the chapter terminates, as it manifestly should have done also in the English Bible. And the leading purport of what is said is to make known the mingled goodness and severity with which the Lord was now going to deal with them, to the end that he might thoroughly wean them from their abominations, and bring them into a state in which he could return to bless them and do them good.

The chief peculiarity in the representation consists in the historical form into which it is thrown; what was to be is exhibited as a doing over again of what had already been done in the earlier periods of their history. A striking example of this species of representation has previously come under our notice, when at chap. 4 we found the prophet disclosing the awful period of iniquity-bearing, or chastisement for sins, that was ready to befall them, under the double form of a return of Egyptian bondage and oppression, and of the sojourn in the wilderness. Here, again, it is precisely the same periods that are represented as returning, but under a somewhat different aspect – not so much as ages of gloom and desolation rolling over them, as rather successive stages of providential dealing, of the same nature, but more perfect in their kind than those formerly experienced. In the carnal and idolatrous state into which they had sunk, they were beginning to think of abandoning all their distinctive privileges and hopes, as the chosen people of God, and amalgamating themselves with the heathen nations around them. This was what formerly had, to a large extent, been done in the land of Egypt, where, as we had occasion already to notice, the distinction in a spiritual respect between Israel and their oppressors became in process of time all but obliterated. The Lord declares, however, he will not suffer this contemplated amalgamation to take place – he will no more do so now than he did formerly; and to prevent it, he will resort to the same kind of stern and wholesome discipline. *"As I live, saith the Lord Jehovah, surely with a strong hand, and with a stretched out arm, and with fury poured out, will I rule over you."* And being thus held under the grasp of Almightiness, and made to feel in their peeled and scattered condition how powerful a Sovereign ruled over them, and was reckoning with them for their iniquities, they were also to know for what holy and beneficent ends he held them bound by this special lordship. *"And I will bring you out from among the peoples* (it is pre-supposed that they had been dispersed among these), *and will gather you out of the countries wherein ye are scattered, with a strong hand, and with a stretched out arm, and with fury poured out. And I will bring you into the wilderness of the peoples, and there will I contend with you face to face. Likeas I contended with your fathers in the wilderness of the land of Egypt, so will I contend with you, saith the Lord Jehovah. And I will cause you to pass under the rod* (the shepherd rod or staff of the Lord), *and I will bring you into the bond* (or discipline) *of the covenant, And I will purge out from among you the rebels, and them that transgress against me. And I will bring them forth out of the country where they sojourn, and they shall not enter into the land of Israel; and ye shall know that I am Jehovah"* (vers. 34-38).

Here the state of dispersion and exile, which was soon to be consummated, and which was of necessity a state of subjection and trouble, corresponds to the period of affliction in Egypt; on which account also the region of exile is in the last verse called *"the country of their sojourn,"* the very common designation of Egypt in the Pentateuch (Ex. 12:40; Lev. 19:33,34; Deut. 26:5; Ps. 105:23, etc).[7] And between the calling out of the people from this Egyptian-like condition, between the termination of their sojourn in the enemies' land and their entrance into their own land, lies now, just as of old, a temporary abode in the wilderness, where the Lord enters into very close and special dealing with them, refines them as in the fire, purges out from among them the rebels, who, though delivered from the land of exile, are not suffered to come into the land of blessing, and so prepares the people for fulfilling aright their covenant obligations. Now, what precisely is to be understood by this wilderness? The prophet expressly distinguishes it from the *"wilderness of the land of Egypt,"* in which of old the people had been thus dealt with by God; so that we are not to think of an actual return to the desert that lay between Egypt and Canaan. He further calls it *"the wilderness of the peoples,"* or nations, which many, and still some of the latest interpreters (most recently, Hitzig), understand of the desert that lies between Babylon and Judea, on account of its being frequented by wandering tribes; – as if the wilderness on the other side, between Judea and Egypt, were not equally and even more frequented by such! The correct view is given by Hengstenberg in his Christology, on Hos. 2:16, where God's future dealings with his people are presented under the very same image of a re-enacting of the scenes of the wilderness: "I will bring you into the wilderness of the nations, stands in direct reference to, I will bring you out from the nations. Hence it appears that the peoples to whom the Israelites were brought could be no other than those out of the midst of whom they were to be led forth. In the earlier leading of the Israelites, the two spiritual conditions also outwardly existed; the first belonged to Egypt, the second to the desert. But it is not to be so in the above-predicted repetition of this leading. At the commencement of the second condition, the Israelites are only spiritually led forth out of the midst of the people, among whom outwardly they still remain. The desert is in the second Egypt itself. The residence in the desert repeated only as to its essential, not its accidental outward form. Hence we acquire the important result, that the leading of God predicted here is not limited to one place." So far from that, it was to be looked for on as extensive a scale as the dispersion itself; this was to bring them into the wilderness of the nations, and while they were there – no matter whether locally in Babylon or in Egypt, on the banks of the

Chebar, or in the cities of Greece or Rome – the Lord was to meet with them for the purpose of judgment, separation, and cleansing.

But such being the case – the wilderness in this new aspect of Jehovah's dealings being, as to its outward position, identified with the new Egypt out of which they were to be delivered – it would evidently be to put an entirely false construction upon such a prediction to surround it on every side with local and definite landmarks, as if all now must have the same outward and ostensible realization as of old. The prophet has guarded against this error by throwing the wilderness and Egypt, as it were, together; so that it would be impossible to mark precisely where the one ended and the other began. And as thus a certain degree of indefiniteness was made to inhere in the prediction in one respect, the same might also to some extent be looked for in others; the more especially as we see indications of it at the very outset. According to the representation of the prophet, the new Egypt-state of bondage and affliction is the exile into other countries; and yet how plainly did such a state begin before the exile was actually consummated! It did not take place all at once, as the descent of old into Egypt, but by many successive strokes and fresh removals. Even before some of the later deportations, the remnant that still existed in the land of Canaan, enfeebled and sore broken as it was, crippled in its resources, and overridden by the might of heathen powers, had become in a manner subject to the yoke of Egypt. And if, in point of fact, Egypt did thus begin in Canaan, and the wilderness was to begin while they still continued to reside in the countries of their dispersion, might not this wilderness-condition (i.e. the period of trial, discipline, and purification) be prolonged also beyond the outward sojourn in the nations, and extend into Canaan again? It is not precise boundaries the prophet seeks to determine, but rather successive spiritual conditions on the part of the people, and corresponding methods of dealing on the part of God. Hence, as Calvin justly remarks, they might even be in exile, though in the land of Judea itself; and in reality, God did come anew to plead with them after he had led them back thither from the Babylonish exile. The writings of the three last prophets, but especially those of Malachi, conclusively show, that as the Egypt-state began before they left Canaan, so the wilderness-state, to a large extent, continued even after the return. The separation between the precious and the vile was still far from being complete, and the bond of the covenant was never more than imperfectly entered into. Canaan could not, therefore, properly be to them what it is described in the word of promise; for in spirit they had not properly emerged from the wilderness, and God could not be present with the full bestowal of his gifts and blessings. Nay, as if scarcely anything in these respects had yet been done, Malachi, after severe but comparatively ineffectual reproofs against the prevailing evils, hands over the returned remnant of the children of the covenant generally to the searching ministry of the Baptist, and the personal dealings of the Lord himself, who were still to find them as in the wilderness, and were to effect, in another manner than hitherto, the still needed separation between sin and holiness among the people.

But Ezekiel, in the passage before us, does not go into detail. He merely sketches the general outline. The children of Israel, he virtually says, by reason of their sinful craving after heathenish pollutions, must have the old things in their history revived again, only with such variations in outward form as the altered circumstances of time might require. They are already sinking anew into the bondage and affliction of Egypt, out of which they shall in process of time be brought, that they may be sifted and purged and prepared for the heritage of Jacob by earnest pleadings and sharp discipline, such as belonged of old to the period of Israel's sojourn in the wilderness. Then shall they reach the state of peace and rest which they desire, and then shall they be in a condition for attaining to the blessed end of their calling. Therefore, on the ground of this fixed determination of God, and in the prospect of this coming good, the prophet addresses himself to the present generation: "*As for you, O house of Israel, thus saith the Lord God, Go ye, serve ye every one his idols* (do so, if you have a mind; I am prepared to expect no better from you); *but afterwards, surely ye will hearken unto me, and ye will not pollute my holy name with your gifts and your idols. For* (this is the reason why they should not do so – the Lord will accomplish his gracious purpose) *in my holy mountain, in the mountain of the height of Israel* (high, because holy, spiritually, not outwardly pre-eminent; see chap. 17:23), *there shall all the house of Israel, all of them in the land, serve me: there will I accept them, and there will I require your offerings, and the first-fruits of your oblations, with all your holy things,"* etc.(vers. 39-44.)

Thus the perfected condition to which matters were to be brought, takes also to the prophet's view the form of a revival of the old; – the regenerated people, the pure and acceptable worship, the glorious inheritance of blessing, presented themselves as the return, and more than the return, of the best in the past – it was to be the full realization of what should have been, yet never was more than in part. How far, however, similar qualifications to those connected with the other points in the prediction were to have place here, could only be determined by the event. But since such a compass was given in the earlier part to the wilderness, there can be no reason, from the nature of the prophecy, why a like enlargement might not also be given to the land, and mountain, and people of the latter part. By the new and better state of things introduced through the gospel, Mount Zion has risen to a nobler elevation that of old, and Canaan has burst its ancient bounds, and the elect people have spread themselves far and wide in the earth. Wherever there is a true believer in Christ, there also is a genuine member of the house of Israel, a pure worshipper coming to Mount Zion, a free-born citizen, who feeds on the heritage of Jacob his father; for they who are Christ's are Abraham's seed, and heirs according to the promise. But other and more fitting opportunities will occur for considering how far the promised good to Israel is to be understood as merging in the good of the Christian Church. See especially at chap. 34, and at the beginning of chap. 40, where the principles of interpretation applicable to such prophecies are more fully discussed.

CHAPTER XX. 45-49, XXI.

THE VISION OF THE LORD'S FIRE AND SWORD.

The five concluding verses in chap. 20, as already noticed, should evidently have been connected with chap. 21, and are justly regarded by interpreters as a kind of general introduction to what follows, or a brief delineation under one aspect of what is afterwards more fully and explicitly described under another. The leading import of the vision is plain enough; but it is written throughout in a style so singularly abrupt, and in some parts so utterly enigmatical, that it may certainly be considered, as a whole, one of the darkest portions of Ezekiel's writings. Even Horsley, who was not scrupulous in forcing a way where none naturally presented itself, has here simply left a record of his inability to proceed, in the brief note, ("The difficulties of this passage are to me insuperable.") For once, at least, his ready resort to a change in the text proved insufficient to bring the necessary relief. Various emendations of the text have been suggested by late authors; but these, being of an entirely arbitrary and conjectural character, are incapable of yielding satisfaction, and are seldom even deserving of notice. I cannot, certainly, pretend to say that I see my way through all the obscurities of the passage, as it stands, and shall not hesitate to state my doubts as to the real meaning, where I have failed to get them removed. But the portions of this kind are not, after all, very numerous, and will be found to interfere comparatively little with the general import of the prophet's communication.

For the greater facility and clearness of interpretation, we shall take the passage in successive portions.

[45]And the word of the LORD came to me, saying,

[46]Son of man, set your face toward the south and drop *your word* toward the south, and prophesy against the forest of the south field.

[47]And say to the forest of the south, Hear the word of the LORD. Thus says the Lord GOD: Behold, I will kindle a fire in you, and it shall burn up every green tree in you, and every dry tree. The flaming flame shall not be put out, and all faces from the south to the north shall be burned in it.

[48]And all flesh shall see that I the LORD have kindled it. It shall not be put out.

[49]Then I said, Ah, Lord GOD! They say of me, Does he not speak parables?

In this portion there is an obscurity, but it is an obscurity that arises simply from the want of precision in defining the exact sphere of the vision. That it indicates a severe and consuming judgment from the Lord upon some land and people, situated somewhere to the south of the prophet, admits of no doubt. For the substitution in one place of faces instead of trees, as the subjects of the burning, renders it manifest that the vision has respect to the inhabitants of a country. And when the conflagration is represented as falling upon every tree, the green as well as the dry, those that were apparently not fit as well as those that were fit fuel for the flame, this could only be meant to express the fearfully comprehensive character of the coming judgment, as not sparing even the better part, who might seem undeserving of such a visitation. It is in the same way, and with reference, doubtless, to this part of the vision, that our Lord, pointing from the troubles that were befalling himself, to those which were soon to befall the Jewish people, said, *"For if they do these things in a green tree, what shall be done in the dry?"* (Luke 23:31); if such things befall one who has done nothing to provoke them, what may be expected for those who are the fit objects of Heaven's vengeance? or, if the righteous suffer thus, what must be the measure of severity that is preparing to overtake the wicked? So that by the green trees can only be understood the more righteous, and by the dry trees the more wicked portions of the community; they were all alike to be involved in the coming desolation. But who precisely were the people thus to be visited, or by what kind of instrumentality the desolation was to be brought upon them, the vision so far is entirely silent; and it might truly be said in this respect, that the prophet was speaking in parables. He notices the complaint that was sometimes made respecting the parabolical character of his communications, as if on this occasion, at least, it might justly be complained of. And he presently obtains from the Lord what may be called a duplicate of the vision, only of such a kind as served to make perfectly intelligible both who the objects of the foreseen calamity were, and who also were to be the instruments of inflicting these upon them.

CHAP. XXI.

[1]And the word of the LORD came to me, saying,

[2]Son of man, set your face toward Jerusalem and drop *your word* toward the holy places, and prophesy against the land of Israel.

[3]And say to the land of Israel, Thus says the LORD: Behold, I am against you and will draw out My sword from its sheath and will cut off from you the righteous and the wicked.

[4]Since then I will cut off the righteous and the wicked from you, therefore My sword shall go out of its sheath against all flesh from the south to the north,

[5]so that all flesh may know that I the LORD have drawn out My sword from its sheath. It shall not return any more.

[6]Therefore sigh, son of man, with the breaking of *your* loins; and sigh with bitterness before their eyes.

[7]And when they say to you, Why do you sigh? You shall answer, Because of the news. Because it is coming; and every heart shall melt, and all hands shall be feeble, and every spirit shall faint, and all knees shall be weak *as* water. Behold, it comes, and *it* shall be brought to pass, says the Lord GOD.

Here the darkness and ambiguity that hung over the earlier part of the vision, so far as the precise locality is concerned, is entirely removed. The region of judgment and desolation is now expressly determined to be the land of Israel, and more especially Jerusalem and its holy places. And if any doubt had remained as to the extent of meaning indicated in the former vision by the burning up of *"every green and every dry tree,"* the declaration that the sword to be presently drawn was to cut off both *"the righteous and the wicked,"* must have set it completely at rest. But the announcement that there was going to be such an indiscriminate and unsparing execution of judgment in Judea is startling, and presents an apparent contrariety to the command given in an earlier vision (chap. 9:4), to seal the foreheads of the righteous, as persons set apart and entrusted to the safe custody of God against the coming evil. It was, no doubt, the stumbling-block of this seeming contrariety which prompted the translator in the Septuagint to make a violent change in the text, so as to express the sense, *"I will destroy out of thee the lawless and unjust"* (ἐξολοθρεύσω ἐκ σοῦ ἄνομον καὶ ἄδικον). But it is only on a superficial consideration that the one passage will appear at all contradictory to the other. For here, as is manifest from the whole nature of the representation, it is the merely external aspect of the visitation which the prophet has in his eye. The sword of the Lord's judgment, he announced, was to pass throught the land, and accomplish such a sweeping overthrow, that all, without exception, would be made to suffer in the fearful catastrophe. This did not prevent, however, but that there might be, in the midst of the outward calamities which were thus to burst like a mighty tempest over the land, a vigilant oversight maintained, and special interpositions of Providence exercised, in behalf of the pious remnant who still continued faithful to the covenant of God. It was this distinguishing goodness to some, even amid the horrors of a general desolation, which, as we showed before, was the real object of that sealing of God's servants on the forehead in a former vision; while here, on the other hand, it is merely the general desolation itself which is contemplated by the prophet. And the very circumstance that he should now have looked so exclusively on the outward scene of carnage and distress, which he described in the approaching future, seemed to say that this was to be the grand feature of the time, and that the special interpositions which were to be put forth in behalf of the better portion would be so few that they scarcely required to be taken into account. It is obvious, too, that the description given even of the general desolation must be understood with some limitation. For, that the sword should literally be unsheathed against all flesh from north to south in the land, and should cut off or destroy all within its borders, whether righteous or wicked, would not only be at variance with the other prophecies of Ezekiel, but would even not consist with the sequel of this prediction itself, which, as we shall see, still speaks of a purpose of mercy in behalf of the covenant-people. But undoubtedly he wished to convey the impression of a very fearful and overwhelming destruction. The immediate prospect of this national disaster had called his mind back again from the bright vision of distant glory he had unfolded at the close of the preceding communication, and as seeing all now overshadowed with gloom, his soul was filled with the deepest trouble and anguish. Agitated and rent, as he thus was, with the most painful and violent emotions, he naturally proceeds to give utterance to his feelings in abrupt sentences and plaintive reiterations.

8 Again the word of the LORD came to me, saying,

9 Son of man, prophesy and say, Thus says the LORD. Say, A sword! A sword is sharpened and also polished!

10 It is sharpened to make a grievous slaughter; it is polished so that it may flash like lightning.[3] Should we then rejoice? It despises the rod of My son, along with every tree.[4]

11 And He has given it to be polished so that it may be handled. This sword is sharpened, and it is polished, to give it into the hand of the slayer.

12 Cry and howl, son of man. For it shall be on My people. It shall be on all the princes of Israel. Because of the sword,[5] terrors shall be on My people. Therefore strike on *your* thigh.

13 Because it is a trial, and what if *the sword* even despises the rod of power? It shall not be any more, says the Lord GOD.

14 Therefore, son of man, prophesy and strike *your* hands together. And let the sword be doubled the third time, the sword of the slain. It is the sword of the great men who are slain, which enters into their secret rooms.

15 I have set the point of the sword against all their gates, that *their* heart may faint and *their* ruins may be multiplied. Ah, *it* is ready to flash like the lightning; it is wrapped up for the slaughter.

16 Go one way or the other, either on the right hand or on the left, wherever your face is set.

17 I will also strike My hands together, and I will cause My fury to rest. I the LORD have spoken.

While these verses abound with critical difficulties, there is very little that calls for special remark in respect to the train of thought. The passage, as a whole, is descriptive of the fearful devastation that was to be made by the Lord's sword of vengeance, and of the painful and agitated feelings thence produced in the bosom of the prophet. The coming judgment is represented as a sweeping calamity taking the circuit of the whole land, and reaching even to the highest personages within it, its king and princes. And as if the desolation were already proceeding under the eye of the prophet, he is called upon to howl and strike his hands together – the natural indications of excessive and violent grief. But in this he acted only as the representative of God, and so Jehovah himself is spoken of as in like manner striking his hands together, on account of the mournful desolations that had taken place; while still there was no excess of evil, when viewed in respect to the occasion that called it forth, all was needed in order to make the Lord's fury, or his indignation on account of sin, to cease.

The prophet now proceeds to indicate more expressly the nature of the visitation which was to be employed as the Lord's sword of vengeance. And the connection in this respect, as well in regard to the subsequent as to the preceding context, is so justly stated by Havernick, that we shall here simply translate his words: "The question might now naturally arise, Whither shall the sword of Jehovah turn itself? Shall the punishment be altogether confined to the theocracy? Shall the enemies of this escape? An opportunity was thus furnished to the prophet for drawing a parallel between Judah and Ammon. This parallel exhibits the punishment in respect to its more internal and profound meaning, by discovering wherein these two nations resembled each other, and wherein they differed: Judah has, like Ammon, become an enemy of God, therefore the same judgment alights on both. Nay, the apostate covenant-people first fall under the stroke of the Divine sword. By God's command, Nebuchadnezzar, the instrument of Jehovah's anger, must first be sent against Jerusalem, and then against Ammon. Both fall through the hand of one slayer. A sword lights upon their head that had long been destined to this end by God. Again, both similarly despised the threatening judgment, held God's hand to be mere delusion and vanity (vers. 23 and 29); they show themselves after the same manner, sinners and daring rebels against God. Judah's sin is brought into remembrance even by the Chaldean monarch; for Ammon, the theocracy is an object only of scorn and emnity (vers. 23,28, and 30). So that in both alike the measure of iniquity is full: the end must come to them. But this very end is what also marks the great difference between the two. The theocracy is devoted to the sword, robbed of its splendor and its king; but still the old promises do not on that account perish. Through the awful process of deep humiliation and indescribable misery, Judah reaches the consummation of its height and glory. But the end of Ammon stands in sharp contrast to this; it perishes without hope; its end is an end of terrors, out of which no new state arises; it is devoted to the absolute destruction."

18 The word of the LORD came to me again, saying,

19 Also, son of man, choose yourself two ways that the sword of the king of Babylon may come. Both of them shall come out of one land. And choose a place, choose *it* at the head of the *highway* to the city.

20 Choose a way that the sword may enter into Rab-bah of the Am-mon-ites and into Judah, into fortified Jerusalem.

21 For the king of Babylon stood at the parting of the way, at the head of the two highways, to ask of images. He made arrows bright; he asked of images; he looked in the liver.

22 At his right hand was the divining for Jerusalem, to choose captains, to open the mouth in the slaughter, to lift up the voice with shouting, to choose *battering* rams against the gates, to cast a mound and to build a fort.

23 And it shall be to them as a false divining in their sight, to those who have sworn oaths. But he will call iniquity to memory, that they may be taken.

24 Therefore thus says the Lord GOD: Because you have made your iniquity to be remembered, in that your transgressions are discovered so that your sins are revealed in all your doings; because you have come to memory, you shall be taken with the hand.

25 And you, ungodly, wicked king of Israel, whose day has come when iniquity shall have an end,

26 Thus says the Lord GOD: Remove the diadem and take off the crown. This shall not be as it was. Lift up the low one and put down the high one.

27 I will overturn, overturn, overturn it! And this shall never again be until the coming of Him whose is the right. And I will give it *to Him.*

This remarkable passage, in its earlier part representing Nebuchadnezzar as hesitating whether he was to take the road that led to Rabbath or that to Jerusalem, and brought ultimately to decide upon the latter by the usual appliances of divination, contains as to its form a striking specimen of Ezekiel's manner. He does not simply announce the event that was to happen, as the prophets generally do, but gives it life and motion; exhibits the springs of action as actually at work before our eyes. It were entirely to mistake the character of the representation (however commonly it is done), to suppose that the scene here described, as it appeared to the illuminated sense of the prophet, was in real life to take place precisely after this form; not less than it would be to maintain that the two ways toward Jerusalem and Rabbath, with the directing sign at the point of divergence, must have been actually constructed by the prophet's hand. The whole is a delineation in a vision of what, as to the substance, was to happen in the regular course of things. All would occur precisely as if the lively scene here described were to pass into reality. Nebuchadnezzar would assuredly move toward the south with his hosts and implements of war, and, advancing under the auspices of his religion, would as assuredly direct his march, in the first instance, toward Jerusalem. What a sublime proof of the overruling providence and controlling agency of Jehovah! The mightiest monarch of the world, travelling at the head of almost unnumbered legions, and himself consciously owning no other direction than that furnished by the blind instruments of his own superstition, yet having his path marked out to him beforehand by this servant of the living God! How strikingly did it show that the greatest potentates on earth, and even the spiritual wickednesses in high places, have their bounds appointed to them by the hand of God, and that however magisterially they may seem to conduct themselves, still they cannot overstep the prescribed limits, and must be kept in all their operations subservient to the higher purposes of Heaven!

The chief point, however, in the representation, is the view that is given in the concluding part of the senseless security of the people at Jerusalem while the portentous cloud was gathering in the north, and of the tremendous fury with which it was soon to discharge itself upon their heads. They who were ready to believe every divination among themselves that fell in with their own vain and corrupt imaginations, would pay no regard either to the oracles of superstition, or to the solemn utterances of God's Spirit, when these told against the infatuated and perilous course they were pursuing. Remaining confident and secure to the last, the evil was destined to come upon them as a resistless whirlwind of destruction. And to show how in this fearful convulsion all was to be really of God, while human instruments alone outwardly appeared – to show that the approaching storm of violence and uproar was to be all directed by the hand of him whom they had so long offended and provoked by their sins – the king of Babylon and his forces are now in a manner lost sight of, and Jehovah alone seems to speak and act. It is he who brings into remembrance the transgressions of the people, and punishes them for their sin; he who utterly subverts the order of things then existing, because of the prevailing and incorrigible wickedness; yet so as, at the same time, not to involve all in complete and final destruction, but only to level with the dust what had become so offensive to the eye of his holiness, and hold the prospect of a new and better destiny in reserve for one who could accomplish it in righteousness.

It is from this change in the mode of representation – from the Lord himself being here again brought directly upon the stage, that we are to account for the peculiar language employed, especially in regard to king Zedekiah. But a lively and energetic turn in the discourse, the prophet passes from the people at large to address himself immediately to Zedekiah, and styles him not only wicked, but also pierced through; although, it is well known, he was not actually slain in the calamities that ensued. But it is not exactly what was to be done by the external sword of the Babylonians that comes here into view; it is the execution of the Lord's judgment, under the same form and aspect of severity as that which had been presented in the former part of the vision – the terrors of his drawn sword. This sword is but an image of the judgment itself, precisely as the devouring fire had been in the vision immediately preceding; and it is not the less true that Zedekiah fell under its powerful stroke, though he personally survived the catastrophe. Driven ignominiously from his throne, doomed to see his family slain before his eyes, to have these eyes themselves put out, and to be led as a miserable and helpless captive in chains to Babylon, he might with the most perfect propriety be regarded as the grand victim of the Lord's sword – already, in a manner, pierced through with it; for, to the strongly idealistic spirit of the prophet, the wickedness and the sword, the sin and its punishment, appear inseparably connected together. The overthrow to which he was destined seemed to the prophet's eye at once so inevitable and so near, that he could speak of it no otherwise than as a thing already in existence.

But it was to be no merely personal loss and degradation; the overthrow to be accomplished on Zedekiah was to draw along with it the complete subversion of the present state of things. Therefore, while the prophet represents the day of visitation as coming upon him, he also speaks of it as being at the time when sin generally had reached its consummation, and the completeness of the guilt was to have its parallel in the complete and terminal character of the judgment. All must now be made desolate; the mitre of the high priest (the emblem of his official dignity and honor, as the representative of a consecrated and priestly people), as well as the crown of the king, was to be put away, and everything turned upside down. Such a convulsed and disorganized state of things was approaching, that, as it is said, *"this should no longer be this;"* in other words, nothing should be allowed to remain what it had been, it should be another thing than formerly; as is presently explained in what follows, *"the low is exalted and the high is brought down,"* – a general revolution, in which the outward relations of things should be made to change places, in just retaliation upon the people for having so grossly perverted the moral relations of things.[18] Yet the agents and participators in these revolutions are warned not to expect any settled condition to come out of them; *"this also,"* it is said, *"shall not be,"* it shall not attain to permanence and security. And so overthrow is to follow overthrow; "nowhere shall there be rest, nowhere security, all things shall be in a state of fluctuation, until the appearing of the great restorer and prince of peace."[19]

When the passage is viewed thus in its proper connection and comprehensive import, the objections vanish which have been raised (by Pradus and others) against the mention of the high priest's insignia, and in justification of their understanding all of the king – such as, that it is the king alone who is personally addressed in the proceding context, and the priesthood is not immediately contemplated in any other part of the discourse. But the king himself, who is expressly named, is not introduced as if he alone were concerned in what is said; he comes thus prominently into notice only as the political head and representative of the covenant-people; and the day of his calamity was to be for them also the time of the end, as regarded their existing privileges and comforts. The loss of these could not be more strikingly represented than by the removal, at one blow, of the distinctions of the high priest and the king; for what should become of all that peculiarly belonged to them as a people, if there was no one either to hold the reins of government, or to make intercession with Heaven! Everything, in such a case, must be in a state of prostration and ruin.

Yet only for a time, and as regarded the existing order of things; the period of trouble and desolation was to have a limit; it was only to last till one should come, who would prevail to rectify the disorder and retrieve the ruin. We can have no hesitation in understanding by this person the Messiah, whether we translate, *"till he comes to whom the right is,"* or, *"till he comes to whom the judgment belongs;"*[20] *"and I give it to him."* It is not expressly said what was to be given him, and should stand waiting for its proper possessor till he should come; but the context plainly forbids us to understand anything less than what was taken away – the things represented by the priestly mitre and the royal crown. The true priestly dignity and the proper regal glory were to be gone for a time into abeyance; some partial, temporary, and fluctuating possession of them might be regained, but nothing more; the adequate and permanent realization was only to be found in the person of Messiah, because in him alone was there to be a fitting representation of the Divine righteousness. It is true there was something like a restoration of the standing and honor of the priesthood after the return from the Babylonish exile; and if the ideas currently entertained upon the subject were correct, there might appear in that a failure of the prophecy. But there was no right restoration of the priestly, any more than of the regal dignity at the time specified; it was but a shadow of the original glory. For there was no longer the distinctive prerogative of the Urim and Thummim, nor the ark of the covenant, nor the glory overshadowing the mercy-seat; all was in a depressed and mutilated condition, and even that subject to many interferences from the encroachments of foreign powers. So much only was given, both in respect to the priesthood and the kingdom, as to show that the Lord had not forsaken his people, and to serve as pledge of the coming glory. But it was to the still prospective, rather than the present state of things, that the eye of faith was directed to look for the proper restoration. And lest any should expect otherwise, the prophet Zechariah, after the return from Babylon, took up the matter, as it were, where Ezekiel had left it, and intimated in the plainest manner that what was then accomplished was scarcely worth taking into account; it was, at the most, but doing in a figure what could only find its real accomplishment in the person and work of Messiah. Especially at chap. 6:14: *"And he* (the branch) *shall build the temple of the Lord, and he shall bear the glory; and shall sit and rule upon his throne, and he shall be a priest upon his throne."* Thus the mitre and the crown were both to meet in him, and the temple in its noblest sense he built, and the glory be obtained, such as it became the Lord's anointed to possess. Meanwhile, all was but preparatory and imperfect.

But now, with this glimpse of coming revival and future glory peering through the dark cloud of judgment and tribulation, which for the present hung around the covenant-people, let us listen to the prophet's announcement of the doom of Ammon, in which there is no such perspective of future recovery.

[28]And, son of man, prophesy and say, Thus says the Lord GOD concerning the Am-mon-ites and as to their shame. Even say: The sword, the sword is drawn,[21] polished to flash like lightning and to destroy –

[29]while they see false visions for you, while they divine a lie to you, to bring you on the necks of *the* slain, of the wicked whose day has come when iniquity shall have an end.[22]

[30]Shall I cause it to return into its sheath? I will judge you in the place where you were created, in the land of your birth.[23]

[31]And I will pour out My fury on you. I

31 And I will pour out My fury on you. I will blow the fire of My wrath against you, and deliver you into the hands of beastly men, able to destroy.

32 You shall be as fuel for the fire. Your blood shall be in the midst of the land. You shall be remembered no more. For I the LORD have spoken.

Here all is darkness, trouble, and desolation. The Ammonites had not only sinned, like other heathen nations, but they had also taken up a taunt and reproach against the covenant-people in the time of their declension, and had pressed forward, and, in the proud spirit of conquerors, spread themselves over a part of Israel's territory (Zeph. 2:8; Jer. 49:1). They might, therefore, be fitly taken here as representatives of the enemies generally of the people of God. And in them the Lord was going to show, by a palpable demonstration, that while Israel could not escape this righteous judgment, when they walked like the heathen, their fall would be no gain to the heathen adversaries, but only the forerunner of a still more severe, even a remediless destruction. A germ of life and blessing still existed in the one, which Babylon with all its might could not extirpate; but in the other there was no such divine element, and when the sword of vengeance was drawn, it must accomplish a final end. So was it with the Ammonites as a people. A few years after the fall of Jerusalem, the arms of the king of Babylon were turned against them, and desolated their country. But this was only the beginning of their troubles, for they never attained again to political power and importance; they gradually dwindled away, till their separate existence ceased, and their place was no more known. *"So let all thine enemies perish, O Lord* (so shall they indeed perish – in the destruction of these aliens and scorners the doom of all is reflected); *but let them that love thee be as the sun when he goeth forth in his strength."*

CHAPTER XXII.

THE LORD'S JUDGMENT UPON THE ALL-PERVADING SINFULNESS OF JERUSALEM.

1 And the word of the LORD came to me, saying,

2 Now, son of man, will you judge, will you judge the bloody city? Yes, you shall make her know all her idolatries.

3 Then say, Thus says the Lord GOD: The city sheds blood in its midst that her time may come, and makes idols against herself to defile herself.

4 You have become guilty in your blood that you have shed; and *you* have defiled yourself in your idols which you have made. And you have caused your days to draw near, and have come to your years. Therefore I have made you a reproach to the heathen and a mocking to all countries.

5 Those who are near and those who are far from you shall mock against you, O defiled of name and troubled one.[1]

6 Behold, the princes of Israel, every one according to his might, has been in you to shed blood.

7 In you they have despised father and mother. In your midst they have dealt with the stranger by oppression. In you they have troubled the orphan and the widow.

8 You have despised My holy things and have profaned My sabbaths.

9 In you are men who carry tales to shed blood; and in you they eat on the mountains; in your midst they commit fornication.

10 In you they have discovered their fathers' nakedness; in you they have humbled her who was set apart because of uncleanness.

11 And one has committed abomination with his neighbor's wife; and another had wickedly defiled his daughter-in-law; and another in you has humbled his sister, his father's daughter.

12 In you they have taken gifts to shed blood. You have taken usury and increase, and you have greedily gained of your neighbors by extortion, and have forgotten Me, says the Lord GOD.

13 Behold, therefore I have beaten My hand because of your unjust gain which you have made, and at your blood which has been in your midst.

14 Can your heart endure, or can your hands be strong, in the day that I shall deal with you? I the LORD have spoken and will act.

15 And I will scatter you among the nations

and disperse you in the countries, and will destroy your uncleanness out of you.

[16]And you shall take your inheritance in yourself[2] in the sight of the nations, and you shall know that I am the LORD.

[17]And the word of the LORD came to me, saying,

[18]Son of man, the house of Israel has become dross to Me. All of them are copper, and tin, and iron, and lead, in the middle of the furnace; they are the dross of silver.

[19] Therefore thus says the Lord GOD: Because you have all become dross, behold, then I will gather you into the middle of Jerusalem.

[20]*As* they gather silver, and copper, and iron, and lead and tin into the middle of the furnace, to blow the fire on it to melt it, so I will gather *you* in My anger and in My fury, and I will leave *you* there and melt you.

[21]Yes, I will gather you and blow on you in the fire of My wrath, and you shall be melted in the middle of it.

[22]As silver is melted in the middle of the furnace, so you shall be melted in the middle of it. And you shall know that I the LORD have poured out My fury on you.

[23]And the word of the LORD came to me, saying,

[24]Son of man, say to her: You are the land that is not cleansed or rained on in the day of fury.

[25]A plot by her prophets is in her midst, like a roaring lion tearing the prey. They have devoured souls; they have taken the treasure and precious things; they multiplied her many widows in her midst.

[26]Her priests have broken My law[3] and have defiled My holy things. They have put no difference between the holy and the common, nor have they shown *difference* between the unclean and the clean. And *they* have hidden their eyes from My sabbaths, and I am defiled among them.

[27]Her princes in her midst are like wolves tearing the prey, to shed blood, to destroy souls, to get unjust gain.

[28]And her prophets have daubed themselves with whitewash, seeing vanity and divining lies to them, saying, Thus says the Lord GOD – when the LORD has not spoken.

[29]The people of the land have used oppression and practiced robbery, and they have troubled the poor and needy. Yes, they have oppressed the stranger without right.

[30]And I sought for a man among them who should make up the wall for the land, and stand in the break before me, that I should not destroy it. But I did not find one.

[31]Therefore I have poured out My fury on them. I have burned them up with the fire of My wrath. I have given them their own way on their heads, says the Lord GOD.

A very few remarks will suffice on this chapter, as it presents scarcely any difficulty in interpretation, and in its theme differs very little from some portions that have already passed under consideration. It stands closely related, however, to the last chapter, and may fitly be regarded as supplementary to it; the former having presented a striking delineation of the Lord's purpose to execute the severity of his displeasure upon the people of Jerusalem, while this returns to lay open the fearful mass of corruption on account of which such severity was to be inflicted. In what is written here, there is nothing properly new; in its general purport, it is a repetition of the charges which were urged in chap. 20; and so the chapter begins much in the same way, with a call upon the prophet to judge the people, and set before them their iniquities. There, however, the charge took the form of an historical review, for the purpose of connecting the present state of wickedness with the past, and showing how continuously the stream of corruption had flowed through all periods of their national existence. Here, on the other hand, the prophet looks exclusively to the present, and brings out in fearful array the many henious and rampant sins which were crying in Heaven's ear for vengeance.

The first section, reaching to the end of ver. 16, is chiefly occupied with detailing the various kinds of transgression that were practised in the land, – the idolatry, revelry, and lust, the selfishness, treachery, oppression, and bloodshed, with which all were polluted. The dark picture is drawn so as to exhibit a sharp contrast between the impure condition to which Israel had now come, and the pure one which Moses had of old represented them as called to maintain (Lev. 18-20). In all that was holy, virtuous, and good, they were to stand honorably apart from the heathen nations, while in reality they had sunk to a level with these in the practice of every species of enormity. Hence the necessity of a dealing in judgment – not utterly to exterminate them as a people, but to purge out the corruptions

which were defeating the design of their calling and election of God. *"And I will scatter thee among the heathen,"* is the closing denunciation of this part, *"and disperse thee in the countries, and will consume thy filthiness out of thee. And thou art polluted by thyself (i.e.) by thy own sinful doings, and the judgments these have deservedly brought down on thee) in the eyes of the heathen; and thou shalt know that I am Jehovah."*

The next section, vers. 17-22, is a sort of figurative episode, in which the prophet, as if impatient to see so much wickedness visited with its due chastisement, introduces a description of the righteous judgment that was ready to be executed upon them. The nation is represented as a miserable compound of the baser metals and of the dross of silver – silver that has become dross; for it is the degeneracy from good to bad, as well as the actual state of corruption, which the prophet would have us to mark. They were, therefore, to be thrown into the burning furnace of the Lord's anger, so as to be blown upon, and melted; that the bad – a result implied, though not actually expressed – might be consumed, and the good separated and preserved. It was in Jerusalem this refining process was to be undergone; so that the doom threatened is but another form of the evil already announced under the images of a devouring fire and a piercing sword. It was, in other words, the desolations to be accomplished by the king of Babylon.

In the last and concluding section (vers. 23-31), the prophet again returns to the charge of guilt, but with a more especial reference to the different ranks and orders of society in the land, showing how each had corrupted their ways, and, as it were, conspired together to bring on the catastrophe. The land, as a whole, presents itself to his eye as a polluted region, and, as such, not to be blessed – not to be rained upon (one of the great covenant-blessings) in the day of indignation. The prophets have acted like beasts of prey, intent only on their personal gain (ver. 25); the priests have done violence to the law, wrested it to improper ends, and have practically allowed the distinctions between good and evil, clean and unclean, to go into desuetude (ver. 26); the princes have exercised cruelty and oppression, countenanced and encouraged by the prophets (vers. 27,28); the people at large have followed in the footsteps of their leaders, and done iniquity as they could, each one against his neighbor (ver. 29). *"And I sought,"* it is added, *"for a man among them that should make up the wall, and stand in the breach before me for the land, that I might not destroy it; but I found none."* It does not mean that there was literally not a righteous man in it; for Jeremiah was still there, and doubtless others of a kindred spirit beside him. But Jeremiah had been discharged from praying for the people (chap. 11:14), as being now doomed to destruction; and the meaning here is, that no one now, knowing the state to which things had come, and understanding the Lord's mind concerning them, would any longer undertake to do the part of a repairer of the breach, so as to have matters brought right again. *"Therefore,"* the inevitable conclusion follows, *"I pour out my indignation upon them; I consume them in the fire of my wrath; I recompense their way upon their head, saith the Lord Jehovah."*

CHAPTER XXIII.

THE STORY OF ISRAEL'S SIN AND PUNISHMENT PARABOLICALLY EXHIBITED UNDER THE NAMES OF AHOLAH AND AHOLIBAH.

[1] The word of the LORD came again to me,

[2] Son of man, there were two women, the daughters of one mother.

[3] And they committed fornications in Egypt. They committed fornications in their youth. There their breasts were handled, and there they bruised their virgin breasts.

[4] And their names were A-ho-lah, the oldest, and A-hol-i-bah, her sister. And they were Mine, and they bore sons and daughters. These were their names: Samaria is A-ho-lah, and Jerusalem is A-hol-i-bah.

[5] And A-ho-lah played the harlot when she was Mine. And she worshiped her lovers, the Assyrians *her* neighbors,[1]

[6] clothed with blue, captains and rulers, all of them desirable young men, horsemen riding on horses.

[7] So she committed her adulteries with them, with all those, the chosen men of Assyria, and with all those she adored. She defiled herself with all their idols.

8 Nor did she leave her fornications from Egypt. For in her youth they lay with her, and they bruised her virgin breasts, and poured their fornication on her.

9 Therefore I have delivered her into the hand of her lovers, into the hand of the Assyrians whom she adored.

10 These uncovered her nakedness. They took her sons and her daughters and killed her with the sword. And she became famous among women, for they had executed judgment on her.

11 And when her sister A-hol-i-bah saw, she was more corrupt in her lust than she had been, and her fornications were beyond the fornications of her sister.

12 She worshiped the Assyrians *her* neighbors, captains and rulers clothed most perfectly, horsemen riding on horses, all of them desirable young men.

13 Then I saw that she was defiled; both of them in the same way.

14 And she multiplied her fornications. For when she saw men carved on the wall – the images of the Chal-de-ans painted with vermilion,

15 clothed with girdles on their loins, with flowing turbans on their heads,[2] all of them looking like princes, according to the custom of the Babylonians of Chal-de-a, the land of their birth –

16 and when she saw them with her eyes, she lusted after them and sent messengers to them into Chal-de-a.

17 And the Babylonians came to her into the bed of love, and they defiled her with their fornications. And she was defiled with them, and her mind was alienated from them.

18 So she uncovered her lustful desires and uncovered her nakedness. Then My mind was alienated from her just as My mind was alienated from her sister.

19 Yet she multiplied her fornications in calling to memory the days of her youth in which she had played the harlot in the land of Egypt.

20 For she lusted after her lovers, whose flesh is *like* the flesh of asses, and whose issue is *like* the issue of horses.

21 So you looked for the wickedness of your youth, when the E-gyp-tians bruised your breasts, for the sake of your youth.

22 Therefore, O A-hol-i-bah, thus says the Lord GOD: Behold, I will raise up against you your lovers from whom your mind is alienated. And I will bring them against you on every side:

23 the Babylonians, and all the Chal-de-ans, Pe-kod, and Shoa, and Koa,[3] all the Assyrians with them – all of them desirable young men, captains and rulers, great and famous lords, all of them riding on horses.

24 And they shall come against you with chariots, wagons and wheels, and with an assembly of people who shall set against you buckler and shield and helmet all around. And I will set judgment before them, and they shall judge you according to their judgments.

25 And I will set My jealousy against you, and they shall deal with you in fury. They shall take away your nose and your ears, and the rest of you shall fall by the sword. They shall take away your sons and your daughters, and the rest of you shall be devoured by the fire.

26 They shall also strip you out of your clothes and take away your beautiful jewels.

27 So I will make your wickedness to cease from you, even your fornication from the land of Egypt, so that you shall not lift up your eyes to them nor remember Egypt any more.

28 For thus says the Lord GOD: Behold, I will deliver you into the hand *of those* you hate, into the hand *of those* from whom your mind is torn away.

29 And they shall deal with you hatefully and shall take away all your labor, and *they* shall leave you naked and bare. And the nakedness of your fornications shall be uncovered, both your wickedness and your fornications.

30 I will do these to you because you have gone lusting after the heathen, because you are defiled with their idols.

31 You have walked in the way of your sister. So I will give her cup into your hand.

32 Thus says the Lord GOD: You shall drink of your sister's cup deep and large; you shall be laughed to scorn and mocked, for it holds much.

33 You shall be filled with drunkenness and sorrow, with the cup of dumbness and shame with the cup of your sister Samaria.

34 You shall even drink it and empty it. And you shall break its pieces and tear out your own breasts.[4] For I have spoken, says the Lord GOD.

35 Therefore thus says the Lord GOD: Because you have forgotten Me and cast Me behind your back, therefore bear also your wickedness and your fornications.

36 And the LORD said to me: Son of man, will you judge A-ho-lah and A-hol-i-bah? Yes, declare to them their idolatries,

37 that they have committed adultery, and blood is in their hands. And they have committed adultery with their idols and have also caused their sons whom they bore to Me

to pass through *the fire* for them, to destroy *them.*

[38]And they have done this to Me: They have defiled My sanctuary in the same day, and have defiled My sabbaths.

[39]For when they had slain their children to their idols, then they came the same day into My sanctuary to defile it. And lo, so they have done in the middle of My house.

[40]And they have even sent for men to come from a distance, to whom a messenger was sent. And, lo, they came. You washed yourself for *them,* painted your eyes and adorned yourself with ornaments,

[41]and you sat on a stately bed *with* a table prepared before it, on which you set My incense and My oil.

[42]And the voice of a careless multitude was with her; and with the men of the common sort were brought Sa-be-ans from the wilderness, who put bracelets on their hands and beautiful crowns on their heads.

[43]Then I said to *her who was* old in adulteries, Will they now commit fornications with her, and she *with them?*

[44]Yet they went in to her, as they go in to a woman who plays the harlot; so they went in to A-ho-lah and to A-hol-i-bah, the wicked women.

[45]And the righteous men, they shall judge them with the judgment of adulteresses, the judgment of women who shed blood; because they are adulteresses, and blood is in their hands.

[46]For thus says the Lord GOD: I will bring up a company on them and will give them to be removed and stripped.

[47]And the company shall stone them with stones and point them out with their swords. They shall kill their sons and their daughters and burn up their houses with fire.

[48]So I will cause wickedness to cease out of the land, that all women may be taught not to go after your wickedness.

[49]And they shall put your wickedness on you, and you shall bear the sins of your idols. And you shall know that I am the Lord GOD.

The figure employed, and the train of thought presented under it in this chapter, are so much akin to those already contained in chap. 16, that I deem it unnecessary to give more than the briefest outline of the subject. The nature of the representation also forbids any minuteness of detail. It is the covenant-people in both its branches, Israel and Judah, and not the latter merely, as in chap. 16, that the prophet here has in view. Hence there are two women, the daughters of one mother – the name of the one Aholah (her tent, her being taken in the sense of her own), of the other Aholibah (my tent in her). The former represents, we are told, Samaria, or the portion of the covenant-people whose capital Samaria was, and the latter Jerusalem, or that other portion whose capital was there. The names of the two divisions respectively were evidently chosen for the purpose of expressing the relation in which each stood to God; – the one, Samaria, having, at the very commencement of her separate existence, apostatized from Jehovah, and set up a tent or standard for herself; while the other, Jerusalem, still had in her the tabernacle of God, the true symbols of worship, and the divinely appointed means of obtaining God's favor and blessing. This difference, however, vanishes in the sequel; at least, no further appears than in the precedence in guilt and punishment ascribed to Samaria, on which account also she is called the elder sister. Iniquity in her reached its maturity earlier, and sooner also received its deserved recompense; but without the effect of deterring the other sister from pursuing the same infatuated course; she was of a kindred spirit, and came in process of time to the same miserable end.

It is to be noted here also, in respect to the representation on both sides, that the breach of conjugal fidelity charged against the daughters has reference not so much to their idolatrous practices as to their worldly spirit – their disposition to form alliances with heathen nations, and to look to them, instead of God, for their protection and safety. The one, no doubt, was very closely connected with the other, and was no more, indeed, than its natural outgoing and result. Hitzig plainly carries the matter too far, when he denies that there is any reference whatever here to the idols of the heathen, and that the heathen nations themselves are alone the idols. This obliges him to hold the last clause in ver. 7, "*with all their idols she defiled herself,*" to be a corruption; and it also overlooks the inseparable connection between the two false directions. The spirit of heathenish idolatry, situated as Israel was, naturally led to the copying after heathenish manners, and the forming of heathenish alliances; and with every step taken in the one direction, the other was sure to follow. We cannot, therefore, suppose that the prophet should have entirely omitted any reference to the idolatrous spirit which formed the root of the evil. At the same time, it is undoubtedly the other direction which he has throughout chiefly in view; partly because the former one had already received very strong and repeated delineations (especially in chap. 16 and 20), and partly because the prophet wished to make the people understand how God had in righteous judgment resolved to turn their false confidences into the immediate instruments of their ruin. It was their crime to have sought after such lovers, and it was to be their punishment that these lovers should become their destroyers.

In the case of Aholah, or the kingdom of Israel, the apostatizing disposition is represented as discovering itself not only in the foulness they contracted in Egypt, and their still hankering after that when they were settled in Canaan, but also in that they became enamoured of the Assyrians. These Assyrians are called their neighbors (ver. 5), as they are also of the other division of the covenant-people (ver. 12); and are described as having the gallant appearance and the gay attire which were fitted to work upon such light and inconstant hearts. The meaning simply is, that they saw in that great neighboring power all the elements of worldly rank and prosperity which they desired to possess themselves, and trusted to their connection with it, rather than their interest in God, for the strength they needed. The notices which the historical books contain respecting the commencement of this connection are so brief, that it would be improper to refer to them for complete information on the subject.

The first express mention of the Assyrians in connection with the kingdom of Israel, in the reign of Menahem, when Pul is said to have come against the land (2 Kings 15:19), has all the appearance of a notice depending upon something going before – a prior connection, which gave him, as he thought, a right to interfere amid the troubles that then prevailed. The word of the prophet seems plainly to imply that the first movement in this direction was on the part of Israel – that she herself courted the alliance; and there can be no doubt, as well from the history as from the word of the prophet, that the connection ended most disastrously for Israel; that she was indeed given up by God into the hands of that heathen power, to be humbled, and smitten, and brought to desolation.

In regard to the people of Judah, represented by Aholibah, the delineation is quite similar, only that their folly and guilt were aggravated by having before them the ruin which befell the kingdom of Israel. They are described as being captivated and allured by the Assyrians first, and then by the Babylonians, so that their heart departed from the Lord to lean upon an arm of flesh. The historical notices regarding this portion of Judah's course, from the time of Ahaz downwards, which are much fuller than those given of the like period of Israel's history, amply bear out the language of the prophet. And how completely the remaining part of the description was also verified, how intense a loathing was created between the two parties, and how utter a destruction was brought upon the people of Judah by those objects of their former confidence and admiration, it is needless at present to relate.

The closing part of the description represents the two women, and especially the one that personated the people of Judah, as persevering to the last in their wicked and profligate courses. Like persons in the final stages of abandonment, they went on rioting in the ways of evil, unchecked by all the troubles and humiliations they had experienced in the past; and now, therefore, as utterly reprobate and hardened and hopeless, they must be adjudged to the doom appointed against such incorrigible and shameless offenders. So the doleful story ends. The prophet looks only, from first to last, to the course of crime and its deserved recompense; and he allows the curtain to drop without one gleam of hope as to the future. He sees that the hammer of the law in its strongest form is needed to break the hard and stony heart of the people. So urgent was the call for a work of conviction, and so great the danger of that not being effectually wrought, that he would not drop a word which might lighten the impression of guilt upon their minds, or afford the least excuse for delay. His message was, Now or never. Judged by the sense of right and wrong current among men, your conduct toward God calls for judgment without mercy. And if there be not immediately awakened the contrition of sincere repentance, you have nothing to expect but the most unsparing visitations of wrath.

CHAPTER XXIV.

THE VISION OF THE BOILING CALDRON, AND OF THE DEATH OF EZEKIEL'S WIFE.

[1]Again in the ninth year, in the tenth month, in the tenth *day* of the month, the word of the LORD came to me, saying,

[2]Son of man, write the name of the day, of this same day. The king of Babylon set himself against Jerusalem this same day.

[3]And speak a parable to the rebellious GOD: Set on a pot; set on and also pour water into it.

[4]Gather its pieces into it, every good piece, the thigh and the shoulder. Fill *it* with the choice bones.

[5]Take the choice of the flock and also burn the bones under it; make it boil high, and let them boil its bones in it.

[6]Therefore thus says the Lord GOD: Woe to the bloody city, to the pot whose scum is in it, and whose scum has not gone out of it! Bring it out piece by piece, let no lot fall on it.

[7]For her blood is in her midst; she set it on the top of a rock. She did not pour it on the ground, to cover it with dust,

[8]that it might cause fury to come up to take vengeance. I have set her blood on the top of a rock, that it should not be covered.

[9]Therefore thus says the Lord GOD: Woe to the bloody city! I will even make the pile great for fire.

[10]Heap on wood, kindle the fire, burn up the flesh, and spice it well, and let the bones be burned.

[11]Then set it empty on its coals, so that its copper may be hot and may burn and its uncleanness may be melted in it, *that* the scum of it may be gone.

[12]She has wearied *herself* with lies, and her great scum did not go forth out of her. Her scum shall be in the fire.

[13]In your uncleanness is wickedness. Because I have purged you and you were not purged, you shall not be purged from your uncleanness any more, until I have caused My fury to rest on you.

[14]I the LORD have spoken. It shall happen, and I will do *it*. I will not go back. I will not spare. I will not repent. According to your ways, and according to your doings, they shall judge you, says the Lord GOD.

These fourteen verses contain the first part of the message given to Ezekiel on this occasion. The occasion was a melancholy one, being marked by the actual investiture of Jerusalem by the armies of Nebuchadnezzar. It was the ninth year of Jehoiachin's captivity, and the tenth day of the tenth month. This is noted in other passages (2 Kings 25:1; Jer. 39:1) as the day and time on which the siege properly commenced. And that this fact should have been communicated to Ezekiel among the Babylonian exiles, and announced by him immediately after, must have been to afford another proof of his true prophetical character. By such an announcement he put his Divine commission in pledge, as he did still further, and more remarkably, by the clear delineation of the disastrous results in which he declared the siege thus begun was sure to terminate.

The image which is chosen for the purpose of unfolding the message to be delivered on this painful subject, that of a caldron set upon the fire to boil, with the best pieces of the meat in it, and the bones piled underneath, was evidently suggested by the proverb formerly noticed as having been bandied about among the people: *"The city is the caldron and we are the flesh"* (chap. 11:3). In a proud feeling of fancied security they had spoken thus; but they were now to find, in bitter experience, that there was a dreadful truth couched in the image, which was to rebuke their senseless folly. So far from the city proving to them a place of secure strength, like the iron ribs of a strong caldron, it was to be set as a seething-pot upon the fire; and the people, like so many pieces of meat destined to be devoured were to be put into it and subjected to a boiling heat. None were to be spared; the mighty and the noble, as well as the comparatively poor and mean, were to suffer in the calamity; the only difference should be like that between consumption in the fire at once – the punishment of the poorer sort – and perishing by the somewhat slower and more lingering process of boiling, from which the rich could not escape.

After having briefly given the ground of the parabolical description, the prophet proceeds, in vers. 6-14, to make special and pointed application of it. His leading object is to show that it was the excessive and inveterate wickedness of the people which provoked, and even rendered necessary, the severe dealing to which they were now subjected.

All measures of a less extreme kind had been tried in vain; those were now exhausted; and as the iniquity appeared to be entwined with the whole fabric and constitution of things, nothing remained but to subject all to the crucible of a severe and overwhelming catastrophe. This is represented by keeping the caldron on the fire till its contents were stewed away, the very bones burnt. And as if even this were not enough, as if something more were necessary to avenge and purge out such scandalous wickedness, the caldron itself must be kept hot and burning till the pollution should be thoroughly consumed out of it. The wicked city must be laid in ruins. It is the very same thought which occurs in Isa. 4:4, where the filth of the daughters of Zion is said to be washed away, and the blood of Jerusalem to be purged from the midst of it, by the spirit of judgment and the spirit of burning; only, after the manner of our prophet, the image is extended to many minute and particular details. In plain terms, the Lord was no longer going to deal with them by half-measures; their condition called for the greatest degree of severity compatible with their preservation as a distinct and separate people, and so the indignation of the Lord was to rest on them till a separation was effected between them and sin.

As to the principle of dealing, there is no essential difference between what God did then with Israel and what he still does with those who stand in a similar relation to him and pursue a similar course. Where there is the profession of a belief in God's word and a regard to God's authority, though intermingled with much that is false in sentiment or unrighteous in conduct, there must still be dealings of severity and rebuke, to bring the professor, if possible, to a sense of his sinfulness, and lead him to renounce it; but failing this, to vindicate concerning him the righteousness of God, and leave him without excuse if his iniquity should prove his ruin. In the case of sincere, God-fearing people, the severity exercised will always be attended with salutary results; for they have the root of the matter in them, and are sure to profit by the chastening of the Lord. But with those who have the profession only, without the principle of true godliness, the iniquity is clung to in spite of all the severity that is exercised, until the wrath falls on them to the uttermost. There is enough in New Testament Scripture, and the experience of men under the present dispensation, to warrant us to expect so far a similarity in God's method of procedure to the representation here given of his conduct toward Israel. But, on the other hand, a difference may also be expected, in so far as his dealings now, in accordance with the genius of the new dispensation, respect men more as individuals, less as public communities, and bear more immediately upon their inward state and spiritual relations. He who would regard aright the operations of the Lord's hand, and profit by the corrections of his rod of chastisement, must keep a watchful eye upon the things that concern his own experience and history. There may be signs of the Divine displeasure, sufficient to startle the tender conscience and call for deep humiliation of spirit, while nothing appears outwardly wrong, and all may even wear a smiling aspect, as far as regards social and public relations. Should there be a restraining of Divine grace within, an absence of spiritual refreshments, a felt discomfort of mind, or an obvious withdrawal of spiritual privileges, there is beyond the commencement of a work of judgment; and if such marks of God's displeasure are slighted, others of a more severe and alarming kind may assuredly be looked for. But as men's tempers and circumstances in life are infinitely varied, so there is a corresponding variety in the methods employed by God to check the risings of sin and expel its poison from the heart. And it is the part of spiritual wisdom to seek for the wakeful ear and the discerning eye, which may enable one to catch even the earliest intimations of God's displeasure, and so improve these as to render unnecessary the heavier visitations of wrath.

The second part of the vision which Ezekiel saw on this occasion bore respect more immediately to himself, although it was really a revelation to the people.

15 Also the word of the LORD came to me, saying,

16 Son of man, behold, I take away from you the desire of your eyes with a stroke. Yet you shall not mourn or weep, nor shall your tears run down.

17 Be silent. Make no mourning for the dead.[8] Tie your bonnet on your head and put your shoes on yur feet, and do not cover *your* lips, and do not eat the bread of men.

18 So I spoke to the people in the morning. And in the evening my wife died, and I did in the morning as I was commanded.

19 And the people said to me, Will you not tell us what these *mean* to us, that *which* you do?[9]

20 Then I answered them, The word of the LORD came to me, saying,

21 Speak to the house of Israel. Thus says the Lord GOD: Behold, I will defile My sanctuary, the glory of your strength, the desire of your eyes, and that which your soul pities. And your sons and your daughters whom you have left shall fall by the sword.

22 And you shall do as I have done. You shall not cover *your* lips nor eat the bread of men.

23 And your bonnets shall be on your heads and your shoes on your feet. You shall not mourn or weep; but you shall pine away for your iniquities and mourn to one another.

24 Thus E-zek-i-el is a sign to you. According to all that he has done, you shall do. And when this comes, you shall know that I am the Lord GOD.

25 Also, son of man, in the day when I take from them their strength, the joy of their glory, the desire of their eyes, and that on which they set their minds, their sons and their daughters,

26 shall it not *be that* he who escapes in that day shall come to you to cause *you* to hear with your ears?

27 In that day your mouth shall be open to him who has escaped, and you shall speak and no longer be dumb. And you shall be a sign to them, and they shall know that I am the LORD.

The portion of these verses which relates to the personal experiance and behavior of the prophet was well fitted to strike both himself and others. In ordinary circumstances such a calamity as the sudden death of a beloved wife would naturally have called forth, and would also have justified, the most affecting demonstrations of grief, – doleful cries and lamentations, mourning attire, the uncovering of the feet (2 Sam. 15:30; Isa. 20:2); uncovering also the head in the case of one who, like Ezekiel was a priest, and wore a peculiar head-dress (comp. Lev. 10:7, 21:10,12; Josh. 7:6; 2 Sam. 13:19; Esth. 4:1,3; Isa. 61:3, etc.),[10] putting a cloth on the chin (Lev. 13:45; Micah 3:7), and eating the bread of sorrow. But not one of these things was the prophet to be permitted to do. He was neither to shed a tear nor to raise a cry, not to make dead-persons' mourning – the mourning which was wont to be made in honor of the dead – nor throw aside his priestly head-dress, nor put off his shoes, nor cover his chin, nor eat the bread which it was customary for men to eat in seasons of calamity and distress.

No reason is given for these singular restrictions as regards the prophet's own case. He simply hears the word of the Lord, telling him what was to happen, and how he was to conduct himself when it did happen. Then he relates that in the evening his wife died, and that in obedience to the Divine command, he abstained from all the usual expressions of grief and mourning. The people, he further relates, came next day to inquire what these Things signified to them. Not really in the outward transactions of life for what we have here is not a historical narrative in the ordinary sense, but the account of a Divine communication between God and the prophet's own soul. The things all took place in the sense and feeling of the prophet, and are recorded as transactions that he personally witnessed and took part in; but, as in the case of all his other visions, the scene of the transactions lay in the ideal, not in the actual world, in that spiritual sphere in which as a prophet he communed with God. Hence, as showing that he still was in that region, and was there dealing directly with heaven, at ver. 25, immediately after the explanation given to the people of the sign, he is addressed by God with what is but a continuation of the message: *"And thou, son of man, shall it not be,"* etc. The whole account, therefore, belongs to that spiritual sphere in which the prophets lived and acted when they received communications from above; and it stands upon the same footing as the narrative of the caldron in the earlier part of the chapter, the vision of the iniquity-bearing in the fourth, or indeed any of the preceding communications in this book. What was done and said in his case, as immediately transacting with God, was an acted lesson for the people, to give force and distinctness to the instructions to be delivered respecting themselves. So they are given to understand in the application of what took place. They were soon actually to lose what was pre-eminently dear to them – the sanctuary of the Lord, which is called, first, *"the pride of their strength,"* because in connection with it, to a large extent, had grown up their feelings of false security (Jer. 7:4); then, *"the desire of their eyes and that which their soul pitied,"* or yearned over, because it was what they peculiarly delighted in and clung to with a kind of conjugal regard. But now it was to be profaned, which, in the circumstances, could only mean laid in the dust, like the prophet's wife. And not only that, but also their sons and their daughters, whom they had left behind them in Judea, were to be given up to the sword. Yet with such singular occasions of grief, the usual signs of affliction were not to be found in them – they were neither to mourn nor to weep, their accustomed dress was to be retained, and their ordinary fare partaken of; but not as if their spirits were unmoved by what should have taken place, and no feeling of gloom sat upon their bosoms; on the contrary, *"they should pine away in their sins, and bemoan themselves one toward another."* (ver. 23).

It appears to us almost unaccountable how any person of ordinary discernment should understand the prophet here to mean, that those Jews were to receive the coming catastrophe in a callous and indifferent manner, sullenly yielding to their fate, but without any sensible movement of the springs of sorrow and regret. Yet such is the view taken of the passage by some leading commentators abroad (in particular, by Eichhorn, Ewald, Hitzig), although the express declaration at the close, and the whole character of the representation, plainly lead to an opposite conclusion. In the typical part of the delineation, it was not because the prophet was insensible to the loss he sustained by the death of his wife that he was to abstain from the habiliments and usages of mourning, but because there was another source of grief behind of which this was but the sign and presage, and in itself so much greater and more appalling that his spirit, instead of venting itself in expressions of sorrow at the immediate and ostensible calamity, was rather to brood in silent agony and concern over the more distressing evil it foreshadowed. And in like manner with the people, when all their fond hopes and visions were finally exploded, when the destruction of their beautiful temple and the slaughter of their sons and daughters came home to them as dreadful realities, they could only refrain from bewailing the loss of what had so deep a hold on their desires and affections, by having come to discern in this the sign of what was still greatly more dreadful and appalling. And what might that be but the blood-stained guilt of their iniquities, which had brought on the catastrophe? Had it been that portion of the people who dwelt at Jerusalem that the prophet here more immediately referred to, there might have been some room for supposing (with Pradus and others) that he pointed merely to the overawing terror of the enemy, and to the breathless horror and astonishment connected with the capture of the city, when he spake of such an arrest being laid on the common outgoings of grief. But it is the captives at Chebar of whom he more immediately speaks, who he well knew would be living in outward quiet, far removed from the scene of uproar and destruction. It could not, in their case, be the presence of a Babylonian host, or the turmoil and consternation caused by the success of the Babylonian arms, which should check the customary expressions of grief; it would be the overwhelming sense that should then break in upon them of the iniquities to which they had clung with such fatal perverseness, absorbing their spirits, and turning their moanings into a new and higher direction. The agonies of breavement would be in a manner lost under the self-inflicted pains of contrition and remorse (comp. chap. 7:16).

Yet while this seems obviously the meaning of the prophet's announcement – of the not mourning in one way, and still pining away with distress and sorrow in another – the description must be understood with certain qualifications, and, indeed, is to be viewed as the somewhat ideal delineation of a state of things that should be found, rather than the exact and literal description of what was actually to take place. The representation would otherwise stand in palpable contrariety, as well with undoubted facts, as with statements elsewhere made both by Ezekiel and by his great contemporary in Judea. That many on the fall of Jerusalem did really exhibit the usual signs of mourning, and give the fullest vent to their feelings of distress, may be inferred with the utmost certainty from what is written in the Lamentations of Jeremiah, where we read of all the common symptoms and appliances of grief, – *"elders sitting upon the ground, casting dust upon their heads, girding themselves with sackcloth,"* and the prophet himself, though he had been told not to lament or bemoan (chap. 16:5), weeping till *"his eyes failed with tears, and his liver was poured on the earth, for the destruction of the daughter of his people."* Nay, while Ezekiel here speaks as if all the indications of mourning should be restrained at the destruction of Jerusalem, he had previously spoken of the people being so filled with distress on account of it that *"they should gird themselves with sackcloth, and have baldness upon their heads"* (chap. 7:18), and had himself also been instructed to howl and cry in contemplation of the approaching troubles (chap. 21:12). There can be no doubt, also, on the other side, that the conscience of sin, however powerfully it might work in some bosoms and absorb other feelings, would be very far from being universally felt as it ought to have been. The prophets were by no means disposed to cherish exaggerated views on the subject. Jeremiah had even spoken of the people carrying their iniquities with them into other lands, and there serving other gods day and night (chap. 16:13). And Ezekiel himself, in chap. 20, represents them as still needing, after they had been all scattered among the nations, to be brought as into the wilderness, that they might there be dealt with for iniquities not yet forsaken, and purged from still remaining abominations.

It is clear, therefore, that the description in the passage before us must not be understood in the absolute sense, as if it were intended to portray what was certainly to be realized among the people at large on the taking of Jerusalem. It is what should have been realized in all, but what, in point of fact, was to have its realization only in part. The people should, on the occurrence of such a fearful catastrophe, have sunk under an overpowering sense of their guilt and folly, and, like the prophet, turned the tide of their grief and mourning rather against the gigantic evil that lay behind, seen only in the chambers of imagery, than what outwardly appeared; they should have bewailed the enormous sins that had provoked the righteous displeasure of God, rather than the present troubles in which that displeasure had taken effect. Their sorrow should have chiefly flowed in this more inward and spiritual direction, for it was here pre-eminently that the evil stood. And such, undoubtedly, was the case with the better and more enlightened portion of the people; but many still cleaved to their idols, and would not receive the instruction given them, either by the prophet's parabolical example or by the reality of God's afflicting dispensations.

But if in respect to the people we see the ideal here exhibited of a suitable and appropriate behavior still destined to be marred by the prevalence of sin, the light in which the prophet himself appears in this vision is every way befitting his character and calling. With solemn and affecting grandeur it closes the first period of his high ministry!

He had entered on this ministry under the most appalling discouragements, in a time of peculiar depression, and with the clear understanding that, as to immediate results, it was to be at once a thankless and a hopeless task which was given him to do. But not the less did he imbibe the spirit of his office, and throw his energetic soul into the work of reformation. Message after message came forth from him, charged with the weightiest tidings and breathing throughout the lively feelings of an affectionate and earnest heart; but without the slightest effect in arresting the fatal current that was bearing Israel onwards to the gulf of ruin. And now, when all remonstrance had failed, when it was found that warnings had been uttered and counsels given only that they might be treated with cold indifference or insolent contempt, the man of God is made in spirit to anticipate the now inevitable doom, and undergoes in his communings with God the same affecting experience of evil which was soon to be the common lot of his countrymen; thus showing, that although he was not a partaker in their sins, he was yet a fellow-sufferer in their condition, and made their case in a manner his own.

But here, for the present, Ezekiel ceases from his labors for the good of Israel. He has exhausted his commission in respect to the disclosure of the people's sins, and the revelation of the Lord's judgments. He has done all that could be done to impress on men's minds the necessity and the nearness of the Divine retribution, and laid open the every side the purposes of God in connection with it. He must now, therefore, cease from his activity in this direction, and wait in silence the mournful issue. And so the word spoken to him at the commencement of his labors passes into fulfilment: *"And I will make thy tongue cleave to the roof of thy mouth, and thou shalt be dumb, and shalt not be to them a reprover; for they are a rebellious house"* (chap. 3:26). But this was only to be for a season. When the calamity had actually come, and the escaped remnant of the people of Jerusalem had joined their brethren on the banks of the Chebar, *"in that day his mouth* (it was said) *should be opened to him that is escaped, and he should speak, and be no more dumb."* A new series of communications, suited to the altered circumstances of his people, was then to be given him, and he would yet do for them the part of a faithful friend and comforter in the time of their greatest desolation.

CHAPTER XXV.

THE JUDGMENT OF ISRAEL'S IMMEDIATE NEIGHBORS AND RIVALS – AMMON, MOAB, EDOM, AND THE PHILISTINES.

The period of Ezekiel's silence toward Israel is broken for the first time by the word contained in chap. 33; and the eight intervening chapters are filled with intimations of Divine judgment against the surrounding heathen, accompanied by delineations of their guilt. The prophetic agency of Ezekiel did not cease; it only turned into a new direction – from what immediately concerned his own countrymen to what concerned the communities and nations around. This was precisely the place for such a series of judgments respecting the worldly kingdoms coming in. The prophet has finished his work, as God's representative, in pronouncing judgment on Israel. And now, therefore, is the time to make it manifest to all, that if the judgment begins there, it must proceed onwards and envelop the ungodly world, – that if the covenant-people fall under the stroke of Divine justice, their fall, so far from being the gain of the world, is but the sure presage and forerunner of its doom. It was necessary, as matters then stood, that God should employ heathen instruments in executing his displeasure upon Jerusalem and scattering the strength and glory of her people; so that in her humiliation she could not but appear for a time in a worse condition than her enemies. But the heathen nations were not to be left with the idea that they really held a position of greater security and permanence than that which belonged to Israel; they must be taught that their doom also was written in heaven, and that the downfall of that kingdom with which God had peculiarly associated his name rung, in a manner, the knell of their perdition, as it proclaimed God's high determination to take vengeance on sin wherever it might be found, and, consequently, to destroy the nations that were wholly devoted to its interests; – worse with them still than with Israel, because they had not, like her, the saving health of Divine truth mingling with their corruption; their downfall should be complete, without the prospect of any future recovery. This essential difference between Israel and the heathen nations is frequently referred to by the prophets, and by Jeremiah in particular is very strongly expressed, when, in the midst of desolating judgments ready to alight on others, he exclaims, *"But fear thou not, O Jacob, my servant, saith the Lord, for I am with thee; for I will make a full end of all the nations whither I have driven thee; but I will not make a full end of thee, but will correct thee in measure, and will not make thee utterly clean,"* or desolate (for so the last clause should be rendered), chap. 46:28.

It cannot be regarded as accidental that the heathen nations who came here within the range of the prophet's vision for judgment are precisely seven; forst four, who are briefly disposed of in chap. 25, and then three, whose case is spread over the seven following chapters. Considering the use that is made generally in Scripture, and particularly in some portions of prophetical Scripture (such as Daniel, Zechariah, the Apocalypse), of the number seven as a symbol of completeness, we may not unreasonably suppose that the prophet named those seven on the present occasion with some reference to this symbolical import of the number. And in that case he must be understood to intimate that the Divine judgment would not exhaust itself on those, but would also take effect on others who were similarly situated, – that in process of time the execution of God's vengeance on sin would traverse the entire round of its domain in the world. We may the rather adopt this supposition, as in the second division we find Sidon named separately from Tyre, though properly but a part of the same maritime power; and yet on another account there was not wanting a reason for the special mention of Sidon, as we shall see when we come to the place. The rest were all such as might have been expected, and, with one grand exception, the whole, perhaps, that might have been expected in a catalogue like the present: Ammon, Moab, Edom, the Philistines – all the immediate neighbors and hereditary rivals and enemies of Israel; and, less hostilely affected, but still occupying somewhat of the same unfriendly relation, Tyre, Sidon, and Egypt. What we specially miss in Babylon herself – in Ezekiel's time the great impersonation of the world's sinfulness and power, and above all others the enemy of Israel's pre-eminence among the nations; yet neither here nor elsewhere in this prophet's writings is she expressly named as an object of vengeance. It is obviously impossible to account for such an ommission from a desire not to exceed the number seven, for had this been all, some inferior state could easily have been sacrificed to make room for Babylon. Nor could the omission have arisen from Ezekiel's residence in Chaldea, as if he was too near the throne of the kingdom to announce its coming downfall, – a supposition which the fearless character of the prophet forbids us to make, to say nothing of the fact of Daniel's once and again proclaiming, in the very presence of the Chaldean monarch, the certain and not very distant overthrow of his empire. The reason most probably was, that as Babylon is constantly viewed by the prophet as the rod of God's vengeance, it stood in some sense apart from the nations of the earth, and seemed too closely connected with the present execution of God's purposes to be fitly represented as an object of his retributive justice. The more especially may such a consideration have weighed with the prophet, as one of the prevailing tendencies of the time was to overlook the hand of God in the present elevation of Babylon to its high ascendancy, and to fret against the dominion which God for a season had given her over the nations. Her final desolation, however, in common with that of all earthly dominions, was included in the prophecy already considered (chap. 17:22-24), and, as we shall see, is still more distinctly embraced in some subsequent predictions. But to proceed now with the denunciations contained in this chapter.

I. The judgment of Ammon (vers. 1-7).

1 The word of the LORD came again to me, saying,

2 Son of man, set your face against the Am-mon-ites and prophesy against them.

3 And say to the Am-mon-ites, Hear the word of the Lord GOD. Thus says the Lord GOD: Because you said, Aha, against My sanctuary when it was defiled, and against the land of Israel when it was ruined, and against the house of Judah when they went into captivity –

4 therefore, behold, I will deliver you to the men of the east for a possession. And they shall set their palaces in you and make their dwellings in you. They shall eat your fruit, and they shall drink your milk.

5 And I will make Rab-bah a stable for camels, and the Am-mon-ites a crouching-place for flocks. And you shall know that I am the LORD.

6 For thus says the Lord GOD: Because you have clapped *your* hands and stamped your feet, and rejoiced in heart with all your spite against the land of Israel,

7 behold, therefore I will stretch out My hand on you and will deliver you as a prize to the nations. And I will cut you off from the people, and I will cause you to perish out of the countries. I will destroy you, and you shall know that I am the LORD.

The feelings attributed to the Ammonites in these verses are evidently those of bitter hostility toward the covenant-people, and that mainly on religious grounds. The first element in their joy respecting the desolations of Israel was because the sanctuary of God was profaned, seeing in that, as they thought, the triumph of heathenism over the rival claims of Jehovah. At an earlier period, most probably in the time of Jehoshaphat, we find this feeling ascribed to them in its most offensive form in Ps. 83, where the combined enemies of Judah, headed by Ammon and Moab (for it is said of the others merely, that *"they stretched out the hand of the children of Lot"*), are represented as saying: *"Let us cut them off from being a nation, that the name of Israel may be no more in remembrance; let us take the houses of God for a possession."* Now, at length, this impious wish was for the present realized. The long-cherished grudge against the chosen seed is gratified; and, as persons in an ecstasy of delight at what they greatly desired, but hardly expected to see accomplished, they clapped their hands and shouted their huzzas over the prostrate and captive foe. It would appear also, from 2 Kings 24:2, that they took an active part, along with the Chaldeans, in accomplishing the destruction.

Viewed, therefore, in respect to their state of feeling, the Ammonites were, in the strictest sense, enemies of God; they were warring with the purposes of Heaven; and expressly on this account is the judgment here denounced against them, – a judgment which declared that their then fertile and cultivated region should be overrun by the children of the East (the sons of Ishmael, Arabians), that their lands and cities should be pastured by flocks, and their name as a separate people become utterly extinct. The prediction began very soon to be fulfilled, for the territory of Ammon was a portion of the lands which were shortly afterwards ravaged by the armies of Nebuchadnezzar (Jer. 49:28, etc.; Josephus, Ant. 10:9. 1). And though the Ammonites still existed as a separate people when the Jews returned from Babylon, and gave indications of their old hostility, yet they appear to have been in an enfeebled condition. Some generations later they became subject, with other tribes in that district, to the Ptolemies of Egypt; and one of the Ptolemies (Philadelphus) found their capital Rabbah in so ruined a state that he caused it to be built anew, and called it after himself Philadelphia. The Ammonites are never afterwards heard of as a separate and independent people, and seem to have become gradually merged in the general Arab population. There is enough surely in these facts to justify the prediction of Ezekiel; and to point to the desolations of that region, as described by travelers in the present day, seems to us somewhat beside the purpose; for the region has long since ceased to be the territory of the children of Ammon, and it was simply as connected with them that any judgment was pronounced against it. The moment it became a desolation for the people then inhabiting it, and they themselves became scattered and dispersed, the word of Ezekiel was fulfilled; then God's displeasure against their enmity had taken full effect. It mattered little what might subsequently become of the region; and if under new occupants and a settled government it should again rise into fertility and cultivation, the word uttered by Ezekiel would not in the least be affected by it.

II. The judgment of Moab (vers. 8-11).

[8]Thus says the Lord GOD: Because Moab and Seir say, Behold, the house of Judah is like all the nations,

[9]therefore, behold, I will open the side of Moab from the cities, from his cities on his borders, the glory of the country: Beth-jesh-i-moth, Baal-me-on and Kir-i-a-tha-im,

[10]to the men of the east with the Am-mon-ites. And *I* will give them in possession so that the Am-mon-ites may not be remembered among the nations.

[11]And I will execute judgments on Moab. And they shall know that I am the LORD.

There is a certain degree of indistinctness in this sentence upon Moab, arising chiefly from the manner in which it is mixed up with Seir and Ammon. Yet we have no reason to think there is any corruption in the text. In regard to Seir, which is coupled with Moab at the beginning as joining in the congratulation that it was no better with Judah than the rest of the nations, Hitzig, in his usual smart and somewhat flippant way, declares it to be out of place, as it is also omitted in the LXX, and supposes it to have been introduced by some ignorant emendator, probably from chap. 35:10. It is quite unnecessary to resort to any such supposition. Ammon, Moab, and Edom were all contiguous countries, stretching from the land of Gilead on the north, in an unbroken line, to the shores of the Red Sea, and acted very much in concert in their hostile feelings and operations toward the covenant-people. It was not, therefore, unnatural, though it might be somewhat out of the most exact order, for the prophet to connect the two latter of these together in the expression of delight over the downfall of Judah, to show how generally the sentiment was participated in. And that Moab and Ammon should toward the close be coupled together as together – this is not to be wondered at, considering that the two tribes were originally of each other by any very definite landmarks. It was inevitable that the same destroying wave which swallowed up the one of these nations should also sweep over the other.

It would seem that the territory of Moab was, upon the whole, of a richer and more cultivated character than that of Ammon. It comprehended the district which goes by the name of the Belka, and which, even in the present times, is described by travellers as the best in all the southern parts of Syria, and on that account is the scene of many a contest among the Bedawin. Hence it is called here by the prophet a glorious land (literally, an ornament of a land); and hence also he makes particular mention of the cities belonging to it – natural indications of prosperity, and, in times of danger, important means of defence. Yet the prophet declares, these should not protect them against the coming desolation; for the Lord was going to lay open the side of border of Moab from the cities – those cities belonging to him upon his end, or extremity – viz. the extreme north-western border, where the cities here specially mentioned lay, considerably beyond the river Arnon (the old boundary of the kingdom in that direction), and even within the territory usually assigned to Ammon. These cities, with various others in the same region, were among those apportioned to Reuben in Joshua (chap. 13:15-21), but had again fallen into the hands of their original owners. Yet only for a time. The men of the East were to come down from Ammon, through the cities on the frontier, and were to waste the land of Moab, till it had ceased to be an independent nation, and had melted away among the hordes of the desert.

Of the precise manner and period of the accomplishment of this prophecy we have no record. We know that the country was overrun by the arms of Nebuchadnezzar, and must consequently have become impaired in strength. But it was chiefly by the encroachments of the men of the East, the wandering Bedawin, the great enemies of civilised and settled life, that the desolation was to be produced. And so completely had this been done, that long before the time of Christ all traces had ceased of Moab's separate existence as a people; and for many an age their country has worn the bare and ruined aspect which are the unfailing characteristics of an Arabian ascendancy.

III. The judgment of Edom (vers. 12-14).

[12]Thus says the Lord GOD: Because Edom has dealt against the house of Judah by taking vengeance, and has greatly offended and revenged himself on them,

[13]therefore thus says the Lord GOD: I will also stretch out My hand on Edom and will cut man and beast off from it; and I will make it a waste from Te-man, and those of De-dan shall fall by the sword.

[14]And I will lay My vengeance on Edom by the hand of My people Israel. And they shall do in Edom according to My anger and according to My fury. And they shall know My vengeance, says the Lord GOD.

Here, as in the prophets generally, the specific sin charged against Edom is not that simply of hatred or opposition to the covenant-people, but of deep, brooding, implacable vengeance. It was the hereditary spirit of wickedness which descended from their father Esau, who could not forgive his brother Jacob for getting precedence in regard to the blessing, but nursed for many a year his deadly purpose of revenge. It yielded at last to the unexpected and extraordinary kindness of Jacob, accompanied by the blessing of him with whom Jacob wrestled to the dawning of the day; and the two brothers appear to have spent their latter days in peace and amity. When Israel, however, grew to be a great people under God's fostering care in Egypt, and marched, with his mighty power on their side, to take possession of the land of Canaan, the old spirit revived in the posterity of Esau. They could not bear to see the younger branch rising to the pre-eminence in rank and glory, which they thought belonged of right to themselves. And thenceforth every opportunity was seized to wreak their vengeance on the children of Israel – for the most part only to draw down a deeper humiliation upon themselves, and never more than with a partial and temporary triumph – till the great period of the Babylonian conquest, when, with the fall of Jerusalem, they supposed that their object was for ever gained. So intense then was their spirit of malignity, that they are represented as not merely taking part with the Babylonians in the last catastrophe, but even as hounding on these ruthless conquerors to consummate the work of destruction, and watching along the byways to cut off the poor fugitives who fled from the presence of the enemy to seek an asylum in other lands. (Comp. especially Ps. 137; Amos. 1:11; Obad. 5:11).

Neither the vengeful spite of Edom, however, nor the might of the Babylonian conqueror, could defeat the purposes of God; and according to the Divine word, it proved that though Israel was sore broken and depressed by these calamities, she was not destroyed. Edom's malicious joy was but of short continuance; for he had the mortification of seeing his old enemy return to occupy the former habitation, and from comparatively small beginnings rise again to the position of a formidable power. The children of Edom had meanwhile been moving northwards (having been themselves gradually dispossessed in the south by the Nabathaeans), and occupied the territory of Judah as far as Hebron. But this greater proximity to the seed of Israel, and partial encroachment on their possessions, only paved the way for their utter extinction as a nation; for after many hostile encounters between the two races, the Edomites were finally subdued by John Hyrcanus, who compelled them to be circumcised, that they might be incorporated with the Jewish people. The amalgamation of course could only take place gradually; but the circumstance of the Herodian family, who were of Idumean origin, reigning as Jews over the entire region occupied by the two races, is abundant proof that it had been substantially effected about the commencement of the Christian era. From that time they ceased to be known as a distinct people, and shared partly in the fortunes of the Jews and partly in those of the neighboring Arab population.

In this external subjection of Edom to the power and dominion of Israel, there was a certain measure of fulfilment given to the word: *"I lay my vengeance upon Edom by the hand of my people;"* a word which clearly pointed to the original promise, *"The older shall serve the younger,"* and virtually declared that still God's purpose should stand – Israel is the divinely constituted governor of Edom. But it is only in a certain limited and imperfect measure that we see in such external victories and forced compliances the fulfilment of this and similar predictions. These were but the shadow and symbol of what should be accomplished, when in Israel the characteristic of the *"my people"* came to be fully realized – when they rose, in Christ and the New Testament Church, to be the head of all authority and power and dominion in the world. Viewed in respect to that elevated position, all Edomite rivalry and spite, all carnal opposition and counter-dominion, is doomed to give way, for, in Christ, Israel is governor among the nations; all must serve him, and the nation which does not serve him must perish. So there is what may be called a twofold revenge. There is first the noble revenge, of which Jacob's victory over Esau, by means of prayer and personal kindness, was the type – the revenge that melts enmity into love, and overcomes evil with good; or, according to the process described by Obadiah, *"deliverance arising first on Mount Zion,"* and then *"saviors coming up there to judge the mount of Esau,"* making Esau's offspring partakers in Jacob's blessing, whereby both alike became members of that kingdom which is the Lord's (vers. 17,21). But in so far as this blessed result fails, in so far as Edom still retains the old hatred, and refuses to bow the neck to the yoke of Jesus, then there inevitably comes the vengeance of deserved and final destruction – a vengeance executed no longer in human passion or for selfish aggrandizement, but, as here expressed, in full accordance with the Lord's mind and purpose, *"according to his anger and fury."*

This mode of understanding the prophecy satisfies to the full all its requirements, for on both sides it brings the matter into connection with the perfect adjustments of God's kingdom in Christ; but we are at a loss to see how it can otherwise meet with any adequate fulfilment. For since it speaks of the Edomites as a people, and these have long since ceased to be a people, the work of complete and perfect retribution it announces must either have taken effect in the manner now described, or it never can be accomplished. The people being gone, no changes upon the land they once occupied can satisfy the conditions of the prophecy.

IV. The judgment of the Philistines (vers. 15-17).

[15]Thus says the Lord GOD: Because the Philistines have taken vengeance; yes, have taken vengeance with a spiteful heart, to destroy for the old hatred,

[16]therefore thus says the Lord GOD: Behold, I will stretch out My hand on the Philistines and I will cut off the Cher-e-thim and will destroy the rest of the sea coast.

[17]And I will execute great vengeance on them with angry rebukes. And they shall know that I am the LORD, when I shall lay My vengeance on them.

Little requires to be said on this part of the prediction. The Philistines were the immediate neighbors of the people of Judah, on the opposite side to that occupied by Ammon and Moab. Their hereditary enmity to the covenant-people is sufficiently known. In the later times of the Hebrew commonwealth, they appear to have been in a very reduced condition, and to be quite unable to cope with Judah even in its comparatively enfeebled state. They were discomfited by Uzziah, and had their chief towns dismantled (2 Chron. 26:6). They were still further humbled and subdued in the days of Hezekiah (2 Kings 18:8). From that time we hear nothing more of them in the historical books of Scripture; but as they still retained their enmity to the cause and people of God, they were made the subject of severe denunciations in the prophets; not, however, without some prospects being intermingled of coming good, and even of an interest in the peculiar blessings of the covenant (comp. especially Zech. 9:7). As the country lay on the direct route from Egypt to Chaldea, it suffered exceedingly in the wars that were carried on between these rival kingdoms, and was the scene of some bloody conflicts. The wandering Arabs also gradually spread themselves over the district, and produced the usual results. Even at the Christian era it no longer appears as the residence of a separate and independent people; so that the vengeance threatened might even then be said to have reached its completion. Gaza alone, from its favorable position, has been able to retain something of its ancient importance, yet merely as a place of comparative wealth and commerce, and was for centuries the seat of a Christian bishop. In every way, both in respect to the evil and the good, the word of the Lord has taken full effect; and while Israel has risen aloft by being the root out of which has come the world's Deliverer and heaven-appointed King, the Philistines have become the heirs only of trouble and desolation, excepting in so far as they yielded themselves to the sway of the King of Zion, and partook, as spiritual Israelites, of the blessings of the kingdom.

CHAPTER XXVI.

THE JUDGMENT OF TYRE.

The relative importance of the prophet's communication in respect to Tyre is marked at the commencement by his prefixing the date, while in the four preceding cases the judgments alone are recorded, without any express mention of the time of their communication. The date given in the case before us has this peculiarity, that it omits the month, and mentions only the year and the day: *"the eleventh year, and the first day of the month."* Various conjuctures have been made to account for or supply this omission. Havernick supposes that the month which might be regarded such by way of distinction was meant – the month, namely, in which Jerusalem was taken and destroyed by the Chaldeans. This, however, is open to the objection (which indeed is urged by Hitzig), that the event in question, as appears from the history, was spread over two months – Jerusalem having been taken in the fourth month, but not actually reduced to ashes till the fifth (Jer. 52:6,12). Some recent commentators (Ewald, Hitzig) think the month has dropped out of the text, but that it must have been one near the close of the year, by which time the report of what had taken place in Judea may have reached the banks of the Chebar. The more probable supposition is that thrown out by the Rabbi David, and followed by Pradus, Grotius, and others, that as the prophet immediately refers to the language of Tyre at the fall of Jerusalem, and takes that as the ground of his communication to Tyre, the month most fitly to be understood is the fifth; since Jerusalem having been taken in the fourth, and Tyre being situated in the immediate neighborhood, she may well be conceived to have uttered her taunt before the close of the same month, while on the first day of the next the prophet meets it with a reply from heaven. This seems to me the most probable opinion, but certainty is unattainable, and it is a matter of comparatively little moment. That the communication was given in the eleventh year determines the period of its announcement to be very nearly contemporaneous with the fall of Jerusalem; the doom of Tyre was pronounced during the same year that witnessed the overthrow of Jerusalem.

It is well known that there were properly two Tyres, – one situated on the mainland of the Phoenician coast, in a rich and fertile plain, commonly called Palaetyrus, or Old Tyre; and another on a rocky isle, lying immediately opposite, and less than half a mile distant from the shore, which was sometimes also called New Tyre. The opinion has been very generally entertained, and is expressed in many of our most approved works (for example, Prideaux's Connection, Lowth's Commentary, Jahn's Hebrew Commonwealth), that the city upon the mainland was the only one that existed down to the time of Nebuchadnezzar; that while he was besieging this the inhabitants removed their property to the adjacent island, where they built and fortified the new and much stronger city; and that as it had been the continental Tyre before, so afterwards it was the insular Tyre which was renowned for its commercial greatness and prosperity. More accurate investigations, however, have shown the groundlessness of this opinion. Vitringa (on Isa. 23), who is also followed by Bishop Newton on the Prophecies, has produced authorities to show that both the cities existed at a time considerably prior to that of our prophet, and that insular Tyre appears, from the earliest accounts, to have laid claim to a very remote antiquity. He understands Josephus to speak of this Tyre, when he says that it was built 240 years before the Temple of Solomon (Antiq. 8:3. 1). Besides, it is evident from the passage quoted by Josephus out of Menander (Antiq. 9:14), a passage avowedly taken from the Tyrian archives, that it was not the continental but the insular city which Shalmaneser, king of Assyria, besieged for five years, and with so little success that he was obliged to relinquish the attempt. At that time, therefore, nearly a century and a half before the destruction of Jerusalem, it not only existed, but had reached such maturity of strength that it could withstand the whole might of the Assyrian empire.

Indeed, the evidences that remain of the strength and importance of ancient Tyre seem all to point to the insular rather than the continental city. The name also, צוֹר, Zor, rock, rock-city, suits exactly the insular, but not the continental one, which was built on a smooth plain. Hence some have recently maintained (in particular, Hengstenberg, De Rebus Tyriorum, also Havernick here) that the insular Tyre was the original, as it certainly was the chief city, and that Palaetyrus was a more recent and inferior place, though closely connected with the other, and rather a suburb of it than an entirely separate and independent city. This view obtains some confirmation from what is known of the procedure of many of the early Grecian colonists in founding maritime settlements. "An island close adjoining to the coast, or an outlying tongue of land connected with the continent by a narrow isthmus, and presenting some hill sufficient for an acropolis, seems to have been considered as the most favorable situation for Grecian colonial settlement."[1] Possibly enough the Tyrian settlers would not, at the very outset of their career, resort to the island to lay the foundations of their future greatness; it is more in accordance with the laws of probability, and with the natural course of things, to suppose that a city existed first upon the shore, and that the island only came to be occupied after a considerable degree of prosperity had already been reached, and when the advantages of its position for security and defence had been fully ascertained. But it is quite compatible with this opinion that the rock-island may have given to both places the name by which they are known to history; first, because the protection and harborage it afforded were of prime importance even to the continental city, and then because in process of time the other actually became the chief seat of government and commerce. Such is the view maintained at great length by Movers (Das Phonizische Alterthum, I. 100. 6), who believes continental Tyre to have been actually the oldest and, till the time, at least, of the Assyrian empire, the greatest of the two; but holds that they were properly but one city, and were often so viewed by ancient writers, who under the general name of Tyre sometimes refer more to the one, sometimes more to the other, or include both.

But leaving the question of the comparative priority of the two cities, which is of no practical moment, the fact chiefly to be borne in mind when proceeding to consider the prophecy on Tyre is, that there actually were two cities which then went by the name of Tyre, and that the insular one is kept prominently in view. In some parts of the description reference is made to a population and cities upon the land; but there can be no doubt that the Tyre spoken of as the seat of commercial power and greatness is the sea-grit rock and city, perched, as it were, in pride and security among the waters. Keeping in view this as the actual state of things, we shall have no difficulty in seeing the property of the different parts of the prophet's delineation, and we shall also find that the judgment denounced is in perfect accordance with the historical results in respect to the state and cities of Tyre.

The word uttered by Ezekiel on the subject falls into three parts, which are distributed into so many chapters. The first, contained in chap. 26, records specifically the sin on account of which Tyre was destined to become the object of Divine retribution, the severe and terrible overthrow that was to be brought upon her greatness, and the means and instruments that were to be employed in effecting it. The second, which occupies the whole of chap. 27, is a lamentation over the downfall and prostration of so much earthly magnificence, busy merchandise, and long-continued prosperity. And the last, which takes up nearly the whole of chap. 28, consists of another lamentation, more immediately addressed to the king, and forming a sort of elegy upon the humiliation and dishonor which were to come over all the pride and vain-glory that in him had towered aloft above everything human, and had even vaunted itself against the Most High. The prophecy in its entire compass affords a most characteristic specimen of the peculiarities of Ezekiel's manner, especially in regard to the singularly life-like character of his representations, his tendency to crowd the picture by a multiplicity of minute details, and his disposition to see the old reviving itself again in the new. There is also this further peculiarity, which pervades all Ezekiel's predictions regarding the heathen kingdoms, that the dark side only is exhibited to our view. The judgments he utters are judgments without mercy, reigning to complete destruction, because the kingdoms are contemplated by him simply in their relation of hostility to the cause and kingdom of the Lord. He would lead us to behold in them so many exemplifications of the fall and doom of heathendom, in contrast to the destiny of Israel, to which belonged the resurrection and the life, the dominion and the glory. Hence he looks no farther here than to the ruin of Tyre; while in the closely-related and earlier prophecy of Isaiah (chap. 23), the prospect is held out at the close of a period of blessing, when, partially recovered from her desolations, Tyre should turn to the Lord, and her merchandise and her hire should be holiness to him.

The word contained in this 26th chapter naturally falls into four divisions: – The sin of Tyre; her coming doom; the instruments and means of executing it; and the effect to be produced on other nations by her sad reverse and miserable downfall.

The first of these divisions is despatched in a single verse:

[1] And in the eleventh year, in the first *day* of the month, the word of the LORD came to me, saying,

[2] Son of man, because Tyre has said against Jerusalem, Aha! She *who was* the gates of the people is broken; she has turned to me; she is laid waste, I shall be filled.

The mind of Tyre is uttered in a few broken sentences, but these plainly enough indicating her satisfaction at the destruction of Jerusalem, and the hope she entertained of turning it to good account. Tyre being a city of merchants, all bent on the one object of plying their worldly interest and increasing their gains, she is represented as contemplating the fall of Jerusalem in a merely commercial light. To some extent Jerusalem had been a rival, as her gate – in Oriental cities the common resort for business as well as justice – had been a market-place, where the inland traders of different countries had been wont to meet for traffic. And it appeared a matter of congratulation to Tyre that this should no longer be the case; for the tide of merchandise which had hitherto flowed in that direction would now, she expected, find its way to her; she would obtain a still more exclusive command of the Syrian trade, and so would get her own coffers more abundantly replenished by means of the desolation that was alighting on Jerusalem.

It does not appear that there was anything like direct hostility between Tyre or the people of Phoenicia generally, and the inhabitants of Judah. It would rather seem that the relation between the two regions was throughout a peaceful character; as it was connected with mutual advantage. Even in the days of David and Solomon, when Israel was at the very summit of her glory, there is no appearance of bitter animosity or jealous rivalry on the part of the Tyrians, such as was displayed by other surrounding nations; but on the contrary, a ready cooperation in the transactions of business, and a neighborly interchange of the civilities of life. This is no more than what might have been expected, as the Phoenicians were chiefly devoted to commerce; and being possessed of a small land-territory, it was their obvious interest to cultivate friendly relations with the Jews and the other inhabitants of Syria, from whom they derived their principal supplies of corn. It was impossible, however, that there should have been an intimate and cordial agreement between them and Israel, so long as the worship of Jehovah was not altogether proscribed at Jerusalem. One of the most formidable adversaries with which that worship ever had to contend had sprung from the Phoenician territory, – the infamous Jezebel having been a daughter of the king of Zidon. And there can be no doubt that the commercial intercourse that subsisted between the Phoenicians and the covenant-people, considering the strong idolatrous tendencies of the latter, must often have proved a snare to their souls, or even a direct source of corruption. This, indeed, is plainly intimated by Ezekiel, when, in immediate connection with the desolating judgments that were to be executed upon the Phoenicians,, he brings out the result, that a pricking *"brier should no longer be found in the house of Israel, nor a grieving thorn in those that were round about them"* (chap. 28:24).

Yet we must distinguish between this kind of latent antipathy and the avowed hostility, the persecuting bitterness, manifested by the nations whose doom is recorded in the preceding chapter. Nothing of the latter description is here, or anywhere else, charged upon Tyre. It was her intense worldly-mindedness, her all-engrossing pursuit of the interest of merchandise, and the selfish avarice and pride engendered by her commercial greatness and political strength, – it was simply this, though viewed also as having its sinfulness aggravated by her heartless indifference regarding the fate of Jerusalem, her hope of being able to turn even that to personal advantage, and subsequently, an actual trafficking in the lives and liberties of the vanquished Jews (Amos. 1:9; Joel 3:6), that constituted the peculiar guilt of Tyre, and called for the righteous retributions of Heaven. In that particular region where God had been pleased to set up his kingdom, she stood pre-eminently the world's representative, in its towering ambition, its fleshly confidences, and its eager prosecution of selfish ends and purposes, in utter disregard or proud defiance of the will and glory of Jehovah. And being such, in a situation where she might have learned better things, it was her just doom that she should be made a perpetual monument of the instability and emptiness of all that the world can secure for its most successful votaries. *"The Lord of hosts hath purposed it, to stain the pride of all glory, and to bring into contempt all the honorable of the earth"* (Isa. 23:9).

This coming doom of Tyre is described with graphic energy, and, in respect to its last issues, in four simple verses:

[3]Therefore thus says the Lord GOD: Behold, I am against you, O Tyre. And *I* will cause many nations to come up against you, as the sea causes its waves to come up.

[4]And they shall destroy the walls of Tyre and break down her towers. I will also scrape her dust from her and make her like the top of a rock.

[5]It shall be *for* the spreading of nets in the middle of the sea. For I have spoken, says the Lord GOD. And it shall become a spoil to the nations.

[6]And her daughters who are in the field shall be killed by the sword; and they shall know that I am the LORD.

There is nowhere to be found in prophecy so striking and minute a description of the melancholy reverse which was to take place in the fortunes of Tyre, and of the utter prostration to which she was to be reduced. But before looking at the particular parts of the description, and inquiring how far it corresponds with the facts of history, we must bring into view the next section, which connects with the coming desolation the instruments that were to be employed in producing it.

[7]For thus says the Lord GOD: Behold, I will bring Neb-u-chad-nez-zar king of Babylon on Tyre, a king of kings from the north, with horses and with chariots and with horsemen and with companies and many people.

[8]He shall kill your daughters with the sword in the field. And he shall make a fort against you and cast a mound against you and lift up a shield against you.

[9]And he shall set engines of war against your walls, and with his axes he shall break down your towers.

[10]Because of his many horses, their dust shall cover you. Your walls shall shake at the noise of the horsemen, and of the wheels,

and of the chariots, when he shall enter into your gates, as men enter into a city in which a break is made.

11 With the hoofs of his horses he shall trample all your streets. He shall kill your people by the sword, and your strong troops shall go down to the ground.

12 And they shall make a spoil of your riches, and make a prey of your merchandise. And they shall break down your walls and destroy your desirable houses. And they shall lay your stones and your timber and your dust in the midst of the water.

13 And I will cause the noise of your songs to cease; and the sound of your harps shall not be heard any more.

14 And I will make you like the top of a rock. You shall be *a place* to spread nets upon; you shall be built no more. For I the LORD have spoken, says the Lord GOD.

It is necessary here, first of all, to look to the part which Nebuchadnezzar was predicted to take in the punishment of Tyre; for it admits of no doubt that the prophet represents the victorious assault of that monarch as the commencement of Tyre's degradation. But to what extent precisely do the terms of the prediction warrant us to carry the result of Nebuchadnezzar's hostility? Does it positively ascribe to him both the capture and the complete destruction of the city? Unquestionably the capture of it, and, of course, along with that the destruction, to some extent, of its power and splendor; but not necessarily anything further. It is plainly foretold that Nebuchadnezzar and his army should enter the city by storm, spread terror and dismay among its inhabitants, and generally inflict a blow on the strength and prosperity of the state. But no one even moderately acquainted with the characteristics of the prophetic style, can be ignorant how usual it is to connect a delineation of events with some grand starting-point, as if all were to spring immediately from it, while ages, perhaps, were needed to consummate the process. Thus Isaiah, in announcing the doom of Babylon (chap. 13), introduces the Medes as the instruments of her coming fall; and without a break, without an intimation of any future conquerors or any other adverse influences, goes on to paint, in the strongest terms, her utter ruin and desolation, though this end was not to be reached till many a century had revolved after the conquest by the Medes, and many a hostile element besides had played its part on the devoted city. But still it was neither mistake nor caprice to connect the result so peculiarly with the Median conquest; for that was the first link in the long chain of evil – the first deadly blow that was never to be properly healed again; it was such a beginning or sorrows as already foreboded the coming end. In like manner Jeremiah, speaking of the Philistines (with whom he also couples those of Tyre and Sidon), and foretelling the destined prostration of the country, even to a state of hopeless exhaustion, points merely to the destructive agency of the king of Babylon, as if he saw in that the fountainhead of the whole evil. How many similar examples also might be referred to of predictions entirely opposite as to their substance, but perfectly alike as to the mode of representation – predictions of good and not of evil, but which connect with a particular event (such as the birth of Christ) a long line of operations or issues which many an age should be required to develope? In all such cases, the Omniscient Spirit that animated the prophets perceived in the particular fact specified the commencement of the entire series of related events; so that from the outset he made known this as the germinant force – the sure sign and earnest of all that might otherwise be needed to accomplish the predicted result.[8]

Such, there can be no reasonable doubt , is the manner in which the prophecy respecting Tyre ought to be interpreted. The prophet distinctly announces Nebuchadnezzar as the beginner of the work of judgment, but not on that account its sole and final executor. It would have been to act against all probability, in despite of the commonest rules and lessons of experience, if he had given it forth as his conviction that one individual should extinguish the very existence of Tyre, and, as by a single stroke, reduce her from being the first commercial power in the world to the condition of a shattered fortress and a nearly unpeopled rock. Common sense alone, apart from the principles of the prophetic style, might satisfy us that such could not be the meaning of the prophet; and the change in the narration at ver. 12, from the individual to the general, gives no obscure intimation of the real import of the description. Up to that point it is Nebuchadnezzar who does it all; he who storms the city, effects a breach in its walls, slays and subdues and triumphs. But as if what he did only served to pave the way for what was to be carried forward by many other hands, the language then becomes quite general: "*And they shall spoil thy wealth, and make a prey on thy merchandise,*" etc.; in short, a progressive work of spoliation and trouble, until she becomes a helpless and a hopeless ruin.

We shall not say it is for the purpose of fastening upon the prophet a more distinct charge of error, when Hitzig alleges it as certain that the passage ascribes to Nebuchadnezzar the total destruction of Tyre, – a thing "which notoriously was not accomplished" (p. 227), – but we have no hesitation in saying that such an assertion is made in palpable disregard of one of the commonest principles of prophetical interpretation. The whole that the prophet can in fairness be understood to declare is, that Nebuchadnezzar should by violent means become master of Tyre, and thus commence the process of her downfall – a process which might be delayed, but would never altogether cease till the period of her complete destruction. But the question still remains: Did the king of Babylon actually do what is here affirmed of him? Did he in truth gain possession of the city, and subject Tyre to his dominion? This is now positively denied (by Hitzig, first in his Commentary on Isaiah, chap. 23, and again in his
indicates nothing as to the result of the expedition against Tyre, excepting that it yielded
before the world as a self-contrived imposter? Or, if he was so regardless himself about
contest. And how likely that, before the close, they would take the precaution of securing
assertion, since at chap. 29:18 he makes mention of the Divine commission to Nebuchadnezzar to go against Egypt, because "*he had served a great service against Tyre, yet had he no wages for his army.*" This is construed into a virtual confession that he had not taken and spoiled Tyre, but had been obliged to desist from the undertaking after the loss of much time and treasure. But it is manifestly a hasty conclusion; for the passage indicates nothing as to the result of the expedition against Tyre, excepting that it yielded no booty as a recompense adequate to the toil and labor that had been spent in it. And surely this might well have been the case, even if the expedition had been successful, considering that it lasted for the extraordinary period of thirteen years. For how much of the available wealth of the Tyrians must have been wasted during such a protracted contest. And how likely that, before the close, they would take the precaution of securing what was left in their ships or their colonies. This is what Jerome expressly affirms to have been done;[9] and it is also what we know to have happened to a very considerable extent in connection with the next great siege Tyre sustained, though it only lasted as many months as the other did years – that, namely, conducted by Alexander the Great (Quint. Cur. 4:3; Diod. Sic. 17:41).

It is, therefore, to adduce that subsequent passage in Ezekiel for more than it can fairly substantiate, when it is produced as a counter testimony to the one before us; for anything that it contains, Nebuchadnezzar may have executed to the full what is here ascribed to him respecting Tyre. And this oracle is so far borne out by the evidence of collateral testimony, that both Menander of Ephesus and Philostratus report, from the Phoenician annals, a thirteen years' seige of Tyre by Nebuchadnezzar (Josephus, 100. Apion, 1:20; Ant. 10:11. 1). True, but then it is one thing to besiege, and another to carry the siege; these profane authors make no mention of this, and that no-mention is held as a proof by those who would fain detect some flaw in the evidence, that the city was not taken by the king of Babylon. One would have thought that, on the supposition of only selfish principles influencing the mind of Ezekiel – allowing him but a measure of common sense, to say nothing of any higher endowments – he would have cancelled that portion of his writings which had announced Nebuchadnezzar as the conqueror of Tyre if the word had palpably proved a mistaken augury. Could he possibly wish to appear before the world as a self-convicted imposter? Or, if he was so regardless himself about the character of his own consistency, how certainly would Ezra and the elders, when making up the Jewish canon, have rejected an oracle which events, still fresh in the recollection of all, had proved to be false! The supposition is every way incredible; and besides, there in not an entire want of external evidence that Nebuchadnezzar succeeded in his attempts against Tyre, for both the heathen writers above referred to, in the passages quoted by Josephus from their abstract of Phoenician affairs, represent the king of Babylon as having made himself master of all Phoenicia, which could with no propriety have been done if the principal Phoenician state had successfully withstood his assault. And it admits too much of no doubt that in the history of the period the Phoenician interest is presently afterwards found in a depressed condition, the hereditary monarchy of Tyre ceases, and she is first goverened by a joint magistracy, then gets a king from Babylon; also during the Persian dynasty, which very soon supplanted that of Babylon, Tyre is named after Zidon, as if it had become the second in rank, and both Tyre and Zidon appear in the train of the new lords of the world as tributary states, – all plainly implying some great work of conquest going before, and compelling the proud mistress of the seas to take this inferior place. To say that the long siege of thirteen years may have so far wasted her resources as to render it politic or necessary for her to descend to such a subordinate position, is an assumption alike gratuitous and improbable, since nothing could have contributed so much to foster the pride and confirm the ascendancy of Tyre as the circumstance of having so long, if she had but successfully, defied the mighty conqueror of nations. Not her successful resistance, but only her subjection, could account for so altered a turn in her affairs.[10]

In regard to the future. fortunes of Tyre, all is matter of well-known and ascertained history; and the result has been a remarkable verification of the words of the prophet. After the times of Nebuchadnezzar, the next great blow struck at its greatness and prosperity, was the conquest of it by Alexander, which took place about 322 years before the Chistian era, and which was only gained after he had, with incredible pains, connected the mainland with the island by a mound or causeway. The stones of old Tyre were all used in the construction of this huge work of art; and so well compacted had it been from the first, that in continued ever afterwards to stand, and in the course of time has grown, by the gradual accumulations of sand, to the breadth of about half a mile. The site of Tyre, therefore, ceased from the time of Alexander to be an isolated rock, and became, what it still remains, a peninsula. It again, however, endured a long siege in the time of Antigonus, one of Alexander's successors, but was obliged to yield at last. Still, even in New Testament times, it had not altogether lost its prosperity. It was even then a place of considerable traffic, and was known in the first centuries as the seat of a Christian bishop. Though nothing compared with what it had been in former ages, it continued to be a place of considerable importance and great strength. The Crusaders in 1124 only got possession of it after a siege of nearly five months, and were surprised at the splendor of its houses and the strength of its fortifications. Though it continued for a long period to withstand the arms of the Saracens, yet ultimately (about the beginning of the 14th century) it fell into their hands, and they appear to have soon razed its fortifications, as they did also those of Sidon and Beirut; for shortly afterwards Abulfeda speaks of it as being in a state of desolation and ruin. The travellers who in more recent times have been on the spot, have all delivered an unvarying testimony concerning it, describing it as a heap of ruins, "not so much as one entire house left, and only a few poor fishermen haboring themselves in the vaults" (Maundrell). The growth and export of tobacco to Egypt has tended slightly to improve its condition during the present century; but the accumulation of sand in its harbors, which has rendered them too shallow for large vessels, and the more favorable position of Beirut at a short distance, prevent the hope of Tyre's ancient glory ever returning to her. The remains of her former magnificence lie for ever too much buried in the deep, and she can never again be the homestead of merchant princes, but only at most the abode of fishermen and a resort for the smaller craft of traders. So surely does the word of God travel on to its accomplishment, though ages may elapse in the process, and seeming impossibilities have to be vanquished before the destined result can be reached.

The remaining verses in the chapter (vers. 15-21) have respect to the impression which the overthrow of Tyre was fitted to produce upon other maritime nations, and more especially her own colonial possessions.

[15]Thus says the Lord GOD to Tyre: Shall not the isles shake at the sound of your fall, when the wounded cry, when the slaughter is made in your midst?

[16]Then all the princes of the sea shall come down from their thrones and lay away their robes and put off their embroidered garments. They shall clothe themselves with trembling; they shall sit on the ground and shall tremble at *every* moment, and be amazed at you.

[17]And they shall take up a mourning for you, and say to you, How you are destroyed, *you who* lived by the sea," the famous city which was strong in the sea, she and her people who caused their terror to be on all who lived in it! [12]

[18]Now the isles shall tremble in the day of your fall. Yes, the isles that are in the sea shall be troubled at your end.

[19]For thus says the Lord GOD: When I shall make you a ruined city, like the cities that have no people; when I shall bring up the deep on you, and great waters cover you;

[20]when I shall bring you down with those who go down into the pit, with the people of old time, and shall set you in the low parts of the earth, in places ruined in days of old, with those who go down to the pit, so that you have no people – and *when* I shall set glory in the land of the living – [13]

[21]I will make you a terror, and you shall not be. Though you are sought for, yet you shall never be found again, says the Lord GOD.

By the isles or sea-coasts, and princes of the sea, in the earlier part of this passage, are chiefly to be understood the maritime powers in different places, colonies of Tyre, with which she traded and kept up a very close connection.[14] Even the greatest and most influential of these, Carthage in Africa, was accustomed to send a yearly present of gifts to the temple of the Tyrian Hercules; and, as the mother-city, Tyre still had the honor of giving high-priests to here colonial dependencies. Being thus connected by the sacred tie of religion, as well as by the regular intercourse of trade with these maritime settlements along the coasts of the Mediterranean, we can easily understand how her humiliation would send a thrill of distress through all the affiliated states, and make them fear also for their own prosperity. The description given of this, however, evidently partakes to a considerable extent of the ideal; and we are not to suppose that the rulers of these states were actually to divest themselves of their royal garments, and sit as mourners upon the ground: what is meant is, that the effect produced would be of a kind that would have its just and fitting expression in such natural indications of sorrow. The prophet seems to have before his eye the account of Nineveh's repentance at the preaching of Jonah. And the feeling of trouble and dismay which then pervaded that great city, when it seemed to stand on the verge of destruction, was now, in like manner, to pervade the colonial settlements and trading associates of Tyre when they heard the report of her overthrow.

What is said of Tyre herself at the close is also entirely figurative. She is described as a person going to be submerged under the waters that encompassed her, and sent from the land of the living to tenant the lower regions of the dead, the land of gloom and forgetfulness, where the departed of primeval time had their abode. In plain terms, Tyre (like the king of Babylon, in the 14th chapter of Isaiah) was to take rank with the dead, and be no more numbered with the living. But, of course, it is the Tyre that then was which is meant – the proud, imperial mistress of the seas; as such, she was to cease to have a local habitation and a name in the earth, she was to be found only among the departed. That there should still be a Tyre on the same spot where the ancient city stood, is nothing against the description; for this poor and shrivelled thing is no longer the Tyre of the prophet – that is gone, never to return again. And to apply such expressions as *"she shall be no more," "she shall be sought for, but not be found,"* only to old Tyre, as we find modern travellers very commonly doing, – because the very site of this is not precisely known, – is to misapprehend the nature of the description, it is to turn a figurative into a literal delineation, and to apply only to a portion of the city what was plainly meant of the whole. It is of Tyre in her completeness, insular as well as continental, that the prophet speaks, and she is long since written among the dead.

CHAPTER XXVII.

THE LAMENTATION UPON TYRE, WITH AN ACCOUNT OF HER FORMER GREATNESS AND PROSPERITY.

It seems somewhat like a freak of fancy in Ezekiel to dwell at such length, as he does in this chapter, on the commercial greatness of Tyre; and to point out, with such elaborate minuteness, both the circumstances connected with her thriving and wide-spread merchandise, and the notes of lamentation and pity that should be raised over her coming ruin. It is the mark, certainly, of a somewhat peculiar cast of mind, and has no exact parallel in any of the other prophets, who usually present us with only a few general and characteristic traits, when they have occasion to speak of the existing condition of a state or people, as contrasted with what they may be destined to become. Yet the prophet, in this singular delineation, was not the less guided by the Spirit of God in what he wrote, nor was the delineation itself less fitted to serve the ends for which such prophecies were written. It was just Ezekiel's way – the way peculiarly suited to his lively and realistic cast of thought – of conveying a distinct and deep impression concerning the things of Tyre; first, her pre-eminent greatness at the centre of the world's wealth and merchandise, and then her complete annihilation in respect to all that had formerly distinguished her; that so the omniscient eye of God, in foretelling what was to happen, and his overruling providence in accomplishing it, might be more strikingly exhibited. With so full and lively a picture before us of what Tyre was in the prophet's own time, we can the more easily discern the hand of God in rendering her what she has become, and also the Divine foresight which so long beforehand declared that it was certainly to be.

In regard to the form of the delineation, it is a trope. Tyre's existing condition and coming destiny are exhibited under the figure of a ship, constructed of the best materials, manned and equipped in the first style, trading in all mercantile commodities, and with all parts of the commercial world; but at length brought into tempestuous seas, shipwrecked, and involved in irrecoverable ruin. This is the general character of the description; but, as usually happens in the more lengthened tropes of the prophet, the figure occasionally gives place to the reality; the desire to be clear and graphic breaks in, at various points, on the uniformity of the representation. This is particularly the case at ver. 9, where all the ships of the sea are represented as having a place in this figurative vessel; and at ver. 11, where towns and walls, and an armed force, as of a city, are mentioned. But for so long a description the figure is wonderfully sustained, though it has in several places been marred by wrong translations. We shall simply present a translation of the whole, and subjoin a few explanatory remarks on those parts which are more obscure deeming it unnecessary to enter at any length into the historical points referred to in the description as regards the commercial relations of antiquity. These have more in them of an antiquarian than of a religious interest, and may be examined by such as have Movers, or what is now more accessible, Heeren's Historical Researches, where the trade and policy of the Phoenicians have received due attention.

[1]The word of the LORD came to me, saying,

[2]Now, son of man, take up a mourning for Tyre.

[3]And say to Tyre, O you who are placed at the entrance of the sea, a merchant of the people for many isles, thus says the Lord GOD: O Tyre, you have said, I am of perfect beauty.

[4]Your borders are in the middle of the seas, your builders have perfected your beauty.

5 They have made all your *ship* boards of fir-trees of Se-nir; they have taken cedars from Leb-a-non to make masts for you.

6 They have made the oaks of Ba-shan your oars; the company of the Ash-u-rites have made your benches of ivory from the isles of Chit-tim.

7 Fine linen with embroidered work from Egypt was what you spread out to be your sail; blue and purple from the isles of E-li-shah was what covered you.

8 The people of Sidon and Arvad were your seamen. Your wise ones, O Tyre, *who* were in you, were your pilots.

9 The elders of Ge-bal and her wise men were your calkers in you. All the ships of the sea with their seamen were in you to do business with your merchandise.

10 Those of Persia and of Lud and of Phut were in your army, your men of war. They hung the shield and helmet in you. They set forth your glory.

11 The men of Arvad were with your army on your walls all around, and short swordsmen were in your towers. They hung their shields on your walls all around. They have made your beauty perfect.

12 Tar-shish was your merchant because of the multitude of all riches; with silver, iron, tin, and lead, they traded in your fairs.

13 Javan, Tubal and Me-shech were your merchants. They traded the persons of men and vessels of copper in your markets.

14 Those of the house of To-gar-mah traded in your fairs with horses and horsemen and mules.

15 The men of De-dan were your merchants; many isles took the merchandise of your hand. They brought you horns of ivory and ebony *for* a present.

16 Syria was your merchant because of the multitude of your works. They did business in your fairs with emeralds, purple and embroidered work, and fine linen, and coral, and agate.

17 Judah and the land of Israel were your merchants. They traded in your market wheat from Min-nith and Pan-nag, and honey, and oil and balm.

18 Damascus was your merchant in the multitude of your works, for the multitude of all riches, in the wine of Hel-bon and white wool.

19 Dan and Javan also, going here and there, traded in your fairs; bright iron, cas-si-a, and cal-a-mus were in your market.

20 De-dan was your merchant in precious clothes for chariots.

21 Arabia, and all the princes of Kedar traded with you in lambs and rams and goats. In these *they were* your merchants.

22 The merchants of Sheba and Ra-a-mah were your merchants. They traded in your fairs with all the best spices, and with all precious stones and gold.

23 Haran, and Can-neh and Eden, the merchants of Sheba, Assh-ur *and* Chil-mad were your merchants.

24 These were your merchants in all sorts of things, in blue clothing and embroidered work and rich clothing in chests tied with cords and made of cedar, among your merchandise.

25 The ships of Tar-shish sang of you in your market. And you were filled and made very glorious in the middle of the sea.

26 Your rowers have brought you into great waters; the east wind has broken you in the middle of the sea.

27 Your riches, and your fairs, your merchandise, your seamen, and your pilots, your calkers and the traders of your merchandise, and all your men of war who are in you, and all your company which is in your midst shall fall into the middle of the sea in the day of your ruin.

28 The waves shall shake at the sound of the cry of your pilots.

29 And all who handle the oar, the mariners, all the pilots of the sea, shall come down from their ships. They shall stand on the land,

30 and shall cause their voice to be heard against you, and shall cry bitterly, and shall throw dust on their heads. They shall wallow themselves in the ashes.

31 And they shall make themselves bald for you and clothe themselves with sackcloth, and they shall weep for you with bitterness of heart and bitter wailing.

32 And in their wailing they shall take up a weeping for you and weep over you, *saying,* What *city* is like Tyre, like the *city* destroyed in the middle of the sea?

33 When your goods went forth out of the seas, you filled many people. You made the kings of the earth rich with the multitude of your riches and of your goods.

34 In the time *when* you shall be broken by the seas in the depths of the waters, your goods and all your company in your midst shall fall.

35 All the people of the isles shall be amazed at you, and their kings shall be grievously afraid; their faces shall be troubled.

36 The merchants among the people shall hiss at you You shall be a terror and shall never be any more.

It may be noted that the remark made at the close of last chapter is equally applicable here. The coming destruction of Tyre is viewed in contrast with her existing greatness; and as it was her commercial prosperity which made her what she was, so the loss of this, which the prophet foresaw was certainly to take place, would in a manner terminate her existence. It is, of course, quite consistent with this, that some remains of a city may still be found; it is plainly implied in other parts of the prophecy that such should be the case, as when she is spoken of as a spreading-ground for nets; for who were to spread these but the fishermen still frequenting her ports, and still dwelling among her ruins? But the Tyre of antiquity no longer exists; her place is no more found; and a voice of lamentation over her fallen and irrecoverable greatness is naturally raised by those who contemplate her condition.

CHAPTER XXVIII. 1-19.

THE CRIMINATORY ADDRESS TO THE KING OF TYRE, AND THE LAMENTATION OVER HIS COMING DOWNFALL.

The portion of chap. 28 which relates to Tyre, may be regarded as a kind of episode to the prophecy of the two preceding chapters. It properly adds nothing to the great theme of the prophecy, but only presents it in a somewhat new aspect, by bringing prominently forward the king of Tyre, and viewing all – the prosperity, the self-elation it produced, the condemnation thence arising, and the subsequent desolation and ruin – as embodied in his personal condition and history. It is rather a matter of surprise to find that a state so thoroughly commercial as Tyre, and possessed of so limited a territory, should have had a king at all; nut in the regions of the East, and, indeed, generally in the earlier ages of the world, royalty seems to have been regarded as an indispensable element to the right management and proper dignity of a state. In such an active, bustling, and enterprising state as Tyre, however, it could not exist in the same absolute and despotic form, nor could it surround itself with the same circumstances of imposing grandeur and majesty as usually distinguished it in the larger monarchies of the East.

That proper scope and security might be found for the active energies of the Tyrians, it was necessary that a certain amount of freedom should be enjoyed by the citizens, and even a considerably share obtained in the administration of civil affairs. The king there must have been a limited, not a despotic sovereign, and could only rule as a prince among merchants, who were themselves princes.

It is not only certain that there was a hereditary king in Tyre, but the fragments of Phoenician history already referred to in the preceding chapters have also preserved the name of the king who at that precise time occupied the throne – Ithobal II. And in the king, as the natural head and representative of the whole state, the prophet sees the full embodiment, the extreme culmination, of the spirit by which the state in general was pervaded – the spirit of self-sufficiency, carnal security, and immoderate pride. These feelings, the natural product of unsanctified prosperity, penetrated the whole community of Tyre; but in the bosom of its monarch they might justly be supposed to find their chosen seat, and their ripest development. And assuming, as they necessarily did, an attitude of lofty indifference, or even of high disdain, in respect to the God of Israel, whose cause seemed then to be sinking amid deep waters while Tyre still held on her majestic course, the prophet's bosom heaved with violent emotion, and in a vein of severe and cutting irony, he exhibits the fancied superhuman greatness, the godlike independence and ascendancy of the king of Tyre, that he might magnify the more the infinite power and supremacy of him whose overruling providence was to lay all prostrate in the dust. It is substantially the same form of representation with that which was adopted by Isaiah respecting the king of Babylon, in the 14th chapter of his writings, where the proud heart of that aspiring monarch is described as scaling the very heavens and claiming to be as the Most High, but only that it might be cast down to the stones of the pit, and trodden upon as a carcase under feet of men. But here, as usual, our prophet is not satisfied with depicting in a few lively strokes the towering ambition of the earthly prince; he ransacks alike the past and the present for the most varied and striking imagery, under which to body forth its pretensions, that so he might present, in more vivid contrast, what is impiously aspired to be, with what it really was. While it was neither new nor peculiar to our prophet to speak in ironical language on such a subject, there is no single passage of Scripture, either in the Old or in the New Testament, where the irony is of so detailed a form, and is cast in altogether so peculiar a mould. Yet it is the Spirit of God that breathes in the words, revealing to our souls the impiety of all ambition, and the vanity of all greatness, which seeks its foundation and support elsewhere than in the power and goodness of the Eternal.

[1] The word of the LORD came again to me, saying,

[2] Son of man, say to the prince of Tyre. Thus says the Lord GOD: Because your heart is lifted up and you have said, I am a god, I sit in the seat of God in the middle of the seas (yet you are a man and not God, though you set your heart as the heart of God;

[3] behold, you are wiser than Daniel; there is no secret that they can hide from you!

[4] With your wisdom and with your understanding you have gotten riches for yourselves, and have gotten gold and silver into your treasuries.

[5] By your great wisdom and by your trade you have multiplied your riches, and your heart is lifted up because of your riches.)

It is the feeling of superhuman might and strength which the prophet evidently means to ascribe to the king of Tyre in the first part of this representation. Hence it is God as the El, the Supreme in power, the Mighty One, whose name and prerogative he is described as impiously arrogating to himself. And the idea is further expanded by the thought that he sits as a God, or occupies a God's seat in the midst of the seas; holding his place, as it were, in impregnable security amid the stormiest elements of nature, and knowing how to wield and control them so as to render them subservient to his own ends and interests. To ascribe this sentiment, with Hitzig, to the king of Tyre, *"because his residence juts up out of the water, much as the palace of God does out of the heavenly ocean above"* (Ps. 104:3), is indescribably flat, and a palpable misapplication besides of the passage of Scripture referred to. The Psalmist is there speaking not of the throne or habitation of God standing out from the boundless ocean of immensity (of which there is nowhere a word of Scripture), but of his constructing a sort of visible habitation for himself out of the watery vapours of the sky – the clouds, which he makes his chariots. The idea also of Havernick, though in better taste than that of Hitzig, that respect is had, in the language here ascribed to the king of Tyre, to the species of Divine honor paid to Oriental monarchs (notice of which is taken in Curtius, 10:11. 1; Josephus, 9:6. 1), is fanciful. It was scarcely possible in a city like Tyre, where the subjects necessarily pressed so close upon the king, that he could be the subject of properly religious homage. There was no room there for those wonderful personal exploits, or that mysterious seclusion and grandeur, which always formed the ground and nutriment of such profound veneration. What is here spoken as from the heart of the king of Tyre, is the proud consciousness of strength and security, which was engendered by the naturally strong position and the immense maritime resources of the state over which he reigned. This gave him such a sense of elevation and independence, as is only put into words when he is represented as claiming for himself the name and posture of Deity. It might certainly tend to foster and strengthen this feeling, as Havernick not improbably conceives, that the island, which was the seat and stronghold of the Tyrian state, possessed somewhat of a sacred character. and was regarded as peculiarly connected with the powers above. It is expressly called *"the holy island"* by Sanconiathon (p. 36, ed. Orelli); and, as already noticed, was so distinguished for the worship of Hercules, that the Tyrian colonies all reverenced it as the mother-city of their religion, not less than the original source of their political existence.

And it was only in the spirit of ancient heathenism to conclude that a state, which was considered to stand in so close a connection with the Divine, might be warranted in claiming, through its head, exemption from the common casualties of fortune, and even something like supernatural strength and absolute perpetuity of being.

In the succeeding verses (vers. 3-5) the prophet merely follows out, and ironically applies the thought which he had already ascribed to the king of Tyre. Exalting himself as a God, he was of course, in his own imagination, superior in intelligence and sagacity to the wisest of mortals; wiser even than Daniel, who, by special assistance received from Heaven, was known far and wide to have put to shame the renowned wisdom of Chaldea; and so unerring in counsel, so far-reaching in discernment, as to have surrounded the smallest territory with the most extensive commerce and the amplest resources. Not perceiving that this is spoken ironically by the prophet, and for the purpose merely of giving a tongue to the foolish thoughts which swelled the heart of the king of Tyre, that their folly and wickedness might appear to all, the ancient interpreters have given some of the sentences are interrogative turn: Art thou wiser? etc.; and most of the earlier commentators have supposed that the words here, and afterwards in vers. 12-14, were not properly used of Tyre, but were rather to be understood mystically of Satan.[1] It is not necessary now, however, to defend the plain sense of Scriptures from such arbitrary modes of interpretation, which need only to be applied to other portions, to extract from the Bible any doctrine or meaning that the capricious fancies of men might wish to find in it. Even Jerome silently admits as much; for however differently he has expressed himself elsewhere, when he comes to write his commentary on the passage he understands the whole discourse of the prince of Tyre, though he still could very imperfectly find his way to a correct explanation of the import. Let only the real character of the description be borne in mind, and there will be no difficulty in perceiving its fitting application to the king of Tyre. It belongs to that species of composition common to all languages, and frequently resorted to, especially by those who have to deal with the errors and delusions of men, in which – instead of directly disputing the mistaken views they hold, or arguing with the false spirit that actuates them – such a graphic representation is given of these as carries its own exposure or refutation along with it. Thus, here, when the prophet has asserted of the king of Tyre that while he was but a man he bore himself as God, and then proceeds to give utterance to the sentiments that necessarily grew out of this absurd and impious pretension, – that he was wiser than Daniel, that he could reveal all secrets, that his own intelligence and sagacity had secured for him the possession of all his wealth, – this could not fail to convey to every reflecting mind an impression of the thoroughly profane and godless spirit that reigned in the bosom of the king of Tyre, and of his ripeness for the judgment of Heaven. The carcase manifestly was there; now, therefore, must the eagles be gathered together.

[6]Therefore thus says the Lord GOD: Because you have set your heart as the heart of God,
[7]behold, therefore I will bring strangers on you, the terrible of the nations. And they shall draw their swords against the beauty of your wisdom, and they shall defile your brightness.
[8]They shall bring you down to the pit, and you shall die the deaths[2] of the slain in the middle of the seas.
[9]Will you yet say before him who kills you, I am God? But you shall be a man, and no god, in the hand of him who kills you.
[10]You shall die the deaths of the uncircumcised by the hand of strangers. For I have spoken, says the Lord GOD.

The judgment to be executed on the king of Tyre was thus to be exactly adapted to his guilt; it was to be such as would force on him the conviction that he had not the might and wisdom of God at his command, but, like other frail and erring mortals, was liable to be overcome and brought to destruction. This judgment, it is simply declared, was going to be executed by the hand of strangers, the terrible ones of the nations – an epithet elsewhere given to the Chaldeans (chap. 30:11, 31:12); though there is no necessity here for absolutely confining it to them. Here it only intimates that terrible instruments of vengeance should be provided, fit for executing the Divine purpose of retribution; so that destruction would surely come in its appointed time – the death, as of persons given up to the slaughter, or as of the uncircumcised, who had no interest in the covenant of Heaven, and were doomed to perish.

The delineation we have considered, first of the high presumption and peerless glory of the king of Tyre, and then of his Divine chastisement and utter ruin, is followed by another in which precisely the same topics are again handled, and in the same order. The representation, however, at the beginning, of the king's greatness and glory, while it is drawn in the same ironical vein as in the former case, is cast in an entirely different mould, and is intended to exhibit this proud monarch as a kind of normal or primeval man, the type of humanity in its best and most divine-like form; but only for the purpose of showing how incapable he was of bearing the glory, and how necessary it was that he should be visited with Divine chastisement, and brought to final ruin. The passage is not without its difficulties; but these have often been greatly aggravated by not perceiving the exact point of view from which the delineation is drawn; and hence, from the LXX. downwards, all manner of liberties have been taken with the original.

[11]And the word of the LORD came to me, saying,

[12]Son of man, take up a mourning on the king of Tyre and say to him, Thus says the Lord GOD: You fill up the measure,[3] full of wisdom and perfect in beauty.

[13]You have been in Eden the garden of God; every precious stone was your covering, the sardius, topaz, and the diamond, the beryl, the onyx, and the jasper, the sapphire, the emerald, and the carbuncle and gold.[4] The workmanship of your tabrets and of your pipes was prepared in you in the day that you were created.[5]

[14]You are the anointed cherub that covers, and I have chosen you *so*. You were on the holy mountain of God. You have walked up and down in the middle of the stones of fire.[6]

[15]You were perfect in your ways from the day that you were created, until iniquity was found in you.

[16]By the multitude of your goods they have filled your midst with violence, and you have sinned. Therefore I will cast you out of the mountain of God as defiled, and I will destroy you, O covering cherub, from the midst of the stones of fire.[7]

[17]Your heart was lifted up because of your beauty; you have spoiled your wisdom because of your brightness. I will throw you to the ground. I will lay you before kings, that they may see you.

[18]You have defiled your holy places by the multitude of your iniquities, by the iniquity of your trade. Therefore I will bring forth a fire from your midst; it shall devour you, and I will bring you to ashes on the earth in the sight of all those who see you.

[19]All those among the people who know you shall be astonished at you; you shall be a terror, and you shall never be any more.

It is clear from the very commencement of this singular passage, from the mention made here of the garden of Eden, that the representation contained in it is of an ideal character; that it is, in short, an historical parable. The kings of Tyre are first personified as one individual – an ideal man, and one complete in all natural excellence, perfect manhood. Not unnaturally so, since Tyre having sprung from a barren rock, and grown till she had become the mistress of the world's commerce, was a kind of new creation in the earth – as a state the most singular product in existence of human energy and enterprising skill. Therefore this ideal man, the representative of whatever there was of greatness and glory in Tyre, and in whom, consequently, the Tyrian spirit of self-elation and pride appear in full efflorescence, is ironically viewed by the prophet as a type of humanity in its highest states of existence upon earth. All that is best and noblest in the history of the past he sees, in imagination, meeting in this so-called beau-ideal of humanity. It was he who in primeval time trod the hallowed walks of paradise, and used at will its manifold treasures, and regaled himself with its corporeal delights. It was he who afterwards assumed the form of a cherub – ideal compound of the highest kinds of animal existence – type of humanity in its predestined state of ultimate completeness and glory; and as such, had a place assigned him among the consecrated symbols of God's sanctuary in the holy mount, where, in the immediate presence of the Most High, he overshadowed the mercy-seat. Thus occupying the highest spheres of created life, and familiar even with the sight of the Divine glory, he knew what it was to dwell amidst the consuming fire, and to walk as on burning stones of sapphire. Whatever humanity has had, or has been typified to have, of dignity and honor in the past history of God's administration, it has been thine to possess. So thou thinkest, thou ideal man, thou concentration of human excellence, thou quintessence of human greatness and pride. Thou thinkest that manhood's divinest qualities, and most honorable conditions of being, belong peculiarly to thyself, since thou dost nobly peer above all and standest alone in thy glory. Let it be so. But thou art still a man, and, like humanity itself in its most favored conditions, thou hast not been perfect before God, thou hast yielded thyself a servant to corruption. With creaturely waywardness and inconstancy thou hast gone astray on thy high places, and hast abused to the gratification of thine own lust and vanity the ample gifts and resources which should have been all employed in subservience to the will and glory of God. Therefore thou must be cast down from thy proud elevation; thou must lose thy cherubic nearness to God; the sacred and blissful haunts which thou hast defiled with thy abominations shall no longer know thee; and thou shalt henceforth be a monument to all of forfeited honors, abused privileges, and hopeless ruin.

Such we take to be the style and import of this vision. It is one of the most highly figurative representations in prophecy, and is only to be compared with Isaiah's lamentation (in chap. 14) over the downfall of the king of Babylon. It characteristically differs from this, however, in that while it moves with equal boldness and freedom in an ideal world, it clothes the ideal according to the usage of our prophet in an historical drapery, and beholds the past revived again in the personified existence of which it treats. But it is no wild play of fancy, or arbitrary indulgence of a lawless imagination. A sublime moral runs through the parable. It reads over again the great lesson of man's weakness and degeneracy, and shows how inevitably the good, when unaccompanied by a really Divine element, turns in him to corruption and ruin. In the royal head of the state of Tyre a new trial was made of humanity with the greatest earthly advantages, he being endowed with the amplest resources of wealth and art, and placed on the loftiest pinnacle of the world's wisdom and prosperity. But all in vain. The good only served, as in other cases, to feed the well-spring of human depravity; and the day of retribution could not fail to come with its recompenses of evil, and God's justice be as conspicuously displayed in the overthrow of Tyre as his goodness had been in her singular rise and prosperity. So that the cry which the prophet would utter through this parabolical history in the ears of all is, that man in his best estate – with everything that art or nature can bring to his aid – is still corruption and vanity. The flesh can win nothing for itself that it really and permanently good. It carries in its bosom a principle of self-destruction, and the more that it can surround itself with the comforts and luxuries of life, the more does it pamper the godless pride of nature, and draw down upon itself calamity and destruction. Therefore *"let not the wise man glory in his wisdom, neither let the mighty man glory in his might; let not the rich man glory in his riches; but let him that glorieth glory in this, that he understandeth and knoweth me, that I am the Lord which exercises loving-kindness, judgment, and righteousness in the earth; for in these things I delight, saith the Lord."*

CHAPTER XXVIII. 20-26.

THE JUDGMENT OF SIDON, AND THE ULTIMATE PEACE OF ISRAEL.

We have already remarked, in the introduction to this series of prophecies, that Sidon was not so properly an independent state, as rather an integral portion of the great maritime power of which Tyre was the centre. Hence in the description given by the prophet in chap. 27 of the resources of Tyre, Sidon is mentioned as contributing of her mariners to man the Tyrian vessels. Though thus, however, politically merged in Tyre, Sidon had possessed a religious connection with the covenant-people, which does not appear to have extended to Tyre, and which furnished an historical reason for the separate mention of Sidon, in addition to the circumstance of its being necessary to complete the number seven. Whether it arose from Sidon being the elder city, or from her citizens having more frequent intercourse with the Israelites, or finally, from the character of the religion prevalent in Sidon being of a more seductive and infectious character, the fact is certain, that a corrupting influence flowed in upon Israel from Sidon such as is never mentioned in connection with Tyre. So early as the time of the Judges, the gods of Sidon are named among the false deities that had acquired an ascendency over the children of Israel (Judg. 10:6). In the days of Solomon, the worship of Ashtoreth, the goddess of the Sidonians, was again openly practised (1 Kings 11:33). And that this influence never became wholly extinct, and continued even to the times of the prophet, is evident from the scene described in chap. 8, of women sitting in the attitude of mourners, and weeping for Tammuz. This was undoubtedly an importation from the territory of Sidon, where the Tammuz or Adonis-worship had its origin. And that the circumstance now referred to was not without its weight in determining the prophet to give a separate place to Sidon, may be certainly inferred, not only from the strongly historical bias of the prophet's mind, but also from the express mention at the close, of the freedom that was to be acquired for Israel, by the overthrow of such neighbors as the Sidonians, from the corrupting influences that had vexed and troubled them in times past.

The prophecy itself against Sidon is of the most general description:

[20]Again the word of the LORD came to me, saying,
[21]Son of man, set your face against Si-don and prophesy against it.
[22]And say, Thus says the Lord GOD: Behold, I am against you, O Si-don, and I will be glorified in your midst. And they shall know that I am the LORD, when I have executed judgments in her and have revealed *My* holiness in her.
[23]For I will send a plague into her, and blood into her streets. And the wounded shall be judged in her midst by the sword on her on every side. And they shall know that I am the LORD.

It was the less necessary to enter here into particulars, as from the nature of Sidon's relation to Tyre it would naturally be understood that the fortunes of the larger city must be shared in by the less. If Tyre was to fall before the adverse influences that were to assail her, and become a scene of desolation, much more should Sidon, which had far inferior resources to meet the danger. It passed through many a siege, and consequently suffered many successive blows; and though it has never altogether ceased to be an inhabited place, it has possessed for ages nothing of the relative greatness and importance which belonged to it in the time of Ezekiel. God has indeed been sanctified in her by means of the humiliating reverses she has been made to undergo.

And now the prophet turns from these scenes of desolation to the prospect of better days to come for the covenant-people, to whom the downfall of these neighboring heathen powers betokened good, as it indicated the purpose of God to rid them of what had hitherto vexed and troubled their condition.

[24]And the house of Israel shall never again have a pricking brier[1] or a wounding thorn from any of those who are all around them, who despised them. And they shall know that I am the Lord GOD.
[25]Thus says the Lord GOD: When I have gathered the house of Israel from the people among whom they are scattered, and have been sanctified in them in the sight of the nations, then they shall dwell in their land that I have given to My servant Jacob.
[26]And they shall dwell safely in it and

shall build houses and plant vineyards. Yea, they shall live safely when I have executed judgments on all those who despise them all around them. And they shall know that I am the LORD their God.

This concluding part of the prophecy evidently has respect to what was said by Moses, in Num. 33:35, regarding such of the original inhabitants of Canaan as the Israelites in their unfaithfulness might fail to drive out: *"They shall be pricks in your eyes, and thorns in your sides, and shall vex you in the land wherein you dwell."* Such in sad experience they found to be the case, and in regard to the Sidonians not less than others. The territory of Sidon lay within the bounds of the tribe of Asher; and it is expressly recorded that this tribe could not dispossess the inhabitants of Sidon (Judg l:3l). A peaceful relation in process of time sprung up between the Sidonians and their Israelitish neighbors; but this only opened the way, as we have seen, to a more pernicious and destructive influence than the open assaults of war. In leading them to depart from the pure worship of Jehovah, by the introduction of the foul rites of Ashtoreth and Adonis the Sidonians proved in the worst sense thorns in the side of the covenant-people. But the result of those judgments which God was now going to execute should be to put an end to these vexations and perverting influences. What the people themselves had failed to do, on account of their unfaithfulness to the covenant, the faithful Jehovah would accomplish by the execution of his judgments; he would extirpate these annoying briers and thorns, and allow the people to enjoy in undisturbed freedom and repose the heritage he had given in covenant to their father Jacob.

The latter part of the prediction which foretells a future period of peace and security to Israel, is a promise of coming good thrown into the form of the past – a prophecy cast in the mould of history. That the good would be realized to the full extent promised, we must certainly hold; but not, therefore, that it would be realized to the full in the precise form here adopted. For if our past investigations into the meaning of this prophet have taught us anything, it is that we must know how to distinguish between the form and the reality. Even the immediately preceding vision respecting the king of Tyre is remarkable for nothing so much as the tendency displayed in it to use the historical as the merely ideal form of the thoughts and feelings sought to be conveyed by the prophet. In the earlier part of it a completely ideal representation is given us, though under the form of history, of the pre-eminent greatness and glory of the king of Tyre; while in the latter part the form is changed, and is neither so boldly figurative nor is it thrown into the historical type. How far, therefore, in this concluding prophecy regarding Israel the historical form should be regarded, cannot be pronounced on with absolute certainty from the words themselves, but must be gathered from the course of Divine providence. The positive element in the promise – that which must be found in history, otherwise the word fails – is, that God's future dealings with his covenant-people should be such as to rid them from the annoyance and the danger to which in past times they had been exposed from the worldly greatness and the idolatrous spirit of their immediate neighbors; so that they should enjoy the peculiar blessing of the covenant in comparative peace and security. And doubtless the Lord might fulfil this promise, while all the ancient relations were allowed to stand – Israel restored to their proper territory, and the surrounding nations either entirely driven from their possessions, or so completely changed in their feelings toward Israel, and so reduced in outward circumstances, as to be no longer snares to Israel's peace and prosperity. To a very considerable extent this was the case. Such of the people as afterwards returned from their dispersions, and settled in the land of Canaan, had comparatively few struggles with their old neighbors, either as political or religious adversaries. Those neighbors had themselves become too broken and enfeebled by the reverses they experienced to exert religious adversaries. Those neighbors had themselves become too broken and enfeebled by the reverses they experienced to exert religiously the deleterious influence, or politically to inflict the evils which in their former flourishing condition they were quite able to produce. And though for a period there were trials and contests which Israel was obliged to maintain with them, yet these proved only occasional interruptions to the general peace; and for generations before the coming of our Lord it might justly be said, that Israel had no longer a thorn or a brier to plague them in their immediate neighbors. In a religious point of view – which is the one here chiefly meant – the Jews were even enabled to make reprisals upon the heathen; and it was not so much the worship of Jehovah that had to be afraid of the corrupting influence of heathenism, as rather the religions of heathenism that were endangered by the knowledge and worship of Jehovah. For instead of melting away, as of old, under the pernicious agency of surrounding idolatries and corruptions, Judaism could number its converts out of all lands, rescued from the crumbling superstitions of heathendom.

It thus appears that even in regard to the historical form of this prediction, it received a very striking and wonderful degree of fulfilment ages after he who uttered it had slept with his fathers. The Lord did bring back Israel to their own land, and by reason of the judgments he executed upon those who in past ages had troubled and vexed them, they were permitted to dwell in comparative peace, and even attained to a place of relative strength and moral ascendancy. But the prophecy should not be limited to that temporary and partial fulfilment. We see its full extent and compass of meaning only when, looking through the historical drapery and the shell of ancient relations, we contemplate Israel rising in Christ and the Church of the New Testament to be the head and centre of all that is great, permanent, and good in the world, before which everything that is adverse must fall. The heritage of Jacob is now no longer the narrow stripe of territory which was given to the seed of blessing as a temporary type and earnest, but the whole ransomed earth, which to its uttermost bounds is the destined possession of Christ and his Israel offspring. Till this great consummation is reached, the prophecy still waits for its full realization. And believing that it shall be realized, that it is the purpose of God to humble and destory every adverse power, and exalt the saints with Christ to possess the kingdom, let the Church of God ply with every means at her command the blessed work of the world's regeneration, and "*bate not a jot in heart or hope*" on account of the evil influences against her. Since it is the cause of truth and righteousness for which she contends, the victory cannot fail to be ultimately on her side.

CHAP. XXIX.
THE JUDGMENT OF EGYPT – ITS DESOLATION FOR FORTY YEARS, AND SUBSEQUENT DEGRADATION – THE FIRST INSTRUMENT OF CHASTISEMENT, NEBUCHADNEZZAR.

We come now to the last of the worldly kingdoms against which in this series the prophet was commissioned to utter the judgments of the Lord. It is also the one that occupies the largest space in the visions of the prophet, as might not unnaturally have been expected from the relative importance of Egypt, and the position it had so long occupied in the world's history. Though standing as to local situation at a much greater distance from the children of Israel than Tyre, it yet held as a kingdom a much closer connection with them, and sought to obtain the same ascendancy in the dominion of the world that Tyre did in its commerce. It was with this view, and not from any desire to benefit the little kingdom of Judah, that the king of Egypt began, about the time now under consideration, to cultivate a friendly understanding with Zedekiah, and by sending an army to his relief, obliged the Chaldeans for a time to raise the siege against Jerusalem (Jer. 37:7-11). The real object of the king of Egypt was to create a diversion against the Babylonian monarch, and, if possible, arrest the victorious career of that dangerous rival. The monarch who then sat upon the throne of Egypt was Apries, the commencement of whose reign was prosperous, and he was considered "the most fortunate monarch who had hitherto ruled in Egypt, next to his grandfather Psammitichus. He sent an expedition against the island of Cyprus, besieged and took Gaza (Jer. 47:1) and the city of Sidon, engaged and vanquished the king of Tyre by sea, and, being uniformly successful, he made himself master of Phoenicia and Palestine, recovering much of the territory and that influence in Syria which had been taken from Egypt by the victories of

Nebuchadnezzar,"[1] especially the great victory at Carchemish, in the fourth year of the reign of Jehoiakim (Jer. 46:2; 2 Kings 24:7). So proud was this king of his successes, and so secure did he think himself of his power and dominion, that he is reported to have said, not even a god could deprive him of his kingdom.[2]

It was while such a king held the sceptre of Egypt, and while he still was in the noontide of his prosperity, that Ezekiel began to utter the prophecies here recorded against him. We can therefore the more easily understand how these prophecies should speak so strongly of the pride and lordly bearing of Egypt and her king, as if an absolute and independent power had become enthroned there. And we may also understand how divine was the insight of Ezekiel, which enabled him at such a time to announce the downfall of Egypt from her high pre-eminence, and her final destination of a comparatively low place among the nations of the earth. It could not be human sagacity which, against all present appearances, spake so fearlessly of the coming future; it was the unerring foresight of the Spirit of God. The prophecy consists of four separate pieces, which have each their respective dates; the first coinciding with the tenth year of the prophet's captivity, and the last in the order of insertion with the close of the twelfth. But one is introduced between the first and second, of a much later date, not having been given till the twenty-seventh year (chap. 29:17; 30:19), and which had its place assigned there as the most appropriate position in respect to its contents. The first in order is a general announcement, in parabolical style, of the punishment of the king of Egypt on account of his intolerable self-sufficiency and pride.

1 In the tenth year, in the tenth *month*, in the twelfth *day* of the month, the word of the LORD came to me, saying,

2 Son of man, set your face against Pharaoh king of Egypt, and prophesy against him and against all Egypt.

3 Speak and say, Thus says the Lord GOD: Behold, I am against you, Pharaoh king of Egypt, the great dragon who lies in the middle of his rivers, who has said, My river is my own and I have made *it* for myself.

4 But I will put hooks in your jaws, and I will cause the fish of your rivers to stick to your scales, and I will bring you up out of the middle of your rivers, and all the fish of your rivers shall stick to your scales.

5 And I will leave you in the wilderness, you and all the fish of your rivers. You shall fall on the open fields. You shall not be brought together or gathered. I have given you for food to the beasts of the field and to the bird of the sky.

6 And all the people of Egypt shall know that I am the LORD, because they have been a staff of reed to the house of Israel.

7 When they took hold of you by your hand, you broke and tore all their shoulder. And when they leaned on you, you broke and made all their loins come to a stand.

This passage represents, under striking and appropriate imagery, the high sense the king of Egypt had of his invincible might and glory, and the state of utter helplessness and ruin to which he should be reduced; as also the damage that should be sustained by those who were dependent upon him for help. It was the old controversy which had formerly been waged in the land of Egypt itself, only under a somewhat modified form, and with altered relations in respect to the covenant-people. The Pharaoh of Moses' time stepped forth into open rivalry with God, and sought in personal conflict to contend with him for the mastery. The Pharaoh of Ezekiel's time, presuming on his godlike sufficiency, gave himself out as not only able to stand his own ground against all powerful assailants, but as also qualified to take the place of God in regard to the covenant-people, and minister help to them in the hour of need. But never could the means of Israel's deliverance come from that old house of bondage; and the very attempt to seek it there was to be met with the rod of chastisement. So far, indeed, the resorting of Zedekiah and his people to such an helper did avail them, as it caused the Babylonians to raise for a time the siege of Jerusalem; but it was only to provoke these powerful adversaries to a severer vengeance, and to accelerate the day of calamity. The staff altogether failed them, when they were especially desiring to lean on it; and they were left a helpless prey in the hands of their ruthless conquerors. But this proved insufficiency on the part of Pharoah to give efficient aid was only the prelude to his own overthrow; and the mournful reverses which were to befall him and his land were to be such as would effectually prevent him from ever henceforth presuming to act – as he had been impiously doing in the past – the part of God. This, however, is more plainly disclosed in the verses that follow: –

8 Therefore thus says the Lord GOD: Behold, I will bring a sword on you and cut off man and animal out of you.

9 And the land of Egypt shall be a desert and waste; and they shall know that I am the LORD, because he has said, The river is mine and I have made *it*.

10 Behold, therefore I am against you and against your rivers, and I will make the land of Egypt a complete waste and ruin, from Mig-dol to Sy-e-ne, even to the border of E-thi-o-pi-a.[7]

11 No foot of man shall pass through it; no foot of beast shall pass through it; no one shall live in it for forty years.

12 And I will make the land of Egypt a ruin in the middle of the countries that are wasted; and her cities shall be deserted forty years among the cities laid waste. And I will scatter the Egyptians among the nations and will scatter them through the countries.

13 Yet thus says the Lord GOD: At the end of forty years I will gather the Egyptians from the people where they were scattered.

14 And I will bring again the captivity of Egypt, and will cause them to return to the land of Path-ros, into their homeland.[8] And they shall be a low kingdom there.

15 It shall be the lowest of the kingdoms and shall no more exalt itself above the nations. For I will make them so few that they shall no longer rule over the nations.

16 And it shall never again be the hope of the house of Israel, which brings their iniquity[9] to mind because they turned after them. And they shall know that I am the Lord GOD.

In this part of the prophecy we have another very peculiar exemplification of the characteristic style of our prophet, in respect to his disposition to serve himself to hisory for the particular hue and form of his announcements. But as we cannot properly elucidate the meaning, and exhibit the fulfilment of this portion, without referring to the additional portion which occupies the remainder of the chapter, and which may fitly be regarded as the complement of the one before us, we shall first give this, that we may have the whole in our view at once.

17 And in the twenty-seventh year, in the first *month,* in the first *day* of the month, the word of the LORD came to me, saying,

18 Son of man, Neb-u-chad-nez-zar king of Babylon caused his army to serve a great service against Tyre. Every head was made bald, and every shoulder was peeled. Yet neither he or his army had any pay for Tyre, for the service that he had served against it.[10]

19 Therefore thus says the Lord GOD: Behold, I will give the land of Egypt to Neb-u-chad-nez-zar king of Babylon. And he shall take her multitude,[11] and take her spoil, and take her prey. And it shall be the wages for his army.

20 I have given him the land of Egypt *for* his labor with which he served against it, because they worked for Me, says the Lord GOD.

21 In that day I will cause the horn of the house of Israel to bud forth, and I will give you the opening of the mouth in the midst of them. And they shall know that I am the LORD.

Viewing this prophecy on Egypt in a general light, and with respect more especially to the part assigned in it to Nebuchadnezzar, there is a certain amount of fulfilment which it is not very difficult to establish. Take for example the distinct and so far satisfactory explanation of the matter by Sir G. Wilkinson. He had previously related the earlier sucessess of Apries, then the reverses that began to come upon him, issuing in the revolt of Amasis, and defeat and ultimately the death of Apries. Having stated that the information on these points is given on the authority of Herodotus, who professed to have derived it from the Egyptian priests, he proceeds: "But no mention was made of the signal defeat their army experienced, or of that loss of territory in Syria, which resulted from the successes of the victorious Nebuchadnezzar. It is therefore reasonable to conclude, they disguised the truth from the Greek historian; and without mentioning the disgrace which had befallen their country, and the interposition of a foreign power, attributed the change in the succession, and the elevation of Amasis to the throne, solely to his ambition and the choice of the Egyptian soldiery. Megasthenes and Berosus affirm that Nebuchadnezzar conquered a great part of Africa, and having invaded Egypt, took many captives, who were committed to the charge of persons appointed to conduct them after him to Babylon. But as this is said to have happened at the period of his father's death, and consequently in the reign of Necho, it cannot refer to the point in question. Josephus, however, expressly states that the Chaldean monarch *'led an army into Coelo-Syria, of which he obtained possession, and then waged war on the Ammonites and Moabites. These being subdued he invaded and conquered Egypt, and having put the king of that country to death, he appointed another in his stead'* (Antiq. 10:9. 7). If Josephus be correct in his statement, there is reason to suppose he alludes to Apries being deposed and succeeded by Amasis; and we can readily imagine that the Assyrians, having extended their conquests to the extremity of Palestine, would, on the rumor of intestine commotions in Egypt, hasten to take advantage of the opportunity thus afforded them of attacking the country. And the civil war and the fatal consequences of the disturbed state of Egypt appear to be noticed by Isaiah in the following prophecy: – *'I will set the Egyptians against the Egyptians, and they shall fight every one against his brother, and every one against his neighbor, city against city, and kingdom against kingdom;... and the Egyptians will I give over into the hand of a cruel lord, and a fierce king shall rule over them"?* (chap. 19:2,11).

"From a comparison of all these authorities, I conclude that the civil war between Apries and Amasis did not terminate in the single conflict at Momemphis, but lasted several years; and that either Amasis solicited the aid and intervention of Nebuchadnezzar, or this prince, availing himself of the disordered state of the country, of his own accord invaded it, deposed the rightful sovereign, and placed Amasis on the throne, on condition of paying tribute to the Assyrians. The injury done to the land of Egypt by this invasion, and the disgrace with which the Egyptians felt themselves overwhelmed after such an event, would justify the account given in the Bible of the fall of Egypt; and to witness many of their compatriots taken captive to Babylon, and to become tributary to an enemy whom they held in abhorrence, would be considered by the Egyptians the greatest calamity, as though they had for ever lost their station in the scale of nations."[12]

It is quite sufficient, in a general point of view, to justify the prediction uttered by Ezekiel, regarding the adverse change that was presently to be brought over the affairs of Egypt by the hand of Nebuchadnezzar. And it may still further be confirmed by the nearly contemporary word of Jeremiah, which was spoken after he had been violently carried to Egypt, and in the immediate prospect of the troubles it foretold. Had the troubles not actually come, it certainly would never have been allowed to stand among his writings: *"Behold, I will send and take Nebuchadnezzar, the king of Babylon, my servant, and will set his throne upon these stones that I have hid; and he shall spread his royal pavilion over them. And he comes, he smites the land of Egypt – such as are for death, to death; and such as are for captivity, to captivity; and such as are for the sword, to the sword. And I kindle a fire in the houses of the gods of Egypt; and he burns them, and carries them away captives; and he clothes himself with the land of Egypt as a shepherd puts on his garments; and he goes forth from it in peace"* (chap. 43:10-12).

But it is obvious, admitting all this, that a wide chasm still exists between the terms of Ezekiel's prophecy, and the recorded or even probable facts of history, if the prophecy is to be taken in the simply literal sense. For what it predicts respecting the land of Egypt is a forty years' desolation, during which it should not so much as be trodden by man or beast – should be, in fact, in a wilderness condition; while the inhabitants also should be dispersed into other countries, and only restored again after the forty years had run their course. What is there in the annals of ancient Egypt to bear out such statements? "We cannot prove," says Bishop Newton in his work on the Prophecies, "from heathen authors that this desolation of the country continued exactly forty years, though it is likely enough that this as well as the other conquered countries did not shake off the Babylonian yoke till the time of Cyrus, which was about forty years after the conquest of Egypt by Nebuchadnezzar." But even if we could prove what is thus held to have been within the bounds of the probable, it would still avail little to the point under consideration; for the word of prophecy is an absolute and determinate thing – it cannot be verified by halves. It is either wholly true, – namely, in the sense of its real import, – or it is not entitled to rank as prophecy at all. And such a subjection as the Bishop notices of Egypt to Babylon, even supposing it to have lasted precisely forty years, comes very far short of that blighted and desolate condition, as of an untrodden wilderness, coupled with the general dispersion of her people, of which the prophet speaks. It is as certain as anything in ancient history can be, that a sweeping desolation of this kind never in reality took place in Egypt during the period of Chaldean ascendancy. And we cannot but express our wonder how interpreters, with this palpable fact staring them in the face, should be able to glide over the surface of what is written in the easy manner they do, as if they needed to look no farther than to the literal sense of the words. Literalism here, in the hands of a fair and honest interpreter, can lead but to one result – the manifest failure of the prediction. But it is just or reasonable to deal after this fashion with a prophet, whose representations usually partake so much of the ideal, and with whom the ideal so frequently clothes itself in the garb of history? Were it not more in accordance with the true interpreting spirit to inquire whether the definite terms and external conditions of the prophecy might not be here also used in a historico-ideal sense, symbolical and not literal, expressive of the nature rather than the precise bounds and limits of the predicted events? Such a course is the more called for on the present occasion, as the period of forty years is one that stands out so prominently in the history of God's dispensations, and one that on this account had already been employed by the prophet in an ideal manner respecting the future treatment of the covenant-people. In the vision of the iniquity bearing, in chap. 4, he had been commanded to lie forty days on his right side as typical of the forty years during which they were to be dealt with in chastisement for their sins; a word, as we there showed, which could mean nothing else than that another season was to pass over them, similar in its character as a time of chastisement and discipline to that of the forty years' sojourn in the wilderness, but by no means corresponding to it in duration. So again, we have seen (at chap. 20:35, etc.) that, without mentioning the years, the prophet names the wilderness condition, with its stringent dealings and sifting trials, as what must be undergone by Israel anew, while he not obscurely intimates that what was to be should not be the mere copy of what had been – not the literal repetition of the wilderness life, but the substantial renewal of its spiritual treatment. And why should it be thought that the reference here to the same great period is to be understood otherwise? Even Jerome, however he failed in making a right application of the idea, could not overlook the respect had to the import of the number forty: *"which,"* he says, *"is always the number of chastisement and affliction. Whence also Moses, and Elias, and the Savior himself, fasted forty days and nights, and for forty years the people were kept in solitude."* Let the prophet thus be taken as his own interpreter, and we shall naturally conclude that what he meant by Egypt becoming a desolation and a wilderness for forty years, was that a season of severe chastisement and hard discipline should be made to pass over them, similar to what in days of yore had passed over Israel when inhabiting the desert. It was to be with these proud and fleshly Egyptians precisely as it had then been with the proud and fleshly Israelites; their pleasant land was, as it were, to be converted into a lonesome wilderness – a field of trial, where *"alone they must strive with God,"* and be brought down from their self-complacent trust, to learn and realize their own nothingness. So that it is not the precise number of years that we are to look to – these only served to indicate, through their historical value, the character of the predicted dealings; and if something like an external correspondence may be described in the first period of Egypt's calamities with that particular number of years, it should only be regarded as a sign in Providence to help to the deeper import of the prophecy.

There is indeed some sort of outward correspondence discernible, though not in the way noticed by Bishop Newton. From what has been already mentioned, there is good ground for believing that the invasion of Nebuchadnezzar took place about the commencement of the reign of Amasis. Now this monarch, it is known, occupied the throne for a very long period – according to Herodotus, for 44 years, and according to Diodorus, 55 years; and it is also known, both from the historical reports and from the character of the monuments erected by him, that Egypt enjoyed a high degree of prosperity in his reign, which in the circumstances must have chiefly belonged to the later portion of it, after Egypt had recovered to some extent from the blow of the Chaldean conquest, consequently somewhere toward the completion of the forty years. But as this point is incapable of proper proof, so it is not to be pressed; nothing material depends on it. It is of necessity the character of the approaching troubles, not their precise duration, of which we are chiefly to think under the forty years' wilderness desolation; the more especially as the dealing of severity referred to was not confined to one period, but was often repeated and in the time of Cambyses, it returned with still more painful and humiliating circumstances, than in the days of Nebuchadnezzar. In like manner, what is said in the prophecy of the scattering and the gathering again of the people of Egypt, is another point in Israel's history – one, as a chastisement, entirely similar in nature to that of the sojourn in the wilderness – which was also to have its parallel in the treatment of Egypt; and the very circumstance of the two being coupled together – the scattering among the nations being represented as coinciding with the forty years' wilderness condition – is itself a clear indication that this as well as the other must be understood as an ideal representation. It was not the few captives that were carried away by the Chaldeans to Babylon of which the prophet spake, that was nothing more than the external sign of the far worse calamity which his words properly express; they intimated that the same shattering was ready to befall the power of Egypt, which was accomplished on Israel by their dispersion among the Gentiles; that though still, perhaps, resident within the boundaries of the land, their independence was to be as much broken, and their forces as scattered, as if they were literally driven into exile. In short, Egypt in her approaching calamities was to become a sort of shadow of Israel – the judgments which befell the one were in substance to have their echo in the other; and hence the unspeakable folly (for to this grand lesson the whole points) of Israel going to lean on a power which was utterly impotent to help itself, which was destined to travel through the same, sore visitations of disaster and trouble that brought Israel to the dust.

Nay, there was a difference in the cases, as well as an agreement, which still more strongly marked the folly of such behavior on the part of Israel. For Egypt, the prophet intimates, though not to be entirely destroyed, was yet never to regain her former position; she was to recover from the extreme depression awaiting her, but still only to be in a low condition – lower than the other kingdoms of the earth, that is, than its larger monarchies. In the evil only was it to stand parallel with Israel, but not in the good. For in Israel, by reason of the covenant, there was a germ of strength and glory which belonged peculiarly to herself, and which the very downfall of Egypt and such temporal monarchies would only serve to develope. Therefore it is said at the close, *"in that day I shall make a horn to bud forth to the house of Israel"* – in the very time of Egypt's humiliation, and in consequence of it, shall the Divine power inherent in the covenant-people spring up into new vigor. As the false worldly element goes down, of which Egypt was the representative, the true spiritual element shall rise up afresh. A truth for all times! May the Spirit write it in our hearts! It is only as the rod of the flesh and the world is broken, that the Divine kingdom of Jesus flourishes in the soul or in the world. The more always that the Egypt falls in us, the more will the horn of Israel bud forth; so that we also, like the prophet, shall get the opening of the mouth, to speak of the Lord's doings and to show forth his praise among men. And co-eval with the putting down of all power and authority and dominion that is of man, shall be the triumph of the kingdom of

Christ, and the complete establishment of righteousness, peace, and joy in the Holy Ghost.

The explanation now given of this prophecy, proceeding on the characteristic style of Ezekiel as exemplified in other portions of his writings, will be seen to be very different from the view of those who would resolve the peculiar language employed into mere hyperbole.[13] As for the opposite class, who will hear of nothing but literalisms – whose key-note here as elsewhere is, it is a literal Egypt that was to be desolated, and a literal Nebuchadnezzar that was to desolate it, and why not also a literal forty years and a literal dispersion? Is it enough to say that the method of Ezekiel in other places shows how he is and that for many wise and important reasons God has not chosen to make his prophetic communications always run in a style the meaning of which lies on the surface; indeed, has seldom done so. And let such literalists themselves show how the infidel is to be answered, when he tells them that the literality they contend for palpably wants its requisite verification in the facts of history. With their style of interpretation we should feel constrained to abandon the veracity of the prediciton.

We shall only advert, in conclusion, to the loose application sometimes made in popular works on prophecy of the language employed in this prediction regarding the desolation of Egypt, to its circumstances in the present day. It ought to be borne in mind that this is not strictly warranted by the language itself, which speaks only of what was to be done to humble the power of Egypt, and to reduce it from the proud elevation of a world monarchy – a rival to the kingdom of God, and a temptation to his people to depart from him. When Egypt finally ceased to occupy, or to be in circumstances to aspire after that condition, the prophecy might be said to have taken full effect – the desolations were accomplished. Now that the relations are so completely changed, and Egypt might be anything so far as the cause of God generally is concerned, the territory is in a manner gone on which the prophecy moved; and if Egypt were to become ever so prosperous, it would not in the least affect the truth of what is here written concerning it. The contrary and, as I think, mistaken view naturally leads those who adopt it to present exaggerated accounts of the difference between ancient and modern Egypt in population and resources – to represent the latter as nothing in comparison of the former. There is undoubtedly a considerable inferiority, yet by no means such as to justify us in regarding the one as a desolation compared with the other. Late investigations have satisfactorily proved that the available ground for cultivation in modern Egypt is not smaller, but probably somewhat larger than it was in ancient times.[14] Yet the entire area of the country is only about 11,000 square miles, not quite a fifth of England and Wales, and the arable portion scarcely exceeds 2300, while in England and Wales there are upwards of 40,000 of arable and meadow land. Small as the area of Egypt is, it is understood to have contained, till within a recent period, not far from 3,000,000 inhabitants – a population fully equal to that of Great Britain in proportion to extent of surface, and at least three times as great in proportion to the extent of arable ground. But ancient writers (Diodorus and Josephus) speak of it as having had a population of more than twice as much – of 7,000,000 – at a period shortly before the Christian era – a most incredible number, unless, as Wilkinson suggests, we should include in the reckoning some of the neighboring provinces belonging to Egypt. And they speak also of 30,000 towns and villages in it, which, even taking the population at 7,000,000 for the whole country, would yield the round sum of 330 to each. Notable towns and villages indeed! or as Herodotus calls them, "populous cities!" It is manifest that the statements of ancient writers on this head are of the most random and exaggerated character; and it may well be doubted if the population of Egypt proper ever exceeded four or five millions. Its arable ground, if all cultivated, is thought equal, at least in good years, to the support of seven or eight millions; but the produce is far from being uniform, and Egypt from the earliest times was always an exporting country in grain. She had to a considerable extent to supply surrounding countries – a circumstance overlooked by Mr. Lane in his Modern Egyptians, when he accredits the ancient statements respecting the populousness of the country under the Pharaohs. We throw out these remarks merely to show how unwise it is to point to the existing condition of Egypt in connection with the prophecy under consideration; and to recall attention to what was its real object – the downfall of Egypt as one of the great ancient monarchies, and its reduction to a comparatively inferior place – a place in which it could have no power to withstand the advancement of God's kingdom, or withdraw the allegiance of its members from the covenant of God. This, which we hold to be the real import of the prediction, has beyond all question been most completely verified.

CHAPTER XXX.

CONTINUATION OF EGYPT'S JUDGMENT.

This chapter is composed of two distinct messages, the first of which reaches to the close of ver. 19, and is merely, as to its substance, a repetition of what had already been announced in chap. 29:1-16, only carried out into much greater fulness of detail. It is another proof how congenial it was to the peculiar temperament of Ezekiel to have the prophetic outline filled up by a great variety of particulars, so as to give a lifelike distinctness and body to the picture. His spirit was not satisfied till the representation had been clothed, as it were, with flesh and blood, and it was seen in all its variety of parts. This is the more striking here, as the vision does not appear to have been given till long after that of which it forms the detailed sequel. The date at chap. 29:17 is most naturally regarded as extending to this portion; as also the commencement of the message, by declaring the day of the Lord to be near for Egypt, suits better to the time when Nebuchadnezzar, having finished his operations at Tyre, was on the eve of marching against Egypt.

The other vision in the chapter was of a much earlier date, having been communicated on the seventh of the first month of the eleventh year; not quite a year after the first date in chap. 29, and about three months before the taking of Jerusalem by the Chaldeans. It relates directly to Pharaoh, and, from some reverses already experienced by him, proceeds to announce the entire overthrow of his kingdom. The general subject being the same in both parts as in the immediately preceding chapter, we shall do little more than give a translation of the original, with some explanatory notes where such are required.

[1] The word of the LORD came again to me, saying,

[2] Son of man, prophesy and say, Thus says the Lord GOD: Howl, Woe is the day!

[3] For the day is near, even the day of the LORD is near, a cloudy day. It shall be the time of the nations.

[4] And the sword shall come on Egypt, and great pain shall be in E-thi-o-pi-a, when the slain shall fall in Egypt, and they shall take away her multitude; and her foundations shall be broken down.

[5] E-thi-o-pi-a and Lib-ya and Lyd-i-a, and all the mixed people, and Chub, and the men of the land who are in covenant with them shall fall with them by the sword.

[6] Thus says the LORD: Those who uphold Egypt shall also fall, and the pride of her power shall come down. From Mig-dol to Sy-e-ne they shall fall in it by the sword, says the Lord GOD.

[7] And they shall be ruined in the middle of the wasted countries, and her cities shall be in the midst of the wasted cities.

[8] And they shall know that I am the LORD, when I have set a fire in Egypt and all her helpers shall be destroyed.

[9] In that day messengers shall go out from Me in ships to make the bold E-thi-o-pi-ans afraid, and great pain shall come on them, as in the day of Egypt; for lo, it is coming.

[10] Thus says the Lord GOD: I will also make the multitude of Egypt to cease by the hand of Neb-u-chad-nez-zar king of Babylon.

[11] He and his people with them, the fearful of the nations, shall be brought to destroy the land. And they shall draw their swords against Egypt and fill the land with the slain.

[12] And I will dry up the rivers, and sell the land into the hand of the wicked. And I will make the land waste, and all that is in it, by strangers' hands. I the LORD have spoken.

[13]Thus says the Lord GOD: I will also destroy the idols, and I will cause images to cease out of Noph. And there shall no longer be a prince in the land of Egypt. And I will put a fear in the land of Egypt.

[14]And I will make Path-ros a ruin and will set fire in Zoan, and will do judgments in No.

[15]And I will pour My fury on Sin, the strength of Egypt. And I will cut off the multitude of No.

[16]And I will set fire in Egypt: Sin shall have great pain, and No shall be torn in pieces, and calamities shall fall on Noph daily.

[17]The young men of Aven and of Pi-be-seth shall fall by the sword; and these *cities* shall go into captivity.

[18]At Te-haph-ne-hes also the day shall be darkened, when I shall break the yokes of Egypt there. And the pride of her strength shall cease in her; as forher, a cloud shall cover her, and her daughters shall go into captivity.

[19]Thus I will do judgments in Egypt. And they shall know that I am the LORD.

[20]And in the eleventh year in the first *month*, in the seventh *day* of the month, the word of the LORD came to me, saying,

[21]Son of man, I have broken the arm of Pharaoh king of Egypt. And, lo, it shall not be bound up to be healed, to put a bandage to bind it, to make it strong to hold he sword.

[22]Therefore thus says the Lord GOD: Behold, I am against Pharaoh king of Egypt and will break his arms, the strong one and the broken one. And I will cause the sword to fall out of his hand.

[23]And I will scatter the Egyptians among the nations, and will scatter them through the countries.

[24]And I will strengthen the arms of the king of Babylon, and put My sword in his hand. But I will break Pharaoh's arms, and he shall groan before him with the groanings of one who is stabbed.

[25]But I will strenthen the arms of the king of Babylon, and the arms of Pharaoh shall fall down. And they shall know that I am the LORD, when I shall put My sword into the hand of the king of Babylon, and he shall stretch it on the land of Egypt.

[26]And I will scatter the Egyptians among the nations, and scatter them among the countries. And they shall know that I am the LORD.

This word against Pharaoh appears to have been occasioned by some reverse he had experienced, which was like the breaking of one of his arms, and which the prophet regarded as the sign of his coming downfall. What the reverse was we can have little doubt when we refer to Jer. 37, and find that the army of Pharaoh had unsuccessfully attempted to deliver Jerusalem from the hand of the Chaldeans. On the appearance of the Egyptian army the Chaldeans raised the siege for a time, and marched against the Egyptians, who, however, durst not give battle, but retired again to their own country, leaving the Jews to the mercy of their adversaries. This pusillanimous or prudent retreat the prophet here regards as tantamount to a discomfiture of the Egyptians by Nebuchadnezzar; it was like the breaking of one of his arms, which was not again to be healed, but only broken anew, and the other also with it, by the conquests of the Chaldeans. It is, of course, the breaking of the power of the king of Egypt, and the subjection of his kingdom to a foreign yoke, that is meant by the prophet, and not any injuries that might be done to his person. And it is no more necessary here, than in the similar language used of the king of Judah in chap. 21:25, to suppose that Pharaoh must have been corporeally wounded and pierced by the sword of the king of Babylon, and fallen before him in the agonies of death. As king of Egypt, he was smitten to death, and his empire scattered and destroyed, when his forces were vanquished by the king of Babylon, and he and all his kingdom lay at the feet of the conqueror. And in the same relative sense must be understood the ceasing of a prince from Memphis in the former part (ver. 13); it indicates, not the absolute non-existence of any one of princely rank, but the comparative failure of such – no prince now as had been formerly, no strictly independent monarch.

CHAPTER XXXI.

THE CERTAINTY OF PHARAOH'S DOOM CONFIRMED BY A PARABOLICAL RELATION OF ASSYRIA'S GREATNESS AND DESTRUCTION.

The discourse in this chapter, which is dated two months later than the concluding portion of the immediately preceding one, is formally an address to Pharoadh; but in its great object and design it is a confirmation of the doom already pronounced upon Pharaoh and his kingdom, by a reference to what had befallen the once magnificent king and empire of Assyria. To the eye of reason it seemed a very bold and scarcely credible announcement that such a kingdom as Egypt, so ancient in its origin, so strong in its foundations, so extensive in its dominion and resources, was destined to fall from its proud ascendancy, and become, compared with what it had been, a desolation and a ruin. Therefore the prophet seeks to establish the faith of God's people in what had been spoken respecting Egypt, by directing their attention to the parallel case of Assyria, which within a comparatively recent period had been a vast and flourishing empire, while now its place was no more found in the earth. And having thus told the story of Assyria's past greatness and present desolation, he concludes with declaring that what had been Assyria's fate shall now be Egypt's; the same mournful reverse, and the same instrument too in accomplishing it. It was the Chaldean sword which had given the fatal blow to the Assyrian monarchy, and the same sword was to prostrate the power and the glory of Pharaoh Thus the past contributed to establish the certainty of the future.

It will easily be understood that it is only in the general that the resemblance between the two monarchies is here traced. The Assyrian empire was entirely supplanted by the Babylonian, and not a fragment, we may say, remained of its existence as an empire. But in respect to Egypt, the prophet had already declared that the desolation was not to be by any means so complete; that it was not to cease altogether to be a kingdom, but was to lose for ever its ascendancy in the affairs of the world, and to sink into a low and enfeebled condition. So far as its grand ambition was concerned – of ruling the destinies of the world – it was to vanish even as Assyria had done; its Pharaohs were no longer to bear sway as great masters of empire. But the kingdom within its own narrow limits was still to be prolonged, and depression, not annihilation, was to be the portion of its cup. The comparison, therefore, must be understood with this obvious difference.

It is scarcely necessary to add that the whole of the present chapter, with the exception of the last verse, has immediate respect only to Assyria. There have not been wanting commentators who have understood the prophet as speaking throughout of Egypt, under the image of an Assyrian, or some particular kind of cedar. But this is so palpably against the sense and connection of the passage, that it has never received any general concurrence.[1] The cedar is unquestionably the king of Assyria; and the parabolical representation under this image is one of the most striking and beautiful in Ezekiel though not without the occasional intermixtures of the real with the figurative, which usually occur in the parabolical delineations of our prophet. Bishop Lowth says of it, that, "if we consider the image itself, none can be found more appropriate or graceful; if the features and coloring, none more elegant or more polished; though the prophet has introduced some literalities into the figure (vers. 11,14-16), whether from the nature of this sort of parable admitting it, or from his own fervent disposition leading him to disregard perfect accuracy of style, I can scarcely take upon me to say" (Praelec. 10).

[1]And in the eleventh year, in the third *month,* in the first *day* of the month, the word of the LORD came to me, saying,

[2]Son of man, speak to Pharaoh king of Egypt and to his multitude: Whome are you like in your greatness?

[3]Behold, the Assyrian was *like* a cedar in Leb-a-non, with fair branches and with a

forest-like shade, andof great height. And his top was among the thick boughs. 2

[4]The waters made him great; the deep set him up on high with her rivers to all the trees of the field.

[5]Therefore his height was lifted up above all the trees of the field, and his boughs were multiplied, and his branches became long because of the multitude of waters, when he shot forth.

[6]All the birds of the sky made their nests in his boughs, and under his branches all the beasts of the field brought forth their young, and under his shadow dwelt all great nations.

[7]So he was beautiful in his greatness, in the length of his branches. For his root was by great waters.

[8]The cedars in the garden of God could not hide him; the fir trees were not like his boughs, and the chestnut trees were not like his branches. Nor was any tree in the garden of God like him in his beauty.

[9]I have made him beautiful by the multitude of his branches, so that all the trees of Eden that were in the garden of God were jealous of him.

[10]Therefore thus says the Lord GOD: Becauseyou have lifted yourself up in height, and he has shot up his top among the thick boughs, and his heart is lifted up in his height;

[11]I have therefore delivered him into the hand of the mighty one[3] of the nations. He shall surely deal with him; I have driven him out for his wickedness.

[12]And strangers, the fearful *ones* of the nations, have cut him off and have left him. On the mountains and in all the valleys his branches have fallen, and his boughs have been broken by the rivers of the land. And all the people of the earth have gone down from his shadow, and have left him.

[13]On his ruin shall all the birds of the sky remain, and all the beasts of the field shall be on his branches,

[14]to the end that none of all the trees by the waters *should* lift themselves up because of their height, nor shoot up their top among the thick boughs. Nor *should* their trees stand up in their height, all that drink water.[4] For they are all delivered to death, to the lower parts of the earth, in the midst of the children of men, with those who go down to the pit.

[15]Thus says the Lord GOD: In the day when he went down to the grave, I caused a mourning. I covered the deep for him, and I held back its floods, and the great waters were held back. And I caused Leb-a-non to mourn for him, and all the trees of the field fainted because of him.

[16]I made the nations shake at the sound of his fall, when I cast him down to hell with those who go down into thepit. And all the trees of Eden, the choice and best of Leb-a-non, all that drink water, shall be comforted in the lower parts of the earth.

[17]They also went down into hell with him to *those who are* slain with the sword, and *those who were* his arm, who lived under his shadow in the midst of the nations.[5]

[18]So to whom are you like in glory and in greatness among the trees of Eden? Yet you shall be brought down with the trees of Eden to the lower parts of the earth. You shall lie in the midst of the uncircumcised with *the* slain by the sword. This is Pharaoh and all his multitude, says the Lord GOD.

This parabolical representation, it will be observed, is marked by the same peculiarity which we had occasion to notice in the ideal delineation of the king of Tyre; it combines the historical with the figurative. While the cedar that represents the king of Assyria is called a cedar in Lebanon, – Lebanon being by way of eminence the region of cedars, – it is presently transferred in the prophet's imagination to the land of primeval beauty and perfection, the Eden in which was the garden that God had planted. There this cedar is described as flourishing, and growing till it overtopt in magnificence and beauty all the trees of the field around it; because fed in a manner quite peculiar with the waters of that deep flood which, rising somewhere in Eden, divided itself into four branches and watered the whole garden. Thus happily circumstanced, the exuberance and glory of paradise appeared to revive in this singular tree, and none even there could be compared with it. But it was only that it might afford another specimen of that instability and transitoriness which belongs to all on earth, when the good bestowed by Heaven is abused to purposes of selfishness, and the creature begins to thrust himself into the place of his Creator. Thus the incomparable cedar, forgetting as it were its own place, is given to destruction, and its place is no more found.

Transferred to the king of Assyria, whom the cedar represented, this parabolical history tells us, in the first instance, of his unparalleled greatness; he was the head and centre of a vast monarchy, which was fed by the tributary streams of surrounding nations, and gathered within its ample bosom the resources of the civilised world. But its peerless grandeur proved the occasion of its overthrow; for it only served to nurse into fatal maturity that *"pride which goeth before a fall."* How thoroughly the loftiness of spirit in the head of that monarchy kept pace with the growth and magnitude of his dominion, may be seen from the heaven-daring language of Sennacherib to Hezekiah, when before the gates of Jerusalem his servants openly blasphemed and defied the God of Israel. Most truly was his heart lifted up in his greatness; and the hand of a righteous God must cast him down. When God's purpose is formed, the proper instrument is sure to be forthcoming at the appointed time; and in an amazing brief period the mighty fabric of Assyrian glory fell, an irrecoverable ruin. It was a lesson on a gigantic scale to the world that then was, how God in his providence abases the proud, and scatters the mighty from their seats; how all power and glory that is of the world is destined to vanish away as a dream of the night! And connected, as it here is, with guilt and the doom of Pharaoh, it was to him, and to those who knew the will of God concerning him, an instructive warning and example of that which certainly awaited him; for in the government of an unchangeable God, that which has been is the sure index to what in like circumstances shall again be.

CHAPTER XXXII.

SONGS OF LAMENTATION OVER THE FALL OF PHARAOH AND HIS KINGDOM.

This chapter is composed of two closely related parts, though the visions contained in them were given at two different periods – the one on the first, the other on the fifteenth day of the twelfth month of the twelfth year. They are both elegies, or songs of lamentation over the coming fall of Pharaoh and his kingdom; not entirely, however, in the same strain, but with certain marked differences in the one as compared with the other, which will appear as we proceed. They afford striking examples of that feature in the prophet's mental constitution, which delighted in amplifying his subject, and following it out to all, even the most minute and varied particulars. He would leave nothing to be supplied by the reader's own fancy, but would place every circumstance and result distinctly before his view.

The first vision reaches to the close of ver. 16, and is as follows: –

[1] And in the twelfth year, in the twelfth month, on the first of the month, the word of the LORD came to me, saying,

[2] Son of man, take up a mourning for Pharaoh king of Egypt, and say to him, You are like a young lion of the nations, and you are like a crocodile in the waters. And you came forth with your rivers, and troubled the waters with your feet, and fouled their rivers.[1]

[3] Thus says the Lord GOD: I will therefore spread out My net over you with a company of many people; and they shall bring you up in My net.

[4] Then I will leave you on the land; I will cast you forth on the open field, and will cause all the birds of the sky to remain on you, and I will fill the beasts of the whole earth with you.

[5] And I will lay your flesh on the mountains and fill the valleys with your height.[2]

[6] I will also water with your blood the land in which you swim, *even* to the mountains; and the rivers shall be full of you.[3]

[7] And when I shall put you out, I will cover the heaven and make its stars dark; I will cover the sun with a cloud, and the moon shall not give her light.

[8] I will make all the bright lights of heaven dark over you and will set darkness on your land, says the Lord GOD.[4]

[9] I will also trouble the hearts of many people, when I shall bring your ruin among the nations,[5] into the countries which you have not known.

[10] Yes, I will make many people amazed at you, and their kings shall be horribly afraid for you, when I shall brandish My sword before them. And they shall tremble at every moment, each man for his own life, in the

day of your fall.
[11]For thus says the Lord GOD: The sword of the king of Babylon shall come on you.
[12]By the swords of the mighty, I will cause your multitudes to fall, the fearful of the nations, all of them. And they shall spoil the pride of Egypt, and all the multitude of it shall be destroyed.
[13]I will also destroy all the beasts of it from beside the great waters. The foot of man shall not trouble them any more, nor shall the hoofs of animals trouble them.
[14]Then I will make their waters deep, and cause their rivers to run like oil, says the Lord GOD.[6]
[15]When I shall make the land of Egypt a ruin, and the country shall be stripped of its fullness; when I shall strike all those who dwell in it; then they shall know that I am the LORD.
[16]This is the mourning with which they shall mourn her. The daughters of the nations shall mourn her. They shall mourn for her, for Egypt and for all her multitude, says the Lord GOD.

In this first song of lamentation there is a gradual transition from the strictly figurative to the more literal. It begins with parabolical representations of the coming destruction of Pharaoh's greatness: the huge monster, that had moved at will and troubled all around him becomes himself a helpless prey in the hands of the might; and his mortal remains are spread forth over hill and dale, so that they everywhere meet the eyes of men, and cover with the monuments of his fall the whole extent of his kingdom. This is the main idea intended to be conveyed by the details of this part of the description. It was not to be as if the proud monarch, after being slain, were buried out of sight, and no more seen nor thought of among men. The circumstances connected with his overthrow should be ordered so as to keep fully before them his fallen greatness, that they might neither forget him nor the sad change that had taken place in his condition. And the idea is still further expanded by the introduction of a new image – the extinguishing of the light of that portion of the world, so as to make it, instead of a bright and illuminated region, a land of darkness, striking horror into the minds of those who should behold it. Then becoming more literal in his delineations, the prophet exhibits the kingdom of Egypt as a general wreck; its people scattered in fragments among the nations; its riches given up as a spoil to the hand of enemies; its waters no more frequented by man or beast, and themselves shrivelled into smaller dimensions, and running smooth and calm in their channels, as if they were no longer able to overflow their banks and saturate the fields with the means of fruitfulness and plenty.

We see thus a gradual change from the more to the less figurative, from the ideal to the real. And yet, to the very last, the representation is of an ideal character; and like many other portions of this book, is utterly at variance with that bald and meagre species of interpretation which insists upon reading prophecy as literally as it does history. To apply such a principle here, would manifestly be to take this passage out of the category alike of prophecy and history. For there certainly never has been, and, so long as the general course of nature stands as it is, there never will be, a period in the history of Egypt when the settled drought upon its waters and the still quiet and desolation throughout its borders, spoken of by the prophet, may be found according to the letter of the description. And this very circumstance, that when Egypt is viewed in a merely natural light its fertility and abundance must ever continue, because the waters of its river will still overflow and supply the land with productive moisture, – this might alone satisfy us that the prophet could not intend under such language to speak of any merely natural revolutions, but that through the image of the natural he sought to shadow forth the moral. It is of what Egypt was to be as an empire, as the seat of a monarchy that had once extensively ruled, and still wished to rule in the affairs of men, that the description must be understood. And in this respect he tells us that the result would be as if the land were to be enveloped in darkness and desolation, the springs of its fertility dried up, and its people scattered to the winds. So it happened. The political ascendancy of Egypt began with the Chaldean conquest finally to decline; the arm of its power was for ever broken; its monarch could no more move about as he pleased, and trouble the nations; he was henceforth to reside in comparatively still and peaceful waters, himself on every hand restrained and hemmed in by superior force, and all his pride and glory, as the head of the empire, reduced to perpetual desolation. It is in this higher point of view that the whole prophecy contemplates Egypt and its monarch – this alone; and so the entire forsaking of its waters, here mentioned, by man and beast, and other symptoms of outward destruction, are perfectly compatible with what was said in a previous chapter, of its always continuing to be a kingdom, though in a depressed condition. In truth, when rightly understood, the one means no more than the other for it is Egypt's doom as a kingdom, not the mere condition of its soil and surface, that the prophet throughout has in view. And if we keep our eye distinctly upon that, we shall easily find our way both to the import of the prediction and the reality of its fulfilment.

That the representation is to be understood in the manner now described – as having respect chiefly to the position of Egypt in its political power and relations, to Egypt as a kingdom, and not simply as a natural region of the earth – is still further evident from the next vision, which fills up the remainder of the chapter, and closes the whole of this series of Divine judgments. There the prophet utters another lamentation over the fallen power, and sings, as it were, its funeral song, accompanying the departed into the world of spirits, and surrounding him there with other prostrate monuments of human greatness. Manifestly the inditing of such a funeral song proceeds on the supposition that it is a great worldly power that is meant, personified in its political head, and ideally represented as undergoing the changes to which humanity itself is subject. The introduction of Egypt, in the person of its destroyed head and people, into the shadowy mansions of the nether world, is easily understood if viewed simply as a mode of presenting distinctly before our view the irrecoverable prostration of the great monarchy; for it shows us its natural representative as now become a tenant of that region, where the temporary distinctions of this life are unknown, and where, as regards power and influence among men, the small and the great are reduced to one sad level. To represent Egypt with her king and her mighty forces as transferred thither, was all one with saying that their sway on earth was finished; it was numbered for ever with the things that are past and gone. But let this be kept steadily in view as the one grand object of the representation, in the other parts of the prophecy as well as here. We cannot otherwise give a consistent interpretation to what is written, but must find our path checked by inextricable difficulties. Read from the right point of view, the vision is plain in its meaning, and in all its forebodings is again re-echoed by the facts of history; but if placed in a wrong position, and contemplated in a false light, it ceases to give the sure and unerring instruction we expect to find in a word of God.

[17]It was also in the twelfth year, in the fifteenth of the month,[7] the word of the LORD came to me, saying,

[18]Son of man, wail for the multitude of Egypt and throw them down, her and the daughters of the famous nations, to the lower parts of the earth, with those who go down into the pit.[8]

[19]Whom do you excel in beauty? Go down and be laid with the uncircumcised.[9]

[20]They shall fall in the midst of *the* slain by the sword. She is delivered to the sword; draw her and all her multitudes.[10]

[21]The strong among the mighty shall speak to him out of the midst of hell with those who help him. They have gone down, they lie uncircumcised, slain by the sword.

[22]Assh-ur is there and all her company; his graves are around him; all of them are slain, fallen by the sword;

[23]*their* graves are set in the sides of the pit, and her company is all around her grave. All of them are slain, fallen by the sword, *those* who caused terror in the land of the living.[11]

[24]There is Elam and her multitude all around her grave. All of them are slain, fallen by the sword, who have gone down uncircumcised into the lower parts of the earth, who caused their terror in the land of the living. Yet they have borne their shame with those who go down to the pit.[12]

[25]They have set her a bed in the middle of the slain, with all her multitude. Her graves are all around him; all of them uncircum-

cised, slain by the sword; though their terror was caused in the land of the living,[13] yet they have borne their shame with those who go down to the pit. He is put into their midst.

[26]There is Me-shech, Tubal and all her multitude. Her graves are all around him. All of them are uncircumcised, slain by the sword; they they caused their terror in the land of the living.[14]

[27]And they shall not lie with the mighty *that are* fallen of the uncircumcised, who have gone down to hell with their weapons of war. And they have laid their swords under their heads, but their sins shall be on their bones, though *they were* the terror of the mighty in the land of the living.[15]

[28]Yes, you shall be broken in the midst of the uncircumcised and shall lie with *those* slain with the sword.

[29]There is Edom, her kings and all her princes, who with their might are laid by *those* slain by the sword. They shall lie with the uncircumcised and with those who go down to the pit.

[30]There are the princes of the north, all of them, and all the Si-do-ni-ans, who have gone down with the slain in their terror. They are ashamed of their might. And they lie uncircumcised with *those* slain by the sword, and bear their shame with those who go down to the pit.

[31]Pharaoh shall see them and shall be comforted over all his multitude; Pharaoh and all his army killed by the sword, says the Lord GOD.

[32]For I have caused My terror to be in the land of the living. And he shall be laid in the midst of the uncircumcised with *those* slain with the sword, Pharaoh and all his multitude, says the Lord GOD.[16]

Thus closes the Divine word against Pharaoh and his kingdom; they go down to the land of forgetfulness, in common with all the surrounding heathen who stood in a position of rivalry or antagonism to Israel. Throughout the whole series of the predictions we find the one grand point of difference between the two parties kept steadily in view; the judgment that lights on Israel is only partial and temporary, the power and dominion again return to him and settle in everlasting possession; while the neighboring kingdoms, that in turn aspired to the supremacy, fall to rise no more. Viewed in respect to its substance, the series is merely an expansion, with a fuller application to particular cases, of what was uttered at the commencement of the national history of Israel by Balaam; "*I see him, but not now; I behold him, but not nigh; there comes forth a star out of Jacob, and a sceptre rises out of Israel, and shatters the territory of Moab, and destroys all the children of tumult. And Edom is possessed, and Seir, his enemy, is possessed; and Israel gains strength. And out of Jacob comes the ruler, and he destroys what is left from the city*" (Num. 24:17-19). Thus early was the issue of the contest indicated; it was announced that the supremacy must belong to Israel, because with him was the covenant of blessing, and out of him was to be the one in whom, as the messenger and head of the covenant, all power, blessing, and glory were to reside. The question virtually discussed in all such predictions is this: Who shall give law to the world? Israel, or the rival nations of heathendom? And the answer returned, though with manifold variety of form, is perpetually the same: All other dominions are destined to pass away; that alone of Israel becomes permanent and universal.

We see both sides of the representation attaining to a certain measure of realization, even before the old relations altogether ceased to exist. The antipathies of the surrounding nations failed to extirpate Israel and their struggles for dominion in every case issued in natural decay or ruin. Not one of them succeeded in making good its ambitious designs, or could even preserve its own natural independence and authority; and before Israel was finally dispersed among the nations, all his ancient rivals had fallen from their former greatness and lost their national personality: Israel stood his ground much better than any of them. But that relative prosperity was rather the earnest of the great distinction pointed to in the prophecies, than its ultimate and proper development. This is to be sought only in Christ, in whom all that peculiarly belonged to Israel concentrates itself and rises to its proper perfection. In him, therefore, it is that the pre-eminence destined for Israel has its accomplishment; and all the external victories gained over the surrounding heathen, or the advantages granted to Israel in preference to them, were but the sign and prelude of that glorious ascendancy over the whole earth, which in right is already Christ's, and in due time shall also be his in actual possession. Such is the unrivalled honor of Israel among the nations; hers alone is the glory that abides; and from her must spring all that the world is to have, that is permanently great and good! It is she who in Christ has become the new life of humanity; she also who has acquired the right to reign over all the tribes of men and all the regions of the earth; and however long may be the struggle, however severe the conflict, the result is certain, that the kingdoms of this world must one and all become the kingdoms of our Lord and his Christ.

CHAPTER XXXIII.

RENEWAL OF EZEKIEL'S COMMISSION – HIS OFFICE AS WATCHMAN.

[1] Again the word of the LORD came to me, saying,

[2] Son of man, speak to the children of your people and say to them: When I bring the sword on a land, if the people of the land take a man of their borders and set him for their watchman,

[3] if, when he sees the sword come on the land, he blows the trumpet and warns the people,

[4] then whoever hears the trumpet's sound and does not take warning, if the sword does come and take him away, his blood shall be on his own head.

[5] He heard the trumpet's sound and did not take warning. His blood shall be on himself. But he who takes warning shall deliver his soul.

[6] But if the watchman sees the sword coming and does not blow the trumpet, and the people are not warned, if the sword comes and takes *any* person from among them, he is taken away in his iniquity. But I will require his blood at the watchman's hand.

[7] So, O son of man, I have set you a watchman to the house of Israel. Therefore you shall hear the word in My mouth and warn them from Me.

[8] When I say to the wicked, O wicked one you shall surely die – if you do not speak to warn the wicked from his way, that wicked one shall die in his iniquity. But I will require his blood at your hand.

[9] But if you warn the wicked of his way, to turn from it; if he does not turn from his way, he shall die in his iniquity. But you have delivered your soul.

[10] Therefore, O son of man, speak to the house of Israel. So you have spoken, saying, When our transgressions and our sins are on us, and we are wasting away in them, how then shall we live?

[11] Say to them: As I live, says the Lord GOD, I have no pleasure in the death of the wicked, but that the wicked turn from his way and live. Turn, turn from your evil ways; for why will you die, O house of Israel?

[12] Therefore, son of man, say to the children of your people: The righteousness of the righteous shall not deliver him in the day of his transgression. As for the wickedness of the wicked, he shall not fall by it in the day he turns from his wickedness. Nor shall the righteous be able to live for his *righteousness* in the day that he sins.

[13] When I shall say to the righteous *that* he shall surely live – if he trusts in his own righteousness and commits iniquity, all his righteousnesses shall not be remembered – but for his iniquity that he has committed, he shall die for it.

[14] Again, when I say to the wicked, You shall surely die – if he turns from his sin and does that which is lawful and right;

[15] *if* the wicked gives back the pledge, gives again what he had robbed, walks in the statutes of life without committing iniquity – he shall surely live; he shall not die.

[16] None of his sins that he has committed shall be called to his memory. He has done that which is lawful and right; he shall surely live.

[17] Yet the children of your people say, The way of the Lord is not equal. But as for them, their way is not equal.

[18] When the righteous turns from his righteousness and commits iniquity, he shall even die by it.

[19] But if the wicked turns from his wickedness and does that which is lawful and right, he shall live by it.

[20] Yet you say, The way of the Lord is not equal. O house of Israel, I will judge you, each one according to his ways.

[21] And in the twelfth year of our captivity, in the tenth *month,* in the fifth of the month, one who had escaped out of Jerusalem came to me, saying, The city is stricken.

[22]Then the hand of the LORD was on me in the evening, before he who had escaped came. And He had opened my mouth until he came to me in the morning; and my mouth was opened, and I was no longer dumb.

[23]Then the word of the LORD came to me, saying,

[24]Son of man, those who live in those wastes of the land of Israel are speaking, saying, Abraham was one, and he inherited the land. But we are many; the land is given to us for inheritance.

[25]Therefore say to them, Thus says the Lord GOD: You eat with the blood, and lift up your eyes to your idols, and shed blood. And shall you *then* possess the land?

[26]You stand on your sword, you work hateful things, each one of you defiling his neighbor's wife. And shall you possess the land?

[27]Speak to them in this way, Thus says the Lord GOD: As I live, surely those who are in the wastes shall fall by the sword, and I will give him who is in the open field to the beasts to be eaten up, and those who are in the forts and in the caves shall die of the plague.

[28]For I have made the land a ruin, and the pride of her strength has ceased. And the mountains of Israel shall be a waste, so that none shall pass through.

[29]Then they shall know that I am the LORD, when I have made the land a ruin because of all their idolatries which they have committed.

[30]Also, son of man, the children of your people are still talking about you by the walls and in the doors of the houses, and speaking to one another, each one to his brother, saying, I ask you, come and hear what is the word which comes forth from the LORD.

[31]And they come to you as the people comes, and they sit before you as My people, and they hear your words. But they will not do them. For with their mouth they show much love, *but* their heart goes after their unjust gain.

[32]And, lo, you are to them as a very lovely song of one who has a pleasant voice and can play well on an instrument – for they hear your words, but they do not do them.

[33]And when this happens; lo, it will come; then they shall know that a prophet has been among them.

An entirely new department of Ezekiel's labors begins here. After a period of suspended animation, the prophetic Spirit again returns to breathe in his soul, and prompts him to a new discharge of his prophetical function. Hitherto it has been chiefly the comminatory part that he has fulfilled, now it is to be the consolatory. He has labored in vain to avert the stroke of Jerusalem's overthrow, and the utter prostration of the tabernacle of David. The calamity, so often foretold and warned against, has come; and he must now address himself. to the more agreeable task of reviving the hopes of the fallen, by disclosing to them the prospect of a glorious future. For judgment cannot rest for ever on the house of God. The night of sorrow must give way to the morning of joy; and when the period of lowest depression has been reached, the moment has assuredly come for the commencement of a new and better position.

It was not till the evil had got to its worst stage of judicial destruction, that the prophet was permitted to enter on this more cheering strain of announcements. At the close of chap. 24, he was instructed to remain silent till the catastrophe had occurred; for till then neither should God be disposed to give, nor the people be prepared to receive, the word of comfort and encouragement. He was not to open his mouth to Israel again till the escaped from Jerusalem's desolations came to him, as a witness that the work of judgment was completed, that the false foundations were thoroughly swept away (chap. 24:26,27). And in vers. 21 and 22 of this chapter he states the fact of such having actually come, with the additional intelligence that already on the evening previous the hand of God had begun to operate on his soul, and had reopened his closed lips.

It was in the eleventh year of Zedekiah's reign, or Ezekiel's captivity, the fourth month, that Jerusalem was taken by the Chaldeans, and on the following month was reduced to ashes. It would seem, therefore, that a whole year and five months had elapsed before this appearance of the escaped before Ezekiel – too long, Hitzig thinks, for the communication of so important a piece of intelligence to the captivity at Chebar, and therefore he would substitute the eleventh for the twelfth year; as Ewald also does, though without assigning any reason. Not too long, however, Havernick judges, considering the turmoil and confusion which must necessarily have ensued on the destruction of Jerusalem, and the existing state of things in Judea. If it were simply, indeed, the communication of the tidings of what had taken place that was meant, seventeen months would certainly be a very long period for the conveyance of such intelligence over a distance so comparatively short. But there is no need for supposing that. The expression *"he that has escaped,"* or *"the escaped,"* is very often used in a collective sense, to denote generally the remnant that survived any great catastrophe.[3] And it is the more probable that such should be the meaning of the term here, as the reopening of the prophet's mouth, and that for the special purpose of speaking the word of consolation and hope, would most naturally be deferred till the last deportation had taken place, and the number of the captives was complete. But in that case we can easily suppose the period of seventeen months to have elapsed, as all the arrangements connected with the settlement of affairs in Judea, and the transportation of a considerable band of captives to Chebar, must necessarily have occupied much time.

Such, then, being the case, – the time having arrived when, by the appearance of an escaped remnant from Jerusalem, the prophet was again to open his mouth in new and more encouraging strains to his countrymen, – the prophetic spirit began to prepare him for the work by descending on him the night before; thus graciously anticipating the circumstances, and giving practical proof of his readiness to meet them by suitable communications from above. What the Spirit actually communicated to the prophet on that preceding night, with what tidings his mind was filled or what words his mouth was opened to speak, we are not expressly told. But the natural supposition is, that the message contained in the earlier part of the chapter (vers. 1-20) forms the substance of his first communication; while that contained in the latter part (vers. 23-33), which is very much like a resumption and practical application of the former, constitutes what the prophet delivered after the escaped had actually come. We thus most naturally account for the first part standing without any intimation of the time or occasion prefixed – this was more fitly reserved for the arrival of the escaped on the following day. And it also affords an easy explanation of the close connection as to substance between the two divisions of the chapter, the one being indeed properly the continuation of the other, with a more special reference to the existing circumstances of the people.

1. In regard to the first part of the communication – that which we suppose to have been made to the prophet on the preceding night – there is no need to dwell at any length, as it consists of representations which have already in substance passed under our notice. The first nine verses exhibit anew the prophet's calling and office, under the same character in which it was presented at the outset, in chap. 3:16-21, as that of a spiritual watchmen; only here the description commences with a detailed account of the responsibilities and duties of such an office, when it has respect merely to common evils, and when the person exercising it is the delegate simply of his fellow-men. This distinct reference to human affairs, and minute delineation of a watchman's calling, is doubtless introduced for the purpose of impressing upon those with whom Ezekiel had to do the paramount importance of faithfulness in the discharge of his ministerial function. For who does not know that faithfulness is the one grand prerequisite in him who is chosen to do the part of a watchman in times of peril or alarm? He must have his eye intent simply on the realities of things, whether these may be agreeable or not to men's feelings; nay, all the more intent on these the more they are fraught with danger and distress; that those for whom he watches may learn from him the true position of affairs, and know how to provide against the coming evil. For such an one to slumber at his post, or to conceal the danger he descries, is to incur the highest guilt; as, on the other hand, for them to neglect and slight the faithful warning, is to exhibit the most reckless folly. Now the people had only to transfer such reflections from the earthly to the spiritual region, in order to acquit Ezekiel in the judgment of their own minds, and condemn themselves. He had received, not from man, but from God, the charge to do the part of a watchman to his countrymen; so that faithfulness was pre-eminently required of him. Nor had it been

wanting. He had most zealously and devotedly done his part. He had sounded the trumpet of alarm over every cause of disquietude, and at every appearance of danger; but it was only to deaf ears and incredulous hearts. The dreaded calamities had come, sending multitudes to destruction, and involving all in the deep waters of affliction and sorrow. The blood of souls to a fearful extent has been incurred – but not on the part of the prophet; his hands are clean; it rests upon the head of the people themselves.

But now that the worst has come, is there nothing more to be done? Has the office of Heaven's watchman ceased when the cloud of Heaven's vengeance has burst on the guilty? Has he no commission to speak to those who are sinking under the stroke of judgment – the miserable remnant that have escaped absolute destruction, but are still shivering on the brink of ruin? Yes; and it is here that a new sphere of labor presents itself to the prophet, and that a new call comes to him to enter on it. *"Therefore, O thou son of man,"* or rather, as it literally is, *"And thou, son of man,"* – since by thy past watchings and warnings thou hast but delivered thy own soul, and the children of thy people are involved in the just desert of their sins, – *"say to the house of Israel, Thus ye speak, saying, 'For our transgressions and our sins are upon us, and we pine away in them; and how should we live? Say to them, As I live, saith the Lord Jehovah, I have no pleasure in the death of the wicked, but that the wicked turn from his way and live: turn ye, turn ye from your evil ways; and why will ye die, O house of Israel?"* (vers. 10,11.)

A yearning tenderness here manifests itself, still seeking, notwithstanding all that has taken place, the return of those who survived to the way of peace. But with that tenderness, what a stern and unflinching holiness! There can be no relaxation or abatement mentioned in respect to this, not even amid the moanings of pain and cries of distress which arose from the people, – no return to life possible but through a return to righteousness. God is anxious, as a kind and affectionate parent, to see them restored to a happy and prosperous condition; he would not have them ignorant of that. But they must also know that in God's sight there was a higher thing still, which he could on no account sacrifice for the sake of the other; he must maintain in his dealings with them the honor of his authority and the rectitude of his government; and only if they turn from their wicked ways, can he turn from his fierce displeasure. Here, therefore, stands the one door-way of escape; and the prophet, in entering upon the second department of his ministerial calling, must begin by reiterating the message with which he entered on the first (chap. 3:18-21), and which he had also subsequently repeated and enlarged upon (chap. 18) – the message, namely, that each should be dealt with according to his ways. The righteousness of the righteous should not deliver him if he turned aside to transgression; but neither would the wickedness of the wicked prove his destruction, if he sincerely repented of his sins and laid hold of the covenant of God. These are God's terms now, as they have been all along; the Lord's servant has no other to offer; and if they are not concurred in, recovery is impossible.

There was something too, especially since matters had come to the worst, in the individual and personal character of God's communication to the prophet. It not only disclosed the righteous nature in general of the Divine administration, but the close adaptation of its righteousness to each particular case; the righteous, the wicked – the righteous lapsed into a transgressor, the wicked reclaimed from the paths of transgression – each according to their state and conduct were to receive at the hands of God. The people, therefore, must be done with the imagination that outward political changes were to avail them much; that their fortunes were to be determined, as it were, in the lump; and that it should matter little what they might be in their single and separate conditions. But on the other hand, every encouragement was held out to the penitent and believing as it was God's settled purpose to distinguish in his dealings between the righteous and the wicked, and so to do it that such as were inclined to submit to the righteousness of God might be sure it would go well with them whether in Chaldea or in Canaan – they at least should be made to experience the loving-kindness of God.

2. So much, then, for the first communication, received immediately before the arrival

of the escaped from Jerusalem. And that which came immediately afterwards, and fills up the concluding part of the chapter, is so far an application of the former, as it shows, in the case of two distinct portions of the people, how opposed they still generally were to the righteousness of God, and consequently how far from salvation.

The first portion are those who remained in Judea, the miserable fraction who dwelt among its desolations, and who, notwithstanding all they had seen and suffered of the righteous judgments of God, were still wedded to their sinful ways and cherishing the most groundless hopes. They are represented as continuing much in the same condition, and practising the same enormities as those which had brought down the judgments of God upon the land. The particular sins specified – eating with blood, lawless murder, adultery, and continued adherence to the practices of idolatry – are evidently given as individualizing examples of the corruption prevalent among the remnant in Judea: not only was sin unrepented of, but sins of the worst kind – crying enormities – were still openly practised. And that this was but too faithful a description of the state of matters in desolate Judea, is abundantly confirmed by the historical notices in Jeremiah (chap. 40-43), which exhibit a degree of spiritual blindness, resolute opposition to the will of God, reckless disregard of consequences, and inveterate attachment to the soul-destroying errors of idolatry, which, considering the circumstances, have few parallels in the records of human guilt. Yet, with such apparent contempt for everything sacred, the people still seemed anxious to keep up a hypocritical show of piety. They sought advice of Jeremiah, though, when obtained, they refused to follow it in anything that crossed their own inclinations; and here they are represented as appealing in the most confident manner to their connection with Abraham, and on that ground assuring themselves of their right to possess the land of Canaan. He, though but one, got the land for an inheritance; and we his descendants, who, however reduced in numbers, are still a greatly larger company than he could boast of, may not we justly expect to be kept in possession of it? Strange infatuation! that when the signs of God's displeasure had been so strikingly displayed against them for their sins, scattering all their vain confidences to the wind, they should still, without abandoning those sins, hope for the peculiar tokens of the Divine favor! Yet in a more subtle and refined form we find the same flagrant inconsistence practised by the Jews of our Lord's time, who in like manner reckoned with confidence on their being children of Abraham, as if that alone were enough to secure them in all covenant blessings, while he charged them with being in spirit children of the devil, and consequently entitled only to look for the portion of the lost (John 8:33-44). Indeed the folly, in one form or another, is common to all ages – though the carnal Jews were more peculiarly in danger of falling into it, as their external connection with Abraham formed a strong temptation in that particular direction. In their case the title to blessing was held by a double tie, a natural and a spiritual one – the spiritual, however, being of necessity the one of chiefest and most essential moment in the estimation and reckoning of God – that without which the other was in a manner nothing. Oneness with Abraham in faith and obedience could alone in his account carry any title to Abraham's heritage of blessing. But on the other hand, with the carnal portion of his posterity the tendency always was, in proportion as they receded from the right spiritual position, to cling to the mere outward tie of a corporeal descent, and to rest their views and prospects on simply natural considerations. And it is not a disadvantage as compared with them, but a great and important boon, a freedom from one of the most insidious and powerful temptations to which human nature can be exposed, that the believer's title to blessing under the gospel rests so exclusively on spiritual grounds, and that no assurance of the Divine favor can be found apart from continuance in faith and holiness before God. Could men know, as they would often fain do, their election of God in an absolute manner, – were it to be held by them as a simple piece of information, derived from supernatural insight into the purposes of Deity, – it would be their misfortune rather than a privilege, for it would immensely increase the danger of their falling into spiritual inactivity or presumption. That assurance only can be safe which is the fruit of a living faith and a righteous behavior.

The small remnant in Judea being so far from righteousness, the prophet could only speak to them as a minister of condemnation: they had not turned from their evil ways, and they could not live. What they had to expect was only judgment still more severe and exterminating than what yet had been appointed. For them the desolations of the land must become still more desolate, and new horrors be inflicted by the sword, the pestilence, and the wild beast. All must be reduced to the condition of a howling wilderness, as it really was, that the new hope for Israel might spring from another and better root, and that the people might know how impossible it was to attain to blessing from God without first separating from sin.

But unfortunately these were not the only persons who still stood in irreconcilable opposition to the righteousness of God; there were others, close beside the prophet, – apparently, indeed, the great mass of the exiles on the banks of the Chebar, – who, though less flagrantly at variance with the mind of God in ourward conduct, were actuated at heart by the same wayward and refractory spirit. Referring now to this class, the word of the Lord says to the prophet: *"And thou, son of man, the children of thy people, who speak against thee beside the walls and at the doors of their houses, and talk one to another, each man to his neighbor, saying, 'Come now, and let us hear what the word is that proceedeth from the Lord.' And they come to thee like a gathering of the people, and they sit before thee as my people, and they hear thy words, but they do them not; for with their mouths they act the part of lovers, after their gain their heart goes. And lo! thou art to them like a lover's song, with a pleasant voice, and playing well on an instrument; and they hear thy words, and do them not: And when it comes – lo! it is come; and they know that a prophet is among them"* (vers. 30-33).

The description forms a continuous and incomplete sentence. The Lord does not say what the prophet was to do, though he begins with the address to him, *"And thou, son of man."* But there can be no doubt as to what is meant. He is furnished with a delineation of the people, as to their real state and conduct, and especially of the false and hypocritical manner in which they had acted toward him as the Lord's messenger; ending with the conclusion, that now, at least, – now that the great catastrophe had come, and that they had living evidence before them of the fact in the presence of the escaped from Jerusalem, – they could no longer treat his communications with the disbelief, nor speak of himself with the disrespect they had done. They must at length be convinced in their minds that a true prophet is among them. And this conviction, of course, would be for him like a higher vantage-ground from which to address them in his future ministrations.

It will be understood that the description here given of the people properly applies to the past. During the period of the prophet's former ministrations their bearing had been that of those who, with a certain degree of deference to the prophet's character, continued to retain and manifest the most settled antipathy to the spiritual object he had in view. His high vocation as an ambassador of Heaven they durst not altogether disavow; the manner in which he fulfilled it bore on it too distinctly the impress of Heaven's majesty and earnestness; and they even professed to seek with desire after the communications he had been receiving from above. In respect to these they had done, as it were, a lover's part with their mouths, exciting one another to go and learn what might recorded in the earlier part of the Book, on which they appeared before the prophet as avowed inquirers respecting the will or purposes of Heaven. Not only so, but even while receiving the prophet's message, there was nothing irreverent or unbecoming in their manner; they listened to his communications as if they felt really interested in the matter – hearing it with lovers' ears, as with lovers' lips they had prompted one another to go where it might be heard. But still it was only as persons floating on the surface of things – dealing as with a lover's song pleasantly chanted, and set off with fit accompaniments of music. Their hearts remained impenetrably shut against the substance of the tidings brought to them, because inveterately attached to their own fond imaginations and foolish conceits. And, as natural consequence, they talked among themselves against the prophet, both more privately at the doors of their houses, and also in their more public haunts around the walls of the city. They noticed in a hostile spirit everything that was peculiar in his manner, or enigmatical in the style of his communications, with the view of excusing themselves from giving an implicit reception to his testimony, or yielding a hearty obedience to his commands. Precisely as in another age their descendants took refuge in the distinctive characteristics of our Lord and his forerunner; alleging, in excuse of their impenitance, that the one was a wine-bibber, and that the other had a devil. In all such cases, which are unfortunately confined to no age or country, the make-shift can only last for a time; sooner or later the spell of delusion must be broken – God's word proves to be true, and every man that sets at naught its counsel a liar. So now it fared with those exiles on the Chebar: the gain they were each looking for, by a speedy return to Judea, perished; the often reiterated, but as often discredited, announcement of Jerusalem's fall and desolation, took effect. With all the prophet's peculiarities, and notwithstanding everything they could say against him, the seal of Heaven is at length given to his testimony, in such a manner as to put all doubt and disbelief to silence, – wisdom is justified in him as one of her true witnesses and most faithful children. So that here again the lesson comes forth with loud and impressive warnings for all times, that *"the word of the Lord is pure, like silver purified seven times."* Whatever exceptions men may be able to take against the casket in which it is presented, or the characteristic properties of the instrument that wields it, the truth it contains is great, and must prevail: *"The counsel of the Lord standeth for ever, the thoughts of his heart to all generations;"* while *"he brings the counsel of the heathen to nought, he maes the devices of the people of none effect."* In making use of human agents to reveal his will to men, the Lord teaches us to look for no external perfection. There may be found all the diversities of manner, and nearly, too, all the imperfections which distinguish ordinary speakers among men, in his most special instruments of working; for the Spirit, even in his highest operations, must still leave free play to native peculiarities of thought and utterance. But in regard to its substance, God's word is perfect, and stands nobly apart from all that is of man. Let it even be ours, therefore, to hear it with reverance, and bow to its requirements with child-like submission. It is we that must fall in with its terms, not it that must accomodate itself to ours. And whatever is opposed to it, either in the imaginations of the heart or in the course of life outwardly pursued, must sooner or later be brought to nought. They only find the true wisdom who have learned to prove what is the holy and acceptable will of God; for theirs is the *"way everlasting."*

CHAPTER XXXIV.

THE PROMISE OF THE TRUE SHEPHERD, AFTER THE FALSE SHEPHERDS HAVE BEEN PUNISHED AND REMOVED.

In the preceding chapter the prophet has announced the first condition of an improved state of things, in reiterating the call to a hearty submission on the part of the people to the demands of God's righteousness. So long as this was postponed, nothing could be looked for of good. But that position being laid down as the first preliminary to a better future, the way now opened itself for the promise of another – the appointment of a good shepherd, one who should be emphatically the good shepherd, to rule over and feed them, in the room of the false ones, who had but sought their own interests and oppressed and ruined the flock. The chapter falls naturally into two parts; in the first of which the misrule of the false shepherds is described, with the fatal results to which it had led; and in the second, the gracious interposition of God, to undo the evils that had arisen from the presidency under which the people had been placed, and set over them one whose benign and careful superintendence would ensure the best and most lasting good.

[1] And the word of the LORD came to me, saying,

[2] Son of man, prophesy against the shepherds of Israel. Prophesy and say to them, Thus says the Lord GOD to the shepherds: Woe to the shepherds of Israel who feed themselves! Should not the shepherds feed the flocks?

[3] You eat the fat and clothe yourselves with the wool. You kill those who are fed, *but* you do not feed the flock.

[4] You have not made the weak strong, nor have you healed the sick,[1] nor have you bound up the broken. You have not brought again that which was driven away, nor have you sought that which was lost. But you have ruled them with force and with cruelty.[2]

[5] And they were scattered because *there is* no shepherd. And they became food to all the beasts of the field when they were scattered.

[6] My sheep wandered through all the mountains and on every high hill. Yea, My flock was scattered on all the face of the earth, and none searched or sought *for them*.[3]

[7] Therefore, shepherds, hear the word of the LORD:

[8] *As* I live, says the Lord GOD, surely My flock became a prey, and My flock became food to every beast of the field, because *there was* no shepherd. My shepherds did not search for My flock, but the shepherds fed themselves and did not feed my flock,

[9] therefore, O shepherds, hear the word of the LORD.

[10] Thus says the Lord GOD: Behold, I am against the shepherds and I will require My flock at their hand and cause them to cease from feeding the flock. Nor shall the shepherds feed themselves any more, for I will deliver My flock from their mouth, that they may not be food for them.

This passage evidently points, both as to its subject and the language it employs, to a quite similar and earlier prophecy of Jeremiah (chap. 23:1-6), where in like manner the false shepherds are denounced and judged, that the way might be opened up for the appearance of the Lord's true shepherd. In both prophecies alike, what is meant by the shepherds is manifestly not priests or prophets, but kings and rulers – the supreme head of the commonwealth, in the first instance, though not without respect also to the subordinate rulers of the kingdom. This admits of no reasonable doubt, even from what is said of the false shepherds themselves – violent, selfish, and oppressive dealing toward the flock being the crimes charged against them. They were rulers who acted towards their subjects with senseless rigor and cruelty. And it is rendered perfectly certain by the promise in the second part of the prophecy, where the special counteractive to the past evil is declared to be the raising up of David as the shepherd that was henceforth to feed them. Such also is the usual meaning of shepherd in the Old Testament Scripture. It has plainly this meaning in the 23d chapter of Jeremiah. And in an earlier chapter of that prophet, the shepherds are distinguished alike from priests and prophets, leaving no other class of persons to be embraced in the designation but rulers: *"The priests said not, Where is the Lord? And they that handle the law knew me not; and the shepherds transgressed against me, and the prophets prophesied by Baal"* (chap. 2:8). This mode of representation originated in the case of David, and had respect partly to the natural employment from which he was taken, and partly also to the essentially pastoral character, when rightly understood, of the higher employment to which he was called. Thus we find the leaders of the people, who came to David at Hebron to invite him to assume the undivided sovereignty of the kingdom, knew perfectly how to connect the lower with the higher in his history: *"Also in time past, when Saul was king over us, thou wast he who leddest out and broughtest in Israel: and the Lord said to thee, Thou shalt feed my people Israel, and thou shall be a captain over Israel"* (2 Sam. 5:2). And still more expressly is the double reference brought into notice in Ps. 88:70,71: *"And he chose David his servant, and took him from the sheepfolds, from following the ewes great with young: he brought him to feed Jacob his people, and Israel his inheritance."*

The connection between the natural and the spiritual here was certainly not accidental – no more than in the case of our Lord's first disciples, who, from being fishers on the lake of Galilee, were called to fishers of men. It was intended to be to David himself, and afterwards to his successors in office, a perpetual monitor, reminding them of the kind, watchful, and paternal character of the administration which they were called to exercise in Israel. For the earthly kingdom set up there was not to be after the pattern of the kingdoms of this world, in which everything is too often managed for the gratification of a single man's ambition, and the purposes of his own selfish aggrandizement. Samuel had foretold it would in all probability grow into this, but at the same time protested against such an abuse, as an entire frustration of the purposes for which the Lord allowed it to be established. The king of Israel was to be the deputy of Jehovah, *"ruling in the fear of God,"* nay, occupying the throne *"in the name of the Lord his God;"* with the law of God before him as his only statute-book (Deut. 17:18,19), and the promotion of a general conformity to its requirements among the people as the great object of his administration. The office of such a king must therefore have materially differed from that of the merely civil ruler of an earthly kingdom. He was the head of a theocracy which, from its very nature, was predominantly spiritual in its aim, and sought nothing in comparison of the moral and religious interests of the people. He was consequently bound to act in all things, not as the organ and representative of the popular will, but as peculiarly the servant of God; as the land over which he presided was the Lord's heritage, and the people he governed were the flock of the Lord's pasture. How much David understood this to be his high calling is manifest, not only from his last words in Samuel (2 Sam. 23:1-6), but also from the conflict he maintained through life with the sons of Belial, the efforts he made to revive the cause and regulate the worship of God, and the beautiful identification of himself, in all his sorrows and his joys, his struggles and his prospects, with the truth and the Church of God. In these respects he showed himself, above all others, to be the man after God's own heart – the man who made the cause of Heaven so much his own, that he might be said to live and reign for it; and who has left in the recorded experience of his spiritual desires and earnest contendings for the truth one of the richest legacies every bequeathed to the household of faith. Some of his successors copied after his example, but none of them came near to him as the representative of God's heart and mind, in this intense zeal for the interests of righteousness and supreme regard for the good of Zion.

Bearing this in mind, as to the end for which the Lord appointed an earthly head over Israel, we have a sufficient explanation of what seems at first sight a peculiarity in the passage before us – its charging upon the kings all the evils that had befallen the heritage of the Lord. It was they who, by their selfish, cruel, and unrighteous administration, had caused the people to become a prey to the ills of life, and to be scattered abroad as the refuse of the earth. We are not to understand from the representation that the people themselves had done nothing to incur these calamities; that had been to belie a large proportion of the earlier part of the Book, and even to contradict the leading purport of the message contained in the chapter immediately preceding. The people had been smitten with the rod of chastisement, because their continued guilt and impenitence had provoked the Lord's anger against them. But the persons who should have set themselves against this waywardness of the people, who, by a vigilant oversight and a faithful discipline, should have ever checked the evil, and labored for the establishment of truth and righteousness, – those who should thus have done the part of real shepherds of the people, – were the very persons who had been most influential in speeding forward the progress of iniquity. Instead of acting as the guardians and regenerators of society, they had, by their selfish indifference and shameful profligacy, fed and nourished its corruptions. So that comparing what they should have done, as exemplified in the case of David, with what they had actually done, the prophet might justly lay at their door, in the first instance, the guilt of all the disorders and desolations that had taken place. If such rulers as David had always occupied the throne of justice, such calamities as they had now to bewail would never have happened.

The judgment of such bad shepherds, therefore, must lie at the foundation of all reasonable expectation of a better future. And so the prospect which God begins here to open up of such a future, starts with the punishment of the shepherds (vers. 7-10). Mercy to the flock imperatively required the execution of judgment upon those who had

betrayed and injured them. And this being done, as it was in great part at least by the terrible things in righteousness in which God had manifested himself toward them, the way was now prepared for the gracious interposition of God to restore and rectify all: which forms the second and main part of the prophecy.

[11]For thus says the Lord GOD: Behold, I, *even* I, will both search My sheep and seek them out.

[12]As a shepherd seeks out his flock in the day that he is among his scattered sheep, so I will seek out My sheep and will deliver them out of all places where they have been scattered in the cloudy and dark day.

[13]And I will bring them out from the people, and gather them from the countries, and will bring them to their own land and feed them on the mountain of Israel by the rivers, and in all the places of the country where people live.

[14]I will feed them in a good pasture, and their fold shall be on the high mountains of Israel.[4] There they shall lie in a good fold, and *in* a fat pasture they shall feed on the mountains of Israel.

[15]I will feed My flock, and I will cause them to lie down, says the Lord GOD.

[16]I will seek that which was lost and bring again that which was driven away. And *I* will bind up the broken and will strengthen that which was sick. But I will destroy the fat and the strong. I will feed them with judgment.

[17]And you, O My flock, says the Lord GOD, behold, I judge between cattle and cattle, between the rams and the he-goats.[5]

[18]Does it seem a small thing to you to have eaten up the good pasture, but you must *also* trample the rest of your pastures with your feet? And you have drunk of the deep waters, but you must foul the rest with your feet.

[19]And *as for* My flock, they eat that which you have trampled with your feet, and they drink that which you have fouled with your feet.

[20]Therefore thus says the Lord GOD to them: Behold I, *even* I, will judge between the fat cattle and the lean cattle.

[21]Because you have thrust with side and with shoulder, and have pushed all the sick with your horns until you have scattered them abroad.

[22]therefore I will save My flock, and they shall no longer be a prey. And I will judge between cattle and cattle.

[23]And I will set up one Shepherd[6] over them. And He shall feed them, My servant David. He shall feed them, and He shall be their Shepherd.

[24]And I the LORD will be their God, and My servant David a prince among them. I the LORD have spoken.

[25]And I will make a covenant of peace with them, and will send the evil beasts out of the land. And they shall live safely in the wilderness and sleep in the woods.

[26]And I will make them, and the places around My hill, a blessing. And I will cause the shower to come down in its season. There shall be showers of blessing.
the shower to come down in its season. There shall be showers of blessing.[7]

[27]And the tree of the field shall yield her fruit, and the earth shall yield her increase. And they shall be safe in their land, and they shall know that I am the LORD, when I have broken the bands of their yoke and have delivered them out of the hands of those who used them as slaves.

[28]And no more shall they be a prey to the nations, nor shall the beast of the land eat them. But they shall live safely, and no one shall make *them* afraid.

[29]And I will raise up for them a famous Plant, and they shall never again be destroyed with hunger in the land, nor bear the shame of the nations any more.[8]

[30]So they shall know that I, the LORD their God, am with them, and that they, the house of Israel, are My people, says the Lord GOD.

[31]And you My flock, the flock of My pasture, are men, and I am your God, says the Lord GOD.[9]

A succession of blessings is promised to the covenant-people in this glowing delineation. First, the evils were to be rectified that had sprung from the former misrule and corruption – the scattered flock gathered again from its dispersions, and restored to the good pasturage of the mountains of Israel. Then the internal disorders that had been allowed to exist and grow, like festering sores, among the flock themselves, – the selfishness and fraud and violence which had so greatly marred the mutual flow and interchange of good, and aggravated every evil, – these were now to be rooted out; for

the persons indulging in such unrighteous dispositions were to be judged by God, and henceforth denied a place in his kingdom. Then again, in lieu of the false shepherds who had formerly wasted and devoured the flock, there was to be raised up one, the pre-eminently good shepherd, the Lord's servant David, who by his wise and faithful administration should prevent such disorders and misrule from again arising, and should establish throughout the whole land, even to its wilderness and forests, perfect security and peace. Finally, in fit correspondence with this happy state of internal order and settled righteousness, all was to be smiling and prosperous outwardly – refreshing showers of rain to fertilize the ground, fruitful fields, cultivated by a free and joyous people, crops everywhere yielding their produce, and trees their fruit in due season – all exhibiting the delightful spectacle of a flock pastured by God himself, or a people enjoying the noble distinction of having him for their God, and sharing in the richest manifestations of his goodness.

In principle, it will be observed, this promise of future good is precisely similar to what has already so frequently appeared in the threatenings of judgment. It takes the form of a renewal of the old, with such modifications and changes as might adapt it to the altered circumstances of the time to come. When judgment was the prophet's theme, the Spirit led him to predict the return of the years of former troubles and desolations, not only of the more general calamities often experienced, of famine and sword and pestilence, but even of the more peculiar afflictions of the Egypt-state of bondage and oppression, and the dreary sojourn in the wilderness. So germane to the prophet's cast of mind is this mode of representation that even when he passes out of the territory of Israel, and speaks of what was to befall the nations of the earth – there, too, when the delineation is of a lengthened and minute description (as in the cases of Tyre and Egypt), it is as a recurrence of the past that he delights to present the evil to our view: the history of Tyre's head and representative is a kind of rehearsal of the best and the worst in the general history of man; and Egypt is spoken of as passing through Israel's peculiar experiences of evil – her bondage, her dispersion, and even her forty years' sojourn in the wilderness. Not that in any of these cases of threatened judgment there was to be the exact reproduction of the old, but only a renewal of its general character and design – a repetition of it in its essential moral features. And in each case peculiar traits, we found, were introduced into the delineation, as if on purpose to indicate that not the literal recurrence of the past was intended, but only what chiefly characterised it as a dispensation of God. Now the correspondence in form between those threatenings of evil and this promise of good, warrants us in applying to it the same principle of interpretation; and indeed the earlier here, as in all similar cases, must be taken as the key to the latter. The uniformity that we expect to characterise the productions of the same hand demand that it be so taken. Nor can we fail to perceive here also the introduction of such an ideal trait as was sufficient to show that the past only in character, not in the precise forms and outward conditions of being was to be expected. For while we are told of a recovered possession of the mountains of Israel, and a secure habitation there as in the best periods of the past, and a fruitful inheritance and a united people dwelling under the peculiar favor and blessing of Jehovah, we are at the same time told of David being the shepherd under whose invigorating influence and paternal oversight the Lord's flock were to rise to such a height of peace and prosperity. But David has long ago slept with his fathers, having *"served his own generation according to the will of God;"* and not the literal David restored to life again, but a distinguished scion of David's house, as our prophet had himself already announced (chap. 17:22, 21:27), was to be the future head and leader of the Lord's people. Shall we therefore consider the name of the father here put for the name of the son? shall we merely substitute the Messiah for David, and hold that with this exception the whole description must be understood according to the letter? This is what is commonly done, but it is manifestly quite arbitrary; and we can see no reason in the nature of things why the literal and the non-literal should be thus made to alternate and be confounded with each other.

The proper view rather is, not that this individual trait merely, but that the description throughout is of an ideal kind: the prophet foretells simply the nature of the coming future under the form of the old landmarks and well-known relations. The best of the past shall revive again; more than revive, it shall appear free from the defects that formerly intermingled with it, clothed with a perfection and a completeness hitherto unknown. But while the substance should thus coincide in the new and the old, it is not obscurely intimated that the shell would materially differ; for certainly the literal David should not be the prince in whom the promise was to stand, but one unspeakably greater than he. And if the other things in the description should receive a corresponding elevation, ought it to have been a matter of surprise to any? would the terms of the prediction have been thereby contravened? would there not rather have been given to them a wider range of meaning and a nobler realization? Unquestionably, up to the time that the new David came to accomplish the predicted good, believers were bound to look for a fulfilment in the nearest possible accordance with the letter of the description. They would thus get the highest idea of the expected good they were then capable of entertaining. But when the personal manifestation of the promised shepherd gave a new turn and aspect to affairs – when he proved to be as much superior to David as the builder of the house is to the house itself – when he was found to be the glorious and mighty Lord to whom, as David in the Spirit foresaw, the heritage, not of Canaan, but of all lands and all nations belonged – when the flock of the Lord's pasture thus saw how sublime a turn was given to what may be called the key-note of the prediction, – then it behoved them to conclude that all the rest must receive a corresponding enlargement: the region, the people, the inheritance of blessing, must severally be what the old but represented and typified; therefore no longer confined to the ancient landmarks and conditions, but found wherever Christ himself is, and reaching as far and as high as the blessings of his great redemption extend. And what Canaan would have been with its David restored again, and all its covenant blessings enjoyed in richest profusion, such, in the new and higher sphere of the Messiah's kingdom, shall the whole domain be over which he is Lord, when this promise of good things to come attains to it full and final accomplishment. Nothings shall be left in it that can hurt or offend; it shall be the inheritance of the saints in light.

Such, it seems manifest, is the only consistent mode of handling a prophecy like the one before us – the only style of interpretation that brings it into harmonious agreement with other predictions that resemble it in form, and binds together its several parts by a common principle of union. But if still it should seem strange to any that the Spirit of God should have led his servant to give forth a prediction of coming good so deeply encased in the liberalities of the old land and people of the covenant, while not these precisely, but things far higher and greater, were to constitute the proper fulfilment, let them seriously consider and resolve the question whether it could have been otherwise. It is easy for persons now – since the realities of the Messiah's dispensation have come – to say, that if these had been chiefly meant in the promise, they would have been more plainly described, the promise would not have run so exclusively in the form of blessings announced to the land and people of Israel. But the question to be fairly met and determined is, Could the promise of the Messiah, and of the affairs connected with his work and kingdom, have been unfolded to the Church beforehand, with any degree of detail, excepting under the form and shadow of Old Testament relation? We unhesitatingly answer, No; not unless the Spirit of God had violently controlled the minds of the prophets, and superseded the free exercise of their faculties; which, again, would have interfered with the essential principles of his working in inspiration, as well as in the commoner operations of grace.

In conceiving of the higher, and anticipating the future things of God's kingdom, the mind must always serve itself of the objects and relations of the present; these are the ladders by which it must rise, the leading-strings by which it must feel its way to what is above and beyond. Man is the highest form of intelligent and animated being with which we are conversant on earth; and it is solely by means of his powers and organs – indefinitely expanded, indeed, in the idea, but still be means of these as the forms and elements of thought – that we are enabled to think of the higher creatures of God's universe, and even of God himself. We can ascribe no perfection to God; we cannot, even in imagination, conceive of any belonging to him but what in an infinitely smaller degree we ourselves possess. And so also in regard to the concerns of God's kingdom, the future must always take shape in our minds from the present or the past, the unknown from the known. We are scarcely sensible how much this is the case, so long as we confine ourselves to a few vague and general ideas; but whenever we attempt to go into detail, our impotence presently betrays itself. Let the purest and loftiest mind under the present dispensation begin to particularize in its thoughts and words respecting the coming dispensation of glory, and what can it do but tell of the removal of existing evils, or the accumulation and enhancement of present blessings? It imagines to itself a state in which there are no longer to be found sin and corruption, sorrow and sighing, bodily diseases, mental infirmities, the numberless evils and disorders of life, or the wide-wasting desolation of death, now so universally experienced; but instead of these, undecaying health and beauty, purity unalloyed, the splendors of an eternal day, rivers of pleasure, feasts of joy, pavements of gold, sceptres, crowns, thrones of glory; – what can we say more? and when we have said them, what are they but the best and greatest things that the world, as it now is, presents to our view? And yet we know, that as flesh and blood cannot inherit that world of incorruption, so there shall be no place there for such carnal elements of grandeur and delight. But we have no other means to help out our apprehensions of what is to be hereafter, no other forms and conditions of being under which to shape and fashion our ideas respecting it; and inspired teachers, as well as others, have no alternative but to resort to them. The things that cannot be exhibited thus are things for the present unutterable (2 Cor. 12:4).

But the position which we now occupy in regard to the more glorious future is precisely that which God's servants of old occupied in regard to our present. And nearly all the difficulty that is experienced, as also nearly all the misapprehensions that have arisen, in reading the descriptions they have penned of what was to take place in Messianic times, springs from the necessity of realizing their exact position (which requires some effort of mind), and surveying the prospects they delineated from their, and not from our, point of observation. To get a correct understanding of what they wrote, it must be borne in mind that all was conceived and uttered by them under the bond of the old shadows and relations, the impress of whose imperfect image and superscription necessarily appears in what they wrote. It might, no doubt, have been possible for them, without any marked reference to these older forms of things, to have given forth a few vague and general statements respecting the future dispensation of the Gospel – such as, that a great Savior was to achieved for the good of the church, or a general diffusion was to appear, or a glorious work was to take place of peace and blessing throughout the world. But such announcements could not of themselves have served the great ends of prophecy; they could not have met the emergencies that arose in the Church's history, nor provided for a weak and dim-eyed faith what it required for support and nourishment. Particular and even lengthened descriptions were indispensable. But these could only be presented under the existing form of things, by telling, as is done here, how the present evils should be abolished, or the past good restored; by filling up the picture with pleasing views of Canaan, Jerusalem, Zion, hills of holiness, sacrifices of righteousness, a seed of blessing, a king and a commonwealth every way worthy of the goodness and majesty of Heaven; by employing, in short, and at the same time expanding and improving upon the old forms and relations, so as to make out of them the picture of a glorious future – a picture perfectly true when viewed in respect to its substance, but necessarily imperfect when considered as to its external conditions. One of two things was inevitable; either there must have been no detailed predictions extending into Gospel times, or those given must have been cast into the mould and pattern of what existed in the times going before. And for any one to insist now on having a fulfilment, which shall preserve entire the very forms of the prophetical representations, is just to repeat on the field of prophecy the error of those in apostolic times who, in respect to the things of salvation themselves, sought to retain the shadow along with the substance – who clung with childish fondness to the weak and beggarly elements of typical ordinances, after the Divine reality had come and burst the narrow shell, because it then required a larger room and a nobler elevation.

Does any enlightened Christian doubt that the prophecy of the sacrificial types has been really fulfilled in Christ, though he formally offered himself on no external altar, and sprinkled no actual mercy-seat with his blood? Does he not readily understand, that however necessary it might be to present the coming redemption under such aspects before, yet, when the redemption itself came, it was too grand to be wrapt up in these little swaddling-bands? And why should we judge otherwise of a prophecy like the one before us – a prophecy in detail, and as such, necessarily written out in the language of the Old Testament times? In that language it made promise of a glorious future under Heaven's anointed King. It told the heart of faith, even in the darkest season, not to despair; for the evils then prevailing should be abolished. The kingdom of God should rise from its depression, and the territory of kingdom yet become, to its utmost bounds, a region of righteousness and peace and blessing. We see the word beginning to take effect, even before Messiah came, in the partial re-establishment of the Divine kingdom within the ancient bounds, and, as far as was needed, for the higher purposes of the kingdom. We see it advancing afterwards toward its riper fulfilment, when the great object of the prediction came and did the part of the Good Shepherd, by avenging for ever the cause of his elect, and laying the sure foundation of his everlasting inheritance. And we see it still travelling on to its full and destined realization, in every victim that is won from the power of Satan and every conquest that is made by the truth of God over the darkness and corruption of the world.

Thus understood, the prophecy is consistent with itself, and in accordance with others of a like kind in the earlier portions of the Book; while in the form it assumes it bears the natural impress of the time to which it belonged. But if any, determined to hear of nothing but the letter, will still hold by the watchword of literality, – will maintain that as it is a literal Israel that is the subject of promise, a literal Canaan, a literal dispersion, and a literal return from it, such too must be all that is to come, – then, we say, let them carry it out, and the shepherd by whom the good is to be accomplished must be the literal David, for David alone is expressly named in the promise; and so the Messiah altogether vanishes from the word of which he is the very heart and centre, and there must be no advance in the Divine dispensations, nothing but the formal reproduction of the past. Such is the result of a slavish adherence to the letter; it ends in shutting up the new wine of the Messiah's kingdom in the old bottles of a transitory and provisional economy. It was necessary that the spirit of prophecy should serve itself of such old things, so long as the old lasted; but it it otherwise now, since the greater and better things have come – things so great and good, that *"eye hath not seen them, nor ear heard, nor had they entered into the mind of man."* And we do no more than make due allowance for the change that the introduction of these has brought into the Divine kingdom, when we say, that as the new David in the prophecy before us was to be one to whom the heritage, not of Canaan, but of the whole earth belonged, so the flock which he presides over and blesses must be the saints of God, gathered from every region by his grace, and feeding in security on his good pasturage; and that the full realization of the word of promise shall be found only when these saints with him shall possess the kingdom, and the ends of the earth shall be blessed in Christ.

CHAPTER XXXV.

THE JUDGMENT OF EDOM.

Superficial readers will be disposed to ask, What has Edom to do here? The Lord's judgment has already been pronounced against Edom (chap. 25:12-14), among the enemies of the covenant-people; and this fresh denunciation against it is inserted among predictions which, both before and after, have immediate respect to the covenant-people themselves. It is, however, in its proper place; and brings out another element in the prosperity which the Lord promises to his Church and people. It gives body and prominence to the thought expressed in ver. 28 of the preceding chapter, that *"they should no more be a prey to the heathen."* So far from it, the prophet now declares that the worst and bitterest of all the heathen shall be utterly destroyed and made desolate, and that those who were then rejoicing over Israel's calamities must themselves become a spoil, without any prospect of recovery.

[1]And the word of the LORD came to me, saying,

[2]Son of man, set your face against Mount Seir and prophesy against it.

[3]And say to it, Thus says the Lord GOD: Behold, O Mount Seir, I am against you, and I will stretch out My hand against you, and I will make you a ruin.

[4]I will lay your cities waste, and you shall be ruined, and you shall know that I am the LORD.

[5]Because you have had a never-ending hatred and have shed *the blood of* the children of Israel by the force of the sword[1] in the time of their calamity, in the time iniquity had an end,

[6]therefore, as I live, says the Lord GOD, I will yield you up to blood, and blood shall pursue you. Since you have not hated blood, even blood shall pursue you.[2]

[7]So I will make Mount Seir a ruin and cut off from it him who passes out and him who returns.

[8]And I will fill his mountains with his dead. In your hills, and in your valleys, and in all your rivers, those who are slain with the sword shall fall.

[9]I will make you ruins forever, and your cities shall not return. And you shall know that I am the LORD.

[10]Because you have said, These two nations and these two countries shall be mine, and we shall possess it – yet the LORD was there –[3]

[11]therefore, *as* I live, says the Lord GOD, I will even do according to your anger and according to your envy which you have shown out of your hatred against them. And I will make Myself known among them when I have judged you.

[12]And you shall know that I am the LORD. I have heard all your blasphemies which you have spoken against the mountains of Israel, saying, They are laid waste, they are given to us for food.

[13]So with your mouth you have boasted against Me, and have multiplied your words against Me. I have heard.

[14]Thus says the Lord GOD: When the whole earth rejoices, I will make you a ruin.[4]

[15]As you rejoiced at the inheritance of the house of Israel because it was a ruin, so I will do to you. You shall be a ruin, O Mount Seir and all I-du-me-a, *even* all of it. And they shall know that I am the LORD.

The leading object of this severe and unsparing denunciation against Edom, is plainly to exhibit in sharp contrast the things that concerned them with those which belonged to the covenant-people. There was an apparent superiority on the side of Edom at the time of Ezekiel wrote, but the real advantage was with Israel. In the latter, amid all their desolations, there still was a seed of blessing, the Divine germ of a glorious future; but in the other no such germ existed – nothing wrought there but enmity to God and holiness, and nothing was to be expected but unrelieved desolation. In the earlier prediction (chap. 25), while the Edomites were declared to be the objects of the Lord's vengeance, it was also said that *"his people Israel"* were to be the instruments of executing it. Here, however, nothing is mentioned as to the way by which the work of desolation was to be accomplished: the thoughts chiefly pressed are, that Edom's own destructive policy was to be meted back to her in full measure, and that the destruction in her case was to be singularly complete. So far from being allowed, as the children of Edom themselves thought, to step into the room of Israel and occupy what they had lost, they should not be able to retain their own: their prospects for the future looked out upon blank and dreary desolation.

It is necessary, however, to understand this, not absolutely of the Edomites as men, but only in their character as the hereditary and sworn enemies of the covenant-people – the people whom the Lord had chosen and blessed. For it is in this character that they are here introduced; and only when understood as applying to them thus, is the word found to consist either with the facts of history or with the prophecy of Amos (chap. 9:12), which makes mention of a remnant of Edom over whom, as well as other heathen, God's name should be called. But as a nation set with relentless hatred against the truth and people of God, the Edomites were doomed to utter destruction, and, as we said before, they actually experienced it. While Israel rose in Christ to the supremacy of the world, Edom vanished from the face of history – their memorial perished, their envy and cruel hatred were for ever buried among the ruins of the nations.

But why in this connection should Edom have alone been singled out for destruction by the prophet? Not as if her people only were appointed to suffer vengeance at the hand of God; but because in the bitterness of their spite, and the intensity of their hatred to the cause and people of God, they stood pre-eminent among the nations; and so were fitly chosen as the representatives of the whole. It is precisely what was done also by Isaiah in his sixty-third chapter, and still more strikingly in the thirty-fourth, when speaking of the Lord's controversy with the heathen, and the fury that he was to pour forth on the nations, it is all represented as concentrating itself on Edom, and taking end there in one fearful outburst of overwhelming vengeance. The region where the greatest enmity reigned is the ideal territory where the final recompenses of judgment take place. And that it is on the same account such peculiar prominence is here also given to Edom, is clear, not only from the connection and character of the prophecy itself, but also from what is written in ver. 5 of the next chapter, where it is said, that *"the Lord had spoken in the fire of his jealousy against the remnant of the heathen, and against all Edom."* While speaking against Edom, he had in reality spoken against all the heathen; for it was simply as heathen of the worst and most inveterate stamp,, that he had spoken as he did against Edom. So that wherever the same elements of evil might be found, the same judgment from the Lord might be expected.

This also, it will be seen, confirms the view we took of the promise to Israel in the preceding chapter. The coming good and evil are alike pictured forth under the old relations, as if these were always, and these only, to exist; while yet the word is pregnant with meaning for all nations and all times. The heathen at large are represented in Edom; and hence, by parity of reason, the whole elect family of God in Israel. Edom's doom as here delineated is the fate of heathendom; and Israel's promised blessedness and glory under the good shepherd carries in its bosom the high and happy destiny of the Church of the living God. As formerly in the case of Isaac and Ishmael (Gal. 4:22-31), so here in Israel and Edom, the whole human family have their representation – in the one all that are of the Spirit, in the other all that are of the flesh. The old relations in both cases alike have passed, and can never be recalled again; but the truth couched under them eternally abides. And in that truth, as set forth in the prophecy before us, there is embodied the solemn testimony, that the Edomite spirit, the carnal, unbelieving, rebellious spirit, is most surely doomed to perdition: enmity to the cause and kingdom of Christ is marked out in the councils of Heaven for irretrievable ruin. They who are of it cannot overthrow the Church, but must themselves be overthrown and fall under the stroke of vengeance.

CHAPTER XXXVI.

ISRAEL REVENGED AND COMFORTED – THE NEW HEART AND THE BLISSFUL HERITAGE.

In this chapter we have a continuation of the present great theme of the prophet: Israel's prospective revival and prosperity as the Lord's covenant-people. But it treats of this under different aspects. In the first section (vers. 1-15) the prophet unfolds the essential distinction between Israel and Edom with the other nations of heathendom, in that the former had, what the others had not, an interest in the power and faithfulness of God, in consequence of which Israel's heritage must revive and flourish, and the hopes of the heathen concerning it must be disappointed. In the next section (vers. 16-21) the reason is given why the Lord had for a time acted toward his land and people as if their connection with him was an evil rather than a blessing; it is traced up to the incorrigible wickedness of the people, and the necessity of God's vindicating the cause of his holiness by exercising upon them the severity of his displeasure. Then in another section (vers. 22-33) the purpose of the Lord for their future good is unfolded – his purpose for his own name's sake to revive his cause among his people, and that in the most effectual manner, by first renewing their hearts to holiness, and then by restoring them to a flourishing condition outwardly. And in a short concluding section (vers. 34-38) the general result is summed up, and the impressions noticed which the whole was fitted to produce upon the minds of others. We shall take up the chapter in these successive portions.

[1]Also, son of man, prophesy to the mountains of Israel and say, Mountains of Israel, hear the word of the LORD.

[2]Thus says the Lord GOD: Because the enemy has said against you, Aha! Even the old high places have become ours to possess.

[3]Therefore prophesy and say, Thus says the Lord GOD: Because they have wasted you and have panted after you on every side,[2] so that you might be a possession to the rest of the nations, and you have been taken up into the lips of talkers[3] and the gossip of the people;

[4]therefore, mountains of Israel, hear the word of the Lord GOD. Thus says the Lord GOD to the mountains, and to the hills, to the rivers, and to the valleys, to the deserted wastes, and to the cities that are forsaken, which became a prey and a mockery to the rest of the nations that are all around.

[5]Therefore thus says the Lord GOD: Surely in the fire of My jealousy I have spoken against the rest of the nations, and against all I-du-me-a,[4] who have given My land to themselves for a possession with the joy of all *their* heart, with scorning minds, that its casting out might be for a prey.[5]

[6]Therefore prophesy concerning the land of Israel, and say to the mountains and to the hills, to the rivers and to the valleys, Thus says the Lord GOD: Behold, I have spoken in My jealousy and in My fury, because you have borne the shame of the nations.

[7]Therefore thus says the Lord GOD: I have lifted up My hand, surely the nations that are around you shall bear their shame.

[8]But you, O mountains of Israel, you shall shoot out your branches and yield your fruit to My people Israel. For they have drawn near to come.

[9]For, behold, I am for you, and I will turn to you, and you shall be tilled and sown.

[10]And I will multiply men on you, all the house of Israel, all of it. And the cities shall have people, and the wastes shall be built.

[11]And I will multiply man and beast on you, and they shall increase and bring fruit. And I will settle you as in your old estates, and will do better than at your beginnings. And you shall know that I am the LORD.

[12]Yes, I will cause men to walk on you – My people Israel. And they shall possess you, and you shall be their inheritance, and you shall never again make them childless from now on.

[13]Thus says the Lord GOD: Because they say to you, You are a devourer of men, and you make your nations childless,

[14]therefore you shall devour men no more, nor shall you make your nations childless any more,[6] says the Lord GOD.

[15]I will not cause *men* to hear the shame of the nations in you any more, nor shall you bear the shame of the people any longer, nor shall you cause your nations to fall any more, says the Lord GOD.

This first section is mainly intended to exhibit the contrast that still existed, notwithstanding all appearances to the contrary, between Israel and the surrounding heathen. As matters now stood, it seemed to the eye of flesh that the dominion and the power were connected with heathenism, as if the conquering and predominating element were there, not with Israel. For at present the most depressed and desolate region in all that neighborhood was the land of Israel; what should have been pre-eminently the land of blessing had now become emphatically the land of emptiness and desolation; instead of cherishing and supporting, it had, as it were, ejected its inhabitants, as if weary of their presence, or opened its bosom to become their common sepulchre. It lay now like a defenceless prey before the Edomite and other heathen adversaries, who had so long waited and longed for the day of evil, and who therefore rejoiced over the fall of Israel as their greatest triumph. But this triumph, the Lord here declares by his servant, would be short; nay, it was the very reason why he must soon bring on a change, and reverse the present aspect and condition of things. Because the name of Jehovah was associated with Israel, he cannot allow this appearance of impotence in Israel, and power in the adversaries, to continue; he cannot give up his people to the scorn of the wicked, or his land to be divided by them at pleasure as their proper inheritance; he must restore everything again to its appropriate place, and settle in due order the relations of things. And he will presently do it. Israel shall again return and possess the land, whose prosperity and fulness shall be restored as at first, even more than restored, – for a higher state of felicity awaited them in the future than had been experienced in the past; and the reproach would be for ever taken away of the land proving the death-region of its inhabitants.

It is clear, from the whole tenor of this prophecy, that the good it contemplates and promises for Israel must have begun at an early period to be realized; for not only is it expressly said that it was near to come, or nigh at hand, but the Edomites and other heathen neighbors are represented as still occupying the same relations towards Israel as they had done – only henceforth themselves bearing the reproach which they were then casting upon Israel, and incapable of any longer speaking scornfully of the covenant land and people. I should hold it to be a dishonest shift, first to take the terms of the prophecy in their literal import, and then say there has as yet been no fulfilment in the past, but there shall be one in the future – a literal Israel shall yet find the literal Canaan all that is here predicted. For if there has been no fulfilment in the past of a literal kind, neither can there be in the future; there shall certainly want two most essential elements of literality: first, the nearness of accomplishment spoken of by the prophet; and the existence of the Edomites and other heathen neighbors, who for the present rejoiced in Canaan as lying at their feet, but were again to find its reproach and humiliation become their own, while it and Israel were exalted. These ancient adversaries are for ever gone; the external relations of that olden time have entirely ceased; and if Israel were restored to-morrow, it would be necessary to take this part of the prophecy in another than the literal sense.

But we do, on the other hand, hold by nothing literal in the interpretation, and look for nothing literal in the fulfilment? By no means. We regard the passage as a prophecy of the full return of prosperity and blessing to the Lord's covenant-people, and even the perpetual enjoyment of this – exhibited under the form of the Old Testament relations, the only ones lying within the ken of the prophet. As soon as the prophecy was uttered, it was the duty of the Lord's people to deal with him respecting the fulfilment of the word, and to look for the fulfilment in the most exact and literal manner. There can be no question that some amongst them did this; and, within a period that might justly be called near, the Lord showed, by a marvellous turn in providence, how ready he was on his part to accomplish what was promised, and how he laid open to them the way of a speedy return to national greatness and prosperity. The opportunity was not embraced as it should have been by the children of the dispersion: only a comparatively small number of them actually returned to the land of their fathers when the opening was presented to them; and of those who did, many still wanted the spirit of piety, which alone God promised to bless. Still, with all the shortcomings and imperfections that existed, a certain fulfilment of the most literal kind began at an early period to be given to the prophecy. People of the stock of Israel did again possess the land of their fathers; by them the mountains of Israel were again cultivated, and for them the land yielded its fruit; there again, as of old, the seed of man and of beast did greatly increase and multiply, so that the region was known for ages as one of the most fertile and prosperous in Asia; and that too while the old and hereditary enemies of Israel in the neighborhood sank into comparative insignificance, and lost their original place in the scale of nations. Had Israel but seen in all this the hand of God, and viewed the whole in connection with his unchangeable righteousness, there should certainly have been nothing wanting to complete the correspondence between the description of the prophet and the facts of history; the fulfilment would have been, not partial and temporary, but full and permanent, while the old relations lasted; and even when they changed, the good for the natural Israel, so far from ceasing would only have risen to a higher sphere, and passed into a nobler realization.

So long, therefore, as the relations of the prophet's time existed – that is, so long as the kingdom of God was connected with the people of Israel as a distinct nation, with the land of Canaan as their proper inheritance, and heathen rivals and enemies for their neighbors – so long as this was the case, we hold that as nothing but a literal fulfilment should have been looked for, so a very considerable fulfilment of this nature, and one that sufficiently marked the hand of God, did take place. Still all was then marred with imperfection. The religion itself of the covenant-people was such, it could make nothing perfect; and we can only look for the promised good being realized in any degree of completeness when the better things of the new dispensation come in. But then, at the same time, the old relations of necessity give way: the outward Israel are no longer distinctively the covenant-people; all the children of faith of every land become the seed of blessing, and heirs according to the promise. And while it is only under the Gospel dispensation that we can expect the perfect realization of the promised good, we must now no longer expect it after the old form, or according to the simply literal interpretation. The good is too great and expansive to be now shut up within such narrow limits; for since wherever there is a royal priesthood offering up spiritual services to God, there the incense and offerings of the temple are perpetuated (Mal. 1:11; 1 Pet. 2:5); so wherever there are members of Christ, there also are the mountains of Canaan, there are the people who have the promise of all things for their portion, on whom descends the blessing - life for evermore. Nor can the old evils properly return again; for the good is avowedly connected with nothing but a spiritual qualification, and is entirely dissevered from a merely ancestral relationship or a political existence in the world.

We can see nothing fanciful or arbitrary in this mode of interpretation, and are persuaded that it rests upon an indispensable necessity, partly in the nature of things, and partly in the operations of the human mind. For the grounds of this we refer to the remarks on the preceding chapter, and proceed to the next section of the prophecy.

[16]And the word of the LORD came to me, saying,

[17]Son of man, when the house of Israel lived in their own land, they defiled it by their own way and by their doings. Their way was like the uncleanness of a woman set apart before Me.

[18]Therefore I poured My fury on them because of the blood that they had shed on the land, and for their idols *with* which they had defiled it.

[19]And I scattered them among the nations, and they were scattered through the countries. I judged them according to their way and according to their doings.

[20]And when they entered into the nations where they went, they defiled My holy name when they said of them, These are the people of the LORD, and have gone forth out of His land.

[21]But I had pity for My holy name, which the house of Israel had defiled among the nations where they went.[7]

The passage, it will be observed, is of an unfinished and incomplete nature, being chiefly intended to form a sort of preamble to the great promise contained in the next section. It assigns the reason of all the severities which had been exercised by God upon the covenant-people; which it traces to their own sinful ways, viewed in connection with the holiness of God. Because of this he had banished them from his presence, and driven them as exiles into foreign lands. And even then so inveterate was their attachment to sin, they still continued to follow their forbidden practices; and by so doing, as also by the abject condition in which they appeared, they still further brought reproach upon the holy name of God. Had he therefore sought merely in them the reason of his procedure, nothing could have been expected but a continuance of the severity until they were utterly consumed. But a higher reason presented itself to the mind of God in regard to his own name, which he must vindicate from the dishonor thus brought upon it; and which, situated as matters were, he could only effectually do by accomplishing a change to the better in their condition. But this change must be no superficial one. The evil had its seat in the opposition between them and the righteousness of God, and the first grand step to an effectual and permanent recovery must consist in their thorough renewal of heart to the Divine image. This is what is promised in the verses that follow.

[22]Therefore say to the house of Israel, Thus says the Lord GOD: I do not do *this* for your sakes, O house of Israel but for My holy name's sake, which you have defiled among the nations where you went.
[23]And I will sanctify My great name, which was defiled among the nations, which you have defiled in their midst. And the nations shall know that I am the LORD, says the Lord GOD, when I shall be sanctified in you before their eyes.
[24]For I will take you from among the nations and gather you out of all countries, and will gather you into your own land.[8]
[25]Then I will sprinkle clean water on you, and you shall be clean. I will cleanse you from all your filthiness and from your idols.
[26]I will also give you a new heart, and I will put a new spirit within you. And I will take away the stony heart out of your flesh, and I will give you a heart of flesh.
[27]And I will put My Spirit within you and cause you to walk in My statutes, and you shall keep and do My judgments.
[28]And you shall live in the land that I gave to your fathers. And you shall be My people, and I will be your God.
[29]I will also save you from all your uncleannesses, and I will call for the grain and will increase it, and I will lay no famine on you.
[30]And I will multiply the fruits of the tree and the increase of the field, so that you shall never again receive the curse of famine among the heathen.
[31]Then you shall remember your own evil ways, and your doings that were not good, and shall despise yourselves in your own sight for your iniquities and for your idolatries.
[32]I do not do *this* for your sakes, says the Lord GOD, be it known to you. Be ashamed and blush for your own ways, O house of Israel.

In this rich and encouraging promise of good things to come there is, first, a very strong asseveration as to the ground on which God's contemplated interference for Israel's behoof was to proceed; negatively, not on their own account, – positively, on account of his own name, which they had profaned. Looking simply to their state and conduct, the Lord, it is declared, could find occasion only for continued severity of dealing, and they themselves for profound humiliation and silent shame. The axe was here, therefore, laid at the root of all self-righteous boasting and fleshly confidences. Just as at first, when Moses said to their fathers, *"Not for thy righteousness or for the uprightness of thy heart dost thou go to possess this land, for thou art a stiff-necked people"* (Deut. 9:5,6); so here the prophet disclosed the utter absence of any personal claim on the Divine goodness, and showed that whatever might henceforth be experienced, it must proceed from the upper spring of God's own grace and righteousness. In himself alone could the Lord find the motive of benevolent action. And while this laid all human merit in the dust, it furnished at the same time a rich ground of consolation and hope, such as could not be found in any inferior consideration or fleshly confidence. For it carried the humble heart of faith above the very sins and backslidings which had caused the judgments of Heaven to alight, and presented to it a source of life and blessing which even these could not stanch. And need we say, that as this was then the only hope of Israel, so now it is the one fountain-head of all the salvation that is experienced by the Christian? *"Not by works of righteousness which we have done, but by his mercy, he saved us,"* is the truth which is written on the threshold of faith, and which must pass into the experience of every sinner as he enters therein. No real life is attainable but such as carries in its bosom the death of all self-trust, and the renunciation of every personal claim on the goodness of God. And mortifying as this is to human pride, it yet provides the only solid and abiding peace for those who have come rightly to know the evil of sin; for it draws the soul up to God, and teaches it to form its expectations of good, not by any merit or demerit of its own, but by the large measures of God's own free and spontaneous beneficence, and the eternal principles of his high administration. The creature thus exchanges the vanity of a human ground for the infinite sufficiency of a Divine one, and the feebleness of an arm of flesh for the all-prevailing might of omnipotence.

But in regard to the promise before us, it is to be considered not only that God finds the ground of action solely in himself, but in himself with respect to his own glory, or the vindication of his name before the world. By what has happened in Israel, and what is still proceeding among them, this name is blasphemed; for it seems as if Jehovah, the God of Israel, were unable to stand before the might of heathenism, and protect and bless his people. Such thoughts, however naturally arising in the circumstances, proceeded on a partial and mistaken view of the character of Jehovah, and especially from an ignorance of his essential righteousness. The heathen judged of Jehovah from their own idol-gods, and hence had no way of accounting for the desolations that had befallen the land and people of Canaan but the comparative impotence of Him in whom they trusted. Therefore, in wiping away this foul reproach, the Lord must act in such a manner as would serve to bring clearly out in the light of day the righteousness which forms the most distinguishing element of his character, and which required only to be understood, both to explain what had taken place of evil, and secure the introduction of the contrary good. But how could such a manifestation of the Divine righteousness be given? It must plainly begin where the evil had its rise – in the hearts of the people with whom God's name was associated. The love of sin there was the polluted fountain-head from which the whole succession of troubles and disasters had sprung; and nothing could effectually reach the evil which did not provide for the re-establishment of holiness in their hearts. Therefore Israel must first of all be made a holy people, – their pollutions must be done away, their hearts subdued and wrought into a conformity to God's holiness, – that they might be known to be his chosen ones from the bright reflection seen in them of his own pure and righteous character. Then, understanding from the regenerated state and exemplary lives of his people what sort of being Jehovah is, the heathen would find a ready explanation of all the tribulations that he had brought upon Israel in the past; they would perceive these to be only the necessary vindications of Jehovah's righteousness on a people who refused to yield themselves to his authority and comply with his will. At the same time, also, the way would be opened for the introduction of a more blessed and glorious future; for the people now entering with their very hearts into the righteousness of God, became capable of the highest outward good from his hand; and all the peculiar blessings of the covenant in a land replenished with the bountifulness of heaven would once more become their portion. Thus God would vindicate the glory of his name by first forming his people to the possession of his own holiness, and then by treating them, as thus renewed and sanctified, to the richest outward tokens of his favor and goodness.[9]

Keeping in view the distinctive character of the prophecy as now explained, no difficulty can be found in regard to its particular expressions. Thus the expression in ver. 23, *"I sanctify my name,"* is at once seen to refer, not to what this name is in itself, but to the reflection given of it in his people. It had been profaned by their wickedness and misery, it must again be sanctified by their returning to holiness and blessing; for God is sanctified when what he is in himself becomes apparent in the world, especially in those who stand nearest to him. So also the expression at the close of the same verse, *"when I sanctify myself in you before your eyes;"* for which many critical authorities, both ancient and modern, would substitute, *"before their eyes,"* namely, those of the heathen. This expression creates no difficulty to a person who enters thoroughly into the import of the passage, for it points to the fact that Israel as well as the heathen needed the manifestation in question of Jehovah's righteousness. It must be done first before the eyes of the people, who by their depravity had lost sight of God's real character; and then what was seen by them experimentally would also be seen reflectively by the heathen who dwelt around. This twofold perception of God's character is also brought out in other passages of our prophet; as in chap. 20:41,42: *"And I will be sanctified in you before the eyes of the heathen, and ye shall know that I am Jehovah."* Finally, the mention, in ver. 25, of clean water to be sprinkled on the people as the means of purification can only be understood symbolically; it does not refer to any mere external rite, or to any specific ordinance of the old covenant, such as the lustration ceremony with water and the ashes of the red heifer (Rosenmuller, Hengs.), or to the ablutions connected with the consecration of the Levites (Havernick); it is rather to be viewed in reference to the purifications by water collectively, which were all, in one respect or another, symbolical of the removal of impurity, and the establishment of the worshipper in a sound and acceptable condition. This was no more of a merely formal and outward character in Old Testament times than it is now, as we may learn from the whole tenor of this prophecy. It was by their moral pollutions most of all that the people of Israel had profaned God's name and drawn down his displeasure; and the purification, which was to undo the evil and again to sanctify the name of God, could be nothing short of a conformity to God's own righteousness, which throughout all ages is the same. The whole of the water-lustrations of the Jews were symbolical of this purity of heart and conduct; and in referring to them here the prophet simply expresses in symbolical language a great spiritual promise – the Lord would make Israel in reality what under the law was outwardly denoted by a sprinkling with clean water. He gives himself, indeed, the interpretation in the verses that follow, where the change is described by the Lord's imparting to them a new heart, and putting his own Spirit within them. In short, the peculiar blessing promised for the future was their being raised to the participation of God's holiness, precisely as in the past the great evil was their having become morally so unlike him.

The last section, as was noticed before, is merely a gathering up of the general result, with some reference to the impressions it was fitted to produce upon the minds of others.

[33]Thus says the Lord GOD: In the day that I shall have cleansed you from all your iniquities, I will also cause *you* to dwell in the cities, and the wastes shall be built.

[34]And the waste land shall be tilled, instead of laying waste in the sight of all who passed by.

[35]And they shall say, This land that was wasted has become like the garden of Eden. And the waste and deserted and ruined cities now are walled and have people in them.

[36]Then the nations that are left all around you shall know that I the LORD build the ruined *places and* plant that which was wasted. I the LORD have spoken and I will act.

[37]Thus says the Lord GOD: I will yet *for* this be inquired of by the house of Israel to do it for them. I will increase them with men like a flock.

[38]As the holy flock, as the flock of Jerusalem in her solemn feasts; so shall the waste cities be filled with flocks of men. And they shall know that I am the LORD.

The general meaning is, that the purpose of God was to accomplish an entire change in the outward as well as the inward condition of his people. They would be as remarkably distinguished for prosperity and blessing as they had been for distress and desolation, so that even the passing stranger could not fail to notice the happy revolution that had taken place in their circumstances; but still not as a matter of fixed and inevitable necessity, nor in any way that might supersede the obligation resting on themselves personally to seek and serve the Lord. Hence the intimation is made at ver. 37, that for this the Lord would *"yet be inquired of by the house of Israel to do it for them."* On former occasions he had refused to be inquired of by them (chap. 14:3, 20:3), that is, sought after in such a manner as to be found ready to perform what was expected, because the inquirers were not in a condition to receive any token of his favor and blessing. Only, therefore, in so far as they attained to a better condition, and stood morally on right terms with God, they were warranted to look for the happy and flourishing state described in the promise. And the higher always they rose in the one respect, the higher also might they expect God to raise them in the other.

Such promises as those contained in this chapter cannot therefore be taken in an absolute sense; they must be understood to some extent conditionally. They reveal the kind propensions of God towards his people – what he is disposed and ready to do toward them – rather than what he will for certain accomplish at any one stage or period of their history. So far the word contains an absolute element, as God certainly pledges himself to make provision for securing, in a larger measure than formerly, a proper regeneration of heart and conduct in his people, and also for giving palpable proof of this in their more flourishing and prosperous condition generally. The goodness of God was certainly to manifest itself for these ends; but it would do so to the full extent represented, only if they continued in his goodness. In the case of God's threatenings, even when most particular and express, it was always possible by a change of mind to the better to escape the evil; according to the word in Jeremiah: *"At what instant I speak concerning a kingdom to pluck up, and to pull down, and to destroy; if that nation against whom I have pronounced turn from their evil, I will repent of the evil that I thought to do unto them"* (chap. 18:7). And there is no reason why we should not expect the same rule to hold in respect to the promises. Here also there would be but a partial realization of what was announced, if the spiritual condition on which it proceeded was not complied with, and those to whom the promise was given set themselves to resist the grace of God. The possibility of their doing this is plainly implied in the accomplishment of the promise being so specially connected with their inquiring of God concerning it; and it was still more distinctly indicated in another passage, where they are commanded to do for themselves what the Lord here promised to do for them, – *"make you a new heart and a new spirit"* (chap. 18:31), – as much as to say, Do not expect the good as an absolute and inalienable heritage of blessing; like all spiritual blessing, it stands inseparably connected with your own earnestness of purpose and diligence in working.

The question, no doubt, may still be asked, Since God himself undertakes to give to Israel as a people the new heart and the right spirit, on which all depends, how could there be any failure of what was promised without unfaithfulness in God? The question, however, touches on the secret things, which belong not to us, but to God himself. For it may as well be asked, Why is there only a partial renewal in the case of any individual Christian, seeing he has the Omnipotent Spirit dwelling in him? or, Why, since the Lord promised the Spirit to convince the world of sin, righteousness, and judgment, is the world still so imperfectly convinced? Had the Spirit continued to work universally, as he did on the day of Pentecost, or with sinners individually, as he did in the case of Saul of Tarsus, the world would long ere now have been converted to the truth of Christ. But somehow there are elements at work, and ends higher even than salvation, though closely connected with it, which still limit, though they cannot altogether prevent, the realization of the good unfolded in the promises. Were we to look simply to the good exhibited in these, we might have expected to see in Israel before the coming of Messiah a people all righteous, and a land replenished through all its bounds with fruitfulness and blessing; as after his coming we might equally have expected to find a Church instinct in every part with the Spirit of life and holiness, and ordinances of grace operating with resistless might to the diffusion of light and blessing in the world. But in both respects alike the good promised on the part of God is qualified by the evil that works in the world; and though the good must ultimately triumph because it has Omnipotence on its side, yet till the last issues of Providence are brought in, we may still expect it to be to some extent countervailed by the intermingling evil. So far, then, the matter admits of an explanation, and that of a kind fitted to abase and silence man, as it charges on his own culpable negligence and waywardness whatever shortcoming may appear in the good that is realized, as compared with the larger good that is promised. But when we rise to the higher region of Divine grace, sovereignty, and power, and begin to inquire why these operate no farther, or not otherwise than they do, we soon reach an insurmountable barrier; for with our present imperfect powers of discernment we have no way of explaining how the good that is in God, the good even that is expressed in his promises of blessing, should not prevail more effectually than it does over the evil that is in man. In this respect God gives no account of his matters; and remembering that we now see but in part, it becomes us to be silent, or to say only with our blessed Lord: *"Even so, Father, for so it seemeth good in thy sight."*

CHAPTER XXXVII.

THE VISION OF THE DRY BONES RESTORED TO LIFE AGAIN, AS SYMBOLICAL OF ISRAEL'S DEATH AND RESURRECTION.

The preceding prophecies have unfolded, in all essential particulars, the future salvation of Israel as God's covenant-people – on what conditions it was to proceed, and in what respects it was to develope itself. "The prophet's eye," however – to use the words of Ewald – "still dwells upon the manner in which it is to unfold itself, and beholds with rapture how it arises, how it grows, how it becomes insuperably great. Three stages here present themselves in vivid colors to the vision of the prophet: 1. The new awakening of the people, the resurrection of the dead (chap. 37:1-14); 2. Then the reunion of the formerly hostile members of the community, through whose contentions the whole had suffered (chap. 37:15-28); Finally, 3. The strength of the community thus again restored, so as to be able to meet the formidable danger which was to come from the hostile assault of God with all the inimical heathen forces of the earth" (chapters 38,39). This is a brief outline of the leading subjects now immediately before us, and of the relations in which they stand to each other.

[1]The hand of the LORD was on me and carried me out of the Spirit of the LORD and set me down in the midst of a valley[1] which was full of bones,

[2]and caused me to pass by them all around. And, behold, *there were* very many in the open valley. And, lo, *they were* very dry.

[3]And He said to me, Son of man, can these bones live? And I answered, O Lord GOD, You know.

[4]Again He said to me, Prophesy to these bones and say to them, O dry bones, hear the word of the LORD.

[5]Thus says the Lord GOD to these bones. Behold, I will cause breath to enter into you, and you shall live.

[6]And I will lay sinews on you and will bring up flesh on you and cover you with skin, and put breath in you, and you shall live. And you shall know that I am the LORD.

[7]So I prophesied as I was commanded. And as I prophesied, there was a noise. And, behold, a shaking! And the bones came together, bone to its bone.

[8]And I watched. Behold! The sinews and the flesh came on them, and the skin covered them above. But no breath *was* in them.

[9]Then He said to me, Prophesy to the Spirit; prophesy, son of man and say to the Spirit, Thus says the Lord GOD: Come from the four winds, O Spirit, and breathe on these dead ones so that they may live.[2]

[10]So I prophesied as He commanded me, and the Spirit came into them, and they lived and stood on their feet, a very great army.[3]

[11]Then He said to me, Son of man, these bones are the whole house of Israel. Behold, they say, Our bones are dried and our hope is lost – we are cut off by ourselves. [4]

[12]Therefore prophesy and say to them, Thus says the Lord GOD: Behold, O My

people, I will open your graves and cause you to come up out of your graves and will bring you into the land of Israel.

[13]And you shall know that I am the LORD, when I have opened your graves, O My people, and have brought you up out of your graves.

[14]And I shall put My Spirit in you, and you shall live, and I will place you in your own land. Then you shall know that I the LORD have spoken and have done *it*, says the LORD.

There can be no reasonable doubt as to the leading scope and purpose of this remarkable vision. It is intended to counteract the feeling of despair which had now succeeded to the opposite one of carnal security and presumptuous confidence which, at an earlier period, had wrought so disastrously among the people. Now that they were reduced to so hapless and shattered a condition, the glowing delineations the prophet had been drawing of a happy future seemed as visionary to their minds as formerly had appeared his dark forebodings of impending distress and ruin. They felt as if they had become like bones dried and scattered at the grave's mouth, and destitute of everything on which they could build any reasonable prospect of restored felicity. The prophet therefore meets them on their own ground. He admits that, as compared with the elevated prospects he had been unfolding, they were in themselves no better than lifeless skeletons; but at the same time shows that even this could raise no barrier against the realization of the better future, since they had to do with the word of him who is equally able to make alive as to kill. Carried in spirit into a valley of destruction, he there sees the whole ground covered with bones, the skeletons of slaughtered men, so thoroughly bleached and dried by long exposure to the atmosphere that all apparent capability of life had left them; and when asked whether such bones should live, he could only refer the matter to God, as one that exclusively belonged to his grace and power. But presently, on being commanded to prophesy to them, or to proclaim God's purpose to endow them anew with the powers and properties of life, the word is no sooner uttered than it begins to take effect. The rushing sound of God's mighty working is heard, – bone is seen starting up and joining itself to its fellow; immediately they are clothed upon with sinews, and flesh, and skin; and then, in obedience to another word of God, the breath of life from his creative Spirit penetrates the whole mass, and transforms them into a host of valiant men, instinct with the animation and braced with the healthful freshness and energy of life. Such is the wonderful scene that took place in vision before the eyes of the prophet; and in the application that is made of it, he is told that these bones are (i.e., represent) the whole house of Israel, who were then indeed, as to all that could be called life according to the covenant of God, in a lost condition – in a manner dead and buried; but he is assured they should be again resuscitated by the word of God, brought up from their present temporary graves, and resettled in their own land to enjoy once more the blessings of the covenant.

Considered in this natural manner, there is no difficulty in the passage. It is merely intended, in the most lively and effectual way, to remove the despondency that hung over the minds of the people, by exhibiting before them an exercise of Divine power, similar that which was needed to retrieve their ruined fortunes, and put them in a condition to inherit all the good of which Ezekiel had spoken. In the visions of God – the proper region of the prophet's activity – he shows them an effect of the Divine Spirit adequate to the full wants and necessities of their state; so that they might the more readily reassure their hearts, and encourage themselves in God as to the issue. If we keep this one definite object of the vision in view, we are in little danger of misapprehending the representation. It was certainly doing a kind of violence to it as furnishing in itself a direct and explicit proof of the resurrection (for example, Tertul. de Resur. Car. 100:30; Jerome, in loco; Augustine, de Genes. ad lit. 10:8), in which they have been followed by many distinguished modern divines. The greater part indeed hold, after the manner of Jerome, that the resurrection here is introduced only, by way of similitude, as an image of Israel's restoration, which it could not have been unless the resurrection itself had been considered certain.[5] Calov, however, maintains that, down to the close of ver. 10, the passage treats distinctly of the resurrection from the dead in the literal sense, and that what follows is entirely another discourse, in which God's promised goodness to Israel is presented under the analogy of that literal resurrection.

This last view is manifestly untenable, as it breaks into two separate parts what obviously but one discourse, and regards as an independent action what was done only with a view to its intended application. Even the other and more common view is not strictly tenable. For it is not properly a similitude that Ezekiel uses in the vision, as if from the certain fact of a general future resurrection he would fortify Israel in the belief and expectation of their own political resuscitation; but it is this resuscitation itself exhibited now in vision, that they might be prepared to look for it afterwards in the reality. The mere circumstance of such a resurrection-scene being thus employed by the prophet for such a specific purpose, could not of itself prove the doctrine of a future general resurrection of the dead, – no more than his employing the machinery of cherubim and wheels of peculiar structure in his opening vision is a proof of the actual existence of such objects, either in the past or the future, in heaven or on earth. In both cases alike, what was exhibited in the vision was a representation in symbol of something corresponding that might be expected in the transactions of life and the events of providence; but whether that symbol might have any separate and substantial existence of its own was not determined by such an employment of it, and, in fact, was quite immaterial as regarded the end in view. The resurrection-scene here is simply a prophecy in action, to render more palpable to the view and more credible to the apprehension of the people the corresponding prophecy in word, and stands parallel to the prophetic actions of the sealing vision in chap. 9, or the prophet's going into exile in chap. 12.

At the same time, while the mere employment of such a scene in a symbolical vision cannot justly be regarded as of itself establishing the doctrine of the resurrection, it should undoubtedly have a place assigned it among the collateral proofs of the doctrine. Its introduction in such a free and familiar manner clearly bespoke it to be one of the loftier anticipations with which the servants of God sought to accustom the minds of the people; which they would have them take, in a manner, for granted, as things destined one day to be actually realized. It may justly be classed with such brief and familiar allusions as those in Isaiah 25:8, *"He will swallow up death in victory;"* and chap. 26:19, *"Thy dead men shall live, together with my dead body shall they arise: awake and sing, ye that dwell in dust;"* also Dan. 12:2, *"And many of them that sleep in the dust of the earth shall awake."* And then the principle on which, as its very basis, the whole vision rests, is one that carries in its bosom the hope of the resurrection to all the family of God. For it is the relation of the people, whom those bones represented, to God himself, securing for them an interest in the vital energy and omnipotent working of his hand, on which everything is made to hang. The resurrection must take place, because the living God cannot let death work in those who are related to him as his own – those in regard to whom he can say, my people. But this, of course, holds good of the literal resurrection from the dead, not less than of any temporary revival out of death-like bondage and degradation; and is, in truth, the very kernel of the argument used by our Lord against the Sadducees, when, from the declaration of God to Moses at the bush, *"I am the God of Abraham, of Isaac, and of Jacob,"* he showed that the dead are raised, because *"God is not a God of the dead, but of the living; for all live unto him."* An argument not so subtle and profound as many would represent it, but level to the apprehension even of the commonest believers! It is simply this: that God having owned himself the God of those patriarchs, their bodies cannot be lost, they must live again; because, by taking to himself the name of their God, he undertook to do for them whatever Omnipotence itself could perform. Just as if one were to adopt a helpless orphan into his family, and promise to be a father to it, should he not warrant the child to expect everything that paternal love or fidelity could do for it? So when God said to Abraham, *"I am thy God,"* he virtually said, Whatever a God can do for thee, that thou mayest look for at my hands.

But cannot God – he who at first formed Abraham of the dust of the ground, and afterwards breathed life into his dead soul – cannot he also breathe the life of immortality into Abraham's mouldering body? Doubtless he can, and because he can he will – he must. He is the ever-living God, and life must be the property of all that are his. He who would have been ashamed to be called their God if he had not provided for them a city, would much more have been ashamed to be called their God if their very body, an essential part of their nature, were to be for ever left rotting in the dust. This would not have been to do to them the part of their God.

It is precisely this relation to God, so pregnant with blessing to those who possess it, on which the promise of good in the word before us is founded. And it must have been impossible for any thoughtful and pious Israelite to enter into the application made of it, to the temporal resuscitation of Israel's prostrate condition, without perceiving how it also involved, for all true believers, the future resurrection of their bodies from the power of death.[6] But along with this higher instruction enwrapped in the prophecy, let us not overlook the honor ascribed in it to the Divine word, as whose proclamation from the lips of a man of God the dead hear, the scattered bones move into their proper places, the spirit of life breathes and quickens. How does the Lord here show that he magnifies that word above all his name! It is his peculiar and chosen instrument of working. Where it alights, there darkness becomes light – death itself is again turned into life. *"For the word of God is quick and powerful, and sharper than a two-edged sword."* When he really *"speaks, it is done; when he commands, it stands fast."*

We turn now to the second part of the prophecy, which occupies the remaining verses of the chapter, and points especially to the reunion of the formerly hostile members of the community.

[15]The word of the LORD came again to me, saying,

[16]And, son of man, take a stick and write on it, For Judah and for the children of Israel who are his companions. Then take another stick and write on it, For Joseph, the stick of Ephraim, and all the house of Israel who are his companions.

[17]And join them to one another into one stick. And they shall become one in your hand.

[18]And when the children of your people shall speak to you, saying, Will you not show us what you *mean* by these?

[19]Say to them, Thus says the Lord GOD: Behold, I will take the stick of Joseph, which is in the hand of Ephraim, and the tribes of Israel who are his companions, and I will put them with him, with the stick of Judah, and will make them one stick, and they shall be one in My hand.[7]

[20]And the sticks on which you write shall be in your hand before their eyes.

[21]And say to them, Thus says the Lord GOD: Behold, I will take the children of Israel from among the nations where they have gone, and will gather them on every side, and will bring them into their own land.

[22]And I will make them one nation in the land on the mountains of Israel, and one king shall be king to them all. And they shall never again be two nations, nor shall they be divided into two kingdoms any more at all.

[23]They shall not defile themselves any more with their idols, nor with their hateful things, nor with any of their transgressions. But I will save them out of all their dwelling places in which they have sinned, and will cleanse them. So they shall be My people, and I will be their God.

[24]And David My servant shall be king over them. And they shall all have one Shepherd. They shall also walk in My judgments and obey My laws, and do them.

[25]And they shall dwell in the land that I have given to Jacob My servant, the *land* in which your fathers have lived. And they shall live in it, they and their children, and their children's children forever. And My servant David shall be their king forever.

[26]And I will make a covenant of peace with them. It shall be an everlasting covenant with them. And I will place them[8] and multiply them, and I will set My sanctuary in their midst forevermore.

[27]Also My tabernacle shall be with them.[9] Yes, I will be their God, and they shall be My people.

[28]And the nations shall know that I the LORD sanctify Israel, when My sanctuary shall be in their midst forevermore.

Here, precisely as in the resurrection-scene of the earlier part, the action with the rods, first writing on them the name of the two ancient divisions of the covenant-people, and then pressing them together into one, is employed merely as a symbol of what was to take place with the people themselves – a prophecy in action, to give distinctness and credibility to the immediately following prophecy in word. And for the direct import of the communication, the close and brotherly union among the members of the covenant that forms the substance of it, is here presented to our view as an immediate and certain effect of the manifestation of God's power to revive and bless them, and as the necessary condition to their complete and final establishment. The whole people of Israel had been represented as participating in the regenerating efficacy of the spirit of life, which was to be given from above; and as the direct result of this was to unite them to God, so its secondary operation could not fail to be to unite them in brotherly concord with each other. For the true covenant-people must form but one body, as they can only have one Head; and hence, as the necessary shell for preserving this great truth, it was so strictly enjoined of old that they should have put one temple, one high priest, one king, and one common-wealth. The breaking up of this united brotherhood by the revolt of the ten tribes under Jeroboam, however needful at the time as a salutary chastisement to the house of David, is constantly represented as a sad dismemberment of the household of God, and the source, to a large extent, of the more overwhelming tide of evils which thenceforth set in upon the land, and at last laid it desolate. As soon, therefore, as there might be produced a revived and healthful condition among the covenant-people, there must be a return to the brotherly union, and that in connection with the house of David; for to this house had been committed, by an irrevocable decree, the right to rule over the heritage of God; and to abide in separation from it was to continue in rebellion against Heaven. Nay, not only must the brotherly union find its centre in the house of David, but David himself must again preside over the united brotherhood; since he is pre-eminently that servant of God whose grand end in ruling was to do the will of God; and promote the ends of his righteous government. This God-honoring king must reign for ever; his rule shall be perpetuated through all generations; that the covenant of peace also may be perpetual, and that God's sanctuary may constantly abide among the people, and his name be magnified through their pure and prosperous condition. Thus, the order of God being re-established and made sure, there should be nothing any more to interrupt the flow of the Divine blessing; God would be most really present with his people; and the inheritance of good promised in the covenant, hitherto found only in part, be fully and for ever realized.

There is nothing absolutely new in the prophecy. It is substantially a fresh exhibition of the prospect already unfolded in chapters 34 and 36; but rendering prominent what was there implied rather than broadly asserted, the formal union of the covenant-people, along with their sanctification and blessedness, under the presidency of David. That there has been no adequate fulfilment of the prophecy in what may be called the literal sense of its terms, is too plain to require any lengthened proof. Some advances were of old made towards it – that is all that can be said. There was a return to some extent of the covenant-people, chiefly indeed of the house of Judah, though not without representa- from the other tribes; a visible display of union among such as did return; a partial repossession of the land of the covenant; and an external reconstruction of the temple and its worship, – enough to show that God had not forgotten his word, and that he was ready to bless to the full, if his people had been willing to seek to him for the blessing. But still all, not excepting even the things connected with the temple (see on chap. 21:26), were found in a very imperfect and mutilated condition – not after the bright pattern furnished here by the hand of the prophet. And the most characteristic part of the description – the cementing, strengthening, benignant rule of David – had not even the appearance of a literal fulfilment in the post-Babylonish history of Israel. The prophecy, therefore, has not been accomplished according to the letter in the past; and with so strong and prominent a feature of an ideal sort as the eternal presidency of David, it seems amazing that any one should expect it to be realized after that manner in the ages to come. For to that end it were indispensable that the literal David should be raised from the dead, and again set over the heritage of God, vested there even with perpetual sovereignty; notwithstanding that Christ has expressly received, by Divine appointment, the throne of his father David. The prophecy is a detailed picture of coming good, drawn, as such a picture must have been, under the form of the old covenant relations. It exhibits the prospective good, as a revival of Israel's best periods, freed from their still remaining defects and oft-intermingling judgments; and a picture that could be realized only in part while the old covenant stood, both from its own inherent imperfections and from the wilful neglect and obstinacy of its people. Not till the new covenant enters does the comparatively perfect begin to develope itself. For with the coming of Messiah, the head and centre of the new, as David was of the old, everything connected with God's kingdom takes a loftier flight and a wider range: the shadows vanish away, being supplanted by the substance; and that which before was partial and restricted presents now the aspect of an expansive freedom and a universal adaptation. The whole earth is as much Christ's rightful heritage as the territory and people of Canaan were David's; and only when it becomes his actual possession can the prophecy respecting him as the New Testament David reach its destined accomplishment. So that to speak now of the prophecy still requiring for its fulfilment a literal Israel, a literal Canaan, a literal tabernacle, with the many outward and fleshly conditions therewith connected, and that too in the face of the palpable incongruity in the heart of the prophecy of a non-literal David, is as if one were to reduce the lofty tree again to the puny dimensions of the plant, or send the man of full-grown stature back to his cradle – as if, in short, against all the experience of the past, which is ever moving on to something higher and better, we should expect the chariot-wheels of God's providence to return to their former courses, and keep within the ancient landmarks.

It was the peerless glory of Israel as a nation to give to the world the new David, who was to be for humanity the one child of hope, and to furnish to his hand the first builders of that spiritual house which was to be formed of renewed souls, and reared on the foundation of his perfected redemption. But there their destinctive honor ceases – not as if their real privileges and blessings were lost, but because these must henceforth be shared in common by the household of faith. The very mother that bore Jesus, and his nearest kindred, could attain to no peculiar place in his kingdom by reason of their earthly connection with him: not these, he said, but every one that heareth the word, and doeth the will of my Father in heaven, is my mother and sister and brother. Thus the fleshly bond was broken at the centre, and it must vanish to the farthest circumference; everything founded on natural relationships and genealogical descent was, with the handwriting of ordinances, nailed to the cross of Christ and buried in his grave, as a part of that bondage to the elements of the world from which the Church had at length escaped, and which should never more be heard of in her borders. The one relationship to be accounted of is union to Christ, which renders all who possess it children of Abraham, and heirs according to the promise – heirs, that is, of all that was given to Abraham in promise; more even, if more could be, for they are heirs of God and joint heirs with Christ himself. Therefore it is folly to speak of robbing the Jew by putting him on a level with the believer in Christ; for to put him there is to raise him to the highest standing that a child of humanity can enjoy, and give him a share in that which, being large enough for all, is not diminished, but rather enhanced by the numbers who partake in it. And for the Church herself, seeing that her exalted Head is now at the right hand of the Majesty on high, with power and authority to make the whole earth his possession, instead of seeking to revive the old distinctions, which have served their day, or hanging her hopes on effete outward arrangements, it is alike her wisdom and her duty to press forward the spiritual conquest of the world – plying with unwearied diligence the means of its regeneration, and withal waiting and praying for the time when, nature itself being regenerated, the earth shall become the fit abode of manifested Deity, and all shall be full of the knowledge, and resplendent with the glory, of the Lord. Then in the fullest sense shall the vision of our prophet be realized; for then the entire territory of the new covenant shall be reclaimed for righteousness, and the tabernacle of the Lord most truly be with men.

In closing this section, we present a brief outline of the view that has been taken of the prophecies contained in the three closely related chapters, 34, 36, 37; and which in substance applies equally to many other portions of the prophetical Scriptures. 1. They were originally given to revive and animate the hearts of God's covenant-people, by holding out to them the assured prospect of a reversion from the present evil, and their still certain destination in God's purpose to the highest and most honorable place on the earth. 2. It was the duty of those to whom such prophecies were delivered, at once to believe the word spoken to them, and apply themselves in earnest to do what was needed to secure its accomplishment; and had they only done this, a far larger measure of the promised good would have been reaped than they actually experienced: this later prospect of blessing, like the earlier, given before entering Canaan, greatly failed through their own sinful unbelief. 3. But there being manifestly ideal features introduced into the delineation, especially the good spoken of being so peculiarly connected with the rule and presidency of David, clearly betokens a kind and degree of blessing which could not have been completely fulfilled under the old covenant, nor intended to be altogether fulfilled any time according to the letter. It shows the prophecies in question to be, like several of an earlier kind in Ezekiel, descriptions of the future under the form and image of the past – not as if the past were actually to return again, but that its general spirit and character were to revive. 4. The new things thus to be looked for in the future could only meet with their full and adequate accomplishment in Christ, who is certainly the David of the promise. They are consequently of a higher and more comprehensive nature than any that could be enjoyed under the old covenant, when the kingdom of God was so straitened in its dimensions and so outward and earthly in its visible constitution. But still, they were of necessity described under the hue and aspect of the things belonging to the old covenant – as if it were these only returning again, or these with certain alterations and improvements, such as might give the future a pre-eminence in glory over the past. For only by means of what belonged to existing or previous dispensations of God could the prophet have given any detailed exhibition of what might be expected under another and higher dispensation. The details of the future must have been cast into the mould of things already perceived or known. 5. Therefore in forming one's conceptions now of the real import of such prophecies, now that the transition has been made into the new and higher dispensation, we must throw ourselves back upon the narrower and more imperfect relations amid which they were written, and thence judge of what is still to come. Thus, as the David of the promise is Christ, so the covenant-people are no longer the Jews distinctively, but the faithful in Christ; and the territory of blessing no longer Canaan, but the region of which Christ is king and lord. What was spoken immediately of the one class of personages and relations, may most fully be applied to the other; and by such a method of interpretation alone do we get a uniform and consistent principle to carry us through the whole. While those, on the other hand, who would find a literal Israel and a non-literal David, or a literal restoration in Christian times and a non-literal tabernacle and ritual of worship, arbitrarily confound together things dissimilar and incongruous, and render certainty of interpretation absolutely impossible. 6. Sixthly, the view thus given is confirmed by the reproduction of some of these prophecies in the field of the New Testament Church, set free, as was to be expected, from the outward distinctions and limits of the Old. Thus, in particular, the resurrection-scene of this 37th chapter substantially recurs in the 20th chapter of Revelation, and is followed precisely as here by the attack from the embattled forces of Gog and Magog; while not a word is said which would confine the things spoken to the land of Canaan or the literal Israel: it is the Church and people of Christ at large that are discoursed of. We say nothing respecting the probable time and nature of the events there referred to, but simply point to the identity in character of what is written with the prophecies before us. In those visions of the Apocalypse the inspired Evangelist stretches out the hand to Ezekiel, and shows how the word spoken so long before by that servant of God, freed from the peculiarities of its Jewish form, is to find its application to the Christian Church. The shell has gone, but the substance remains. 7. We may add, lastly, that the common interpretation, which understands Christ by David, and takes all the rest literally, must inevitably tend to justify the Jew in his unbelief. For he naturally says, Your Messiah has not done the thing you yourselves hold must be done, to fulfil the prophecy: he has not set up his throne in Canaan, and gathered Israel there, and re-established the old worship in its purity; this was the very purpose for which he was to appear, and we must wait till he comes to do it. On the basis of the literal interpretation, there seems no satisfactory answer to this; and it is well-known that since it has become prevalent, many Jews believe that Christians are coming over to their view of the matter. We are not surprised to hear, as we have heard, of converted Jews declaring that such a mode of interpretation would carry them back to Judaism.

CHAPTERS XXXVIII, XXXIX.

THE ASSAULT OF GOG, AND HIS DESTRUCTION.

The last portion of the prophecy, which began at chap. 37, stretches through these two next chapters, which properly form but one piece. It is one of the most remarkable predictions in the book of Ezekiel; and before offering any remarks on its general purport and design, we shall present an exact translation of the whole, with such explanatory notes as may be needed to elucidate the meaning, that the subject in its entire compass may be distinctly in view.

[1] And the word of the LORD came to me, saying,

[2] Son of man, set your face against Gog, the land of Magog,[1] the chief prince[2] of Me-shech and Tu-bal, and prophesy against him.

[3] And say, Thus says the Lord GOD: Behold, I am against you, O Gog, the chief prince of Me-shech and Tu-bal.

[4] And I will turn you back[3] and put hooks into your jaws, and I will bring you forth, and all your army, horses and horsemen, all of them clothed with all kinds, a great company *with* bucklers and shields, all of them handling swords –

[5] Persia, E-thi-o-pi-a and Lib-y-a with them, all of them with shield and helmet –

[6] Go-mer and all his bands; the house of To-gar-mah of the north quarters and all his bands; and many people with you.[4]

[7] Be prepared, and prepare for yourself, you and all your company that are gathered to you, and be a guard to them.

[8] After many days you shall be visited. In the latter years you shall come into the land *that is* brought back from the sword, *and* gathered out of many people. You shall come against the mountains of Israel which have always been waste. (But they have been brought forth out of the nations, and they shall live safely, all of them.)[5]

[9] You shall go up, coming up like a storm. You shall be like a cloud to cover the land, you and all your bands, and many people with you.

[10] Thus says the Lord GOD: And it shall be in that day *that* things shall come into your mind, and you shall think an evil thought.

[11] And you shall say, I will go up to the land of unwalled villages. I will go to those who are at rest, who live safely, all of them living without walls and have neither bars or gates,

[12] in order to take a spoil, and in order to take a prey – to turn your hand on the waste places *that now* have people in them, and on the people gathered out of the nations, who have gotten cattle and goods, who live in the midst of the land.[6]

[13] Sheba and De-dan, and the merchants of Tar-shish, with all their young lions, shall say to you, Have you come to take a spoil? Have you gathered your company to take a prey, to carry away silver and gold, to take away cattle and goods, to take a great spoil?[7]

[14] Therefore, son of man, prophesy and say to Gog, Thus says the Lord GOD: In that day when My people of Israel lives safely, shall you not know?

[15] And you shall come from your place out of the north parts, you and many people with you, all of them riding on horses, a great company and a mighty army.

[16] And you shall come up against My people Israel like a cloud, to cover the land. It shall be in the last days, and I will bring

you against My land, so that the heathen may know Me when I shall be sanctified in you, O Gog, before their eyes.

17 Thus says the Lord GOD: Are you he of whom I have spoken in old time by My servants the prophets of Israel, who prophesied in those days *many* years that I would bring you against them? [8]

18 And at the same time when Gog shall come against the land of Israel, says the Lord GOD, My fury shall come up in My face.

19 For in My jealousy and in the fire of My wrath I have spoken, Surely in that day there shall be a great shaking in the land of Israel, [9]

20 so that the fishes of the sea, and the birds of the sky, and the beasts of the field, and all creeping things that creep on the earth, and all the men that are on the face of the earth, shall shake at My presence. And the mountains shall be thrown down, and the steep places shall fall, and every wall shall fall to the ground.

21 And I will call for a sword against him throughout all My mountains, says the Lord GOD. Each man's sword shall be against his brother. [10]

22 And I will judge him with plagues and with blood. And I will rain on him, and on his bands, and on the many people who are with him, an overflowing rain and great hailstones, fire and brimstone.

23 So I will magnify Myself and sanctify Myself. And I will be known in the eyes of many nations, and they shall know that I am the LORD.

CHAPTER 39

1 Therefore, son of man, prophesy against Gog and say, Thus says the Lord GOD: Behold, I am against you, O Gog, the chief prince of Me-shech and Tu-bal.

2 And I will turn you back [11] and leave but the sixth part of you. And I will cause you to come up from the north parts and will bring you on the mountains of Israel.

3 And I will strike your bow outof your left hand, and will cause your arrows to fall out of your right hand.

4 You shall fall on the mountains of Israel, you and all your bands, and the people that is with you. I will give you to the birds of prey of every kind, and *to* the beasts of the field to be eaten up.

5 You shall fall on the open field, for I have spoken, says the Lord GOD.

6 And I will send a fire on Magog, and among those who live carelessly in the isles. And they shall know that I am the LORD. [12]

7 So I will make My holy name known in the midst of My people Israel. And I will not *let them* defile My holy name any more. And the heathen shall know that I am the LORD, the Holy One of Israel.

8 Behold, it has come and it is done, says the Lord GOD. This is the day of which I have spoken.

9 And those who live in the cities of Israel shall go out and shall set on fire and burn the weapons, both the shields and the bucklers, the bows and the arrows, and the javelins, and the spears. And they shall burn them with fire seven years. [13]

10 So that they shall take no wood out of the field, nor cut down out of the forests; for they shall burn the weapons for fire. And they shall plunder those who plundered them, and rob those who robbed them, says the Lord GOD.

11 And in that day I will give to Gog a place of memorial for graves in Israel, the valley of those who pass by on the east of the sea. [14] And it shall stop the *noses* of those who pass by. And there they shall bury Gog and all his multitude. And they shall call *it* the valley of Ha-mon–gog.

12 And the house of Israel shall be seven months burying them, that they may cleanse the land.

13 Yes, all the people of the land shall bury *them.* And it shall be a famous date to them, that I should be glorified, says the Lord GOD.

14 And they shall separate men for continual employment, passing through the land to bury those who remain on the face of the earth, in order to cleanse it, along with those who pass by. After the end of seven months they shall search.

15 And those who pass by, passing through the land, when *any* sees a man's bone, then he shall set a sign by it, until the buriers have buried it in the valley of Ha-mon–gog. [15]

16 And also the name of the city shall be Ha-mo-nah. [16] Thus they shall cleanse the land.

17 And, son of man, Thus says the Lord GOD. Speak to every feathered fowl, and to every beast of the field: Gather yourselves and come; gather yourselves on every side to My sacrifice which I sacrifice for you, a great sacrifice on the mountains of Israel, so that you may eat flesh and drink blood.

18 You shall eat the flesh of the mighty and drink the blood of the princes of the earth, of rams, of lambs, and of goats, of bulls, all of them fatlings of Ba-shan.

19 And you shall eat fat until you are full,

and drink blood until you are drunk, of My sacrifice which I have sacrificed for you.[17]

[20]So you shall be filled at My table with horses and chariots,[18] with mighty men and with all men of war, says the Lord GOD.

[21]And I will set My glory among the nations, and all the nations shall see My judgments which I have done, and My hand that I have laid on them.

[22]So the house of Israel shall know that I am the LORD their God from that day and forward.

[23]And the nations shall know that the house of Israel went into captivity for their iniquity. Because they sinned against Me, therefore I hid My face from them and gave them into the hand of their enemies. So they all fell by the sword.

[24]According to their uncleanness and according to their sins I have done to them, and have hidden My face from them.

[25]Therefore thus says the Lord GOD: Now I will bring again the captivity of Jacob, and will have mercy on the whole house of Israel, and will be jealous for My holy name;

[26]after they have borne their shame[19] and all their sins by which they have sinned against Me, when they lived safely in their land and no one made *them* afraid.

[27]When I have brought them again from the people, and have gathered them out of their enemies' lands, and am sanctified in them in the sight ofmany nations;

[28]then they shall know that I am the LORD their God who caused them to be led into captivity among the heathen. But I have gathered them to their own land, and have left none of them there any more.

[29]Neither will I hide My face from them any more, for I have poured out My Spirit on the house of Israel, says the Lord GOD.

Now, with this remarkable prophecy fully before us, let us ask how it is as a whole to be explained and understood. Are we to regard it as simply an anticipated history of transactions that were to take place precisely in the form and manner here described; or rather as an ideal delineation of what, as to the substance, might certainly be expected to happen, though possibly under aspects and relations widely different from those to be found in the prophet's description? For a satisfactory answer to this question we must look especially to the leading features of the description itself.

1. And the first thing that strikes us there is the name given to the leader of the hostile party – Gog. From the very mode of its formation this discovers itself at once as an ideal name; it is simply the root of Magog, the only related name known to history. And this Magog is itself the name of a very indefinite territory and people, as appears not only from the want of any express landmarks connected with them here or elsewhere, but also from the parties most closely associated with Gog, as his natural and proper subjects. Of the land of Magog, he is also the prince of Rosh, Meshech and Tubal – tribes that seem to have been contiguous in territory, as they were probably also related in their origin, but which were never, that we know of, actually united into one kingdom, and have long since disappeared as distinct races. When, therefore, we find the prophet giving to the head of the great movement and ideal name, derived from a sort of indefinite,obscurely known territory, it is scarcely possible to avoid the impression at the outset, that the description is intended to possess an ideal, not a real character. 2. Another thing that presently comes into consideration is the singular combination of the party which this Gog is represented as heading. The nations mentioned are all selected from the distance – remote, in the first instance, from the land of Israel, in the extremities of the earth, and also many of them far apart from one another, and consequently the most unlike naturally to act in concert for any particular purpose. Beside the Scythian tribes, with whom the head of the movement was more immediately connected, there are the Persians, Armenians, the other inhabitants of the far north in Asia and Europe; and then, passing to the opposite extreme, and overleaping all the intermediate regions, he names the Ethiopians and

Libyans of Africa, – the people, in short, occupying the most distant and remote territories of the then known world. The principle of assortment and union is evidently the very reverse of the natural one – not nearness, but remoteness of position, as well to the land of Israel as to the associated parties themselves. But this entire omission of the near, and conjunction only of the remote and distant, is so very peculiar a characteristic, and so contrary to all real combinations, that it is impossible to avoid thinking that here also we have but the clothing of an idea – not a literal reality, but the pictorial delineation of one. 3. Then the huge numbers of this combined party are to be taken into account, in connection with the object for which it was avowedly formed. According to the description, it was to be a marauding host, breaking in like a mighty inundation upon the land of Israel, and again departing after it had enriched itself with the spoil and booty there obtained (chap. 38:12,13). That is, myriads of people were to be gathered from the most distant regions of the earth, combining and acting together against all the known principles of human nature: and for what? To spoil and plunder a land which could not, had they got all it contained, have been a handful to tithe of their number – could not have served to maintain the invaders for a single day! One would think it is impossible in such a case for the most aerial fancy to dream of literality; and when the prophet is spoken of as furnishing here a plain historical description, one is tempted to ask whether he is supposed to have written for the amusement of children or for the belief and instruction of persons of mature understanding? 4. This impression is still further increased when we look to the fruits of the victory. The wood of the adversaries' weapons was to serve for fuel to all Israel for seven years! and all Israel were to be employed for seven months in burying the dead! It would be but a very moderate allowance, on the literal supposition, to say that a million of men would thus be engaged, and that on an average each would consign two corpses to the tomb in one day; which, for the 180 working days of the seven months, would make an aggregate of 360,000,000 of corpses! Then the putrefaction, the pestilential vapors arising from such masses of slain victims before they were all buried! Who could live at such a time? It bids defiance to all the laws of nature, as well as the known principles of human action; and to insist on such a description being understood according to the letter, is to make it take rank with the most extravagant tales of romance, or the most absurd legends of Popery. 5. Further, on the ground of a literal description, there is the collateral consideration of its becoming utterly impossible to make out a prophetical harmony; the prophets in that case do not mutually confirm, but, on the contrary, oppose and contradict each other. Here the great controversy, which finally adjudges the cause of heathendom, is represented as taking issue on the mountains of Israel, and covering the whole land with the slain. In Isaiah 34 we have, to all appearance, the same controversy – the controversy of the Lord's judgment upon Zion's adversaries, when his indignation was to be *"upon all nations, and his fury upon all their armies"* – determined upon the mountains of Edom. In Joel, again, it takes place in the valley of Jehoshaphat, or the valley of decision (chap. 3:12,14); and in Zechariah (chap. 14) in the immediate neighborhood of Jerusalem, as also in the Apocalypse (chap. 20) around the camp of the saints and the beloved city. Thus we have three or four distinct localities, each represented as the scene of a last conflict, ending in a final triumph to the cause of God over the leagued hostility of the world. If held to be literal descriptions, they of course mutually destroy one another; for the localities being different (as also many of the accompanying circumstances), they must either be ideal delineations under various aspects of what was to happen, or they are literal and contradictory descriptions. 6. Finally, pointing, as all these prophetical descriptions do, and the one before us in particular, to the latter ages of the world – to the times of the Messiah – the gross carnality of the representation in respect to God's dealing with the adversaries demands a non-literal interpretation. Under the old covenant, when the Church was still in its childhood, it was necessary to employ to a large extent the outward and material; carnal elements had a prominent place in the immediate service of God, and they could not fail to be much resorted to in the administration of the kingdom, so long as it had a political existence in the world. His people had then often to defend themselves with a carnal sword, and often in the successful exercise of this did God's power and goodness appear to his people. But the revelation of God in the person and work of Christ introduced an entire change in this respect. The spiritual element in the Divine character came thereby into fuller manifestation, and, as a necessary consequence, everything carnal fell into the background. Not that the Lord's people must therefore cease to operate upon the outward and material things around them, but that in doing so they must bring more into exercise the higher elements of power, and no longer lean upon the more gross and imperfect instruments of working. The carnal sword, in particular, must henceforth be sheathed, and weapons of violence for ever put aside. The glorious Head of the Church showed himself strong only in the truth of God, and conquered by suffering in its behalf. It was thus that he gained unspeakably the noblest victory recorded in the annals of time. And never would he permit his followers to entertain the thought of winning any triumphs over the ignorance and malice of the world, otherwise than by their standing like him in the truth of God, and holding it fast, even unto death. How, then, would such conflicts and victories as those described here, if literally understood, comport with this new and more elevated posture of affairs? Precisely as the imperfections of childhood with the higher developments of mature age. They would exhibit a Church again in bondage to the elements of the world, wielding the artillery of brute force instead of the nobler weapons of her spiritual armor, and so losing infinitely more than she would gain by such a method of achieving her conquests. The spirit of prophecy never could intend by such delineations of the far-distant future to indicate so humiliating a result, or give birth to anticipations so directly opposed to the teaching of Christ; the less so, as it was Christ's Spirit that guided the prophets of the Old Testament in their prospective delineations (1 Pet. 1:11). And therefore, in addition to all the other impossibilities standing in the way of the literal interpretation of this vision, there is that which arises from the false and degrading position in which it would put the Church, sending her back, after she has attained to the spiritual light and privileges of the Gospel, to her old fleshly weapons and worldly entanglements.

Persons who in the face of all these considerations can still cling to the literal view of this prophecy, must be left to themselves; they must have principles of interpretation or grounds of conviction with which it is impossible to deal in the way of argument. Their views, also, respecting the position and calling of the Old Testament prophets, as to the revelation of the future, must be altogether erroneous. They must suppose that the object of these was to delineate beforehand, with historical exactness, the coming events of Providence; whereas it often consisted much more in disclosing how the great truths and principles of the Divine government should appear in the administration of the affairs of men. In doing this it was necessary for them to throw their delineations, even when referring to the last periods of time, into the form of existing relations and known circumstances – for such alone it was competent to them to use; but they could, and they did, sometimes use these in such strange assortments and grotesque combinations, as might in a sense compel thoughtful minds to look beyond the surface, and feel that in the things written they had but the form and drapery of what should be; that the reality itself lay deeper, and could meanwhile be but dimly apprehended. Such, certainly, is the manner in which the description of the prophet here ought from the first to have been understood. He was going, through the Spirit, to present a picture of what might be expected in the last scenes of the world's history; and according to the native bent and constitution of his mind, the picture must be lifelike. Not only must it be formed of the materials of existing relations, but it must also be formed into a perspective with manifold and intricate details; yet so constructed and arranged, that while nothing but the most superficial eye could look for a literal realization, the great truths and prospects embodied in it should be patent to the view of all. What, then, are these? Let it be remembered at what point it is in Ezekiel's prospective exhibitions that this prophecy is brought in. He has already represented the covenant-people as recovered from all their existing troubles, and made victorious over all their surrounding enemies. The best in the past has again revived in their experience, freed even from its former imperfections, and secured against its ever-recurring evils. For the new David, the all-perfect and continually-abiding Shepherd, presides over them, and at once prevents the outbreaking of internal disorders, and shields them from the attacks of hostile neighbors. All around, therefore, is peace and quietness; the old enemies vanish from the field Israel dwells securely in his habitation. But let it not be supposed that the conflict is over, and that the victory is finally won; it is a world-wide dominion which this David is destined to wield, and the kingdom of righteousness and peace established at the centre must expand and grow till it embrace the entire circumference of the globe. But will Satan yield his empire without a struggle? Will he not rather, when he sees the kingdom of God taking firmer root and rising to a higher elevation, seek to effect its dismemberment or its downfall, by stirring up in hostile array against it the multitudinous and gigantic forces that lie scattered in the extremities of the earth? Assuredly he will do so; and God also will direct events into this channel, in order to break effectually the power of the adversary, and secure the diffusion of Jehovah's truth and the glory of his name to the remotest regions. A conflict, therefore, must ensue between the embattled forces of heathenism, gathered out of their far-distant territories, and the nation that holds the truth of God. But the issue is certain. For God's people being now holiness to him, he cannot but fight with them and give success to their endeavors. So that the arm of heathenism shall be completely broken. Its mightiest efforts only end in the more signal display of its own weakness, as compared with the truth and cause of God; and the name of God as the Holy One of Israel is magnified and feared to the utmost bounds of the earth.

Such is the general course and issue of things as marked out in this prophecy, under the form and aspect of what belonged to the old covenant, and its relation to the world as then existing. But, stripping the vision of this merely temporary and imperfect exterior, since now the higher objects and relations of the new covenant have come, we find in the prophecy the following series of important and salutary truths. 1. In the first place, while the appearance of the new David to take the rule and presidency over God's heritage would have the effect of setting his people free from the old troubles and dangers which had hitherto assailed them, and laying sure and broad the foundations of their peace, it should be very far from securing them against all future conflicts with evil; it would rather tend to call up other adversaries, and enlarge the field of conflict, so as to make it embrace the most distant and barbarous regions of the earth. For the whole earth is Christ's heritage, and sooner or later it must come to an issue between the adherents of his cause and the children of error and corruption. Though the latter might have no thought of interfering with the affairs of Christ's kingdom, and would rather wish to pursue their own courses undisturbed (see on 38:4), yet the Lord will not permit them to do so. He must bring the light of heaven into contact with their darkness; so as to necessitate a trial of strength between the powers of evil working in them, and the truth and grace of God as displayed in the kingdom of Christ. 2. From the very nature of the case, this trial would fall to be made on a very large scale, and with most gigantic resources; for the battlefield now is the world to its farthest extremities; and the question to be practically determined is, whether God's truth or man's sin is to have possession of the field? So that all preceding contests should appear small, and vanish out of sight, in comparison of this last great struggle, in which the world's destiny was to be decided for good or evil. Hence it seemed in the distance as if not thousands, as formerly, but myriads upon myriads, numbers without number, were to stand here in battle array. 3. Though the odds in this conflict could not but appear beforehand very great against the people and cause of Christ, yet the result should be entirely on their side; and simply because with them is the truth and the might of Jehovah. Had it been only carnal resources that were to be brought into play on either side, victory must inevitably have been with those whose numbers were so overwhelmingly great. But these being only flesh, and not spirit, they must fall before the omnipotent energy of the living God, who can make his people more than conquerors over all that is against them. And so in this mighty conflict, in which all that the powers of darkness could muster from the world was to stand, as it were, front to front with the people of God, there were to be found remaining only, on the part of the adversaries, the signs of defeat and ruin. 4. Lastly, as all originated in the claim of Messiah and his truth to the entire possession of the world, so the whole is represented as ending in the complete establishment of the claim. The kingdom through every region of the earth becomes the Lord's. He is now universally known and sanctified as the God of truth and holiness. It is understood at last that it was his zeal for the interests of righteousness which led him to chastise in former times his own professing people; and that the same now has induced him to render them triumphant over every form and agency of evil. And now, all counter rule and authority being put down, all disturbing elements finally hushed to rest, the prospect stretches out before the Church of eternal peace and blessedness, in what have at length become the new heavens and the new earth, wherein dwelleth righteousness.

It may still, perhaps, seem strange to some, if this be the real meaning and import of the vision, that the prophet should have presented it under the aspect of a single individual, gathering immense forces from particular regions, and at the head of these fighting in single conflict, and falling on the land of Israel. They may feel it difficult to believe that a form so concrete and fully developed should have been adopted, if nothing more local and specific had been intended. But let such persons look back to other portions of this Book, especially to what is written of the king of Tyre in chap. 28 (which in form, perhaps, most nearly resembles the prophecy before us), and judge from the shape and aspect there given to the past, whether it is not in perfect accordance with the ascertained characteristics of Ezekiel's style, to find him giving here such a detailed and fleshly appearance to the future. There Tyre is not only viewed as personified in her political head, but that head is represented as passing through all the experiences of the best and highest of humanity. It is, as we showed, a historical parable, in which every feature is admirable chosen and pregnant with meaning, but all of an ideal and not a literal or prosaic kind. And what is the present vision, as now explained, but a prophetical parable, in which, again, every trait in the delineation is full of important meaning, only couched in the language of a symbolical representation? Surely we must concede to the prophet what we would never think of withholding from a mere literary author, that he has a right to employ his own method; and that the surest way of ascertaining this is to compare one part of his writings with another, so as to make the better known reflect light upon the less known – the delineations of the past upon the visions of the future.

At the same time let us not be understood as declaring for certain, that the delineation in this prophecy must have nothing to do with any particular crisis, or decisive moment, in the Church's history. It is perfectly possible that in this case, as in most others, there may be a culminating point, at which the spiritual controversy is to rise to a gigantic magnitude and virtually range on either side all that is good and all that is evil in the world. It may be so; I see nothing against such a supposition in the nature of the prophecy, but, I must add, I see nothing conclusively for it. For when we look back to the other prophecy just referred to, we find the work of judgment represented as taking effect upon Tyre, precisely as if it were one individual that was concerned, and one brief period of his history; while still we know blow after blow was required, and even age after age, to carry forward and consummate the process. Perfectly similar, too, was the case of Babylon, as described in the 13th and 14th chapters of Isaiah; it seems as if almost one act were to do the whole, yet how many instruments had a hand in it! and over how many centuries was the work of destruction spread! We see no necessity in the form of the representation, or in the nature of things, why it should be otherwise here; none at least why a different mode of reaching the result should be expected as certain. We believe that as the judgment of Tyre began when the first breach was made in the walls by Nebuchadnezzar, and as the judgment of Babylon began when the Medes and Persians entered her two-leaved gates, so the controversy with Gog and his heathenish forces has been proceeding since Chirst, the new David, came to lay the everlasting foundations of his kingdom, and asserted his claim to the dominion of the earth as his purchased possession. Every stroke that has been dealt since against the idolatry and corruption of the world, is a part of that great conflict which the prophet in vision saw collected as into a single locality and accomplished in a moment of time. He would thus more clearly assure us of the certainty of the result. And though, from the vast extent of the field and the many imperfections that still cleave to the Church, there may be much delay and many partial reverses experienced in the process, – though there may, too, at particular times be more desperate struggles than usual between the powers of evil in the world and the confessors of the truth, when the controversy assumes a gigantic aspect, – yet the prophecy is at all times proceeding onwards in its accomplishment. Let the Church, therefore, do her part, and be faithful to her calling; let her grasp with a firm hand the banner of truth, and in all lands display it in the name of her risen Lord. And whichever way he may choose to finish and consummate the process, – whether by giving fresh impulses to the hearts of his people, and more signally blessing the work of their hands, or by shining forth in visible manifestations of his power and glory, such as may at once and for ever shame into confusion the adversaries of his cause and kingdom, – leaving this to himself, to whom it properly belongs, let the blessed hope of a triumphant issue animate every Christian bosom and nerve every Christian arm to maintain the conflict, and do all that zeal and love can accomplish to hasten forward the final result.

In the preceding remarks we had deemed it unnecessary to take any special notice of such interpretations as seek the accomplishment of the prophecy in particular and partial occurrences of the past: for example, the conflicts of the Maccabees with Antiochus (Grotius, Dathe, Jahn), the invasion and overthrow of the Chaldeans (Ewald), the temporary successes and destined overthrow of the Turks (Luther). All such interpretations are obviously unsatisfactory and inadequate. And we simply add, further, in case of misapprehension, that while we have no hesitation in regarding the vision respecting Gog and Magog in the Apocalypse to be in substance a re-announcement of the prophecy before us, it does not therefore follow that the prophecy in the Apocalypse has exactly the same compass as in Ezekiel. It plainly, indeed, has not. Ezekiel contemplates the great conflict in a more general light, as what was certainly to be connected with the times of Messiah, and should come then to its last decisive issues. John, on the other hand, writing from the commencement of the Messiah's times, breaks up these into distinct portions (how far successive or contemporaneous, we pretend not to say), and giving the vision respecting Gog and his forces the same relative place that it had in the visions of Ezekiel, he describes under it the last struggles and victories of the cause of Christ. In each case alike the vision is appropriated to describe the final workings of the world's evil, and its results in connection with the kingdom of God: only, the starting-point is placed farther in advance in the one case than in the other. Therefore, as found in Ezekiel, it can throw no light on the chronological arrangement of the Apocalypse.

CHAPTER XL. – XLVIII.

PRELIMINARY REMARKS ON THE VISION IN CHAP. XL. – XLVIII., WITH RESPECT TO THE PRINCIPLES ON WHICH IT OUGHT TO BE INTERPRETED.

We have now, with God's help, reached the closing vision of Ezekiel's prophecies; but so far from seeing all difficulties behind us, we find ourselves in front of the darkest, and in several respects the most singular and characteristic vision of the whole book. For all that is most peculiar, and much also that is most difficult in the manner of our prophet, concentrates itself here; and whatever need there may have been of the Spirit's aid to guide our steps through the earlier visions, the same need exists, in yet greater force, with respect to this concluding revelation. May the aid so required not be withheld! May the Spirit of Truth himself direct our inquiries, and shine for our instruction on his own handwriting! May no blinding prejudice, or narrow purpose of our own, prevent us from following the path of enlightened research and honest interpretation; so that the views to be propounded may, at least in all that is essential, bear the impress of soberness and truth!

Leaving out of view some minor shades of opinion, which are too unimportant to deserve any special notice, the views that have been entertained upon the vision generally, and in particular the description contained in it respecting the temple, may be ranged under four classes.

1. The first is what may be called the historico-literal; which takes all as a prosaic description of what had existed in the times immediately before the captivity, in connection with that temple which is usually called Solomon's. Ezekiel just delineated, it is thought by those who hold this view, what he had himself seen at Jerusalem, that the remembrance of the former state of things might be preserved, and that the people on their return might restore it as nearly as they could. Such is the opinion sought by a huge apparatus of learning to be maintained by Villalpandus; and he is substantially follwed by Grotius, Calmet, Secker, in part also by the elder Lowth, Adam Clarke,[1] Bottcher, Thenius, etc. Those, however, who adopt this view find it necessary, against the natural order and connection, to separate between what is written respecting the construction of the temple, and the distribution of the land, as well as some other things which are known to have been quite different in the times before the exile. And even in regard to the temple itself, and the things immediately connected with it, making due allowance for any changes that may have been introduced, there are many, and some of them most palpable contrarieties between what is known to have existed in the times before the exile, and the scheme of things delineated by the prophet. These will fall to be noticed in the sequel.

2. The straining required to maintain this view, and its utterly unsatisfactory nature, gave rise to another, which may be called the historico-ideal. According to it, the pattern exhibited to Ezekiel differed materially from anything that previously existed, and presented for the first time what should have been after the return from the captivity, though, from the remissness and corruption of the people, it never was properly realized. "The temple described by Ezekiel should have been built by the new colonists; the customs and usages which he orders should have been observed by them; the division of the country should have been followed by them. That the temple did not arise out of its ruins according to his model, and that his orders were in no manner obeyed, was the fault of Israel. How far were they behind the orders of their first lawgiver, Moses! What wonder, therefore, that they as little regarded their second lawgiver, Ezekiel?" So wrote Eichhorn, and of the same mind were Dathe and Herder. But it is a view entirely at variance with the dimensions assigned to the temple, the mode of the distribution of the land and the description of the river, all of which were connected with physical impossibilities to the new colonists. Some, therefore, who hold substantially the same general view, so far modify it as to admit that there were things in the prophet's delineation which could never have been intended to receive a literal accomplishment, yet conceive that the prophet did not the less design to present in it a perfect draught of what it was desirable and proper for the people to aim at. In so far as the actual state of things fell short of this, there was a failure – but only in the realization, not in the idea; and it was simply this last, not the other, which was properly any concern of the prophet's. So various of the older rationalists (among others, Doederlein), and in the present day, Hitzig. The view manifestly proceeds on an abandonment of the strictly prophetical character of the vision, and reduces its announcements to a sort of vague and well-meaning anticipation of some future good, such as a strong faith and lively hope might cherish, and thrown into any form the writer's own fancy might suggest. It cannot

therefore be concurred in by any one who believes that the prophet spake as he was moved by the Holy Ghost, and uttered what, according to its genuine import, must be strictly fulfilled.

3. The Jewish-carnal view is the one we shall next advert to; in its main character the opposite extreme of the last mentioned. It is the opinion of some Jewish writers that the description of Ezekiel was actually followed by the children of the captivity as far as their circumstances would allow, and that Herod also, when he renovated and enlarged it, copied after the same pattern. (Lightfoot, Desc. Templi, 100:10). But they further hold, that as this was necessarily done in a very imperfect manner, it waits to be properly accomplished by the Messiah, who, when he appears, shall cause the temple to be reared precisely as here described, and carry out all the other subordinate arrangements. A considerable party has of late years been springing up in the Christian Church, especially in England, who entirely concur in these Jewish anticipations, with no further difference than that, believing Jesus to be the Messiah, they expect the vision to receive a complete and literal fulfilment at the period of his second coming. The whole seed of Israel, they believe, shall then be restored to possess anew the land of Canaan, where they shall become, with Christ at their head, the centre of the light and glory of the world; the temple shall be rebuilt after the magnificent pattern shown to Ezekiel, the rites and ordinances of worship set up, and the land apportioned to the tribes of Israel, – all as described in the closing chapters of this book.[2] This opinion has also found its advocates on the Continent; Hofmann, for example,[3] and Hess in his letters on the Apocalypse, who says: "So then it shall come to pass that our Lord, who once was rejected and crucified by his own countrymen, shall by the same be publicly and formally acknowledged, and in the restored temple shall be honored; and that as Israel of old was often made to do service to the nations for the rejection of his God and Messiah, so now the nations shall be subjected to him when acknowledging his Messiah and confiding in his God."[4]

4. The last view is the Christian-spiritual, or typical one, according to which the whole representation was not intended to find either in Jewish or Christian times an express and formal realization, but was a grand, complicated symbol of the good God had in reserve for his Church, especially under the coming dispensation of the Gospel. From the Fathers downwards this has been the prevailing view in the Christian Church. The greater part have held it to the exclusion of every other; in particular, among the Reformers, and their successors, Luther, Calvin, Capellus, Cocceius, Pfeiffer, followed by the majority of evangelical divines of our own country. But not a few also have combined it with one or more of the other opinions specified. Thus Diodati, joining it with the first, says: "Now the Lord showeth the prophet the frame of Solomon's temple, which had been destroyed by the Chaldeans, that the memory of its incomparable magnificence might be preserved in the Church, for a figure and assistance of her spiritual temple in this world, but especially in the celestial glory." To the same effect Lowth, in his Commentary – and Lightfoot only differs in so far as he rather couples the second view with the last – regards the vision as intended to "encourage the Jews with the prospect of having a temple again," though the temple and its ordinances were neither formed after Solomon's nor designed to be actually set up, but prefigured "the enlargement spiritual beauty, and glory of the Church under the Gospel." This is also the view adopted by Greenhill in his work on Ezekiel, who supposes, indeed, that the vision "represented the restitution of the Jewish Church, their temple, city, and worship, after the captivity; yet not simply, but as they were types of the Church under the Gospel; for as we must not exclude these, so we must know this is not the principal thing intended; that which the vision doth chiefly hold out to us in the building of the Christian temple, with the worship thereof, under Jewish expressions, which began to be accomplished in the apostle's days" (Acts 15:16).

It is not to be denied that this last writer, as generally the writers of the class and period to which he belonged, failed in a correct appreciation of the nature of the vision, and of the distinctive principles which ought to be kept in view in its interpretation. Consequently much of an arbitrary and fanciful kind entered into the explanations they gave of particular parts. The basis must first be laid of the proper line to be pursued, by distinguishing correctly the character of this species of composition, and the relation in which the vision stands to other portions of Ezekiel's writings. Let us now endeavor to prepare the way by a careful consideration of what bears on these points.

1. First of all, it is to be borne in mind that the description purports to be a vision – a scheme of things exhibited to the mental eye of the prophet *"in the visions of God."* This alone marks it to be of an ideal character, as contradistinguished from anything that ever had been, or ever was to be found in actual existence, after the precise form given to it in the description. Such we have uniformly seen to be the character of the earlier visions imparted to the prophet. The things described in chapters 1-3 and 8-11, which were seen by him *"in the visions of God,"* were all of this nature. They presented a vivid picture of what either then actually existed or was soon to take place, but in a form quite different from the external reality. Not the very image or the formal appearance of things was given, but rather a compressed delineation of their inward being and substance. And such, too, was found to be the case with other portions, which are of an entirely similar nature, though not expressly designated visions; such, for example, as chapters 4, 12, 21, all containing delineations and precepts, as if speaking of what was to be done and transacted in real life; and yet it is necessary to understand them as ideal representations, exhibiting the character, but not the precise form and lineaments of the coming transactions. Had this ideal nature of the description been rightly understood, it would have afforded for the vision before us an easy solution of what Dathe has thought inexplicable on any supposition but that of the literal character of the description, viz. the preceptive cast into which it is thrown. "He appears not to promise, but to command; not to show what sort of structure would be raised, and what arrangement made in connection with it, but to order what should be done." This is precisely what appears also in the earlier visions referred to; and it is what might have been expected in the present vision, on the supposition of its being an ideal representation of things belonging to the kingdom of God, – but not otherwise. Rightly understood, the preceptive form of the revelation is an evidence of the non-realistic character of what was communicated, especially when viewed in connection with the variations it presents to the handwriting of Moses. Never at any period of his Church has God given laws and ordinances to it simply by vision; and when Moses was commissioned to give such in the wilderness, his authority to do so was formally based on the ground of his office being different from the ordinarily prophetical, and of his instructions being communicated otherwise than by vision (Num. 12:6). So that to speak by way of vision, and at the same time in the form of precept, as if enjoining laws and ordinances materially differing from those of Moses, was itself a palpable and incontrovertible proof of the ideal character of the revelation. It was a distinct testimony that Ezekiel was no new lawgiver coming to modify or supplant what had been written by him with whom God spake face to face upon the mount.

2. What has been said respecting the form of the prophet's communication, is confirmed by the substance of it; as there is much in this that seems obviously designed to force on us the conviction of its ideal character. There are things in the description which, taken literally, are in the highest degree improbable, and even involve natural impossibilities. This was long ago marked by Lightfoot, in regard to the dimensions of the temple and city: "And now, if any one will take up the full circuit of the wall that encompassed the holy ground, according to our English measure, it will amount to half a mile and about 166 yards. And whosoever likewise will measure the square of Ezek. 42:20, he will find it six times as large as this, the whole amounting to three miles and a half and about 140 yards – a compass incomparably greater than Mount Moriah divers times over. And by this very thing is showed that that is spiritually and mystically to be understood . . . As for a literal respondency of that city and temple (viz. those which were to be built after the return from Babylon) to all the particulars of this description, it is so far from it, that

Ezekiel's temple is delineated larger than all the earthly Jerusalem, and his Jerusalem larger than all the land of Canaan. And thereby the scope of the Holy Spirit in that ichnography is clearly held out to be, to signify the great enlarging of the spiritual Jerusalem and temple, the Church under the Gospel, the spiritual beauty and glory of it, – as well as to certify captived Israel of hopes of an earthly city and temple to be rebuilt; which came to pass upon the return under Cyrus."[5]

What in this passage is called the city, it must be borne in mind, includes the oblation of holy ground set apart for the prince, the priests, and the Levites, whose residence was to be in immediate connection with the city. Taken thus, the statement of Lightfoot is not far from the truth. Referring to the notes on the particular verses for the proof of what we say, we simply announce at present the general result; which is that, according to the most exact modes of computation, the prophet's measurements give for the outer wall of the temple a square of an English mile, and about a seventh on each side, and for the whole city a space of between three and four thousand square miles. There is no reason to suppose that the boundaries of the ancient city exceeded two miles and a half in circumference (see Robinson's Researches, vol. 1); while here the circumference of the wall of the temple is nearly twice as much. So that the first part of Lightfoot's statement, that the bounds of Ezekiel's temple exceed those of the whole city, is perfectly correct; but in regard to the other part, in which he asserts the bounds of the city to be greater than those of the whole land of Canaan, some exception must be taken, if by Canaan he meant the whole that Israel ever possessed on both sides of Jordan, which is computed at fully double of Ezekiel's square – somewhere between ten and eleven thousand square miles. If understood of Canaan Proper, the land lying between Jordan and the Mediterranean Sea, the portion here allotted for the city might in that case equal the whole land. But taking the land at the largest, the allotment of a portion nearly equal to one-half of the whole for the prince, the priests, and Levites, is a manifest proof of the ideal character of the representation; the more especially when we consider that that sacred portion is laid off in a regular square, with the temple on Mount Zion in the centre. For then the one-half of it, extending to nearly thirty miles in length, and lying to the south of Jerusalem, must have covered nearly the whole southern territory,, which only reached as far as the Dead Sea (chap. 47:19); while yet by another provision five of the twelve tribes were to have their inheritance on that side of Jerusalem beyond the sacred portion (chap. 48:23-28). Such manifest incongruities on the literal understanding of the passage have led to alterations in the text; some transcribers and ancient translators, as well as modern commentators, putting so many cubits instead of reeds for the boundaries of the temple and the city. But there is no foundation for the change; it is the easy, arbitrarily way of getting rid of a difficulty by removing the occasion of it; we might as well adjust other parts to suit our own fancies, or expunge the vision altogether. The measurements of the prophet were made to involve a literal incongruity, as did also the literal extravagances of the vision in chapters 38, 39, that men might be forced to look for something else than a literal accomplishment. And in utter misapprehension of the prophet's design, the proposed alterations are resorted to for the purpose of bringing the plan within the bounds of probability, as a scheme of things that might one day be actually realized.[6]

3. Some, perhaps, may be disposed to imagine that, as they expect certain physical changes to be effected upon the land before the prophecy can be carried into fulfilment, these may be adjusted in such a manner as to admit of the prophet's measurements being literally applied. It is impossible, however, to admit such a supposition. For the boundaries of the land itself are given, not new boundaries of the prophet's own, but those originally laid down by Moses. And as the measurements of the temple and city are out of all proportion to these, no alterations can be made on the physical condition of the country that could bring the one into proper agreement with the other. Then there are other things in the description which, if they could not of themselves so conclusively prove the impossibility of a literal sense as the consideration arising from the measure-

ments, lend great force to this consideration, and on any other supposition than their being parts of an ideal representation, must wear an improbably and fanciful aspect. Of this kind is the distribution of the remainder of the land in equal portions among the twelve tribes in parallel sections, running straight across from east to west, without any respect to the particular circumstances of each, or their relative numbers; more especially the assignment of five of these parallel sections to the south of the city, which, after making allowance for the sacred portion, would leave at the farthest a breadth of only three or four miles a piece! Of the same kind also is the supposed separate existence of the twelve tribes, which now, at least, can scarcely be regarded otherwise than a natural impossibility, since it is an ascertained fact that such separate tribeships no longer exist; the course of providence has been ordered so as to destroy them, and once destroyed, they cannot possibly be reproduced. If a man is dead, he may be brought to life again; but if the once separate lines of his posterity have come to be fused together, no power in nature can resolve them again into their primary elements. Of the same kind, further, is *"the very high mountain"* on which the vision of the temple was presented to the eye of the prophet; for as this unquestionably refers to the old site of the temple, the little eminence on which it stood could only be designated thus in a moral or ideal and not in a literal sense.[7] Finally, of the same kind is the account given of the stream issuing from the eastern threshold of the temple and flowing into the Dead Sea, which, both for the rapidity of its increase and for the quality of its waters, is unlike anything that ever was known in Judea or in any other region of the world. Putting all together, it seems as if the prophet had taken every possible precaution, by the general character of the delineation, to debar the expectation of a literal fulfilment; and I should despair of being able in any case to draw the line of demarcation between the ideal and the literal, if the circumstances now mentioned did not warrant us in looking for something else than a fulfilment according to the letter of the vision.

4. Yet there is the further consideration to be mentioned – which, however some minds of peculiar temperament or sophistical tendencies may contrive to evade it, will surely prevail with the great mass of Bible Christians – that the vision of the prophet, as it must, if understood literally, imply the ultimate restoration of the ceremonials of Judaism, so it inevitable places the prophet in direct contradiction to the writers of the New Testament. The entire and total cessation of the peculiarities of Jewish worship is as plainly taught by our Lord and his apostles as language could do it, and on grounds which are not of temporary, but of permanent validity and force. The word of Christ to the woman of Samaria – *"Woman, believe me, the hour cometh when ye shall neither in this mountain, nor yet at Jerusalem, worship the Father"* – is alone conclusive of the matter; for if it means anything worthy of so solemn an asseveration, it indicates that Jerusalem was presently to lose its distinctive character, and a mode of worship to be introduced capable of being celebrated in any other place as well as there. But when we find the apostles afterwards contending for the cessation of the Jewish ritual, because suited only to a Church *"in bondage to the elements of the world,"* and consisting of what were comparatively but *"weak and beggarly elements,"* – and when in the Epistle to the Hebrews we also find the disannulling of the old covenant with its Aaronic priesthood and carnal ordinances argued at length, and especially *"because of the weakness and unprofitableness thereof,"* that is, its own inherent imperfections, – we must certainly hold either that the shadowy services of Judaism are finally and for ever gone, or that these sacred writers very much misrepresented their Master's mind regarding them. No intelligent and sincere Christian can adopt the latter alternative; he ought therefore to rest in the former. And he will do so in the rational persuasion, that as in the wise administration of God there must ever be a conformity in the condition of men to the laws and ordinances under which they are placed, so the carnal institutions, which were adapted to the Church's pupilage, can never, in the nature of things, be in proper correspondence with her state of manhood, perfection, and millennial glory. To regard the prophet here as exhibiting a prospect founded on such an unnatural conjunction, is to

ascribe to him the foolish part of seeking to have the new wine of the kingdom put back into the old bottles again; and while occupying himself with the highest hopes of the Church, treating her only to a showy spectacle of carnal superficialities. We have far too high ideas of the spiritual insight and calling of an Old Testament prophet, to believe that it was possible for him to act so unseemly a part, or contemplate a state of things so utterly anomalous. And we are perfectly justified by the explicit statement of Scripture in saying, that "a temple with sacrifices now would be the most daring denial of the all-sufficiency of the sacrifice of Chirst, and of the efficacy of the blood of his atonement. He who sacrificed before, confessed the Messiah; he who should sacrifice now, would most solemnly and sacrilegiously deny him."[8]

5. Holding the description, then, in this last vision to be conclusively of an ideal character, we advance a step farther, and affirm that the idealism here is precisely of the same kind as that which appeared in some of the earlier visions – visions that must necessarily have already passed into fulfilment, and which therefore may justly be regarded as furnishing a key to the right understanding of the one before us. The leading characteristic of those earlier visions, which coincide in nature with this, we have found to be the historical cast of their idealism. The representation of things to come is thrown into the mould of something similar in the past, and presented as simply a reproduction of the old, or a returning back again of what is past, only with such diversities as might be necessary to adapt it to the altered circumstances contemplated; while still the thing meant was, not that the outward form, but that the essential nature of the past should revive. Thus, in the vision of the iniquity-bearing in chap. 4, the judgments described as alighting or destined to alight on the houses of Israel and Judah, are represented under a return of the periods of time spent of old in Egypt and the wilderness; yet as certain things in the description not doubtfully indicated, and as the event itself clearly proved, it was the return, not of those precise periods of time, but of similar afflictive and disciplinary methods of dealing that were there predicted. So again in the description of chap. 20, quite similar in its announcement of coming evils to the prediction just noticed, the prophet speaks of a repetition of the sojourn in the wilderness, with its severe and humbling dispensations, but calls it now *"the wilderness of the peoples,"* to distinguish it from *"the wilderness of Egypt,"* thereby intimating that something different from a literal re-enacting of the old scenes was intended. There was the same method of treatment to be pursued, the same and even higher spiritual results to be aimed at, but amid circumstances outwardly dissimilar. Again, in the ideal representation given of the king of Tyre (chap. 28:11-19), first as to his pre-eminent greatness, and then his appointed downfall, the whole is made to assume a historical aspect; as if it were humanity itself, first enjoying a paradisiacal honor and glory, then received into the inmost sanctuary of Jehovah's presence, but only to be cast down as a polluted creature to shame and contempt and ruin; so that the Tyrian monarch's history was to be like a renewal of man's in its best and its worst experiences. Once more, in the prediction of Egypt's humiliation (chap. 29:1-16), a humiliation that was to take its beginning from the hand of Nebuchadnezzar, the doom is represented as a passing over the most afflictive and humbling part of Israel's experience upon Egypt: she who had presumed to do the part of Israel's God must have trial of Israel's forty years' wilderness sojourn, and scattering among the nations; in short, as to judgment and depression, she must become a second Israel herself.

Now in all these cases of an apparent, we should entirely err if we looked for an actual, repetition of the past. It is the nature of the transactions and events, not their precise form or external conditions that is unfolded to our view. The representation is of an ideal kind, and the history of the past merely supplies the mould into which it is cast. The spiritual eye of the prophet discerned the old, as to its real character, becoming alive again in the new. He saw substantially the same procedure followed again, and the unchangeable Jehovah must display the uniformity of his character and dealings by visiting it with substantially the same treatment.

If now we bring the light furnished by those earlier revelations of the prophet, in respect to which we can compare the prediction with the fulfilment, so as to read by its help and according to its instruction the vision before us, we shall only be giving the prophet the benefit of the common rule, of interpreting a writer by a special respect to his own peculiar method, and explaining the more obscure by the more intelligible parts of his writings. In all the other cases referred to, where his representation takes the form of a revival of the past, we see it is the spirit and not the letter of the representation that is mainly to be regarded; and why should we expect it to be otherwise here? In this remarkable vision we have the old produced again, in respect to what was most excellent and glorious in Israel's past condition – its temple, with every necessary accompaniment of sacredness and attraction – the symbol of the Divine presence within – the ministrations and ordinances proceeding in due order without – the prince and the priesthood: everything, in short, required to constitute the beau-ideal of a sacred commonwealth according to the ancient patterns of things. But at the same time there are such changes and alterations superinduced upon the old, as sufficiently indicate that something far greater and better than the past was concealed under this antiquated form. Not the coming realities, in their exact nature and glorious fulness – not even the very image of these things – could the prophet as yet distinctly unfold. While the old dispensation lasted, they must be thrown into the narrow and imperfect shell of its earthly relations. But those who lived under that dispensation might get the liveliest idea they were able to obtain of the brighter future, by simply letting their minds rest on the past, as here modified and shaped anew by the prophet, just as now the highest notions we can form to ourselves of the state of glory, is by conceiving the best of the Church's present condition refined and elevated to heavenly perfection. Exhibited at the time the vision was, and constructed as it is, one should no more expect to see a visible temple realizing the conditions, and a reoccupied Canaan after the regular squares and parallelograms, of the prophet, than in the case of Tyre to find her monarch literally dwelling in Eden and as a cherub occupying the immediate presence of God, or to behold Israel sent back again to make trial of Egyptian bondage and the troubles of the desert. Whatever might be granted in providence of an outward conformity to the plan of the vision, it should only be regarded as a pledge of the far greater good really contemplated, and a help to faith in waiting for its proper accomplishment.

6. But still, looking to the manifold and minute particulars given in the description, some may be disposed to think it highly improbable that anything short of an exact and literal fulfilment should have been intended. Had it been only a general sketch of a city and temple, as in the 60th chapter of Isaiah, and other portions of prophecy, they could more easily enter into the ideal character of the description, and understand how it might chiefly point to the better things of the Gospel dispensation. But with so many exact measurements before them, and such an infinite variety of particulars of all sorts, they cannot conceive how there can be a proper fulfilment without corresponding objective realities. It is precisely here, however, that we are met by another very marked characteristic of our prophet. Above all the prophetical writers he is distinguished, as we have seen, for his numberless particularisms. What Isaiah depicts in a few bold and graphic strokes, as in the case of Tyre for example, Ezekiel spreads over a series of chapters, filling up the picture with all manner of details not only telling us of her singular greatness, but also of every element, far and near, that contributed to produce it; and not only predicting her downfall, but coupling with it every conceivable circumstance that might add to its mortification and completeness. We have seen the same features strikingly exhibited in the prophecy on Egypt, in the description of Jerusalem's condition and punishment under the images of the boiling caldron (chap. 24), and the exposed infant (chap. 16), in the vision of the iniquity-bearing (chap. 4), in the typical representation of going into exile (chap. 13), and indeed in all the more important delineations of the prophet, which, even when descriptive of ideal scenes, are characterised by such minute and varied details, as to give them the appearance of a most

definitely shaped and lifelike reality.

Let this, then, be borne in mind respecting the distinctive character of our prophet's delineations generally, and there will be no difficulty felt in regard to the number and variety of particulars in this concluding vision. Considering his peculiar manner, it was no more than might have been expected, that, when going to present a grand outline of the good in store for God's Church and people, the picture should be drawn with the fullest detail. If he has done so on similar but less important occasions, he could not fail to do it here, when rising to the very top and climax of all his revelations. For it is pre-eminently by means of the minuteness and completeness of his descriptions that he seeks to impress our minds with a feeling of the Divine certainty of the truth disclosed in them, and to give, as it were, weight and body to our apprehensions.

7. In further support of the view we have given, it may also be asked, whether the feeling against a spiritual understanding of the vision, and a demand for outward scenes and objects literally corresponding to it, does not spring to a large extent from false notions regarding the ancient temple, and its ministrations and ordinances of worship, as if these possessed an independent value apart from the spiritual truths they symbolically expressed? On the contrary, the temple, with all that belonged to it, was an embodied representation of Divine realities. It presented to the eye of worshippers a manifold and varied instruction respecting the things of God's kingdom. And it was by what they saw embodied in those visible forms and external transactions, that the people were to learn how they should think of God, and act toward him in the different relations and scenes of life – when they were absent from the temple, as well as when they were near and around it. It was an image and emblem of the kingdom of God itself, whether viewed in respect to the temporary dispensation then present, or to the grander development everything was to receive at the advent of Christ. And it was one of the capital errors of the Jews, in all periods of their history, to pay too exclusive a regard to the mere externals of the temple and its worship, without discerning the spiritual truths and principles that lay concealed under them.

But such being the case, the necessity for an outward and literal realization of Ezekiel's plan obviously falls to the ground. For if all connected with it was ordered and arranged chiefly for its symbolical value at any rate, why might not the description itself be given forth for the edification and comfort of the Church on account of what it contained of symbolical instruction? Even if the plan had been fitted and designed for being actually reduced to practice, it would still have been principally with a view to its being a mirror, in which to see reflected the mind and purposes of God. But if so, why might not the delineation itself be made to serve for such a mirror? In other words, why might not God have spoken to his Church of good things to come by the wise adjustment of a symbolical plan? And when commentators like Hitzig, or writers of a more spiritual cast, incredulously ask what is the symbolical meaning of this small particular or that, we might reply by putting the like question regarding the temple of Solomon or the tabernacle of Moses; while yet nothing can be better established on grounds of Scripture, than that these sacred fabrics were constructed so as to embody and represent the leading truths of God's character and kingdom. This, of course, does not preclude – when rightly considered, it rather requires that the several parts should be viewed in subordination to the general design, and that many things must enter into the scheme, which, taken by themselves, could have no independent or satisfactory meaning. But let the same rules be applied to the interpretation of Ezekiel's visionary temple which on the express warrant of Scripture we apply to Solomon's literal one, and it will be impossible to show why, so far as the ends of instruction are concerned, the same great purposes might not be served by the simple delineation of the one, as by the actual construction of the other.[9]

It is also not to be overlooked, in support of this line of reflection, that in other and earlier communications Ezekiel makes much account of the symbolical character of the temple, and the things belonging to it. It is as a priest, he gives us to understand at the outset, and for the purpose of doing priest-like service for the covenant-people, that he received his prophetical calling, and had visions of God disclosed to him (see on chap. 1:1-3). In the series of visions contained in chapters 8-11, the guilt of the people was represented as concentrating itself there, and determining God's procedure in regard to it. By the Divine glory being seen to leave the temple, was symbolized the withdrawing of God's gracious presence from Jerusalem; and by his promising to become for a little sanctuary to the pious remnant in Chaldea, it was virtually said that the temple, as to its spiritual reality, was going to be transferred thither. This closing vision comes now as the happy counterpart of those earlier ones, giving promise of a complete rectification of preceding evils and disorders. It assured the Church that all should yet be set right again; nay, that greater and better things should be found in the future than had ever been known in the past; things too great and good to be presented merely under the old symbolical forms, – these must be modelled and adjusted anew to adapt them to the higher objects in prospect.

Nor is Ezekiel at all singular in this. The other prophets represent the coming future with a reference to the symbolical places and ordinances of the past, adjusting and modifying these to suit their immediate design. Thus Jeremiah says, in chap. 31:38-40: *"Behold, the days come, saith the Lord, that the city shall be built to the Lord from the gate of Hananeel to the corner gate. And the measuring line shall go forth opposite to it still farther over the hill Gareb (the hill of the leprous,), and shall compass about to Goah (the place of execution). And the whole valley of the dead bodies, and of the ashes, and all the fields to the brook Kedron, unto the corner of the horse-gate toward the east, shall be holy to the Lord."* That is, there shall be a rebuilt Jerusalem in token of the revival of God's cause, in consequence of which even the places formerly unclean shall become holiness to the Lord: not only shall the loss be recovered, but also the evil inherent in the past purged out, and the cause of righteousness made completely triumphant. The sublime passage in Isaiah 60 is entirely parallel as to its general import. And in the two last chapters of Revelation we have a quite similar vision to the one before us, employed to set forth the ultimate condition of the redeemed Church. There are differences in the one as compared with the other, precisely as in the vision of Ezekiel there are differences as compared with anything that existed under the old covenant. In particular while the temple forms the very heart and centre of Ezekiel's plan, in John's no temple whatever was to be seen. But in the two descriptions the same truth is symbolized, though in the last it appears in a state of more perfect development than in the other. The temple in Ezekiel, with God's glory returned to it, bespoke God's presence among his people to sanctify and bless them the no-temple in John indicated that such a select spot was no longer needed, that the gracious presence of God was everywhere seen and felt. It is the same truth in both, only in the latter represented, in accordance with the genius of the new dispensation, as less connected with the circumstantials of place and form.

8. It only remains to be stated that in the interpretation of the vision we must keep carefully in mind the circumstances in which it was given, and look at it, not as from a New, but as from an Old Testament point of view; we must throw ourselves back as far as possible into the position of the prophet himself; we must think of him as having just seen the Divine fabric which had been reared in the sacred and civil constitution of Israel dashed in pieces, and apparently become a hopeless wreck. But in strong faith on Jehovah's word, and with Divine insight into his future purposes, he sees that that never can perish which carries in its bosom the element of God's unchangeableness; that the hand of the Spirit will assuredly be applied to raise up the old anew; and not only that, but also that it shall be inspired with fresh life and vigor, enabling it to burst the former limits, and rise into a greatness and perfection and majesty never known or conceived of in the past. He speaks, therefore, chiefly of Gospel times, but as one still dwelling under the veil and uttering the language of legal times. And of the substance of his communication, both as to its general correspondence with the past and its difference in particular parts, we submit the following summary as given by Havernick: – "1. In the Gospel part of Jehovah a solemn occupation anew of his sanctuary, in which the entire fulness of

the Divine glory shall dwell and manifest itself. At the last there is to rise a new temple, diverse from the old, to be made every way suitable to that grand and lofty intention, and worthy of it; in particular, of vast compass for the new community, and with a holiness stretching over the entire extent of the temple, so that in this respect there should no longer be any distinction between the different parts. Throughout everything is subjected to the most exact and particular appointments; individual parts, and especially such as had formerly remained indeterminate, obtain now an immediate Divine sanction; so that every idea of any kind of arbitrariness must be altogether excluded from this temple. Accordingly this sanctuary is the thoroughly sufficient, perfect manifestation of God for the salvation of his people (chapters 40-43:12). 2. From this sanctuary, as from the new centre of all religious life, there gushes forth an unbounded fulness of blessings upon the people, who in consequence attain to a new condition. There comes also into being a new glorious worship, a truly acceptable priesthood and theocratical ruler; and equity and righteousness reign among the entire community, who, being purified from all stains, rise indeed to possess the life that is in God (chap. 43:13, 47:12). 3. To the people who have become renewed by such blessings, the Lord gives the land of promise; Canaan is a second time divided among them, where, in perfect harmony and blessed fellowship, they serve the living God, who abides and manifests himself among them" (chap. 47:13, 48).[10]

CHAPTER XL.

THE POSITION, WALLS, GATES, AND COURTS OF THE TEMPLE.

It is not our purpose to go into greater length on the details of this closing vision, than is absolutely necessary to convey a pretty distinct idea of the revelation contained in it. And as the readiest and most satisfactory way of handling it, we shall take it in covenient successive portions; first giving a translation, with explanatory notes where such may be required, and on each section presenting a brief view of the general import.

[1]In the twenty-fifth year of our captivity, in the beginning of the year,[1] in the tenth of the month, in the fourteenth year after the city was stricken, in the same day the hand of the LORD was on me and brought me there.[2]

[2]In the visions of God He brought me into the land of Israel and set me on a very high mountain, on which *was* the frame of a city on the south.[3]

[3]And He brought me there. And, behold, a man whose look was like the look of bronze, with a line of flax in his hand, and a measuring reed! And he stood in the gate.

[4]And the man said to me, Son of man, look with your eyes and hear with your ears, and set your heart on all that I shall show you. For you are brought here so that I might show *them* to you. Declare all that you see to the house of Israel.

These verses form the introduction to the whole concluding section, and call for little in the way of general remark. We observe in them so far a resemblance between the commencement and the close of the book, that in each alike the prophet is borne away by a Divine hand, and placed amid the visions of God. There are, however, two characteristic differences between the earlier and the later. First, in respect to the region where these ideal manifestations of Divine truth and glory were given – formerly on the banks of the Chebar, as if the glory of Jehovah had forsaken its old haunts, and now on what was emphatically the mount of God, as if he were again returned thither, and had even already raised it to a far nobler elevation. The substance of the visions, too, very strikingly differed; for while that on the Chebar was fitted chiefly to awaken thoughts of terror and solemn awe in the bosom, this, on the other hand, was calculated to produce feelings of the liveliest confidence and the most exalted hopes. The heavens seemed now, in a sense, cleared of all their stormier elements, and were radiant with the sunshine of the Divine favor. The man with the appearance of brass (bright, furbished brass is to be understood) must, of course, be considered a representative of the higher world, a special messenger of God; and the two instruments in his hand, the linen tape and the measuring rod, were for taking the dimensions – the first the larger, the second the less. It is also quite in unison with the prophet's strongly ideal and realistic cast of mind, that he should not simply have given the pattern and dimensions, but should have presented the Divine messenger in the attitude of going to take all the measurements before his eyes.

5 And, behold, a wall on the outside of the house all around, and in the man's hand was a measuring reed of six cubits, by the cubit and a hand breadth![4] So he measured the breadth of the building, one reed; and the height, one reed.

6 Then he came to the gate which looked toward the east, and went up its stairs, and measured the threshold of the gate, one reed broad. And the other threshold, one reed broad.[5]

7 And *each* little room was one reed long and one reed broad. And between the little rooms were five cubits. And the threshold of the gate by the porch of the gate within was one reed.

8 He also measured the porch of the gate inside, one reed.

9 Then he measured the porch of the gate, eight cubits. And its post was two cubits. And the porch of the gate was inward.

10 And the little rooms of the gate eastward were three on this side, and three on that side. The three of them were of one measure; and the posts were of the same size on this side and on that side.

11 And he measured the breadth of the entry of the gate, ten cubits. The length of the gate was thirteen cubits.

12 The space also in front of the little rooms was one cubit on this side, and the space was one cubit on that side. And the little rooms were six cubits on this side and six cubits on that side.

13 Then he measured the gate from the roof of *one* little room to the roof of another. The breadth was twenty-five cubits, door against door.

14 He also made posts of sixty cubits, even to the post of the court all around the gate.

15 And from the face of the gate of the entrance to the face of the porch of the inner gate was fifty cubits.

16 And narrow windows to the little rooms and to their posts inside the gate all around, and likewise to the porches – and windows were all around inside. And on *each* post were palm trees.[6]

In this description, as stated in the note below, there are obscurities in regard to several of the particulars mentioned which we have not the means of satisfactorily clearing up. But we may not the less apprehend the general import of this part of the description. It marks a very decided superiority in the new pattern presented to the eye of Ezekiel over that which had previously existed; the imperfections of the one should have no place in the other. And this, first, in regard to the wall that enclosed the sacred edifice. It is probable that the temple of Solomon was surrounded by such a boundary wall, as something of this kind was customary in ancient temples; but there is no appearance of that having formed part of the Divine plan, or possessing strictly a sacred character. Hence various alterations were made from time to time in that respect, and new gates opened (2 Kings 15:35; Jer. 36:10), for the purpose, no doubt, of suiting more fully the convenience of the worshippers. Something of an irregular, adventitious, of a common or profane character was thus brought into close contact with the affairs of the temple and on this account no scruple was made of turning apartments in the buildings raised on these sacred precincts to the commonest uses. It was in one of these that Jeremiah was detained as in a prison (chap. 20:2, 29:26). But now, according to the new and better state of things seen in vision by the prophet, this imperfection and arbitrariness were to be done away. The whole summit of the temple mount was to be set off as an holy place to the Lord; and the wall enclosing it, and the gates and erections connected with it, were all, equally with the temple itself, to bear on them the stamp of Divine perfection.

The wall, as described by the prophet, does not seem to have been planned with any other view than to convey this impression of sacredness. As usual in Divine measurements (for example, the most holy place in the sanctuary, and the city in Rev. 21:16), it bears the square form, as broad as it is high but this being only twelve feet at the utmost, it was manifestly not designed to present by its altitude an imposing aspect, or by its strength to constitute a bulwark of safety. In these respects it could not for a moment be compared with many of the mural erections which existed in antiquity. But as the boundary line between the sacred and the profane, which, being drawn by the hand of God, must therefore remain free from all interference on the part of man, it is precisely such as might have been expected. Something more, however, needed to be expressed in the construction of the gates. These being the channels of intercourse with what was within – the doorways out and in to what might be called emphatically the city of the living God – they must be formed so as adequately to provide for the due preservation of the sacred character of the house. This is the point chiefly brought out in the plans and measurements connected with them. There are not wanting in the description signs of beauty and magnificence – porticoes, pillars, turrets, carved and ornamented, so as to convey the impression that the way through them conducted to the palace of the great King. But furnished as they were so amply with guard-chambers for those who should be charged with maintaining the sanctity of the house (chap. 44:11,14), they were formed more especially with a view to the holiness, which must be the all-pervading characteristic of the place. It was imprinting on the architecture of this portion of the buildings the solemn truth *"that there shall in nowise enter into it anything that defileth, neither worketh abomination, or maketh a lie"* (Rev. 21:27) – a truth which in past times, partly from defective arrangements, partly from the wilful disregard of such as existed, had been most greviously suffered to fall into abeyance. But henceforth it must be made known to all that holiness becometh God's house, and that they only who possess this shall be allowed to come and minister before him.

While this character attaches substantially to each of the four gates, it is brought out most especially and distinctly in connection with the eastern gate, because this was the one that looked straight to the door of the temple, and to it, therefore belonged a place of pre-eminence. It was through that gate that the prophet in a former vision had seen the glory of the Lord departing (chap. 11:23), and through this also it was to return; whence the access through it was to be reserved for special occasions (chap. 44:2,3). The more intimate connection between this and the peculiar manifestations of Deity imparted to it a character of deeper sacredness.

[17]Then he brought me into the outer court. And, lo, rooms and a pavement made for the court all around! Thirty rooms were on the pavement.

[18]And the pavement by the side of the gates across from the length of the gates was the lower pavement.

[19]Then he measured the breadth from the front of the lower gate to the front of the inner court outside, a hundred cubits eastward and northward.

In this brief description of the outer court there is properly no difficulty in the terms, or any of the particular parts, but still there is an indefiniteness which would leave us at sea if we were going to draw out the plan. For what was the position of the thirty rooms or cells spoken of in this space? Did they appear immediately in front when one entered the east gate (as Havernick contends), or were they placed at a side (as Bottcher and Hitzig affirm?) Did the measurement of an hundred cubits apply merely to the buildings, or to the court itself? Here, again, is room for difference of opinion. It is foolish for us to fix and determine what the prophet has left indeterminate. I think the natural impression is, that the prophet means to represent the whole outer court as laid with a smooth and polished pavement round and round as far as this court reached; that on the pavement, but to the north or right, as one entered, there was a large building of thirty rooms covering the whole width of the court in that direction (for why otherwise should he have given the measurement on the east and north merely, and yet have made it reach from the lower gate to the outer part of the inner court?) so that the measurement given indicated at once the extent of the buildings and the width of the court. (Havernick disputes this, but without any just reason; he would make the court larger.) Such is the impression I take up from the description, but there can be no absolute certainty in regard to the relative positions and adjustments – itself a proof that nothing depends on them. The determinate things in the description are, that the compass of the outer court was exactly defined, and hundred cubits; that it was finely paved, as a place which should be trodden only by clean feet (emblem of internal purity); and that the erections belonging to it were to be a square of an hundred cubits, and consisting of thirty apartments. So that here also nothing was left to men's caprice or corrupt fancies, as had been the case of old. While from the first there appears to have been an outer court connected with Solomon's temple, it seems to have been left to a certain extent open to alterations, as well as the intrusion of idolatrous inventions hence we read in 2 Chron. 20:5 of *"a new court,"* and in 2 Kings 23:11,12 of the profanation of the place by some of the worst things of heathenish idolatry being set up there, for which, no doubt, the innovators would plead the absence of any express statutes determining what should or should not belong to it. Now, however, there should be no room for such displays of human arbitrariness and corruption; a more perfect state of things was to be brought in, and even all in the outer court was to be regulated by God's hand, and bear the impress of his holiness. This too must be hallowed ground, fashioned and ruled in all its parts after the perfect measures of the Divine mind and the just requirements of his service; therefore – such was evidently the practical result aimed at – let not the ungodly and profane any longer presume to tread such courts (Isa. 1:12), or desecrate them by the introduction of their own unwarranted inventions. Let all feel that in coming here they have to do with a God of purer eyes than to behold iniquity.

Now follows a brief description of the north and south gates:

[20]And the gate of the outer court that looked toward the north, he measured its length and its breadth.

[21]And the little rooms of it were three on this side and three on that side. And its posts and its porches were according to the measure of the first gate. The length of it was fifty cubits, and its breadth was twenty-five cubits.

[22]And their windows, and their porches, and their palm trees were according to the measure of the gate that looks toward the east. And they went up to it by seven steps; and its porches were before them.

[23]And the gate of the inner court was across from the gate toward the north and toward the east. And he measured from gate to gate a hundred cubits.

[24]After that he brought me toward the south, and behold a gate toward the south. And he measured its posts and its porches according to these measures.

[25]And windows *were* in it and in its porches all around, like those windows. The length was fifty cubits, and the breadth was twenty-five cubits. And seven steps to go up to it and its porches were before them.

[26]And it had palm trees, one on this side and another on that side, on its posts.

[27]And a gate *was* in the inner court toward the south. And he measured from gate to gate toward the south a hundred cubits.

These directions regarding the north and south divisions merely intimate a correspondence in the plan between the different approaches, expecting that in the case of these two other gates no mention is made of the building with its thirty chambers, which was found on the eastern side. Probably because only one was needed, and it was assigned to the eastern quarter, as being the more peculiarly sacred; and being intended for the officiating priests, it might be most conveniently situated there. Having thus finished the boundary wall and the outer court, he comes to the inner court:

[28]And he brought me to the inner court by the south gate. And he measured the south gate according to these measures.

[29]And its little rooms and its posts and its posts *were* according to these measures. And windows *were* in it and in its porches all

around. *It was* fifty cubits long and twenty-five cubits broad.

[30]And the arches all around were twenty-five cubits long and five cubits broad.[7]

[31]And its porches were toward the outer court. And palm trees were on its posts. And its stairway had eight steps.

[32]And he brought me into the inner court toward the east. And he measured the gate according to these measures.

[33]And the little rooms of it, and its posts, and its porches *were* according to these measures. And windows *were* in it and in its porches all around. *It was* fifty cubits long and twenty-five cubits broad.

[34]And its porches were toward the outer court. And palm trees were on its posts, on this side and on that side. And its stairway had eight steps.

[35]And he brought me to the north gate and measured according to these measures;

[36]its little rooms, its posts, and its porches, and its windows all around. The length was fifty cubits, and the breadth twenty-five cubits.

[37]And its posts were toward the outer court. And palm trees were on its posts, on this side and on that side. And its stairway had eight steps.

[38]And the rooms and their doors were by the posts of the gates, where they washed the burnt offering.

[39]And in the porch of the gate were two tables on this side and two tables on that side, for the killing of the burnt offering and the sin offering and the trespass offering.

[40]And at the side outside, as one goes up tothe entrance of the north gate, were two tables. And on the other side, which was at the porch of the gate, were two tables.

[41]Four tables were on this side and four tables were on that side, by the side of the gate: eight tables on which they killed.

[42]And the four tables were of cut stone for the burnt offering, of a cubit and a half long, and a cubit and a half broad, and one cubit high. On *these* they also laid the instruments with which they killed the burnt offering and the sacrifices.

[43]And inside were hooks, a hand broad, fastened all around. And on the tables was the flesh of the offering.

The provison here made for killing and washing the sacrifice appears evidently to have been connected with only one of the gates; and yet the passage at the commencement speaks of *"the pillars of the gates,"* as if it were something in common to them all. But by the original direction (Lev. 1:11), the sacrifices were all to be killed on the north side of the altar; and there is no reason to think that that regulation was generally departed from in the ministrations of the old temple. It seems to have been with respect to that custom that Ezekiel himself (chap. 8:5) calls the north gate *"the gate of the altar,"* that gate being on the account of the sacrifices specially connected with the altar. Hence here it is in immediate connection with the north gate that the description is introduced about the preparation of the sacrifices; and the particular mention of the *"north"* in ver. 40 seems still more decisively to point out the north gate as the quarter to which these arrangements belonged. It appears quite arbitrary, therefore, to substitute (as Ewald and Hitzig here do) the east for the north gate; the more especially as the east gate was to be shut to the mass of worshippers, and must consequently have been the most unsuitable for such a purpose. The description itself, as to its general import, is of the same nature as the preceding. Everything connected even with the killing and preparing of victims must now be regulated by the word of God. Even there all is to have an impress of sacredness, such as has not hitherto been found, in consequence of the higher elevation to which the Divine kingdom was to attain.

[44]And outside the inner gate were the rooms of the singers in the inner court, which was at the side of the north gate. And their view was toward the south: at the side of the east gate one *had* the view toward the north.

[45]And he said to me, This room, whose view is toward the south, is for the priests, the keepers of the charge of the house.

[46]And the room whose view is toward the north is for the priests, the keepers of the charge of the altar. These are the sons of Za-dok among the sons of Levi, who come near the LORD to minister to Him.

[47]So he measured the court: *it was* square, a hundred cubits long and a hundred cubits broad; and *he measured* the altar *that was* before the house.

The two remaining verses properly belong to the next chapter, which treats of the temple itself; with which, therefore, we shall couple them. The court mentioned in the last verse, which measured an hundred cubits square, must not be confounded with what in the preceding verses is called the inner court. The inner court was the court of Israel, which was open to all who had sacrifices and offerings to bring; and it went round the three sides of the sacred territory, of the breadth of an hundred cubits, or two hundred feet. But this court was precisely an hundred cubits square, and had the altar standing in it, in front of the temple. It was the court of the priests; and hence is mentioned in connection with those who had charge of the house, the altar, and the sacred music. The description here is more brief, as the things connected with this portion had from the first been made matter of Divine regulation.

CHAPTER XL. 48, 49, XLI.

THE TEMPLE ITSELF.

48 And he brought me to the porch of the house and measured *each* post of the porch five cubits on this side and five cubits on that side. And the breadth of the gate was three cubits on this side and three cubits on that side.

49 The length of the porch was twenty cubits, and the breadth eleven cubits. And *he brought me* by the steps by which they went up to it. And *there were* pillars by the posts, one on this side and another on that side.[1]

1 Afterward he brought me to the temple and measured the posts, six cubits broad on the one side and six cubits broad on the other side, the breadth of the tabernacle.[2]

2 And the breadth of the door was ten cubits. And the sides of the door was five cubits on the one side and five cubits on the other side. And he measured the length of it, forty cubits, and the breadth, twenty cubits.

3 Then he went inside and measured the post of the door, two cubits; andthe door was six cubits, and its breadth seven cubits.

4 So he measured the length of it, twenty cubits; and the breadth, twenty cubits, before the temple.[3] And he said to me, This is the most holy place.

5 Afterwards he measured the wall of the house, six cubits; and the breadth of *each* side room was four cubits, all around the house on every side.

6 And the side rooms were three, one over another, and thirty in a row. And they entered into the wall which was of the house for the side rooms all around, so that they might have a support, but they did not have a support in the wall of the house.[4]

7 And *there was* a broadening, and a winding about still upward to the side rooms. For the winding around of the house went still upward, all around the house. Therefore the breadth of the house was still upward, and so increased *from* the lowest to the highest by the middle.

8 I also saw the height of the house all around. The foundations of the side rooms were a full reed of six large cubits.[5]

9 The thickness of the wall, which was for the side room outside, was five cubits. And what was left was the place of the side rooms that were inside.

10 And between the rooms was the width of twenty cubits, all around the house, on every side.

11 And the doors of the side rooms were toward *the* left, one door toward the north and another door toward the south. And the breadth of the place that was left was five cubits all around.

There is considerable minuteness in the description of these side-chambers, as compared, at least, with the original description in 1 Kings 6, where the whole that is said of them is comprised in two verses. And yet with the advantage of the greater minuteness here, it would be impossible to construct an architectural plan without taking a good deal for granted that has no place in the prophet's delineation. One can easily understand how there might be a winding stair within, leading up through the several stories, but how should this have been accompanied with an enlarging or widening of the house itself? What is meant by the foundations being a full rod of six cubits, – some underground buildings on which they rested, or the ground itself on which they were raised? (Both have their advocates). What was the object of the unoccupied place of five cubits? and how did it differ from the space of twenty cubits lying between the side-chambers and the halls of the priests? Very different answers might be and have been given to these questions, and the greatest liberties taken with the text to lighten the difficulties connected with the account. But we deem it needless to enter into these, or to attempt fixing what the prophet himself has left vague and obscure. He never intended that a structure should be reared precisely according to the plan and measurements he furnishes; otherwise he would have been still more minute in his delineations. He has given enough, however, for his great object, which was chiefly to show that in the Divine purpose respecting the future there was to be a full and every-way complete reconstruction of the house of God – if not in the outward and material sense, yet in the higher things, which that represented and symbolized; and with the effect of securing a far purer and more elevated condition for the covenant-people. It is this last point which throughout he seeks to render prominent by the nature of his descriptions. Hence, in marked contrast to the earlier delineations respecting the tabernacle and Solomon's temple, he passes rapidly over the things that more immediately respected God, and dwells upon those which bore on the state and condition of the people. The temple itself, in its two important divisions, is hastily sketched, and nothing scarcely said of its sacred furniture, not even the slightest notice taken of the ark of the covenant, the heart and centre of the whole in former times; while the most lengthened details are given of all that concerned the chambers of the priests, and the courts which were to be frequented by the worshippers. The prophet would thus teach that there was to be in the future a conformity to the Divine idea, where there had been but little before; that while Jehovah should remain the same in all his essential attributes and manifestations as formerly, he should be otherwise known and glorified by his people; their dwellings should all become true sanctuaries, and their services fragrant with the odor of living piety. In the excellent words of Havernick, "Jehovah will dwell among a new people; and accordingly he must do so in a new manner, though one still analogous to the old. The most essential and indispensable condition of this new indwelling of Jehovah among his people is the due elevation of the Divine community; hence the importance and high significance attached by the prophet to the otherwise much inferior and outward parts of the temple buildings. The description now advances to the preparation of the proper centre of those external forms. No longer, as in the old sanctuary, will Jehovah manifest himself in an imperfect manner, but in the full splendor of his glory, as at chap. 43:1-12. The interior of the temple there stands empty, waiting for the entrance of the Lord, that he may come and fill it with his glory. It is the same temple, but the courts of it have become different, in order to accommodate a far more numerous people; and all the provisions and arrangements here bespeak the sincerity and the zeal with which they now seek and serve the Lord. The entire compass of the temple-mount has become a holy of holies (chap. 42:12); consequently every thing now rises to a higher, to its true dignity and importance. On this account the ark of the covenant had no place in this temple; the full display of the Divine Shechinah has come into its room. And so Ezekiel treads very closely in the footsteps of his predecessor Jeremiah – who, under the dark foreboding of the near loss of the sacred ark, consoles the people with the glorious promise, that what might seem in a natural point of view to be an irreparable loss, was going to be compensated by an unparalleled manifestation of the immediate glory of Jehovah: *'In those days they shall say no more, The ark of the covenant of the Lord. and it shall not come to mind; neither shall it be missed; and another shall not be made. At that time they shall call Jerusalem the throne of the Lord'* (Jer. 3:16,17). This thought is merely carried out by Ezekiel after his own manner."

[12]Now the building that was before the separate place at the end toward the west was seventy cubits broad. And the wall of the building was five cubits thick all around, and its length was ninety cubits.

[13]So he measured the house, a hundred

cubits long. And the separate place, and the building with its wall were a hundred cubits long.

[14]Also the breadth of the house and of the separate place toward the east was a hundred cubits.

[15]And he measured the length of the building across from the separate place which was behind it, and its balconies on the one side and on the other side, a hundred cubits,[6] with the inner temple and the porches of the court,

[16]the door posts, and the narrow windows, and the balconies all around on their three stories, across from the door, with wood ceilings all around, and from the ground up to the windows – and the windows were covered –

[17]to that above the door, even to the inner house, and outside, and by all the wall around inside and outside, by measure.

[18]And *it* was made with cherubims and palm trees, so that a palm tree was between a cherub and a cherub. And *each* cherub had two faces,

[19]so that the face of a man was toward the palm tree on the one side, and the face of a young lion toward the palm tree on the other side. *It was* made through all the house all around.

[20]From the ground to above the door were cherubims and palm trees made, and on the wall of the temple.

[21]The posts of the temple were squared, the face of the sanctuary. The looks *of the one* was like the looks *of the other.*

[22]The altar of wood was three cubits high, and its length was two cubits. And its corners, andits length, and its walls were of wood. And he said to me, This is the table that is before the LORD.

[23]And the temple and the sanctuary had two doors.

[24]And the doors had two leaves, two turning leaves – two for the one door, and two leaves for the other.

[25]And on them, on the doors of the temple *were* made cherubims and palm trees like those made on the walls; and thick planks were on the front of the porch outside.

[26]And narrow windows and palm trees *were* on the one side and on the other side, on the sides of the porch and the side rooms of the house, and thick planks.

The latter part of the description has reference chiefly to the ornamental work which was done upon the walls of the temple, and which is also mentioned in 1 Kings 6. The account here is fuller, though it makes no mention of the flowers and the overlaying with gold, which are found there. What is meant by the עָב in ver. 25 and 26 is quite uncertain, but has been conjecturally understood to be some sort of sill-piece or plank about the threshold. Some later writers (Ewald, Hitzig) incline rather to understand it of some peculiar kind of carved work, or settings in the outer porch; but opinions may vary as much as the fancies of men. It will be observed, too, that the only article of sacred furniture mentioned, the altar of incense, is called the Lord's table; and it is again also, at chap. 44:16, referred to under this name: *"They shall enter into my sanctuary, and they shall come near to my table, to minister unto me."* It was at the incense altar, and not at the table of show-bread, that the daily and regular ministrations of the priesthood in the sanctuary proceeded; and it was of this also, which stood in immediate front of the veil, that it could with special propriety be said that it was *"before the Lord."* Its being called a table probably referred to the satisfaction and delight with which the Lord was to regard the services, which were henceforth to be offered to him by his renewed people. And possibly on this account, too, the dimensions are given larger than of old – three cubits in height and two in breadth, instead of two and one. But the most peculiar part of the description is what relates to the buildings connected with the separate place, so closely adjoining to the temple, in the unoccupied ground on the west, and so much resembling it in size. Nothing is said of their exact intention, nor is there even any particular description of the internal construction. The account as to details is remarkably general and obscure and why then given at all? To show, as it would seem, that there was now to be no place left, as of old, which might not be held to be sacred ground. It appears to have been there that in Manesseh's time the horses were kept which were consecrated to the sun (2 Kings 23:11), called *"the suburbs of the temple."* But all excuse was henceforth to be taken away for such abominations; the Lord laid claim to all for his peculiar service, and had this also filled up with sacred erections.

CHAPTER XLII.

CHAMBERS OF THE TEMPLE AND ITS BOUNDARY WALLS.

[1]Then he brought me out into the outer-court, the way toward the north. And he brought me into the room that was across from the separate place and which was in front of the building to the north.

[2]Before the length of a hundred cubits was the north door, and the breadth was fifty cubits.

[3]Across from the twenty which were for the inner court, and across from the pavement which was for the outer court, balcony was on balcony in three *stories.*

[4]And before the rooms was a walk of ten cubits breadth inward, a way of one cubit. And their doors were toward the north.

[5]Now the upper rooms were shorter; for the balconies were higher than these, than the lower, yet *higher* than the middle of the building.

[6]For they were in three *stories,* but did not have pillars like the pillars of the courts. So *the building* was made narrower than the lower and the middle stories from the ground.

[7]And the wall that was outside across from the rooms toward the outer court on the front part of the rooms, its length was fifty cubits.

[8]For the length of the rooms that were in the outer court was fifty cubits. And, lo, in front of the temple was a hundred cubits

[9]And under these rooms was the entrance on the east side, as one goes into them from the outer court.

[10]The rooms were in the thickness of the wall of the court toward the east, across from the separate place and across from the building.

[11]And the passageway in front of them looked like the rooms which were toward the north, as long as they were, and as broad as they were. And all their doors were both according to their patterns and according to their entrances.

[12]And according to the doors of the rooms that were toward the south was a door in the head of the way, the way directly in front of the wall eastward, as one enters them.

[13]Then he said to me, The north rooms and the south rooms which are in front of the separate place, they are holy rooms, where the priests who approach to the LORD shall eat the most holy things. There they shall lay the most holy things, and the meal offering, and the sin offering and the trespass offering. For the place is holy.

[14]When the priests enter into it, then they shall not go out of the holy *place* into the outer court, but there they shall lay their clothes in which they minister, for they are holy; and shall put on other clothes, and shall approach *those thingss* which are for the people.

This part of chap. 42 is taken up with describing the apartments, or chambers, which were reserved for the officiating priests. That this was their particular destination, is expressly stated in the two last verses. The aim and object of the buildings, therefore, is quite accurately defined they were for the priests, that they might be able in their ministrations to treat with due solemnity the sacred things of the Lord, and keep broad the distinction between the holy and the corrupt, the Divine and the human so that the particularizing here is in perfect accordance with the great design of the prophet, in exhibiting a restored community and worship purified from the corruptions which had hitherto cleaved to them. And as he had before (chap. 40:44-46) spoken of apartments on the north and south gates of the inner court for the officiating priests, it seems quite necessary to understand what is said here of the same the prophet merely returns, after having seen and described what belonged to the temple, to take a second and more exact view of these sacerdotal chambers. But why they should be said to stand over against the separate place and the building belonging to it rather than the temple itself (vers. 1-10), does not appear. Nor is the description generally of such a kind that we could hope to make it more intelligible to an English reader by any lengthened observations. It seems impossible to ascertain distinctly the pattern, without either making considerable alterations in the text of filling up many blanks from imagination. It is enough for us to know that the prophet saw in vision all the subordinate provisions made which were necessary to the full and efficient discharge of the duties of the priesthood. He thus obtained for the Church the assurance that the service of God would yet be performed so as to meet God's perfect approval. We therefore pass on to the closing verses, which give the dimensions of the boundary wall.

15 Now when he finished measuring the inner house, he brought me forth toward the gate whose view is toward the east, and measured it all around.

16 He measured the east side with the measuring reed, five hundred reeds with the measuring reed, all around.

17 He measured the north side, five hundred reeds with the measuring reed all around.

18 He measured the south side, five hundred reeds with the measuring reed.

19 He turned around to the west side, measuring five hundred reeds with the measuring reed.

20 He measured it by the four sides. It had a wall all around, five hundred *reeds* long and five hundred broad, to make a separation between the holy place and the common place.

We cannot but note the particularity with which these measurements are given, – the rod as the measuring instrument, and the number of lengths on each side, being successively stated in regard to each. This plainly shows the importance which the prophet attached to the external dimensions, while the frequent occurrence also of the terms employed more fully certifies us of their exact amount. Yet from an early period a disposition has been shown to tamper with the numbers. The Septuagint substitutes cubits for rods, and the great mass of modern commentators (still also Ewald, Hitzig, Bottcher, Thenius, the latter in his *Anhang* to the Com. on Kings) have thought it necessary to adopt the same alteration. The chief reasons for this are, first, the apparently extravagant compass assigned to the sacred buildings – a square of 500 rods, or 3000 cubits, and these cubits about two feet each (chap. 40:5), making in all a square of fully 1 1/7 of a mile. There can be no doubt that this exceeded the limits of all ancient Jerusalem; and so, it is thought, the prophet could never intend to give such enormous bounds to his new temple; he must have meant cubits only, and not rods. Then it is also alleged that the particular measurements in the preceding portion do not require a space larger than a square of 500 cubits, and that the adoption of rods here instead of cubits would necessarily leave an immense space of unappropriated ground. Havernick has tried to evade this argument by denying that the 100 cubits mentioned in connection with the outer and inner courts (chap. 40:23,27) are given as the measures of the whole breadth of these, and contending that they apply only to the distance between one gate and another in the same court. I cannot concur in this, for I think the natural supposition is, that the gates between which the distances in question lay were simply those of the two courts respectively. But if by rejecting that method of relief we seem to have far too much space on hand, by adopting the smaller measures of cubits instead of rods we should have decidedly too little. I think this might be proved by reckoning up the different items of the several measures connected with the temple itself and the separate place. But as we should thus inevitably get into intricacies where few would follow, we prefer establishing our position by a simpler process. In the central part to the east of the temple there was a square of 100 cubits, the court of the priests. But if on three sides of an entire square of 500 cubits you take off first 100 cubits for the outer court, then 100 for the inner, with nothing intervening, there would be left precisely this square of 100 more for the court of the priests. But where, then, was the space to be found for the broad outermost wall, outside of which the measurement of 500 was made – six cubits all round? Where, again, for the seven steps leading up to the gate of the inner court, and the breadth of the wall dividing it from the outer? And where, once again, space for the eight steps leading up to the court of the priests, and the buildings of many chambers for them? There is evidently no room for these on the cubit hypothesis, which would require the different courts to be enclosed, and separated from each other by strictly mathematical lines; so that the objection of too much ground by the measurements of the text may fairly be met by the too little of the hypothesis.

In truth, we have here another of those traits which render manifest, and, I believe, were intended to render manifest and palpable, the ideal character of the whole description. It is of a nature throughout which defies all attempts to bring it within the bounds of the real. Those who have endeavored so to deal with it have always been obliged to resort to numberless arbitrary suppositions and violent adjustments. And, in particular, the vast compass the prophet so explicitly and distinctly assigns to the whole area, involving a sort of natural incongruity, like the promise of the new David in the prophecies of the restoration, must ever be regarded as an inseparable obstacle to their superficial literalism. It is an incontrovertible evidence that the prophet had something else in his eye than the masonry of stone and lime erections, and was laboring with conceptions which could only find their embodiment in the high realities of God's everlasting kingdom.

We abide, then, by the Hebrew text as the true handwriting of the prophet, the very difficulties of which are a proof of their correctness; and we regard the immense extent of the sacred area as a symbol of the vast enlargement that was to be given to the kingdom of God in the times of Messiah. It was immeasurably to surpass the old in the extent of its territory, and in the number of its adherents, as well as in the purity of its worship. The wall that surrounded the sacred buildings is expressly said, in ver. 20, to have been for separating between the holy and profane; not, therefore, as in Rev. 21:12, and very commonly elsewhere, for defence and safety, as indeed its comparative want of elevation might seem to render it unfit for such a purpose. But its square form, and the square appearance of the entire buildings (as in John's city, Rev. 21:16), betokened the strength and solidity of the whole, along with a vast increase in extent and number. A perfect cube, it was the emblem of a kingdom that could not be shaken or removed. And thus every way it exhibited to the eye of faith the true ideal of that pure and glorious temple which, resting on the foundation of the eternal Son, and girt round by all the perfections of Godhead, shall shine forth the best and noblest workmanship of Heaven.

CHAPTER XLIII.

THE LORD'S RETURN TO THE TEMPLE.

In the preceding part of the vision, the external things belonging to the Lord's house have been exhibited in their vast proportions and manifold arrangements. Everything has become ready for the Lord himself taking formal possession of it, by the visible manifestations of his glory. This was now, as of old, to constitute the peculiar distinction of the place; and was to belong to this temple in a degree so much higher than formerly, as the general plan transcended what had existed in the past. The prophet had seen in vision the glory of the Lord depart from the old temple (chap. 11), by the way of the east, and rest over the Mount of Olives, as it were to watch upon the destruction which must thenceforth alight on the devoted city. And now, again, when the work of judgment has run its course, and due preparation has been made for the return of Jehovah to bless his people, a manifestation of the Divine glory appears to the prophet similar to what he had seen on the banks of the Chebar, and also in the old temple courts (vers. 1-3); and by the very same approach through which it had departed it comes back, and fills the whole house. The prophet is then caught up by the Spirit of the Lord, and placed in the inner court, where as a priest his proper position was; and he heard the voice of God speaking to him from within, while the interpreting angel beside him gives utterance to the message meant to be conveyed.

[1] Afterward he brought me to the gate, the gate that faces toward the east.

[2] And, behold, the glory of the God of Israel came from the way of the east. And His voice was like the noise[1] of many waters. And the earth shone with His glory.

[3]And it looked the same as the vision which I saw, according to the vision which I saw when I came to destroy the city.[2] And the visions were like the vision that I saw by the river Che-bar. And I fell on my face.

[4]And the glory of the LORD came into the house by the way of the gate whose view is toward the east.

[5]So the Spirit took me up and brought me into the inner room. And, behold, the glory of the LORD filled the house.

[6]And I heard *Him* speaking to me out of the house; and the man stood beside me.

[7]And He said to me, Son of man, the house of Israel shall no more defile the place of My throne[3] and the place of the soles of My feet, where I will dwell in the midst of the children of Israel forever – they, nor their kings, by their fornication, nor by the dead bodies of their kings in their high places.[4]

[8]In their setting of their doorstep by My doorsteps, and their posts by My posts, and the wall between Me and them, they have even defiled My holy name by their idolatries that they have committed. Therefore I destroyed them in My anger.

[9]Now let them put away their fornication, and the dead bodies of their kings, far from Me, and I will dwell in their midst forever.

[10]Son of man, show the house to the house of Israel, so that they may be ashamed of their iniquities. And let them measure the pattern.

[11]And if they are ashamed of all that they have done, show them the form of the house, and its pattern, and its exits and its entrances, and all its forms, and all its ordinances and all their forms, and all its laws. And write *it* in their sight, so that they may keep the whole form of it, and all its ordinances, and do them.

[12]This is the law of the house. On the top of the mountain, its whole boundary all around shall be most holy. Behold, this is the law of the house!

In this striking passage we are first of all to note the character in which the Lord now appears to dwell and manifest himself among his people. It is as their Divine king, occupying that house as the throne of his kingdom. God has always claimed this position, and had at first resisted their desires to have an earthly sovereign, because this virtually implied a rejection of him as the proper head of the state. Even when he consented to their request, it was with a solemn and earnest protest against the person chosen ruling in his own name, and for selfish purposes, or in any other way than as the Lord's vicegerent. The protest, however, was soon forgotten. The king looked upon himself, and the people also looked upon him, as possessing an absolute title to the throne, and the earthly head came very much to occupy in men's eyes the place of the true and proper king. But in the new and more perfect order of things now unfolded in vision to the prophet, this flagrant perversion of the past must be rectified; God must be known and honored as alone properly *"king in Jeshurun."* And hence, not only here does he declare that he had come to occupy his throne in the house, but, as mentioned in the note on ver. 7, the earthly head, when spoken of in a subsequent chapter, is simply called *"the prince."* The supremacy and glory of Jehovah were henceforth to appear in their full splendor. We have further to notice in the preceding passage the essentially moral character of all that was here displayed in vision respecting the future things of God's kingdom. It was not a pattern which God was going to carry out anyhow, and accomplish as by a simple fiat of Omnipotence. It depended upon the condition of the people; and only if they agreed to put away sin from among them, and give God the supreme place in their hearts, could he manifest himself toward them in the manner described. And, finally, while the whole scheme was fraught with lessons of instruction, and inlaid with principles of holiness, the grand and distinguishing peculiarity of this pattern of the future as compared with the past, we are expressly informed, was to be a general and all-pervading sanctity. The law of the house – what was pre-eminently entitled to be called the law – consisted in the whole region of the temple mount being most holy. Not, as hitherto, was this characteristic to be confined to a single apartment of the temple; it was to embrace the entire circumference occupied by the symbolical institutions of the kingdom, – the chambers allotted to the priest, and even the courts trodden by the people, as well as the immediate dwelling-place of Jehovah. All were to have one character of sacredness, because all connected with them were to occupy a like position of felt nearness to God, and equally to enjoy the privilege of access to him. So that the pattern delineated is that

of a true theocracy, having God himself for king, with the community in all its members for true denizens of the kingdom, and acceptable ministers of righteousness before the Lord.

The remaining verses of this chapter (vers. 13-27), which contain a description of the altar of burnt-offering, and of the necessary rites of consecration connected with it, seem at first view somewhat out of place. But there is an historical reason for such a description being given here. Now that the Lord has taken possession of the house, the prophet goes on to show how the work of fellowship and communion with him is to proceed on the part of the people. It must, as it were, commence anew; and of course be conducted after the old manner, for no other could here come into contemplation. But in ancient times the grand medium of Divine intercourse was the altar, at which all gifts and sacrifices were to be presented for the Divine favor and blessing. And therefore the prophet here, to show that the way was open, and that the people might have free access to the fellowship of God, after having briefly sketched the dimensions of the altar, gives instructions for its consecration and the consecration of the priesthood, which was all that was needed to complete the arrangements. There is no need for going into the particulars either of the dimensions of the altar or of the prescribed services, as nothing peculiar seems to belong to them. The dimensions named have usually been thought to differ materially from those of the altar made by Solomon, which was ten cubits high, and twenty in length and breadth; but the probability is that they are the same, though it is scarcely possible to show the agreement without a diagram. The curious may see it done in Thenius (Bucher, der Konige, Anhang, p. 42). The seven days' purification services for the altar have respect to the original directions of Moses for the same purpose, in Ex. 29:37; and are simply a preparation for the great end aimed at – that God might accept the sacrifices of the people, and be gracious to them (ver. 27). This indispensably required that there should first be a consecrated way of access – a holy altar, and a holy priesthood to minister at it.

[13]And these are the measures of the altar by the cubits. The cubit is a cubit and a hand breadth: even the bottom shall be a cubit, and the breadth a cubit, and its border by its edge all around shall be a span. And this shall be the higher place of the altar.

[14]And from the bottom *on* the ground *even* to the lower ledge shall be two cubits, and the breadth one cubit. And from the smaller ledge to the greater ledge shall be four cubits, and the breadth one cubit.

[15]So the altar shall be four cubits, and from the altar and upward shall be four horns.[5]

[16]And the altar shall be twelve *cubits* long, twelve broad, square in its four squares.

[17]And the ledge shall be fourteen *cubits* long and fourteen broad in its four squares. And the border around it shall be half a cubit, and its bottom shall be half a cubit around. And its stairs shall look toward the east.

[18]And He said to me, Son of man, thus says the Lord GOD: These are the ordinances of the altar in the day when they shall make it, to offer burnt offerings on it and to sprinkle blood on it.

[19]And you shall give a young bull for a sin offering to the priests the Levites, who are of the seed of Za-dok, who approach Me to minister to Me, says the Lord GOD.

[20]And you shall take of its blood and put *it* on the four horns of it, and on the four corners of the ledge, and on the border all around. So you shall cleanse and purge it.

[21]You shall also take the bull of the sin offering, and he shall burn it in the appointed place of the house, outside the sanctuary.

[22]And on the second day you shall offer a kid of the goats without blemish for a sin offering. And they shall cleanse the altar as they cleansed *it* with the bull.

[23]And when you have finished cleansing *it*, you shall offer a young bull without blemish and a ram out of the flock without blemish.

[24]And you shall offer them before the LORD, and the priests shall cast salt on them, and they shall offer them up for a burnt offering to the LORD.

[25]Every day *for* seven days you shall prepare a goat *for* a sin offering. They also shall prepare a young bull, and a ram out of the flock, without blemish.

[26]They shall purge and purify the altar seven days; and they shall consecrate themselves.

[27]And when these days are expired, it shall be *that* on the eighth day and forward, the priests shall make your burnt offerings before the altar, and your peace offerings. And I will accept you, says the Lord GOD.

CHAPTER XLIV.

ORDINANCES FOR THE PRINCE AND THE PRIESTHOOD.

[1]Then he brought me back by the way of the gate of the outer sanctuary which looks toward the east. And It was shut.

[2]Then the LORD said to me, This gate shall be shut; it shall not be opened, and no man shall enter in by it. Because the LORD, the God of Israel, has entered in by it, therefore it shall be shut.

[3]*It is* for the prince. The prince shall sit in it to eat bread before the LORD. He shall enter by the way of the porch of *that* gate, and shall go out by the same way.

[4]Then he brought me by the way of the north gate before the house. And I looked, and, behold! The glory of the LORD filled the house of the LORD! And I fell on my face.

[5]And the LORD said to me, Son of man, note carefully: see with your eyes and hear with your ears all that I say to you concerning all the ordinances of the house of the LORD, and all its laws. And note carefully the entrance of the house, with every exit of the sanctuary.

[6]And you shall say to the rebellious, to the house of Israel, Thus says the Lord GOD: O house of Israel, let it be more than enough for you, of all your hateful deeds,

[7]that you have brought strangers, uncircumcised in heart and uncircumcised in flesh, to be in My sanctuary, to defile it – My house, when you offer My bread, the fat and the blood. And they have broken My covenant because of all your idolatries.

[8]And you have not kept the charge of My holy things, but you have set keepers of My charge in My sanctuary for themselves.

[9]Thus says the Lord GOD: No stranger, uncircumcised in heart or uncircumcised in flesh, shall enter into My sanctuary, or any stranger that is among the children of Israel.

[10]And the Levites who have gone far away from Me, when Israel went astray – who went astray from Me after their idols – they shall even bear their iniquity.

[11]Yet they shall be ministers in My sanctuary, *having* charge at the gates of the house and ministering to the house. They shall kill the burnt offering and the sacrifice for the people, and they shall stand before them to minister to them.

[12]Because they ministered to them before their idols, and caused the house of Israel to fall into iniquity, therefore I have lifted up My hand against them, says the Lord GOD, and they shall bear their iniquity.

[13]And they shall not come near Me, to do the office of a priest to Me, nor to come near any of My holy things, in the most holy place – but they shall bear their shame and their idolatries which they have committed.

[14]But I will make them keepers of the charge of the house for all its service, and for all that shall be done in it.

[15]But the priests the Levites, the sons of Za-dok, who kept the charge of My sanctuary when the children of Israel went astray from Me, they shall come near Me to minister to Me, and they shall stand before Me to offer to Me the fat and the blood, says the Lord GOD.

[16]They shall enter My sanctuary, and they shall come near My table, tominister to Me, and they shall keep My charge.

[17]And when they enter in at the gates of the court, they shall be clothed with linen clothing. And no wool shall come on them while they minister in the gates of the inner court, and inside.

[18]They shall have linen bonnets on their heads and shall have linen breeches on their loins. They shall not dress with anything that causes sweat.

[19]And when they go out into the outer court, into the outer court of the people, they shall put off their clothes in which they ministered, and lay them in the holy rooms. And they shall put on other clothes, so that they shall not sanctify the people with their own clothes.

[20]They shall not shave their heads or allow their hair to grow long. They shall only trim their heads.

[21]No priest shall drink wine when they enter the inner court.

[22]They shall not take for their wives a widow or her who is put away. But they shall take virgins of the seed of the house of Israel, or a widow who had a priest before.

[23]And they shall teach My people *the* difference between the holy and common, and cause them to tell the difference between the unclean and the clean.

[24]And in arguments they shall stand in judgment – they shall judge it according to My judgments. And they shall keep My laws and My statutes in all My assemblies; and they shall keep My sabbaths holy.

[25]And they shall not come near any dead

person to defile themselves; but they may defile themselves for father, or for mother, or for son, or for daughter, for brother, or for sister who has had no husband.

[26]And after he is cleansed, they shall count seven days for him.

[27]And in the day that he goes into the sanctuary, to the inner court, to minister in the sanctuary, he shall offer his sin offering, says the Lord GOD.

[28]And it shall be to them for an inheritance. I am their inheritance. And you shall give them no possession in Israel. I am their possession.

[29]They shall eat the meal offering, and the sin offering and the trespass offering; and every dedicated thing in Israel shall be theirs.

[30]And the first of all the first-fruits of all, and every offering of all, of every *kind* of your sacrifices, shall be the priest's, you shall also give the priest the first of your dough, so that he may cause the blessing to rest in your house.

[31]The priests shall not eat of anything that died of itself, or *is* torn, whether it is bird or animal.

As the preceding chapter had disclosed the purpose of God to re-occupy, and that for ever, this new temple, and had described the necessary means and rites of consecration in order to its being a source of blessing to his people, so the present chapter lays down regulations for preventing any new desecration of the house, such as might again compel God to withdraw his gracious presence. These regulations refer successively to the prince and the priesthood – the two classes through whom directly the former pollutions had been introduced into the house of God.

In regard to the former, who is simply called the prince (for the reason stated under last chapter), it is impossible for us to think of any one but the royal head, as he is throughout spoken of as an individual, and in the next chapter is directed *"to prepare for himself, and for all the people of the land,"* a sin-offering (chap. 45:22). So that the idea of Havernick, that the word is used collectively for the rulers and presidents generally of the people, is quite untenable. And not less so is the opinion, that by the expression is simply to be understood the Messiah; for this is utterly irreconcileable with all the prescriptions given, and in particular with those requiring the presentation of sacrifices and sin-offerings for the prince. It is to be explained precisely as the whole delineation here and in the preceding visions (chapters 34-39), by viewing it as a part of an ideal description of coming realities under the form and aspect of the old relations. And no more than we expect other parts of the vision to find their accomplishment under the Gospel by a restoration of the carnal sacrifices and institutions of Judaism, should we look here for an actual prince to follow the regulations prescribed. Standing on the position he did, the prophet must speak of the future under the image of the past; and as it was by means of the earthly head of the Jewish state that many of the former corruptions had been introduced, he now shows how a repetition of such evils is to be guarded against in the future. Whether the kingly power should ever again be concentrated in one person, or should be shared by many, is of no moment as regards the substance of the truth here unfolded.

What is said in the present chapter on this subject is very little, and relates to but one point, the connection between the prince and the east gate (vers. 1-3). Because the Lord had appeared in the vision returning by this gate, a peculiar stamp of sacredness was put upon it. It was therefore not to be open for ordinary worshippers, but only for the prince; he was to enter by it, and sit there and eat bread before the Lord. What could this import, but that the prince should feel he now occupied a place of peculiar nearness to God? As God's vicegerent and deputy among the people, it became him to be the most distinguished representative in public life of God's holiness, – to tread the higher walks of spiritual communion and fellowship with Heaven, and stand pre-eminent in his zeal for the interests of truth and righteousness. Far now from usurping the authority that belonged to God, and abusing to selfish ends and purposes the power which was given by him for higher ends, all authority and power in Israel should be exercised – if this Divine ideal were reduced to practice – in a solemn feeling of subordination to God's majesty, and with an unfeigned desire for his glory.

2. The prophet dwells at much greater length on the priesthood, as this class had more

immediately to do with God's sanctuary, and in their condition and behavior were reflected those generally of the covenant-people. It is on account of this close connection, first between the priesthood and the sanctuary, and then between the priesthood and those whom they represented in Israel, that the prophet appears at the commencement of the passage to identify the apostacy of the nation at large with the desecrations of God's house by the priesthood. He says (ver. 6, etc.): *"Thus saith the Lord Jehovah, Let it suffice you of all your abominations, O house of Israel; in that you brought strangers uncircumcised in heart and uncircumcised in flesh to be in my sanctuary, to pollute it, my house; in that ye made them offer my bread, the fat and the blood: and they broke my covenant to* (in addition to) *all our abominations. And ye did not keep my holy charge, but set for keepers of my charge in my sanctuary for yourselves."* The children of Israel are spoken of as doing all this because the corrupt priesthood was inseparably connected with the sins of the people – the one continually acting and re-acting on the other. And the corruption in the priesthood, it will be observed, is expressed as if persons had been put into the office who were not of the tribe of Levi, or even of the seed of Israel, but uncircumcised heathen. Not that literally persons of this description had been admitted into the priestly office; that did not take place, not even the kingdom of Israel, where still the Israelites were employed, though not of the family of Aaron. But the prophet is viewing all in a spiritual light, he is reading forth the import of the outward transactions as they appeared to the eye of God; and as in that respect the officiating priesthood had been no better than uncircumcised strangers, so he speaks of them as having actually been such. And if thus in regard to the past the prophet expresses the reality in the language of symbol, and must be understood according to the spiritual import, not the mere letter, of the description, it cannot certainly be otherwise when he points to the future. In reference to this he says: Not any of these uncircumcised strangers of the children of Israel, not any of the Levites who took part in the idolatrous services which had formerly been practised in the house of God – not these, but only the sons of Zadok, who had stood faithful, and kept the charge of the Lord when others fell into impurities, were henceforth to minister in the Lord's house; the rest were at the most to be employed about the subordinate ministrations of the temple courts. The instruction points back to 1 Sam. 2:32,35, where the priesthood of the line of Ithamar was discharged from the office of ministering in the Lord's house, on account of its corruption, in order that another line might be chosen, who should perform the work after the Lord's mind and heart. This new line was found in Zadok and his house (1 Kings 2:35, 1 Chron. 24:3), whose name also (the righteous) was significant of what was expected at their hand. In later times they lost the distinction implied in this name, and took part in the general apostacy; but the prophet keeps his eye upon their original state, and speaks of them as they appeared when first chosen to the office. The promise, therefore, of a priesthood of the house of Zadok, entirely corresponded to the promise of a shepherd with the name of David. It simply indicated a race of faithful and devoted servants, in whom the outward and the inward, the name and the idea, should properly coincide – a priesthood serving God in newness of spirit, not in the oldness of the letter; as the people whom they represented should also have become true Israelites, themselves a royal priesthood offering up spiritual sacrifices to the Lord. In truth, it is the raising up of a people who should be such a priesthood that is meant by the description, and the sons of Zadok came into notice only because in connection with them there was an historical ground for taking them as representatives of a right-hearted spiritual community. So that it is the same truth, only under a different outward clothing, which is exhibited by Isaiah, when he speaks of the Lord's people generally in the more glorious future being taken to be priests and Levites (Isa. 61:6, 66:21). All was to rise into a new and higher sphere; first the kingdom of God itself, and then the people who enjoyed its distinctive privileges and experienced its blessings.

Having given promise of such a true spiritual priesthood, under the old names and historical relations, the prophet proceeds to describe, after the same manner, how the sanctity of the priesthood was to be preserved and manifested. The true import of the symbolical regulations in the law was now to be reached; and he therefore describes what was to be done under the observance of these regulations: They should wear only linen garments (emblems of cleanliness and purity), they should neither shave their heads (as mourners did), nor let their hair grow uncut (as persons unfit for active service), nor drink wine when engaged in the service of the sanctuary, lest they should be unfit for the spiritual actions required of them; nor, in short, do any of the things which under the outward restrictions of a symbolical ritual betokened a want of inward purity. Holiness to the Lord should be expressed in their whole state and procedure, as well as in the ministrations of their public service; and one pervading characteristic be found in God's house, and the servants who belonged to it.

CHAPTER XLV.

THE SACRED ALLOTMENTS IN LAND AND GIFTS.

[1] And when you shall divide the land by lot for inheritance, you shall offer an offering to the LORD, a holy piece of the land. The length shall be the length of twenty-five thousand *reeds,* and the breadth shall be ten thousand. This shall be holy in all its borders all around.

[2] Of this there shall be five hundred *reeds* for the sanctuary, with five hundred *reeds wide,* square all around. And fifty cubits around shall be for its suburbs.

[3] And this measure you shall measure the length of twenty-five thousand, and the breadth of ten thousand. And in it shall be the sanctuary, the most holy *place.*

[4] The holy *part* of the land shall be for the priests, the ministers of the sanctuary, who shall come near to minister to the LORD. And it shall be a place for their houses and a holy place for the sanctuary.

[5] And the twenty-five thousand of length, and the ten thousand of breadth, shall also be for the Levites, the ministers of the house, for themselves for a possession for twenty rooms.

[6] And you shall appoint the possession of the city five thousand broad, and twenty-five thousand long, opposite the offering of the holy *part.* It shall be for the whole house of Israel.

[7] And *a piece shall be* for the prince on the one side and on the other side of the offering of the holy *part,* and of the possession of the city; in front of the offering of the holy *part,* and in front of the possession of the city, from the west side westward and from the east side eastward. And the length shall be across from one of the pieces, from the west border to the east border.

[8] In the land shall be his possession in Israel. And My princes shall never again ill-treat My people. And *the rest of* the land they shall give to the house of Israel according to their tribes.

[9] Thus says the Lord GOD: Let it be enough for you, O princes of Israel. Remove violence and spoil and do judgment and justice. Take away your demands on My people, says the Lord GOD.

[10] You shall have just balances, a just ephah and a just bath.

[11] The ephah and the bath shall be of one measure, that the bath may contain the tenth part of a homer, and the ephah the tenth part of a homer. Its measure shall be according to the homer.

[12] And the shekel shall be twenty gerahs. Twenty shekels, twenty-five shekels, fifteen shekels, shall be your maneh.[1]

[13] This is the offering that you shall offer: you shall give the sixth part of an ephah of a homer of wheat and the sixth part of an ephah of a homer of barley.

[14] Concerning the ordinance of oil, the bath of oil, *you shall offer* the tenth part of a bath out of the cor (a homer of ten baths – for ten baths are a homer);[2]

[15] and one lamb out of the flock, out of two hundred, out of the fat pasture of Israel; for a meal offering, and for a burnt offering, and for peace offerings, to make atonement for them, says the Lord GOD.

[16] All the people of the land shall give this offering for the prince in Israel.

[17] And it shall be the prince's part to *give* burnt offerings and meal offerings and drink offerings, in the feasts, and in the new moons, and in the sabbaths, in all solemn seasons of the house of Israel. He shall prepare the sin offering and the meal offering and the burnt offering and the peace offerings, to make atonement for the house of Israel.

[18] Thus says the Lord GOD: In the first

month, in the first *day* of the month, you shall take a young bull without blemish and cleanse the sanctuary.

[19]And the priest shall take of the blood of the sin offering and put *it* on the posts of the house, and on the four corners of the ledge of the altar, and on the posts of the gate of the inner court.

[20]And so you shall do the seventh *day* of the month for everyone who errs, and for *the* simple one. So you shall purify the house.

[21]In the first *month,* in the fourteenth day of the month, you shall have the Passover, a feast of seven days. Unleavened bread shall be eaten.

[22]And on that day shall the priest prepare for himself and for all the people of the land a bull *for* a sin offering.

[23]And seven days of the feast he shall prepare a burnt offering to the LORD, seven bulls and seven rams without blemish daily for the seven days, and a kid of the goats daily *for* a sin offering.

[24]And he shall prepare a meal offering of an ephah for a bull, and an ephah for a ram, and a hin of oil for an ephah.

[25]In the seventh *month,* in the fifteenth day of the month, he shall do the same in the feast of the seven days, according to the sin offering, according to the burnt offering, and according to the meal offering, and according to the oil.

The prophet passes here to what may be called the outer territory, and presents a pattern of things in beautiful accordance with the inner and more sacred. There must be a new distribution of the land, and a new adjustment as to giving and receiving between prince and people, in order that the old heats and discords might be avoided, and no pretext any longer found for arbitrary appointments and oppressive exactions. In regard to the new distribution of the land, what is mentioned here (vers. 1-7) has respect merely to the central portion, which was to be set apart for the temple, the priesthood, the prince, and the city (the remainder is treated of in chap. 47). And this altogether was to form a square of 25,000 – it is not said of what; and hence many insert cubits, as at chap. 42:16 they substituted cubits for rods. We showed the proposed change there to be unwarranted and arbitrary; and as the present passage is merely a continuation of the other, the same reasons which obliged us to abide by rods there render it necessary for us to understand these also here. Besides, the express mention of so many cubits for the suburbs of the sanctuary (ver. 2) clearly implies, that in all the other measures, not cubits, but rods are intended; for why should cubits have been named only there, unless it was because there alone such were to be understood? It might also be shown, were it necessary, that, on the supposition of cubits being meant, the portion of land would be immensely too small for the purpose indicated (only about eight miles square), – a space of ground in that case not nearly so large as is possessed by many a modern nobleman being assigned for the support of the whole priesthood, the prince and his household, and the people of the city. Holding it, then, to be rods by which the dimensions are given, and taking each rod, as before, at about twelve feet, the entire area of the central portion of land would be a square of somewhere about sixty miles on each side. Of this area a large part was to be of a sacred character, and is hence called *"an holy portion, offered to the Lord"* (ver. 1). It embraced the whole length, but only two-fifths of the breadth; and was to be appropriated thus: – 500 rods square for the temple, with 50 cubits outside additional (that other buildings might not come too close upon those of so sacred a character), and all that remained of the 10,000 in breadth by 25,000 in length was to be for a possession to the priesthood, allowing, however, as much as might be needed for the erection of twenty apartments to the Levites who for the time being happened to minister at the temple. It is plainly of such sort of chambers that mention is made in ver. 5, and not ordinary dwellings; they were to be for the ministering Levites what the chambers within the temple grounds were for the officiating priests. The other part of the central portion was to be assigned for the city and the prince – 5000 in breadth for the city itself, and the remaining 10,000 for a possession to the people of the city and to the prince to supply them with food, but in what relative proportions is not stated, either here or in chap. 48. It is merely said respecting the prince, that his possession was to be taken out of this civic portion, and was to consist of two halves, – the one on the west and the other on the east side of the sacred territory. For thus again the prophet would

set forth the close relation in which the prince, as head of so holy a community, should stand to the sanctuary. His possession must on each side adjoin that which was to be peculiarly the Lord's.

That the whole ground for the priesthood, the prince, and the people of the city was to form together a square, betokened the perfect harmony and agreement which should subsist between these different classes, as well as the settled order and stability that should distinguish the sacred commonwealth, in which they held the highest place. That the priesthood were to occupy what was emphatically holy ground, was a symbol of the singular degree of holiness which should characterize those who stood, in their official position, the nearest to the Lord. And that the prince was to have a separate possession assigned him, was to cut off all occasion for his lawlessly interfering with the possessions of the people, and to exhibit the friendly bearing and upright administration which was to be expected of him. Hence, in immediate connection with the assignment of such a portion, it is said (ver. 8): *"And my princes shall no more oppress my people, and the land shall they give to the house of Israel according to their tribes."* And not only must he personally abstain from all oppressive behavior, but, as the divinely constituted head of a righteous commonwealth, he must take effective measures for establishing judgment and justice throughout the whole. Particular examples are given of this in regard to the using of just weights and measures in the transactions of business (vers. 9-12).

Then follow directions respecting the contributions to be made by the people to the prince (ver. 13-17), – the sixtieth part of their wheat, the hundredth of their oil, and of the young of their flocks the two hundredth part. These were to be regularly given to the prince as the representative of the people, that he might provide out of them the suitable offerings to be presented to the Lord for the community, especially at the stated solemnities. They would therefore be perpetual remembrancers to the prince of the sacred character he maintained as the head of such a people, and would supply him, by Divine enactment, with what was needed to fulfil this part of his office, without needing to have resort to any arbitrary and oppressive measures. Expressed more generally, it was a symbol of the perfect harmony and mutual co-operation which should exist in such a holy community in regard to the public service and glory of God; without constraint or any sort of jarring, the several classes would freely and faithfully do their parts.

As it was more especially in connection with the stated and yearly festivals that the prince had to represent the people in the public service of God, so the prophet takes a rapid glance of these, and refers particularly to the first and the last. But he first mentions a consecration service, with which the year was always to begin, and of which no mention whatever was made in the law (vers. 18-20). On the first, and again on the seventh day of the first month, the sanctuary was always to be cleansed, that the year might be commenced in sacredness, and that all might be in preparation for the Feast of the Passover on the fourteenth day of the month. As the prophet has introduced a new solemnity before the Passover, so for the Passover itself he appoints quite different sacrifices from those named by Moses; instead of one ram and seven lambs for the daily burnt-offering, he has seven bullocks and seven rams; and the meat-offerings also vary. And while there were quite peculiar offerings prescribed in the law for the Feast of Tabernacles, constantly diminishing as the days of the feast proceeded, here, on the other hand, the prophet appoints the same as in the case of the Passover. This shows how free a use was made by the prophet of the Old Testament ritual, and how he only employed it as a cover for the great spiritual truths he sought to unfold. They were not permanently fixed and immutable things, he virtually said, those external services of Judaism, as if they had an absolute and independent value of their own, so that precisely those and no other should be thought of; they were all symbolical of the spiritual and eternal truths of God's kingdom, and may be variously adjusted, as in now done, in order to make them more distinctly expressive of the greater degree of holiness and purity that is in future times to distinguish the people and service of God over all that has been in the past.

CHAPTER XLVI.

ADDITIONAL ORDINANCES FOR THE PRINCE AND PEOPLE.

The instructions contained in this chapter are merely a following out into some subordinate details of the subject handled in the chapter immediately preceding. The first section (vers. 1-8) refers more immediately to the prince in his worship. To him, it was already said, belonged the distinction of entering for worship by the east gate. But this gate, to mark more distinctly its peculiar sacredness, was to be shut during the six days of the week, and opened only on Sabbath-days and those of the new moon. On these occasions the prince was to go through this gate to the porch of the inner court (for such is undoubtedly meant by the gate in ver. 2), but no farther; he had no right to advance into the court of the priests. There, as the head and representative of the people, and as such in a state of peculiar nearness to God, he should present his offerings to the Lord; while at a greater distance, at the outer gate of the same entrance, the people were to stand worshipping without. The offerings he is here appointed to bring on Sabbaths and on new moons are considerably larger than those mentioned in the law of Moses; and hence serve to show that the worship of God in the future was to be conducted in a more complete and glorious manner than formerly, and that as both prince and people were to rise to a higher place in connection with the kingdom of God, so they would express this in more liberal and generous manifestations of pious feeling.

The next section (vers. 9-15) exhibits the order that should be observed in the great festivals. On those occasions the prince was to depart from the state of isolation which it was proper for him to observe at other times, and, at the head of the people, join in the great throng of worshippers that were to pass through the temple courts from one side to another. It reminds us of David, who in this was doubtless the exemplar in the eye of the prophet: *"I had gone with the multitude, I went with them to the house of God, with the voice of joy and praise, with a multitude that kept holiday."* A beautiful picture of a religious people, – the highest in rank freely mingling with the mass of worshippers, and inspiring their devotions by the elevating influence of his presence and example. But to show that his worship was not merely to be of public and official nature, that it should spring from a heart truly alive to Divine things, and itself delighting in fellowship with God, the prophet passes from those holiday services to the voluntary offerings and the daily morning sacrifice, which the prince was also to present to the Lord. In a word, the proper head of a religious people, he was to surpass them all, and be an example to them all in the multitude and variety of his acts of homage and adoration.

A short section follows (vers. 16-18), respecting the inalienable nature of the prince's possession, and the sacred regard he must pay to the people's. He might give his own sons an inheritance with himself, but if he should give a grant of any portion of it to a servant, it must revert to the royal house at the year of jubilee; in order that no temptation might exist to spoil the people of their proper inheritances, as had been too often done in the days that were past. It is the exhibition, by an individual trait, of the pure righteousness and settled order which should pervade the kingdom of God when set up in its new and more perfect form. Everything should now be ruled by the principles of eternal rectitude, and no licence given, no occasion even, or pretext afforded, for the usurpations of tyrannical violence.

The closing verses (vers. 19-24) refer to a matter which is certainly not immediately connected with what precedes, but which the prophet adds as necessary to complete the picture he had been drawing of a well-ordered, sacred community. It respects the preparation made in the temple building for the officiating priests eating, with due regard to the sanctity of the food, the portion that fell to them of the sacred offerings. For this purpose there were provided, in connection with the chambers of the priests, cooking apartments at the several corners, where the flesh of the sacrifices should be boiled, and the meat-offering prepared, so that they might eat them before again mingling with the people. A distinction is even made in regard to one portion of the sacred food and another. For the sin and trespass-offerings being of a higher class than the peace-offerings (in the participation of which latter, the people according to the law shared with the priesthood), therefore two sets of chambers were to be provided for cooking, – one at the corners of the inner court, reserved for the flesh of the sin and trespass-offerings, which was *"a holy of holies,"* to be eaten only by the priests (Lev. 6:25, 7:7); and another at the corners of the outer court, where the flesh of the peace-offerings was to be prepared. The arrangement indicates, as by an additional stroke, the peculiar sacredness that should now attach in men's feelings to everything that bore on it the impress of the Lord's name. No longer confounding together the common and unclean, the Divine and human, theyshouldin all things give to God the pre-eminent glory which is due, and the nearer they stood to him, be always the more jealous of his honor. A truly royal priesthood! following even to the minutest particulars the rule of the apostle: *"Whether they might eat or drink, or whatsoever they might do, doing all to the glory of God."*

CHAPTER XLVII. 1-12.

VISION OF THE TEMPLE WATERS.

It is necessary to take the first part of this chapter apart from the second, which relates to a different subject, – the new division of the land, – and which ought to have formed part of chap. 48. The vision contained in the first twelve verses of this chapter is a thing by itself, although it stands in close connection with what precedes, and springs naturally out of it. The prophet has been exhibiting, by means of a variety of detailed representations, the blessed results to the Lord's people of his re-occupying his temple. The way now stands open to them for a free and elevating communion with the Lord, and the work proceeds on their part by the regular employment of all spiritual privileges and the faithful discharge of holy ministrations; God is duly glorified in his people, and his people are blessed in the enjoyment of his gracious presence and the benefit of his fatherly administration. But what is to be the nature of the kingdom in this new form, in respect to the world without? Is it to be of a restrictive or expansive character? Is the good it discloses and provides for a regenerated people to be confined, as of old, to a select spot, or is it to spread forth and communicate itself abroad forthe salvation of the world at large? In an earlier prophecy (chap. 17), when speaking of the future head of the Divine kingdom, under the image of the future head of the Divine kingdom,under the image of a little twig, plucked from the top of a cedar in Lebanon and planted upon a lofty mountain in Israel, the prophet has represented this not only as growing and taking root there, but as winning the regard of all the trees of the field, and gathering under its ample foliage beasts of every kind and birds of every wing. The kingdom of God, as thus exhibited, seemed to carry a benign and diffusive aspect toward the entire world. And should it be otherwise now, when presented under the different but more detailed and variegated form of a spiritual house, with the living God himself for the glorious inhabitant, and a royal priesthood for its ministering servants? No; it is for humanity, mankind as a whole, that God was thus seen dwelling with men; and though everything presents itself, according to the relations then existing, as connected with a local habitation and circumscribed bounds, yet the good in store was to be confined within no such narrow limits; it was to flow forth with healthful and restorative energy, even upon the waste and dead places of the earth, and invest them with the freshness of life and beauty.

This fine idea is presented by the prophet under a pleasing natural image. He is brought back by the angel from the outer court, where he was standing, to the door of the temple on the east; and there he sees a stream of water gushing from beneath the threshold, and running in the direction of south-east, so as to pass the altar on the south. He is then brought outside by the north gate, and carried round to where the waters appeared beyond the temple grounds, that he might witness the measurements that were to be made of them, and the genial effects they produced. But let us take his own account of it.

[1]Afterward he brought me again to the door of the house. And, behold, waters came out from under the doorsill of the house eastward. For the front of the house *was* toward the east, and the waters came down from under the right side of the house, at the south of the altar.

[2]Then he brought me out by the way of the gate northward and led me around the way outside, to the outer gate, by the way that looks eastward. And, behold, waters ran out on the right side.

[3]And when the man who had the line in his hand went out eastward, he measured a thousand cubits, and he brought me through the waters. Thewaters were to the ankles.

[4]Again he measured a thousand *cubits,* and brought me through the waters. The waters were to the knees. Again he measured a thousand and brought me through; the waters were to the loins.

[5]Afterward he measured a thousand; *and it was* a river that I could not pass over; for the waters had risen, waters to swim in, a river that could not be passed over.

[6]And he said to me, Son of man, have you seen? Then he brought me and caused me to return to the edge of the river.

[7]Now when I had returned, behold, very many trees *were* on the one side and on the other.

[8]Then he said to me, These waters go out toward the east country, and go down into the desert,[1] and go into the sea. Being brought out into the sea, the waters shall be healed.

[9]And everything that lives, which moves, wherever the rivers shall come,[2] shall live. And there shall be a very great multitude of fish, because these waters shall come there. For they shall be healed. And everything shall live where the river comes.

[10]And the fisherman shall stand on it from En-ge-di even to En-eg-la-im.[3] There shall be a *place* to spread out nets; their fish shall be according to their kinds, like the fish of the Great Sea, a very great many.

[11]But its muddy places, and its marshes shall not be healed; they shall be given to salt.[4]

[12]And by the river on its bank, on this side and on that side, shall grow all trees for food, whose leaf shall not fade, nor its fruit fail. It shall bring forth new fruit according to its months, because there their waters come out of the sanctuary. And its fruit shall be for food, and its leaf for healing.

That the description given of this stream and its effect must be understood in an ideal manner, not of any actual river, but, like all the rest of the vision, of spiritual things shadowed forth under it, is so evident as scarcely to require any proof. The source of it alone (the summit of an elevated mountain), and the manner of its increase, should put this beyond a doubt with all who would not convert the Bible into a nursery of extravagance and credulity. For a natural river like this would of necessity be in a contravention of the established laws of nature, and could only exist as a perpetual miracle. Supposing that by some new adjustment of the land a stream might be made to rise on the top of Mount Zion, yet a stream feeding itself as described in the vision, and growing with such rapid strides, is utterly at variance with the known laws of the material world. For, it is to be observed, the increase here comes from no extraneous and incidental sources; it is all along the temple waters that form the river, and at last empty themselves into the sea; and yet, from being at first but a small streamlet, these grow, by self-production, in the space of little more than a mile, into an unfordable river! To expect such a prodigy as this on the outward territory of nature is plainly to identify the natural with the miraculous, and confound the hopes of faith with the dreams of superstition. The Bible does teach us to look for things above nature, but never for merely natural things against the ascertained laws of nature.

Issuing as this stream does from the threshold of the temple, from the very foot of the throne of God (comp. Rev. 22:1), it must be, like all the special manifestations of God to his Church, itself of a spiritual nature, and only in its effects productive of outward material good. It is just the efflux of that infinite fulness of life and blessing which is treasured up in his spiritual temple, and continually pours itself forth as the operations of his grace proceed among men. It is emphatically a river of life. Wherever it is experienced, the barren soil of nature fructifies, the dead live again, the soul is replenished with joy and gladness. And instead of spending, like the streams of nature, as it advances through the moral deserts of the world, it still multiplies and grows; for it diffuses itself from heart to heart, from family to family. Every true recipient of grace becomes a channel and instrument of grace to those around him; so that the more who partake of the blessing, the more always does the region expand over which the kingdom developes its resources. And in proportion as these are developed, everything around wears a smiling and joyous aspect; the evils and disorders of nature are rectified; peace and order reign where before were the favorite haunts of wretchedness and crime; the very field of judgment becomes a region of life and blessing; until at last corruption itself is changed into incorruption, mortality is swallowed up in life, and the earth, which God had cursed for men's sin, is transformed into the inheritance of the saints in light.

Such, we have no doubt, is the general import of the vision before us; and to this we must confine ourselves. It must be contemplated as a whole, and not broken up into fragments; as if we should inquire what is to be understood specially by the fish, what by the fishers, what by the trees, and so on. A life-giving and ever increasing stream of heavenly influence, proceeding from the centre of the Divine kingdom, and diffusing itself far and wide among men, is what the prophet intends to exhibit to our mind; and to give this idea form and shape to our apprehensions, he must fill up the picture with the appropriate signs and manifestations of life. But to take these up one by one, and adapt them to particular things in the present or future dispensations of God, can only be an exercise of fancy, as likely to mislead as to conduct to sound and legitimate conclusions. Let us rest in the great reality; let us rejoice in the thought that the Spirit of God should have coupled, with all the other exhibitions of the Divine kingdom given to the prophet, so encouraging a prospect of its vivifying, restorative, and expanding energies; and let it deepen the blessed conviction in our bosom, that the purpose of God in grace is fixed; and that mighty as the obstacles are which everywhere present themselves to withstand its progress, it shall certainly not fail to make good its triumph over all the disorders and corruption of the world.

We simply add, in regard to the relation of this prophecy to others in Scripture, that there is undoubtedly a reference in the whole passage to the description in Gen. 2 of the garden of Eden; although it seems rather pushing the allusion too far, when Hengstenberg, on Rev. 22:2, maintains the trees here mentioned to be simply the tree of life. The mention of every kind of tree for food in ver. 12, and the prominence given also to the abundance of fish in the waters, show that there is no servile copying of the description in Genesis; while still it is impossible not to see that a kind of new paradise was evidently intended to be described by the prophet. Then as he has, after his own manner, enlarged and amplified the thought which is contained in such passages as Joel 3:18; Zech. 14:8, so his delineation is again taken up by the Evangelist John, and in his peculiar manner accommodated to express the last grand issues of God's kingdom towards man: *"And he showed me a pure river of water of life, clear as crystal, proceeding out of the throne of God and the Lamb. In the midst of the street of it, and on either side of the river, was there the tree of life, which bare twelve manner of fruits, and yielded her fruit every month (for which Ezekiel has all manner of fruit trees, bearing monthly); and the leaves of the tree are for the healing of the nations. And there shall be no more curse (corresponding in Ezekiel to the beneficient change wrought on the doomed region of the Dead Sea); but the throne of God and of the Lamb shall be in it, and his servants shall serve him"* (Rev. 22:1-3).

CHAPTER XLVII. 13-23, XLVIII.

THE BOUNDARIES AND RE-DISTRIBUTION OF THE LAND.

As the whole of the representations contained in the preceding parts of the vision proceed on the basis for the old covenant, the series naturally closes with the re-occupation of the land of Canaan, which formed the great objective promise of the covenant. A people settled in the inheritance of their God is the proper result of the re-establishment of the covenant, and the renewal of their souls after its principles of righteousness. There is, of course, no more reason for understanding this portion according to the letter than those which went before. The whole vision is of a piece, – a pictorial representation of the future things of God's kingdom under the image of the past, yet so altered and adjusted as to indicate the vast superiority of what was to come compared with what hitherto had been. To say, as many in effect do, that the part of the vision which refers to the temple and its worship is figurative, while this, which makes mention of a re-occupation of the land by the tribes of Israel, must be understood literally, is to bring complete arbitrariness and confusion into the interpretation of the prophecy. There is the very same reason for holding that the Old Testament ritual of worship, with all its carnal ordinances, and more than its carnal display of outward pomp, shall again be set up, as for holding that the natural Israel shall again be restored to the possession of Canaan, so as to form a peculiar commonwealth of believers. And if to maintain the one be to place the prophets of the Old Testament in palpable contrariety to the apostles of the New, to maintain the other by itself is not less evidently to mutilate the prophetic record, and place one part of the prophetic testimony in virtual opposition to another.

[13]Thus says the Lord GOD: This shall be the border by which you shall inherit the land according to the twelve tribes of Israel. Joseph shall have *two* parts.

[14]And you shall inherit it, one as well as another, *as to* which I lifted up My hand to give it to your fathers; and this land shall fall to you for an inheritance.

[15]And this shall be the border of the land toward the north side, from the Great Sea, the way of Heth-lon, as men go to Ze-dad,

[16]Ha-math, Be-ro-thah, Sib-ra-im, which is between the border of Damascus and the border of Ha-math; Ha-zar–hat-ti-con, which is by the border of Hau-ran.

[17]And the border from the sea shall be Ha-zar–e-nan, the border of Damascus and the north northward, and the border of Ha-math. And *this is* the north side.

[18]And you shall measure the east side from Hau-ran, and from Damascus, and from Gilead, and from the land of Israel by Jordan, from the border to the east sea. And *this is* the east side.

[19]And the south side is southward from Ta-mar, to the waters of Mer-i-bath–ka-desh, the river to the Great Sea. and this is the south side southward.

[20]The west side also is the Great Sea from the border, until a man come over against Ha-math. This is the west side.

[21]So you shall divide this land to yourselves according to the tribes of Israel.

[22]And you shall divide it by lot for an inheritance to yourselves, and to the strangers who live among you, who shall father children among you. And they shall be to you as those born in the country among the children of Israel. They shall have inheritance with you among the tribes of Israel.

[23]And in whatever tribe the stranger lives there you shall give him his inheritance, says the Lord GOD.

CHAPTER 48

[1]Now these are the names of the tribes. From the north end to the coast of the way of Heth-lon, as one goes to Ha-math, Ha-zar–e-nan, the border of Damascus northward to the coast of Ha-math – for these are its sides east and west – one part for Dan.

[2]And by the border of Dan, from the east to the west side, one *part for* Asher.

[3]And by the border of Asher, from the east side even to the west side, one *for* Naph-ta-li.

[4]And by the border of Naph-ta-li from the east side to the west side, one *for* Ma-nas-seh.

[5]And by the border of Ma-nas-seh, from the east side to the west side, one *for* Ephraim.

[6]And by the border of Ephraim, from the east side even to the west side, one *for* Reuben.

[7]And by the border of Reuben from the east side to the west side, one *for* Judah.

[8]And by the border of Judah, from the east side to the west side, shall be the offering which you shall offer of twenty-five thousand *reeds* breadth, and in length as one of the other parts, from the east side to the west side. And the sanctuary shall be in

the middle of it.

[9]The offering that you shall offer to the LORD shall be of twenty-five thousand *reeds* in length and of ten thousand in breadth.

[10]And for them, for the priests, shall this holy offering be – toward the north twenty-five thousand, and toward the west ten thousand in breadth, and toward the east ten thousand in breadth, and toward the south twenty-five thousand in length. And the sanctuary of the LORD shall be in the middle of it.

[11]*It shall be* for the priests who are sanctified, of the sons of Za-dok, who have kept My charge, who did not go astray when the children of Israel went astray, as the Levites went astray.

[12]And *this* offering of the land that is offered shall be to them a thing most holy by the border of the Levites.

[13]And over across from the border of the priests, the Levites *shall have* twenty-five thousand in length and ten thousand in breadth. All the length shall be twenty-five thousand, and the breadth ten thousand.

[14]And they shall not sell *any* of it, or trade it, or cause the first-fruits of the land to pass away. For it is holy to the LORD.

[15]And the five thousand that are left in the breadth over across from the twenty-five thousand shall be a common *place* for the city, for living and for suburbs. And the city shall be in its middle.

[16]And these shall be its measures: the north side, four thousand and five hundred; and the south side, four thousand and five hundred; and on the east side, four thousand and five hundred; and the west side, four thousand and five hundred.

[17]And the suburbs of the city shall be toward the north, two hundred and fifty; and toward the south, two hundred and fifty; and toward the east, two hundred and fifty, and toward the west, two hundred and fifty.

[18]And the rest in length opposite the offering of the holy *part* shall be ten thousand eastward and ten thousand westward. And it shall be opposite the offering of the holy *part*. And the produce of it shall be for food to those who serve the city.

[19]And they who serve the city shall serve it out of all the tribes of Israel.

[20]All the offering shall be twenty-five thousand by twenty-five thousand. You shall offer the holy offering four-square, with the possession of the city.

[21]And the rest shall be for the prince, on the one side and on the other of the holy offering, and of the possession of the city, opposite the twenty-five thousand of the offering toward the east border, and westward across from the twenty-five thousand toward the west border; across from the lots of the prince. And it shall be a holy offering. And the sanctuary of the house shall be in its middle.

[22]And from the possessions of the Levites, and from the possession of the city, being in the midst *of that* which is the prince's between the border of Judah and the border of Benjamin, shall be for the prince.

[23]As for the rest of the tribes, from the east side to the west side, Benjamin shall have one *part*.

[24]And by the border of Benjamin,from the east side to the west side, Simeon shall have one *part*.

[25]And by the border of Simeon, from the east side to the west side, Is-sa-char shall have one *part*.

[26]And by the border of Is-sa-char, from the east side to the west side, Ze-bu-lun shall have one *part*.

[27]And by the border of Ze-bu-lun, from the east side to the west side, Gad shall have one *part*.

[28]And by Gad's border, at the south side southward, the border shall be even from Ta-mar to the waters of Mer-i-bath–ka-desh, to the river toward the Great Sea.

[29]This is the land which you shall divide by lot to the tribes of Israel for inheritance, and these are their parts, says the Lord GOD.

[30]And these are the exits of the city on the north side, four thousand and five hundred measures.

[31]And the gates of the city shall be according to the names of the tribes of Israel: three gates northward, one gate of Reuben, one gate of Judah, one gate of Levi.

[32]And at the east side four thousand and five hundred, and three gates: and one gate of Joseph, one gate of Benjamin, one gate of Dan.

[33]And at the south side four thousand and five hundred measures, and three gates: one gate of Simeon, one gate of Is-sa-char, one gate of Ze-bu-lun.

[34]And at the west side four thousand and five hundred, their three gates: one gate of Gad, one gate of Asher, one gate of Naph-ta-li.

[35]*It was* eighteen thousand *measures* all around. And the name of the city from *that* day shall be, THE LORD IS THERE

The concluding portion of chap. 47 is nearly all occupied with the boundaries of the

land, which seem to be substantially the same with those originally given by Moses in Num. 34, though the names mentioned to some extent differ. It is to be noted, however, that in the fair and natural construction of the words, it is only Canaan proper, exclusive of what was given to the two tribes and a half beyond Jordan, which forms here the inheritance to be divided. For the eastern boundary runs (ver. 18) *"from between Hauran and Damascus, and from between Gilead and the land of Israel, the Jordan, from the border unto the east sea."* We can make no intelligible sense of this, unless it means that the boundary-line on the east was to be cut off by Hauran and Gilead, and go straight down to the Dead Sea by the valley of Jordan. And this is confirmed by comparing Num. 34:11,12, where the border is also said to go down by Jordan and the Salt Sea; while immediately afterwards (ver. 13), it is stated that the land thus bounded is what was to be allotted to the nine tribes and a half. What the prophet here, therefore, describes as the land, is strictly and properly Canaan within Jordan, which was the original inheritance promised. We did not urge this point in our preliminary remarks on this last vision, lest we should seem to press the matter too far, but allowed that the prophet might include all that Israel every occupied. There is really, however, no ground for supposing this; and if we abide by what seems the plain boundary-line of the prophet, the statement of Lightfoot becomes in both parts quite correct, – that the site of the prophet's temple is larger than all ancient Jerusalem, and his central portion for the city, prince, and priesthood larger than all the land of Canaan as described by himself.

The territory to be divided being thus obviously viewed in an ideal light, the division itself is conducted in the same manner, - not as it ever could have taken place in the reality, but after rule and measure, in exact and regular portions running along-side of each other the whole breadth from west to east, and standing in a common relation to the temple in the centre. Seven of the tribes have their portions on the north, on account of the greater stretch of the land in that direction with respect to the actual Jerusalem, and in the following order: – Dan, Asher, Naphtali, Manasseh, Ephriam, Reuben, Judah; the latter having its place close by the central portion on the north, as Benjamin had on its south. This honor appears to have been given to these two tribes in consideration of their relative historical superiority, having so long adhered to the temple and ordinances of God, when the others deserted them. Dan, on the contrary, was placed at the extreme north, on account of the low religious character of the tribe, precisely as John, in representing the whole elect church by twelve thousand from the several tribes of Israel, leaves Dan out altogether (Rev. 7). As there were actually thirteen tribes, he finds his 12 times 12 by omitting Dan, whose idolatrous and semi-heathen character made it border morally, as it did locally, on the Gentiles. Here the two tribes of Joseph are thrown into one, to admit of Dan's having a place, but it is still the lowest place in the ideal territory of a blessed world. With these exceptions, we can discern no specific grounds for the particular places assigned to the tribes respectively. The order on the south side was, Benjamin, Simeon, Issachar, Zebulon, Gad. But the city, the temple, the prince, and priesthood, with their respective portions, being situated precisely in the middle, and not within the boundaries of any of the tribes, was intended to intimate that all were now to be regarded as having a common interest in them, and that the miserable and mischievous jealousies which had of old exercised so disastrous an influence, especially between Judah and Ephraim, should finally and for ever cease. All now should stand related as a united and compact brotherhood to the sanctuary of the Lord, from which, as a central fountainhead of life and blessing, there should continually stream forth manifestations of grace to all the people.[3]

The desire of giving due prominence to the sacred portions in the centre leads the prophet again to enter into some statements regarding the Terumah, or oblation, and its subdivisions. Nothing of importance is added to what was said before, except that the 5000 rods apportioned out of the 25,000 square to the city is here laid off in a square of 4500, with the 250 all round for suburbs. This space for the city was not strictly holy ground, in the sense that the sacerdotal portions were, and hence it is called profane or common. But being thus immediately connected with the sacred portions, and standing apart from the individual tribes, the city built on it formed a fit and proper centre to the whole land, – in its position and its structure the beau-ideal of a theocratic capital, encompassed by the most hallowed influences, and fitted to exert a uniting and healthful effect upon the entire community. Hence the prophet closes the description by the mention of some things regarding the city which might serve more deeply to impress the feeling of its being the suitable representative and common centre of the community. Itself occupying a central position, and immediately in front of the house of God, it was also to have twelve gates, bearing the names of the twelve tribes of the children of Israel, in token that all the family of faith had their representation in it, and, as if they were actually resident in it, stood before the Lord for the enjoyment of his favor and blessing. He specifies, again, the entire circumference of the city, 18,000 rods (between twenty and thirty miles), as a symbol of the immense numbers of the covenant-people under the new and better dispensation of the future, immeasurably transcending what has existed under the old. And to exhibit the character of the city itself, as representative of the community at large and indicative of its own relative position, it was to bear from that day, namely, from the period of the beginning of this new and better order of things, the honorable name of *"Jehovah-Shammah"* – not, as has been already stated, Jehovah-there, but Jehovah-thither, or thereupon; for it was in the temple, rather than in the city, that the Lord was represented as having his peculiar dwelling place. But his eyes were to be ever from the temple toward the city, and again from the city toward the whole land. The manifestations of his love and goodness were to radiate from the chosen seat of the kingdom through all its borders: he in all, and all united and blessed in him. So that the consummation of this vision substantially corresponds with the object prayed for by our Lord when he sought respecting his people that they might be where he was, and that they might be all one, as he and the Father are one, – he in them and they in him, that they might be made perfect in one.

Thus ends the marvellous vision of the prophet, – alike marvellous whether we look to the lofty pattern (true in the spirit, though unavoidably wearing the garb of imperfect forms and shadowy relations) which it embodied of better things to come in God's kingdom, or to the time chosen for presenting this to the Church of God. The cause of Heaven was then at its lowest ebb. The temple that had been, together with the kingdom it symbolized and represented, were laid in ruins; they were to be seen only in broken fragments and mournful dilapidations, as if smitten with the powerful curse of an irrecoverable perdition. Yet from the midst of these howling desolations, as from the very "suburbs of hell," the prophet ascends, with assured step, the mount of vision, and has there exhibited to his view, not, indeed, the very image of better things to come, but the ideal pattern after which the blessed and glorious future was to be fashioned. He even sees it as already present; and, with such imperfect materials of thought and utterance as then stood at his command, he gives it forth to the Church and the world as a thing which his own eyes had beheld, showing how God would certainly dwell with his people in a manner he had never done before, – how he would at once immeasurably extend the sphere of his kingdom and greatly elevate the condition of those who belonged to it, – and how, through the copious effusions of his life-giving Spirit, the former imperfections should be done away, the most remote regions of the Divine territory hallowed and blessed, and even the peculiar haunts of cursing and desolation made to rejoice and blossom like the rose.

> "O scenes surpassing fable, and yet true!
> Scenes of accomplished bliss! which who can see,
> Though but in distant prospect, and not feel
> His soul refreshed with foretaste of the joy?"

That such scenes should have been described with such assured confidence, and at a time so deeply overspread with gloom, was indeed an ennobling triumph of faith over sight. It gave a most illustrious proof of the height in spiritual discernment and far-reaching insight into the purposes of Heaven which is sometimes imparted in the hour of greatest need, especially to the more select instruments of the Spirit's working. And surely the children of the kingdom now must be chargeable with neglecting an important privilege, if they fail to profit by so inspiriting an example. Here the heart of faith is taught never to despair, – not even in the darkest seasons. And when it is seen how much of the scheme delineated in the prophetic vision has already been accomplished, should not believers feel encouraged to look and strive for its complete realization, assured that God is ready to hear their cry, and to second with the aid of his Spirit the efforts that are made to dispossess and drive out the hostile powers that continue to linger in his kingdom. It is theirs, if they feel thus, not only to contend in the best of causes, but also with the surest prospect of success; for the Lord himself is upon their side, and his word of promise must be established.

"Thus heavenward all things tend. For all were once
Perfect, and all must be at length restored.
So God has greatly purposed; who would else
In his dishonored works himself endure
Dishonor, and be wronged without redress!
– Come, then, and, added to thy many crowns,
Receive yet one as radiant as the rest,
Due to thy last and most effectual work,
Thy word fulfilled, the conquest of a world."

FOOTNOTES

INTRODUCTION

[1] We are glad to see that there is a growing recognition of the fitness of this in regard to the exposition of Scripture generally. Hengstenberg, in the preface to his Commentary on the Apocalypse, expresses it as his opinion, that the present times demand a kind of exposition of Scripture which is in accordance with its great doctrinal and practical design. And Stier, in his preface to the 4th vol. of his Reden Jesu, thus vindicates his adoption of such a form of commentary: "Our older expositors, as is well known, gave to their exegesis very much of the same form, in respect to edification; it is only in the present age, in our unhappy divorce between the Church and the professorial chair, that such can appear to be of a mongrel character. Intentionally and on principle I abandon the wholly unpractical manner of the schools, which coldly and stiffly guards itself against the use of any word that might speak from heart to heart, and which must always carry an unnatural and unseemly appearance in every, even the most learned, treatment of the living word of God."

[2] Miscel. Sac. i. p. 243.

CHAPTER I

[1] We have here, at the outset, a striking example of our prophet's love of emphasis. He does not say simply, after the usual manner, the word of Jehovah was or came הָיָה to him; but הָיֹה הָיָה, using the infinitive absol. along with the verb, according to a common Hebrew usage, to strengthen the meaning. The Authorized Version employs the adverb *expressly* to bring out the force of this peculiar construction; but it is rather the felt assurance with which the revelation came, than its expressness, which is indicated.

[2] Ezekiel, composed of יְחַזֵּק אֵל, God will strengthen.

[3] Dan. i. 1. In 2 Kings xxiv. 1 it is merely said that Nebuchadnezzar king of Babylon came up and besieged Jerusalem, and Jehoiakim became his servant. Daniel places his deportation by Nebuchadnezzar in the third year of Jehoiakim, while Jeremiah (chap. xxv. 1) says that the fourth year of Jehoiakim was coincident with the first of Nebuchadnezzar, in which same year, he also states, Nebuchadnezzar gained a victory over the Egyptians at Carchemish. The probability is, that it was shortly before this battle, in the end of the third year of Jehoiakim, that Nebuchadnezzar came against Jerusalem and took away some captives (among others Daniel). If his assault on Jerusalem was after the battle, the Jews at Jerusalem and those in Chaldea must have dated the commencement of his reign differently.

[4] Hengstenberg's Christol. vol. iii. p. 450, Eng. Trans.

[5] This fourth verse is peculiar in almost every one of the expressions contained in it. The אֵשׁ מִתְלַקַּחַת is literally, fire catching itself; but the

only definite meaning we can attach to this is, that of fire kindling itself—self-communicating from one part to another. The expression occurs only in another passage (Ex. ix. 24), where it is plainly used to denote, as here, the awful intensity and living force of the fire. The two *its*, being of different genders in the original, plainly refer, the one to the cloud, the other to the fire; and I have marked this by inserting the words for the two objects respectively. The כְּעֵין הַחַשְׁמַל is rendered by our translators, "as the colour of amber." But עַיִן is not properly *colour;* it is the eye, the look, the glance, such as the eye itself or anything brilliant gives forth. *Amber* also is not the right word here for *Chashmal.* The derivation of the word is uncertain, but it is generally understood to denote a sort of mixed metal, a composition of gold and silver, which is expressed by the ἤλεκτρον of the LXX. Gesenius, however, takes it as equivalent to the *Nehosheth Kâlâl*, furbished or glittering brass, of ver. 7. The glance of this glittering metal in the midst of so intense a fire suggests the highest possible splendour. And as it is this quality of it that the prophet here has in view, it is, for us, better to give prominence to the *shining* than the *mixed* character of the metal. The appearance of this fiery cloud is said to have been from the north, we believe simply on natural grounds; it was of the nature of a storm, hence it seemed to come from the hilly Caucasian region to the north—the natural region of clouds and tempests. We regard it as quite fanciful in Häv. to suppose that the prophet conceives himself in the temple, and points to the north as the quarter from which the instruments of God's displeasure, the Chaldeans, were to come. Besides, there is mercy as well as judgment indicated in the vision.

[6] Hitzig would translate this last expression, *molten brass* or metal, deriving קָלָל from קָלָה, to roast or burn in the fire. But the transition from roast to melt does not appear at all easier, in respect to such an article as brass, than from to be light to make light (the common meaning of קָלַל), to furbish or brighten. For nothing is more usual than to say of any piece of metal, it is heavy or light in appearance, according as it is well or ill polished. I therefore retain the common meaning, which was quite correctly given by Stephanus in his Thes. as "*refulgens*, a consequenti tamen, cum proprie *politum* ac *tersum* declaret."

[7] The import of what is said in this 11th verse regarding their faces and wings is, that they were each separate or distinct both in regard to their heads and wings, but that the tips of the two outstretched wings reached to one another, while the other two wings, in token of humble and reverential awe, formed a sort of veil or covering for the middle or lower parts of their bodies. Very commonly the first clause is rendered, "and their faces and their wings were expanded from above," or spread forth upwards. But one does not see how that could properly be said of the faces, as well as the wings, and the verb בַּרָד is never used but in the sense of separating, dispersing, or scattering. The Septuagint leave out the faces altogether, in order, apparently, to make the sense of expanding (ἐκτεταμέναι) more suitable.

[8] The בָּזָק here, which I render by the *meteor-flash*, is not found in Heb. as a verb, but has in Arabic and Syriac the sense of to scatter, spread; hence Häv. prefers the meaning of spark-fire. But this hardly comes up to

what seems to be required here; and something of the same nature as lightning, only more diffuse and sporadic in its appearance, must be understood. Such is meteor or sheet-lightning; and such is at least one of the meanings ascribed to the word by Ephraim: either a flash of lightning, or a meteor, falling-star. Many in ancient and modern times prefer the first; but we should then have expected בָּרָק, which occurs in the verse immediately before.

The leading features of the description so far are, first, the portentous cloud, radiant round about, and within glowing with the fervour and brightness of a living self-fed flame. Then, in the midst of this awful heat and lightning-splendour, the four living creatures, in whom the general form and appearance was that of a man, though conjoined with this were also the likenesses of a lion, an ox, and an eagle—each looking to its own quarter—a face each way, so that wherever the living creatures moved, they did not need to turn; there was a face in that direction. Each were separate in respect to the others, yet by the two wings that were expanded for flying, they were in immediate juxtaposition above; and were all moved and animated by one living spirit, by whose mighty impulse they shot like meteors from place to place, and in all their movements and appearance reflected the bright, burning splendour of the fiery element in which they were seen to exist. At chap. x. 1 they are expressly called cherubim.

[9] Our translators have given *beryl* as the stone here meant; but it is now more commonly regarded as the chrysolite of the ancients, though this also is not quite certain.

[10] Both Häv. and Hitzig here render רוּחַ הַחַיָּה the spirit or breath of life, the living principle, holding that if the living creatures had been meant, the usual term חַיּוֹת would have been used. But in the very next verse except one, we have the same word as here for what must mean the living creatures —"the heads of the living creatures;" and there Hitzig, as usual, is obliged to suppose a corruption in the text, and correct from the LXX. But in both places the word is most naturally taken collectively, just as in Gen. vii. 14, viii. 1, for living creatures: that which has life, the living creature-hood, for the living creatures. So here the prophet has spoken of the creatures separately; he now views them collectively, as being together the aggregate creaturely forms in which the spirit resided and manifested itself. The clause in the middle of the verse, "the spirit was for going," seems to have been thrown in for greater explicitness, to indicate expressly that it was not the wheels themselves, but the spirit working in them, that was the source of motion. I see no need, therefore, for rejecting the clause.

The description in this second part of the vision is to the following effect: By the side of each cherub (that is, apparently, on the same side and exterior to the cherub) there was a gigantic wheel, or more properly a double wheel —one within another, going through each other transversely; for the wheels, like the cherubim with their four faces, did not need to turn when they moved from one direction to another; and this could only be effected by a sort of double wheel to every cherub, each running transversely through the other, so that to whichever quarter the movement might point, there could be a motion of the wheel towards it. The felloes or outer rings of these wheels were set round with eyes, and were each also instinct with the same spirit of life and power that wrought in the cherubim, so that the motions of all were simultaneous.

[11] This looks somewhat like a contradiction to what was said in ver. 11, where simply four wings were assigned to each cherub, two for flying and two for covering their bodies. Here it seems as if each had four for covering their bodies. But, possibly, what is meant is, not that four wings existed specially for this purpose, but that the use of the four wings altogether was such as to act like a covering for the body; the whole body was overshadowed by them, and kept out of sight.

[12] A tumultuous noise, קוֹל הֲמֻלָּה, so the expression is now commonly understood. Our translators have given to the phrase the meaning of "the voice of speech." But this hardly makes sense, and is also against the pointing. The only other passage where the word occurs is in Jer. xi. 16, and there our translators have rendered *tumult*, and the connection here evidently requires something of that description. The LXX. omits the clause, as it does various others in this chapter, but the Vulgate translates: "sonus multitudinis." The expression here, therefore, may be regarded as equivalent in meaning to the very similar one קול המון, which is more frequently employed. (Dan. x. 6; Isa. xiii. 4. See Ges. Lex.)

The description in this third and last part, which is that of manifested Godhead in the likeness of enthroned humanity, closely resembles the description given in Ex. xxiv. 10, only more extended and particular. Here, as there, we have the sky-blue sapphire-stone, and the heavens' crystal clearness, emblem of Divine splendour, only here the splendour is of a more dreadful aspect; and there is seen not merely a pavement, but a throne also as of sapphire, while the glorious being that sat on it was radiant with the bright lustre of celestial fire. From that throned firmament also were heard voices of terrific majesty and power, at the utterance of which the cherubic forms continually let down their wings, as in the attitude of reverent and listening silence.

[13] The Typology of Scripture, 3d ed. vol. i. pp. 229-248, where the whole subject of the cherubim is fully investigated.

CHAPTER II., III. 1–11.

Hävernick, after many leading commentators, both ancient and modern, still lays stress on this expression, "son of man," so frequently applied to Ezekiel, and regards it as containing a perpetual admonition to him of his own weakness and frailty. It seems rather strange, however, that this prophet alone should be so often plied with such an admonition, and that it should have been conveyed under so general a form. We are rather disposed to concur with Lightfoot: "This expression is of frequent use in Scripture, in the Hebrew Rabbins, but more especially in the Chaldean and Syrian tongues. . . . Why Ezekiel and no other prophet should have been so often styled thus, has been ascribed to different reasons by different commentators. To me, at least, who am much inferior to them all, the principal reason appears to be this, that as his prophecy was written during the Babylonish captivity, he naturally made use of the Chaldean phrase, *Son of man*—that is, O man. The same phrase was also used by Daniel in Chaldea, chap. x. 16." Erubim, chap. iv.

[2] It is, literally, to peoples, the rebellious ones—Israel being not only called peoples (גּוֹיִם, the common epithet of the heathen), but with the additional epithet of the rebellious. They were thus virtually put on a level with the heathen, who might be addressed by God as Loammi, not my people; with the additional aggravation, that they had brought themselves into that condition after having been in covenant with God. The Septuagint, with its characteristic laxity, altogether omits the expression.

[3] The precise meaning of סָרָבִים is involved in some doubt. The sense of rebellious or refractory has often been ascribed to it, which it bears in the Chaldee; but this would not suit here, being coupled with thorns, and hence that of pricking briers or nettles has been adopted. Gesenius, however, still prefers *rebels.*

[4] **The expressions are literally, "deep of lip, and heavy of tongue," which can only mean obscurity of speech, and language hard to be understood—a foreign tongue.**

[5] Vitringa in Apoc. p. 441, on chap. x. 8-11.

CHAPTER III. 12–27.

[1] This clause has from an early period been felt to be a difficulty, and given rise to different modes of solution. The Jewish critics could not find their way to the interpretation, as is evident by their suggesting for וָאֲשֶׁר of the text, the Kri וָאֵשֵׁב which has been adopted by our translators: "And I sat where they sat." Various conjectures, though not of a satisfactory kind, have been resorted to, with a view of making out a somewhat similar meaning from the text. Rosenmüller, for example, by ascribing to אשר the sense of the Chaldean שרא, and Maurer's, who would identify it with אסר. Hävernick would take it simply for the relative, and renders the clause, "And those who were settled there," that is, as he supposes, the older class of settlers, as contradistinguished from the more recent ones, who were mentioned in the preceding clause as sitting down or settling beside the Chebar. But the distinction, it must be confessed, is very faintly marked, if two separate companies were meant, and there is no difference of time noted in the verbs. I incline, on the whole, to agree with Hitzig, that the pointing should be וָאָשֻׁר, from the verb שׁוּר, to view or behold. (For similar cases he refers to 1 Kings iii. 21; Zech. vi. 1; Lev. xx. 23; and for הֵמָּה, in the sense of *them*, Jer. xlvi. 5.) The prophet first went to them, then observed their condition, and lastly sat down in pensive solitude, giving vent to his grief; for such the verb שָׁמֵם imports, rather than being astonished. As for the idea of Häv., that the older settlers, whom he supposes to be mentioned here, were the captives of the ten tribes, and that the Habor in 2 Kings xvii. 6 is but another name for the Chaboras, it is against all probablity. The region of the captivity of the ten tribes is said to have been in the "cities of the Medes," and by "the river Gozan," viz. the Kissilozan, that runs into the Caspian.

CHAPTER IV.

The sense of *fort*, which, in the received translation, as in most earlier versions and commentators, was ascribed here to דָּיֵק, is now generally abandoned, and it is most commonly taken in the sense of watch-tower, such as besiegers were wont to erect in front of a city, for the purpose of descrying the motions of the besieged. So it is taken by the Syriac, and though the Septuagint has here περίτειχος, yet, in chap. xxvi. 8, it uses προφυλακή for the same word. So, too, Gesenius, in his Thes., and latterly in Lex., also Hävernick, Henderson (on Jer. lvi. 4), and Maurer. The last, however, hesitates between this sense, according to which the word is derived from דוק to look out, *speculari*, still found in the Aramaic, and that of a battering machine, from דָּקַק.

[2] Instead of battering-rams, Hävernick would render כָּרִים *through-borers*, or *through-breakers*, on the ground that כַּר does not signify ram, but lamb, and in particular a fat lamb. He would, therefore, take it as a noun from כָּרָה, to dig or bore through. The thing indicated, however, is still much the same; and, allowing the derivation, which cannot be regarded as certain, there seems no need for altering the translation, which gives the usual term for the old warlike instrument referred to. The Targum gives the same sense, and Kimchi explains, "iron rams to batter down the walls." The LXX., however, render by the more general term βελοστάσεις, engines for throwing some sort of missiles.

[3] The expression, "a day for a year," is twice used, as in Num. xiv. 34, instead of a day for every year, in order to render the reference to the passage in Numbers more manifest.

[4] The allowance of provisions specified would form, if reduced to English measure, about a pound weight of bread per day, and from a pint and a half to two pints of water—barely enough to support life.

[5] Dr. Pradus and others have sought to lengthen out the time between the two periods given at the beginning of this and the eighth chap., by resorting to the fiction of an intercalary month. But shifts of this kind, to say the least, are always unsatisfactory, and the defective time, taken along with the other considerations mentioned, are quite conclusive against a literal understanding of the vision.

[6] It is scarcely worth while, perhaps, to refer to a recent small publication of Mr. Galloway on this chapter, in which he admits the expression "*sometimes* has the force of bearing the punishment of iniquity." We affirm it *always* has so in the passages which are at all parallel to the one before us. For to bring in here, as Mr. G. does, the idea of *bearing* in the sense of *atoning* is entirely out of place, since there is nothing here of expiation by sacrifice, the only valid means of atonement; and to bear or atone by doing penance, which would with his views be the sense really imposed on the passage, is utterly foreign to our prophet, and to Scripture generally.

[7] It is by the neglect of the considerations adduced above that the false interpretations of the vision—which unfortunately comprehend all that have been current in this country—have gone so much astray. They all lose

themselves in unsatisfactory and needless attempts to show, partly how the number of days assigned to the prophet for lying on his side coincided with the time consumed in the siege of Jerusalem, and partly how the 390 years for the house of Israel, and the 40 for the house of Judah, corresponded with the respective periods of transgression, down to the taking of Jerusalem. The Duke of Manchester, in his Times of Daniel, p. 20, etc., has recently produced some calculations of his own on the subject, and dates the 390 years from the first public defalcation of Rehoboam, a little before the revolt of the ten tribes, the usual starting-point, in order to make the time square more exactly with the 390 of the prophet; and the 40 years he transfers altogether to another age,—to the period between John the Baptist's public appearance and the destruction of Jerusalem by the Romans. It is needless to go into such calculations and conjectures, as they proceed on an entire misconception of the subject, and refer the prophetic periods to times of God's forbearance with iniquity, instead of times of direct and formal chastisement for its guilt.

[8] Of course it will be understood that the two periods of 430 years for Egypt, and 40 for the desert, are referred to as well-known periods of chastisement and trouble, marked historical periods of that description, although in reality a portion of each of them was not exactly of that description. Their leading character as great passages in God's dealings with his people is constantly presented in that light. There is, therefore, no necessity for raising the question, whether the whole 430 years were actually spent by the children of Israel in Egypt, or whether this period did not also comprehend the previous sojourning of the patriarchs in the land of Canaan. The Samaritan Pentateuch and the Septuagint translation have both changed the text

[9] It may not be improper to note further, that it is the prophet's desire to make quite plain the reference for Judah to the 40 years' sojourn in the wilderness, and the modified character of the evil this suggested, that an explanation arises of an apparent anomaly, of which no express notice has been taken above. At ver. 9 he is ordered to "make bread according to the number of the days that he should lie upon his side; three hundred and ninety days shalt thou eat thereof." Here the 40 days are left out, although during them also he was to lie upon his side,—not, as commentators generally, and still also Hävernick, suppose, from the first period being by much the larger of the two, and as such standing for the whole; but to keep the reference clear to the distinctive character of the wilderness-period, which was the point chiefly to be had in view by the Jewish exiles. The eating of polluted bread as a symbol properly implied a constrained residence in a Gentile country—an unclean region; hence, in the explanation given of the symbol at ver. 13, it is declared of the house of Israel, that "they shall eat their defiled bread *among the Gentiles*." But in the wilderness Israel stood quite separate from the Gentiles, though still under penal treatment, and in a sense still connected with Egypt (hence "the wilderness of Egypt," xx. 36); and so they who were in a manner to return to that state again were merely to "eat bread by weight, and with care, and drink water by measure, and in desolateness;" *i.e.* a state of chastisement and trouble, but not by any means so heathen-like, so depressed and helpless, as the other.—It is proper to state that the path to the right interpretation of the vision as a whole began to be opened up by Hengstenberg in his Christology and his work on the

Pentateuch, though without any special reference to this passage of Ezekiel. Hävernick has taken the right course in regard to its general character; but by understanding the first part of an actual siege of Jerusalem, and the eating of defiled bread only of subsequent calamities, he has greatly embarrassed his interpretation; he has also failed to bring fully out the application of the periods of chastisement to Israel and Judah respectively.

CHAPTER V., VI.

[1] The Authorized Version, along with some, both ancient and modern, expositors, have rendered this clause, "And hath changed my judgments into wickedness." But the verb מָרָה never signifies to change; it is always used in the sense of resisting, rebelling against, or something similar, and is often, as here, coupled with the accusative of the object against which the resistance is made,—the Lord's word or statutes, Num. xx. 24; 1 Sam. xii. 15; Jer. iv. 17, etc. The sin of the Israelites lay, not in changing the Lord's statutes, but, from their prevailing wickedness, setting them aside, and so exceeding the heathen in guilt.

[2] Probably the precise meaning of הֲמָנְכֶם here is that given by Gesenius in his Thes.: "tumultuamini," ye tumultuate; and this sense we substantially adopt, though the meaning given in the received translation is entitled to regard, and makes an intelligible sense. The children of Israel had "multiplied," or heaped up, in the line here referred to by the prophet, above the heathen; that it had outdone them in iniquity. The verb certainly is not found in this sense, but its derivative הָמוֹן is often used for multitude or heaps, only with the collateral idea of noise or turmoil. And as it seems probable that the tendency of a multitude to cause such noise or turmoil was the reason of the noun coming to have the sense of multitude, we rather incline to take the verb in the same sense. It also agrees well with what was said before about their doing the part of rebels; as such they raged, or did outrageously.

[3] This is the proper meaning of the verb גָּרַע; and though it may seem here to be used somewhat abruptly, yet if viewed, as it should be, with reference to Deut. iv. 2, where the people were forbidden to withdraw anything from God's statutes, its propriety and force will be manifest. They had now withdrawn from God's sanctuary all its sacredness, and in return he withdraws from them—namely, his favour and protection, life and blessing.

[4] Very characteristic, in the latter part of this chapter, of Ezekiel's style, are the frequent transitions from the objective to the subjective, and inversely,—they and you, it and thou, alternating with each other; also the tendency to repeat over and over again the same thought, and even the same expressions, for the sake of deepening the impression.

[5] It is not certain what precise district is referred to by the name of Diblath. We read elsewhere of the cities that had Diblathaim as part of their names (Num. xxxiii. 46; Jer. xlviii. 22), but not of any wilderness so designated. It is needless to notice the different conjectures which have been thrown out upon the subject, for no certain result has been attained.

[6] See also chap. xvii. 21, where the remnant of the people of the very king that Nebuchadnezzar was to carry to Babylon is expressly said to be scattered to all the winds of heaven.

CHAPTER VII.

[1] It might be rendered *singular*, or remarkable evil, for in that sense אַחַת is here plainly taken, as of a thing by itself, *sui generis*. So also at Job xxiii. 12; Cant. vi. 9.

[2] The *morning*, צְפִירָה; this is a word of very doubtful import and derivation, and there is great diversity among commentators as to the proper way of rendering it. The most probable sense, however, is that adopted by our translators, *aurora*, the morning—a sense which has been preserved both in the Syriac and the Chaldee. Gesenius renders, The turn comes to thee, which makes a suitable meaning.

[3] *No brightness upon the mountains:* taking הֵד, with Hävernick, for an unusual form of הוֹד, splendour, brightness. This also was the rendering of Jerome, who supports himself by the authority of Theodotion. The whole passage bears a close resemblance to Joel ii. 2: 'A day of darkness and gloominess, a day of clouds and of thick darkness, as the morning spread upon the mountains."

[4] What is meant here by the "rod that sprouts," "the pride, or proud one, that blossoms," and "the violence that rises into a rod of the wicked," is not the evil proceeding to its utmost length *within* Israel, but the evil *without* ripening into an instrument of vengeance for Israel,—the Babylonish power. It is God's rod of chastisement for punishing the wicked, and now, under His superintending providence, fast assuming that appearance of towering pride and conquering energy which would speedily put in execution the judgments written.

The הָמוֹן in ver. 11, which we render *store* rather than *multitude*, originally signifies noise or tumult, but is used also of a multitude of persons, or of heaps of riches that are gotten by noisy, bustling activity. It is in this latter sense that it appears to be used by the prophet in this and the two following verses. The word *store*, which suggests something of care and trouble with what is possessed, expresses the meaning more nearly, perhaps, than any other word in our language. The next and closely related word, הֶמֵהֶם, is best understood as a derivative from הָמָה, to make a noise or tumult; hence, restless application, careful solicitude or anxiety. The last word, נֹהַ, is now commonly taken in the sense of attraction or beauty. (See Ges. Lex.)

[5] The idea expressed in vers. 12 and 13 can only be understood by keeping in view the law respecting the year of jubilee, as recorded in Lev. xxv. According to that law, all buying and selling of possessions in Israel was bounded by this ever-recurring season of release; for then every one returned to his proper possession, though he might in the interval have been obliged to part with it. But now, says the prophet, there is to be a suspension of all such transactions: neither may the purchaser rejoice in what he has got, nor the

distressed debtor mourn over what he has been constrained to sell; the vision of coming wrath stretches over all that can be made matter of merchandise; and even though the seller may live to see the year of jubilee, yet he shall not be able to return to his sold possession, for one Sabbath of rest alone remains for the land,—that which it is to enjoy in the absence of all its inhabitants (Lev. xxvi. 34, etc.; 2 Chron. xxxvi. 21). "And no one," adds this prophet, in words that have seldom been correctly rendered, from the allusion not having been distinctly apprehended, "no one by his iniquity shall invigorate (or strengthen) his life." The Sabbaths of the Lord generally, and in particular the Sabbath of the year of jubilee, brought a kind of revivification to the whole commonwealth of Israel; the disorders and troubles that from time to time crept in were then rectified, and the enervated or diseased state of the body politic sprung up again into renewed health and vigour. But what the Lord thus provided for being done by His own beneficent arrangements, let no one think *he* can himself do by his iniquity; from such a source no such strengthening or invigoration of life can be derived; on the contrary, it is this very iniquity which is bringing all to desolation and ruin.

[6] "Let them blow with the trumpet," etc. The meaning is: when the moment of danger arrives that is now at hand, they may set themselves to meet it with warlike preparation; let them do so if they please, it will be of no avail; for the face of the Lord is set against them, and He will strike terror into the hearts of their men of war, and render all their efforts fruitless. The coming desolation was inevitable, and it would be the part of wisdom to consult for safety by flight, not by resistance; even that a few only would be able to accomplish, and in the midst of deep lamentations and manifold distresses.

[7] In vers. 19–24, a threefold example is given of the Divine *lex talionis.* But we must first explain, in regard to the צְבִי עֶדְיוֹ in ver. 20, his beautiful ornament, that we differ from Häv. and Hitzig, and indeed the majority of recent commentators, and agree with some earlier ones and Hengstenberg (on Dan. ix. 27), who understand it of the temple. The gold and riches generally of the people might doubtless have had such an expression applied to them; but, as used here, it seems plainly to point to something that, by way of eminence, was the glory and ornament of the nation, and which, undoubtedly, was the temple. This, it is said here, they used לְגָאוֹן, for the nourishment of pride; and much the same thing is again said in chap. xxiv. 21, where the temple is expressly called "the pride of their strength." What is said here, too, that "in it they made (or did) their abominations," exactly applies to the temple; while the threatened retaliation of *profaning* it, at the close of ver. 21, alone suits the temple. In itself it was their beautiful ornament; but they had first turned it into an occasion of carnal glorying, and then had defiled it with their impurities, whence God must outwardly desecrate it. The retaliation then proceeds thus:—The people have abused their wealth, by making idols of gold and silver, and all manner of ornaments for vainglorious display, so that it has become "the stumbling-block of their iniquity;" now, it was to be seized as a spoil by the enemy, and, in respect to their deliverance, should be found worthless as the mire of the streets. They have carried their abominations into God's sanctuary,

and defiled the secret place of the Most High; now, the whole is to be laid open to the unhallowed feet of the stranger, and robbers are to be sent to walk at liberty where saints only should have been permitted to enter. They, by their daring wickedness, have made the land full of violence and blood; therefore shall they themselves be bound with a chain by the ungodly heathen, and their best possessions be turned into the prey of the lawless and the profane. "*Their* holy places shall be defiled," as they have already defiled *mine.* So truly was God to do to them according to their ways, and judge them according to their judgments.

CHAPTER VIII.

[1] Our translators have here taken עָתָר as an adjective, rendering it *thick.* But it is evidently a noun, and must be understood either generally in the sense of worship, or more specially in that of prayer. To supplicate or pray is the common meaning of the verb, and in Zeph. iii. 10, where it occurs as a noun, it is in the sense of "suppliant," or worshipper. It is here explanatory of the offering of incense, which was a symbol of the highest act of worship, believing prayer, which those elders were prostituting to the basest idolatry.

[2] The chambers of imagery were so called from being painted all round with the images referred to in ver. 10; and they are called each man's chambers of imagery, or the chambers of *his* imagery, because the idolatrous spirit of each had its representation there, and made the chambers what they were in pollution.

[3] The persons mentioned in this 16th verse are said to have been in number כְּעֶשְׂרִים, about twenty, as it is usually put; but in such a description, in numbers and names alike have a significance, it is not to be supposed that the number here was meant to be left indefinite. The כְּ of similitude, therefore, must be taken in its more exact sense of likeness in such a manner or to such an extent; he saw the appearance as of twenty men, as many as that. To express the act of homage in which these men were engaged, the Hebrew text has a peculiar, a sort of corrupt form: not מִשְׁתַּחֲוִים, but מִשְׁתַּחֲוִיתֶם—a slip of the pen, says Ewald, and after him Hitzig. But with more reverence and better taste, Lightfoot, in the very form of the word, saw a reference to the monstrous abominations the men were practising. To him also Hävernick assents, perceiving in the word a strong irony; as if the prophet was so impressed with the corruptness of the service he was describing that he instinctively corrupted the word usually employed to express acts of homage and obeisance.

[4] It is impossible to determine precisely the meaning of this singular expression, "they put the branch to their nose." The Septuagint translator evidently took it for a proverbial expression, indicating a scornful or contemptuous behaviour: "And lo! these are as persons turning up the nose" (or scorning). The other more ancient translators seem also to have understood it as expressive of insolent or contemptuous feelings, though the exact rendering is different; but Jerome took it literally, and supposed it to refer to the use of palm branches in the worship of the sun. Various devices

have been fallen upon to extract a plain and satisfactory meaning from the words, but with so little success that we deem it enough to refer to the two last. Hävernick views it as a pointing to the Adonis-festival; and changing the usual meaning of the two principal words, translates: "And lo! they send forth the mournful ditty to their anger" (viz. the anger they are provoking against themselves). But Hitzig, who justly rejects this fanciful interpretation, and takes זְמוֹרָה in the sense, not of a branch, but of a pruning-knife, renders: "And lo! they are applying the knife to their nose,"—the people being silently likened to a vine, and their nose to a branch, which they were themselves by their infatuated policy cutting off! Had it been their throat or their head to which the knife was applied, one could have seen some shadow of probability in the idea, but none as it is. Besides, the sense ascribed to the word in question is quite arbitrary, as it never occurs but in the sense of a branch, especially a vine-branch, as in chap. xv. 2. From the connection in which the clause stands, one would expect it to denote something that rendered their sinful ways peculiarly obnoxious to God; and as nothing would more readily do this than feelings of fancied security or insolent scorn, so the likelihood is, as the Septuagint understood, that the "putting the branch to the nose," was a proverbial expression for something of that nature.

[5] Entirely similar in principle, though differing in the particular form, as also much briefer in detail, is the representation given in Amos ix. 1: "I saw the Lord standing upon the altar; and he said, Smite the lintel of the door, that the posts may shake: and cut them in the head all of them," etc., where, though the work of judgment had respect to the house of Israel as well as Judah—to the whole covenant-people—yet it is upon the one altar at Jerusalem that the Lord is seen in vision coming forth to execute it, and as if the people were all assembled there, appearing to bring the temple in ruins upon them. The reason is that there, as the services of the people should have been ever coming up for acceptance and blessing, so now their abominations were lying unpardoned, and crying for vengeance, though in reality, and in point of space, they had mostly been committed elsewhere. Therefore from that, as from the place of collective guilt, the work of judgment proceeds, both in Amos and here also in the next chapter; only, while Amos simply supposes the sins to be all clustered around the altar and temple, Ezekiel first gives an embodied representation of them as all appearing and nestling there. Compare also the visions of a somewhat marked description, such as Jacob's (Gen. xxviii. xxxi. 11-13); Pharaoh's (Gen. xli.); Daniel's and Nebuchadnezzar's (Dan. ii. iv. vii.); in all of which there was given an ideal picture, not a prosaic account of the things to which they referred.

[6] How little the commentators have succeeded in giving any satisfactory explanation of the leading points above noticed, on the simply literal plan, may be learned from the solutions of the latest of them, Hitzig. He admits a side chamber could hardly be supposed large enough to hold seventy worshippers at once, but then it was only in spirit the prophet saw them there together! That the entrance was closed up by a wall was a still remaining proof of Josiah's reformation; but, no doubt, the elders had some private door to enter by—as if the prophet could not have discovered that, and as if

now, amid the corruptions of Zedekiah's time, they needed to go about the matter so stealthily! And then, in regard to what is said of every man's doing so "in the chambers of his imagery," as this seems to point to separate scenes of idol-worship enacted in private, why, most likely the text is corrupt; it should have been simply, what each one did in that one chamber in the dark!! With such an elastic style of interpretation, what convenient or wished-for meaning may not be extracted from the sacred text?

CHAPTER IX.

[1] The language in this opening verse, as well as the communication that follows, shows that what is said here is merely the continuation and proper sequel of the preceding vision. In the last words of the eighth chapter, mention was made of a cry being heard in the Lord's ears, a loud cry for mercy from the doomed city; and now the prophet is made to hear in *his* ears a loud cry for vengeance—in itself a sign how fruitless the other cry should be. The persons addressed, ideal executioners of justice, are called פְּקֻדּוֹת, which properly means *offices*, but it is also used concretely for those holding office, or having charge—for example, Isa. lx. 17; 2 Chron. xxiv 11.

[2] Christology, on Amos ix. 1.

[3] The practice of imprinting marks upon men in a religious connection was in ancient times not unknown in real life, as we learn from Herodotus (ii. 113), who says in respect to a temple of Hercules in Egypt, "that if the slave of any one takes refuge there, and has sacred marks impressed upon him, it is not lawful to lay hands on him." In opposition, however, to what is said above, and apparently under the idea that an actual mark was to be made on the persons in question, some of the Fathers (Tertullian, Origen, Jerome), and the Roman Catholic writers generally, have strenuously contended for the specific sign of the cross as being the mark intended. The chief philological ground for this idea is, that as the word used for *mark* is *tau*, the name of the last letter of the alphabet, the old form of that letter was a *cross.* On this ground, though without respect to the use made of it by the Catholics, Hitzig translates: "mark a cross." But the more ancient versions, the Sept., Aq., and Symm., all render generally a *mark.* And Vitringa justly observes, that "nowhere throughout Scripture are those words, which are now employed as names of the letters of the alphabet, and several of which occur, ever used to denote those letters themselves or their figures. Besides, there is connected with the word *tau* in this text the verb תָּוָה, from which the other is derived. And as among the Hebrews such conjunctions of verbs with nouns sprung from them are common, it is probable that the *tau* here is of the same meaning with the verb with which it is joined. Is it not also the case that in the parallel passage (Rev. vii. 3), where a fact of the same kind is recorded, no mention is made of any special mark? We therefore gladly embrace the version of the Septuagint, which accords with the interpretations of the most eminent Jews, and simply render: *mark a sign.*"—Obs. Sac. lib. ii. chap. xv. sec. 8.

CHAPTER X.

[1] This has been unhappily rendered in the authorized version, O wheel. In the original there are two words used in this chapter, which we can scarcely avoid translating by the same word, wheel,—אוֹפָן, which strictly means a wheel; and גַּלְגַּל, which comprehends the entire machinery of wheel-work, wheel within wheel, so called from its quick, whirlwind-like movements. This is what the word properly means, anything having a swift rotatory motion; whence it denotes a whirlwind, Ps. lxxvii. 18. It was this last word which was here proclaimed in the prophet's ears, for the purpose partly of indicating their nature, and partly of calling them to put themselves in motion. For by their rapid energetic motion they symbolized the resistless speed and certainty with which the Divine agency accomplishes its purposes. Bottcher, quoted by Maurer, renders: "To the wheels, to these was it always cried in my ears, the Roll—Roll;" meaning that they were called to be continually revolving. The Septuagint is still more literal, for it simply gives the original word, Γελγέλ.

[2] The peculiarity in this description of the personal aspect of the cherubim is, that while they are said to have had each four faces, that is, to have combined in their visage the fourfold aspect of ox, man, lion, and eagle, the first is represented as having simply the appearance of a cherub, and the others that of a man, a lion, and an eagle respectively. Some commentators, as Maurer, confess that they see no proper way of explaining this; many more pass on without offering any explanation; and others, comparing the passage with chap. i. 10, where the ox is mentioned as the fourth component element in the composition of the cherub, take cherub here for ox, and suppose that the cherubic structure had some peculiar affinity with the form of the ox, on account of which the name of cherub might be substituted for that of ox. But this is without any foundation, and, indeed, contrary to the description in chap. i., according to which, as formerly stated, the form of man was undoubtedly predominant in the appearance. The explanation I take to be this: the prophet simply describing what he saw, and standing at the time right in front of one of the cherubim, the one who gave the live coals to the angel, could not say in regard to this cherub which particular form was prominent, the *whole* cherubic figures appeared in the face; while, having only a *side* view of the others, they each presented to his eye the different forms he specifies.

CHAPTER XI.

[1] This is the plain import of the original here, and, as will be shown afterwards, gives the best sense. The meaning adopted by Calvin, and followed by the authorized version and many commentators, is, "It is not near (viz. the destruction of the city); let us build houses;" or, "to build houses." Let us proceed to that, and we can do so with safety. This, as Maurer has justly objected, would have required the inf. absol.; not בְּנוֹת, but בָּנֹה. Ewald would take the words interrogatively, "Is it not in the nearness to build houses?" *i.e.* Cannot we do so with perfect safety? Grammatically, the

interpretation is admissible; but it does not give a natural sense, nor the one best fitted to explicate the meaning; rather, indeed, the reverse.

2 The state of mind implied in the speech here put into the mouth of the priests is vividly represented, and with substantial accuracy, by Calvin. He also perceived a reference to both the passages in Jeremiah above noticed; though, as formerly stated, he gave an untenable view of the first part, and understood it of the security the people now thought they had to build houses in Jerusalem. Various other modes of explanation have been adopted,—of which none, certainly, are more ridiculous than one of the last, that of Hitzig, who puts into the mouth of the priesthood the very tame and quite inappropriate sentiment: "War is at hand, we are going to revolt; it is therefore not a time for building houses, but rather for laying in provisions!" That of Hävernick, which we have followed, is the only one which at once gives to the words their proper rendering, and extracts from them a sentiment entirely suited to the occasion.

CHAPTER XII.

1 The expression כְּלֵי גוֹלָה does not mean properly "stuff for removing," but the articles or implements which are proper to a person going as an exile or captive to a distant land; in particular, a staff, a scrip, and a knapsack, with a few supplies of food and clothing. The word הַגּוֹלָה, which is so often used by Ezekiel to denote the collected body of the exiles, is so used (as has been shown by Hengstenberg on Zech. xiv. 2) by way of personification, the captives being viewed collectively in the light of a female humbled and depressed. The same kind of personification is applied, and carried out at considerable length, in reference to Babylon, in Isa. xlvii. Hence those who returned to Jerusalem are, in Ezra viii. 35, not only said to have "come out of captivity," but also to be "the children of the captivity," *i.e.* of the captives. Denoting properly a captive or exiled state, it may, of course, be understood of any in that state, whether one or many. The same phrase as in our text is used by Jeremiah, chap. xlvi. 19, of Egypt, where the marginal reading in our Bibles is, "make thee instruments of captivity."

2 The expression בָּעֲלָטָה is so seldom used, that there might be some dubiety as to its exact meaning, were it not for the passage Gen. xv. 17, where the word certainly means the thick darkness of night. We may suppose it here to refer to any part of the night, though naturally to the earlier part; but to the night as enveloping the person in a deep shade, and so affording the opportunity of a secret escape.

3 *Portent* seems to come nearer to the import of מוֹפֵת than *sign*. It is properly a wonder, a miracle, then something extraordinary and ominous—here, ominous of evil—a portent. What was now done by Ezekiel in vision typically foreshadowed fearful transactions of a like kind in real life.

4 The pouncing at once here on the *prince* in Jerusalem, as the foremost object in the prophetic burden, is very emphatic; it proclaimed aloud that the man in whom they were trusting for safety was himself to be the chief sufferer in the impending calamities.

CHAPTER XIII.

[1] This last clause is rendered in the authorized version, "and they made *others* to hope, that they would confirm the word." But יָחַל with לְ, as Hävernick remarks, always means to expect or hope for something. The correct interpretation, therefore, is that which refers the hope to the prophets themselves. Secker: "They hoped to establish the word." Michaelis: "They hoped that their words would be fulfilled." Hitzig's attempt to change the reference—"Jehovah has not sent them, that they should hope for the confirmation of their words"—is quite arbitrary, and has been resorted to merely because he thought the prophets could not be so self-deceived. But there are sufficient grounds, as we shall show, for holding that they were so. And such expressions as those in Jeremiah: "I have not sent these prophets, yet they ran; I have not spoken by them, yet the people said," "They say the burden of the Lord" (chap. xxiii. 21, 34), betoken the working of a strong spirit of delusion.

[2] "Daub with untempered mortar," is the phrase used for this operation in the authorized version, as in many others, ancient and modern. It partly, however, suggests a false idea. The word תָּפֵל, when used in a physical sense, is simply *coating* or *whitewash*, such as is usually laid on the outside of walls. Jarchi: *est terra similis calci.* Hitzig renders expressly, and not improperly, *chalk.* The idea intended is, that the false prophets, countenancing the people in their delusions, sought merely to make the outside fair—to give to the fabric the people raised a showy and promising appearance, while still there was no real solidity or inherent strength. Hence St. Paul's word to the high priest, "Thou whited wall," Acts xxiii. 3, and the "whited sepulchre" of our Lord in Matt. xxiii. 27.

[3] The verb בָּקַע commonly signifies to cleave or rend asunder; in the Piel, to cleave, for example, wood, or tear an object like a wild beast. Hence it has here commonly been understood of rending or breaking down the wall. But the object of the rending is not expressed; and in ver. 13 it seems plainly to be applied in the casual form to the wind itself: I make it rend or break forth. It is best, therefore, to understand it in the same sense also in ver. 11. The Latins use the quite similar phrase, *ventus frangit*, for a violent gale. In Greek also, ῥήγνυμι is often applied to the breaking forth of storms and showers.

[4] It is scarcely possible to make out with certainty the precise meaning of some of the expressions in this verse, reference being made to customs of which we have no exact description. What is meant by the cushions, or pillows (as it is in the common translation, and in the Rabbins *pulvinar longius*), was probably some sort of soft covering or tapestry used for purposes of luxury. They are said to have been sewed for "all the joints of the hands"—so the words literally mean; referring, probably, to the wrists and elbow-joints. By comparing Jer. xxxviii. 12 and xli. 9, we learn that it was used of shoulder or elbow-joints; and in ver. 20 here, the articles of dress are spoken of as going to be torn from the *arms* of the wearers. The head-dresses or kerchiefs on every stature seem to be the mantles or coverings with which the women of the East envelop their heads, and which are sometimes made both of large dimensions and of costly workmanship. And as it

would certainly be a peculiar expression, "coverings upon the head of every stature," if by every stature were meant persons of different heights, it is better, perhaps, with Hävernick, to regard "coverings upon the head" as a complex phrase, like "head-coverings," qualified by the "every stature" or size, to denote the different conditions and ages of persons who had such articles of seduction provided and fitted for them. The persons who are described as doing such things are obviously represented as plying the arts of seduction proper to the most abandoned characters; and in ver. 19 are still further assimilated to them by seeking for their reward only "handfuls of barley and pieces of bread,"—the smallest pittances.

[5] I retain the rendering of לְפֹרְחוֹת given in the authorized version; which is that also adopted by Gesenius for this passage, and is supported by the Syriac. It certainly, however, does not yield a very distinct or plain meaning. The sense in which the word is commonly found is that of *sprouting* or *flourishing*—in which sense it occurs also in Ezekiel at chap. xvii. 24. Gussetius would retain that sense here, and renders, *ut efflorescant*, that they may flourish or be prosperous. But it is somewhat incongruous to apply such a term to those who are represented immediately before under the image of snared birds. The Septuagint renders εἰς διασκορπισμὸν, for scattering or dispersion—probably understanding the sort of flying meant to be that of a forced flight to other and distant regions. Ewald interprets: "as if they were birds of passage;" differing little from the sense given by old Pradus: "with which ye catch souls for birds, *i.e.* as if they were birds —*animas volantes*." This mode of interpretation, which seems competent, would make the flying an indication of the light and unstable character of the persons so caught. But probably the more natural meaning is, to regard it as pointing to the result, expressed so as to indicate, with a certain degree of irony, the contrariety between what was promised and what actually happened. The souls were caught like silly birds, expecting to get as it were new wings to fly aloft in ample freedom and prosperity; but it was only to fly away from their native home to the land of captivity. Hävernick's interpretation of diversions (wanton pleasures) is without any proper foundation, and has only certain analogies to support it.

[6] Delitzsch, Der Prophet Habakkuk ausgelegt, p. 3.

CHAPTER XIV.

[1] This last clause is given in the authorized version, as by many others, "I the Lord will answer him that cometh according to the multitude of his idols," following the Kri, which has נַעֲנֵיתִי בָא instead of נַעֲנֵיתִי בָה. There is no need, however, for such a change. Reading בָּהּ (which ought to be the pointing), we have, as Hävernick remarks, a perfectly common Aramaic construction, according to which the subject expressed in the following noun is anticipated by a pronoun going before, so that the latter is not a mere pleonasm, but employed for the purpose of giving increased emphasis to the following substantive: "I the Lord will answer him according to it, according to the multitude of his idols." The use of the Niphal of עָנָה in the sense of *answering*, or *making answer*, is certainly a peculiarity, as elsewhere the

common meaning is, to be answered, or to receive answer. Both Ewald and Hävernick have tried to establish new renderings, but without any satisfactory result. The context plainly obliges us to adhere to the general and common import of the verb. Literally, "I the Lord am answered to him, according to it;" or reflectively, as the Niphal is often used, "I the Lord answer myself (or, for myself) to him, according to it." The same sentiment, with a very slight variation, is repeated in ver. 7: "And cometh to the prophet to inquire of him concerning me (בִּי), I Jehovah will answer him myself concerning me (בִּי)." The בִּי should in each case be alike rendered "concerning me," and not in the latter case, as in the common version, "by myself." For the meaning is not, as most commentators, and among others Hävernick, seem to suppose, that God would give an answer directly and personally, as from himself, without the intervention of a prophet; for in the very next verse but one, the case is supposed of a deceived prophet giving to such persons a wrong answer, while the Lord affirms that even such answer would be from him. Such would be, at least, one of the modes of his meeting these hypocritical inquirers. But the Lord would show, by the *kind* of answer given, however it might be communicated, that he had taken the matter into his own hand, and that he dealt with them not according to their desires and expectations, but to their deserts. He would take them, as it is said in ver. 5, in their own heart, or would make them feel that he was cognisant of their great idolatries and perverse ways.

2 The "how much more when" here, which we retain as it is in the English Bible, expresses rather the thought indicated than the exact force of the original—אַף כִּי. The prophet had announced what would take place on each of the supposed cases separately; and he comes now to say, Surely shall it be so now, when I send, etc. The particles are strongly affirmative, and intimate the much greater necessity that existed for what was now to be declared.

3 Olshausen on 2 Thess. ii. 11, 12.

4 Exception has been taken very unreasonably against the mention of Daniel along with Noah and Job, and an argument raised out of it against the authenticity of Daniel's history. But at the time Ezekiel now wrote, Daniel had been at least fourteen years in Babylon, and the circumstances which first spread abroad his fame so much—those recorded in the two first chapters of his book—are understood to have occurred very shortly after his going to Babylon. There was, therefore, ample time for his extraordinary worth to be generally known and familiarly referred to; the more so, as the Jews would naturally, in their present low condition, think with pride of one who had acquired so much glory for their nation at the very seat of empire, and would probably even be disposed to count unduly upon the benefits to be derived from his virtues and influence. See Hengstenberg's Beitr. i. pp. 70-72.

CHAPTER XVI.

1 Hävernick would render here: the place of thy production and the place of thy birth. But no instance can be produced in which the terms are used

distinctly to express the locality in which the action or event took place. And if it had been the locality that was here pointed to, what follows would have been not *of*, but *in*, the land of Canaan. The words are literally, thy diggings, or originatings, and thy bringings forth, to which substantially correspond thy origin and thy birth.

[2] Not simply *an* Amorite and *a* Hittite, but these two tribes themselves personified; as if all the peculiarities respectively belonging to them united in the parentage of the Israelitish people.

[3] The use of water is here said to be 'לְמִשְׁעִ—which occurs only here, and has been very commonly rendered "for suppling," as from שָׁעַע, to stroke or smear. Gesenius gives cleansing as the meaning, which, with most recent authorities, we adopt. The latter is certainly the more natural sense. In the Septuagint the word is altogether omitted. The application of salt to new-born infants in ancient times is known to have been a common practice, supposed to have been used medicinally, for the purpose of hardening the skin; but probably, also, not without reference to the symbolical import of salt, as an emblem of purity and incorruption. Jerome says on the passage: "The tender bodies of infants, while they still retain the heat of the womb, and by their cries give evidence of the first commencement of this toilsome life, are wont to be sprinkled with salt by the nurses, to make them more dry and firm." Galen speaks of it, De Sanit. i. 7.

[4] "With contempt of thy life," seems to come nearer to the idea here expressed than the "loathing of thy person." For נֶפֶשׁ, though often used for *life*, never precisely means *person;* and when the treatment is said to have been done with loathing of this, it is much the same as we would express by contempt, or disdainful indifference, to the life.

[5] It is literally, "and didst come to ornament of ornaments." The word עֲדִי has no other well-ascertained meaning; and the attempts of Hävernick and Hitzig to change the sense are both quite unsuccessful. See Hengstenberg on Ps. xxxii. 9. It is there also used somewhat peculiarly,—of the bit and bridle of a horse, "whose ornaments are bit and bridle," meaning that the nature of a horse is such as to require decorations of that sort.

[6] The meaning of this last clause is much obscured in the Authorized Version, by giving the conjunction *and* the adversative force of *whereas*, thereby making the nakedness and bareness here mentioned point to a condition prior to that described in the preceding terms. But it is only the literal rendering that conveys the proper idea. The prophet means to say, that even when grown to womanhood and ripe for marriage, she was still naked and bare; beautiful, indeed, in person, but as to other things in an unfurnished and poor condition.

[7] This expression, of "throwing the skirt over her," as appears also from what immediately follows, is synonymous with entering into the marriage relation. It is taken from Ruth iii. 9: "Spread thy skirt over thine handmaid; for thou art a near kinsman." It gives a very feeble sense when explained, as it often is, of taking under the wing of Divine protection and support. The passage in Ruth, and collateral passages in the law (Deut. xxii. 30, xxvii. 20), fully bear out the other and more specific meaning. Nor are similar expressions wanting in the Greek poets for indicating the marriage union;

as in Sophocles' Trachin, v. 536. See also Grotius here.

[8] It is not ascertained with certainty what was meant by *tachash;* it is always used in connection with skin, or articles made of skin; for example, the tabernacle was covered with tachash skins, Ex. xxv. 5. The ancient versions understood it to denote the colour of the skins, red or blue; but the Talmudists and Hebrew interpreters take it for the name of the animal from which the skins were obtained, probably the badger or seal; and this is now generally acquiesced in.

[9] The most literal rendering here is to be preferred. Hävernick's, "against thy name," with a reference to Judg. xix. 2, is rather forced. She played the wanton upon her name, because her renown, with the riches and honour on which it was grounded, carried her away into sin.

[10] It seems probable that what is meant here by גַּב is such a chamber as the Latins denoted by *fornix*, here suitably rendered by the Septuagint οἴκημα πορνικόν—a class of apartments too frequently associated with the impure religions of antiquity.

[11] This epithet, "great of flesh," applied to the Egyptians, seems to point to the gross and lustful character of their religion (comp. chap. xxiii. 20). How much the Egyptian religion partook of such a character has been abundantly established. See, for example, Hengstenberg on the Pentateuch, ii. p. 118 sq.; also Herod. ii. 46. It may be doubted, however, whether committing adultery with the Egyptians means worshipping their idols. We would rather understand it, with Calvin, of their improper trust in the power of Egypt, which was itself an act of unfaithfulness toward God. So also may be understood what is said of the Assyrians.

[12] "The daughters of the Philistines" seem here to be taken generally as a name for heathen adversaries. They were not actually the parties to whom Israel was given up, when her allowance was diminished, or her inheritance curtailed; but those to whom they were given up might be called daughters of the Philistines, from their character and position.

[13] The meaning of this fresh charge, which we render quite literally, seems to be this, that the people multiplied still further their backslidings and pollutions, such as belonged to the land of Canaan under its original inhabitants, and that by going even to Chaldea; bringing in Chaldea to aggravate the Canaanitish character of their evil ways. We greatly prefer this sense to taking Canaan as an appellative, and rendering, "the merchant-land to Chaldea."

[14] The practice of harlots is referred to, scoffing at or scorning the offered hire, in order to obtain more. Unlike such, worse even than those profligates, Israel seemed to be indifferent to the result of her procedure; she did not care whether she got much or little—heedlessly bent on the way of ruin. The rendering of this clause by the Vulgate is particularly happy: *Nec facta es sicut meretrix fastidio augens pretium.*

[15] The common version misses the exact import of this verse, by rendering, "taketh strangers instead of her husband." The sin charged is that of taking or receiving strangers while under the law of her husband. It refers to Num. v. 19, 20, 29, where the rendering should be, "goeth aside under her husband," *i.e.* turns aside to another while properly under him.

[16] This last clause is very commonly, and also in the Authorized Version, rendered, "And thou shalt not commit this lewdness above all thy abominations"—but what lewdness? Nothing had been mentioned separate from the abominations themselves. The verse treats of God's proceedings, not Israel's, and this clause is plainly a continuation of what he declared it his purpose to do to Israel. He will deal with her according to her sins, and will not be guilty of the scandalous part (such is the precise import of the phrase) of encouraging her in her sinful courses. The expression refers to the conduct of a father who should encourage his daughter to play the harlot, as recorded in Lev. xix. 29. The very same term is also used there.

[17] The expression here has been misunderstood, from not perceiving that it refers to Gen. xviii. 21, where the Lord said to Abraham, that he would go down and would *see* whether the iniquity of Sodom was according to the cry that came into his ears: he did according to what he saw.

[18] The proper meaning of the verb פָּלַל seems to be to *judge for*, to undertake or vindicate the cause of any one, and in this sense it is plainly used in 1 Sam. ii. 25. It is used also in Piel in the sense of judging generally; but most commonly in Hithpael in the sense of entreating for, or supplicating—a sense very naturally arising out of what we suppose to be the primary one of judging, for the purpose of establishing the cause or right of any one. Here the meaning is, that Israel by her greater guilt had, as it were, given judgment in favour of her less guilty neighbours.

[19] I adhere to the common rendering of the phrase שׁוּב שְׁבוּת, in preference to that so strenuously contended for by Hengstenberg in his Beitr. ii. p. 104, and again on Ps. xiv. 6. It is quite true, that in other expressions the verb is used intransitively—to turn back to, or return to anything. That, however, does not conclusively prove it may not be used actively in a proverbial expression like this; indeed, the אֵת here between the verb and the noun, pointing out the one as the object of the other, seems to demand the active sense; and in Jer. xlix. 6 the Hiphil form is employed, to render the force of the expression more apparent: "I will cause to return—*i.e.* I will bring back—the captivity of the children of Ammon." See also Nah. ii. 3. The difference, however, between the two interpretations is merely philological; it respects simply the original import of the words, whether they mean precisely a turning back of the captivity, or a turning back to it, viz. on the Lord's part, with a view to its removal. The meaning is still, in either case, substantially the same. The expression is a proverbial one, to denote the undoing of an existing evil, and is often used of cases where there was no real captivity, as in Job xlii. 10, and Jer. xxx. 18.

[20] Thus, in Gen. xv. 16, "The iniquity of the Amorites is not yet full," evidently meaning the inhabitants of Canaan generally. (Comp. also Amos ii. 9.) So again in Jos. i. 4, "All the land of the Hittites" is used as a designation of the whole land of Canaan. In naming a Hittite mother, an allusion is doubtless intended to Esau's wives, daughters of Heth, whose ways vexed the heart of Rebekah (Gen. xxvi. 46).

[21] The same figure was in familiar use among the Greeks and Latins: "Sons of Hercules," "Daughters of Apollo," etc.; and in Virgil the much stronger expression, which finds a parentage in the most senseless part of

inanimate nature, "Duris genuit te cautibus horrens Caucasus" (Æn. iv. 366).

[22] Lev. xx. 10, which, though it simply mentions putting to death, is yet to be connected with ver. 1 as to the manner of inflicting the punishment. Also John viii. 5, which shows the Jewish mind on the subject. And, indeed, generally, stoning to death appears to have been the only legal form of capital punishment for individual sins.

[23] Hengstenberg's Christol. on Hos. ii. 12; also Isa. xlvii. 3; Jer. xiii. 26; Nah. iii. 6, in all which the same idea is unfolded, only less fully and broadly.

[24] Such must be held to be the meaning here. The "not by thy covenant" cannot possibly refer to the old covenant made with Israel, as contradistinguished from the new, for God had already traced to that covenant, as its fountain-head, all the grace and blessing that was to be conferred. And, as Calvin justly remarks here, while there were important differences between the two covenants, as noticed by Jeremiah in chap. xxxi. and xxxii., yet the new covenant so sprung from the old, that it is well-nigh the same in substance, though different in form.

CHAPTER XVII.

[1] The term צַמֶּרֶת is peculiar to Ezekiel, but from the use of it here, and in chap. xxxi. 3-14, there can be no doubt that it means the summit, or topmost branch—the woolly part of the tree at the farthest extremity.

[2] We have here also another word peculiar to Ezekiel, צַפְצָפָה, which is usually rendered *willow*, and in that sense has the support of Jewish authority. Indeed, this is the only Rabbinical meaning of the term. If any modification whatever were allowable, it might be supposed, with Hitzig, to denote generally a water-plant, a shrub or tree naturally growing in or beside waters. It was probably applied as a designation of the willow on this account, being derived from צוּף, to flood or overflow. Set where it was, the cedar-twig became a willow for growth, and a spreading luxuriant vine for fruitfulness.

[3] The time lies between the two dates, that of the 6th month of the 6th year of Zedekiah's reign, or Jehoiachin's captivity, in chap. viii., and that of the 5th month of the 7th year, in chap. xx.

[4] "There can be no doubt," says Calvin, "that God means Mount Zion, which in itself was a little hill. But Isaiah gives us the reason of its being lofty, when he shows it should surpass every elevation in the world in dignity and excellence. The supereminence, indeed, was not to be patent to the eye, for the prophet declares, at the same time, it should consist in this, that the law should go forth from Zion and the word of God from Jerusalem. Accordingly we see Mount Zion, though little among the hills, yet raised aloft above the highest mountains; because from it shone forth the glory of God, which has been seen even to the farthest bounds of the earth."

CHAPTER XVIII.

[1] The *vau* here must plainly be taken as an example of the inferential use of the conjunction—*so then therefore* (Ges. Gr. sec. 152, 1*d*).

[2] How little the Jews of modern times have learned from what was spoken to their ancestors, may be gathered from the defence Orobius makes, as noticed by Warburton in his Dedication to the Jews, for the evils of their long dispersion: "They suffer," says he, "not for their own sins, but for the sins of their forefathers."

[3] It is a striking proof of the loose and arbitrary manner in which subjects of this kind were handled half a century ago in this country, that such a man as Paley could deliberately, and with apparent satisfaction, state, "that the only way of reconciling them (the principle set forth in the second commandment, and that in this passage of Ezekiel) together, is by supposing that the second commandment related solely to temporal, or rather family adversity and prosperity, and Ezekiel's chapter to the rewards and punishments of a future life" (Serm. xiii.). As if the very point under debate in this chapter were not why the covenant-people were subjected to their *present* temporal troubles and misfortunes. Drop this, and there is no question agitated between them and the prophet. As for the view of Warburton, that the principle of the second commandment was introduced to supply the want of a future state, and that the word by Ezekiel amounted to a virtual abrogation of it, now that the hope of immortality was going to be brought in, it can only be characterised as an utterly groundless assertion, proceeding on a mistaken view of the Divine dispensations. The idea of an innocent posterity suffering for a guilty parentage is justly designated by Hävernick as a heathenish one. "When men lost the faith of a *living* God, they were impelled to the worship of a blind Nemesis—a fate pregnant with mischief. The sentiments uttered by the people here are precisely what we find in those words of Solon with Stobæus (Ecl. ix. p. 100), 'Αλλ' *ὁ μὲν αὐτικ ἔτισεν*, etc., and in the well-known passage of Horace's Delicta majorum immeritus lues, Romane (Od. iii. 6. 1, comp. iii. 2. 30). See also Homer, Il. iv. 161 ss."

[4] The general feelings of remote antiquity perfectly harmonized with those expressed in the Jewish law. Usury was unknown among the ancient Germans (Tacit. Ger. 26). Even in Greece, Aristotle and other superior men pronounced it unworthy of an honourable citizen to lend money on interest; and at Rome, Cato went so far as to denounce the practice as a heinous crime. They regarded it as among the discreditable tricks of trade, and left it to the lower class of citizens. See Grote's Greece, iii. pp. 145-7.

CHAPTER XIX.

[1] In the rendering of this clause, there is only a choice of difficulties, and it is impossible to obtain anything like satisfaction. According to the natural construction, both the verbs should refer to the *hope* as their object; and this construction, I think, must be retained. But then there is no well ascertained meaning of the first of the two verbs, נוֹחֲלָה, which altogether makes sense.

It properly means to wait or hope for anything; but, undoubtedly, what presents itself as a thing to be waited for has, to an ardent mind, a deferred and almost forlorn appearance. The transition to this sense cannot be regarded as unnatural or harsh. In Gen. viii. 12 it occurs very nearly in that sense, importing simply a putting off or delaying from one period to another. I prefer, therefore, with Hävernick, to render as in the text, and deem both improbable and unnecessary the other derivations and senses which have been adopted. The LXX. seem to have had or made a different text; and Hitzig, as very commonly, prefers following them.

[2] The literal rendering here is: And he knew their widows—but the sense is that given above. There is no good authority for ascribing to אַלְמְנוֹת the meaning of *palaces*, or any other than that of *widows*. Of course the image is violated by the lion being spoken of thus in connection with widows; the reality breaks through the veil; but that is no uncommon thing, as we have seen, with Ezekiel; various examples of it occur in chap. xvi.

[3] Our translators have here inserted in the margin two other meanings for *in thy blood:* in thy quietness, in thy likeness. The former of these two is the one adopted by Hävernick, deriving דָּם here from דּוּם, דָּמָה, to be silent, to be at rest; a state of repose or rest, therefore, is what he understands to be indicated. Ewald and Hitzig prefer, in thy likeness. The LXX. appear to have read כְּרִמּוֹן, a pomegranate, and are followed by Newcome and others. But there is really no need for any change in the received text, or departing from the most natural and simplest rendering; especially since the prophet, in chap xvi., had once and again used the same expression, "in thy blood," for denoting the earliest stage of existence. In his peculiar phraseology, it was all one with saying, "When thou wast in the very infancy of thy being," even then the mother of the royal house was like a vine planted beside waters, full of strength and vigour; she could look for great things for her offspring.

[4] A sudden change of gender takes place here in the original, from the feminine to the masculine, which I have not thought it necessary to imitate. Ezekiel uses considerable freedom in that way. A similar anomaly occurs again in the latter part of ver. 12. The expression עַל בֵּין עֲבֹתִים ought certainly to be "up," or "aloft among the clouds" (comp. chap. xxxi. 3, 10, 14). There it evidently denotes the highest elevation, and "among the thick branches" will not make sense. The later interpreters agree in this result, but differ somewhat in their way of reaching it. Ewald and Hengstenberg regarding עָבוֹת, clouds, as one of those nouns which came gradually to lose their plural meaning; and so Ezekiel forms a new plural by adding ים; while Hävernick, we think with less probability, supposes an interchange to have taken place between the meanings of עב and עבות, so that the latter, in the plural, was used, not for thickets, but for thicket-clouds.

CHAPTER XX.

[1] The interrogative has here the force of a command, the הֲ being equivalent to the usual הֲלֹא, Wilt thou not? And the interrogation is repeated to show the strength of feeling on the part of God, and the urgency of the oc-

casion: Wilt thou not do it? Wilt thou not do it? Why delay? There is here the loudest call for the exercise of judgment; do it promptly.

[2] It is, literally, the *ornament* or *beauty* of all lands; and from being applied to Canaan before the Israelites took possession of it, the epithet must, of course, be understood in its natural sense, as denoting the native excellence and desirableness of the country. The same epithet is applied in Isa. xiii. 19 to Babylon as a kingdom, and several times in Daniel to Palestine (chap. viii. 9, xi. 16). We may understand by it, not so properly the absolute superiority of Canaan, as its relative superiority, considered as the abode and heritage of the Lord's people.

[3] The expression here, of "making to pass over," does not refer to the horrid practice of making children pass through the fire to Moloch, as our translators have unhappily understood it. That was a later abomination, and as such is mentioned in ver. 31, where subsequent corruptions are historically related; but what is here meant, is the consecration of the firstborn to the Lord. It is the same term that is used to express the act of consecration in Ex. xiii. 12, where the original ordinance is given: "The firstborn shall all be made to pass over to the Lord." Here, however, *to the Lord* is omitted, and on purpose. As if to say: They kept up the ceremony, indeed, the outward service was still gone through; but I did not own it as done to me, since it was mingled with such pollutions.

[4] Such is the literal translation of this passage, and that also which yields the best meaning. Various interpretations and renderings have been given. Hävernick would regard it as charging them with having confounded the difference between God's temple and other places of worship; but it seems rather to indicate what God himself held their worship to be: he gave the name *Bamah* to every place of their worship, and held by that as the proper name, for the worship was essentially of a polluted and heathenish character. Quite parallel is Hos. iv. 15, where Bethel, God's house, is changed into Bethaven, the House of Iniquity.

[5] *Καλέεται δὲ ὅ τε τράγος, καὶ ὁ Πὰν αἰγυπτιστὶ, Μένδης* (Herod. ii. 46). And this Pan was one of the chief gods of Egypt, viewed as personified, incarnate in the he-goat, which was hence deemed sacred. (See Hengst. Beitr. ii. p. 119.)

[6] We cannot help noticing with regret, that Hävernick here contents himself with expressing his concurrence in the view of Bähr, who regards the Jewish Sabbath as simply a day of outward rest, in memorial of creation, and in token of the people's looking to God as the final resting-place of their souls. But something of a more positive nature was necessary to secure the design of the Sabbath; it required *spiritual* employments and holy convocations. See Typology of Scripture, vol. ii. p. 118, where the subject is more fully discussed. Herbert only expressed the sentiment that pervades the bosoms of pious men in every age when he wrote:

> "Sundays the pillars are
> On which heaven's palace arched lies;
> The other days fill up the spare
> And hollow room with vanities.
> They are the fruitful beds and borders

In God's rich garden : that is bare
Which parts their ranks and orders."

By a strange misapprehension of this part of the description, Hävernick supposes here a reference to the sojournings of the patriarchs in the land of Canaan, and considers the land of exile to be called "the country of their sojourn" by a bitter irony. A very forced and unnatural idea. Egypt, in such a connection as this, was manifestly the historical place of the people's sojourn.

CHAPTER XX. 45–49, XXI.

[1] The two words here used, לַהֶבֶת שַׁלְהֶבֶת, are very like in sound, and also not very different in meaning, although they are not quite so synonymous as our translators have taken them to be. The second rather means ardent, glowing heat, than flame in the ordinary sense. What is meant is evidently a flame of intense fervency.

[2] Here, as not unfrequently with Ezekiel, the figure is dropt, or rather, figure and reality are mingled together. He lets out the secret, that men are represented by the trees, when he speaks of all faces being burnt. (See similar violations in chap. xix. 7, and various passages in chap. xvi.)

[3] Literally, that the lightning-flash may belong to it. It was to *look* terrible, as well as to execute fearful desolations. The language evidently has respect to Deut. xxxii. 41, where the Lord also speaks of "whetting his glittering sword, and his hand taking hold of judgment."

[4] We have here only a choice of difficulties. The sentence is so enigmatical, that the greater part of commentators have supposed the text to be corrupted, and suggest alterations of various kinds. The LXX. express an entirely different sense from what can be made out by any construction from the present text. But the arbitrary change made at ver. 3 clearly shows that the Greek translator was not scrupulous in *making* a plain sense when he thought the original did not afford it. He renders here, *σφάζε, ἐξουδένει ἀπόθου πᾶν ξύλον*, slay, set at nought, despise every tree. Jerome notices this strange rendering of the LXX., and himself translates with more regard to the Hebrew, but still with some licence, *qui moves sceptrum filii mei, succidisti omne lignum*,—thou that shakest the sceptre of my son, hast felled all wood. The modern versions are endlessly varied. Of those which take the text as it stands, perhaps the nearest to our authorized version is De Wette's,—"or shall we rejoice ourselves? the rod of my son despises all wood;" a rendering, however, which is grammatically inadmissible, and, besides, makes no very intelligible sense. Hävernick translates, "or shall, on the other hand, my son's sceptre bear itself proudly, else despising every wood?" not only coupling the masculine שֵׁבֶט with the feminine מֹאֶסֶת, but giving also a quite arbitrary meaning to נָשִׂישׂ. The meaning I have given has, at least, the merit of doing no violence to the existing text, or to the received import of the words: "perchance (a quite common meaning of אוֹ) the sceptre (rod) of my son rejoiceth," or is glad—spoken, as I take it, ironically, as if the king of Judah, proudly presuming on being God's son (2 Sam. vii. 12, 14), could afford to exult at the display of God's sword,

because either expecting it to be drawn on behalf of his throne, or so, at least, as not to overthrow it. But the vain confidence is dispelled as soon as conceived. It (the sword, חֶרֶב, the only feminine nominative in the preceding context to agree with מָאֶסֶת) despises every tree, or all wood. It has no respect to the rod or sceptre of Judah, no more than if it were a piece of ordinary wood. And accordingly he goes on to say, that it is to be used against both the princes and the people of Judah.

[5] The word מְגוּרֵי, as is now commonly admitted, is the participle from מָגַר, to fall to, or throw. The princes of Israel were thrown to the sword, or given up to it.

[6] Here, again, the expression is very abrupt and difficult. Numberless modes of solution have been proposed, which it is needless to recount. The rendering adopted above is at once the simplest and the most easily understood. According to it, the prophet represents the sword of the Lord as the instrument by which all were to be subjected to a stern ordeal; such an ordeal as would not respect the very sceptre of the king, and hence would bring it to nothing. This, no more than other things, could stand the severe process of judgment, but should be made to disappear.

[7] I have simply given the literal rendering of the passage; but it is hard to say what is meant by the doubling of the sword threefold. De Wette gives, "Let it be repeated for the third time;" and Häv., "Let it be multiplied into threefold." But כָּפַל occurs elsewhere only in the sense of doubling (Ex. xxvi. 9, xxviii. 16), etc. Perhaps it may be taken as a pregnant construction,—The sword shall be doubled, shall even go into threefold, שְׁלִישִׁתָה—the ה indicating motion towards, the tendency in this direction: into twofold, as far even as threefold, according to the works of judgment to be executed.

[8] So the older Hebrew interpreters substantially understood the expression, הַחֹדֶרֶת לָהֶם. They took the verb as a denominative from חֶדֶר, *penetralia*, or inner chamber; hence gave it the meaning of penetrating into, or reaching within. The explanation has recently been somewhat modified from the Aramaic, where the noun has the import of a shut in, an enclosed place; and so Ewald, and after him Häv., Hitzig, render the expression in the text, "that encloses them." The other seems to me to be more natural, both as suiting the fierce action of the sword, and also because of the preposition ל, which seems to denote motion of some sort *towards*, *up to*.

[9] The expression אִבְחַת־חָרֶב is the glance or whirl of the sword. It occurs nowhere else. But אִבְחַת is understood to be=אִבְכַת, from אָבַךְ, to turn, or involve itself. It may indicate either the whirling glance, or the whirling motion of the sword, as going to be presented at all the gates. The one shade of meaning is preferred by some, and the other by others.

[10] The only ascertained meaning of עָטָה is to veil or cover; hence מְעֻטָּה לְטָבַח should be *covered for the slaughter*. Häv. gives from the Arabic, "drawn for slaughter." The LXX. have *εὖ γέγονεν*. It seems to be used in some secondary sense, denoting fitness or preparation for the terrible work.

[11] Literally, make or engrave a hand, וְיָד בָּרֵא. The old rendering of "appoint a place," is now justly exploded; for neither does יָד ever signify exactly a *place*, or בָּרָא to *appoint*. That the word יָד was sometimes used in much the same sense that our word *hand* is, as something to indicate or point out what was to be observed or known, is evident from 1 Sam. xv. 12, 2 Sam. xviii. 18, where hand-post or index-pillar must be meant. See also Deut. xxiii. 12: "And a hand (or sign-post) shall be to thee without the camp;" and Isa. lvi. 5. That בָּרָא is used in the sense of forming or engraving, needs no proof.

[12] The expressions here are chosen with great care to bring out an impressive sense: This way for the sword of the king of Babylon was not only to lead to Judah, but into Jerusalem, to settle and rest there, in the fortified—what then will its fortifications avail? In such a connection, the *fortified* has a strongly ironical meaning.

[13] The phrase אֵם הַדֶּרֶךְ, mother of the way, is peculiar, but there is no reason to think with Häv. that the Arabic sense of *highway* should be given to it. The point where the king stood was, as it were, the parent of ways. Two directions issued from it; the king hesitated which to take, and the prophet was, as by a finger-post, to indicate his course.

[14] These things are plainly mentioned as the practices that would naturally be followed by an idolater, such as the king of Babylon, in seeking direction regarding the course it was advisable for him to pursue. The inspection of the liver is known to have been particularly resorted to in such cases, even in the later periods of Greek and Roman History. The shaking of the arrows is not mentioned as a practice in divination among ancient European nations, although some earlier commentators, and still also Hitzig, held it to be much the same as the βελομαντία among the Greeks; but it is referred to in some old Arabic writings as formerly in use, Pockocke Specil. Hist. Arab. p. 329, etc.; also Sale's Koran, Prelim. Disc. sec. 5, makes mention of seven arrows kept in the temple at Mecca, for the purpose of divining, though only three were customarily used. The practice is condemned in the Koran among other superstitions (c. 5). In one of the sculptures brought from Nineveh, a representation is given of the king with a cup in his right hand, his left resting upon his bow, and then again with two arrows in his right hand and his bow in the left; and there is reason for supposing that he there appears practising the arts of divination, both by cup and arrows (Bonomi's Nineveh, pp. 263-5). The other action mentioned, inquiring at the teraphim, was an idolatrous practice too frequently resorted to by the covenant-people themselves. Indeed, this is the only passage where the use of teraphim is expressly ascribed to a heathen, although in 1 Sam. xv. 23, it is stigmatized as of an essentially heathen, and consequently obnoxious character, "Stubbornness is as iniquity and teraphim." They first appear as idol-gods of Mesopotamia, whence Rachel brought them by stealth out of her father's house, who expressly styles them "his gods." From the connection in which they are afterwards found, there can be little doubt that they were a sort of household gods, a kind of family talisman, worshipped with the general design of obtaining a blessing on the family, and at times also for the more special purpose of getting direction respecting the

future. There was consequently always a degree of superstition and idolatry connected with their use, and the idea of Horsley (on Hos. iii. 4), that they were probably at first symbolical figures, somewhat like the cherubim, and not improperly used in the worship of Jehovah, is entirely without foundation. The very first mention of them is in the way of disapprobation, as not only did Jacob disown having anything to do with them, but afterwards caused them to be buried under the oak at Shechem (Gen. xxxv. 4). The setting up of teraphim by Micah, as recorded in Judg. xvii. etc., and coupling them with the ephod (made after that of the high priest, by which he inquired of God), is in perfect accordance with what has been said: it indicated a family-worship, considerably corrupt, and closely connected with divination. And so must we regard the use of them here by the king of Babylon, for the purpose of getting direction in his course; the more so as he came from Mesopotamia, the original country of the teraphim. In Zech. x. 2 the false prophets are said to get their lying answers from teraphim.

[15] Here, again, there is room for considerable diversity of opinion. We have adopted the most natural rendering, and understand by the persons who had sworn oaths, the Jews, and by the Babylonians, the *them* to whom they had sworn. It certainly is rather strange that these Babylonians, to whom the *them* in this case refers, had not been previously mentioned, at least no further than as they were represented by the king of Babylon. To avoid this harshness, various other interpretations have been adopted. Häv.: "Oaths of oaths are to them;" meaning, they had very solemn oaths from the Lord, or pledges of his protection and support, on which they falsely relied—a very far-fetched interpretation. Ewald: "They thought they were to have weeks upon weeks"—changing the punctuation. But what even if they thought that? It still would not have evinced the divination to be false in their account. There is more of apparent reason in the interpretation of Jerome and some of the ancients, who take the words in substantially the same sense, but understood them as referring especially to the seventh day: keeping Sabbaths as if they were perfectly secure. But this also is strained and untenable. There can be little doubt, I think, that the words refer to the Jews; the divination which directed the course of Nebuchadnezzar to them, and promised him a successful siege, appear unworthy of credit to them, even as nothingness in their view—though they were in closest compact with the invaders (so I would be inclined to take the allusion, somewhat ironically), had sworn oaths of allegiance to them; these no longer secure unanimity of mind, or suffice to avert the brooding evil, because the iniquity of those who had sworn comes into remembrance for chastisement.

[16] That חָלָל here should be taken in the same sense in which it occurs at ver. 14, seems quite manifest; for it was evidently used there in the singular, and with the additional epithet הַגָּדוֹל, the mighty one, with express allusion to the king. The apparent contrariety between this sense and the actual result in history has led very generally to the adoption of the meaning of *profane*. But the word never properly signifies profane, and the grammatical sense must be retained, whatever consequences follow. The contrariety, however, is only apparent, as we shall show.

[17] מִצְנֶפֶת is never used for the crown of a king, but, as is now on all hands

admitted, denotes the mitre or head ornament of the high priest (Ex. xxviii. 4, etc.). See Ges. Lex., and Hengstenberg's Christol. on this passage.

[18] Quite similar descriptions are given of great revolutions and subversions of the established order of things in the other prophets—for example, Isa. xxiv. 1, ii. 12.

[19] Hengstenberg on the verse.

[20] I am inclined to adopt the latter view; authorities are very nearly equally divided on the matter. But I scarcely think the passages referred to for ascribing to מִשְׁפָּט the sense of right or prerogative, bear out that meaning, especially when used absolutely, as here. The common and usual meaning of the word undoubtedly is judgment, or right objectively, right as administered and done, the execution of righteousness. Now, while this in the full and primary sense is ascribed to God (Deut. i. 17), it is also ascribed, subordinately, to rulers, but especially to Messiah, as the grand representative and revealer of Godhead in the affairs of men (Ps. lxxii.; Isa. ix. 7, etc.). He is held out to men's hopes, in these and many similar passages, as the great avenger of evil, and the administrator of righteousness. Finally, this view appears to suit the connection much better. The contrast between those who then were in office and him that was to come was not as to the right to rule, but to the fitness and power for exercising the right. They had the right, but abused it; he was to exercise it with perfect rectitude; they had put all wrong, he was to put all right. I therefore hold with Hävernick here, in opposition to Hengstenberg, Hitzig, and many others, and believe with him that the promise has some reference to the word in Gen. xlix. 10. The sceptre was not to depart from Judah, nor a lawgiver from between his feet, till Shiloh come; but now, says Ezekiel, there shall be no crown till the Just One comes—a certain withdrawal meanwhile takes place—a mere fragment remains till then.

[21] The literal rendering here (taking לְהָכִיל as the infinitive of כּוּל, which seems the most natural derivation) would be—furbished for what it was capable, or as much as possible; the infinitive of the verb being taken adverbially.

[22] The meaning seems to be, that these Ammonites were to be added to the slain in Judah,—thrown, as it were, upon the decapitated bodies of those wicked men who had there perished in judgment, and whom they had imitated in their foolhardy and sinful ways.

[23] The destruction was to overtake them in their own territory; and the sentence at the beginning of the verse, "Let it return to the scabbard," may be understood thus:—The sword must do the work of destruction for which it is drawn; do not trouble yourselves to move out of your place; let it do its work, and then be sheathed; it is in vain to resist or strive against the doom.

[24] The word here is singular in the Hebrew, מַשְׁחִית, though it scarcely admits of being rendered but in the plural,—forgers of that which destroys —slaughter-weapons. There is an evident allusion to the language in Isa. liv. 16. But compare also Jer. v. 26.

CHAPTER XXII.

[1] These words are best understood as the reproach itself, which the surrounding countries cast against Jerusalem. They held her up to derision as utterly soiled in reputation, and, at the same time, involved in mischief. In name and reality alike evil.

[2] Our translators have here put the proper rendering in the margin, and retained a quite wrong one in the text. Most of the old translators and interpreters give the sense, "And I shall be profaned by thee." Conjectural emendations of the text are resorted to by Ewald and others, but without any necessity. The thought expressed is, that Jerusalem now appeared, from her depraved and miserable condition, as a polluted thing in the eyes of her heathen neighbours; and she had brought the reproach upon herself. It had not come upon her as a calamity, which she had no power to prevent; but she had, with her own hand, made herself vile.

[3] Such, undoubtedly, is the meaning of the expression חָמְסוּ תוֹרָתִי. It does not mean simply, that the priests personally transgressed the law, but that they dealt violently with it—wrested it in a way to suit their own selfish ends.

CHAPTER XXIII.

[1] There is no ground for doubting that קְרוֹבִים was used to express nearness of relation—neighbours; either in respect to juxtaposition, or to closeness of connection, as friends. Ps. xxxviii. 11 alone proves this, and seems also favourable to the meaning *neighbour* in the ordinary sense, rather than to that of relationship. The Assyrians, who at the time referred to were extending their dominions on every side, might properly enough be called, even locally, the neighbours of Israel. On the north-east the one kingdom certainly bordered on the other. Ewald's change of the text, and Hitzig's fanciful analysis to establish the sense *red*, can yield no satisfaction.

[2] Gesenius renders this clause, "redundant with mitres upon their heads," that is, "wearing long turbans hanging down from their heads." In this explanation he omits the idea of dyed or coloured usually connected with the טְבוּלִים, and, we think, without any sufficient reason; for the word is most naturally derived from טָבַל, to dip, whence *dyed* and *coloured* readily flow. It is also matter of historical certainty that the Assyrians delighted not only in loose and flowing, but also in richly coloured dresses. The recent discoveries amid the remains of Nineveh and Babylon have thrown fresh light upon this subject, and supply many illustrations of the description of Ezekiel in this chapter. In respect, generally, to the representations upon the monuments, we find that "the dresses furnish us with a proof of a state of great luxury. The robes of the Assyrians were generally ample and flowing, but differed in form from those of the Egyptians and the Persians. They consisted of tunics or robes varying in length, in mantles of divers shapes, of long fringed scarfs, and of embroidered girdles. Ornaments were scattered with profusion over these dresses, some of which appear to have been emblematic of certain dignities or employments. . . . Cyrus likewise is related by Xenophon to have given each of his superior officers and allies a dress of the Median fashion, *i.e.* long robes of a variety of the brightest colours, and

richly embroidered with gold and silver," etc. (Bonomi's Nineveh, p. 319.) It is needless to adduce quotations in proof of the practice of engraving and painting the figures of men, and especially of war scenes, upon the walls of houses, as it is now familiarly known to all. In these sculptures also the remains have been found of colouring in red, blue, and black.

[3] The chief peculiarity in this part of the description is the accumulation of names respecting the Babylonians, at ver. 23: "Sons of Babel, and all the Chaldeans, Pekod, and Shoa, and Koa;" but it is one in regard to which little information can be given. The LXX. simply give the Hebrew words. That they are designations, in some respect, of the Babylonians generally, and not names of persons or tribes belonging to the empire, seems certain. By a series of transformations, Hitzig brings them to signify different ranks—noble, and prince, and lord; good enough, certainly, if one could only get solid footing as to the ground on which liberties are taken with the particular words. Pekod is used by Jeremiah (chap. l. 21) as a designation of Babylon —*visitation*, punishment, denoting it as peculiarly the land of judgment. Perhaps it is used here to indicate that it was to be punishment in a double sense—first, actively against Judah, as well as afterwards passively in respect to herself. Shoa and Koa are explained by the ancient interpreters to mean much the same thing—rich and noble, or powerful: designations of the Babylonians as possessed of great resources—having all the world's dignity and opulence at their command.

[4] The meaning of this passage is, that she acted after receiving the cup of the Lord's anger, like a person utterly devoid of sense and reason, breaking in pieces the vessel itself from which she had drunk, and tearing her very breasts. The image of the cup in Scripture, as given from the Lord to an enemy, always conveys the idea of utter prostration and helpless impotence. —Comp. Jer. li. 7; Nahum iii. 11; Obad. v. 16; Hab. ii. 15, 16.

CHAPTER XXIV.

[1] The usual meaning of סָמַךְ is to lay against, to lean upon. Michaelis, Gesenius, and others have here imposed a different meaning on the word, and taken it in the sense of drawing near to, approaching. But Häv., Hitzig, properly adhere to the more exact and only ascertained meaning of laying against, or throwing oneself upon.

[2] There is no need for any change in the clause דּוּר הָעֲצָמִים תַּחְתֶּיהָ, either by regarding תַּחְתֶּיהָ, with Dathe, as superfluous, or with Newcome and many others substituting הָעֵצִים, wood, for bones. What the prophet means is, that the best, the fleshiest parts, full of the strongest bones, representing the most exalted and powerful among the people, were to be put within the pot and boiled; but that the rest, the very poorest, were not to escape: these, the mere bones, as it were, were to be thrown as a pile beneath, suffering first, and, by increasing the fire, hastening on the destruction of the others. דּוּר is properly a noun, a pile; literally: And also let there be a pile of the bones underneath. The expression cannot signify, with Häv., a pile of wood for the bones; for דּוּר is simply a pile, not a pile of wood, and when coupled with bones, can only mean a heap of these.

[3] This seems to me the preferable way of understanding the latter part of ver. 6. Most commentators, including Hävernick and Hitzig, render: bring forth piece after piece. But why drop the *it* connected with the verb הוֹצִיאָהּ? Bring it out—then, what it? The only thing made prominent in the preceding context is the poisonous scum; but it does not make sense to speak of bringing it forth piece by piece. This poisonous scum would not go out, the prophet had said, by such dealings as had already been resorted to; let it go out, then, he adds, upon each of the pieces in the pot; let the pot and its contents become alike infected with the corrupting taint: there is to be no lot cast, as if some were to escape; all were to be in the same category of evil. The communication of the poisonous scum is only to prepare the way for the application of the same consuming judgment to the caldron and its contents. And so the prophet immediately goes on to declare how the heaven-daring guilt was within and throughout the city, just as the poisonous scum was all through the pot and its pieces; whence all alike must suffer the vengeance of God's destroying judgment. The confusion here commonly fallen into has arisen chiefly from pressing too closely the reference to chap. xi. 7, where, certainly, the Lord speaks of fetching the people out of the caldron, and giving them up to strangers. But, in the passage before us, the idea throughout is of their being kept in the caldron till they were there utterly wasted and consumed.

[4] Blood is here mentioned as the consummation of all wickedness; that, the existence of which presupposes every other form of guilt. It is also brought specially into notice with a view to Gen. iv. 10, where, even though the ground did receive the blood of Abel, still it cried to Heaven for vengeance. Here the people are represented as, with shameless and hardened effrontery, setting the blood they had shed in the most exposed and prominent place, on the naked rock, where there was nothing to conceal it, or intercept its cry to Heaven. And the Lord says not only that they had spilt it there, but that he himself also had set it there; that is, he had ordered matters so as to make the blood appear thus prominent, that the connection between the guilt and the punishment might be more easily perceived. Hence the proposal of some, after the Septuagint, to change the text in ver. 7, so as to read: upon the parched rock *I* have put it, etc., instead of *she*, proceeds upon a superficial view of the passage. It was the city herself that did so, yet not without the overruling providence of God outwardly turning things into that direction; so that in one respect it might be said, she had set it, and in another, God had set it on the rock.

[5] The radical meaning of the verb רָקַח appears to be the artificial amalgamation of various substances into one, as in the case of the formation of sweet spices or ointments, usually done by pounding and boiling. Hence the meaning here of הַרְקַח הַמֶּרְקָחָה is, let it be sodden into a compound, or reduce it to a pulp. Vulgate: *coquatur universa compositio.*

[6] This is substantially the rendering of the Vulgate: *multo labore sudatum est.* **It indicates the pains or toilsome labours God had taken with Jerusalem to get her purified, but without effect; she had wearied them out, or allowed them to exhaust themselves without parting with her sins. תְּאֻנִים nowhere else occurs in the sense here ascribed to it; but there is**

now a general agreement that it bears this sense here, derived from the root און, which sometimes has the meaning of trouble or distress, and in Arab., of being fatigued.

7 The verb פָּרַע is used with considerable latitude. But the primary meaning seems to be that of uncovering, or making bare, in which sense it occurs in Num. v. 18, and other parts of the Pentateuch. Hence the secondary meaning of loose, relax, or dissolve, in which sense, probably, it is used, Ex. xxxii. 25, for the people were not properly naked, but in a relaxed and dissolute state. I take it in this sense also here. In Prov. i. 25, and other places, it bears the still stronger sense of unbridled, lawless, or contemptuous treatment. It never means to *go back*.

8 The literal rendering here is: dead-persons' mourning thou shalt not do or make. Storr, and after him Hävernick, render: the dead shalt thou not make for mourning, *i.e.* shalt not take for an occasion or object of mourning. A very artificial sort of construction, and liable, besides, to the objection of mentioning dead persons as those for whom the mourning should naturally have been made, while in reality there was only one. The expression is evidently, like all the rest, of a quite general kind, referring to what was wont to take place on such occasions; so that dead-persons' mourning was mourning appropriate to such.

9 "Bread of men" can only mean such bread as men in circumstances of bereavement and distress usually eat; and hence, though it undoubtedly suggests the idea of poor or unsavoury food, yet we are not on that account to render with some: the bread of the mourning, or the wretched.

10 The two first of the passages referred to show that it was a natural and becoming sign of grief in priests to take off their head-dress, at least in times of peculiar distress; while others, it would seem, rather veiled and covered their heads in times of mourning (2 Sam. xv. 30, etc.). The reason, doubtless, was, that the priests had their head-dress given them for ornament, as an appropriate badge of office; and on this account, as well as from being made of fine twined linen, it was unsuitable for a time of mourning. Besides this and other ornaments peculiar to himself, the high priest also had on his head the holy anointing oil, and was therefore forbidden, as mentioned in the second of the above passages, to lay aside his head-dress in *any* case of mourning; since it would have been to dishonour that by which he was specially consecrated to his high office, to disrobe himself of his mitre, and, after the common custom, wrap his head in sackcloth and ashes. The priests generally, however, might do this, though only in the case of the death of their nearest relatives (Lev. xxi. 1–3). It is of course to be understood that the putting off of the mitre or head-band in such cases was in order to the putting on of inferior attire, with the addition of dust or ashes.

CHAPTER XXV.

1 The כִּי in these three clauses ought plainly to be taken in the usual sense, *for*, assigning the cause of the joy and contempt of the Ammonites, and not *when*, as in our common version and many others.

2 The common meaning of טִירָה is undoubtedly a pen or fold for flocks, and is the only suitable meaning here, where the discourse is of shepherd tribes. *Palaces*, the rendering of the Authorized Version, is quite unsuitable.

[3] "Into couching of flocks." I take לְמִרְבַּץ־צֹאן to be a sort of complex phrase, made up of the noun denoting the subject, and the participle indicating the position or attitude; couching flocks, or flocks in a couching position; *couching* being added to render the idea more graphic—flocks for men, and not that merely, but flocks in a state of perfect repose. It makes no proper sense: children of Ammon into a couching-place of flocks; for what sort of revolution could change men into places, lairs for flocks? What the prophet means to declare is evidently that flocks were to take the place of men, or that the fertile parts of the territory were, by changes to the worse, to become pastoral.

[4] The Kri reading here, לְבַז instead of לַבַּג, is almost universally adopted. Häv. defends the text, and would derive the word from the Sanscrit, *bhagga*, *part* or *portion*. This, of course, would render the meaning nearly the same, whichever word were adopted. But as לבג is nowhere else found in Hebrew, and so many codices also read לבז that it has been actually received into the text in the Complutensian Bible, we incline to prefer the latter. The ancient versions express this sense.

[5] The accents are manifestly wrong here, as the *to Dedan* is required after *from Teman* to complete the sense. Our translators, by following them, have confused the meaning of the passage.

[6] There is a paronomasia here in the original, which is preserved in the Vulgate: *interficiam interfectores*, I will slay the slayers—the Philistines being perhaps so designated from their warlike and cruel disposition. But Cherethim is also used as a proper name, the same probably with Cretans —the Philistines being supposed to be of Cretan extraction. (Comp. Jer. xlvii. 4; Amos ix. 7; Deut. ii. 23; Vitringa on Isa. xiv. 28.)

CHAPTER XXVI.

[1] Grote's Hist. of Greece, III. p. 240.

[2] There is here a peculiarity in the construction, דַּלְתוֹת—a plural being coupled with a verb in the singular. We find quite a similar construction in Jer. li. 58, in regard to the walls of Babylon. And here, probably, the plural has reference merely to the folding-leaves of the gates—the single gate composed of two parts, as at chap. xli. 24.

[3] I give here what I take to be the proper meaning of the words, rather than a literal translation. מְחִי is evidently a noun from מָחָה, which, as Hävernick notes, is always used in the sense of destroying, extirpating, etc.; therefore, not *percussio*, as many take it, but rather *extirpatio*, destruction. קְבֵל is anything in front of or opposition to another; hence קָבָלּוֹ is a general designation of what the enemy was to put in hostile array against the walls of Tyre—his enginery. So that the two words together may best be rendered: his enginery of destruction, or the destruction of his enginery.

[4] It certainly sounds rather strange to speak of breaking down towers with swords; and on this account our translators, with the greater part of commentators, substitute axes or hatchets for swords. But חֶרֶב is not elsewhere used of any warlike instrument, except the sword. In Ex. xx. 25, it seems to denote an iron tool for hewing stones; and perhaps the general

meaning of iron or steel might, with Ewald, be adopted here: Thy towers he breaks down with his iron. It is rather against this, however, that the word is plural, and so appears to denote specific instruments. We therefore adhere to the usual meaning, *swords;* believing, with Hävernick, that the coupling of swords with the destruction of towers was intended to heighten the idea of the extraordinary and resistless character of the Babylonians, who, as God's instruments of vengeance, would do with their swords what common warriors could not attempt. Compare as a like mark of the peculiar and extraordinary, though on a different account, the lines in the ode on Sir John Moore:—

> "We buried him darkly by dead of night,
> The sods with our bayonets turning."

[5] It seems evident from the use of גַּלְגַּל here, and in chap. xxiii. 24, also x. 13, that it is employed by our author not in the ordinary sense of *wheels*, as part of a conveyance, but for a separate conveyance or instrument of operations. He means by it some sort of wheelwork, whether as a car for riding on, or for the operations of the siege.

[6] *Imbreached*, if we had such a word, would be the exact meaning of the original here. The prophet intimates, that strong and impregnable as the fortifications of Tyre were deemed, a breach would be made in them, through which, as in other vanquished cities, the army should enter. Even Tyre's sea-girt position, and massy walls to the water's edge, would not be sufficient to prevent the catastrophe.

[7] I adhere to the usual meaning of מַצֵּבָה, a statue or pillar. It is nowhere found in the sense of garrison, as a thing that could be thrown down,—a military fort or building. It is commonly used of sacred or monumental pillars. And possibly some allusion is made here to the famous pillars in the temple of Hercules (Herod. ii. 44).

[8] Cautious and reverential students of the prophetic word have in every age noted the peculiarity above referred to, though they have not always made a judicious use of it. Even Abarbinel has the following remark concerning it: *morem hunc esse prophetarum*, etc., "that it is the custom of the prophets in their predictions to have respect at once to a near and a remote period; so that prophecies pointing to very distant times are found amongst others which relate to the immediate future. Whence we may the more certainly conclude, that God might threaten the Tyrians with the destruction of their city, though it might be brought on at different times and by gradual advances."

[9] "Quod quum viderent Tyrii jam jamque perfectum, et percussione arietum, murorum fundamenta quaterentur, quidquid pretiosum in auro, argento, vestibusque, et varia supellectili nobilitas habuit, impositum navibus ad insulas asportavit; ita ut capta urbe, nihil dignum labore suo inveniret Nebuchodonosor" (on chap. xxix. 18).

[10] For the proof of the facts last referred to, see the passages from Menander and Philostratus in Josephus; also Ezra, iii. 7; Herod. vii. 99, 100; viii. 67; or Movers' Das Phönizische Alterthum, c. 11, where the matter is fully investigated. Even Gesenius, on Isa. xxiii., holds it as certain that the Tyrians, if not actually overthrown, must have been brought to terms by Nebuchadnezzar, "as we see that subsequently the Tyrians sent to Babylon

to fetch Merbal, one of their later kings" (referring to Jos. c. Ap. i. 21). In a matter of this kind, it is only the broader statements of history that should be brought into notice, especially as the historical fragments to be depended on are from the pen, not of contemporary writers, but of persons who lived two or more centuries after the events in question, and who merely wrote compends of history. In such a case it is unwise to urge little points, as it only gives the adversary an opportunity of pressing improbabilities or inconsistencies in the accounts relied on. Hengstenberg, and in part also Hävernick, have in this way laid themselves open, at various points, to the attacks of a sharp and unsparing writer like Hitzig, who has a quick eye for any small discrepance or mistake, but does not know often how to estimate things of greater moment. It is unwise, also, to speculate about the probable way which Nebuchadnezzar took to carry the siege of Tyre, whether by mounds, floats, or ships, or by any other means. No information has come down to us on the subject; but surely it is not to be supposed that such a monarch as Nebuchadnezzar, accustomed to such gigantic undertakings, was to conduct a thirteen years' siege without resorting to prodigious appliances of some sort. See for proof of such in Movers, p. 446, sq.

[11] Literally, Thou that art inhabited from the seas. The rendering adopted by our translators, "inhabited of sea-faring men," though supported by Grotius and others, is quite untenable, as it arbitrarily substitutes sea-farers for seas, and regards such sea-farers, persons merely coming for traffic to Tyre, as its proper inhabitants. The Targum and the Peschito already give the correct meaning, *habitatrix marium;* the Vulgate, not quite so correctly, *quæ habitas in mari.* It denotes Tyre as a prosperous city rising out of the seas, appearing as if she had got thence her very inhabitants, being peopled so closely down to the waters. The rendering of the LXX., which gives, "destroyed out of the sea," is another specimen of the loose character of their translation of Ezekiel. They evidently mistook the verb for a part of שָׁבַת.

[12] Hitzig, with some reason, ridicules the very forced and artificial construction adopted by Hävernick of this clause: Tyre's inhabitants (her home-people), who kept in terror all the inhabitants (namely, the inhabitants of her colonies, who might still be called her own). Understood thus, it is certainly, as Hävernick styles it, "a somewhat enigmatical sentence." Hitzig supposes, as very commonly, a corruption in the text, and would prefer the more abbreviated reading of the LXX.: "the renowned city that put her terror on all her inhabitants"—finding *inhabitants* only once in the passage. But there is no need for this change. When the prophet had said that Tyre was strong in the sea, he specifies both the city itself and its inhabitants as sharing in this strength; and then adds, that they (the people and city viewed complexly—the state) put their terror upon all her inhabitants—that is, not only were, as a whole, objects of fear to others, but communicated of this to every one of her people; causing the name of a Tyrian to be everywhere dreaded.

[13] The negative in this verse ought undoubtedly to be applied to both clauses: not be inhabited, and not set as an ornament. The Chaldee, and those who followed it, understood the last clause to refer to Judah, and hence took it positively. But the LXX. properly understood both clauses of Tyre,

and took both negatively. The *because* or *in that*, at the beginning of the whole passage, is to be explained as a construction *ad sensum*. The reason is here given of what goes before.

[14] For the extraordinary number and extent of these colonial possessions of Tyre, see Heeren, Phœnicians, chap. ii.

CHAPTER XXVII.

[1] The מְבוֹאֹת יָם are the openings, the inlets or outlets, by which one finds communication with the sea, in going and coming; hence its ports (as from the Latin *porta*, the gate that opens out and in to a city, there is *portus*, that does the same to the sea). Insular Tyre was remarkable for its good harbours: ancient writers specially notice two—one on the north, and another on the south.

[2] Senir was the Sidonian name for Hermon (Deut. iii. 9). Instead of fir-trees, some read cypresses, which is countenanced by Sirach, xxiv. 13, where the cypress is named as the peculiar production of Hermon. The names of trees, in Scripture, are not very accurately defined. The cedar of Lebanon is well known from its height, durability, and strength; hence, well adapted for the purpose here mentioned—making masts. It is also matter of history that the Tyrians obtained wood for their costlier buildings from these mountains. See especially Josephus, Antiq. viii. 5.

[3] Instead of the punctuation of the Hebrew text, making two words of בַּת־אֲשֻׁרִים, the junction of the two, long ago proposed by the Chaldee: *asseres buxeos ebore obductos*, also adopted by Rabbi Solomon, has been sanctioned by Bochart, and is now, indeed, generally acquiesced in. It becomes then, *with bashurim*, a sort of trees. But instead of the box-tree, Ges. Thes. would understand a species of cedar to be meant; the same as תְּאַשּׁוּר in Isa. xli. 19, lx. 13—though here he retains the received text, and renders *transtra tua fecerunt ex ebore, filia cedorum, i.e. cedro incluso.* He refers for a parallel to Virgil, Aen. x. 137, *inclusum buxo ebur.* By the קַרְשֵׁךְ have very commonly been understood, the benches on which the rowers sat; but as there were tiers of these at each side of the vessel, the singular is rather against the supposition. It is more probably the deck, as Hitzig suggests, that is meant, which was one piece, though made up of separate parts.

[4] The meaning of the verse is, that the fine quality of the sailcloth, and the embroidery upon it, was instead of a pennant or standard; it served the purpose of this. Several of the plates in Wilkinson's Egypt show what expense was sometimes gone into by the ancients in decorating their sails. There is a general agreement among commentators that by Elisha Greece is to be understood, but they differ in the mode of explanation—some identifying it with Elis in the Peloponesus; others, with Hellas. Laconian purple was renowned.

[5] When the men of Zidon and Arvad (Aradus) are mentioned as oarsmen in the ships of Tyre, it denotes the relative superiority of Tyre; these also were very important Phœnician cities, yet their men sought employment in the merchant vessels of Tyre, certainly not working as slaves, but with the view of bettering their condition.

[6] The people of Lud and Phut are not certainly known, but most probably were Lydians and Libyans. See at ch. xxx. 5, where the words again occur.

[7] The *Gammadims* of our version ought to be translated; there is no trace whatever of such a people; and the position which the persons in question are said to have occupied, that of keeping watch in the towers, is one that would never have been entrusted to foreigners. The sense also adopted by Hitzig and some others, *deserters* (namely, from other countries) is arbitrary and unsuitable. I follow those, among whom is Hävernick, who, from the Arabic, obtain the sense of hardy, strong, daring, or enterprising. The stout-hearted and daring occupied her watch-towers.

[8] נָתְנוּ עִזְבוֹנָיִךְ, not as in the received translation, "they traded in thy fairs;" but, they made thy exchanges, or did barter with thee. The noun is from the verb עָזַב, to leave; hence, "that which you leave to any one, for something else given you by him in regular barter" (Gussetius). So also Ewald, Hävernick, and others. The richness of Tarshish, the Latin Tartessus, and that part of Spain in which it was situated, in the precious metals mentioned in this part of the text, is well known.

[9] Javan, the Ionians or Greeks; Mesech, the Moschi, in the Moschian mountains, between Armenia, Iberia, and Colchis, a rough and warlike race; Tubal, the Tibareni in Pontus; all, in short, of Greece, or connected with it. The souls of men, in which these races are said to have trafficked with Tyre, are the slaves which, when obtained from certain parts of Greece and the surrounding countries, were particularly prized in ancient times.

[10] The פָּרָשִׁים must here mean a certain kind of horses—horses for riding; as it could not be the prophet's design to class horsemen with horses and mules as articles of trade. That the word has this meaning also in other passages, see Gesenius, Lex. Togarmah is Armenia.

[11] "Horns of ivory," were so called because of the resemblance of ivory, in its original state, to horns; not, as some have gratuitously supposed, because the ancients falsely imagined ivory was obtained from the horns of certain animals.

[12] Instead of Syria, Aram, some codices, LXX., Peschito, read Edom; and many commentators prefer this reading. Neither of the two names is unsuitable, though from the connection we might rather have expected Edom than Aram. The precious stone meant by נֹפֶךְ, according to the most ancient authorities, was carbuncle, not emerald—so Sept., Josephus, Epiphanius, and the Jer. Talmud. See Ges. Thes.

[13] Minnith was originally an Ammonite city (Judg. xi. 33). Of Pannag we know nothing; hence some translate it here, and give it the meaning of sweet things generally. But if held to be a proper name, then it and Minnith must be regarded as places remarkable for the finest qualities of wheat.

[14] Wine of Chalybon was so famous, that the kings of Persia are reported to have used it in preference to all others.

[15] There is great difficulty in determining how the proper names in this verse ought to be taken. "And Dan," with which the verse begins in our version, is open especially to the two objections—that none of the parts in the prophet's enumeration begin with *And*, and that *Dan* also would be quite out of place here. It seems better, therefore, to read Vedan as one word, and

to understand it of some place unknown. From the products specified, one would expect to find some Arabian cities or people mentioned. The conjecture of Tuch (on Gen. x. 27), that by Javan here might possibly be meant a Greek settlement in Arabia in the neighbourhood of Uzal, a town in Yemen, is not improbable. Yemen was distinguished for its manufacture of fine sword-blades, which may be the wrought or polished iron here specified. The other things were the natural products of Arabia.

[16] When Arabia is mentioned separately, it is commonly the Nomadic portion that is meant; and especially must that be understood here when it is coupled with the princes of Kedar, the heads, in a manner, of the shepherd tribes. Hence the articles of traffic named are of the flocks.

[17] Shebah and Raamah, two ancient places in Arabia (Gen. x. 7).

[18] I follow Horsley in this way of reading the names of the verse, which appears to me decidedly preferable to Hävernick's: "Haran and Canneh and Aden are dealers of Saba; (but) Assur, Chilmad are thy customers." For it seems very unnatural to bring in here those who dealt with Saba, and not less so, to couple all Assyria with some obscure place or district like Chilmad. I think they ought all to be regarded as mentioned here simply on account of their relation to Tyre. The places appear partly to be Arabian and partly Assyrian.

[19] The אֲרֻזִים here is now generally taken for part. pas. of an unused root, in the sense of closely bound together; hence, compact, strong—a sense still retained in the Arabic. In this sense it is a fit designation of the wares spoken of, the בְּרֹמִים—a very doubtful word, found only here, but supposed to mean woven stuffs, made up of various kinds of threads—damasks. If the אֲרֻזִים is taken in the sense of cedars; or, as an adj. *cedrine* (with Ges.), it must qualify not the wares spoken of, but the bundles or chests in which they were put—as if the prophet laid stress on the mere ornamenting of the exterior of the packages.

[20] To call the ships of Tarshish the walls of Tyre, has been thought so peculiar as to justify a departure from the received meaning of שָׁרוֹת. But there is endless diversity in the renderings adopted. The Vulgate: *principes;* our translators: kings; and to mention no more, Hitzig, the last commentator, while on Jer. v. 10, he had proposed for the passage before us *ship-masts*,—he now abandons this, and would read שְׂדוֹתַיִךְ, thy fields: "The fitting out and freighting of ships with goods was, in a manner, the cultivation of the land. The importation of all the treasures, which the ships brought back in return, was the land's produce"!! A strong figure truly! For ourselves, we think the received text, and the ascertained meaning of *walls*, afford a greatly more natural explanation. The ships of Tarshish, meaning by these, perhaps, not so much the ships that belonged to that particular place, as rather ships of the size usually trading thither, the largest and finest merchant-vessels—these were the walls of thy merchandise, or as to thy merchandise; at once the bulwarks of thy commercial greatness, and the means by which its traffic was carried on. To name such ships as peculiarly hers, seemed all one with naming walls of security and defence as to her mercantile prosperity.

CHAPTER XXVIII. 1–19.

[1] Why *deaths* here, and in ver. 10, and not rather *death?* Because, say Origen, Tertullian, Jerome, Ambrose, and Augustine, are carefully brought together in Villalpandus, who himself agrees with those who took a middle course, ascribing what was said partly to the prince of Tyre and partly to Satan.

[2] Why *deaths* here, and in ver. 10, and not rather *death?* Because, say **some, various kinds of death are referred to ; or, because the abstract idea (as made up of the several particulars) is thus denoted when raised to its highest form. No, says Häv., "the plural is only used of death when several persons are spoken of." This is not so clear. Isa. liii. 9 is not quite easily explained on that principle. And certainly the apostle Paul, whose style of thought was quite Hebraistic, used the plural in reference to different kinds, when he says, "in deaths oft."**

[3] Literally, according to the present text and punctuation, which I take to be correct, "Thou art the one sealing exactness." For חוֹתֵם is the participle, and consequently means *obsignans*, sealing, the person sealing. Instead of תָּכְנִית, all the ancients appear to have read תָּבְנִית, as they give the sense of similitude or resemblance, and many moderns still prefer this to the received text. But this, of course, necessitates the further change of חוֹתָם for חוֹתֵם, seal for sealing ; and is to be rejected as arbitrary. The noun is from תָּכַן, to weigh, to measure exactly, to level, etc.; hence applicable to anything that is of an exact or perfect nature. In chap. xliii. 10, the prophet uses it of the complete or perfect pattern he had exhibited of the temple; and here more generally, of what is every way exact or complete. To say of the king of Tyre that he sealed up this, was, in other words, to declare him every way complete: he gave, as it were, the finishing stroke, the seal, to all that constitutes completeness; or, as we would now say it, he was a normal man—one formed after rule and pattern. Hence it is immediately explained by what follows: "full of wisdom and perfect in beauty;" in this stood his sealing completeness. Thus, without any alteration in the text, or even in the punctuation, we get a much more suitable meaning than can be obtained even by conjectural emendations. Take, for example, Hitzig's: "Thou art a curiously wrought seal-ring," a seal-ring full of wisdom. No wonder that, with such a commencement, he should have had to resort to many other alterations, and should have held the whole passage to be very corrupt.

[4] The representation of the king of Tyre as the normal or perfect man, not unnaturally led the prophet back to the garden of Eden, where the man that really was such had his abode; and so he ironically represents this assumed pattern of perfection as having his local habitation there, in the normal land—just as afterwards (chap. xxxi. 8, 9, xxxvi. 35) the garden of Eden is variously employed by him as the region of ideal beauty and perfection. But occupying such a blessed region, all objects of natural preciousness and beauty of course lay at the king's command; and as we are told in Genesis (chap. ii.) of the gold and the jewels with which that land originally abounded, so here the prophet speaks of them as forming the very apparel of the king. How much also Oriental monarchs are in the habit of bespangling and almost literally covering themselves with such things, is well known.

A notion very early prevailed, that the precious stones here mentioned were those of the high-priest's breastplate; and on that account, it is supposed, the LXX. translator made up their number to twelve. Even still Ewald and Hitzig think that respect was had to those sacred gems in this enumeration, and the former even regards the mention of them here as connected with an instrument of oracular wisdom and purposes of divination. The idea in any form is entirely gratuitous and out of place. The rendering of the names for the different jewels is what is now generally adopted. We deem it needless to enter into details.

[5] Endless changes and arbitrary meanings have been resorted to from the earliest times, to lighten the difficulty of this last clause of ver. 13. I adhere to the received text, and the most natural meanings. תֻּפִּים has no other signification in Scripture than *tambourines*, or kettle-drums, an instrument of music in frequent use among the Orientals, and commonly played on by women. נְקָבִים, on the other hand, is never found of a musical instrument, such as *pipes*, the rendering adopted by our translators and many others. Indeed, as a plural word it never occurs at all; and the only single word which can be thought of is נְקֵבָה, female. Elsewhere, however, it is used only to denote the female sex, not precisely women; and there is besides the anomaly of a masculine instead of a feminine termination. Yet this is not without a parallel, as appears from such examples as נשים, women, and on the other side, אבות, fathers, the first with a masculine, the other with a feminine termination. I think, therefore, with Hävernick, that the objects denoted here are the musical instruments, tambourines, and the women who played on them; and that this peculiar word נְקֵבָה, female, rather than any other, was used, because of the reference which the passage bears to Gen. i. 27, "Male and female created he them." Tambourines, and female musicians to play on them, were provided for this king of Tyre on the day of his creation; that is, from the very first, from the period of his being a king, he was surrounded with the customary pleasures, as well as the peculiar treasure, of kings. The royal house of Tyre (for it is of this at large that the discourse must be understood) had not, like many others, to work its way with difficulty and through arduous struggles, but started at once into the full possession of royal power and splendour; no sooner formed than, like Adam, surrounded with fitting attendants and paradisiacal delights. So already Michaelis: "All things poured in around thee which could minister to thy necessities, thy comfort, or even thy pleasure, as they did formerly to Adam in the garden of Eden, which God granted to him."

[6] Here, again, a great many expedients have been resorted to, both in the way of textual alterations, and extraordinary meanings. The chief verbal difficulty hangs on מִמְשַׁח, which nowhere else occurs; and the Vulgate rendering of *extentus* (the LXX. omits it altogether) has led to the supposition that it was derived from some Aramaic root, signifying to extend. But there is no solid ground for this, though it has the anthority of Gesenius. The Chaldaic version gives the sense of *anointing*, taking it as a derivative from מָשַׁח in its usual meaning. And one does not see why there might not be מִמְשַׁח, anointing, from מָשַׁח, as well as מִמְכָּר, sale, from מָכַר, or מִמְשַׁל,

government, from מָשַׁל. Indeed, in this very chapter, in ver. 24, we have a verbal adjective formed in precisely the same way, מַמְאִיר from *hiphil* of מָאַר, bitter or painful, from to make bitter. Cherub of anointing would thus make substantially the same sense as the anointed cherub, כְּרוּב הַמָּשְׁחִית; the cherub that is consecrated to the Lord by the anointing oil. In regard to the next difficulty in the passage, which respects "the holy mountain of God on which he was," Hävernick says, it would indeed be a wonderful representation, if the prophet described the king of Tyre as having been placed on Mount Sion, and he therefore renders *a* holy God's mount, on which he was raised aloft, as a being of a higher nature, as one of those hill-gods, whom the Syrians worshipped (1 Kings xx. 23). But the *holy* hill of God can only be understood of a mount which has been consecrated by peculiar manifestations of Godhead—therefore, either Mount Sinai, or Mount Sion, which is elsewhere named "the holy hill of God." And if the king of Tyre could be placed in God's garden, surely he might also be placed on God's hill. The objection proceeds on a misapprehension of the nature of the representation. Hävernick is no happier in regard to the next expression, the stones of fire, amid which the king is said to have walked. He considers it to have respect to the worship of the Tyrian Hercules as the fire-god, and to the two pillars in his temple, the one of gold, the other of emerald, which were kept shining by night. But as Hitzig justly remarks, these were not stones, but pillars, and only one of them of stone, and even that not fiery, though resplendent. Besides, what a confusion would it make to throw together in one sentence God's holy mount and any emblems of fire-worship in the city of Tyre! The reference seems to be to the description in Ex. xxiv., where Moses and the elders of Israel are said to have gone up to the mount to meet God, and to see "under his feet as it were a paved work of sapphire-stone," while "the sight of the glory of the Lord was like devouring fire on the top of the mount." It is just another mode of expressing the peculiar nearness of the King of Tyre to God: he was on God's holy mount, where he trod, as it were, the very stones that are beneath the feet of God—stones of fire; for all is fire where God has his dwelling.

[7] This 16th verse also contains several difficulties; at least what have been regarded as such. The clause, "they have filled thy midst with violence," which beyond all question is the literal rendering of the text, has been thought to give an unsuitable meaning—one applicable rather to the city as a whole than personally to the king—and hence supposed corruptions in the text, and also violent renderings. We refer only to Hävernick's, who abides by the existing text, but forces it into a meaning strictly applicable to the king; therefore תָּוֶךְ must denote middle in the physical sense of *venter*, belly, or the body with respect to its middle part; and the plural verb must be explained by a peculiar construction, according to which an active is sometimes substituted in the place of a passive, even where it is not quite suitable; thus the sense is obtained, "they have filled thy body," for "thou art filled as to thy body, with violence." It is not sense after all. If it had been *lust*, or wickedness generally, that was represented as filling him, one could have made something of such an interpretation. And so, indeed, Hävernick shoves in *frevel*, wickedness, instead of violence, when he comes to give the

general import, but without any right to do so. The Vulgate long ago gave substantially the same rendering: *in multitudine negotiationis tuæ repleta sunt interiora tua iniquitate.* But besides, no example can be produced of תָּוֶךְ ever signifying either the inward parts of a man or his body in general; though used with great frequency, it is always in the sense of *midst*—the middle of a great city, a people, or such like. Therefore I adopt, as the only natural rendering, "they have filled thy midst with violence;" which undoubtedly has respect to the city, but not, it must be remembered, without at the same time implicating the king. He, as head of the state, is to a certain extent identified with the whole of it; and he is evidently viewed in that light here. For when the prophet says, "by the greatness of thy traffic," he plainly includes the state along with the king; and when he says further, that through this "his midst was filled with violence," what does it indicate but that he had not ruled as he should have done, for righteousness? He had become the head of a state that was filled with violence; and so it is immediately added, "and *thou* hast sinned." Thou hast not restrained the iniquity that prevails around thee; so far from it, thou art thyself also a transgressor. Thus understood, there is quite a natural meaning, and a regular progression of thought. It is admitted on all hands that the מָלוּ of the received text is for מָלְאוּ (which also stands in many codices), as מָלֵתִי for מָלֵאתִי in Job xxxii. 18. The expression, "and I profane thee from the mount of God," is quite similar to, "thou hast profaned his crown to the ground," in Ps. lxxxix. 39. In both cases it is a pregnant construction, and means that the person was dealt with as no longer sacred but profane, and as such was driven from the position of honour he had hitherto held to a despicable place.

[8] The sanctuaries which the king of Tyre is charged with having profaned, are to be understood of the sacred places with which the prophet had in the preceding verses associated him, viz. the holy mount of God, and the garden of God. It is his ideal position there, not his actual position in the city of Tyre, that is meant; for the latter could in no proper sense be called his sanctuary, still less, in the plural, his sanctuaries. And the fire, that is presently afterwards represented as going out of his midst and reducing him to ashes—so different as an instrument of destruction from the violent hands of strangers shortly before mentioned—was doubtless suggested by the stones of fire amid which in those ideal sanctuaries he had his abode. So far from finding it a good thing for him to have dwelt there, now that he had sinned, there would proceed thence, as it were, a consuming fire against him; his very elevation, having been abused, carried with it the element of his destruction.

CHAPTER XXVIII. 20–26.

[1] The only verbal peculiarity in the passage, is in the epithet here applied to brier, מַמְאִיר. Gesenius derives it from מָאַר taken as synonymous with מָרַר, to be bitter; hence the word here, anything causing bitterness, vexing. מַמְאֶרֶת is applied to the leprosy, when found to be fixed and settled (Lev. xiii. 51, 52), where our translators have rendered it *fretting.* The ancient

versions, Vulgate, Syriac, express the sense of bitterness in the passage before us; the noun evidently requires something of that sort.

CHAPTER XXIX.

[1] Wilkinson's Ancient Egyptians, vol. i. p. 169.

[2] Herodotus, ii. 169.

[3] There can be no reasonable doubt that it is the crocodile which is here meant by תַּנִּים. Both it and the word *leviathan* are used in the prophetic Scriptures with considerable latitude, and in a kind of general sense denoting any huge aquatic animal, or the larger species of serpents—monsters, whether of the water or of the dry land. The crocodile was this peculiarly in respect to the Nile, and precisely answers to the description here, being covered with scales, each with a high horned crest, which render the skin almost impenetrable through them, and give to the animal a very formidable appearance. To the ancients generally it was an object of great dread, though in some parts of Egypt it was worshipped as a divinity. More commonly, however, it was killed as an object of horror, and was usually caught by means of hooks. The term *streams* was very often applied to the Nile in antiquity, with reference to the canals and branches that were derived from it, and also probably its various mouths.

[4] The expression here is evidently elliptical, "I have made (it) me," for "I have made (it) to me." The suffix has therefore the force of לִי.

[5] The crocodile is here plainly regarded as the lord of the Nile, just as Pharaoh was of Egypt. The fish, therefore—the smaller inhabitants of the water—are viewed as properly belonging to this monster, and following his fate; so that when he was caught, and laid out as a helpless carcase on the sandy desert, these all came along with him, and lay there too. It intimates that Pharaoh and his people together should be brought forth as victims for slaughter.

[6] That is, as I understand it, lettest them stand the best way they can, stand themselves, if they are able for it—if not, fall. Most modern commentators consider that there is a transposition of the letters, and that הַעֲמַדְתָּ is for הַמְעַדְתָּ, which is used in Ps. lxix. 23, in connection also with loins; so that the sense would be, and dost make all their loins to shake. This seems to have been the view taken by the earlier translators, as the LXX. has συνέκλασας; the Vulgate, *dissolvisti;* the Syr., *concussisti.* Yet I do not feel warranted in resorting to this licence with the text. Besides the meaning obtained is rather flat. The mere crushing of the reed is said to have rent their shoulder by the splinters that flew off from it; and one would naturally expect something more to come from the utter breaking of it than the mere shaking or trembling of their loins. A piercing to death would have been more according to our expectations. The prophet, as I understand him, refrains from expressing this result in so many words; but yet virtually expresses it, by saying that the effect of leaning on the reed was that it broke and left the loins to stand for themselves—loins that felt they could not so stand, and whose worst misfortune was to be thus bereft of the power that had failed them; for falling and destruction then became

inevitable. The image is plainly borrowed from Isa. xxxvi. 6; but is to be understood of present not of former times.

[7] Our translators have obscured the meaning of this clause, by translating Migdol, and rendering, from the tower of Syene. The words mark the two extremities of the land: Migdol, the same as Magdolum, a fortress near Pelusium on the north, and Syene in the farthest south; then across to the borders of Ethiopia.

[8] By Pathros is understood the upper part of Egypt, as distinguished from the lower—the Thebaid. That, it is now generally agreed, was the most ancient part of Egypt, as to civilisation and art—"the school of learning and the parent of Egyptian science," as Wilkinson calls it (vol. i. p. 4). He also afterwards quotes Aristotle's words, "that the Thebaid was formerly called Egypt;" and those of Herodotus, that "Egypt in ancient times was called Thebes." This part of the country in particular is here named the birthplace of the Egyptians, or rather, Egypt under this name is styled the native region of the people; because that district appears to have had the priority over the rest, and now matters had to start as it were from a new beginning.

[9] It was from Egypt setting herself forth, and being accepted by Israel as a ground of confidence, that she was a remembrancer of iniquity; for she thus served as a witness in regard to the people's departure from God. But she was to be too much reduced to do that any more.

[10] I give here the most literal rendering possible, to show that the words do not, as formerly mentioned, imply an utter failure and the loss of all profit in respect to the siege of Tyre, but only one in no degree proportioned to the time and labour expended, and in that respect as good as none. *For the service* is equivalent to *according to the service;* so עַל is used in other places; for example, in Ps. cx. 4, "after (according to) the order of Melchizedec."

[11] הָמוֹן cannot signify *multitude* here in the sense of crowds or masses of people; for in that case נָשָׂא could not have been the verb coupled with it. This plainly denotes that it was property of some sort which Nebuchadnezzar was to take up and carry away with him. It was this also, and not people, which formed a proper reward for him. I therefore take the word here, as in chap. vii. 12, 13, and in chap. xxx. 4, etc., for multitude, in the sense of great possessions—*store.*

[12] Wilkinson's Ancient Egyptians, vol. i. p. 176–8.

[13] This view was adopted by the late Dr. Arnold, who says on the prophecy before us, "This is a striking instance of the hyperbolical language of the prophecies, as far as regards the historical sense of them. The prophecy says, 'I will make the land of Egypt utterly waste,' etc. It is perfectly evident that we are to seek for no literal fulfilment of this. But I think, also, that the expression 'forty years' is no more to be taken literally than the other expressions; and indeed it is inconsistent to seek chronological exactness where there is evidently no historical exactness intended" (Sermons on Prophecy, p. 48). The prophets, however, no more than other writers, must play at random with definite periods and strong descriptions; and if they did not mean by these historical exactness, we may be sure there was exactness of some other kind, which warranted them to write as they did."

[14] Wilkinson's Ancient Egyptians, vol. i. p. 216, and Encyclopædia Britannica, art. Egypt.

CHAPTER XXX.

[1] The commencement is almost precisely in the words of Joel, i. 15; ii. 1, 2. The peculiar expression also, "the day of the heathen," indicates briefly what is described more at large in the last chapter of Joel; it reveals the world-wide import of the judgment to be inflicted on Egypt, which was like the beginning of revenges on the heathen. We find the same representation given by Obadiah (ver. 15) with respect to Edom.

[2] It is not possible to determine with certainity all the countries and people here named. The people of Phut and Lud were formerly mentioned as among the hired soldiers of Tyre (chap. xxvii. 10); and as it is known Egypt relied very much on her mercenary troops at the time before us, it is likely that they are mentioned here in the same character. Indeed, in Jer. xlvi. 9, 21, they are expressly named the hired warriors of Egypt; and are rendered by our translators, Lybians and Lydians. This is a very ancient opinion, and in regard to both countries is concurred in by Gesenius. See Thes., at the words. The people named must have been some warlike races of Asia or Africa, who hired themselves out to other countries for military service. And this holds of both the Lybians and the Lydians. The Chub (or, with a different pointing, Kuf) are wholly unknown. Hävernick would identify them with a people named Kufa on the monuments, and by Wilkinson (vol. i. p. 379) considered to be a people situated considerably to the north of Palestine. But this also is mere conjecture. The LXX. omit the name, as if they did not know what to put for it. The *mixed multitude* are the people from various countries in the pay of Egypt.

[3] Who are to be understood here by "the children of the land of the covenant," or the covenant-land, is also a matter of dispute. Hävernick takes the expression generally: persons in covenant, allies. But the expression, as Hitzig notices, is too definite for that; and *the* covenant-land can hardly be taken for anything but the land of Canaan. So the LXX. took it, and to make the matter plain, put "*my* covenant." So also Jerome and Theodoret understood it of the Jews who migrated to Egypt, as mentioned in Jer. xlii.-xliv.

[4] The sending of messengers to Ethiopia, to rouse it out of its security, is probably mentioned with reference to Isa. xviii. 2. It merely denotes that the tidings of evil would quickly travel from the one country to the other; Egyptians fleeing from before the Lord, in his executions of judgment, would hasten in their vessels to their neighbours in Ethiopia, and would do the part of special messengers. "As the day of Egypt" may either mean that the time of sore visitation would come on them as it had just come on Egypt, or as it had been at some former time in Egypt, the day peculiarly of Egypt's judgment at the smiting of the first-born. Hävernick would refer the expression to the latter event. But this seems unnatural. The connection of the passage is best sustained by understanding *day* of the present time —Egypt's day would shortly be Ethiopia's.

[5] Noph is Memphis, the residence of the kings of Egypt, and the chief seat of its idolatrous worship; hence in connection with it both idol-gods

and princes are named as going to be cut off.

[6] Pathros denotes Upper Egypt, of which No, or No-Ammon, was one of the chief cities; but it is coupled with Zoan, or Tanis, a principal city in Lower Egypt.

[7] Sin is the same with Pelusium, which, on account of its position as a barrier-town, might justly be called the strength of Egypt. Suidas names it the Key of Egypt, because the possession of it opened the way to the whole.

[8] That a difficulty was early felt in rendering this last clause of ver. 16, is evident from the obviously conjectural meaning given by the LXX., "and waters shall be poured out." צָרֵי is either *enemies*, or the *distresses*, *troubles* occasioned by them. So also יוֹמָם is either *by day*, *of the day*, or *daily*, *perpetually*; in which last sense, though rare, it occurs also in Ps. xiii. 3. Hence there are two literal renderings: Noph's enemies shall be in the day, that is, fill her streets in broad daylight; or, Noph shall be distresses perpetually. I prefer the latter, as yielding a better sense, and more in accordance with the immediately preceding clause, in which No is said to be for tearing asunder—given up, as it were, to that. So here Noph is to be made the subject of perpetual distress. Hävernick adopts from the Aramaic the sense of splitting or division, and thus gives to the last clause respecting Noph much the same meaning as the preceding bears respecting No: Noph shall be for perpetual splitting. I don't think the meaning would be improved by this change, even if it could be established; but the entire absence of any countenance to it in the Hebrew is enough to set it aside, considering that the word is one in such common use.

[9] The Aven in this 17th verse is undoubtedly the same as what is elsewhere read On, Heliopolis, a strong and well-fortified city in Lower Egypt, and one of the great seats of Egyptian idolatry. On this account, probably, the prophet, by a slight alteration in the name, marks it as the place of iniquity—the *Aven*. Pi-beseth is rendered Bubastos in the LXX. and Vulgate; and doubtless Bubastos, or Bubastis, was a mere corruption of Pi-bast. The place, situated in lower Egypt near the Pelusiac branch of the Nile, was celebrated for the worship of the goddess Bubastis (Copt. Pasht), regarded as the same with Diana of the Greeks. A beautiful and much-frequented temple stood there in honour of her (Herod. ii. 137, 138). The Persians destroyed the walls of the city, though it continued to be a place of some note long afterwards.

[10] Tehaphnehes, or Tapannes, rendered by the LXX. Taphnæ, is the city Daphne, not far from Pelusium, on the confines of Lower Egypt, a place of considerable strength; hence with its capture the pride or glory of Egypt's strength is said to cease. Jeremiah speaks of Pharaoh having a house there (chap. xliii. 9), which implies that it had been occasionally at least a royal residence. By "breaking the yokes of Egypt" there, appears to be meant her dominion or supremacy which she exercised over many other people in and around her. I see no need for any other view than this simple one. The LXX. (and after them, Ewald, Hitzig, and others) render as if מַטּוֹת were in the text: "the sceptres of Egypt." As if Egypt was made up of several states or kingdoms! The present text gives a better meaning. The idea of Hävernick, hat by the yokes of Egypt reference is made to the Jews who,

according to Jer. xliv. and xlvi., went and settled there, is quite unnatural. In going there, they acted of their own accord, and there was no yoke or bondage of Egypt on them.

CHAPTER XXXI.

[1] The author of this opinion seems to have been one Meimbomius. Horsely speaks of Bishop Lowth as agreeing with it; if he ever did, it must have been in the first edition of his Prælections, for in the second, Michaelis' edition, he expressly refers the cedar to the king of Assyria. Hävernick also quotes Michaelis as supporting the same view. But he renounces it in his note on the passage in Lowth's Tenth Prælec.; he adheres, he there says, to the common view, *Meibomianam deserens.*

[2] See on chap. xix. 11.

[3] The אֵל here has by some been thought too strong, and they would substitute אַיִל a ram, then a powerful person, a leader or prince; so also some MSS. But perhaps the El might rather be chosen to denote the kind of divine-like power of judgment given to Nebuchadnezzar.

[4] Literally: may stand for, or on themselves, because of their greatness. For I agree with Hitzig and some others, that the אֵילֵיהֶם of the text should be pointed thus, אֲלֵיהֶם, so as to make the preposition with the pron. suffix, and not: their *terebinths*, or trees (taking it generally). The latter makes a very awkward and unnatural sense. The meaning is, that the trees were to be taught not to stand as by themselves, upon their own greatness, as if this, with their plentiful supply of water, could do all for them.

[4] The most literal rendering is here the best. Ewald and, after him, Häv. have missed the precise shade of meaning by throwing the two verbs together, and rendering as if it were: and I covered with mourning over him the deep. The prophet rather personifies the deep; God causes it to wrap itself in mourning, to cover up its fulness against him who had abused its treasures, and to withhold the streams which it had hitherto poured forth with joyfulness; for it is of the nature of grief to contract and seal up the flowing streams of plenty.

[5] It cannot be denied that the latter clause of this 17th verse is very peculiar in its construction and obscure in its import. Various emendations have been proposed in the text, but, as usual, with no satisfactory result; so that the last emendator, Hitzig, has still his own to propose, and, we have no hesitation in saying, with no better success than his predecessors. Many, after the LXX., with a slight difference in the punctuation, read *his seed*, for *his arm;* but the king of Assyria, as here considered, had no seed; he was the last of his race. I take: and, his arm, they dwelt, for: even they who as his arm had dwelt, or: though being his arm (the instruments of his power and glory) they had dwelt. Their connection with him was such that they could not but share his fate.

CHAPTER XXXII.

[1] There is a crowding of thought here, and in connection with that a mixture also of images. Pharaoh is like a lion on dry land among the

nations, and a monster, a crocodile, in the rivers. The idea, however, is still the same: Pharaoh was an object of terror, by reason of his great power and dominion. And his breaking forth—for such is undoubtedly the usual, and here quite appropriate, meaning of גִּיחַ; and there is no need for repairing, with Hävernick and Hitzig, to the cognate languages for some other—his breaking forth in the waters, like an impetuous and self-willed monster of the deep, and disturbing them with the commotion he raised, is merely added to strengthen the idea of his formidable character.

[2] With thy hugeness, רָמוּתֶךָ. The verb רוּם commonly signifying, to be high, lifted up, greatened; and the participle, lofty, great of stature; it is a very natural meaning for the noun to bear here, *hugeness*,—such an elevation or magnitude as to fill up the valleys of the land. It might be put more literally: thy prominences, thy projecting heights (referring, perhaps, to the scaly protuberances of the crocodile)—these filling up the valleys, as the flesh was to be spread over the hills. Hävernick's *corrupting corpse*, and Hitzig's *blood*, are quite fanciful, and are without the least shadow of support in Hebrew.

[3] The first part of ver. 6: And I water the earth with, or make the earth to drink, what flows from thee, is evidently the correct rendering, and is now generally adopted; though De Wette still has, "where thou swimmest." But, as Hävernick remarks, the verb צוּף, from which צָפָה comes, never signifies exactly to swim, but rather to flow, or stream out; hence the word here, which is properly a participle, the discharging or streaming of blood that flowed out from the slain creature.

[4] Pharaoh is represented in these two verses as himself a great light of heaven, a star of the first magnitude, at the fall of which the whole heavenly host are put into disorder, and veiled in darkness. A poetical representation, of course; to show the terrible sensation that would naturally be caused in the political heavens by the fall of so great a monarchy: trouble and confusion would seize many a heart.

[5] "Thy ruins," שִׁבְרְךָ, literally, thy breakage or fracture, a strong expression for the broken and ruined people themselves. Shattered and dispersed, they would appear among the nations as one great fracture—the ruins of what they had been.

[6] Our translators give the first part of this verse: Then I will make their waters deep. The verb is, properly, to sink; but this, as applied to a river, may be variously understood, according to the circumstances. When the discourse here is of a diminishing of the resources of Egypt, the most natural sense is, certainly, the subsiding of her waters—make them sink or decrease, so that they should not overflow, but keep easily in their proper channel. To deepen, in the sense of increasing, or to make them clear, are both unsuitable.

[7] The number of the month is here omitted, and only the year and the day announced. But there can be no doubt that the twelfth month is to be supplied from the preceding vision, so that this is separated from the former by an interval of fourteen days.

[8] There is a certain degree of abruptness in the manner in which the lamentation commences: all at once Egypt is coupled with others, in com-

pany with whom she is sent down to the pit, while it is only afterwards we are told who these others are; and both between her and them, and in the use of the person, rapid interchanges are made. The daughters of glorious nations, coupled with Egypt, are undoubtedly those afterwards mentioned by name; not the tributaries of Egypt, but those who, like her, had risen to eminence in the world, and grasped at dominion. Their destiny was bound up with hers. And the prophet is commanded to bring them down; because his word was the expression of God's will, and carried with it the execution of his pleasure.

[9] Egypt was uncircumcised, that is, polluted and corrupt; hence it must share the fate of all such; they are all doomed to perdition, and Egypt can have no exemption from the common lot: she has no ground of endearment above the rest.

[10] This 20th verse describes the common lot of Egypt, and the other nations similarly circumstanced. They are alike destined to fall by the sword; but she, as the more immediate object of the Divine word, has a place of pre-eminence assigned her; she is given up to the sword; and as such, the command is issued to draw her forth as peculiarly devoted to destruction.

[11] In these two verses, 22 and 23, which relate to Assyria (and the same is partly found in some of the other cases), there is a singular rapidity of alternations in the gender of the pronouns: *her* company, *his* graves, then again *her* graves and *her* company. It can only be explained by the circumstance of the party named being, in the prophet's eye, partly as a kingdom, partly as a monarch with his people; so that sometimes the one, sometimes the other, seemed fittest to be specially thought of. The general character of the representation is clear: Assyria and her people not only have gone down to the pit, but as deepest in guilt, they have their graves appointed in its farthest extremities, they occupy its lowest depths, and their graves stand open around them; like profane wretches, they have been denied the rites of burial; the horror they had inspired in others now rests on themselves.

[12] Elam is joined immediately with Assyria, probably as having been connected with it in the way of conquest. The territory of Elam lay in Persia, though the boundaries of it are not distinctly known. Originally it was an independent kingdom, and existed as early as the time of Abraham (Gen. xiv.). Its people were much addicted to war, and were famous for the use of the bow. At the time of Ezekiel they had become amalgamated with the Chaldean empire, as they afterwards were with the Median. The shame they were to bear with others among the dead, is the punishment of their pride and lawless doings among men.

[13] The כִּי here, and in the other passages that follow, is to be taken in the usual meaning of *for*, and not *though*, as in our version. It assigns the reason of the doom to the pit: the power given by God for good had been abused to spread terror through its violent proceedings in the world.

[14] The Mesech and Tubal here mentioned as one people were also named together in chap. xxvii. 13. Some, and among these Ewald, have been disposed to identify them with the Scythians. They were certainly very closely connected with the Scythian tribes, but were themselves properly the Moschi

and Tibareni, whose territory lay between the Black and Caspian Seas, and among the Caucasian Mountains. They appear here as a subdued people, and they are known to have paid tribute to Darius Hyst. (Herod. iii. 94.)

[15] I read this verse with Häv. as an interrogative. I see no other way of understanding the existing text, so as to make sense. It is expressly said of the people in question that they were to dwell with the uncircumcised and slain, and the negative, therefore, at the beginning must be understood interrogatively. Shalt thou not do so? thou who hast been among the most violent—a terror even to heroes, thou must dwell in the midst of them. The going down with weapons of war refers to the ancient practice of burning, or burying the bodies of warriors with their armour. It seems also to be these, the instruments of their iniquitous courses, which are meant by their "iniquity on their bones;" the instrument of iniquity being put, by metonymy, for the iniquity itself. It is certainly, however, a peculiar expression; and one cannot speak with confidence of its meaning.

[16] In these two last verses, Pharaoh's case again comes up as the conclusion of the whole matter—the beginning and the ending of the lamentation. The *his* and *her* here also exchange with each other, in what appears to us extraordinary confusion and disorder. Some of the MSS., to avoid this, retain only the masculine suffix, *his*. But there can be no doubt that the more difficult text is the correct one, and that the variation was made in order to remove the apparent anomaly. I have rendered it as it stands, believing that the alternations arise from the double reference to Egypt as a kingly power, and as a kingdom. The comfort to be got by Pharaoh is spoken ironically; as much as to say, This is the only comfort he is to have, that he is not without companions in his ruin.

CHAPTER XXXIII.

[1] Spencer (De Leg. Heb. ii. 11) has laboured to prove that the expression here עַל־הַדָּם תֹּאכֵלוּ, literally upon or over the blood ye eat, differs materially from that which merely prohibits the eating of blood: Ye shall not eat the blood. He understands the reference here to be to Lev. xix. 26, where the same form of expression is used; and that in both passages what is forbidden is the practice of eating over or near the blood of animals sacrificed in the celebration of magical rites, particularly the rites of evocation. And Horsley speaks of Spencer's exposition being clearly and incontrovertibly proved. To me it seems to fail in the very point to be proved—viz. that the connection between the eating near the blood of slain victims and practising the rites of magic was of so close and peculiar a kind, that the one might be sufficient to indicate the other. It was palpably the reverse: there was no sacrifice at all when the witch of Endor evoked Samuel, and while with Balaam's enchantments there were sacrifices employed, yet, these being holocausts, there was no eating connected with them. Besides, in 1 Sam. xiv. 32–34, where the army of Saul are spoken of as eating with the blood, and where there was no room for enchantments or magical rites of any sort, it is precisely the expression before us that is used. Hence all recent commentators justly regard the sin here charged upon the people as simply a disregard of the Divine prohibition against eating the blood with the flesh.

[2] The word עֲגָבִים, as a noun, only occurs in Jer. iv. 30, besides the double use of it in the present passage, and there it is plainly used in the sense of *lovers*. But in another passage (chap. xxiii. 5) the verb is used by Ezekiel in much the same sense, "She doted upon her lovers," or went after them with fond affection. So that simply lovers or admirers, not much love, as our version, nor jokes, as Ewald, nor lovely, as Hitzig, must be taken as the proper meaning of the word here. Hävernick says it is always used by Ezekiel in the sense of impure love, gallantry (*buhlerei*), and that he is particularly fond of it. But this fondness shows itself no more than three times, and then only as indicative of a strong, though not necessarily a wrong affection. His common word for *lovers* in a bad sense in not this, but מְאַהֲבִים, as it is also of the other prophets. If any subordinate meaning therefore were to be added to the meaning *lovers*, it should simply be that of fond or doting affection.

[3] See, for example, Isa. xv. 9, "the escaped of Moab;" also Isa. xxxvii. 31, 32; Jer. xlviii. 19, "he that is escaped;" Amos ix. 1, "he that escapeth of them;" 1 Kings xix. 17; in all which passages the singular is used collectively for the whole company.

CHAPTER XXXIV.

[1] The two epithets here, נַחְלוֹת and חוֹלָה, can only have their distinctive import determined by the verbs respectively connected with them; strengthening being used with the first, the evil affection referred to must have been feebleness or impotence, the effect of sickness; and healing being the other verb, sickness itself must have been the disorder there to be remedied. That נַחְלוֹת should have been put in the plural, probably arose from a desire to prevent its being mistaken for נַחֲלָה, the inheritance.

[2] In this charge of ruling with force and with cruelty, בְּפֶרֶךְ, there is a reference to Lev. xxv. 43, where this word is used in the instruction given to the judges, as to the way they were not to rule over the people. They had done the very thing which Moses in the law had charged them not to do.

[3] Our translators have missed the precise import of the two verbs here, and indeed have rather transposed them: דָּרַשׁ signifying to be concerned about anything, and make inquiry after it in a general way; somewhat like the Latin *petere;* while בִּקֵּשׁ means more definitely to make search for, nearly corresponding to *quærere*. There was no inquisition and no search made for the lost portion of the flock.

[4] On two former occasions (chap. xvii. 23, xx. 40) the prophet had used the expression, "the mountain of the height of Israel," or its high mountain; but here we have the plural, "the mountains of the height." The reason of the difference is evident: *there* the prophet spoke of the centre of the kingdom, where the king was to have his seat, and the people were to meet for the worship of Jehovah—Mount Zion; but *here* he speaks of the kingdom at large—the entire region occupied by the flock. The mountains on which they roam are still, however, the mountains of the height of Israel, because everything in Israel has a moral elevation—a height, not as per-

ceived by the eye of flesh, but well known and discerned by the eye of faith; for to it the high places of the earth are always those where God's kingdom is.

[5] The parties meant here by the rams and the he-goats are evidently the same as in ver. 16, and are called "the fat and the strong," as contradistinguished from the lean, the weak, and the sick. The Lord would judge between sheep and sheep, the rams and he-goats; that is, between the sheep generally, and this particular class of them, the more robust and headstrong part; for the לְשֶׂה is in apposition with the two expressions that follow,—the rams and he-goats; these form the evil-doers that are to be distinguished from the שֶׂה, the flock generally. Many have erred in supposing that by this fat and robust class are represented the rulers of the people, identifying them with the shepherds in the earlier portion; against the connection, for these have already been judged and disposed of (vers. 10, 11), and also against the natural import of the figure, which treats here of one part of the flock as compared with another. The misconduct of the rulers had been imitated by the stronger and more ungodly portion of the people, who had dealt unkindly with their poorer brethren, and acted as if it would even be an enhancement of their own comforts to oppress and trample on the rights of others. The description given is of a haughty, insolent, and selfish disposition,—the very reverse of that required in the kingdom of God; and hence one that must be judged and punished by him.

[6] The emphasis is here on the singleness of the shepherd, רֹעֶה אֶחָד, a shepherd, one: qualified to exercise an undivided superintendence over the covenant-people, as opposed to the old division, fraught with such unhappy results, into the two kingdoms of Judah and Israel. It implies, of course, the possession of singular qualities in the one who should be appointed to hold such a place; he must be in the fullest sense a shepherd after God's own heart, capable of healing far worse divisions, and rectifying far worse disorders, than those which prevailed when David came to the throne. In this oneness, therefore, of the promised shepherd, an intimation of his pre-eminent excellence lies concealed; as is also presently expressed, in his being called "my servant David"—*my servant*, not pursuing a self-chosen and arbitrary course, as so many of the kings had done, but acting as the faithful administrator of the will of God. In an immense number of passages this appellation is given to David, to indicate his peculiar fitness for the office of ruling in the name of God.

[7] What is meant by *my hill* in the first clause of this verse is undoubtedly Zion, for this was God's hill by way of eminence. But the idea of Hengstenberg, that this hill here designates Israel as the people of God, and that the environs are the heathen who join themselves to Israel, is quite unnatural. The discourse here is simply of Israel, and of the blessings to be conferred on them. They are represented as dwellers on God's hill of Zion, where, as in the seat and centre of all good, they are richly blessed; but not they alone, the blessing streams forth, and all the environs of the hill partake in the beneficence of Heaven. All the suburbs, the pasture grounds (for the allusion is plainly to that), are refreshed from the Lord's presence, as well as the people themselves. And so the idea indicated is

presently expressed more fully by the promise of rain in plentiful abundance, to produce a rich pasturage. In this promise, as well as in the promise of peace and security, allusion is made to Lev. xxvi. 2–6, where these blessings are specially connected with the covenant of God.

[8] By "the plantation for a name," or renown, that the Lord promises in the earlier part of this verse to raise up, is not to be understood Israel itself, but something for Israel's benefit, something that would give them a name of honour among the nations, and take away for ever the reproach of poverty and want. It simply means that the Lord would secure for them a flourishing and prosperous condition, under the image of "a place well planted with fruitful trees, rising aloft and growing through the goodness of God, so that the Israelites should be replenished with the means of nourishment, and be no more impoverished with want" (Gussetius Lex.). An allusion appears to be made, as Hengstenberg and Hävernick suggest, to Gen. ii. 8–11, where the garden of Eden is described with its trees of all kinds good for food and pleasant to the sight: the land of Israel would become such a glorious plantation—a second Eden.

[9] Dathe, Ewald, and others, would understand the declaration in this closing verse as a mere explanation of the parable—that the flock are the men of Israel, and the shepherd is God. But there is evidently an emphasis on the *men:* men are ye; remember your place, you are but men; but remember at the same time that I am your God; so that without me nothing, but with me all. Hitzig prefers the miserable tautology of the LXX.: "ye are my sheep and the sheep of my flock, and I am," etc., and calls it an excellent sense!!

CHAPTER XXXV.

[1] The more literal rendering here is: and hast poured out the children of Israel upon the hands of the sword. It is a strong personification both ways —the children of Israel being likened to water which the Edomites poured out, and the sword upon which they were poured being thought of as a person, a devourer, whose hands were instruments of destruction. When the figure is understood, there is no need for supplying *blood* as the object of the pouring out, as our translators have done. The same expression is used in Jer. xviii. 21, and Ps. lxiii. 11; a very closely-related one also by our prophet at chap. xxi. 17. There, too, at ver. 30, the peculiar phrase of עֲוֹן קֵץ, the end, or consummation of iniquity, occurs.

[2] The whole cast of expression in this verse will appear strange, unless it is understood that there is a play upon the name of Edom, which is very like the Hebrew word for blood. אֱדֹם (Edom) was to be made for דָם (dâm), blood; the former also signifying *red*, which rendered the transition to blood more natural and easy. אֱדֹם also has the signification of *blood* in the cognate dialects. The most peculiar part of the verse, however, is the clause אִם־לֹא דָם שָׂנֵאתָ, which not only our version, but also nearly all commentators, render "since thou hast not hated blood." But no examples can be produced to justify such a rendering; and the remark of Hitzig, that as the words stand they must be regarded by every reader as an affirmative protestation, is quite

correct. Because the clause therefore ascribes to Edom the hating of blood, he rejects it as a gloss—a most unlikely clause to be a gloss—and supports himself by the omission of it in the LXX. I cannot concur with Theodoret, Jerome, Michaelis, and others, that דָּם is to be taken in the sense of *relationship*, and refers to the near affinity between Esau and Jacob, as being both sprung from one father; so that the hating of the Israelites on the part of Edom was like a hating of their own blood. There is no authority for ascribing to the word such a meaning. But taking blood in the usual sense, I do not see why, in a passage so strongly epigrammatic and alliteral as this, the hatred of it might not be affirmed of Edom; for the grand point on which the desires of the Edomites were centred was life, life in themselves, as opposed to the bloody extermination they sought for Israel: the shedding of their blood was what they would on no account think of. I take the meaning to be, therefore: The preservation of thy life is what thou art intent on securing; the thought of blood being shed among thee is what thou art putting far from thee as the object of aversion; but God's purposes are contrary to thine, and what thou hatest he will send—blood shall pursue thee.

[3] The construction in this 10th verse is peculiar, as in broken sentences it expresses the excited feelings which were called forth. It is on this principle we are to account for the אֶת at the beginning of the words put into the mouth of the Edomites; it marks the object uppermost in their thought: these two nations and these two lands. Then they think of the two as one whole, a region to be possessed: And we inherit it. And the last clause, And Jehovah was there! is thrown in by the prophet as an interjection, a sudden flash of light revealing the folly and impiety of their imaginations. They were calculating on doing what they pleased with a land with which Jehovah was peculiarly connected, and which he claimed as specially his own: how vain and presumptuous!

[4] I quite agree with Häv., that כָּל־הָאָרֶץ must here be taken in the restricted sense of all the land, viz. of Edom. For it could scarcely be meant that Edom was to be desolate, while all the earth rejoiced, since in the next chapter the other heathen nations are expressly coupled with Edom in her desolations. The meaning is, that as the whole country had rejoiced in Israel's fall, so it would all be made desolate in turn; according to the joy, so the desolation, as is explained in next verse.

CHAPTER XXXVI.

[1] The prophecy takes the form of an address to the mountains of Israel, partly in allusion to the "Mount Seir" of the preceding prophecy, and partly also with reference to the original prophecy in Gen. xlix. 26, where the peculiar blessings of the covenant are spoken of in connection with the "everlasting hills." The reference to this passage is especially manifest in the words put into the mouth of the adversaries, claiming the everlasting heights for their inheritance; as much as to say, We have seen an end of the blessings to Israel—the heights with which these blessings were connected, and which stood as fixed natural memorials of them, have become ours. Here, too, the adversaries are personified as one—הָאוֹיֵב, the enemy;

for, as was mentioned under last chapter, they were all represented in the Edomite—the name Edom comprehends the whole.

[2] In regard to the second of the two verbs in this clause, שָׁאַף, there is not much diversity of opinion now. It does not properly signify to swallow up, but to snuff up, in the manner of a wild beast, which with a keen and ravenous appetite smells after its prey, in order to seize and devour it. In this sense it is used by the Psalmist (in Ps. lvi. 1, 2) of his cruel enemies: "Be gracious to me, O God, for there snuffs after me man," etc. The other verb, שַׁמּוֹת, is generally derived from שָׁמַם, whose proper signification is, to be made desolate, although here it has sometimes—still also by Ewald and Hävernick—been rendered by, *to make desolate*, *to lay waste*. But this would more appropriately have been ascribed to the Chaldeans, not to the neighbouring enemies, who are regarded here as hunting after the land of Israel as an object of desire. I think therefore, with Hitzig, that the passage is to be explained from Isa. xlii. 14, where the same two verbs are used together, and the אֶשֹּׁם must be taken from the root נָשַׁם, to breathe, of which נְשָׁמָה, breath, is a derivative in very frequent use. Viewed thus, the surrounding enemies are strikingly and quite appropriately represented as breathing and snuffing like wild beasts after Canaan as their prey.

[3] The expression here is best understood as an elliptical one: the lip of the tongue, for, the lip of a man of tongue, בַּעַל לָשׁוֹן, a talker, or speakers generally.

[4] The כַּלָּא is the Chaldaic form, for which many codices have substituted the more regular כַּלָּה. Such a Chaldaic termination, however, was not unnatural.

[5] The common rendering of this latter clause is, "that it may be cast forth as a prey." But this is a very unnatural expression to be used of a land. Therefore taking מִגְרָשָׁהּ, not as an Aramaic inf., but as the substantive, and changing thus the pointing of לָבַז, so as to make it the inf. instead of the noun, we have the sense: in order to plunder its pasturage; a quite suitable meaning. In chap. xxi. 20, we have also לְמַעַן coupled with ל of the infinitive. In this, again, I follow Hitzig.

[6] There is here a play of words in the original which is necessarily lost in the translation. The prophet had mentioned the reproach against the land as being only the grave of its people, devouring and bereaving them, like a cruel unnatural mother. But now in predicting the better future, while he says it should not devour any more, he suddenly changes the other verb, and instead of saying, לֹא תְשַׁכְּלִי, thou shalt not bereave, he says, לֹא תְכַשְּׁלִי, thou shalt not make to stumble or fall. The Kri reading substitutes the former, evidently for the purpose of affording an easy explanation, and the ancient versions also express it. Most modern commentators adopt the Kri, so still Ewald and Hitzig; but Hävernick properly adheres to the text. For the repetition of לֹא תְכַשְּׁלִי in the next verse is a proof that here a change of meaning is introduced, and a change that also very suitably prepares the way for the truths to be declared in the next section (ver. 16, etc.), which unfolds the moral cause of the past

destructions, the sins and defections of the people. Canaan must not only cease to devour and swallow up its people, but even to prove an occasion of stumbling to them. By being this in time past, it had necessarily proved a destroyer; but henceforth both cause and effect should be taken away. Throughout, the land is personified, and represented as doing that which was done on it.

[7] The only peculiar expression in the passage is that in the first clause of this last verse: "I felt pity for my holy name." This is undoubtedly the proper rendering; as the עַל after חָמַל denotes the object in behalf of which the pity is exercised. The LXX., whom Hävernick follows, refer it to the people: I spared them for my holy name. Undoubtedly the people were spared because of the affection indicated here; but the affection itself was one of tender regard, or pitying concern for the Lord's own abused and dishonoured name.

[8] It should be noted that this part of the promise very clearly implied the breaking of the yoke of Babylon, and the precipitation of that power in some way from its present ascendancy. No one could mistake this to be implied in such predictions; but it is only by this sort of implication that the doom of Babylon is referred to in Ezekiel.

[9] Such appears to be the leading design and purport of this prophecy. Hengstenberg, in his Christology, on the passage, has viewed the matter as if it was God's faithfulness to his covenant that was at stake, which required that a seed of blessing should still be found among the people of the covenant, notwithstanding all their sins and defections. That certainly is true, but, as Hävernick justly remarks, not the truth under consideration here. The heathen did not reproach God for want of fidelity to his own covenant; for in truth they did not know what that covenant really was or required. This was precisely the thing to be made plain; God must let them know that here holiness was everything, and that by the possession or the want of it all his outward dealings must be regulated.

CHAPTER XXXVII.

[1] It is literally *the* valley, הַבִּקְעָה, which was also used at chap. iii. 22. But as no particular valley was mentioned, we must use the indefinite article, for the Hebrews sometimes prefixed their definite article to nouns by way of emphasis, when these, though neither previously nor subsequently described, were viewed as definite in the mind of the writer. (Nordheimer, Gr. ii. § 720.)

[2] This passage plainly shows that the spirit, רוּחַ, here and throughout the section, is not to be identified with the *wind*, for the thing wanted was to be called from the four winds. It is the life-breath, the spirit of life, immediate eflux of God, as the source of animated life in the creature.

[3] Ewald renders here, "with very, very great power." But there is no preposition answering to the *with*, so that the clause is most naturally regarded as in apposition with what precedes. At the same time the idea of power is certainly indicated in the original, and the "great army" of our common version does not convey the exact meaning. Our word *force*, however, pre-

cisely corresponds to the Heb. חַיִל, and equally with it is used in the double sense of power, as connected either with numbers or with personal resources and energy. Both references are intended here; the now living skeletons presented the appearance of a vast multitude in full strength and vigour.

[4] The last clause is literally, "we are cut off to ourselves," נִגְזַרְנוּ לָנוּ, that is, cut off from the source of power and influence, and abandoned to ourselves. The "cut off for our parts" in the Authorized Version is scarcely intelligible.

[5] "Nunquam enim poneretur similitudo resurrectionis ad restitutionem Israelitici populi significandam, nisi staret ipsa resurrectio, et futura crederetur; quia nemo de rebus non extantibus incerta confirmat."—*Jerome.*

[6] We might have added, though this is not properly the place to discuss the subject, that many other portions, even the earlier portions of Old Testament Scripture, equally imply the doctrine of the resurrection; and so far from thinking with Hitzig, and Hävernick also, that the belief of that doctrine was not generally diffused among the older Jewish people, we are convinced it was always held by believers—inseparable from a living faith in the Divine word. The first promise involved it; the earliest religion could have imparted no consolation, and inspired no hope, without presupposing it; all the leading promises and dispensations of God contained it, as the vital germ, with the unfolding of which their own final perfection was to be reached; so that the hope of the resurrection, rather than the simple belief of immortality, was the form which the ulterior expectations of God's earlier worshippers took. See this investigated at some length in the Typology of Scripture, vol. i., pp. 173 and 425.

[7] There are two peculiarities in this verse. The first is the apparent anomaly of the rod of Joseph, which had been spoken of as being, along with the other, in the hand of the prophet, being said to be in the hand of Ephraim—of which some far-fetched explanations have been given. The proper explanation evidently is, that the prophet here passes to the meaning of what had been said previously: the staff was the symbol of authority and rule; and this, in the case of Joseph, had been seized and exercised by Ephraim, but now was to be withdrawn from his hand, and united with the other staff into one in God's hand. The two met in God. The other peculiarity is the use of the plural in the second clause: and I put *them* with it, though, properly, the rod of Joseph is the object referred to. It is a construction according to the sense—the rod being identified in the prophet's mind with the ten tribes, who owned its authority.

[8] The expression here is certainly peculiar, though I see no need, with many, for either omitting the clause or emending the text. Hengstenberg follows Venema, who throws this and the following verb together, and renders: *dabo eos multiplicatos*, I will give them multiplied, and supposes there is a reference to the promise to Abraham, "I give thee for nations." But for this reference the expression is greatly too abbreviated. I rather incline to take the verb נָתַן in the sense of appointing or setting, which it certainly often possesses; and understand it as importing that now God himself orders and determines everything concerning them—sets them in opposition to their former fluctuating, because self-ordered, condition.

[9] The expression may possibly have some respect to the elevated position of the temple-mount, which seemed as if it overlooked the land generally; but if so, only to this as an emblem of God's watchful and gracious oversight. His sanctuary was to be in their midst, but his dwelling all over them, for protection and blessing.

CHAPTER XXXVIII.,XXXIX.

[1] The name Magog occurs only once elsewhere in the Old Testament, at Gen. x. 2, among the sons of Japheth; and according to the principles on which the genealogical tables are there constructed, it must be regarded as the name of a land and people, belonging to a branch of Japheth's posterity. The syllable Ma, which in Coptic bears the meaning of *place* (in the Sanscrit, also, Mahâ signifies earth or land), was probably regarded as having respect to the territory; so that Gog would naturally denote the people, or the head who represented both land and people. Gog is clearly a name formed by the prophet from Magog—a representative name, intended to designate the political head of the region. With a like freedom, Gog and Magog are in Rev. xx. used as the names of two separate people.

[2] The two words נְשִׂיא רֹאשׁ are, with various ancient and some modern authorities, connected together in our common version, and rendered *chief prince*. Ewald adheres to this view, on the ground that no people are known in the Bible by the name of Rosh; so also does Hengstenberg on Rev. xx. 7—he regards Gog as having Magog for his original kingdom, though he had also acquired the mastery over Meshech and Tubal, and so might be called their "chief prince." It is certainly possible. But Hitzig justly objects, on the other side, that an epithet formed by the junction of these two words is nowhere else known in the Bible; and that the full title, if it were simply a compound title, should be so formally repeated three several times (ver. 2, 3, xxxix. 1) is rather improbable. Besides, traces have been found of a northern people anciently bearing such a name. The passage especially of Tzetzes, in Gallæus ad Orac. Sibyl. p. 391, quoted by Havernick, in which the Tauri are expressly called Rôs (ἐδήλωσα Ταύρους τοῦς Ρῶς καλεῖσθαι), is a strong proof. Bochart, also (Paleg. iii. 13), has shown that the Araxes had the name of Rhos, rendering it probable that the people in the neighbourhood were called by the same name. There is hence great probability in the opinion, that the people referred to were the Russi, from whom the modern Russians derive their name. The other two names connected with them, Meshech and Tubal, are the Moschi and Tibareni, inhabitants of the regions about Caucasus. The Moschi seem to have formed the chief population in Cappadocia down to classical times, and gave it much of its well-known rough and semi-barbarous character. The Tibareni were their neighbours, and in profane history also are often joined with them; but thier territory is not well ascertained (see Rawlinson's Herod. iv. p. 222–24). So that the people mentioned are northern tribes; and Jerome gives it as the opinion of the Jews in his day, that Magog was a general name for the numberless Scythian tribes.

[3] The usual meaning of the verb suits well enough here, if only it is understood that the aspect under which Gog is contemplated by the prophet

is that of an untamed, fractious wild beast, which thought only of taking its own way and pursuing its lawless career at pleasure, while God was going to direct events into such a channel as would draw it where destruction was sure to overtake it. He would turn it back, bend its lawless and ferocious energies into this one course, in which it must inevitably perish. In the parallel passage (Rev. xx.) the directing impulse is ascribed to the deceptive power of Satan, but to him, of course, as the mere instrumental agent: precisely as in 1 Chron. xxi. 1, where the temptation is ascribed to Satan, which in 2 Sam. xxiv. 1 is represented as coming from God in the exercise of his just displeasure.

[4] We must note respecting the nations that are mentioned as in league with Gog, and under his influence, their great distance from each other, as well as from Canaan. Not only have we the Scythian hordes, but the Persians also; the Ethiopians and Libyans of Africa; Gomer, or the Cimmerians of Crim Tartary; Togarmah, or the Armenians, and the multitudes beyond them that peopled the regions of the far north.

[5] The first clause in this verse has been very differently understood; most commonly, as in our version, made to express the destiny of Gog to punishment: thou art visited or chastised. But to make this sense the preposition עַל, with the person, would have been necessary: to visit upon one, to punish. Hävernick supposes a reference to Isa. xxiv. 22, and renders: for a long time thou art missed; that is, regarded as a lost people, not heard of—a very unnatural idea, and founded on a very unusual sense. I greatly prefer the rendering of De Wette, Rosen., Hitzig: after a long time thou art made leader, or gettest the command. The verb certainly has this sense in Jer. xv. 3, Neh. vii. 1, xii. 44. It was not to be immediately; a long period was to elapse before the assault, headed by Gog, was to take place; but when the time came, he should have the leadership, and everything would seem favourable—the land against which they came apparently an easy prey to their combined and numerous forces, unfortified, and its people dwelling in outward security, without any thought of the sword. The eye of flesh looked only to the want of visible defences, and perceived not the grand security—the invisible shield of Jehovah.

[6] The peculiar expression, "the navel of the earth," is very much the same in meaning as that used in chap. v. 5, where Israel was said to have been set in the midst of the nations. It does not denote, as was shown there, that Jerusalem, or Judea generally, was placed physically in the centre of the world; but that it occupied morally a central position, and one also in every respect advantageously situated for exerting a happy influence on the world. The expression here may include the two points—of a prominent position, and of great fulness of blessing; on both accounts fitted to awaken the envy of others. It is the same idea, though differently expressed, in Rev. xx. 9, where the combined forces are said to "compass the camp of the saints about, and the *beloved city*"—the city which was the object of special favour, and held the pre-eminent place.

[7] The people here represented as speaking thus to Gog and his company, were on his side rather than with the covenant-people. They are representatives of that portion of the world who, though they are not disposed to take any active part against the cause of God, are well pleased to see

others do it. Their worldly feeling makes them disrelish the truth; and they are ready to cheer on those who would make a spoil of its defenders.

[8] Gog and his warlike force are here identified with the enemies of whom former prophets have spoken, when they spake of the conflicts and troubles of the last days. Thinking of those prophecies—prophecies uttered long ago, and spread over many years—such, for example, as those recorded in Num. xxiv. 17–24, Isa. xiv. 28–32, xviii., etc., Joel iii., Dan. ii. 44, 45, etc.,—and seeing now in vision this last grand gathering of the powers of evil under Gog, the prophet asks whether it was not the same that had already so often been announced. It appeared now only in a new form, but the thing itself had been many times described by God's servants.

[9] We find mention made of the earthquake also, though more briefly, in the parallel prophecy of Joel iii. 16; also Isa. xxix. 6. In Rev. xx. 9, the external form differs; there is no earthquake, but fire is said to come down from heaven to consume the adversaries, as here also in ver. 22.

[10] There can be no doubt that this is the proper rendering of the original in this clause; and the translation in the Authorized Version—every man's sword shall be against his brother—suggests a wrong idea, as if the enemies were to turn and fight against each other. The meaning simply is, that God would meet sword with sword; for the sword of the adversary he would provide a brother sword, a fellow, in the hand of his people.

[11] In this rendering of שִׁשֵּׁאתִיךָ, we have the substantial agreement of the ancient translators, who concur in ascribing to it the sense of leading or guiding in some respect; occasionally of leading wrong, decoying. The connection plainly requires some such meaning, and though there is no direct confirmation, there are not wanting analogies to support it, as Hävernick has shown. The rendering, "I will leave but the sixth part of thee," and some others of a like nature, are justly exploded.

[12] From the mention of Magog here, we are not to identify it with Gog; it refers, as before, to the Scythian territory, including the people who occupy it. The anger of God first flames out against the Scythian host, who came against the covenant-people; but it does not stop there, it goes forth in judgment against all belonging to them, and consumes the adversaries out of the earth, wherever they may be found: the Scythians at home, and all of like mind and temper with them.

[13] The burning of the armour here mentioned has nothing to do with any ancient custom, but was evidently introduced for the purpose of conveying the idea that no remnant should be left of the great conflict to pollute the land; the very weapons of the enemy should be utterly consumed. The *seven years* points to the sacredness and completeness of the number *seven*. It was a great work getting the land thoroughly cleansed from all the implements of heathenism, and the people would not rest till the whole was accomplished. How different from the ancient Israelites, who, because they were themselves so imperfectly purified, were content to let, not the implements merely, but the persons of the heathen remain among them! The action here, therefore, is a sign of the people's zeal for purity.

[14] The idea of Hitzig respecting this valley scarcely deserves being mentioned, except as a specimen of the ridiculous. He thinks it should be understood to be the valley of the opposite heights, and supposes it to refer to

the valley in Zech. xiv. 4, formed by the cleaving asunder of Mount Olivet, for which Ezekiel, thinking there must be some use, fell on the happy idea of a burying-ground for Gog's army! That the prophet thought of a valley for such a purpose, arose, we should fancy, from the vast numbers it was to receive; nothing but a deep valley would be sufficient to contain such a mass of dead bodies. He lays it to the east of the sea, by which we naturally understand the Dead Sea, the memorial of one of God's earliest and greatest judgments; so that the final resting-place of those last sinners would be close beside that of their ancient prototypes, the guilty inhabitants of Sodom and Gomorrah. And he calls it first, more generally, the valley of the passers-through, ironically, because the persons buried in it had only intended to pass through the land and return again after they had made all their own, though here they found an effectual stop put to their proceedings; and then, more definitely, the valley of Hamon-gog. The *stopping* is to be taken in reference, not to the noses, but to the persons of the enemies. So Cocceius, in his Lex.: *Et ea (detinet) frænat transeuntes; habenam injicit transeuntibus.*

[15] The process described in vers. 12–15, is the following:—The whole people of the land are engaged burying the corpses in the grave-valley for seven months (the *seven*, as before, the symbol of sacredness and completeness); then, at the end of the seven months, persons are selected to the special and regular work (for such is the force of אַנְשֵׁי תָמִיד) of going through the land to search everywhere for the skeletons of those who might still have been left—the stragglers of the great host. And when they found any such skeletons, they were to set up a mark, that the buriers might go and fetch them to the proper burying-ground. The whole denotes the minute care and business-like alacrity with which the work of purification should be gone about, that every remnant of heathenish impurity might be extirpated.

[16] The thought here is, that an additional memorial of the transaction was to be found in the erection of a city near, called Hamonah (multitude). Pointing שָׁם, and so rendering: "And also there is a city Hamonah," makes fully a better sentence, but leaves the meaning essentially the same.

[17] The representation of a great sacrifice of slain victims lying exposed on the face of the earth, and ready to afford a repast for the beasts of the field and birds of prey, is found also elsewhere: in Isa. xviii. 6 (in chap. xxxiv. 6, there is the representation of a great sacrifice in Idumea, though nothing is said of an invitation to the wild beasts and birds of prey), Zeph. i. 7, Rev. xix. 17, 18. Here it occupies only a secondary place, and hence it is mentioned last, though in point of order it rather belonged to the immediate results of the battle.

[18] The ordinary sense of רֶכֶב will manifestly not suit here, as *chariots* are entirely out of place in a feast. But the word is used in the sense of horsemen, or cavalry, in Isa. xxi. 7, also in 2 Kings ix. 17, though the Masorites have there used a different pointing. Ewald accordingly translates: riders; as did also the Sept., Vulgate, Syriac, Capellus, etc.

[19] נָשׂוּ אֶת־כְּלִמָּתָם, but pointing נָשׁוּ, so as to obtain the sense of *forgetting*. The expression of bearing one's iniquity is always used (as was shown on chap. iv.), of suffering the punishment due to it. But that is quite out of place here, where the people are expressly said to have escaped from all the

consequences of their sins. Nor will it do, with Ewald and Hävernick, to point to such passages as chap. xx. 43, xxxvi. 31, where, after their conversion, the people are said to remember their iniquities. These passages refer to the nearer results of their conversion; this here to the more remote. They would at first be deeply conscious of their sins, and bear the shame of them; but this could with no propriety be said after they were fully settled in the Divine favour and blessing.

CHAPTER XL.–XLVIII.

[1] It was, perhaps, unnecessary to mention the commentary of Dr. Clarke in this connection, as all his notes (so we are told in his Memoirs) on Isaiah, Jeremiah, and Ezekiel, were written in about six weeks. He gives a specimen of the extreme haste with which he wrote, at the commencement of this 40th chapter, when he states, in respect to the view under consideration, that "every biblical critic is of the same opinion;" and tells us that "the Jesuits, Prada and Villalpandus, have given three folio vols. on this temple," etc., though five minutes' inspection would have shown him that of the three one entire vol. had nothing whatever to do with the temple.

[2] See Fry on the Unfulfilled Prophecies, as one of many.

[3] Weissagung und Erf. i. p. 359, where, however, it is only briefly indicated. Baumgarten also seems to incline to the same view in his Comm. on Pent.

[4] Quoted by Delitzsch in his Biblisch-prophetische Theologie, p. 94, but without giving assent to it; and, at p. 308, he seems to mark the opinion as a false extreme in a few remarks on some passages of Baumgarten's.

[5] Description of Temple, pp. 5, 6. Ed. 1650.

[6] The same effect as here is aimed at in the measurements and proportions of St. John's city, Rev. xxi.—the numbers employed being all symbolical of perfection and of immense greatness. The walls are represented as being a perfect square, and on each side 12,000 stadia, or 1200 ordinary miles. This as far surpasses the dimensions of Ezekiel's city, as his did those of ancient Jerusalem.

[7] I am aware some say that the hill of Zion is to be raised in the latter days to an enormous height, and so to become literally above the hills. But this is a groundless assertion; and we appeal in proof to chap. xvii. 22, 23, where the same Mount Zion is designated as the peculiarly high and eminent mountain; and that in a prophecy which *must* refer to the first appearing of Christ. For it speaks of him, not as the great and mighty king, but as the little slender twig, which was to be planted there by God; it speaks of him in his humiliation, not in his glory; and yet the place where he began to take root is called "the mountain of the height of Israel."

[8] Douglas's Structure of Prophecy, p. 71.

[9] See the Typology of Scripture, vol. i., chapters i. and ii., for the establishment of the principles referred to regarding the tabernacle, and vol. ii., part iii., for the application of them to particular parts.

[10] Hävernick, Comm. p. 623.

CHAPTER XL. 1–48.

[1] It is a much debated point, and not yet settled, what is to be understood by the beginning of the year—whether the first month of the ecclesiastical year (Nisan), or the first of what was called the civil year (Tisri), or the first of the year of jubilee, which began on the tenth day of the seventh month. We need not spend either our own time or that of our readers by recounting all the arguments that have been alleged for either of these opinions, and against the others; but deem it enough to state that no satisfactory reasons have ever been produced to show that the Hebrew people generally, before the captivity, or the prophets in particular, were wont to take account in their dates of any year but that usually called the ecclesiastical one. All except this may be said to be mere conjecture. The beginning of the year, in this sense, memorable for its connection with the first beginnings of the people as a nation, was surely a fit period for the Spirit imparting the vision of new and better things to come.

[2] The expression in this clause is striking: brought me *thither*—where? —namely, to that place whither his thoughts and feelings were ever tending as their centre, and which needed not to be more particularly described. It indicates how much the heart of the prophet felt itself at home in that beloved region.

[3] We can have no doubt what is to be understood by the very high mountain on which the prophet was set down in the visions of God. The expression refers back to chap. xvii. 22, xx. 40, where a similar designation is given to that mount, which formed the seat and centre of God's earthly kingdom. That Mount Zion was thus named chiefly in a moral respect, on account of its being the chosen theatre of God's peculiar manifestations to his Church and people, has been already stated on the former of these passages, and again noticed in the introduction to this chapter. And now especially, when the prophet was in the ideal region of God's visions, where all was to be seen and considered in a spiritual respect, it was most fitly presented to his view as a place of high elevation. The last clause is attended with some difficulty, but the most natural rendering seems to be that given above. The *upon it* must necessarily point to the mountain itself on which the prophet stood; and this, as he immediately proceeds to tell us, was the site, not of a city in the proper sense, but of the temple buildings. For what he sees upon the hill is what he proceeds to describe; and it is in regard to the framework he saw that he says, at the beginning of ver. 3, "and he brought me thither." It seems plain, therefore, that the כְּמִבְנֵה־עִיר must be a compound phrase, descriptive of the temple buildings which he saw in vision on the mount. And so I understand it: like the framework of a city, or a city-like building—an erection so vast and varied that it bore the aspect of a city rather than of a single structure. We need not wonder at this, when we consider that the space they occupied was much larger than the entire site of ancient Jerusalem. Then in regard to the remaining word, "to the south," I see no proper difficulty about it, or any necessity for adopting the change suggested by the LXX., and followed by many commentators, and reading מִנֶּגֶד, over-against. The prophet was first brought to the mountain, and somewhere about it, or on it, was set down (he uses the rather indefinite preposition אֶל, at, or by); there he descries the city-like framework a little to the south of him, and then God "brings him thither," *i.e.*, close up to it, that he might see what it was.

[4] The exact proportions of the Hebrew measures of length cannot be ascertained with absolute correctness, as they were derived from parts of the human body, which necessarily vary. But the most careful inquiries have led to the conclusion that the ordinary Hebrew cubit was to a nearness 21 inches; and consequently the one employed here being an handbreadth or 3½ inches more, will make the cubit somewhere about 2 feet of our reckoning, and the rod about 12 feet. This must have been very near the length of each. (See Winer's Real-Wört., art. Elle, and Kitto's Bib. Cyclop., art. Cubit.)

[5] It is impossible to make sense of our English version here, which renders, "and the other threshold of the gate, which was one reed broad." What other threshold? There could be but one sill or threshold to each gate. Ewald arbitrarily substitutes אחר for אֶחָד, and renders, "the back threshold was one rod broad," as if their could properly be two thresholds, or the dimensions behind were to be different from those in front. The true meaning is undoubtedly that adopted by Böttcher, and followed by Häv., that the prophet in this clause calls attention to the ample dimensions of the threshold of the gate, the breadth (one rod, or 12 feet, the height of the wall) being sufficient to let numbers pass and repass at once. There was no break or division; even the one gate had its threshold a rod-breadth.

[6] The whole of these verses (vers. 7–16) are taken up with a description of the east gate, and the buildings connected with it; but from certain obscurities in the terms, and the vagueness in some parts of the description itself, it is not possible to speak definitely and minutely of the plan—not at least without taking great liberties with the text. Some parts of the description are intelligible enough—as that there was a porch with pillars, or some sort of ornamental work, to the gate; that on each side there were three chambers (by which are plainly to be understood guard-chambers, such as also belonged to the old temple buildings, 1 Chron. ix. 26, 27, xxvi. 12; 2 Kings xxii. 4); that these chambers were each a rod or six cubits long by as much in breadth, separated from each other by a wall of five cubits, and having windows somehow fixed in them. These are the more prominent points. But when we ask, how the chambers stood precisely to the gate—whether longitudinally or transversely, projecting altogether outwards from the wall, or altogether inwards, or partly both; how the threshold could be found in ver. 7 one rod or six cubits broad, and in ver. 9 could be said to be eight cubits; what precisely were the אֵילִם, translated pillars, though they are themselves said to have posts (ver. 49), or how they, as well as the guard-chambers, could have had windows, in ver. 16; what could be the use of windows, especially to the porches; how the measurement of the chambers from roof to roof could have been managed so as to make twenty-five cubits; and how the pillars of sixty cubits are to be understood, whether as rising aloft to this enormous height or placed horizontally: these, and several other points, are involved in hopeless obscurity, partly from the terms not being sufficiently understood, and partly from the relative positions of the objects not being distinctly enough marked. Ewald and Hitzig endeavour to make something of it by occasionally altering the text, supporting themselves to some extent by the LXX.; but I prefer saying, I don't find the text such as I can fully explain, to making a text which needs little or no explanation. I have no doubt that the original would have been

more precise and definite if this had been necessary to our getting the instruction it was intended to convey. I deem it, therefore, quite unnecessary to enter into the *minutiæ* of the different terms, which can lead to no satisfactory result.

[7] This seems to contradict what has just been said, that the porch of this inner gate was of the same dimensions with the outer one; it is now made immensely larger. Michaelis, Böttcher, Ewald, Hitzig, etc., consequently reject the text in its present form; Hävernick understands what is said of another porch, one looking inwards towards the temple. It may be so, but there is nothing in the text to determine such to be the meaning.

CHAPTER XL. 48, 49, XLI.

[1] It is not to be denied that there are some peculiarities in this last verse, which look very like corruptions of the text. Thus the *eleven* cubits assigned for the breadth of the porch gate, which do not bear any exact proportion to the length, and which also differ from the dimensions given in 1 Kings vi. 3, of Solomon's temple, while the length agrees. Some would therefore altogether omit the two, and read ten; and others, with the LXX. (changing עַשְׁתֵּי into שְׁתֵּי), would make the number twelve. Again in the clause about the steps, which certainly reads awkwardly as it stands, many substitute עֶשֶׂר for אֲשֶׁר, and render: and by ten steps they go up to it. If the present text is retained, we must supply, "And he measured," or something like it: (he measured) by the steps which they go up to it—the course merely being noticed, but not the exact measurement, as the description here is very brief. It seems intended to show that the porch was much the same as in the old temple of Solomon.

[2] The introducing of the tabernacle has certainly a peculiar appearance in this connection; hence some would regard אֹהֶל as used in an unusual sense for *temple*, while the greater part suppose a corruption of the text, and render "porch," or "projection-work." Häv., however, defends the existing text, and conceives that the prophet, as in the dimensions of the outer porch he had pointed to Solomon's temple, so here in the temple proper he points to the old tabernacle, which being composed in its breadth of eight boards, each one and a half cubit broad, would make in all twelve cubits, as here. This was the breadth externally of the tabernacle, though the interior was only ten cubits. The prophet would thus connect together the two most sacred erections of former times. Such was probably the reason, though the mention of the tabernacle even in such a way looks somewhat artificial.

[3] This expression, "before (or in front of) the temple," is used on account of the peculiar sacredness of the most holy place, which stood in a sense by itself and into which the prophet did not enter with the angel. Hence he had said, not that the angel brought him in thither, but that the angel went in himself, and measured it; so that the most holy place appeared like a separate apartment in front of the portion of the temple which alone was accessible to him (comp. 1 Kings vi. 3, where *temple* is used in the same restricted sense). The dimensions of the two apartments are precisely those of Solomon's temple, which having been fixed of old by Divine direction, are to be regarded as already finally determined.

[4] The meaning of this rather obscure description, as we learn by turning to 1 Kings vi. 6, is that there were rests made in the walls of the temple for supports to the side-chambers; but the temple walls did not thereby become part of this side building, they stood separate from it.

[5] The אַצִּיל here must be regarded as an architectural term, denoting something about the foundations; and as it is used elsewhere in the sense of joints, the natural supposition is that it indicates the point where the foundation of one chamber ceased and another began. Yet, it must be confessed, there is no certainty.

[6] By the אַתִּוּקִים, galleries, are supposed to be meant some sort of terrace building, but the word, being only found in this description of Ezekiel, cannot be defined exactly. Indeed in the account contained in these four verses there is considerable obscurity, so that some have even held, and Böttcher still holds, that it is only the temple that is spoken of. But I think this impossible. The prophet seems plainly to mean, that on the west, or to the back of the temple, there was a separate place occupied as to its greater part by buildings, which were much about the same external dimensions with the temple; both being in their entire compass an hundred cubits square. But in neither case is the description so full as to enable us to make up the different items with anything like certainty.

CHAPTER XLIII

[1] What is meant is not the voice of God, but the sound or noise of the manifested glory of God, as formerly described, chap. i. 24. It is better, therefore, to render "its noise" than "his voice," as the latter seems to point to what is not here intended—a personal speaking on the part of God.

[2] A striking example of the manner in which the prophets identified themselves with him in whose name they spake, and whose word they uttered. Ezekiel came to destroy when he came to utter God's destroying word. Comp. Gen. xlviii. 22; Hos. vi. 5, etc.

[3] The construction is here quite similar to that of chap. xxxv. 10, where, to render the object uppermost in the thoughts particularly prominent, the speech begins with it, preceded by an אֵת. It is as much as to say, This is it—this that you have seen, with which your mind has been so long occupied, is my throne.

[4] By mentioning the "carcases of their kings," the prophet has been very commonly thought to refer to the burying-place of the kings being improperly situated within the temple mount, and, perhaps, to some connection between this and the abominations of idolatry. But there is no evidence of such a thing in the historical or prophetical books. No charge of corruption on this score is even so much as mooted against the people; while it is clear, from the manner it is noticed here, that not only a corruption, but a most flagrant and crying abomination, is referred to. I think, therefore, that we must understand by the expression, the pollutions of idolatry. These are characterised by a strong, yet in the circumstances not unnatural, epithet of contempt and abhorrence. Not unnatural; for God is here presenting himself as the glorious head and monarch of his people—so near to

them that the earthly head, the David, has only the name of the prince (chapters xliv. xxxvi.). God himself occupies the throne; and in what light, then, appeared their old idols? Kings indeed—other kings, but dead and not living; only *carcases of kings.* And to make it more plain that such are really meant, the high places are immediately mentioned, and placed in apposition with these carcases of kings, as but another name for the same thing; for it was with the high places that the idol worship was more especially connected, insomuch that God gave the name of Bamah, high place, to all their worship (see on chap. xx. 29). These rival monarchs, therefore, whose throne was as it were on the high places, but whose foul services had also been brought into the courts of God's house, these must now be put away—must, like carcases, be buried out of sight.

[5] This is the most singular part of the description respecting the altar, and we simply give in the original form the two terms which cause the chief difficulty. Many, including Hävernick, regard these as significant terms applied to the altar, to denote the high security and strength which it was to be the means of imparting to the new community: "And the mount of God is four cubits, and from the lion of God," etc. One can scarcely avoid feeling that such epithets, introduced thus in the middle of dry measurements, have a very fanciful and unnatural appearance. Besides the second of the two, אֲרִאֵיל, is not exactly the same with the אֲרִיאֵל of Isa. xxix. 1. I am therefore inclined to follow Gesenius, Ewald, Hitzig, Thenius, and to regard the words as properly but one, and to take it as a term for the hearth or fire-place of the altar.

CHAPTER XLV

[1] It is scarcely possible to make any intelligible sense of this verse as it stands. The greater part of commentators suppose a corruption of the text here, not excepting Häv., who adopts the meaning given by the Sept.: "And the five shekels shall be five, and the ten shekels shall be ten, and fifty shekels shall be your maneh." It is, of course, quite conjectural. Hitzig prefers understanding the three numbers of the different metals: 20 shekels for the gold maneh, 25 for the silver, and 15 for the brass or copper. Also quite conjectural; the more so as, by comparing 1 Kings x. 17 with 2 Chron. ix. 16, the maneh of gold seems to have been 100 shekels.

[2] In these oblations, from the different kinds of property, there is an evident progression as to the relation between the kind and the quantity. Of the corn there was to be the sixth of a tenth—that is, a 60th part of the quantity specified; of the oil, the tenth of a tenth—that is, an 100th part; and of the flock, one from every 200.

CHAPTER XLVII. 1–12

[1] Perhaps the word should be untranslated, for the Arabah (plain) is the name given at this day to the valley that lies around, and to the south of the Dead Sea (Robinson's Researches, ii. p. 595). We can therefore have no doubt that by the sea is meant the Dead Sea, which also lies in the direction of the stream toward the east.

[2] The dual here, נַחֲלַיִם, double-stream, is peculiar; but there is no reason

for supposing, with some, that it is used with reference to any division in the current into two or more branches; for no mention is made of that, and the word is presently, in the latter part of the verse, and again in ver. 12, used in the singular. It is rather to be understood of the copiousness of the stream; increasing at such a rapid rate, it becomes like rivers, though still really but one.

[3] The former of these two names, Engedi, was applied to the wilderness lying to the west and south of the Dead Sea, where David sought a place of refuge from Saul. A fountain, and the remains of a town, still exist under that name, and have been identified by Robinson (Researches, ii. p. 214). The other place, En-eglaim, no doubt lay somewhere at a considerable distance on the shores of the same sea. The two places appear to be used as boundaries, comprising between them the whole extent of the Dead Sea.

[4] This verse tells us that the sea had certain parts or places about it which did not participate in the general change, and which were given or appointed for salt. But both the things themselves, and the nature of the destination, have been variously understood; and as usual in cases of difficulty, alterations in the text have also been proposed. We must keep in view the general nature and design of the representation. This stream of life, flowing from the dwelling-place of God, images the regenerating efficacy of his grace and word upon a dead world, represented by the barren region through which the stream flows, and the salt waters of the Dead Sea, into which it empties itself. The general result is such, that the barren soil becomes in the highest degree fertile, and even the salt waters of the Dead Sea are sweetened and made capable of sustaining the greatest abundance of fish. But certain parts in the neighbourhood—pits and marshes, such as the region is known to possess, and which it is to be understood the stream from the temple does not reach—remain still unhealed, and are therefore given to salt, the image of what is waste, bitter, and unproductive in nature (Deut. xxix. 23; Ps. cvii. 34; Zeph. ii. 9). So that the meaning is, in so far as there might be any places in the desert world which should not participate in the beneficent influence, these, if any, would remain in their originally bad state—unhealed.

CHAPTER XLVII.13–23, XLVIII

[1] The גֵּה here we take, with our translators, and the greater part of commentators, to be a corruption for זֶה; so also the Septuagint, Vulgate, and Chaldee.

[2] Not precisely "Jehovah there;" for the ָה— cannot be sunk, as Hengstenberg has remarked on Hos. iii. 17. The exact import is thither, or thereupon.

[3] In chap. xlvii. 22, 23, provision is also made for the strangers who should come and join themselves to the Lord: these, it was ordered, should be treated as Israelites, and have an inheritance like the rest. It is merely a trait thrown in to show how the spiritual community of the Lord would now form a point of attraction to others, and how also, instead of repelling these, they were to give them free access to the highest privileges, as the provision to be made was to be large enough for all, and none need envy another.

Easily understood on the spiritual interpretation, but quite inexplicable on the literal; for, as within the bounds mentioned it is impossible to understand how even the members of the different tribes could be accommodated, what room could be found for an influx of strangers? The notice is intelligible only if understood as intimating that the distinction of Jew and Gentile should be abolished, and that the whole believing world should be one, and their name one.

Puritan Commentary Series

S150-00001-7	Matthew Henry's Commentary, unabridged in 3 volumes	35.00
A150-00094-7	Calvin's Commentaries, O.T. & N.T., 45 vols. in 8, unabr.	125.00
A150-00126-5	Keil & Delitzsch Old Testament Commentaries, 25 in 6v.	70.00
S150-00002-9	Puritan Commentary on Ephesians, Goodwin-Bayne	12.00
A150-00003-0	Exposition of I John, R. S. Candlish and A. W. Pink, 2 in 1	7.00
S150-00004-2	Exposition of Hebrews, John Owen 7 volumes in 3, unab.	30.00
S150-00005-4	Exposition of Galatians, John Brown	6.00
S150-00006-6	Exposition of Romans, Robert Haldane	6.00
S150-00007-8	Exposition of the Minor Prophets, George Hutcheson	10.00
S150-00008-X	Exposition of Proverbs, Charles Bridges	8.00
S150-00009-1	Exposition of the Song of Solomon, John Gill	6.00
S150-00010-8	Exposition of Leviticus, A. A. Bonar	6.00
S150-00011-X	Exposition of I Peter, John Brown 3 volumes in 1, unabr.	9.00
S150-00012-1	Exposition of James, Thomas Manton	6.00
S150-00013-3	Exposition of Colossians, John Daille	8.00
S150-00014-5	Exposition of Ezekiel, Patrick Fairbairn	6.00
S150-00015-7	Exposition of II Timothy, John Barlow & Jay Green	8.00
S150-00016-9	Exposition of Job, Joseph Caryl & Jay Green, Vol. I (of 3)	10.00
SA150-00017-0	Treasury of David, C. H. Spurgeon (Psalms), 7 vols. in 2	27.50
S150-00032-7	Exposition of John's Gospel, George Hutcheson	6.00
S150-00100-9	Exposition of Psalm 18 and Isaiah 53, John Brown (This is under the title: Sufferings & Glories of the Messiah)	4.50
S150-00102-2	Exposition of Ruth & Esther, Geo. Lawson & Alex. Carson	5.00
A150-00109-5	Hodge's Commentary on I & II Corinthians, Ephesians	8.00
S150-00120-4	The Epistles of the Apostles, I Cor. thru Rev., Jay Green	8.00
A150-00167-8	Commentary on Galatians, Martin Luther	6.00
A150-00168-X	Exposition of Genesis, R. S. Candlish	7.00
A150-00169-1	Commentary on Genesis, Martin Luther	7.00
A150-00191-5	Commentary on Romans, Martin Luther	5.00
S150-00204-X	Exposition of Titus, Thomas Taylor	7.00
S150-00205-1†	Exposition of Job, Caryl & Jay Green, Volume II (of 3)	10.00
SA150-00229-4	PURITAN COMMENTARY SERIES NO. 714, All 47 of the volumes listed above, if purchased at one time =	469.00

† To be delivered 1 volume per month beginning in May, 1971

OTHER COMMENTARIES AVAILABLE FROM THE PUBLISHERS:

CALVIN'S COMMENTARIES IN INDIVIDUAL VOLUMES AS FOLLOWS:

150-00128-9	Commentary on the Gospels, 5 volumes in 1	16.00
150-00130-7	Commentary on the Penteteuch, 6 volumes in 1	18.00
150-00132-0	Commentary on the Psalms and Joshua, 6 volumes in 1	18.00
150-00143-5	Commentary on Isaiah, 4 volumes in 1	16.00
150-00144-7	Commentary on Jeremiah & Lamentations, 5 vols. in 1	18.00
150-00145-9	Commentary on Ezekiel, 4 volumes in 1	16.00
150-00146-0	Commentary on the Minor Prophets, 5 volumes in 1	18.00
150-00133-2	Commentary on Acts–Jude, 13 volumes in 1	16.00
	ALSO AVAILABLE IN PAPERBACK @ $7.50 Retail	
S150-00052-2	Matthew Henry's Commentary, complete & unabridged in 1 volume, 2000 pages, 8½ x 11"	15.00

Puritan Devotional Library

S150-00018-2	The Complete Works of John Bunyan, 3 volumes	20.00
S150-00019-4	Man's Guiltiness Before God, Thomas Goodwin	7.00
S150-00020-0	The Objects & Acts of Justifying Faith, Thos. Goodwin	8.00
S150-00021-2	Alleine's Alarm to the Unconverted, Joseph Alleine	3.00
S150-00022-4	Christian Love and Its Fruits, Jonathan Edwards	4.50
S150-00023-6	The Existence & Attributes of God, Charnock	10.00
S150-00024-8	The Saints' Everlasting Rest, Richard Baxter	4.00
S150-00025-X	The Reformed Pastor, Richard Baxter	4.00
S150-00026-1	Keeping the Heart, John Flavel	3.00
S150-00027-3	Heaven Opened, Richard and Joseph Alleine	4.00
S150-00028-5	The Five Points of Calvinism, Bonar, Gill, Calvin, Edwards	3.50
S150-00029-7	Reconciliation, A. W. Pink, Thomas Goodwin	4.50
S150-00033-9	Thomas Watson's Body of Divinity, all 3 vols. in 1	10.00
S150-00037-6	Temptation and Sin, John Owen	5.00
S150-00038-8	The Holy Spirit, John Owen 2 volumes in 1	10.00
S150-00039-X	Communion with God, John Owen	5.00
S150-00040-6	Justification by Faith, John Owen	5.00
S150-00041-8	The Saints' Perseverance, Arthur W. Pink	5.00
S150-00042-X	The Religious Affections, Jonathan Edwards	4.00
S150-00047-9	The Impeccable Christ, W. E. Best	3.50
A150-00048-0	Holiness, J. C. Ryle	3.75
A150-00055-8	Beautiful Bible Stories for Little Eyes & Ears, Palmer	3.50
S150-00058-3	The Atonement Acc. to Christ & His Apostles, Smeaton	7.00
A150-00067-4	John Calvin's Institutes of the Christian Religion, 2 v. in 1	7.50
S150-00070-4	John Gill's Body of Divinity	10.00
A150-00095-9	Spurgeon's Morning and Evening	4.50
A150-00098-4	On the Bondage of the Will, Martin Luther	3.50
A150-00099-6	God in Three Persons, Morton Smith & Edw. Bickersteth	3.50
S150-00122-8	The Life & Diary of David Brainerd, Jonathan Edwards	4.50
S150-00137-X	The Afflicted Man's Companion, Willison, Boston, Brooks	6.00
S150-00139-3	Apostasy & Spiritual-Mindedness, John Owen	5.00
S150-00157-5	Christ Our Mediator, Thomas Goodwin	7.00
A150-00160-5	Daily Light on Our Daily Path, from King James II	4.00
A150-00166-6	Foxe's Book of Martyrs, new edition by George Jaffray	5.00
A150-00197-6	Selected Choice Sermons by C. H. Spurgeon	5.00
A150-00199-X	Selected Encouragements to Holiness, C. H. Spurgeon	5.00
A150-00202-6	The Soul-winner, C. H. Spurgeon	3.50
S150-00216-6	A Narrative of Surprising Conversions, Jonathan Edwards	3.50
S150-00220-8	Pilgrim's Progress in Modern English, Bunyan (J.Green, Ed.)	3.00
S150-00221-x	The Holy War in Modern English, Bunyan (Jay Green, Ed.)	5.00
SA150-00031-5	King James II Version of the Bible, trans. by Jay Green	7.50
A150-00183-6	Morning and Evening II, Devotional gems fr. Spurgeon	4.75
S150-00186-1	The Person of Christ, John Owen	5.00
S150-00228-2	THE PURITAN DEVOTIONAL LIBRARY NO. 714, All 45 of the above volumes at this special price =	230.00

STUDENT'S REFERENCE LIBRARY

150-00057-1	Thayer's Greek-English Lexicon	9.50
150-00060-1	Evangelical Creeds & Confessions,deKlerk	4.00
150-00066-2	Miracles, Miraculous Gifts & Scrip.,Green	4.00
150-00084-4	Life & Times of Jesus the Messiah, Alfred Edersheim, 2 vol. in 1	12.00

PAPERBACK CLASSICS

		Retail
150-00034-0p	Prayer & The Return of Prayer, Bunyan–Goodwin	1.25
150-00035-2p	Rare Jewel of Christian Contentment, Burroughs	1.50
150-00036-4p	Precious Remedies Against Satan's Devices, Brooks	1.50
150-00043-1p	The Religious Affections, Jonathan Edwards	2.50
150-00044-3p	The Soul-winner, C. H. Spurgeon	1.50
150-00045-5p	Pilgrim's Progress in Modern English, Bunyan (Green)	1.00
150-00046-7p	The Holy War in Modern English, Bunyan (Jay Green)	2.00
150-00049-2p	Holiness, J. C. Ryle	1.50
150-00051-0p	Synonyms of the New Testament, Trench	2.00
150-00056-Xp	The Reformed Pastor, Richard Baxter	1.50
150-00059-5p	Faith Healing & Faithless Healers, Jay Green	1.00
150-00062-5p	The Cause of God and Truth, John Gill	3.00
150-00064-9p	Keeping the Heart, John Flavel	1.25
150-00065-0p	Augustine's Confessions in Modern English	1.00
150-00069-8p	The Children's King James New Testament (The King James II New Testament plus 117 Bible Stories & Ill.)	3.00
150-00071-6p	The King James II New Testament, kivar binding	1.50
150-00072-8p	An Antidote to Arminianism, Christopher Ness	1.00
150-00073-Xp	The Vanity of Thoughts, Thomas Goodwin	1.25
150-00074-1p	Absolute Predestination, Jerome Zanchius	1.75
150-00076-5p	A History of Redemption, Jonathan Edwards	3.00
150-00077-7p	God's Sovereignty, Elisha Coles	1.75
150-00078-9p	Romans 8 : 28, A Divine Cordial, Thomas Watson	1.25
150-00079-0p	The Woman Taken in Adultery, John Burgon	1.50
150-00080-7p	Death, Samuel Eyles Pierce	1.00
150-00082-0p	Heaven Opened, Richard and Joseph Alleine	1.50
150-00083-2p	Alleine's Alarm to the Unconverted	1.00
150-00090-Xp	Baptism, Its Mode & Subjects, Alexander Carson	2.50
150-00091-1p	God's Everlasting Love, Jay Green	.75
150-00092-3p	The Philadelphia Baptist Confession of Faith	1.50
150-00096-0p	Morning and Evening, C. H. Spurgeon	2.50
150-00103-4p	Women of the Old & New Testaments, Abra. Kuyper	2.50
150-00105-8p	On the Bondage of the Will, Martin Luther	1.50
150-00106-Xp	Sufferings & Glories of the Messiah (Ps. 18,Isa.53), a verse by verse exposition by John Brown	2.50
150-00107-1p	The Trinity, Edward Bickersteth	1.50
150-00108-3p	Commentary on Ephesians, Hodge	1.75
150-00111-3p	On the Preparation & Delivery of Sermons, Broadus	2.00
150-00112-5p	Lectures to My Students, C. H. Spurgeon (unabridg.)	2.00
150-00113-7p	Beautiful Bible Stories for Little Eyes & Ears, Palmer	2.00
150-00114-9p	Calvin's Institutes of the Christian Religion (unabr.)	4.00
150-00115-0p	Temptation and Sin, John Owen	2.50
150-00116-2p	Reconciliation, A. W. Pink and Thomas Goodwin	2.00
150-00117-4p	Exposition of I John, Arthur W. Pink (1 & 2)	2.50
150-00118-6p	Exposition of I John, R. S. Candlish (all 5 chapters)	2.50
150-00119-8p	The Five Points of Calvinism, Bonar, Gill, Calvin, Edwards, Goodwin, Fuller (foreword, Jay Green)	1.50
150-00121-6p	The Epistles of the Apostles, 1 Cor.–Rev., Jay Green	4.00
150-00123-Xp	The Life & Diary of David Brainerd, Jon. Edwards	1.50
150-00135-6p	Animals of the Bible, Burton Goddard	.85
150-00136-8p	Baptism: Baptist vs Reformed Views, Jewett-Feenstra	.50
150-00138-1p	The Afflicted Man's Companion, Willison, Brooks, Bos.	3.00

PAPERBACK CLASSICS (Continued)

		Retail
150-00140-Xp	Apostasy & Spiritual-mindedness, John Owen	2.50
150-00142-3p	A Call to the Unconverted, Richard Baxter	1.50
150-00153-8p	Atonement According to Christ, Smeaton	2.50
150-00154-Xp	The Atonement According to the Apostles, Smeaton	2.50
150-00156-3p	Calvinism Today, Yesterday & Tomorrow, Jay Green	1.00
150-00158-7p	The Christian's Great Interest, William Guthrie	1.75
150-00159-9p	The Crook in the Lot, Thomas Boston	1.00
150-00161-7p	The Dairyman's Daughter and Other Personal Testimonies, Geo. Whitefield, Spurgeon, Others	1.50
150-00162-9p	The Doctrine of Particular Redemption, John Gill	.75
150-00165-4p	The Eternal Sonship of Christ, J. C. Philpot	1.00
150-00170-8p	God's Will, Man's Will and Free Will, H. Bonar, etc.	.75
150-00171-Xp	Human Nature in Its Fourfold State, Thomas Boston	2.25
150-00172-1p	The Holy Spirit, complete 2 vols.in 1, John Owen	4.50
150-00173-3p	The Impeccable Christ, W. E.Best	1.50
150-00175-7p	The Irresistible Grace of God, T. Goodwin, etc.	.75
150-00176-9p	Exposition of John's Gospel, Geo. Hutcheson (unabr.)	3.00
150-00177-0p	Justification by Faith, John Owen	2.50
150-00178-2p	King James II Version of the Bible, Jay Green, kivar	3.75
150-00181-2p	Lectures on Calvinism, Abraham Kuyper	1.50
150-00182-4p	The Moral Law, Ernest Kevan	1.25
150-00184-8p	Morning and Evening II, day by day with Spurgeon	2.50
150-00185-Xp	A Mute Christian Under the Smarting Rod, Brooks	1.50
150-00187-3p	The Person of Christ, John Owen	2.50
150-00189-7p	Principles of Sacred Theology, Abraham Kuyper	3.00
150-00190-3p	Commentary on Revelation, Abraham Kuyper	2.25
150-00192-7p	The Saints' Perseverance, A. W. Pink	2.00
150-00198-8p	Selected Choice Sermons of C. H. Spurgeon	2.50
150-00200-2p	Selected Encouragements to Holiness, C. H. Spurgeon	2.50
150-00201-4p	A Serious Call to a Devout & Holy Life, Wm. Law	1.75
150-00203-8p	Thayer's Greek-English Lexicon of the N.T.	5.00
150-00207-5p	Westminster Confession of Faith in Modern English	1.50
150-00209-9p	The Work of the Holy Spirit, Abraham Kuyper	3.00
150-00210-5p	Work Out Your Own Salvation, John Daille	.85
150-00212-9p	My Sermon Notes, C. H. Spurgeon (unabridged)	4.00
150-00215-4p	Christian Love and Its Fruits, Jonathan Edwards	1.75
150-00217-8p	A Narrative of Surprising Conversions, Edwards	1.50
150-00224-5p	Evangelical Creeds and Confessions, DeKlerk	2.00
150-00225-7p	The Saints' Everlasting Rest, Richard Baxter	1.75
150-00226-9p	Exposition of Ruth and Esther, Lawson–Carson	2.00

THE PAPERBACK PURITAN COMMENTARY SERIES

150-00147-2p	Calvin's Commentaries, 45 vols. in 8, unabridged	$60.00
150-00078-9p	Romans 8:28, A Divine Cordial, Thomas Watson	1.25
150-00106-xp	Psalm 18, Isa. 53, Sufferings and Glories of the Messiah, John Brown (of Edinburgh)	2.50
150-00117-4p	Exposition of I John 1 and 2, Arthur W. Pink	2.50
150-00121-6p	The Epistles of the Apostles, I Cor.-Rev., compiled and put into today's English, from great puritans, Jay Green	4.00
150-00176-9p	Exposition of John's Gospel, George Hutcheson	3.00
150-00226-9p	Exposition of Ruth and Esther, George Lawson	2.00
150-00232-4p	Exposition of James, Thomas Manton	3.00
150-00118-6p	Exposition of I John, R. S. Candlish	2.50
150-00108-3p	Commentary on Ephesians, Charles Hodge	1.75
150-00233-6p	ALL 17 VOLUMES ABOVE	$82.50